THE MAHATMA LETTERS
To A. P. Sinnett

THE
MAHATMA LETTERS

To A. P. SINNETT *from*
THE MAHATMAS M. & K. H.
Transcribed and Compiled by A. T. BARKER

THIRD AND REVISED EDITION
Edited by Christmas Humphreys and Elsie Benjamin

1972
THE THEOSOPHICAL PUBLISHING HOUSE
ADYAR, MADRAS 20, INDIA
68, Great Russell Street, London, WC1B 3BU, England
Post Box 270, Wheaton, Illinois 60187, U.S.A.

First Published	. *December, 1923*
Second Impression . . .	. *May, 1924*
Third Impression . . .	. *June, 1924*
Fourth Impression . .	. *November, 1924*
Second Edition (*Fifth Impression*)	*March, 1926*
Second Edition (*Sixth Impression*)	*January, 1930*
Second Edition (*Seventh Impression*)	*March, 1933*
Second Edition (*Eighth Impression*) .	. *1948*
Third Edition (*Ninth Impression*) .	. *1962*
Third Edition (*Tenth Impression*) .	. *1972*

SBN   7229—7013—7 (U. K.)
ISBN   0-8356—7013—9 (U. S. A)

PRINTED IN INDIA

At the Vasanta Press, The Theosophical Society, Adyar, Madras 20 also to The Occult World, a volume published by the same Author. The reader is asked to believe that the greatest care has been taken with the work of transcription; the whole MS. has been checked word for word with the originals, and everything possible done to ensure accuracy. It would be too much to expect that the printed book will contain no errata. They are almost inevitable. To bear this point steadily in mind the reader is asked as to wonder approximate passage has been copied from the originals, the originals of passage has been ...

COMPILER'S PREFACE

To First Edition

It will be seen, if reference is made to the " Contents ", that the letters have been arranged in 7 Sections and an Appendix. The former contain nothing but Mahatma letters, while in the latter some letters have been added from three pupils of The Mahatmas M. and K.H.—: H. P. Blavatsky, T. Subba Row, and Damodar K. Mavalankar, not only for their intrinsic merit, but because they help to make clear questions arising in the main part of the book which would otherwise be left obscure.

The seven Sections suggest themselves as more or less natural divisions, but it should be remembered that as letters in one section often contain matter which also relates to the other Sections, considerable overlapping is unavoidable. However, an attempt has been made and that is the best that can be said.

The contents of each Section are arranged where possible chronologically, in the order of their receipt. The reader must bear in mind that with only one or two exceptions none of the letters were dated by the writer thereof. On many of them, however, the dates and places of receipt have been noted in Mr. Sinnett's handwriting, and these appear in small type immediately under the Letter Numbers.

It should be understood clearly that *unless otherwise stated*:

1. Each letter has been transcribed direct from the original.
2. Every letter was written to A. P. Sinnett.
3. All footnotes are copies of notes which appear in and belong to the letters themselves, unless signed (Ed.) in which case they have been added by the compiler.

Throughout this volume there are a great many words used which belong to Buddhist, Hindu, and Theosophical terminology. Those who are unfamiliar with such terms are referred to the excellent glossary in H. P. Blavatsky's *Key to Theosophy* and also to *The Theosophical Glossary*, a separate publication by the same author. The reader is asked to believe that the greatest care has been taken in the work of transcription; the whole MS. has been checked word for word with the originals, and everything possible done to prevent errors. It is however probably too much to expect that the printed book will contain no mistakes, they are almost inevitable. In case any doubt should arise in the reader's mind as to whether any particular passage has been correctly copied from the original, the compiler wishes to intimate that he will be happy to deal with any correspondence on the subject addressed to him care of the Publishers.

In conclusion the compiler's thanks are due and most gratefully acknowledged to those who by their assistance have made his task possible of accomplishment.

A. T. B.

PREFACE

To Third Edition

As Trevor Barker wrote in his original Introduction to the first edition of this book:

" It is well known, among students of Theosophy and Occultism, that the philosophical doctrines and ethics which were given to the world through the Theosophical Society during the 16 years immediately following its foundation in 1875, emanated from certain Eastern Teachers said to belong to an Occult Brotherhood living in the trans-Himalayan fastnesses of Tibet. H. P. Blavatsky, who, together with Colonel Olcott founded the Theosophical Society, acknowledged these Eastern Brothers as her Teachers, stating not only that They existed, but that she herself had received training and instruction at their hands during her sojourn in Tibet, and was therefore able to speak from her own knowledge and personal experience.

" It was not until 1880 that further testimony became available. In that year the late A. P. Sinnett, then living in India, was enabled through the agency of Madame Blavatsky, to enter into correspondence with her own Teachers, whom she referred to variously under the terms, ' The Brothers,' ' The Mahatmas,' and later, ' The Masters of Wisdom '. During the course of this correspondence, which extended over the years 1880 to 1884, Mr. Sinnett received many letters from the Mahatmas M. and K.H., the Teachers in question, and it is these original communications which are published in the present volume under the title of ' The Mahatma Letters '. The circumstances attending their receipt were fully dealt with by Mr. Sinnett in his ' Occult World ' and they need not therefore be restated here.

" They are now published with the permission of the Executrix of the late A. P. Sinnett, to whom they were bequeathed solely and unconditionally; she, in her turn, at the suggestion of the writer of this Introduction, allowed him the great privilege of undertaking the whole responsibility for the transcription, arrangement and publication of the Letters in book form ".

This book, under the title, *The Mahatma Letters to A. P. Sinnett*, as transcribed, compiled and edited by A. T. Barker, was first published in London by T. Fisher Unwin in December, 1923. A second edition, as revised by Mr. Barker, was published by Rider and Co., in 1926. In 1939, the Manuscript of the Letters, together with the MSS. which later formed the book, *The Letters of H. P. Blavatsky to A. P. Sinnett*, and other miscellaneous material in the possession of Mr. Sinnett when he died, was irrevocably given to the British Museum. In July, 1941, Mr. Barker died.

Mr. Barker's Executors were his brother and Mr. Christmas Humphreys, but in the absence of the former on war service the latter took over the mass of correspondence, notes and other material relating to the Mahatma Letters which were found among Mr. Barker's effects.

The Executrix of Mr. A. P. Sinnett, who died in 1921, was Miss Maud Hoffman who had, as set out in the quotation from Mr. Barker's Introduction, arranged with him to edit and have published the MSS. of the Letters. Miss Hoffman approved the idea of a third and improved edition of the Letters; but to save herself the editorial and business detail involved in such a task she created by Deed of Trust " The Mahatma Letters Trust " to control the future of the book for the remainder of the copyright. As Trustees she appointed Mr. Christmas Humphreys who, with his wife, had co-operated in a small way in the original publication of the Letters, and Mrs. Elsie Benjamin (née Savage) who was for many years the personal assistant of the late Dr. G. de Purucker.

The two Trustees at once appealed to all members of the Theosophical Movement for suggestions for correction and improvement in the form and matter of the second, current edition. The response to the appeal was very large, and the number of suggestions for correction and improvement so numerous that it became obvious that it would be some years before this Third Edition would be ready for the press. A further reprint of the Second Edition was therefore authorised. Meanwhile the Trustees and their group of willing asistants set to work.

In his own Preface to the Second Edition Mr. Barker expressed " the great regret and concern " at the number of errors in transcription and the like which had appeared in the First Edition; but none who has had the privilege of working on the actual MSS., now in the British Museum, can blame him for such errors. Rather is his name to be remembered for the immense skill and patience which he exercised in transcribing the great quantity of MSS. which filled the wooden box which Mr. Sinnett had made for the Letters in 1890, and much of a tin trunk besides. A great variety of writing material was used, and as great a variety of pen, pencil and crayon; many of the Letters are written on both sides of very thin paper, with the Masters' comments often written over that of another writer, and in many cases the ink has so faded that it is a marvel that the Compiler was able to transcribe the material at all. In these circumstances, even assuming the Letters to have been written in the normal way, it is impossible to be dogmatic over spelling, punctuation or even as to the word used. Even now, all that can be said is that the number of places where the actual meaning is in doubt has been reduced to very few indeed.

In the great task of preparing a third and so far as possible a definitive edition, it was clearly necessary to formulate and work to definite principles. These were agreed between the Trustees, and approved by those who assisted them. Of these the most valuable was the late President of the Theosophical Society, Mr. C. Jinarājadāsa, who on every visit to England gave up long hours of his limited time to going over the actual MSS. in the British Museum with Mr. Humphreys. His wide personal knowledge of the men and women who figured prominently in the early days of the Movement was freely placed at the disposal of the Trustees, as were the resources of the Archives at Adyar and even the readers of *The Theosophist*, to whom appeal was made from time to time for assistance. A second worker was the late Mr. James Graham, who collated and summarized the great volume of suggested corrections and improvements sent in by students, and prepared the entirely new Index for this volume. At a later stage Mr. Boris de Zirkoff, the Compiler of the *H. P. Blavatsky Collected Writings*, gave the Trustees the benefit of his great knowledge of early Theosophical literature, and with the aid of his own unique library and archives in Los Angeles was able again and again to suggest the right interpretation of a disputed passage or clearly incorrect word.

As the responsibility of this editorship is great, and many variations from the Second Edition have in fact been made, it is thought right to reveal the principles adopted in such revision.

The idea of transcribing the material exactly as it appeared was at once abandoned. One reason alone sufficed, that Trevor Barker had already made many corrections in spelling, punctuation and the like, and it was therefore decided to produce a book of the maximum value to students while remaining faithful to the thoughts behind the original.

But voices have been loudly raised in the past about changes in later editions of the works of early Theosophical writers, and it is therefore important to be able to declare, as is now declared, (a) *that in this Work no single word has been added*, save in square brackets to make the sense clear; and (b) *that no single word has been omitted* save in a few cases where its presence was an obvious grammatical error.

The Trustees then had to make decisions on a number of basic suggestions for the new edition. The first was to re-arrange the entire material, and to print the Letters in chronological order. As it was decided, though with regret, that the book would have to be entirely reset, and therefore the pagination altered, this suggestion was carefully considered, and a serious attempt made to collate such a chronology from the six known attempts to produce one. Those of the late Miss Mary K. Neff, Mrs. Margaret G. Conger, Mrs. Beatrice Hastings, and Mr. James Arthur, and two more by Mr. G. N. Slyfield and Mr. K. F. Vania, were carefully considered. All the lists were the fruit of long and careful effort, but when compared, although there was a consensus of opinion on a great many Letters, including, of course, the few actually dated, there remained such a wide divergence of view on the right place for so many of them that it was thought unwise to re-arrange the material in an order which would never satisfy more than a few. In any case, it will be appreciated that the order of writing is only of prime importance in the writing of history; the spiritual and doctrinal teaching of the Letters is largely unimpaired by the order in which they are read. The Letters remain, therefore, in the order in which the late Mr. Trevor Barker first published them and many take the view that, short of an agreed chronological order, this arrangement could not be bettered. The Letters on history, doctrine and probation are here collected together, and students of each can find in them what they need.

Should any material be added? Suggestions fell into three groups, as to further Letters from these Masters, such as those to Mr. W. Q. Judge; that from the Maha Chohan, which Mr. Jina-rājadāsa described to Mr. Humphreys as in his view ' practically a charter for the T.S. through the centuries' ; and notes and comments on the actual material. As to the first, it was thought that other cognate material should be left to a subsequent volume. As to the Letter from the Maha Chohan, it was decided that once any Letters were added which were not contained in the collection in the possession of A. P. Sinnett at his death, it would be difficult to decide where such addition should stop. This Letter may be found as No. I in *Letters From The Masters of The Wisdom*, First Series, edited by Mr. C. Jinarājadāsa, and its history is given in the notes attached thereto.

Should any material be left out? It was thought right to omit from this edition the controversial Appendix by Mr. Barker on " Mars and Mercury ". This, however valuable, has no place in a volume of the Letters themselves, and should in the Editors' view be kept for a later volume of such comment, notes and additions. For the same reason Mr. Barker's original Introduction has been omitted, save the passage quoted at the beginning of this Preface. Much of its contents was comment, but once so much of comment appears there is little reason for not including a great deal more. The few letters to Mr. Sinnett from writers other than the Mahatmas which appear in the Appendix, though in one sense irrelevant, have value as throwing light on the Masters' own letters, and are therefore retained.

In the treatment of the standing text the following principles were applied:

(*a*) Actual corrections in transcription were in all cases made, subject to correction of these as under.

(*b*) The spelling of names, places, non-English phrases and the like has been revised, and attempts made at greater consistency in the use of capital letters and italics. Quotations from books and of foreign phrases have been corrected where errors have been found.

(*c*) No attempt has been made to achieve consistency in the use of diacritical marks. When used they have been left, but none has been added. The Masters' spelling of Sanskrit words is sometimes a North Indian variation of the classical spelling, and the former has not been changed.

(*d*) Footnotes are either as in the text, or those of Mr. Trevor Barker, marked Ed., or those of the present Editors, marked Eds. They have been kept to a minimum.

(*e*) The Editors are grateful for the suggestion, clearly right, that Letter 18 (pp. 115 to 119) and Letter 95 (pp. 423-424) are two parts of one Letter, though on different paper.

(*f*) Finally, there have been many changes in the punctuation. In most cases the corrections were obvious improvements, and in no case made any possible alteration to the meaning. Sometimes, however, it was very difficult to understand a sentence until the addition of a comma, or its removal, suddenly made sense. In those cases such a change has only been made after all concerned agreed that it was necessary to clarify the meaning.

The present Editors, however, had to achieve a delicate balance between leaving much unnecessary and obscuring punctuation, and boldly re-writing the material in modern English. Mr. Sinnett, in his *Occult World* transcription of some of the Letters, adopted the latter course, and Mr. Jinarājadāsa, in his *Early Teachings of the Masters* (*1881-3*), did much the same. But the present Editors respectfully take the view that this is not to the advantage of the best understanding of the Letters. In many cases the somewhat laboured use of dashes and the like has obvious value. The Letters were not written as prose, nor meant to be read as such. They were an extended attempt to teach a willing pupil some of the fundamental principles of doctrines utterly new to him. Hence the deliberate stress and emphasis on words and phrases, the importance of which can best be appreciated if passages are read aloud. Then the dashes, pauses and italics are seen for what they are, a reproduction of the actual teaching, whether written or dictated, of the Masters. For this reason the improvement to the original has not gone far enough to remove the value of this form of punctuation.

But after years of revision there still remain a number of cases where a word in the MSS. cannot be read, or where, though what was written seemed to be clear, no such word existed; and cases where, though the word used was clear, it was obviously not that

which the Master would have used on reflection. In some cases
footnotes have been added to draw attention to such instances;
for the rest, so long as the general meaning is clear the Editors
feel that their task is in the main accomplished.

All suggested alterations, whether or not adopted, and all
material for notes and comments have been filed by the Trustees,
and will be available for future generations.

Such material may one day form a second volume of further
Letters, notes, and comments on all of them, including the right
Chronology of the Letters, or the various attempts at deciding
such a chronology, and, it is hoped, the collection of Mahatma
Letters at Adyar, now available in two small volumes as *Letters
from the Masters of the Wisdom*, edited by Mr. C. Jinarājadāsa.

In 1952 the whole of the Mahatma Letters MSS. given to the
British Museum was microfilmed at the orders of the Trustees. The
Museum authorities had bound the material in seven volumes,
with their usual exquisite skill and care, and the seven volumes
were reduced to four reels of microfilm. Copies of these four
have been sent to various organizations throughout the world,
Theosophical and otherwise, including the Library of Congress in
Washington, thus reducing to a minimum the loss to mankind
should the originals be destroyed in another war. At the same
time the brass-bound wooden box which Mr. Sinnett had made
to contain the Letters was returned to the Trustees, and now
contains the more valuable papers in the possession of the Mahatma
Letters Trust.

The original work of this Trust, as already described, was to
safeguard the interests of the book, of which this is the Third
Edition. But the Trustees at once began to collect all works
which bore on the production, authenticity and history of the
Letters, and this soon grew into a library of early works in
Theosophy, written during the lifetime of H. P. Blavatsky. Then
a number of early workers in the field were contacted and very
valuable annotated copies, notes of talks at classes, photographs
and other such material was given to the Trust for perpetuity.
This is available to all students of the early days of Theosophy,
and has already proved of some value in the compilation of the
Collected Writings of H. P. Blavatsky, edited by Mr. Boris de
Zirkoff and now being published at Adyar. Contributions of such

material, whether books, pamphlets, magazine articles, photographs, relics, letters and the like will be gratefully received by
the Trustees.

The first and second Editions of this work were published in
London. For the third Edition the Trustee-Editors are delighted
that the publisher should be the Theosophical Publishing House
at Adyar, Madras, which is, as none can deny, the early home of
the modern Theosophical Movement. Our knowledge of this
Wisdom called Theosophy sprang from two sources, these Letters
and the writings of H. P. Blavatsky. From these Letters A. P.
Sinnett wrote *The Occult World* and *Esoteric Buddhism*; from the
knowledge gained from these Masters, H. P. Blavatsky gave the
world *Isis Unveiled*, *The Secret Doctrine*, *The Key to Theosophy*, *The
Voice of the Silence*, and much besides.

Later generations may have added to this knowledge. That is
for the individual to decide. But the Letters are their own
authority for the Principles they teach, and that Teaching, whether
of doctrine or as to the inner life and the nature of probation, is
one with that of 'H.P.B.', who was the Founder of the Theosophical Movement, and the Masters' chosen and beloved pupil,
agent, and scribe.

Whatever else, therefore, is studied by the student of Theosophy, these Letters must be read, their teaching digested and
applied and their warnings heeded. For this is Theosophy. From
such a study there may come in time a new understanding of
Theosophy, so wide that it may heal the rifts in the Movement
which in the last fifty years have impeded its development, so
deep that every member of that Movement may rededicate his
life to its service. For these Letters speak not only of the Wisdom
but of the Way which leads to it, and it is for the reader, by inner
conquest and the awakening of compassion, to achieve for himself
the timeless Wisdom which the writers of these Letters sought,
and found, and taught in outline in these pages for the benefit of
all mankind.

Christmas Humphreys
Elsie Benjamin

CONTENTS

SECTION I

THE OCCULT WORLD SERIES

SECTION II

PHILOSOPHICAL AND THEORETICAL TEACHINGS 1881-1883

SECTION III

PROBATION AND CHELASHIP

CONTENTS

CONTENTS   xxxi

SECTION IV

THE PHŒNIX VENTURE AND THE CONDITION OF INDIA

SECTION VII
MISCELLANEOUS LETTERS

APPENDIX

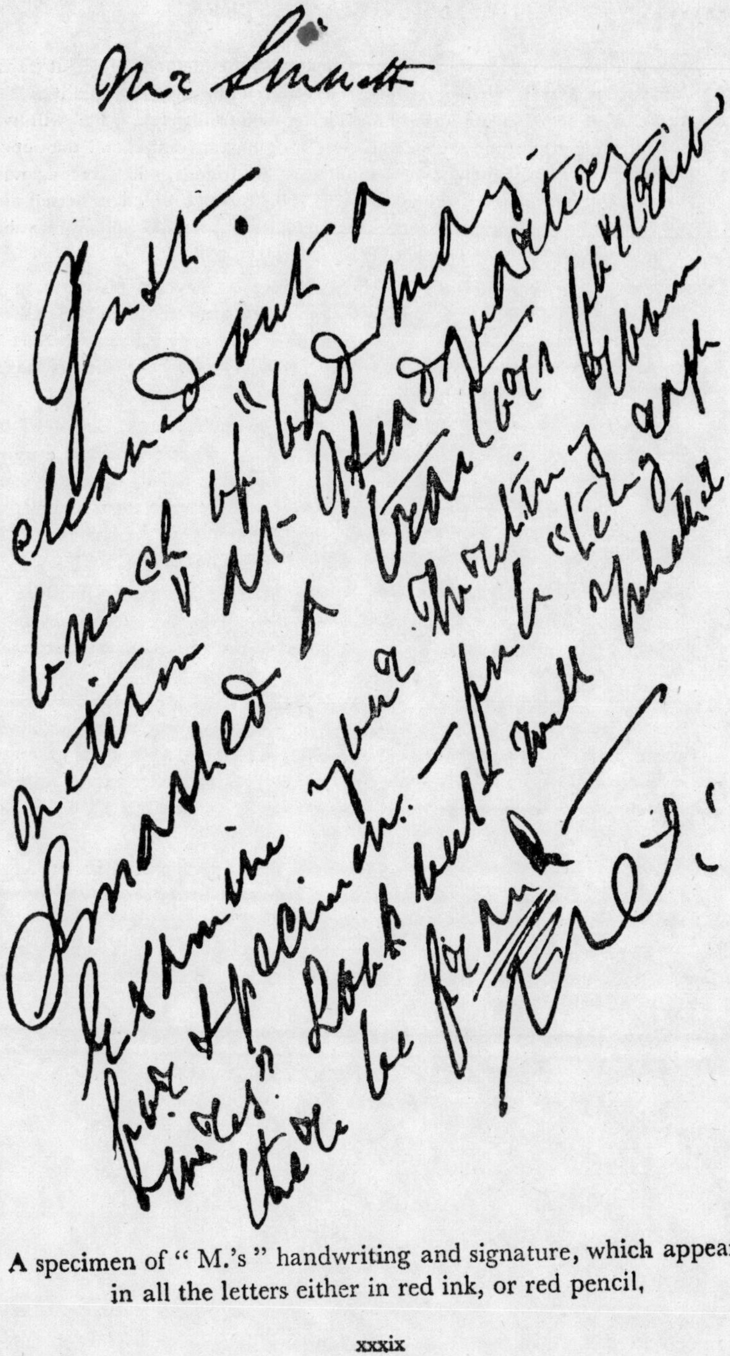
Mr Sinnett

A specimen of " M.'s " handwriting and signature, which appears in all the letters either in red ink, or red pencil,

Respectfully submitted to
the consideration of Mr Sinnett,
under the direct orders of
Brother Koot Hoomi

Damodar K. Mavalankar.

With the Exception of fee — too
Exaggerated — his views are quite
correct. Such is the impression
produced upon the naïve mind.
I trust, my dear friend, that you
add a paragraph showing the
Society in its true light. Listen
to your inner voice, and oblige
once more your's Ever faithfully

K. H.

A specimen of the handwriting of " K.H." precipitated in blue
ink, beneath a note from Damodar K. Mavalankar. The
majority of the " K.H." Letters are written either in blue ink
or blue pencil.

I

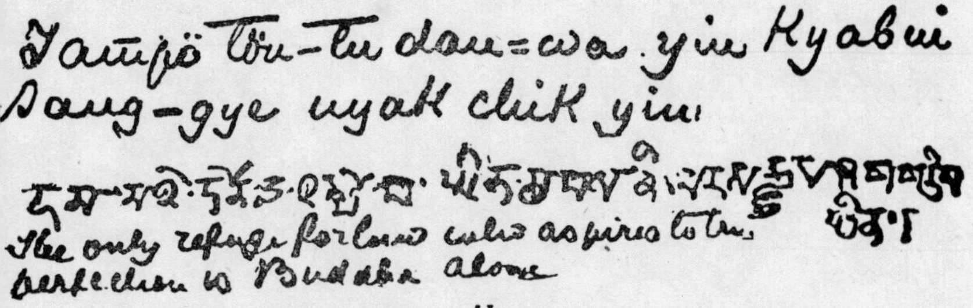

Tam-pö töu-tu dam=wa. yin Kyabui
Sang-gye nyak chik yin.

[handwritten script]

The only refuge for him who aspires to true
perfection is Buddha alone

II

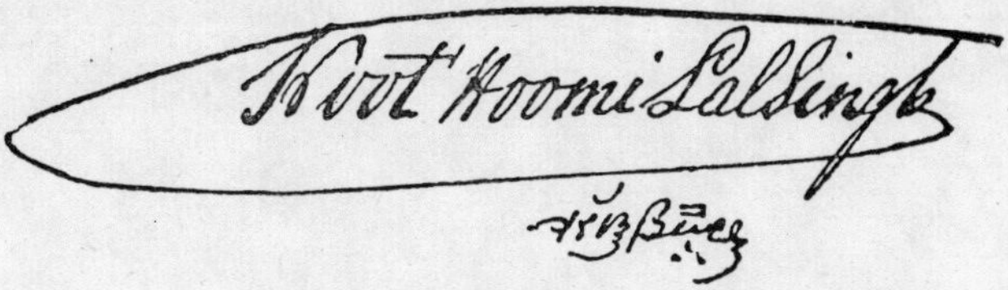

III

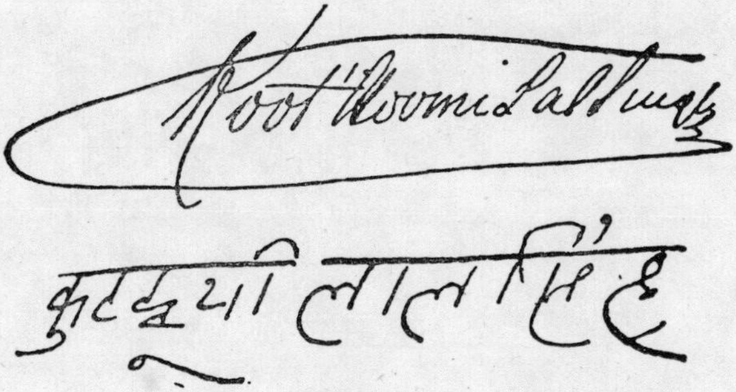

IV

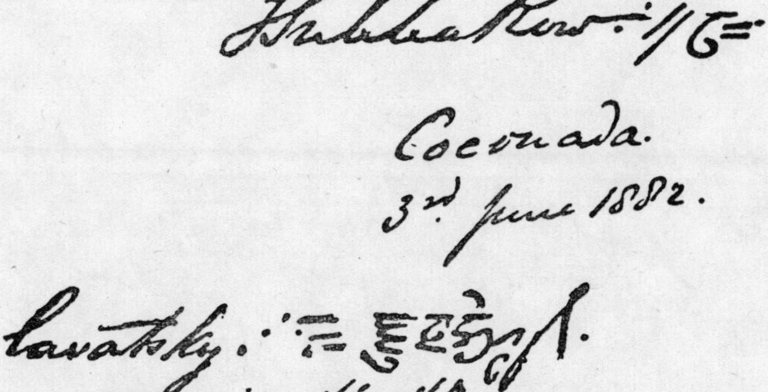

Coconada.
3rd June 1882.

I Fragment found in the envelope of Letter No. 92.

II, III and IV. Reproductions of the signatures of Letters No. 1, 4
and 132 respectively.

THE MAHATMA LETTERS

SECTION I

" THE OCCULT WORLD SERIES "

1880-1881

LETTER No. 1

Received Simla about October 15th, 1880.

Esteemed Brother and Friend,

Precisely because the test of the London newspaper would close the mouths of the skeptics—it is unthinkable. See it in what light you will—the world is yet in its first *stage* of disenthralment if not development, hence—unprepared. Very true, we work by natural not supernatural means and laws. But, as on the one hand Science would find itself unable (in its present *state*) to account for the wonders given in its name, and on the other the ignorant masses would still be left to view the phenomenon in the light of a miracle, everyone who would thus be made a witness to the occurrence would be thrown off his balance and the results would be deplorable. Believe me, it would be so—especially for yourself who originated the idea, and the devoted woman who so foolishly rushes into the wide open door leading to notoriety. This door, shough opened by so friendly a hand as yours, would prove very soon a trap—and a fatal one indeed for her. And such is not surely your object?

Madmen are they, who, speculating but upon the present, wilfully shut their eyes to the past when made already to remain naturally blind to the future! Far be it from me, to number you with the latter—therefore will I endeavour to explain. Were we to accede to your desires know you really what consequences would follow in the trail of success? The inexorable shadow which follows all human innovations moves on, yet few are they who are ever conscious of its approach and dangers. What are then to expect they who would offer the world an innovation which, owing to human ignorance, if believed in, will surely be attributed to

1

those dark agencies the two-thirds of humanity believe in and dread as yet? You say—half London would be converted if you could deliver them a *Pioneer* on its day of publication. I beg to say that if the people believed the thing true they would kill you before you could make the round of Hyde Park; if it were not believed true, the least that could happen would be the loss of your reputation and good name,—for propagating such ideas.

The success of an attempt of such a kind as the one you propose, must be calculated and based upon a thorough knowledge of the people around you. It depends entirely upon the social and moral conditions of the people in their bearing on these deepest and most mysterious questions which can stir the human mind— the *deific* powers in man and the possibilities contained in nature. How many, even of your best friends, of those who surround you, who are more than superficially interested in these abstruse problems? You could count them upon the fingers of your right hand. Your race boasts of having liberated in their century the genius so long imprisoned in the narrow vase of dogmatism and intolerance—the genius of knowledge, wisdom and freethought. It says that in their turn ignorant prejudice and religious bigotry, bottled up like the wicked *Jin* of old, and sealed up by the Solomons of science, rests at the bottom of the sea and can never, escaping to the surface again, reign over the world as it did in days of old; that the public mind is quite free, in short, and ready to accept any demonstrated truth. Aye; but is it verily so, my respected friend? Experimental knowledge does not quite date from 1662, when Bacon, Robert Boyle and the Bishop of Rochester transformed under the royal charter their " Invisible College " into a Society for the promotion of experimental science. Ages before the Royal Society found itself becoming a reality upon the plan of the " Prophetic Scheme " an innate longing for the hidden, a passionate love for and the study of nature had led men in every generation to try and fathom her secrets deeper than their neighbours did. *Roma ante Romulum fuit*—is an axiom taught to us in your English schools. Abstract enquiries into the most puzzling problems did not arise in the brain of Archimedes as a spontaneous and hitherto untouched subject, but rather as a reflection of prior enquiries in the same direction and by men separated from his days by as long a period—and far longer—than the one which separates you from the great Syracusan. The *vril* of the " Coming Race " was the common property of races now extinct. And, as the very existence of those gigantic ancestors of ours is now questioned—though in the *Himavats*, on the very territory belonging to you we have a cave full of the skeletons of these giants—and their huge frames when found are invariably regarded as isolated freaks of nature, so the *vril* or *Akas*—as we call it—is looked upon as an impossibility, a myth. And, without a thorough knowledge of *Akas*, its combinations and properties, how can Science hope to account for such phenomena? We doubt not but the men of your science are open to conviction; yet facts must be first demonstrated to them, they must first have become their own property, have proved amenable to their own modes of investigation, before you find them ready to admit them as *facts*. If you but look into the *Preface* to the " Micrographia " you will find in Hooke's suggestions that the intimate relations of objects were of less account in his eyes than their external operation on the senses —and Newton's fine discoveries found in him their greatest opponent. The modern Hookeses are many. Like this learned but ignorant man of old your modern men of science are less anxious to suggest a physical connexion of facts which might unlock for them many an occult force in nature, than to provide a convenient " classification of scientific experiments "; so that the most essential quality of an hypothesis is not that it should be *true* but only *plausible*—in their opinion.

So far for Science—as much as we know of it. As for human nature in general, it is the same now as it was a million of years ago: Prejudice based upon selfishness; a general unwillingness to give up an established order of things for new modes of life and thought—and occult study requires all that and much more—; pride and stubborn resistance to Truth if it but upset their previous notions of things,—such are the characteristics of your age, and especially of the middle and lower classes. What then would be the results of the most astounding phenomena, supposing we consented to have them produced? However successful, danger would be growing proportionately with success. No choice would soon remain but to go on, ever *crescendo*, or to fall in this endless struggle with prejudice and ignorance killed by your own weapons. Test after test would be required and would have to be furnished; every subsequent phenomenon expected to be more marvellous than the preceding one. Your daily remark is, that one cannot be expected to believe unless he becomes an eye-witness. Would the lifetime of a man suffice to satisfy the whole world of skeptics? It may be an easy matter to increase the original number of believers at Simla to hundreds and thousands. But what of the hundreds of millions of those who could not be made eye-witnesses? The ignorant—unable to grapple with the invisible operators—might some day vent their rage on the visible agents at work; the higher and educated classes would go on disbelieving as ever, tearing you to shreds as before. In common with many, you blame us for our great secrecy. Yet we know something of human nature, for the experience of long centuries—aye, ages—has taught us. And we know, that so long as science has anything to learn, and a shadow of religious dogmatism lingers in the hearts of the multitudes, the world's prejudices have to be conquered step by step, not at a rush. As hoary antiquity had more than one Socrates so the dim Future will give birth to more than one martyr. Enfranchised science contemptuously turned away her face from the Copernican opinion renewing the theories of Aristarchus Samius, who " affirmeth that the earth moveth circularly about her own centre " years before the Church sought to sacrifice Galileo as a holocaust to the Bible. The ablest mathematician at the Court of Edward VI—Robert Recorde—was left to starve in jail by his colleagues, who laughed at his *Castle of Knowledge*, declaring his discoveries " vain phantasies." Wm. Gilbert of Colchester—Queen Elisabeth's physician—died poisoned, only because this real founder of experimental science in England has had the audacity of anticipating Galileo; of pointing out Copernicus' fallacy as to the " third movement," which was gravely alleged to account for the parallelism of the earth's axis of rotation! The enormous learning of the Paracelsi, of the Agrippas and the Dee's was ever doubted. It was science which laid her sacrilegious hand upon the great work " De Magnete ", " The Heavenly White Virgin " (*Akās*) and others. And it was the illustrious " Chancellor of England and of Nature "—Lord Verulam-Bacon—who having won the name of the Father of Inductive Philosophy, permitted himself to speak of such men as the above-named as the " Alchemicians of the Fantastic philosophy."

All this is old history, you will think. Verily so; but the chronicles of our modern days do not differ very essentially from their predecessors. And we have but to bear in mind the recent persecutions of mediums in England, the burning of supposed witches and sorcerers in South America, Russia and the frontiers of Spain—to assure ourselves that the only salvation of the genuine proficients in occult sciences lies in the skepticism of the public: the charlatans and the jugglers are the natural shields of the " adepts." The public safety is only ensured by our keeping secret the terrible weapons which might otherwise be used against it, and which, as you have been told became deadly in the hands of the wicked and selfish.

I conclude by reminding you that such phenomena as you crave, have ever been reserved as a reward for those who have devoted their lives to serve the goddess Saraswati—our Aryan *Isis*. Were they given to the profane what would remain for our faithful ones? Many of your suggestions are highly reasonable and will be attended to. I listened attentively to the conversation which took place at Mr. Hume's. His arguments are perfect from the standpoint of exoteric wisdom. But, when the time comes and he is allowed to have a full glimpse into the world of *esotericism*, with its laws based upon mathematically correct calculations of the future—the necessary results of the causes which we are always at liberty to create and shape at our will but are as unable to control their consequences which thus become our masters—then only will both you and he understand why to the uninitiated our acts must seem often unwise, if not actually foolish.

Your forthcoming letter I will not be able to fully answer without taking the advice of those who generally deal with the European mystics. Moreover the present letter must satisfy you on many points you have better defined in your last; but it will no doubt disappoint you as well. In regard to the production of newly devised and still more startling phenomena demanded of her with our help, as a man well acquainted with strategy you must remain satisfied with the reflection that there is little use in acquiring new positions until those that you have already reached are secured, and your Enemies fully aware of your right to their possession. In other words, you had a greater variety of phenomena produced for yourself and friends than many a regular neophyte has seen in several years. First, notify the public of the production of the note, the cup and the sundry experiments with the cigarette papers, and let them digest these. Get them to work for an explanation. And as except upon the direct and absurd accusation of deceit they will never be able to account for some of these, while the skeptics are quite satisfied with their present hypothesis for the production of the brooch—you will then have done real good to the cause of truth and justice to the woman who is made to suffer for it. Isolated as it is, the case under notice in the *Pioneer* becomes less than worthless—it is positively injurious for all of you—for yourself as the Editor of that paper as much as for anyone else, if you pardon me for offering you that which looks like advice. It is neither fair to yourself nor to her, that, because the number of eye-witnesses does not seem sufficient to warrant the public attention, your and your lady's testimony should go for nothing. Several cases combining to fortify your position as truthful and intelligent witness to the various occurrences, each of these gives you an additional right to assert what you know. It imposes upon you the sacred duty to instruct the public and prepare them for future possibilities by gradually opening their eyes to the truth. The opportunity should not be lost through a lack of as great confidence in your own individual right of assertion as that of Sir Donald Stewart. One witness of well known character outweighs the evidence of ten strangers; and if there is anyone in India who is respected for his trustworthiness it is—the Editor of the *Pioneer*. Remember that there was but one hysterical woman alleged to have been present at the pretended ascension, and that the phenomenon has never been corroborated by repetition. Yet for nearly 2,000 years countless milliards have pinned their faith upon the testimony of that one woman—and she not over trustworthy.

TRY—and first work upon the material you have and then we will be the first to help you to get further evidence. Until then, believe me, always your sincere friend,

KOOT' HOOMI LAL SINGH.

LETTER No. 2

Received Simla, October 19th, 1880.

Much Esteemed Sir and Brother,

We will be at cross purposes in our correspondence until it has been made entirely plain that occult science has its own methods of research as fixed and arbitrary as the methods of its antithesis physical science are in their way. If the latter has its dicta so also has the former; and he who would cross the boundary of the unseen world can no more prescribe how he will proceed than the traveller who tries to penetrate to the inner subterranean recesses of L'Hassa—the blessed, could show the way to his guide. The mysteries never were, never can be, put within the reach of the general public, not, at least, until that longed for day when our religious philosophy becomes universal. At no time have more than a scarcely appreciable minority of men possessed nature's secret, though multitudes have witnessed the practical evidences of the possibility of their possession. The adept is the rare efflorescence of a generation of enquirers; and to become one, he must obey the inward impulse of his soul irrespective of the prudential considerations of worldly science or sagacity. Your desire is to be brought to communicate with one of us directly, without the agency of either Mad. B. or any medium. Your idea would be, as I understand it, to obtain such communications either by letters—as the present one—or by audible words so as to be guided by one of us in the management and principally in the instruction of the Society. You seek all this, and yet, as you say yourself, hitherto you have not found " sufficient reasons " to even give up your " modes of life " directly hostile to such modes of communications. This is hardly reasonable. He who would lift up high the banner of mysticism and proclaim its reign near at hand, must give the example to others. He must be the first to change *his* modes of life; and, regarding the study of the occult mysteries as the upper step in the ladder of Knowledge must loudly proclaim it such despite exact science and the opposition of society. " The Kingdom of Heaven is obtained by force " say the Christian mystics. It is but with armed hand, and ready to either conquer or perish that the modern mystic can hope to achieve his object.

My first answer covered, I believed, most of the questions contained in your second and even third letter. Having then expressed therein my opinion that the world in general was unripe for any too staggering proof of occult power, there but remains to deal with the isolated individuals, who seek like yourself to penetrate behind the veil of matter into the world of primal causes, *i.e.*, we need only consider now the cases of yourself and Mr. Hume. This gentleman also, has done me the great honour to address me by name, offering to me a few questions and stating the conditions upon which he would be willing to work for us seriously. But your motives and aspirations being of diametrically opposite character, and hence—leading to different results, I must reply to each of you separately.

The first and chief consideration in determining us to accept or reject your offer lies in the inner-motive which propels you to seek our instructions, and in a certain sense—our guidance. The latter in all cases under reserve—as I understand it, and therefore remaining a question independent of aught else. Now, what are your motives? I may try to define them in their general aspect, leaving details for further consideration. They are (1) The desire to receive positive and unimpeachable proofs that there really are forces in nature of which science knows nothing; (2) The hope to appropriate them some day—the sooner the better, for you do not like to wait—so as to enable yourself—(*a*) to demonstrate their existence to a few chosen western minds; (*b*) to contemplate future life as an objective reality built upon the rock of Knowledge —not of faith; and (*c*) to finally learn—most important this, among all your motives, perhaps, though the most occult and the best guarded—the whole truth about our Lodges and ourselves; to get, in short, the positive assurance that the " Brothers "—of whom everyone hears so much and sees so little—are real entities, not fictions of a disordered, hallucinated brain. Such, viewed in their best light appear to us your " motives " for addressing me. And in the same spirit do I answer them, hoping that my sincerity will not be interpreted in a wrong way or attributed to anything like an unfriendly spirit.

To our minds then, these motives, sincere and worthy of every serious consideration from the worldly standpoint, appear—*selfish*. (You have to pardon me what you might view as crudeness of language, if your desire really is that which you profess—to learn truth and get instruction from us—who belong to quite a different world from the one you move in.) They are selfish because you must be aware that the chief object of the T.S. is not so much to

gratify individual aspirations as to serve our fellow men; and the
real value of this term " selfish," which may jar upon your ear,
has a peculiar significance with us which it cannot have with you;
therefore, and to begin with, you must not accept it otherwise than
in the former sense.   Perhaps you will better appreciate our meaning when told that in our view the highest aspirations for the welfare of humanity become tainted with selfishness if, in the mind
of the philanthropist, there lurks the shadow of desire for self benefit or a tendency to do injustice, even when these exist unconsciously to himself.   Yet, you have ever discussed but to put down
the idea of a universal Brotherhood, questioned its usefulness, and
advised to remodel the T.S. on the principle of a college for the
special study of occultism.   This, my respected and esteemed
friend and Brother—will never do!

Having disposed of " personal motives," let us analyze your
" terms " for helping us to do public good.   Broadly stated these
terms are—*first*: that an independent Anglo-Indian Theosophical
Society shall be founded through your kind services, in the
management of which neither of our present representatives shall
have any voice; and *second*, that one of us shall take the new
body " under his patronage," be " in free and direct communication with its leaders," and afford them " direct proof that he
really possessed that superior knowledge of the forces of nature
and the attributes of the human soul which would inspire them
with proper confidence in his leadership."   I have copied your
own words, so as to avoid inaccuracy in defining the position.

From your point of view then, those terms may seem so very
reasonable as to provoke no dissent; and, indeed, a majority of
your countrymen—if not of Europeans—might share that opinion.
What, will you say, can be more reasonable than to ask that
teacher—anxious to disseminate his knowledge, and pupil—offering him to do so, should be brought face to face and the one give
the experimental proofs to the other that his instructions were
correct? Man of the world, living in, and in full sympathy with it,
you are undoubtedly right.   But the men of this other world of
ours, untutored in your modes of thought, and who find [it] very
hard at times to follow and appreciate the latter, can hardly be
blamed for not responding as heartily to your suggestions as in your
opinion they deserve.   The first and most important of our objections is to be found in our *Rules*.   True, we have our schools
and teachers, our neophytes and shaberons (superior adepts), and
the door is always opened to the right man who knocks.   And
we invariably welcome the new comer; only, instead of going
over to him he has to come to us.   More than that; unless he has
reached that point in the path of occultism from which return
is impossible, by his having irrevocably pledged himself to our

association, we never—except in cases of utmost moment—visit him or even cross the threshold of his door in visible appearance.

Is any of you so eager for knowledge and the beneficent powers it confers as to be ready to leave your world and come into ours? Then let him come; but he must not think to return until the seal of the mysteries has locked his lips even against the chances of his own weakness or indiscretion. Let him come by all means, as the pupil to the master, and without conditions; or let him wait, as so many others have, and be satisfied with such crumbs of knowledge as may fall in his way.

And supposing you were thus to come—as two of your own countrymen have already—as Mad. B. did, and Mr. O. will; supposing you were to abandon all for the truth; to toil wearily for years up the hard steep road, not daunted by obstacles, firm under every temptation; were to faithfully keep within your heart the secrets entrusted to you as a trial; had worked with all your energy and unselfishly to spread the truth and provoke men to correct thinking and a correct life—would you consider it just, if, after all your efforts, we were to grant to Mad. B. or Mr. O. as "outsiders" the terms you now ask for yourselves? Of these two persons one has already given three-fourths of a life, the other six years of manhood's prime to us, and both will so labour to the close of their days, though ever working for their merited reward, yet never demanding it, nor murmuring when disappointed. Even though they respectively could accomplish far less than they do, would it not be a palpable injustice to ignore them as proposed in an important field of Theosophical effort? Ingratitude is not among our vices, nor do we imagine you would wish to advise it. . . .

Neither of them has the least inclination to interfere with the management of the contemplated Anglo-Indian Branch, nor dictate its officers. But, the new society, if formed at all, must (though bearing a distinctive title of its own) be, in fact, a Branch of the Parent body as is the British Theosophical Society at London, and contribute to its vitality and usefulness by promoting its leading idea of a Universal Brotherhood, and in other practicable ways.

Badly as the phenomena may have been shown, there have still been—as yourself admit—certain ones that are unimpeachable. The "raps on the table when no one touches it," and the "bell sounds in the air" have, you say, "always been regarded as satisfactory," etc., etc. From this, you reason that good "test phenomena" may easily be multiplied *ad infinitum.* So they can—in any place where our magnetic and other conditions are constantly offered; and where we do not have to act with and through an enfeebled female body in which, as we might say, a vital cyclone is raging much of the time. But, imperfect as may be our visible agent—and often most unsatisfactory and imperfect she is—yet she is the best available at present, and her phenomena have for about half a century astounded and baffled some of the cleverest minds of the age. If ignorant of "journalistic etiquette" and the requirements of physical science, we still have an intuition of the effects of causes. Since you have written nothing about the very phenomena you properly regard as so convincing we have the right to infer that much precious power may be wasted without better results. By itself the "brooch" affair is—in the eyes of the world—completely useless, and time will prove me right. Your kind intention has entirely failed.

To conclude: we are ready to continue this correspondence if the view given of occult study as above suits you. Through the ordeal described, each of us, whatever his country, or race, has passed. Meanwhile, hoping in the best—yours faithfully as ever

KOOT' HOOMI LAL SINGH.

LETTER No. 3A.

I saw K. H. in astral form on the night of 19th of October, 1880—waking up for a moment but immediately afterwards being rendered unconscious again (in the body) and conscious out of the body in the adjacent dressing-room where I saw another of the Brothers afterwards identified with one called "Serapis" by Olcott,—"the youngest of the chohans."

The note about the vision came the following morning, and during that day, the 20th, we went for a picnic to Prospect Hill, when the "pillow incident" occurred.

My Good "Brother,"

In dreams and *visions* at least, when rightly interpreted there can hardly be an "element of doubt.". . . . I hope to prove to you my presence near you last night by something I took away with me. Your lady will receive it back on the Hill. I keep no pink paper to write upon, but I trust modest white will do as well for what I have to say.

KOOT' HOOMI LAL SINGH.

LETTER No. 3B.

My "Dear Brother,"

This brooch, No. 2, is placed in this very strange place simply to show to you how very easily a real phenomenon is produced and how still easier it is to suspect its genuineness. Make of it what you like even to classing me with confederates.

The difficulty you spoke of last night with respect to the interchange of our letters I will try to remove. One of our pupils will shortly visit Lahore and the N.W.P. and an address will be sent to you which you can always use; unless, indeed, you really would prefer corresponding through—pillows. Please to remark that the present is not dated from a " Lodge " but from a Kashmir valley.

Yours, more than ever,

KOOT' HOOMI LAL SINGH.

LETTER No. 3c.

A few words more: why should you have felt disappointed at not receiving a direct reply to your last note? It was received in my room about half a minute after the currents for the production of the pillow-*dāk* had been set ready and in full play. And—unless I had assured you that a man of your disposition need have little fear of being " fooled "—there was no necessity for an answer. One favour I will certainly ask of you, and that is, that now that you—the only party to whom anything was ever promised—are satisfied, that you should endeavour to disabuse the mind of the amorous Major and show to him his great folly and injustice.

Yours faithfully,

KOOT' HOOMI LAL SINGH.

LETTER No. 4

Apparently received 5th November.

Madam and Colonel O. arrived at our house, Allahabad, on December the 1st, 1880. Col. O. went to Benares on the 3rd—Madam joined him on the 11th. Both returned to Allahabad on 20th and stayed until 28th.

Amrita Saras,[1] Oct. 29.

My Dear Brother,

I could assuredly make no objection to the style which you have kindly adopted, in addressing me by name, since it is, as you say the outcome of a personal regard even greater than I have as yet deserved at your hands. The conventionalities of the weary world, outside our secluded " Ashrams," trouble us but little at any time; least of all now, when it is men not ceremony-masters, we seek, devotion, not mere observances. More and more a dead formalism is gaining ground, and I am truly happy to find so unexpected an ally in a quarter where, hitherto there have not been too many—among the highly educated classes of English Society. A crisis, in a certain sense, is upon us now, and must be met. I might say two crises—one, the Society's, the other for Tibet. For, I may tell you in confidence, that Russia is gradually massing her forces for a future invasion of that country under the pretext of a Chinese War. If she does not succeed it will be due to us; and herein, at least we will deserve your gratitude. You see then, that we have weightier matters than small societies to think about; yet, the T.S. must not be neglected. The affair has taken

---

[1] Usual English spelling " Amritsar ".—EDS

an impulse, which, if not well guided, might beget very evil issues. Recall to mind the avalanches of your admired Alps, that you have often thought about, and remember that at first their mass is small and their momentum little. A trite comparison you may say, but I cannot think of a better illustration, when viewing the gradual aggregation of trifling events, growing into a menacing destiny for the Theos. Soc. It came quite forcibly upon me the other day as I was coming down the defiles of Kouenlun—Kara-korum you call them—and saw an avalanche tumble. I had gone personally to our chief to submit Mr. Hume's important offer, and was crossing over to Ladakh on my way home. What other speculations might have followed I cannot say. But just as I was taking advantage of the awful stillness which usually follows such cataclysm, to get a clearer view of the present situation and the disposition of the " mystics " at Simla, I was rudely recalled to my senses. A familiar voice, as shrill as the one attributed to Saraswati's peacock—which, if we may credit tradition, frightened off the King of the Nagas—shouted along the currents " Olcott has raised the very devil again! . . . The Englishmen are going crazy. . . . Koot Hoomi, *come quicker* and help me! "—and in her excitement forgot she was speaking English. I must say, that the " Old Lady's " telegrams do strike one like stones from a catapult!

What could I do but come? Argument through space with one who was in cold despair, and in a state of moral chaos was useless. So I determined to emerge from the seclusion of many years and spend some time with her to comfort her as well as I could. But our friend is not one to cause her mind to reflect the philosophical resignation of Marcus Aurelius. The fates never wrote that she could say: " It is a royal thing, when one is doing good to hear evil spoken of himself.". . . I had come for a few days, but now find that I myself cannot endure for any length of time the stifling magnetism even of my own countrymen. I have seen some of our proud old Sikhs drunk and staggering over the marble pavement of their sacred Temple. I have heard an English-speaking Vakil declaim against *Yog Vidya* and Theosophy, as a delusion and a lie, declaring that English Science had emancipated them from such " degrading superstitions," and saying that it was an insult to India to maintain that the dirty Yogees and Sannyasis knew anything about the mysteries of nature; or that any living man can or ever could perform any phenomena! I turn my face homeward to-morrow.

The delivery of this letter may very possibly be delayed for a few days, owing to causes which it will not interest you for me to specify. Meanwhile, however, I have telegraphed you my thanks for your obliging compliance with my wishes in the matters you allude to in your letter of the 24th inst. I see with pleasure, that you have not failed to usher me before the world as a possible "confederate." That makes our number *ten*, I believe? But I must say, that your promise was well and loyally fulfilled. Received at Amritsar on the 27th inst., at 2 p.m., I got your letter about thirty miles beyond Rawalpindi, five minutes later, and had an acknowledgment wired to you from Jhelum at 4 p.m., on the same afternoon. Our modes of accelerated delivery and quick communications are not then, as you will see, to be despised by the Western world, or even the Aryan, English-speaking and skeptical Vakils.

I could not ask a more judicial frame of mind in an ally than that in which you are beginning to find yourself. My Brother, you have already changed your attitude toward us in a distinct degree: what is to prevent a perfect mutual understanding one day!

Mr. Hume's proposition has been duly and carefully considered. He will, no doubt, advise you of the results as expressed in my letter to him. Whether he will give our " modes of action " as fair a trial as yourself—is another question. Our *Maha* (the " Chief ") has allowed me to correspond with both of you, and even—in case an Anglo-Indian Branch is formed—to come some day in personal contact with it. It now depends entirely on you. I *cannot* tell you more. You are quite right as to the standing of our friends in the Anglo-Indian world having been materially improved by the Simla visit; and, it is also true, though you modestly refrain from saying so, that we are mainly indebted to you for this. But quite apart from the unlucky incidents of the Bombay publications, it *is not possible* that there should be much more at best than a benevolent neutrality shown by your people toward ours. There is so very minute a point of contact between the two civilisations they respectively represent, that one might almost say they could not touch at all. Nor would they but for the few—shall I say eccentrics?—who, like you, dream better and bolder dreams than the rest; and provoking thought, bring the two together by their own admirable audacity. Has it occurred to you that the two Bombay publications, if not influenced, may at least have not been prevented, by those who might have done so, because they saw the necessity for that much agitation to effect the double result of making a needed diversion after the Brooch Grenade, and, perhaps, of trying the strength of your personal interest in occultism and theosophy? I do not say it *was* so; I but enquire whether the contingency ever presented itself to your mind. I have already caused it to be intimated to you that if the details given in the stolen letter had been anticipated in the *Pioneer*—a much more appropriate place, and where they would have been handled to better advantage—that document would not have been worth anyone's while to purloin for the *Times of India*, and therefore *no names* would have appeared.

Colonel Olcott is doubtless " out of time [1] with the feelings of English people " of both classes; but nevertheless more in time *with us* than either. Him we can trust under *all* circumstances, and his faithful service is pledged to us come well, come ill. My dear Brother, my voice is the echo of impartial justice. Where can we find an equal devotion? He is one who never questions, but obeys; who may make innumerable mistakes out of excessive zeal but never is unwilling to repair his fault even at the cost of the greatest self-humiliation; who esteems the sacrifice of comfort and even life something to be cheerfully risked whenever necessary; who will eat any food, or even go without; sleep on any bed, work in any place, fraternise with any outcast, endure any privation for the cause. . . . I admit that his connection with an A.I. Branch would be " an evil "—hence, he will have no more to do with it than he has with the British (London Branch). His connection will be purely nominal, and may be made more so, by framing your *Rules* more carefully than theirs; and giving your organization such a self-acting system of Government as would seldom if ever require any outside interference. But to make an independent A.I.B., with the self-same objects, either in whole or a part, as the Parent Society and with the same directors behind the scenes would be not only to deal a mortal blow at the Theos. Soc., but also put upon us a double labour and anxiety without the slightest compensating advantage that any of us can perceive. The Parent S. has never interfered in the slightest degree with the British T.S., nor indeed with any other Branch, whether religious or philosophical. Having formed, or caused to be formed a new branch, the Parent S. charters it (which it cannot now do without our Sanction and signatures), and then usually retires behind the scenes, as you would say. Its further connection with the subject branches is limited to receiving quarterly accounts of their doings and lists of the new Fellows, ratifying expulsions—only when specially called upon as an arbitrator to interfere on account of the Founders' direct connection with us—etc., etc.; it never meddles otherwise in their affairs except when appealed to as a sort of appellate court. And the latter depending on you, what is there to prevent your Society from remaining virtually independent? We are even more generous than you British are to us. We will not force upon, nor even ask you to sanction a Hindu " Resident " in your Society, to watch the interests of the Parent Paramount Power when we have once declared you independent; but will implicitly trust to your loyalty and word of honour. But if you now so dislike the idea of a purely

[1] *Sic.* But see Letter 5, p. 19.—Eds.

nominal executive supervision by Col. Olcott—an American of
your own race—you would surely rebel against dictation from a
Hindu, whose habits and methods are those of his own people, and
whose race, despite your natural benevolence, you have not yet
learnt even to tolerate, let alone to love or respect. Think well
before you ask for our guidance. Our best, most learned, and
holiest adepts are of the races of the " greasy Tibetans ", and the
Punjabi Singhs—you know the lion is proverbially a dirty and
offensive beast, despite his strength and courage. Is it certain
that your good compatriots would more easily forgive our Hindu
solecisms in manners than those of their own kinsmen of
America? If my observations have not misled [me] I should say
this was doubtful. National prejudices are apt to leave one's
spectacles undimmed.[1] You say " how glad we should be, if that
one (to guide you) were yourself," meaning your unworthy correspondent. My good Brother, are you certain, that the pleasant
impression you now may have from our correspondence would not
instantly be destroyed upon seeing me? And which of our holy
Shaberons has had the benefit of even the little university education and inkling of European manners that has fallen to my
share? An instance: I desired Mad. B. to select among the two
or three Aryan Punjabees who study *Yog Vidya*, and are natural
mystics, one whom—without disclosing myself to him too much—I
could designate as an agent between yourself and us, and whom
I was anxious to despatch to you, with a letter of introduction,.
and have him speak to you of *Yoga* and its practical effects. This
young gentleman who is as pure as purity itself, whose aspirations
and thoughts are of the most spiritual ennobling kind, and who
merely through self-exertion is able to penetrate into the
regions of the formless worlds—this young man is not fit for—a
drawing-room. Having explained to him that the greatest good
might result for his country if he helped you to organize a Branch
of English mystics by proving to them *practically* to what wonderful results led the study of Yog, Mad. B. asked him in guarded
and very delicate terms to change his dress and turban before
starting for Allahabad—for, though she did not give him this
reason, they were *very dirty and slovenly.* You are to tell Mr.
Sinnett, she said, that you bring him a letter from our Brother
K., with whom he corresponds, but, if he asks you anything
either of him or the other Brothers, answer him simply and truthfully that you are not allowed to expatiate upon the subject. Speak
of Yog and prove to him what powers you have attained. This
young man, who had consented, wrote later on the following
curious letter: " Madam," he said, " you who preach the highest
standards of morality, of truthfulness, etc., you would have me

[1] Query bedimmed.—EDS.

play the part of an impostor. You ask me to *change my clothes* at the risk of giving a false idea of my personality and mystifying the gentleman you send me to. And what if he asks me if I personally know Koot'hoomi, am I to keep silent and allow him to think I do? This would be a tacit falsehood, and guilty of that, I would be thrown back into the awful whirl of transmigration! " Here is an illustration of the difficulties under which we have to labour. Powerless to send to you a *neophyte* before you have pledged yourself to us—we have to either keep back or despatch to you one who at best would shock if not inspire you at once with disgust! The letter would have been given him by my own hand; he had but to promise to hold his tongue upon matters he knows nothing about and could give but a false idea of, and to make himself look cleaner. Prejudice and dead letter again. For over a thousand years,—says Michelet,—the Christian Saints never washed themselves! For how long will our Saints dread to change their clothes for fear of being taken for Marmaliks [1] and the neophytes of rival and cleaner sects!

But these, our difficulties, ought not to prevent you from beginning your work. Colonel O. and Mad. B. seeming willing to become *personally responsible* for both yourself and Mr. Hume, if you yourself are ready to answer for the fidelity of any man your party may choose as the leader of the A.I.T.S., we are content that the trial shall be made. The field is yours and no one will be allowed to interfere with you except myself on behalf of our Chiefs when you once do me the honour to prefer me to the others. But before one builds the house he makes the plan. Suppose you draft a memorandum as to the constitution and policy of management of the A.I. Society you have in mind and submit it for consideration? If our Chiefs agree to it—and it is not surely they who would show themselves obstructive in the universal onward march, or retard this movement to a higher goal—then you will at once be chartered. But they must first see the plan; and I must ask you to remember that the new Society shall not be allowed to disconnect itself with the Parent Body, though you are at liberty to manage your affairs in your own way without fearing the slightest interference from its President so long as you do not violate the general Rule. And upon this point I refer you to Rule 9. This is the first practical suggestion coming from a *Cis* and *Trans*-Himalayan " cave-dweller " whom you have honoured with your confidence.

And now about yourself personally. Far be it from me to discourage one so willing as yourself by setting up impossible barriers to your progress. We never whine over the inevitable but try to make the best of the worst. And though we neither push nor draw into the mysterious domain of occult nature those who are

[1] Query Mlechchas (barbarians).—EDS.

unwilling; never shrink from expressing our opinions freely
and fearlessly, yet we are ever as ready to assist those who come
to us; even to—*agnostics* who assume the negative position of
" *knowing nothing* but *phenomena and refuse to believe in anything else.*" It is true that the marrried man cannot be an
adept, yet without striving to become " a *Raja* Yogi " he can
acquire certain powers and do as much good to mankind and
often more, by remaining within the precincts of this world of his.
Therefore, shall we not ask you to precipitately change fixed
habits of life, before the full conviction of its necessity and advantage has possessed you. You are a man to be left to lead himself
and may be so left with safety. Your resolution is taken to
deserve much: time will effect the rest. There are more ways
than one for acquiring occult knowledge. " Many are the grains
of incense destined for one and the same altar: one falls sooner
into the fire, the other later—the difference of time is nothing,"
remarked a great man when he was refused admission and
supreme initiation into the mysteries. There is a tone of complaint in your question whether there ever will be a renewal of the
vision you had, the night before the picnic day. Methinks, were
you to have a vision nightly, you would soon cease to " treasure "
them at all. But there is a far weightier reason why you should
not have a surfeit—it would be a waste of our strength. As often
as I, or any of us can communicate with you, whether by dreams,
waking impressions, letters (in or out of pillows) or personal visits
in astral form—it will be done. But remember that Simla is 7,000
feet higher than Allahabad, and the difficulties to be surmounted
at the latter are tremendous. I abstain from encouraging you to
expect too much, for, like yourself, I am loath to promise what,
for various reasons, I may not be able to perform.

The term " Universal Brotherhood " is no idle phrase.
Humanity in the mass has a paramount claim upon us, as I try
to explain in my letter to Mr. Hume, which you had better ask
the loan of. It is the only secure foundation for universal
morality. If it be a dream, it is at least a noble one for mankind:
and it is the aspiration of the *true adept*.

Yours faithfully,
KOOT' HOOMI LAL SINGH.

LETTER No. 5

My Dear Friend,
I have your letter of November 19th, abstracted by our special
osmosis from the envelope at Meerut, and yours to our " old lady "
in its half empty registered shell safely sent on to Cawnpore, to
make her swear at me. . . . . But she is too weak to play at the

astral postman just now. I am sorry to see that she has once more proved inaccurate and led you into error; but this is chiefly my own fault, as I often neglect to give her an extra rub over her poor sick head, now, when she forgets and mixes up things more than usual. I did not ask her to tell you " to give up the idea of the A.I. Branch as nothing would come of it," but—" to give up the idea of the Anglo-Indian Branch *in co-operation with Mr. Hume*, as nothing would come of it." I will send you his answer to my letter and my final epistle and you will judge for yourself. After reading the latter, you will please seal and send it to him, simply stating that you do so on my behalf. Unless he asks the question you better not let him know you have read his letter. He *may* be proud of it, but—*should* not.

My dear, good friend, you must not bear me a grudge for what I say to him of the Eaglish in general. They *are* haughty. To us especially, so that we regard it as a national feature. And, you must not confound your own private views—especially those you have now—with those of your countrymen in general. Few, if any—(of course with such exceptions as yourself, where intensity of aspirations makes one disregard all other considerations)—would ever consent to have " a nigger " for a guide or leader, no more than a modern Desdemona would choose an Indian Othello nowadays. The prejudice of race is intense, and even in free England we are regarded as an " inferior race." And this same tone vibrates in your own remark about " a man of the people unused to refined ways " and " a foreigner but a gentleman," the latter being the man to be preferred. Nor would a Hindu be likely to have such a lack of " refined ways" disregarded in him were he " an adept " twenty times over again; and this very same trait appears prominent in Viscount Amberley's criticism on the " underbred Jesus." Had you paraphrased your sentence and said:—" a foreigner but *no* gentleman " (according to English notions) you could not have added as you did, that he would be thought the fittest. Hence, I say it again, that the majority of our Anglo-Indians, among whom the term " Hindu " or " Asiatic " is generally coupled with a vague yet actual idea of one who uses his fingers instead of a bit of cambric, and who abjures soap—would most certainly prefer an American to " a greasy Tibetan." But you need not tremble for me. Whenever I make my appearance—whether astrally or physically—before my friend A. P. Sinnett, I will not forget to invest a certain sum in a square of the finest Chinese silk to carry in my *chogga* pocket, nor to create an atmosphere of sandal-wood and cashmere roses. This is the least I could do in atonement for my countrymen. But then, you see, I am but a slave of my masters; and if allowed to gratify my own friendly feeling for you, and attend to you *individually*, I may not be permitted to do as much for others. Nay, to tell truth, I *know* I am not permitted to do so, and Mr. Hume's unfortunate letter has contributed much to it.   There is a distinct group or section in our fraternity who attend to our casual and very rare accessions of another race and blood, and who brought across the threshold Captain Remington and two other Englishmen during this century.   And these " Brothers "—do not habitually use floral essences.

So the *test* of the 27th was *no* test phenomenon? Of course, of course.   But did you try to get, as you said you would, the original MS. of the Jhelum dispatch?   Though our hollow but plethoric friend, Mrs. B., were even proved to be my *multum in parvo*, my letter-writer, and to manufacture my epistles, yet, unless she were ubiquitous or had the gift of flying from Amritsar to Jhelum—a distance over 200 miles—in two minutes, how could she have written for me the dispatch in my own hand-writing at Jhelum hardly two hours after your letter was received by her at Amritsar? This is why I was not sorry that you said you would send for it, for, with this dispatch in your possession, no " detractors " would be very strong, nor even the sceptical logic of Mr. Hume prevail.

Naturally you imagine that the " nameless revelation "—which now re-echoes in England—would have been pounced upon far more eagerly than even it was, by the *Times of India*, if it revealed the names.   But here again, I will prove you wrong.   Had you first printed the account, the *T. of I.* could never have published " A day with Madame B.," since that nice bit of American " sensationalism " would not have been written by Olcott at all It would not have had its *raison d'être*.   Anxious to collect for his Society every proof corroborative of the occult powers of what he terms the 1st Section, and seeing that you remained silent, our gallant Colonel felt his hand itch until it brought everything to light, and—plunged everything into darkness and consternation! . . . " Et voici pourquoi nous n'irons plus au bois," as the French song goes.

Did you write " tune "? Well, well; I must ask you to buy me a pair of spectacles in London.   And yet—out of " time " or out of " tune " is all one, as it seems.   But you ought to adopt my old fashioned habit of " little lines " over the " m's."   Those bars are useful, even though " out of tune and time " with modern calligraphy.   Besides, bear in mind, that these my letters, are not written but *impressed* or precipitated and then all mistakes corrected.

We will not discuss, at present, whether your aims and objects are so widely different from those of Mr. Hume's; but if he may be actuated by " a purer and broader philanthropy," the way he sets to work to achieve these aims will never carry him beyond pure theoretical disquisitions upon the subject.   No use now in trying to represent him in any other light. His letter that you will soon read is, as I say to himself, " a monument of pride and unconcious selfishness." He is too just and superior a man to be guilty of petty vanities; but his pride climbs like that of the mythical Lucifer; and, you may believe me—if I have any experience in human nature—when I say, that this is Hume—*au naturel*. It is no hasty conclusion of mine based upon any personal feeling, but the decision of the greatest of our living adepts—the Shaberon of Than-La. On whatever question he touches his treatment is the same; a stubborn determination to make everything either fit his own foregone conclusions or—sweep it away by a rush of ironical and adverse criticism. Mr. Hume is a very able man and—Hume to the core. Such a state of mind offers little attraction, as you will understand, to any of us who might be willing to come and help him.

No; I do not and never will " despise " any " feeling," however it may clash with my own principles, when it is expressed as frankly and openly as yours. You may be, and undoubtedly are, moved by more egotism than broad benevolence for mankind. Yet as you confess it without mounting any philanthropical stilts, I tell you candidly that you have far more chances than Mr. Hume to learn a good bit of occultism. I, for one, will do all I can for you, under the circumstances and restrained as I am by fresh *orders*. I will not tell you to give up this or that, for, unless you exhibit *beyond any doubt* the presence in you of the necessary *germs* it would be as useless as it would be cruel. But I say— TRY. Do not despair. Unite to yourself several determined men and women and make experiments in mesmerism and the usual so-called " spiritual " phenomena. If you act in accordance with prescribed methods you are sure to ultimately obtain results. Apart from this, I will do my best and—who knows! *Strong will creates* and sympathy attracts even adepts, whose laws are antagonistic to their mixing with the uninitiated. If you are willing I will send you an *Essay* showing why in Europe more than anywhere else a *Universal Brotherhood*, i.e., an association of "affinities " of strong magnetic yet dissimilar forces and polarities, centred around one dominant idea, is necessary for successful achievements in occult sciences. What one will fail to do—the combined many will achieve. Of course you will have—in case you organise—to put up with Olcott at the head of the Parent Society, hence—nominally the President of all the existing Branches. But he will be no more your " leader " than he is the leader of the British Theos. Society, which has its own President, its own *Rules* and Bye-laws. You will be chartered by him, and that's all. In some cases he will have to sign a paper or two— 4 times a year the accounts sent in by your Secretary; yet he has *no right* to interfere either with your administration or modes of action, so long as these do not clash with the general *Rules,* and he certainly has neither the ability nor the desire of being your leader. And, of course, you (meaning the whole Society) will have besides your own President chosen by yourselves, " a qualified professor of occultism " to instruct you. But, my good friend, abandon all notion that this " Professor " can bodily appear and instruct you for years to come. *I* may come to you personally— unless you drive me off, as Mr. Hume did—I *cannot* come to ALL. You may get phenomena and proofs, but even were you to fall into the old error and attribute them to " Spirits " we could but show you your mistake by philosophical and logical explanations; no adept would be allowed to attend your meetings.

Of course you ought to write your book. I do not see why in any case it should be impracticable. Do so, by all means, and any help I can give you I will. You ought to put yourself immediately in correspondence with Lord Lindsay, and take the Simla phenomena and your correspondence with me as the subject. He is intensely interested in all such experiments, and being a theosophist and upon the General Council is sure to welcome your overtures. Take the ground that you belong to the T.S., that you are the widely known Editor of the " *Pioneer,*" and that, knowing how great an interest he takes in the " spiritual " phenomena, you submit to his consideration the very extraordinary things which took place at Simla, with such additional details as have not been published. The best of the British Spiritualists could, with proper management, be converted into Theosophists. But neither Dr. Wyld, nor Mr. Massey, seem to have the requisite force. I advise you to confer personally with Lord Lindsay upon the theosophical situation at home and in India. Perhaps you two might work together: the correspondence I now suggest will pave the way.

Even if Madame B. might " be induced " to give the A.I. Society any " practical instruction " I am afraid she has remained too long a time outside the *adytum* to be of much use for practical *explanations.* However, though it does not depend upon me, I will see what I can do in this direction. But I fear she is sadly in need of a few months of recuperative *villegiatura* on the glaciers, with her old Master before she can be entrusted with such a difficult task. Be very cautious with her in case she stops with you on her way down home. Her nervous system is terribly shaken, and she requires every care. Will you please spare me needless trouble by informing me of the year, date, and hour of Mrs. Sinnett's birth?

Ever yours sincerely,
KOOT' HOOMI.

LETTER No. 6

Received at Allahabad about December 10th, 1880.

No—you do not " write too much." I am only sorry to have so little time at my disposal; hence—to find myself unable to answer you as speedily as I otherwise would. Of course *I have to read* every word you write: otherwise I would make a fine mess of it. And whether it be through my physical or spiritual eyes the time required for it is practically the same. As much may be said of my replies. For, whether I " precipitate " or dictate them or write my answers myself, the difference in time saved is very minute. I have to *think* it over, to photograph every word and sentence carefully in my brain before it can be repeated by " precipitation." As the fixing on chemically prepared surfaces of the images formed by the camera requires a previous arrangement within the focus of the object to be represented, for otherwise—as often found in bad photographs—the legs of the sitter might appear out of all proportion with the head, and so on, so we have to first arrange our sentences and impress every letter to appear on paper in our minds before it becomes fit to be read. For the present, it is *all* I can tell you. When science will have learned more about the mystery of the *lithophyl* (or lithobiblion) and how the impress of leaves comes originally to take place on stones, then will I be able to make you better understand the process. But you must know and remember one thing: we but follow and *servilely copy nature* in her works.

No; we need argue no longer upon the unfortunate question of a " Day with Mad. B." It is the more useless, since you say, you have no right to crush and grind your uncivil and often blackguardly opponents in the " *Pioneer* "—even in your own defence—your proprietors objecting to the mention of occultism altogether. As they are Christians it is no matter of great wonder. Let us be charitable and hope they will get their own reward: die and become angels of light and Truth—winged paupers of the Christian heaven.

Unless you join several, and organize somehow or other, I am afraid I will prove but of little help for you practically. My dear friend, I have my " proprietors " also. For reasons best known to themselves they have set their foot upon the idea of teaching isolated individuals. I will correspond with you and give you proof from time to time of my existence and presence. To teach or instruct you—is altogether another question. Hence to sit with your lady is more than useless. Your magnetisms are too similar and—you will get nothing.

I will translate my *Essay* and send it to you as soon as I can. Your idea of corresponding with your friends and fellows is the next best thing to do. But do not fail to write to Lord Lindsay.

I am a little " too hard " upon Hume, you say. Am I? His is a highly intellectual and, I confess, a spiritual nature too. Yet he is every bit of him " Sir Oracle." It may be that it is the very exuberance of that great intellect which seeks issue through every chink, and never loses an opportunity to relieve the fulness of the brain, which overflows with thought. Finding in his quiet daily life too meagre a field with but " Moggy " and Davison to sow upon—his intellect bursts the dam and pounces upon every imagined event, every possible though improbable fact his imagination can suggest, to interpret it in his own conjectural way. Nor do I wonder that such a skilled workman in intellectual mosaic as he, finding suddenly the most fertile of quarries, the most precious of colour-stores in this idea of our Fraternity and the T.S.—should pick out ingredients from it to daub our faces with. Placing us before a mirror which reflects us as he finds us in his own fertile imagination he says: " Now, you mouldy relics of a mouldy Past, look at yourselves how you *really* are! " A very, very excellent man our friend Mr. Hume, but utterly unfit for moulding into an *adept*.

As little, and far less than yourself does he seem to realize our real object in the formation of an A.I. Branch. The truths and mysteries of occultism constitute, indeed, a body of the highest spiritual importance, at once profound and practical for the world at large. Yet, it is not as a mere addition to the tangled mass of theory or speculation in the world of science that they are being given to you, but for their practical bearing on the interests of mankind. The terms " unscientific," " impossible," " hallucination," " impostor," have hitherto been used in a very loose, careless way, as implying in the occult phenomena something either mysterious and abnormal, or a premeditated imposture. And this is why our chiefs have determined to shed upon a few recipient minds more light upon the subject, and to prove to them that such manifestations are as reducible to law as the simplest phenomena of the physical universe. The wiseacres say: " The age of miracles is past," but we answer, " it never existed! " While not unparalelled, or without their counterpart in universal history, these phenomena must and WILL come with an overpowering influence upon the world of sceptics and bigots. They *have* to prove both destructive and constructive—*destructive* in the pernicious errors of the past, in the old creeds and superstitions which suffocate in their poisonous embrace like the Mexican weed nigh all mankind; but *constructive* of new institutions of a genuine, practical Brotherhood of Humanity where all will become co-workers of nature, will work for the good of mankind *with* and *through* the higher *planetary Spirits*—the only " Spirits " we believe in. Phenomenal elements, previously unthought of—undreamt of—will soon begin manifesting themselves day by day with constantly augmented force, and disclose at last the secrets of their mysterious workings. Plato was right[1]: *ideas* rule the world; and, as men's minds will receive *new* ideas, laying aside the old and effete, the world will advance; mighty revolutions will spring from them; creeds and even powers will crumble before their onward march crushed by the irresistible force. It will be just as impossible to resist their influx, when the time comes, as to stay the progress of the tide. But all this will come gradually on, and before it comes we have a duty set before us; that of sweeping away as much as possible the dross left to us by our pious forefathers. New ideas have to be planted on clean places, for these ideas touch upon the most momentous subjects. It is not physical phenomena but these universal ideas that we study, as to comprehend the former, we have to first understand the latter. They touch man's true position in the universe, in relation to his previous and future births; his origin and ultimate destiny; the relation of the mortal to the immortal; of the temporary to the eternal; of the finite to the infinite; ideas larger, grander, more comprehensive, recognising the universal reign of Immutable Law, unchanging and unchangeable in regard to which there is only an ETERNAL Now, while to uninitiated mortals time is past or future as related to their finite existence on this material speck of dirt. This is what we study and what many have solved.

And now it is your province to decide which will you have: the highest philosophy or simple exhibitions of occult powers. Of course this is by far not the last word between us and—you will have time to think it over. The *Chiefs* want a " Brotherhood of Humanity," a real Universal Fraternity started; an institution which would make itself known throughout the world and arrest the attention of the highest minds. I will send you my *Essay*. Will you be my co-worker and patiently wait for minor phenomena? I think I foresee the answer. At all events the holy lamp of spiritual light burning in you (however dimly) there is hope for you, and—for me, also. Yes; put yourself in search after natives if there are no English people to be had. But think you the spirit and power of persecution gone from this enlightened age? Time will prove. Meanwhile, being *human* I have to rest.

I took no sleep for over 60 hours.

Ever yours truly,
KOOT' HOOMI.

---

[1] For passages omitted from the Master's original Letter at this point see pp. 418-9.—EDS.

LETTER No. 7

Enclosed in Mad. B.'s from Bombay.   Received January 30th, 1881.

There is *no* fault on your part in the whole matter.   I am sorry you should think I am imputing any fault to you.   If anything, you might almost feel you had to blame *me* for giving you hopes without having the shadow of such a right.   I ought to have been less optimistic and then you would have been less sanguine in your expectations.   I really feel as if I had wronged you!   Happy, thrice happy and blessed are they, who have never consented to visit the world beyond their snow-capped mountains; whose physical eyes have never lost sight for one day of the endless ranges of hills, and the long unbroken line of eternal snows! Verily and indeed, do they live in, and have found their *Ultima Thule.* . . .

Why say you are a victim of circumstances, since nothing is yet seriously changed and that much, if not all, depends upon future developments?   You were *not* asked or expected to revolutionise your life habits, but at the same time you were warned not to expect too much as you are.   If you read between the lines you must have remarked what I said about the very narrow margin left to me for doing as *I* choose in the matter.   But despond not, for it is all but a matter of time.   The world was not evolved between two monsoons, my good friend.   If you had come to me as a boy of 17, before the world had put its heavy hand upon you, your task would have been twenty-fold easier. And now, we must take you, and you must see yourself as *you are*, not as the ideal human image which our emotional fancy always projects for us upon the glass.   Be patient, friend and brother; and I must repeat again—be our *helpful co-worker*; but in your own sphere, and according to your ripest judgment. Since our venerable Khobilgan has decreed in his wise prevision that I had no right to encourage you to enter a path where you would have to roll the stone of Sisyphus, held back as you surely would be by your previous and most sacred duties—we really must wait.   I know your motives are sincere and true, and that a real change, and in the right direction, has come over you, though even to yourself that change is imperceptible.   And—the chiefs know it too.   But, say they—motives are vapours, as attenuated as the atmospheric moisture; and, as the latter develops its dynamic energy for man's use only when concentrated and applied as steam or hydraulic power, so the practical value of good motives is best seen when they take the form of deeds. . . . " Yes, we will wait and see "—they say.   And now I have told you as much as I ever had the right to say.   You have more than once already helped this Society, even though you did not care for it yourself, and these deeds are upon record. Nay—they are even more meritorious in you than they would [be] in anyone else, considering your well grounded ideas of that poor organization at present. And you have thereby won a friend—one, far higher and better than myself—and one who will in future help me to defend your cause, able as he is to do it far more effectually than I can, for he belongs to the " foreign Section."

I believe I have laid down for you the general lines on which we wish the work of organizing—if possible—the Anglo-Indian Branch to proceed: the details must be left to you—if you are still willing to help me.

If you have anything to say or ask any questions, you better write to me and I will always answer your letters. But, ask for no phenomena for a while, as it is but such paltry manifestations which now stand in your way.

Yours ever truly,

K. H.

LETTER No. 8

Received through Mad. B.   About February 20th, 1881.

My dear friend, you are certainly on the right path; the path of deeds and actions, not mere words—may you live long and keep on! . . . I hope this will not be regarded by you as an encouragement to be " goody goody "—a happy expression which made me laugh—but you indeed step in as a kind of *Kalki Avatar* dispelling the shadows of " Kali-yug," the black night of the perishing T.S., and driving away before you the *fata morgana* of its *Rules*. I must cause the word *fecit* to appear after your name in invisible but indelible characters on the list of the General Council, as it may prove some day a secret door to the heart of the sternest of Khobilgans. . . .

Though a good deal occupied—alas, as usual—I must contrive to send you a somewhat lengthy farewell epistle before you take up a journey that may have most important results—and not alone for our cause. . . . You understand, do you not, that it is no fault of mine if I *cannot* meet you as I would? Nor is it yours, but rather that of your life-long environment and *a special delicate task I have been entrusted with since I knew you*. Do not blame me then, if I do not show myself in more tangible shape, as not you alone but I myself might desire! When I am not permitted to do so for Olcott—who has toiled for us these five years, how could I be for others who have undergone none of his training as yet? This applies equally to the case of the Lord Crawford and Balcarres, an excellent gentleman—imprisoned by the world. His is a sincere and noble, though may be a little too repressed nature. He asks what hope he may have? I say—*every hope.* For he has that within himself that so very few possess, an exhaustless source of magnetic fluid which, if he only had the time, he could call out in torrents and need no other master than himself. His own powers would do the work and his own great experience be a sure guide for him. But, he would have to guard against and avoid every *foreign influence*—especially those antagonistic to the nobler study of MAN as an integral Brahm, the microcosm free and entirely independent of either the help or control of the invisible agencies which the " new dispensation " (bombastic word!) calls " Spirits." His Lordship will understand my meaning without any further explanation: he is welcome to read this if he chooses, if the opinions of an obscure Hindu interest him. Were he a poor man, he might have become an English Dupotet, with the addition of great scientific attainments in exact science. But alas! what the peerage has gained psychology has lost. . . . And yet it is not too late. But see, even after mastering magnetic science and giving his powerful mind to the study of the noblest branches of exact science, how even he has failed to lift more than a small corner of the veil of mystery. Ah! that whirling, showy, glittering world, full of insatiable ambition, where family and the State parcel out between them a man's nobler nature, as two tigers a carcase, and leave him without hope or light! How many recruits could we not have from it, if no sacrifice were exacted! His Lordship's letter to you exhales an influence of sincerity tinged with regret. This is a good man at heart with latent capacity for being a far better and a happier one. Had his lot not been cast as it has, and had his intellectual power all been turned upon Soul-culture, he would have achieved much more than he ever dreamt. Out of such material were adepts made in the days of Aryan glory. But I must dwell no longer upon this case; and I crave his Lordship's pardon if, in the bitterness of my regret I over-stepped in any way the bounds of propriety, in this too free " psychometrical delineation of character " as the American mediums would express it . . . " full measure only bounds excess " but—I dare go no farther. Ah, my too positive and yet impatient friend, if you but had *such* latent capacities!

The " direct communication " with me of which you write in your supplement note, and the " enormous advantage " that it would bring " to the book itself, if it can be conceded," would be so conceded at once, did it depend but on me alone. Though it is not often judicious to repeat oneself, yet I am so anxious that you should realize the present impracticability of such an arrangement, were it even conceded by our Superiors, that I will indulge in a brief retrospect of principles stated.

We might leave out of the question the most vital point—one, you would hesitate perhaps to believe—that the refusal concerns as much *your own salvation* (from the standpoint of your worldly material considerations) as my enforced compliance with our time honoured *Rules*. Again I might cite the case of Olcott (who, had he not been permitted to communicate face to face—and without any intermediary—with us, might have subsequently shown less zeal and devotion but more discretion) and his fate up to the present. But, the comparison would doubtless appear to you strained. Olcott—would you say—is an enthusiast, a stubborn, unreasoning mystic, who goes headlong before him, blindfolded, and who will not allow himself to look forward with his own eyes. While you are a sober, matter-of-fact man of the world, the son of your generation of cool thinkers; ever keeping fancy under the curb, and saying to enthusiasm: " Thus far shalt thou go and no farther." . . . Perhaps you are right—perhaps not. " No Lama knows where the *ber-chhen* will hurt him until he puts it on," says a Tibetan proverb. However, let that pass, for I must tell you now that for opening " direct communication " the only possible means would be: (1) For each of us to meet in our own *physical* bodies. I being where I am, and you in your own quarters, there is a material impediment *for me*. (2) For both to meet in our astral form— which would necessitate your " getting out " of yours, as well as my leaving my body. The spiritual impediment to this is on *your part*. (3) To make you hear my voice either within you or near you as " the old lady " does. This would be feasible in either of two ways: (*a*) My chiefs have but to give me permission to set up the conditions—and this for the present they refuse; or (*b*) for you to hear my voice, *i.e.*, my *natural voice* without any psycho-physiological *tamasha* being employed by me (again as we often do among ourselves). But then, to do this, not only have one's *spiritual* senses to be abnormally opened, but one must himself have mastered the great secret—yet undiscovered by science—of, so to say, abolishing all the impediments of space; of neutralising for the time being the natural obstacle of intermediary particles of air and forcing the waves to strike your ear in reflected sounds or echo. Of the latter you know as yet only enough to regard this as an unscientific absurdity. Your physicists, not having until recently mastered acoustics in this direction, any further than to acquire a perfect (?) knowledge of the vibration of sonorous bodies and of reverberations through tubes, may sneeringly ask: " Where are your indefinitely continued sonorous bodies, to conduct through space the vibrations of the voice? " We answer that our tubes, though invisible, are indestructible and far more perfect than those of modern physicists, by whom the velocity of the transmission of mechanical force through the air is represented as at the rate of 1,100 feet a second and no more—if I mistake not. But then, may there not be people who have found more perfect and rapid means of transmission, from being somewhat better acquainted with the occult powers of air (*akas*) and having *plus* a more cultivated judgment of sounds? But of this we will argue later on.

There is still more serious inconvenience; an almost insurmountable obstacle—for the present, and one, under which I myself am labouring, while even I do no more than correspond with you, a simple thing that any other mortal could do. It is my utter inability to make you understand my meaning in my explanation of even physical phenomena, let alone the spiritual rationale. This is not the first time I mention it. It is, as though a child should ask me to teach him the highest problems of Euclid before he had even begun studying the elementary rules of arithmetic. Only the progress one makes in the study of Arcane knowledge from its rudimental elements, brings him gradually to understand our meaning. Only thus, and not otherwise, does it, strengthening and refining those mysterious links of sympathy between intelligent men—the temporarily isolated fragments of the universal Soul and the cosmic Soul itself—bring them into full rapport. Once this established, then only will these awakened sympathies serve, indeed, to connect MAN with—what for the want of a European scientific word more competent to express the idea, I am again compelled to describe as that energetic chain which binds together the material and Immaterial Kosmos, Past, Present, and Future, and quicken his perceptions so as to clearly grasp, not merely all things of matter, but of Spirit also. I feel even irritated at having to use these three clumsy words—past, present and future! Miserable concepts of the objective phases of the Subjective Whole, they are about as ill adapted for the purpose as an axe for fine carving. Oh, my poor, disappointed friend, that you were already so far advanced on THE PATH, that this simple transmission of ideas should not be encumbered by the conditions of matter, the union of your mind with ours—prevented by its induced incapabilities! Such is unfortunately the inherited and self-acquired grossness of the Western mind; and so greatly have the very phrases expressive of modern thoughts been developed in the line of practical materialism, that it is now next to impossible either for them to comprehend or for us to express in their own languages anything of that delicate seemingly ideal machinery of the Occult Kosmos. To some little extent that faculty can be acquired by the Europeans through study and meditation but—that's all. And here is the bar which has hitherto prevented a conviction of the theosophical truths from gaining wider currency among Western Nations; caused theosophical study to be cast aside as useless and fantastic by Western philosophers. How shall I teach you to read and write or even comprehend a language of which no alphabet *palpable*, or words *audible* to you have yet been invented! How could the phenomena of our modern electrical science be explained to—say, a Greek philosopher of the days of Ptolemy were he suddenly recalled to life—with such an unbridged *hiatus* in discovery as would exist between his and our age? Would not the very technical terms be to him an unintelligible jargon, an abracadabra of meaningless sounds, and the very instruments and apparatuses used but " miraculous " monstrosities? And suppose, for one instant, I were to describe to you the hues of those colour rays that lie *beyond* the so-called " visible spectrum "—rays invisible to all but a very few even among us; to explain, how we can fix in space any one of the so-called subjective or *accidental* colours—the *complement*, (to speak mathematically) *moreover, of any other given colour of a dichromatic body* (which alone sounds like an absurdity), could you comprehend, do you think, their optical effect or even my meaning? And, since you see them not, such rays, nor can know them, nor have you any names for them as yet in Science, if I were to tell you:—" My good friend Sinnett, if you please, without moving from your writing desk, try, search for, and produce before your eyes the whole solar spectrum decomposed into fourteen prismatic colours (seven being complementary), as it is but with the help of that occult light that you can see me from a distance as I see you " . . . What think you, would be your answer? What would you have to reply? Would you not be likely enough to retort by telling me in your own quiet, polite way, that as there never were but seven (now three) primary colours, which, moreover, have never yet by any known physical process been seen decomposed further than the seven prismatic hues—my invitation was as " unscientific " as it was " absurd "? Adding that my offer to search for an imaginary solar " complement " being no compliment to your knowledge of physical science—I had better, perhaps, go and search for my mythical " dichromatic " and solar " pairs " in Tibet, for modern science has hitherto been unable to bring under any theory even so simple a phenomenon as the colours of all such dichromatic bodies. And yet—truth knows— *these* colours are objective enough!

So you see, the insurmountable difficulties in the way of attaining not only *Absolute* but even primary knowledge in Occult Science, for one situated as you are. How could you make yourself understood—*command* in fact, those semi-intelligent Forces, whose means of communicating with us are not through spoken words but through sounds and colours, in correlations between the vibrations of the two? For sound, light and colours are the main factors in forming these grades of Intelligences, these beings, of whose very existence you have no conception, nor *are you allowed* to believe in them—Atheists and Christians, materialists and Spiritualists, all bringing forward their respective arguments against such a belief—Science objecting stronger than either of these to such a " degrading superstition "!

Thus, because *they* cannot with one leap over the boundary walls attain to the pinnacles of Eternity; because *we* cannot take a savage from the centre of Africa and make him comprehend at once the *Principia* of Newton or the " Sociology " of Herbert Spencer; or make an unlettered child write a new Iliad in old Achaian Greek; or an ordinary painter depict scenes in Saturn or sketch the inhabitants of Arcturus—*because of all this our very existence is denied*! Yes; for this reason are believers in us pronounced impostors and fools, and the very science which leads to the highest goal of the highest knowledge, to the real tasting of the Tree of Life and Wisdom—is scouted as a wild flight of Imagination!

Most earnestly do I ask you not to see in the above a mere ventilation of personal feeling. My time is precious and I have none to lose. Still less ought you to see in this an effort to disgust or dissuade you from the noble work you have just begun. Nothing of the kind; for what I now say may avail for as much as it can and no more; but—*vera pro gratiis*—I WARN you, and will say no more, apart from reminding you in a general way, that the task you are so bravely undertaking, that *Missio in partibus infidelium*—is the most ungrateful, perhaps, of all tasks! But, if you believe in my friendship for you, if you value the word *of honour* of one who never—*never* during his whole life polluted his lips with an untruth, then do not forget the words I once wrote to you (see my last letter) *of those who engage themselves in the occult sciences*; he who does it " must either reach the goal or *perish*. Once fairly started on the way to the great Knowledge, to doubt is to risk insanity; to come to a dead stop is to fall; to recede is to tumble backward, headlong into an abyss." Fear not,—if you are sincere, and that you are—*now*. Are you as sure of yourself, as to the *future*?

But I believe it quite time to turn to less transcendental and what you would call less gloomy and more mundane matters. Here, no doubt, you will be much more at home. Your experience, your training, your intellect, your knowledge of the exterior world, in short, all combine to aid you in the accomplishment of the task you have undertaken. For, they place you on an infinitely higher level than myself as regards the consideration of writing a book, after your Society's " own heart." Though the interest I take in it may amaze some who are likely to retort on me and my colleagues with our own arguments, and to remark that our " boasted elevation over the common herd " (our friend Mr. Hume's words) —above the interests and passions of ordinary humanity, must militate against our having any conception of the ordinary affairs of life—yet I confess that I *do* take an interest in this book and its success, as great as in the success in life of its future author.

I hope that at least *you* will understand that we (or most of us) are far from being the heartless, morally dried up mummies some would fancy us to be. " Mejnour " is very well where he is— as an ideal character of a thrilling—in many respects truthful story. Yet, believe me, few of us would care to play the part in life of a desiccated pansy between the leaves of a volume of solemn poetry. We may not be quite the " boys "—to quote Olcott's irreverent expression when speaking of us—yet none of *our* degree are like the stern hero of Bulwer's romance. While the facilities of observation secured to some of us by our condition certainly give a greater breadth of view, a more pronounced and impartial, as a more widely spread humaneness—for answering Addison, we might justly maintain that it *is* " the business of ' magic ' to humanise our natures with compassion " for the whole mankind as all living beings, instead of concentrating and limiting our affections to one predilected race—yet few of us (except such as have attained the final negation of Moksha) can so far enfranchise ourselves from the influence of our earthly connection as to be insusceptible in various degrees to the higher pleasures, emotions, and interests of the common run of humanity. Until final emancipation reabsorbs the *Ego*, it *must* be conscious of the purest sympathies called out by the esthetic effects of high art, its tenderest cords respond to the call of the holier and nobler *human* attachments. Of course, the greater the progress towards deliverance, the less this will be the case, until, to crown all, human and purely individual personal feelings—blood-ties and friendship, patriotism and race predilection—all will give away, to become blended into one universal feeling, the only true and holy, the only unselfish and Eternal one—Love, an Immense Love for humanity—as a *Whole*! For it is " Humanity " which is the great Orphan, the only disinherited one upon this earth, my friend. And it is the duty of every man who is capable of an unselfish impulse to do something, however little, for its welfare. Poor, poor humanity! It reminds me of the old fable of the war between the Body and its members; here too, each limb of this huge " Orphan "—fatherless and motherless—selfishly cares but for itself. The body uncared for suffers eternally, whether the limbs are at war or at rest. Its suffering and agony never cease. ... And who can blame it—as your materialistic philosophers do—if, in this everlasting isolation and neglect it has evolved gods unto whom "it ever cries for help but is not heard!" Thus—

> "Since there is hope for man *only in man*
> I would not let *one* cry whom I could save!..."

Yet I confess that I, individually, am not yet exempt from some of the terrestrial attachments. I am still attracted towards *some* men more than toward others, and philanthropy as preached by our Great Patron—"the Saviour of the World—the Teacher of Nirvana and the Law," has never killed in me either individual preferences of friendship, love for my next of kin, or the ardent feeling of patriotism for the country in which I was last materially individualized. And, in this connection, I may some day, unasked, offer a bit of advice to my friend Mr. Sinnett, to whisper into the ear of the Editor of the PIONEER *en attendant*—"May I beg the former to inform Dr. Wyld, the Prest. of the British T.S., of the few truths concerning us as shown above? Will you kindly undertake to persuade this excellent gentleman, that not one of the humble "dew drops" which, assuming under various pretexts the form of vapour, have at various periods disappeared in the space to congeal in the white Himalayan clouds, have ever tried to slip back into the shining Sea of Nirvana through the unhealthy process of hanging by the legs or by making unto themselves another "coat of skin" out of the sacred cow-dung of the "thrice holy cow"! The British President labours under the most original ideas about us, whom he persists in calling "Yogis," without allowing the slightest margin to the enormous differences which exist even between "Hatha" and "Raj" Yog. This mistake must be laid at the door of Mrs. B.—the able editor of "*The Theosophist*," who fills up her volumes with the practices of divers Sannyasis and other "blessed ones" from the plains, without ever troubling herself with a few additional lines of explanation.

And now, to still more important matters. Time is precious and material (I mean writing material) is still more so. "Precipitation"—in your case having become unlawful; lack of —whether ink or paper—standing no better chance for "Tamasha," and I, being far away from home, and at a place where a stationer's shop is less needed than breathing air, our correspondence threatens to break very abruptly, unless I manage my stock in hand judiciously. A friend promises to supply me in case of great need with a few stray sheets, memento relics of his grandfather's will, by which he disinherited him and thus made his "fortune." But, as he never wrote one line but once, he says—for the last eleven years, except on such "*double* _superfin glacé_ " made at Tibet as you might irreverently mistake for blotting paper in its primitive days, and that the will is drawn upon a like material—we might as well turn to your book at once. Since you do me the favour of asking my opinion, I may tell you that the idea is an excellent one. Theosophy needs such help, and the results will be what you anticipate in England as well. It may also help our friends in Europe—generally.

I lay no restrictions upon your making use of anything I may have written to you or Mr. Hume, having full confidence in your tact and judgment as to what should be printed and how it should be presented. I must only ask you for reasons upon which I must be silent (and I am sure you will respect that silence) _not to use one single word or passage from my last letter to you_—the one written after my long silence, no date, and the first one forwarded to you by our " old lady." I just quoted from it at page 4. Do me the favour, if my poor epistles are worth preserving, to lay it by in a separate and sealed envelope. You may have to unseal it only after a certain period of time has elapsed. As to the rest—I relinquish it to the mangling tooth of criticism. Nor would I interfere with the plan you have roughly sketched out in your mind. But I would strongly recommend you in its execution to lay the greatest stress upon small circumstances— (could you oblige me with some receipt for blue ink?!) which tend to show the impossibility of fraud or conspiracy. Reflect well, how bold a thing it is to endorse phenomena as adeptic which the Spirits[ts.] have already stamped as proofs of mediumship and skeptics as legerdemain. You should not omit one jot or tittle of collateral evidence that supports your position, something you have neglected doing in your " A " letter in the _Pioneer_. For instance, my friend tells me that it was a _thirteenth_ cup and the pattern unmatchable, in Simla at least.[1] The pillow was chosen by yourself—and yet the word " pillow " occurs in my note to you, just as the word " tree " or anything else would have been substituted, had you chosen another depository, instead of the pillow. You will find all such trifles serving you as the most powerful shield for yourself against ridicule and sneers. Then you will of course, aim to show that this Theosophy is no new candidate for the world's attention, but only the restatement of

---

[1] So, at least, Mrs. S. says; I myself did not search the crockery shops; so too, the bottle filled with water I filled with my own hand—was one of the four only that the servants had in the baskets, and these four bottles had but just been brought back empty by these peons from their fruitless search after water, when you sent them to the little brewery with a note. Hoping to be excused for the interference and with my most respectful regards to the lady.

Yours, etc., THE " DISINHERITED." *

* A nickname for Djual Kool.—EDS.

principles which have been recognised from the very infancy of mankind. The historic sequence ought to be succinctly yet graphically traced through the successive evolutions of philosophical schools, and illustrated with accounts of the experimental demonstrations of occult power ascribed to various thaumaturgists. The alternate breakings-out and subsidences of mystical phenomena, as well as their shiftings from one centre to another of population, show the conflicting play of the opposing forces of spirituality and animalism. And lastly it will appear that the present tidal-wave of phenomena, with its varied effects upon human thought and feeling, made the revival of Theosophical enquiry an indispensable necessity. The only problem to solve is the practical one, of how best to promote the necessary study, and give to the spiritualistic movement a needed upward impulse. It is a good beginning to make the inherent capabilities of the inner, living man better comprehended. To lay down the scientific proposition that since *akarsha* (attraction) and *Prshu* (repulsion) are the law of nature, there can be no intercourse or relations between clean and unclean Souls—embodied or disembodied; and hence, ninety-nine hundredths of supposed spiritual communications, are, *prima facie* false. Here is as great a fact to work upon as you can find, and it cannot be made too plain. So, while a better selection might have been made for the *Theosophist* in the way of illustrative anecdotes, as, for instance, well authenticated historical cases, yet the theory of turning the minds of phenomenalists into useful and suggestive channels away from mere mediumistic dogmatism was the correct one.

What I meant by the " Forlorn Hope " was that when one regards the magnitude of the task to be undertaken by our theosophical volunteers, and especially the multitudinous agencies arrayed, and to be arrayed, in opposition, we may well compare it to one of those desperate efforts against overwhelming odds that the true soldier glories to attempt. You have done well to see the " large purpose " in the small beginnings of the T.S. Of course, if we had undertaken to found and direct it in *propria persona* very likely it would have accomplished more and made fewer mistakes, but we could not do this, nor was it the plan: our two agents are given the task and left—as you now are—to do the best they could under the circumstances. And much has been wrought. Under the surface of Spiritualism runs a current that is wearing a broad channel for itself. When it reappears above ground its effects will be apparent. Already many minds like yours are pondering the question of occult law—forced upon the thinking public by this agitation. Like you, they are dissatisfied with what has been hitherto attainable and clamour for better. Let this—encourage you.

It is not quite accurate that by having such minds in the Society they would be " under conditions more favourable for observation " for us. Rather put it, that by the act of joining other sympathisers in this organization they are stimulated to effort and incite each other to investigate. Unity always gives strength: and since Occultism in our days resembles a " Forlorn Hope," union and co-operation are indispensable. Union does indeed imply a concentration of vital and magnetic force against the hostile currents of prejudice and fanaticism.

I wrote a few words in the Maratha boy's letter, only to show you that he was obeying *orders* in submitting his views to you. Apart from his exaggerated idea about *huge fees*, his letter is in a way worth considering. For Damodar is a Hindu—and knows the mind of his people at Bombay; though the Bombay Hindus are about as unspiritual a group as can be found in all India. But, like the devoted enthusiastic lad he is, he jumped after the misty form of his own ideas even before I could give them the right direction. All quick thinkers are hard to impress—in a flash they are out and away in " full cry," before half understanding what one wants to have them think. This is our trouble with both Mrs. B. and O. The frequent failure of the latter to carry out the suggestions he sometimes receives—even when written, is almost wholly due to his own active mentality preventing his distinguishing our impressions from his own conceptions. And *Missus* B.'s trouble is (apart from physical ailment) that she sometimes listens to two or more of our voices at once; *e.g.*, this morning while the " Disinherited," whom I have accommodated with space for a footnote—was talking with her on an important matter, she lent an ear to one of ours, who is passing through Bombay from Cyprus, on his way to Tibet—and so got both in an inextricable confusion. *Women* do lack the power of concentration.

And now, my good friend and co-worker—an irremediable paperless condition obliges me to close. Farewell, until your return, unless you will be content, as hitherto, to pass our correspondence through the accustomed channel. Neither of us would prefer this. But until authority is given to change it must be even so. Were she to die to-day—and she is really sick—you would not receive more than two, or at most three more letters from me (through Damodar or Olcott, or through already established emergent agencies), and then, that reservoir of force being exhausted—our parting would be FINAL. However, I will not anticipate; events *might* bring us together somewhere in Europe. But whether we meet or not, during your trip, be assured that my personal good wishes will attend you. Should you actually need now and again the help of a happy thought as your work progresses, it may, very likely, be *osmosed* into your head—if sherry bars not the way, as it has already done at Allahabad.

May the " deep Sea " deal gently with you and your house.

Ever yours,

K. H.

P.S.—The " friend " of whom the Lord Lindsay speaks in his letter to you, is, I am sorry to say, a true skunk *mephitis*, who managed to perfume himself with ess-bouquet in his presence during their palmy days of friendship, and so avoided being recognised by his natural stench. It is Home—the medium, a convert to Roman Catholicism, then to Protestantism, and finally to the Greek Church. He is the bitterest and most cruel enemy O. and Mad. B. have, though he has never met either of them. For a certain time he succeeded in poisoning the Lord's mind, and prejudiced him against them. I do not like saying anything behind a man's back, for it looks like back-biting. Yet in view of some future events I feel it my duty to warn you, for this one is an exceptionally bad man—hated by the Spiritualists and mediums as much as he is despised by those who have learned to know him. Yours is a work which clashes directly with his. Though a poor sickly cripple, a paralysed wretch, his mental faculties are as fresh and as alive as ever to mischief. He is no man to stop before a slanderous accusation—however vile and lying. So— beware.

K. H.

SECTION II

PHILOSOPHICAL AND THEORETICAL TEACHINGS

1881-1883

LETTER No. 9

From K.H., first letter received on return to India, July 8th, 1881, while staying with Madame B. at Bombay for a few days.

Welcome good friend and brilliant author, welcome back! Your letter at hand, and I am happy to see your personal experience with the " Elect " of London proved so successful. But, I foresee, that more than ever now, you will become an incarnate note of interrogation. Beware! If your questions are found premature by the powers that be, instead of receiving my answers in their pristine purity you may find them transformed into yards of drivel. I am too far gone to feel a hand on my throat whenever trenching on the limits of forbidden topics; not enough to avoid feeling myself—uncomfortably so—like a worm of yesterday before our " Rock of Ages," my Cho-Khan. We must all be *blindfolded* before we can pass onward; or else, we have to remain outside.

And now, what about *the* book? *Le quart d'heure de Rabelais* is striking, and finds me, if not quite insolvent, yet quasi-trembling at the idea that the first instalment offered may be found below the mark; the price claimed—inadequate with my poor resources; myself led *pro bono publico* to trespass beyond the terrible—" hitherto shalt thou go, and no further," and the angry wave of the Cho-Khan's wrath swamping me blue ink and all! I fondly hope you will not make me lose " my situation."

Quite so. For, I have a dim notion that you will be very impatient with me. I have a very clear notion that you need not be. It is one of the unfortunate necessities of life that imperial needs do sometimes force one apparently to *ignore* the claims of friendship, not to violate one's word, but to put off and lay aside for a while the too impatient expectations of neophytes as of inferior importance. One such need that I call imperial is the need of your future welfare; the realization of the dream dreamt by you in company with S.M. That dream—shall we call it a vision?—was that you, and Mrs. K.—why forget the Theos. Soc.?—" are all parts of a large plan for the manifestations of

38

occult philosophy to the world." Yes; the time must come, and it is not far—when all of you will comprehend aright the apparently contradictory phases of such manifestations; forced by the evidence to reconcile them.   The case not being so at present, meanwhile—remember: it is because we are playing a risky game and the stakes are human souls that I ask you to possess yours in patience.   Bearing in mind that I have to look after your "Soul" and mine too, I propose to do so at whatever cost, even at the risk of being misunderstood by you as I was by Mr. Hume.   The work is made the more difficult by my being a lonely labourer in the field, and that, as long as I fail to prove to my superiors that you, at least, mean business; that you—are in right good earnest.   As I am refused higher help, so will you fail to easily find help in that Society in which you move, and which you try to move.   Nor will you find, for a certain time much joy in those directly concerned.   Our old lady is weak and her nerves are worked to a fiddle string; so is her jaded brain.   H. S. O. is far away—in *exile*—fighting his way back to *salvation*—compromised more than you imagine by his Simla indiscretions—and establishing theosoph. schools.   Mr. Hume—who once promised to become a champion fighter in that Battle of Light against Darkness —now preserves a kind of armed neutrality wondrous to behold. Having made the mirific discovery that we are a body of antediluvian Jesuits or fossils—self-crowned with oratorical flourishes, he rested but to accuse us of intercepting his letters to H. P. B.! However, he finds some comfort by thinking " what a jolly argument he shall have *elsewhere* (Angel Linnean ornithological Society, perhaps) with the entity which is represented by the name Koothoomi."   Verily has our very intellectual, once mutual friend, a flood of words at his command which would suffice to float a troop ship of oratorious fallacies.   Nevertheless—I respect him. . . . But who next? C. C. Massey? But then he is the hapless parent of about half a dozen of illegitimate brats.   He is a most charming, devoted friend; a profound mystic; a generous, noble minded man, a gentleman—as they say—every inch of him; tried as gold; every requisite for a *student* of occultism, but none for an *adept*, my good friend.   Be it as it may, his secret is his own, and I have no right to divulge it.   Dr. Wyld?—a christian to the back bone.   Hood?—a sweet nature, as you say; a dreamer, and an idealist in mystic matters, yet—no worker. S. Moses? Ah! here we are.   S.M. has nearly upset the theosoph. ark set afloat three years back: and, he will do his level best to do it over again—our Imperator notwithstanding. You doubt? Listen.

His is a weird, rare nature.   His occult psychical energies are tremendous; but they have lain dormant, folded up within him and unknown to himself, when, some eight years or so, Imperator

threw his eye upon him and bid his spirit soar.   Since then, a new
life has been in him, a dual existence, but his nature could not
be changed.   Brought up as a theological student, his mind was
devoured by doubts.   Earlier, he betook himself to Mount Athos,
where, immuring himself in a monastery, he studied Greek
Eastern religion, and it is there that he was first noticed by his
" *Spirit* guide " (! !) Of course, Greek casuistry failed to solve
his doubts, and he hurried on to Rome,—popery satisfying him as
little.   From thence he wandered to Germany with the same
negative results.   Giving up dry christian theology he did not give
up its presumable founder with all that.   He needed an ideal and
he found it in the latter.   For him Jesus is a reality, a once
embodied, now a disembodied *Spirit*, who, " furnished him with
an evidence of his personal identity "—he thinks,—in no less a
degree than other " Spirits "—Imperator among the rest—have.
Nevertheless, neither the religions of Jesus nor yet his words, as
recorded in the Bible and believed by S.M. authentic—are fully
accepted by that restless Spirit of his. *Imperator*, on whom the
same fate devolved later on, fares no better.   His mind is too
positive.   Once impressed it becomes easier to efface characters
engraved upon *titanium* than impressions made upon his brain.

Whenever under the influence of *Imperator* he is all alive to
the realities of Occultism, and the superiority of our Science over
Spiritualism.   As soon as left alone and under the pernicious
guidance of those he firmly believes having identified with disembodied Souls—all becomes confusion again!   His mind will
yield to no suggestions, no reasonings but his own, and those are
all for Spiritualistic theories.   When the old theological fetters
had dropped off, he imagined himself a free man.   Some months
later, he became the humble slave and tool of the " Spirits "!   It
is but when standing face to face with his *inner Self* that he
realizes the truth that there is something higher and nobler than
the prittle-prattle of pseudo Spirits.   It was at such a moment
that he heard for the first [time] the voice of *Imperator*, and it was, as
he himself puts it: " as the voice of God speaking to his inner
Self."   That voice made itself familiar to him for years, and
yet he very often heeds it not.   A simple query: Were Imper.
what he believes, nay—*knows* him to be, he thinks,—would not
he have made S.M.'s will completely subservient to his own by
this time?   Alone the adepts, *i.e.*, the embodied spirits—are forbidden by our wise and intransgressible laws to completely subject
to themselves another and a weaker will,—that of free born man.
The latter mode of proceeding is the favourite one resorted to
by the " Brothers of the Shadow," the Sorcerers, the Elementary
Spooks, and, as an isolated exception—by the *highest* Planetary
Spirits, those who can no longer err.   But these appear on

Earth but at the origin of every *new* human kind; at the junction of, and close of the two ends of the great cycle. And, they remain with man no longer than the time required for the eternal truths they teach to impress themselves so forcibly upon the plastic minds of the new races as to warrant them from being lost or entirely forgotten in ages hereafter, by the forthcoming generations. The mission of the planetary Spirit is but to strike the KEY NOTE OF TRUTH. Once he has directed the vibration of the latter to run its course uninterruptedly along the catenation of that race and to the end of the cycle—the denizen of the highest inhabited sphere disappears from the surface of our planet—till the following " resurrection of flesh." ·The vibrations of the Primitive Truth are what your philosophers name " innate ideas."

Imperator, then, had repeatedly told him that " in occultism alone he should seek for, and *will* find a phase of truth not yet known to him." But that did not prevent S.M. at all from turning his back upon occultism whenever a theory of it clashed with one of his own preconceived Spiritualistic ideas. To him mediumship appeared as the Charter of his Soul's freedom, as resurrection from Spiritual death. He had been allowed to enjoy it only so far as it was necessary for the confirmation of his faith; promised that the abnormal would yield to the normal; ordered to prepare for the time when the Self within him will become conscious of its spiritual, independent existence, will act and talk face to face with its Instructor, and will lead its life in Spiritual Spheres normally and without external or internal mediumship at all. And yet once conscious of what he terms " external Spirit action " he recognised no more hallucination from truth, the false from the real: confounding at times Elementals and Elementaries, embodied from disembodied Spirit, though he had been oft enough told of, and warned against " those spirits that hover about the Earth's sphere "—by his " Voice of God." With all that he firmly believes to have invariably acted under Imper's direction, and that such spirits as have come to him came by his " guide's " permission. In such a case H. P. B. was there by Imper's consent? And how do you reconcile the following contradictions? Ever since 1876, acting under direct orders, she tried to awake him to the reality of what was going on around and in him. That she must have acted either according to or *against* Imper's will—he must know, as in the latter case she might boast of being stronger, more powerful than his " guide " who never yet protested against the intrusion. Now what happens? Writing to her from Isle of Wight, in 1876, of a vision lasting for over 48 consecutive hours he had, and during which he walked about, talked as usual, but did not preserve the slightest remembrance of anything external, he asks her to tell him whether it was a vision or a hallucination. Why did he not ask $+I\text{-}r$? "You can tell me *for you were there*," he says . . . "You —changed, yet yourself—if you have *a Self* . . . I suppose you have, but into that I do not pry." . . At another time he saw her in his own library looking at him, approaching and giving him some masonic signs of the Lodge he knows. He admits that he " saw her as clearly as he saw Massey—who was there." He saw her on several other occasions, and sometimes knowing it was H. P. B., he could not recognise her. " You seem to me from your appearance as from your letters so different at times, the mental attitudes so various, that it is quite conceivable to me, as I am authoritatively told, that you are a bundle of Entities. . . . I have *absolute* faith in you." In every letter of his he clamoured for a " *living* Brother "; to her unequivocal statement that there was one already having charge of him, he strongly objected. When helped to get free from his *too material* body, absent from it for hours and days sometimes, his empty machine run during that period from afar and by *external, living* influence,—as soon as back, he would begin labouring under the ineradicable impression of having been all that time the vehicle for *another* intelligence, a disembodied not embodied Spirit, *truth* never once flashing across his mind. " Imperator," he wrote to her, " traverses your idea about mediumship. He says there should be no real antagonism between the medium and the adept." Had he used the word " Seer " instead of " medium " the idea would have been rendered more correctly, for a man becomes rarely an adept without being born a natural Seer. Then again. In September, 1875, he knew nothing of the Brothers of the Shadow—our greatest, most cruel, and—why not confess—our most potential [1] Enemies. In that year he actually asked the old lady whether Bulwer had been eating underdone pork chops and dreaming when he described " that hideous Dweller of the Threshold." " Make yourself ready," she answered—" in about twelve months more you will have to face and fight with them." In October, 1876, they had begun their work upon him. " I am fighting "—he wrote—" a hand to hand battle with all the legions of the Fiend for the past three weeks. My nights are made hideous with their torments, temptations and foul suggestions. I see them all around, glaring at me, gabbling, howling, grinning! Every form of filthy suggestion, of bewildering doubt, of mad and shuddering fear is upon me . . . I can understand Zanoni's Dweller now . . . I have not wavered yet . . . and their temptations are fainter, the presence less near, the horror less. . . ."

One night she had prostrated herself before her Superior, one of the few they fear, praying him to wave his hand across the

---

[1] Query, should be powerful.—EDS.

ocean, lest S.M. should die, and the Theos. Soc. lose its best subject. " He must be tried " was the answer. He imagines that + *Imper.* had sent the tempters because he S.M. was one of those Thomases who must *see*; he would *not* believe that + could not help their coming. Watch over him he did—he could not drive them away unless the victim, the neophyte himself, proved the strongest. But did these human fiends in league with the Elementaries prepare him for a new life as he thought they would? Embodiments of those adverse influences which beset the inner Self struggling to be free and to progress, they would never have returned had he successfully conquered them by asserting his own independent WILL, by giving up his mediumship, his *passive* will. Yet they did.

You say of + " Imperator is certainly not his (S.M.'s) astral soul, and assuredly, also, he is not from a lower world than our own—not an earth-bound Spirit." No one ever said he was anything of the kind. H. P. B., never told you he was S.M.'s *astral soul*, but that what he often mistook for + was his own higher *Self*, his divine *atman*—not *linga Sarira* or astral Soul, or the *Kama rupa*, the independent *doppelganger*—again. + cannot contradict himself; + cannot be ignorant of the truth, so often misrepresented by S.M.; + cannot preach the occult Sciences and then defend mediumship, not even in that highest form described by his pupil. Mediumship is abnormal. When in further development the abnormal has given way to the natural, the *controls* are shaken off, and passive obedience is no longer required, then the medium learns to use his will, to exercise his own power, and becomes an adept. The process is one of development and the neophyte has to go to the end. As long as he is subject to occasional trance—he cannot be an adept. S.M. passes the two-thirds of his life in Trance.

To your question—Is Imperator " a Planetary Spirit " and " may a Planetary Spirit have been humanly incarnated," I will first say that there can be no Planetary Spirit that was not once material or what you call human. When our great Buddha—the patron of all the adepts, the reformer and the codifier of the occult system, reached first *Nirvana* on earth, he became a Planetary Spirit; *i.e.*—his spirit could at one and the same time rove the interstellar spaces *in full consciousness*, and continue at will on Earth in his original and individual body. For the divine Self had so completely disfranchised itself from matter that it could create at will an inner substitute for itself, and leaving it in the human form for days, weeks, sometimes years, affect in no wise by the change either the vital principle or the physical mind of its body. By the way, that is the highest form of adeptship man can hope for on our planet. But it is as rare as the Buddhas themselves, the last Khobilgan who reached it being Tsong-ka-pa of Kokonor (XIV Century), the reformer of esoteric as well as of vulgar Lamaism. Many are those who " break through the egg-shell," few who, once out, are able to exercise their *Nirira namastaka* fully, when completely out of the body. *Conscious* life in Spirit is as difficult for some natures as swimming is for some bodies. Though the human frame is lighter in its bulk than water, and though every person is born with the faculty, so few develop in themselves the art of treading water that death by drowning is the most frequent of accidents. The planetary Spirit of that kind (the Buddha like) can pass at will into other bodies—of more or less etherialised matter, inhabiting other regions of the Universe. There are many other grades and orders, but there is no *separate* and eternally constituted order of Planetary Spirits. Whether Imperator is a " planetary " embodied or disembodied, whether he is an adept in flesh or out of it, I am not at liberty to say, any more than he would himself [be] to tell S.M. who I am, or may be, or even who H. P. B. is. If he himself chooses to be silent on that subject S.M. has no right to ask *me*. But then our friend S.M. ought to know. Nay: he firmly believes he does. For in his intercourse with that personage there came a time when not satisfied with + assurances, or content to respect his wishes that he, Imperator & Co. should remain impersonal and unknown save by their assumed titles, S.M. wrestled with him, Jacob-like, for months on the point of that spirit's *identity*. He was the Biblical flim-flam all over again. " I pray thee tell me thy name "—and though answered: " Wherefore is it that thou dost ask after my name? "—what's in a name?—he allowed S.M. to label him like a portmanteau. And so, he is at rest now, for he has " seen God face to face "; who, after wrestling, and seeing that he prevailed not, said " let me go " and was forced to come to the terms offered by Jacob. S. Moses. I strongly advise you for your own information to put that question to your friend. Why should he be " anxiously awaiting " my reply since he knows all about + ? Did not that " Spirit " *tell him a story one day,—a queer story, something that he may not divulge about himself, and forbid him ever mentioning it*? What more does he want? That fact, that he seeks to learn through me the true nature of +, is a pretty good proof in itself that he is not as sure of his identity as he believes he is, or rather would make believe he is. Or is the question a blind?—which?

I may answer you, what I said to G. Th. Fechner one day, when he wanted to know the Hindu view on what he had written— " You are right; . . . ' every diamond, every crystal, every plant and star has its own individual soul, besides man and animal . . .' and, ' there is a hierarchy of souls from the lowest forms of matter up to the World Soul,' but, you are mistaken when adding to the above the assurance that ' the spirits of the departed hold *direct* psychic communication with Souls that are still connected with a human body '—for, they do not." The relative position of the inhabited worlds in our Solar System would alone preclude such a possibility. For I trust you have given up the queer idea —a natural result of early Xtian training—that there can possibly be *human* intelligences inhabiting *purely spiritual* regions? You will then as readily understand the fallacy of the christians— who would burn *immaterial* souls in a *material* physical hell—as the mistake of the more educated spiritualists, who lullaby themselves with the thought that any other but the denizens of the two worlds immediately interlinked with our own can possibly communicate with them? However etherial and purified of gross matter they may be, the pure Spirits are still subject to the physical and universal laws of matter. They *cannot* even if they would span the abyss that separates their worlds from ours. *They can be visited in Spirit*, their Spirit cannot descend and reach us. They attract, they cannot be attracted, their Spiritual polarity being an insuperable difficulty in the way. (By-the-bye you must not trust *Isis* literally. The book is but a tentative effort to divert the attention of the Spiritualists from their preconceptions to the true state of things. The author was made to hint and point out in the true direction, to say what things *are not*, not what they are. Proof reader helping, a few real mistakes have crept in as on page 1, chapter 1, volume 1, where divine Essence is made emanating from Adam instead of the reverse.)

Once fairly started upon that subject, I will endeavour to explain to you still clearer where lies the impossibility. You will thus be answered in regard to both Planetary Spirits and séance room " Spirits."

The cycle of intelligent existences commences at the highest worlds or *planets*—the term " highest " meaning here the most spiritually perfect. Evolving from cosmic matter—which is *akasa*, the primeval not the secondary plastic medium, or Ether of Science instinctively suspected, unproven as the rest—man first evolutes from this *matter* in its most sublimated state, appearing at the threshold of Eternity as a perfectly *Etherial*— not Spiritual Entity, say—a Planetary Spirit. He is but one remove from the universal and Spiritual World Essence—the *Anima Mundi* of the Greeks, or that which humanity in its spiritual decadence has degraded into a mythical personal God. Hence, at that stage, the Spirit-man is at best an *active* Power, an *immutable*, therefore an *unthinking* Principle (the term " immutable " being again used here but to denote that state for the time being, the immutability applying here but to the inner principle which will vanish and disappear as soon as the spark of the material in him will start on its cyclic work of Evolution and transformation). In his subsequent descent, and in proportion to the increase of matter he will assert more and more his activity. Now, the congeries of the star-worlds (including our own planet) inhabited by intelligent beings may be likened to an orb or rather an epicycloid formed of rings like a chain—worlds inter-linked together, the totality representing an imaginary endless ring, or circle. The progress of man throughout the whole—from its starting to its closing points meeting on the highest point of its circumference—is what we call the *Maha Yug* or Great Cycle, the *Kuklos*, whose head is lost in a crown of *absolute* Spirit, and its lowest point of circumference in *absolute* matter—to *viz.* the point of cessation of action of the *active* principle. If using a more familiar term we call the Great Cycle the *Macrokosm* and its component parts or the inter-linked star worlds *Microkosms*, the occultists' meaning in representing each of the latter as perfect copies of the former will become evident. The Great is the Prototype of the smaller cycles: and as such, each star world has in its turn its own cycle of Evolution which starts with a purer and ends with a grosser or more material nature. As they descend, each world presents itself naturally more and more shadowy, becoming at the " antipodes " *absolute* matter. Propelled by the irresistible cyclic impulse the Planetary Spirit has to descend before he can reascend. On his way he has to pass through the whole ladder of Evolution, missing no rung, to halt at every star world as he would at a station; and, besides the unavoidable cycle of that particular and every respective star world, to perform in it his own " *life-cycle* " too, *viz.*: returning and reincarnating as many times as he fails to complete his round of life in it, as he dies on it before reaching the age of reason, as correctly stated in *Isis*. Thus far Mrs. Kingsford's idea that the human Ego is being reincarnated in several successive human bodies is the true one. As to its being reborn in animal forms after *human* incarnation it is the result of her loose way of expressing things and ideas. Another WOMAN—all over again. Why, she confounds " Soul and Spirit," refuses to discriminate between the animal and the spiritual Egos, the *Jiv-atma* (or Linga-Sharir) and the *Kama-Rupa* (or Atma-Rupa), two as different things as body and mind, and—*mind* and *thought* are! That is what happens. After *circling*, so to say, along the arc of the cycle, circling along and within it (the daily and yearly rotation of the Earth is as good an illustration as any) when the Spirit-man reaches our planet, which is one of the lowest, having lost at every station some of the etherial and acquired an increase of material nature, both spirit and matter have become pretty much

equilibrized in him. But then, he has the Earth's cycle to perform; and, as in the process of involution and evolution downward,
matter is ever striving to stifle spirit, when arrived at the lowest
point of his pilgrimage, the once pure Planetary Spirit will be
found dwindled to what Science agrees to call a primitive or
Primordial man—amidst a nature as primordial, speaking geologically, for physical nature keeps pace with the physiological as
well as the spiritual man, in her cyclic career. At that point the
great Law begins its work of selection. Matter found entirely
divorced from spirit is thrown over into the still lower worlds—
into the *sixth* " GATI " or " way of rebirth " of the vegetable and
mineral worlds, and of the primitive animal forms. From thence,
matter ground over in the workshop of nature proceeds *soulless*
back to its Mother Fount; while the *Egos* purified of their dross
are enabled to resume their progress once more onward. It is
here, then, that the laggard *Egos* perish by the millions. It is
the solemn moment of the " survival of the fittest," the annihilation of those unfit. It is but matter (or material man) which is
compelled by its own weight to descend to the very bottom of the
" circle of necessity " to there assume animal form; as to the
winner of that race throughout the worlds—the Spiritual Ego,
he will ascend from star to star, from one world to another,
circling onward to rebecome the once pure planetary Spirit, then
higher still, to finally reach its first starting point, and from thence
—to merge into MYSTERY. No adept has ever penetrated beyond
the veil of primitive Kosmic matter. The highest, the most
perfect vision is limited to the universe of *Form* and *Matter*.

But my explanation does not end here.   You want to know why
it is deemed supremely difficult if not utterly impossible for pure
disembodied Spirits to communicate with men through mediums or
Phantomosophy. I say, because:—

(*a*) On account of the antagonistic atmospheres respectively
surrounding these worlds;

(*b*) Of the entire dissimilarity of physiological and spiritual
conditions; and—

(*c*) Because that chain of worlds I have just been telling you
about, is not only an *epicycloid* but an elliptical orbit of existences,
having, as every ellipse, not one but two points—two *foci*, which
can never approach each other; Man being at one focus of it and
pure Spirit at the other.

To this you might object. I can neither help it, nor change
the fact, but there is still another and far mightier impediment.
Like a rosary composed of white and black beads alternating with
each other, so that concatenation of worlds is made up of worlds
of CAUSES and worlds of EFFECTS, the latter—the direct result produced by the former. Thus it becomes evident that every sphere

of Causes—and our Earth is one—is not only inter-linked with, and surrounded by, but actually separated from its nearest neighbour —the higher sphere of Causality—by an impenetrable atmosphere (in its spiritual sense) of effects bordering on, and even inter-linking, never mixing with—the next sphere: for one is active, the other—passive, the world of causes *positive*, that of effects— *negative*. This passive resistance can be overcome but under conditions of which your most learned Spiritualists have not the faintest idea. All movement is, so to say polar. It is very diffi-cult to convey my meaning to you at this point; but I will go to the end. I am aware of my failure to bring before you these—to us—axiomatical truths in any other form but that of a simple logical postulate—if so much—they being capable of absolute and unequivocal demonstration but to the highest Seers. But, I'll give you food for thinking if nothing else.

The intermediary spheres, being but the projected shadows of the Worlds of Causes—are negatived by [1] the last. They are the great halting places, the stations in which the new *Self-Conscious Egos* to be—the self-begotten progeny of the old and disembodied Egos of our planet—are gestated. Before the new phœnix, reborn of the ashes of its parents can soar higher, to a better, more spiritual, and perfect world—still a world of matter—it has to pass through the process of a new birth, so to say; and, as on our earth, where the two-thirds of infants are either still-born or die in infancy, so in our " world of effects." On earth it is the physiological and mental defects, the sins of the progenitors which are visited upon the issue: in that land of shadows, the new and yet unconscious Ego-foetus becomes the just victim of the trans-gressions of its old *Self*, whose *karma*—merit and demerit—will alone weave out its future destiny. In that world, my good friend, we find but unconscious, self-acting, ex-human machines, souls in their transition state, whose dormant faculties and indi-viduality lie as a butterfly in its chrysalis; and Spiritualists would yet have them talk sense! Caught at times, into the vortex of the abnormal " *mediumistic* " current, they become the uncon-scious echoes of thoughts and ideas crystallized around those present. Every *positive*, well-directed mind is capable of neutralizing such secondary effects in a séance room. The world below ours is worse yet. The former is harmless at least; it is more sinned against by being disturbed, than sinning; the latter allowing the retention of full consciousness as being a hundred-fold more material, is positively dangerous. The notions of hells and purgatory, of paradises and resurrections are all caricatured, distorted echoes of the primeval one Truth, taught humanity in the infancy of its races by every First Messenger—the Planetary

[1] Query, negatives of.—EDS.

Spirit mentioned on the reverse of page the third—and whose remembrance lingered in the memory of man as Elu of the Chaldees,
Osiris the Egyptian, Vishnu, the first Buddhas and so on.

The lower world of effects is the sphere of such distorted
Thoughts; of the most sensual conceptions, and pictures; of
anthropomorphic deities, the out-creations of their creators, the
sensual human minds of people who have never out-grown their
brutehood on earth. Remembering thoughts are things—have
tenacity, coherence, and life,—that they are real entities—the rest
will become plain. Disembodied—the creator is attracted naturally
to its creation and creatures; sucked in—by the Maelstrom dug
out by his own hands. . . . But I must pause, for volumes
would hardly suffice to explain all that was said by me in this
letter.

In reference to your wonder that the views of the three mystics
" are far from being identical," what does the fact prove? Were
they instructed by *disembodied*, pure, and wise Spirits—even by
those of one remove from our earth on the higher plane—would
not the teachings be identical? The question arising: " May not
Spirits as well as men differ in ideas? " Well, then, their teaching—aye, of the highest of them since they are the " guides "
of the three great London Seers—will not be more authoritative
than those of mortal men. " But, they may belong to different
spheres? " Well; if in the different spheres contradictory doctrines are propounded, these doctrines cannot contain the Truth,
for Truth is *One*, and cannot admit of diametrically opposite
views; and pure Spirits who see it *as it is*, with the veil of matter
entirely withdrawn from it—cannot err. Now, if we allow of
different aspects or portions of the Whole Truth being visible to
different agencies or intelligences, each under various conditions,
as for example various portions of the one landscape develop
themselves to various persons, at various distances and from
various standpoints—if we admit the fact of various or different
agencies (individual Brothers for instance) endeavouring to develop the *Egos* of different individuals, without subjecting entirely
their wills to their own (as it is forbidden) but by availing themselves of their physical, moral, and intellectual idiosyncracies; if
we add to this the countless kosmical influences which distort and
deflect all efforts to achieve definite purposes: if we remember,
moreover, the direct hostility of the Brethren of the Shadow
always on the watch to perplex and haze the neophyte's brain, I
think we shall have no difficulty in understanding how even a
definite spiritual advance may to a certain extent lead different
individuals to apparently different conclusions and theories.

Having confessed to you that I had no right to interfere with
Imperator's secrets and plans, I must say that so far, however,

he has proved the wisest of us. Had our policy been the same, had I, for instance allowed you to infer and then believe (without stating anything positive myself) that I was a "disembodied angel"—a Spirit of pellucid electroidal essence, from the Super-Stellar phantasmatical zone—we would both be happier. You—you would not have worried your head as to "whether agencies of that sort will always remain necessary" and I—would not find myself under the disagreeable necessity of having to refuse a friend a "personal interview and *direct* communication." You might have implicitly believed anything coming from me; and I would have felt less responsible for you before my "GUIDES." However, time will show what may or may not be done in that direction. The book is out, and we have to patiently wait for the results of that *first serious shot* at the enemy. *Art Magic* and *Isis* emanating from women and, as it was believed, Spiritualists—could never hope for a serious hearing. Its effects will at first be disastrous enough, for the gun will recoil and the shot rebounding will strike the author and his humble hero, who are not likely to flinch. But it will also graze the old lady, reviving in the Anglo-Indian press last year's outcry. The Thersites and literary Philistines will go hard to work, the flings, squibs and *coups de bec* falling thick upon her—though aimed at you alone, as the Editor of the *Pioneer* is far from being beloved by his colleagues of India. Spiritualistic papers have already opened the campaign in London and the Yankee editors of the Organs of "Angels" will follow suit, the heavenly "Controls" ejaculating their choicest *scandalum magnatum*. Some men of science—least of all their admirers—the parasites who bask in the sun and dream they are themselves that sun—are not likely to forgive you the sentence—really much too flattering—which ranges the comprehension of a poor, unknown Hindoo "So far beyond the science and philosophy of Europe, that only the broadest minded representatives of either will be able to realize the existence of such powers in man, etc." But what of that? It was all foreseen and was to be expected. When the first hum and ding-dong of adverse criticism is hushed, thoughtful men will read and ponder over the book, as they have never pondered over the most scientific efforts of Wallace and Crookes to reconcile modern science with Spirits, and—the little seed will grow and thrive.

In the meantime I do not forget my promises to you. As soon as installed in your sleeping chamber I will try and [1]. . . .

I hope to be permitted to do so much for you. If, for generations we have "shut out the world from the Knowledge of our Knowledge," it is on account of its absolute unfitness; and if,

---

[1] Here three lines in the original letter have been completely erased apparently by the writer thereof.—ED.

notwithstanding proofs given, it still refuses yielding to evidence, then will we at the End of this cycle retire into solitude and our kingdom of silence once more. . . . We have offered to exhume the primeval strata of man's being, his basic nature, and lay bare the wonderful complications of his inner Self—something never to be achieved by physiology or even psychology in its ultimate expression—and demonstrate it scientifically. It matters not to them, if the excavations be so deep, the rocks so rough and sharp, that in diving into that, to them, fathomless ocean, most of us perish in the dangerous exploration; for it is we who were the divers and the pioneers, and the men of science have but to reap where we have sown. It is our mission to plunge and bring the pearls of Truth to the surface; theirs—to clean and set them into scientific jewels. And, if they refuse to touch the ill-shapen oyster-shell, insisting that there is [not], nor *cannot* be any precious pearl inside it, then shall we once more wash our hands of any responsibility before human-kind. For countless generations hath the adept builded a fane of imperishable rocks, a giant's Tower of INFINITE THOUGHT, wherein the Titan dwelt, and will yet, if need be, dwell alone, emerging from it but at the end of every cycle, to invite the elect of mankind to co-operate with him and help in his turn enlighten superstitious man. And we will go on in that periodical work of ours; we will not allow ourselves to be baffled in our philanthropic attempts until that day when the foundations of a new continent of thought are so firmly built that no amount of opposition and ignorant malice guided by the Brethren of the Shadow will be found to prevail.

But until that day of final triumph someone has to be sacrificed —though we accept but voluntary victims. The ungrateful task did lay her low and desolate in the ruins of misery, misapprehension, and isolation: but she will have her reward in the here-after for we never were ungrateful. As regards the Adept—not *one of my kind*, good friend, but far higher—you might have closed your book with those lines of Tennyson's " Wakeful Dreamer "— you knew him not—

> " How could ye know him? Ye were yet within
> The narrower circle; he had well nigh reached
> The last, which with a region of white flame,
> Pure without heat, into a larger air
> Up-burning, and an ether of black blue,
> Investeth and ingirds all other lives. . . ."

I'll close. Remember then on the 17th of July and [1]   . . . . , to you will become the sublimest of realities. Farewell.

Sincerely yours,

K. H.

[1] Here again six lines in the original have been deleted.—ED.

LETTER No. 10 [1]

NOTES BY K. H. ON A " PRELIMINARY CHAPTER " HEADED " GOD "
BY HUME, INTENDED TO PREFACE AN EXPOSITION OF OCCULT
PHILOSOPHY (ABRIDGED).

Received at Simla, Sept. 1882.

Neither our philosophy nor ourselves believe in a God, least of all in one whose pronoun necessitates a capital H. Our philosophy falls under the definition of Hobbes. It is pre-eminently the science of effects by their causes and of causes by their effects, and since it is also the science of things deduced from first principle, as Bacon defines it, before we admit any such principle we must know it, and have no right to admit even its possibility. Your whole explanation is based upon one solitary admission made simply for argument's sake in October last. You were told that our knowledge was limited to this our solar system: ergo as philosophers who desired to remain worthy of the name we could not either deny or affirm the existence of what you termed a supreme, omnipotent, intelligent being of some sort *beyond* the limits of that solar system. But if such an existence is not absolutely impossible, yet unless the uniformity of nature's law breaks at those limits we maintain that it is highly improbable. Nevertheless we deny most emphatically the position of agnosticism in this direction, and as regards the solar system. Our doctrine knows no compromises. It either affirms or denies, for it never teaches but that which it knows to be the truth. Therefore, we deny God both as philosophers and as Buddhists. We know there are planetary and other spiritual lives, and we know there is in our system no such thing as God, either personal or impersonal. Parabrahm is not a God, but absolute immutable law, and Iswar is the effect of Avidya and Maya, ignorance based upon the great delusion. The word " God " was invented to designate the unknown cause of those effects which man has either admired or dreaded without understanding them, and since we claim and that we are able to prove what we claim—*i.e.*, the knowledge of that cause and causes—we are in a position to maintain there is no God or Gods behind them.

The idea of God is not an innate but an acquired notion, and we have but one thing in common with theologies—we reveal the infinite. But while we assign to all the phenomena that proceed from the infinite and limitless space, duration and motion, *material, natural, sensible and known* (to us at least) causes, the theists assign them *spiritual*, super-*natural* and *unintelligible* and

[1] Transcribed from a copy in Mr. Sinnett's handwriting.—ED.

un-known causes. The God of the Theologians is simply an imaginary power, *un loup garou* as d'Holbach expressed it—a power which has never yet manifested itself. Our chief aim is to deliver humanity of this nightmare, to teach man virtue for its own sake, and to walk in life relying on himself instead of leaning on a theological crutch, that for countless ages was the direct cause of nearly all human misery. Pantheistic we may be called—agnostic NEVER. If people are willing to accept and to regard as God our ONE LIFE immutable and unconscious in its eternity they may do so and thus keep to one more gigantic misnomer. But then they will have to say with Spinoza that there is not and that we cannot conceive any other substance than God; or as that famous and unfortunate philosopher says in his fourteenth proposition, " praeter Deum neque dari neque concipi potest substantia "—and thus become Pantheists . . . Who but a Theologian nursed on mystery and the most absurd supernaturalism can imagine a self-existent being of necessity infinite and omnipresent *outside* the manifested *boundless* universe. The word infinite is but a negative which excludes the idea of bounds. It is evident that a being independent and omnipresent cannot be limited by anything which is outside of himself; that there can be nothing exterior to himself—not even vacuum, then where is there room for matter? for that manifested universe even though the latter [be] limited? If we ask the theist is your God vacuum, space or matter, they will reply no. And yet they hold that their God penetrates matter though he is not himself matter. When we speak of our One Life we also say that it penetrates, nay is the essence of every atom of matter; and that therefore it not only has correspondence with matter but has all its properties likewise, etc.—hence *is* material, is *matter itself*. How can intelligence proceed or emanate from non-intelligence—you kept asking last year. How could a highly intelligent humanity, man the crown of reason, be evolved out of blind unintelligent law or force! But once we reason on that line, I may ask in my turn, how could congenital idiots, non-reasoning animals, and the rest of " creation " have been created by or evoluted from, absolute Wisdom, if the latter is a thinking intelligent being, the author and ruler of the Universe? How? says Dr. Clarke in his examination of the proof of the existence of the Divinity. " God who hath made the eye, shall he not see? God who hath made the ear shall he not hear? " But according to this mode of reasoning they would have to admit that in creating an idiot God is an idiot; that he who made so many irrational beings, so many physical and moral monsters, must be an irrational being. . . .

. . . We are not Adwaitees, but our teaching respecting the one life is identical with that of the Adwaitee with regard to Parabrahm.

7

And no true philosophically trained Adwaitee will ever call himself an agnostic, for he knows that he is Parabrahm and identical in every respect with the universal life and soul—the macrocosm is the microcosm and he knows that there is no God apart from himself, no creator as no being. Having found Gnosis we cannot turn our backs on it and become agnostics.

. . . . Were we to admit that even the highest Dhyan Chohans are liable to err under a delusion, then there would be no reality for us indeed and the occult sciences would be as great a chimera as that God. If there is an absurdity in denying that which we do not know it is still more extravagant to assign to it unknown laws.

According to logic " nothing " is that of which everything can truly be denied and nothing can truly be affirmed. The idea therefore either of a finite or infinite nothing is a contradiction in terms. And yet according to theologians " God, the self existent being is a most simple, unchangeable, incorruptible being; without parts, figure, motion, divisibility, or any other such properties as we find in matter. For all such things so plainly and necessarily imply finiteness in their very notion and are utterly inconsistent with complete infinity." Therefore the God here offered to the adoration of the XIXth century lacks every quality upon which man's mind is capable of fixing any judgment. What is this in fact but a being of whom they can affirm *nothing* that is not instantly contradicted. Their own Bible, their Revelation, destroys all the moral perfections they heap upon him, unless indeed they call those qualities perfections that every other man's reason and common sense call imperfections, odious vices and brutal wickedness. Nay more, he who reads our Buddhist scriptures written for the superstitious masses will fail to find in them a *demon* so vindictive, unjust, so cruel and so stupid as the celestial tyrant upon whom the Christians prodigally lavish their servile worship and on whom their theologians heap those perfections that are contradicted on every page of their Bible. Truly and veritably your theology has created her God but to destroy him piecemeal. Your church is the fabulous Saturn, who begets children but to devour them.

(*The Universal Mind*)—A few reflections and arguments ought to support every new idea—for instance we are sure to be taken to task for the following apparent contradictions. (1) We deny the existence of a thinking conscious God, on the grounds that such a God must either be conditioned, limited and subject to change, therefore *not* infinite, or (2) if he is represented to us as an eternal unchangeable and independent being, with not a particle of matter in him, then we answer that it is no being but an immutable blind principle, a law. And yet, they will say, we believe in Dhyans, or Planetaries ("spirits" also), and endow them with a universal mind, *and this must be explained.*

Our reasons may be briefly summed up thus:

(1) We deny the absurd proposition that there can be, even in a boundless and eternal universe—two infinite eternal and omnipresent existences.

(2) Matter we know to be eternal, *i.e.*, having had no beginning (*a*) because matter is Nature herself (*b*) because that which cannot annihilate itself and is indestructible exists necessarily—and therefore it could not begin to be, nor can it cease to be (*c*) because the accumulated experience of countless ages, and that of exact science show to us matter (or nature) acting by her own peculiar energy, of which not an atom is ever in an absolute state of rest, and therefore it must have always existed, *i.e.*, its materials ever changing form, combinations and properties, but its principles or elements being absolutely indestructible.

(3) As to God—since no one has ever or at any time seen him or it—*unless he or it is the very essence and nature of this boundless eternal matter, its energy and motion,* we cannot regard him as either eternal or infinite or yet self existing. We refuse to admit a being or an existence of which we know absolutely nothing; because (*a*) there is no room for him in the presence of that matter whose undeniable properties and qualities we know thoroughly well (*b*) because if he or it is but a part of that matter it is ridiculous to maintain that he is the mover and ruler of that of which he is but a dependent part and (*c*) because if they tell us that God is a self existent pure spirit independent of matter—an extra-cosmic deity, we answer that admitting even the possibility of such an impossibility, *i.e.*, his existence, we yet hold that a purely immaterial spirit cannot be an intelligent conscious ruler nor can he have any of the attributes bestowed upon him by theology, and thus such a God becomes again but a blind force. Intelligence as found in our Dhyan Chohans, is a faculty that can appertain but to organized or animated being—however imponderable or rather *invisible* the materials of their organizations. Intelligence requires the necessity of thinking; to think one must have ideas; ideas suppose senses which are physical material, and how can anything material belong to pure spirit? If it be objected that thought cannot be a property of matter, we will ask the reason why? We must have an unanswerable proof of this assumption, before we can accept it. Of the theologian we would enquire what was there to prevent his God, since he is the alleged creator of all—to endow matter with the faculty of thought; and when answered that evidently it has not pleased Him to do so, that it is a mystery as well as an impossibility, we would insist upon being told why it is more impossible that matter

should produce spirit and thought, than spirit or the thought of God should produce and create matter.

We do not bow our heads in the dust before the mystery of mind—for we *have solved it ages ago*. Rejecting with contempt the theistic theory we reject as much the automaton theory, teaching that states of consciousness are produced by the marshalling of the molecules of the brain; and we feel as little respect for that other hypothesis—the production of molecular motion by consciousness. Then what do we believe in? Well, we believe in the much laughed at *phlogiston* (see article "What is force and what is matter?" *Theosophist*, September), and in what some natural philosophers would call *nisus*, the incessant though perfectly imperceptible (to the ordinary senses) motion or efforts one body is making on another—the pulsations of inert matter— its life. The bodies of the Planetary spirits are formed of that which Priestley and others called Phlogiston and for which we have another name—this essence in its highest seventh state forming that matter of which the organisms of the highest and purest Dhyans are composed, and in its lowest or densest form (so impalpable yet that science calls it energy and force) serving as a cover to the Planetaries of the 1st or lowest degree. In other words we believe in MATTER alone, in matter as visible nature and matter in its invisibility as the invisible omnipresent omnipotent Proteus with its unceasing motion which is its life, and which nature draws from herself since she is the great whole outside of which nothing can exist. For as Bilfinger truly asserts, "motion is a manner of existence that flows necessarily out of the essence of matter; that matter moves by its own peculiar energies; that its motion is due to the force which is inherent in itself; that the variety of motion and the phenomena that result proceed from the diversity of the properties of the qualities and of the combinations which are originally found in the primitive matter" of which nature is the assemblage and of which your science knows less than one of our Tibetan Yak-drivers of Kant's metaphysics.

The existence of matter then is a fact; the existence of motion is another fact, their self existence and eternity or indestructibility is a third fact. And the idea of pure spirit as a Being or an Existence—give it whatever name you will—is a chimera, a gigantic absurdity.

Our ideas on Evil. Evil has no existence *per se* and is but the absence of good and exists but for him who is made its victim. It proceeds from two causes, and no more than good is it an independent cause in nature. Nature is destitute of goodness or malice; she follows only immutable laws when she either gives life and joy, or sends suffering [and] death, and destroys what she has created. Nature has an antidote for every poison and her laws a reward for every suffering. The butterfly devoured by a bird becomes that bird, and the little bird killed by an animal goes into a higher form. It is the blind law of necessity and the eternal fitness of things, and hence cannot be called Evil in Nature. The real evil proceeds from human intelligence and its origin rests entirely with reasoning man who dissociates himself from Nature. Humanity, then, alone is the true source of evil. Evil is the exaggeration of good, the progeny of human selfishness and greediness. Think profoundly and you will find that save death—which is no evil but a necessary law, and accidents which will always find their reward in a future life—the *origin* of every evil whether small or great is in human action, in man whose intelligence makes him the one free agent in Nature. It is not nature that creates diseases, but man. The latter's mission and destiny in the economy of nature is to die his natural death brought by old age; save accident, neither a savage nor a wild (free) animal dies of disease. Food, sexual relations, drink, are all natural necessities of life; yet excess in them brings on disease, misery, suffering, mental and physical, and the latter are transmitted as the greatest evils to future generations, the progeny of the culprits. Ambition, the desire of securing happiness and comfort for those we love, by obtaining honours and riches, are praiseworthy natural feelings, but when they transform man into an ambitious cruel tyrant, a miser, a selfish egotist they bring untold misery on those around him; on nations as well as on individuals. All this then—food, wealth, ambition, and a thousand other things we have to leave unmentioned, becomes the source and cause of evil whether in its abundance or through its absence. Become a glutton, a debauchee, a tyrant, and you become the originator of diseases, of human suffering and misery. Lack all this and you starve, you are despised as a *nobody* and the majority of the herd, your fellow men, make of you a sufferer your whole life. Therefore it is neither nature nor an imaginary Deity that has to be blamed, but human nature made vile by *selfishness*. Think well over these few words; work out every cause of evil you can think of and trace it to its origin and you will have solved *one-third* of the problem of evil. And now, after making due allowance for evils that are natural and cannot be avoided,—and so few are they that I challenge the whole host of Western metaphysicians to call them evils or to trace them directly to an independent cause—I will point out the greatest, the chief cause of nearly two thirds of the evils that pursue humanity ever since that cause became a power. It is religion under whatever form and in whatsoever nation. It is the sacerdotal caste, the priesthood and the churches; it is in those illusions that man looks upon as sacred, that he has to search out

the source of that multitude of evils which is the great curse of
humanity and that almost overwhelms mankind.   Ignorance
created Gods and cunning took advantage of the opportunity.   Look
at India and look at Christendom and Islam, at Judaism and
Fetichism.   It is priestly imposture that rendered these Gods so
terrible to man; it is religion that makes of him the selfish bigot,
the fanatic that hates all mankind out of his own sect without
rendering him any better or more moral for it.   It is belief in
God and Gods that makes two-thirds of humanity the slaves of
a handful of those who deceive them under the false pretence of
saving them.   Is not man ever ready to commit any kind of evil
if told that his God or Gods demand the crime—voluntary victim
of an illusionary God, the abject slave of his crafty ministers?
The Irish, Italian and Slavonian peasant will starve himself and
see his family starving and naked to feed and clothe his padre
and pope.   For two thousand years India groaned under the
weight of caste, Brahmins alone feeding on the fat of the land,.
and to-day the followers of Christ and those of Mahomet are
cutting each other's throats in the names of and for the greater
glory of their respective myths.   Remember the sum of human
misery will never be diminished unto that day when the better
portion of humanity destroys in the name of Truth, morality, and
universal charity, the altars of their false gods.

If it is objected that we too have temples, we too have priests
and that our lamas also live on charity . . . let them know
that the objects above named have in common with their Western
equivalents, but the name.   Thus in our temples there is neither
a god nor gods worshipped, only the thrice sacred memory of the
greatest as the holiest man that ever lived.   If our lamas to
honour the fraternity of the *Bhikkhus* established by our blessed
master himself, go out to be fed by the laity, the latter often to
the number of 5 to 25,000 is fed and taken care of by the
Samgha (the fraternity of lamaic monks), the lamassery providing
for the wants of the poor, the sick, the afflicted.   Our lamas
accept food, never money, and it is in those temples that the
origin of evil is preached and impressed upon the people.   There
they are taught the four noble truths—*ariya* sacca, and the chain
of causation, (the 12 *nidānas*) gives them a solution of the problem
of the origin and destruction of suffering.

Read the Mahavagga and try to understand, not with the prejudiced Western mind but the spirit of intuition and truth what
the Fully Enlightened one says in the 1st Khandhaka.   Allow me
to translate it for you.

  " At the time the blessed Buddha was at Uruvela on the
  shores of the river Neranjara as he rested under the Bodhi
  tree of wisdom after he had become Sambuddha, at the end

of the seventh day having his mind fixed on the chain of causation he spake thus: 'from Ignorance spring the samkharas of threefold nature—productions of body, of speech, of thought. From the samkharas springs consciousness, from consciousness springs name and form, from this spring the six regions (of the six senses, the seventh being the property of but the enlightened); from these springs contact from this sensation; from this springs thirst (or desire, kama, tanha) from thirst attachment, existence, birth, old age and death, grief, lamentation, suffering, dejection and despair. Again by the destruction of ignorance, the samkharas are destroyed, and their consciousness, name and form, the six regions, contact, sensation, thirst, attachment (selfishness), existence, birth, old age, death, grief, lamentation, suffering, dejection, and despair are destroyed. Such is the cessation of this whole mass of suffering.' "

Knowing this the Blessed One uttered this solemn utterance:

" When the real nature of things becomes clear to the meditating Bhikshu, then all his doubts fade away since he has learned what is that nature and what its cause. From ignorance spring all the evils. From knowledge comes the cessation of this mass of misery, and then the meditating Brahmana stands dispelling the hosts of Mara like the sun that illuminates the sky."

Meditation here means the superhuman (not supernatural) qualities, or arhatship in its highest of spiritual powers.

Copied out Simla, Sept. 28, 1882.

LETTER No. 11[1]

Received by A.O.H., June 30th, 1882.

Simple prudence misgives me at the thought of entering upon my new role of an " instructor." If M. satisfied you but little I am afraid of giving you still less satisfaction, since besides being restrained in my explanations—for there are a thousand things I will have to leave unrevealed by my vow of silence—I have far less time at my disposal than he has. However, I'll try my best. Let it not be said that I failed to recognize your present sincere desire to become useful to the Society, hence to Humanity, for I am deeply alive to the fact that none better than yourself in India is calculated to disperse the mists of superstition and popular error by throwing light on the darkest problems. But

[1] Transcribed from a copy in Mr. Sinnett's handwriting.—ED.

before I answer your questions and explain our doctrine any further, I'll have to preface my replies with a long introduction. First of all and again I will draw your attention to the tremendous difficulty of finding appropriate terms in English which would convey to the educated European mind even an approximately correct notion about the various subjects we will have to treat upon. To illustrate my meaning I'll underline in red the technical words adopted and used by your men of Science and which withal are absolutely misleading not only when applied to such transcendental subjects as on hand but even when used by themselves in their own system of thought.

To comprehend my answers you will have first of all to view the eternal *Essence*, the Swabhāvat not as a compound element you call spirit-matter, but as the one element for which the English has no name. It is both passive and active, pure *Spirit Essence* in its absoluteness and repose, pure matter in its finite and conditioned state—even as an imponderable gas or that great unknown which science has pleased to call *Force*. When poets talk of the " shoreless ocean of immutability " we must regard the term but as a jocular parodox, since we maintain that there is no such thing as immutability—not in our Solar system at least. Immutability, say the theists and Christians, " is an attribute of God, " and forthwith they endow that God with every mutable and variable quality and attribute, knowable as unknowable, and believe that they have solved the unsolvable and squared the circle. To this we reply, if *that* which the theists call God, and science " *Force* " and " *Potential Energy*," were to become immutable but for one instant even during the Maha-Pralāya, a period when even Brahm the creative architect of the world is said to have merged into non-being, then there could be no manvantara, and space alone would reign unconscious and supreme in the eternity of time. Nevertheless, Theism when speaking of mutable immutability is no more absurd than materialistic science talking of " *latent* potential energy," and the indestructibility of matter and force. What are we to believe as indestructible? Is it the invisible something that moves matter or the energy of moving bodies! What does modern science know of force proper, or say the forces, the cause or causes of motion? How can there be such a thing as *potential energy, i.e.*, an energy having latent *inactive* power since it is energy *only while it is moving matter*, and that *if it ever ceased to move matter it would cease to be*, and with it matter itself would disappear? Is force any happier term? Some thirty-five years back a Dr. Mayer offered the hypothesis now accepted as an axiom that force, in the sense given it by modern science, like matter, is *indestructible*; namely, when it ceases to be manifest in one form it still exists and has only *passed into some other form.* And yet your men of science have not found a single instance where one *force* is transformed into another, and Mr. Tyndall tells his opponents that " in no case is the force producing the motion annihilated or changed into anything else." Moreover we are indebted to modern science for the novel discovery that there exists a quantitative relation between the dynamic energy producing something and the " something " produced. Undoubtedly there exists a quantitive relation between cause and effect, between the amount of energy used in breaking one's neighbour's nose, and the damage done to that nose, but this does not solve one bit more the mystery of what they are pleased to call correlations, since it can be easily proved (and that on the authority of that same science) that neither motion nor energy is indestructible and that the physical forces are in no way or manner convertible one into another. I will cross-examine them in their own phraseology and we will see whether their theories are calculated to serve as a barrier to our " astounding doctrines." Preparing as I do to propound a teaching diametrically opposed to their own it is but just that I should clear the ground of scientific rubbish lest what I have to say should fall on a too encumbered soil and only bring forth weeds. " This potential and imaginary *materia prima* cannot exist without form," says Raleigh, and he is right in so far that the *materia prima* of science exists but in their imagination. Can they say the same quantity of energy has always been moving the matter of the Universe? Certainly not so long as they teach that when the elements of the material cosmos, elements which had first to manifest themselves in their uncombined gaseous state, were uniting, the quantity of matter-moving energy was a million times greater than it is now when *our globe* is *cooling off.* For where did the heat that was generated by this tremendous process of building up a universe go to? To the unoccupied chambers of space, they say. Very well, but if it is gone for ever from the *material universe* and the energy operative on earth has never and at no time been the same, then how can they try to maintain the " unchangeable quantity of energy," that potential energy which a body may sometimes exert, the FORCE which passes from one body to another producing motion and which is not yet " annihilated or changed into anything else."? " Aye," we are answered, " but we still hold to its indestructibility; while it remains *connected with matter*, it can never cease to be, or less or more." Let us see whether it is so. I throw a brick up to a mason who is busy building the roof of a temple. He catches it and cements it in the roof. Gravity overcame the propelling energy which started the upward motion of the brick, and the dynamic energy of the ascending brick until it *ceased to ascend.* At that moment it was caught and fastened to the roof. No natural force could now move it, therefore it possesses no longer potential energy. The motion and the dynamic energy of the ascending brick are absolutely *annihilated.* Another example from their own text books. You fire a gun upward from the foot of a hill and the ball lodges in a crevice of the rock *on* that hill. No natural force can, for an indefinite period move it, so the ball as much as the brick has lost its potential energy. " All the motion and energy which was taken from the ascending ball by gravity is absolutely annihilated, no other motion or energy succeeds and gravity has received no increase of energy." Is it not true then that energy is indestructible! How then is it that your great authority teaches the world that " in no case is the force producing the motion annihilated or changed into anything else" ?

I am perfectly aware of your answer and give you these illustrations but to show how misleading are the terms used by scientists, how vacillating and uncertain their theories and finally how *incomplete* all their teachings. One more objection and I have done. They teach that all the physical forces rejoicing in specific names such as gravity, inertia, cohesion, light, heat, electricity, magnetism, chemical affinity, are convertible one into another? If so the force producing must cease to be as the force produced becomes manifest. " A flying cannon ball moves only from its own inherent force of inertia." When it strikes it produces heat and other effects but its force of inertia is not the least diminished. It will require as much energy to start it again at the same velocity as it did at first. We may repeat the process a thousand times and as long as the quantity of matter remains the same its force of inertia will remain the same in quantity. The same in the case of gravity. A meteor falls and produces heat. Gravity is to be held to account for this, but the force of gravity upon the fallen body is not diminished. *Chemical attraction* draws and holds the particles of matter together, their collision producing heat. Has the former passed into the latter? Not in the least, since drawing the particles again together whenever these are separated it proves that it, the chemical affinity is *not* decreased, for it will hold them as strongly as ever together. Heat they say generates and produces electricity yet they find no decrease in the heat in the process. Electricity produces heat we are told? Electrometers show that the electrical current passes through some poor conductor, a platinum wire say, and heats the latter. Precisely the same quantity of electricity, there being no loss of electricity, *no decrease.* What then has been converted into heat? Again, electricity is said to produce magnetism. I have on the table before me primitive electrometers in whose vicinity chelas come the whole day to recuperate their nascent powers. I do not find the slightest decrease in the electricity stored. The chelas are magnetized, but their magnetism or rather that of *their rods* is not *that* electricity under a new mask. No more than the flame of a thousand tapers lit at the flame of the *Fo* lamp is the flame of the latter. Therefore if by the uncertain twilight of modern science it is an axiomatic truth " that during vital processes the *conversion* only and never the *creation* of matter or force occurs " (Dr. J. R. Mayer's organic motion in its connection with nutrition)—it is for us but half a truth. It is neither *conversion* nor *creation*, but something for which science has yet no name.

Perhaps now you will be prepared to better understand the difficulty with which we will have to contend. Modern science is our best ally. Yet it is generally that same science which is made the weapon to break our heads with. However, you will have to bear in mind (*a*) that we recognize but *one* element in Nature (whether spiritual or physical) outside which there can be no Nature since it is *Nature* itself,[1] and which as the *Akasa* pervades our solar system, every atom being part of itself, pervades throughout *space* and *is* space in fact, which pulsates as in profound sleep during the pralayas, and [is] the universal Proteus, the ever active Nature during the Manvantaras; (*b*) that consequently spirit and matter are *one*, being but a differentiation of states not *essences*, and that the Greek philosopher who maintained that the Universe was a huge animal penetrated the symbolical significance of the Pythagorean monad (which becomes two, then three △ and finally, having become the tetraktis or the perfect square, thus evolving out of itself *four* and involuting three ◺ , forms the sacred seven—and thus was far in advance of all the scientific men of the present time; (*c*) that our notions of " cosmic matter " are diametrically opposed to those of western science. Perchance if you remember all this we will succeed in imparting to you at least the elementary axioms of our esoteric philosophy more correctly than heretofore. Fear not, my kind brother; your life is not ebbing away and it will not be extinct before you have completed your mission. I can say *no more* except that the Chohan has permitted me to devote my spare time to instruct those who are willing to learn, and you will have work enough to " drop " your Fragments at intervals of two or three months. My time is *very limited* yet I will do what I can. But I can promise *nothing* beyond this. I will have to remain silent as to

[1] Not in the sense of *Natus* " born ", but Nature as the sum total of everything visible and invisible, of forms and minds, the aggregate of the known (and unknown) causes and effects, the universe, in short, infinite and uncreated and endless, as it is without a beginning.

the Dhyan Chohans nor can I impart to you the secrets concerning the men of the seventh round. The recognition of the higher phases of man's being on this planet is not to be attained by mere acquirement of knowledge. Volumes of the most perfectly constructed information cannot reveal to man life in the higher regions. One has to get a knowledge of spiritual facts by personal experience and from actual observation, for as Tyndall puts it, "facts looked directly at are vital, when they pass into words half the sap is taken out of them." And because you recognise this great principle of personal observation, and are not slow to put into practice what you have acquired in the way of useful information, is perhaps the reason why the hitherto implacable Chohan my Master has finally permitted me to devote to a certain extent a portion of my time to the progress of the Eclectic.[1] But I am but *one* and you are many, and none of my Fellow Brothers with the exception of M. will help me in this work, not even our semi-European Greek Brother who but a few days back remarked that when "every one of the Eclectics on the Hill will have become a Zetetic then will he see what he can do for them." And as you are aware there is very little hope for this. Men seek after knowledge until they weary themselves to death, but even they do not feel very impatient to help their neighbour with their knowledge; hence there arises a coldness, a mutual indifference which renders him *who knows* inconsistent with himself and inharmonious with his surroundings. Viewed from our standpoint the evil is far greater on the spiritual than on the material side of man: hence my sincere thanks to you and desire to urge your attention to such a course as shall aid a true progression and achieve wider results by turning your knowledge into a permanent teaching in the form of articles and pamphlets.

But for the attainment of your proposed object, *viz.*, for a clearer comprehension of the extremely abstruse and at first incomprehensible theories of our occult doctrine, never allow the serenity of your mind to be disturbed during your hours of literary labour, nor before you set to work. It is upon the serene and placid surface of the unruffled mind that the visions gathered from the invisible find a representation in the visible world. Otherwise you would vainly seek those visions, those flashes of sudden light which have already helped to solve so many of the minor problems and which alone can bring the truth before the eye of the soul. It is with jealous care that we have to guard our mind-plane from all the adverse influences which daily arise in our passage through earth-life.

Many are the questions you ask me in your several letters, I can answer but few. Concerning Eglinton I will beg you to wait

[1] The Simla Eclectic Theosophical Society.—EDS.

for developments. In regard to your kind lady the question is more serious and I cannot undertake the responsibility of making her change her diet as ABRUPTLY as you suggest. Flesh and meat she can give up at any time as it can never hurt; as for liquor with which Mrs. H. has long been sustaining her system, you yourself know the fatal effects it may produce in an enfeebled constitution were the latter to be suddenly deprived of its stimulant. Her physical life is not a real existence backed by a reserve of vital force, but a factitious one fed upon the spirit of liquor however small the quantity. While a strong constitution might rally after the first shock of such a change as proposed, the chances are that she would fall into a decline. So would she if opium or arsenic were her chief sustenance. Again I promise nothing yet will do in this direction what I can. " Converse with you and teach you through astral light? " Such a development of your psychical powers of hearing, as you name—the Siddhi of hearing occult sounds—would not be at all the easy matter you imagine. It was never done to any one of us, for the iron rule is that what powers one gets *he must himself acquire*. And when acquired and ready for use the powers lie dumb and dormant in their potentiality like the wheels and clockwork inside a musical box; and only then does it become easy to wind up the key and set them in motion. Of course you have *now* more chances before you than my zoophagous friend Mr. Sinnett, who were he even to give up feeding on animals would still feel a craving for such a food, a craving over which he would have no control and,— the impediment would be the same in that case. Yet every earnestly disposed man *may* acquire such powers practically. That is the finality of it; there are no more distinctions of persons in this than there are as to whom the sun shall shine upon or the air give vitality to. There are the powers of all nature before you; *take what you can*.

Your suggestion as to the box I will think over. There would have to be some contrivance to prevent the discharge of power when once the box was charged, whether during transit or subsequently: I will consider and take advice or rather permission. But I must say the idea is utterly repugnant to us as everything else smacking of spirits and mediumship. We would prefer by far using natural means as in the last transmission of my letter to you. It was one of M.'s chelas who left it for you in the flower-shed, where he entered invisible to all yet in his natural body, just as he had entered many a time your museum and other rooms, unknown to you all, during and after the " Old Lady's " stay. But unless he is told to do so by M. he will *never* do it, and that is why your letter to me was left unnoticed. You have an unjust feeling towards my Brother, kind sir, for he is better and more powerful than I—at least he is not as bound and restricted as I am. I have asked H. P. B. to send you a number of philosophical letters from a Dutch Theosophist at Penang—one in whom I take an interest: you ask for more work and here is some.   They are translations, originals of those portions of Schopenhauer which are most in affinity with our *Arhat* doctrines.   The English is not idiomatic but the material is valuable.   Should you be disposed to utilize any portion of it, I would recommend your opening a direct correspondence with Mr. Sanders, F.T.S.—the translator. Schopenhauer's philosophical value is so well known in the western countries that a comparison or connotation of his teachings upon will, etc., with those you have received from ourselves might be instructive.   Yes, I am quite ready to look over your 50 or 60 pages and make notes on the margins; have them set up by all means and send them to me either through little " Deb " or Damodar and Djual Kool will transmit them.   In a very few days, perhaps to-morrow, your two questions will be amply answered by me.

Meanwhile

Yours sincerely,

K. H.

P.S.—The Tibetan translation is not quite ready yet.

LETTER No. 12

Your hypothesis is far nearer the truth than Mr. Hume's.   Two factors must be kept in view—(*a*) a fixed period, and (*b*) a fixed rate of development nicely adjusted to it.   Almost unthinkably long as is a Mahayug, it is still a definite term, and within it must be accomplished the whole order of development, or to state it in occult phraseology, the descent of Spirit into matter and its return to the re-emergence.   A chain of beads, and each bead a world is an illustration already made familiar to you.   You have already pondered over the life impulse beginning with each *Manvantara* to evolve the first of these worlds; to perfect it; to people it successively with all the aerial forms of life.   And after completing on this first world seven cycles—or evolutions of development— in each kingdom, as you know—passing forward down the arc— to similarly evolve the next world in the chain, perfect it, and abandon it.   Then to the next and next and next—until the seven- fold round of world-evolutions along the chain is run through and the Mahayug comes to its end.   Then chaos *again*—the *Pralaya*. As this life-impulse (at the seventh and last round from planet to

planet) moves on it leaves behind it dying and—very soon—" *dead*
planets."

The last seventh round man having passed on to a subsequent
world, the precedent one with all its mineral, vegetable and animal
life (except man) begins to gradually die out, when with the exit
of the last animalcula it is extinguished, or as H. P. B. has it—
snuffed out (*minor* or partial *pralaya*). When the Spirit-man
reaches the last bead of the chain and passes into *final* Nirvana,
this last world also disappears or passes into subjectivity. Thus
are there among the stellar galaxies births and deaths of worlds
ever following each other in the orderly procession of natural Law.
And—as said already—the last bead is strung upon the thread of
the " Mahayuga."

When the last cycle of man-bearing has been completed by that
last fecund earth; and humanity has reached in a mass the stage
of Buddhahood and passed out of the objective existence into the
mystery of Nirvana—then " strikes the hour; " the seen becomes
the unseen, the concrete resumes its pre-cyclic state of atomic
distribution.

But the dead worlds left behind [by] the on-sweeping impulse *do
not* continue *dead*. Motion is the eternal order of things and affinity
or attraction its handmaid of all works. The thrill of life will
again re-unite the atoms, and it will stir again in the inert planet
when the time comes. Though all its forces have remained in *status
quo* and are now asleep, yet little by little it will—when the hour
re-strikes—gather for a new cycle of man-bearing maternity, and
give birth to something still higher as moral and physical types
than during the preceding *manvantara*. And its " cosmic atoms
already in a differentiated state " (*differing*—in the producing
force, in the mechanical sense, of motions *and* effects) remains in *statu
quo* as well as globes and everything else in the process of formation." Such is the " hypothesis fully in accordance with (your)
(my) note." For, as planetary development is as progressive as
human or race evolution, the hour of the Pralaya's coming catches
the series of worlds at successive stages of evolution; (*i.e.*), each
has attained to some one of the periods of evolutionary progress—
each stops there, until the outward impulse of the next *manvantara*
sets it going from that very point—like a stopped time-piece
rewound. Therefore, have I used the word " differentiated."

At the coming of the Pralaya no human, animal, or even
vegetable entity will be alive to see it, but there will be the earth
or globes with their mineral kingdoms; and all these planets will
be physically disintegrated in the pralaya, yet not destroyed; for
they have their places in the sequence of evolution, and their
" privations " coming again out of the subjective, they will find
the exact point from which they have to move on around the chain

of " manifested forms." This, as we know, is repeated endlessly throughout ETERNITY. Each man of us has gone this ceaseless round, and will repeat it for ever and ever. The deviation of each one's course, and his rate of progress from Nirvana to Nirvana is governed by causes which he himself creates out of the exigencies in which he finds himself entangled.

This picture of an eternity of action may appal the mind that has been accustomed to look forward to an existence of ceaseless repose. But their concept is not supported by the analogies of nature, nor—and ignorant though I may be thought of your Western Science, may I not say?—by the teachings of that Science. We know that periods of action and rest follow each other in everything in nature from the macrocosm with its Solar Systems down to man and its parent-earth, which has its seasons of activity followed by those of sleep; and that in short all nature, like her begotten living forms has her time for recuperation. So with the spiritual individuality, the Monad which starts on its downward and upward cyclic rotation. The periods which intervene between each great *manvantarian* " round " are proportionately long to reward for the thousands of existences passed on various globes; while the time given between each " race birth "— or *rings* as you call them—is sufficiently lengthy to compensate for any life of strife and misery during that lapse of time passed in conscious bliss after the re-birth of the *Ego*. To conceive of an *eternity* of bliss or woe, and to offset it to any conceivable deeds of merit or demerit of a being who may have lived a century or even a millenium in the flesh, can only be proposed by one who has never yet grasped the awful reality of the word Eternity, nor pondered upon the law of perfect justice and equilibrium which pervades nature. Further instructions may be given you, which will show how nicely justice is done not to man only but also his subordinates, and throw some light, I hope, upon the vexed question of good and evil.

And now to crown this effort of mine (of writing) I may as well pay an old debt, and answer an old question of yours concerning earth incarnations. Koot'humi answers some of your queries— at least began writing yesterday but was called off by duty— but I may help him anyhow. I trust you will not find much difficulty—not as much as hitherto—in making out my letter. I have become a very plain writer since he reproached me with making you lose your valuable time over my scrawlings. His rebuke struck home, and as you see I have amended my evil ways.

Let us see what your Science has to tell us about Ethnography and other matters. The latest conclusions to which your wise men of the West seem to have arrived briefly stated are the following. The theories even approximately correct I venture to underline with blue.[1]

(1) The earliest traces of man they can find disappear beyond the close of a period of which the rock-fossils furnish the only clue *they possess*.

(2) Starting thence they find four races of men who have successively inhabited Europe (*a*) The race of the river Drift—mighty hunters (perchance Nimrod?) **who dwelt in the then sub-tropical climate of Western Europe,** who used chipped stone implements of the most primitive kind and **were contemporary with the rhinoceros and the mammoth**; (*b*) the so-called cave-men, a race developed during the glacial period **(the Esquimaux being now, they say, its only type)** and which possessed finer weapons and tools of chipped stone since they made with wondrous accuracy pictures of various animals they were familiar with, simply with the aid of sharp pointed flints on the antlers of reindeer and on bones and stones; (*c*) the third race—the men of the Neolithic age are found already *grinding* their stone implements, building houses and boats and making pottery, in short—the lake dwellers of Switzerland; and finally (*d*) appears the fourth race, coming from Central Asia. These are the fair complexioned Aryans who intermarry with the remnant of the dark Iberians—now represented by the swarthy Basques of Spain. This is the race which they consider as the progenitors of you modern peoples of Europe.

(3) They add, moreover, that the men of the river Drift preceded the glacial period known in geology as the *Pleistocene,* and originated some 240,000 years ago, while human beings generally (see Geikie, Dawkins, Fiske and others) inhabited **Europe at least 100,000 years earlier.**

With one solitary exception they are all wrong. They come near enough yet miss the mark in every case. There were not *four* but *five* races; and we are that fifth with remnants of the fourth. (A more perfect evolution or race with each mahacyclic round); while the first race appeared on earth not half a million of years ago (Fiske's theory)—but several millions. The latest scientific theory is that of the German and American professors who say through Fiske: " we see man living on the earth for perhaps half a million years to all *intents and purposes dumb*."

He is both right and wrong. Right about the race having been " dumb," for long ages of silence were required for the evolution and mutual comprehension of speech, from the moans and mutterings of the first remove of man above the highest anthropoid (a race now extinct since " nature shuts the door behind her " as she advances, in more than one sense)—up to

[1] These passages appear in bold type italics.—ED.

8

the first monosyllable-uttering man. But he is wrong in saying all the rest.

By the bye, you ought to come to some agreement as to the terms used when discussing cyclic evolutions. Our terms are untranslatable; and without a good knowledge of our complete system (which cannot be given but to regular initiates) would suggest nothing definite to your perceptions but only be a source of confusion as in the case of the terms " Soul " and " Spirit " with all your metaphysical writers—especially the Spiritualists.

You must have patience with Subba Row. Give him time. He is now at his *tapas* and will not be disturbed. I will tell him not to neglect you but he is very jealous and regards teaching an Englishman as a sacrilege.

Yours M.

P.S.—My writing is good but the paper rather thin for penmanship. Cannot write English with a brush though; would be worse.

LETTER No. 13 [1]

Cosmological Notes. Queries and M.'s Replies. Received Janaury, 1882. Allahabad.

(1) I conceive that at the close of a pralaya the impulse given by the Dhyan Chohans does not develop from chaos, a succession of worlds simultaneously, but seriatim. The comprehension of the manner in which each in succession ensues from its predecessor as the impact of the original impulse might perhaps be better postponed till after I am enabled to realize the working of the whole machine—the cycle of worlds—after all its parts have come into existence.

(1) Correctly conceived. Nothing in nature springs into existence suddenly, all being subjected to the same law of gradual evolution. Realize but once the process of the *maha* cycle, of one sphere and you have realized them all. One man is born like another man, one race evolves, develops, and declines like another and all other races. Nature follows the same groove from the " creation " of a universe down to that of a mosquito. In studying esoteric cosmogony, keep a spiritual eye upon the physiological process of human birth; proceed from cause to effect establishing as you go along, analogies between the birth of a man and that of a

[1] Mr. Sinnett's Queries in ordinary type with M.'s Replies in bold type. —ED.

world. In our doctrine you will find necessary the synthetic method; you will have to embrace the whole—that is to say to blend the *macrocosm* and microcosm together—before you are enabled to study the parts separately or analyze them with profit to your understanding. Cosmology is the physiology of the universe spiritualized, for there is but one law.

(2) Taking the middle of a period of [activity between two pralayas, *i.e.*, of a manvantara—what I understand to happen is this. Atoms are polarized in the highest region of spiritual efflux from behind the veil of primitive cosmic matter. The magnetic impulse which has accomplished this result flits from one mineral form to another within the first sphere till having run the round of existence in that kingdom of the first sphere it descends in a current of attraction to the second sphere.

(2) Polarize themselves during the process of motion and propelled by the irresistible Force at work. In Cosmogony and the work of nature the positive and the negative or the active and passive forces correspond to the male and female principles. Your " spiritual efflux " comes not from " behind the veil " but is the male seed falling *into* the veil of cosmic matter. The active is attracted by the passive principle and the Great Nag, the serpent emblem of the eternity, attracts its tail to its mouth forming thereby a circle (cycles in the eternity) in that incessant pursuit of the negative by the positive. Hence the emblem of the *lingam*, the *phallus* and the *kteis*. The one and chief attribute of the universal spiritual principle—the unconscious but ever active life-giver—is to expand and shed; that of the universal material principle to gather in and fecundate. Unconscious and non-existing when separated, they become consciousness and life when brought together. Hence again—Brahma, from the root " brih " the Sanskrit for " to expand, grow or to fructify," Brahma being but the vivifying *expansive* force of nature in its eternal evolution.

(3) Do worlds of effects intervene between the worlds of activity in the series of descent?

(3) The worlds of effects are not lokas or localities. They are the shadow of the world of causes, their *souls*—worlds having like men their seven principles which develop and grow simultaneously with the body. Thus the *body* of man is wedded to and remains for ever within the body of his planet; his individual *jivatma* life principle, that which is called in physiology *animal spirits* returns after death to its source—*Fohat*; his *linga shariram* will be drawn into *Akasa*; his *Kamarupa* will recommingle with the Universal *Sakti*—the Will-Force, or universal energy; his " animal soul " borrowed from the breath of *Universal Mind* will return to the Dhyan Chohans;

his sixth principle—whether drawn into or ejected from the matrix of the Great Passive Principle must remain in its own sphere—either as part of the crude material or as an individualized entity to be reborn in a higher world of causes. The seventh will carry it from the *Devachan* and follow the new *Ego* to its place of re-birth. . . .

(4) The magnetic impulse which cannot yet be conceived of as an individuality—enters the second sphere in the same (the mineral) kingdom as that to which it belonged in sphere I and runs the round of mineral incarnations there passing on to sphere III. Our earth is still a sphere of necessity for it. Hence it passes into the upward series—and from the highest of these passes into the vegetable kingdom of sphere I.

Without any new impulse of creative force from above, its career round the cycle of worlds as a mineral principle has developed some new attractions or polarization which cause it to assume the lowest vegetable form—in vegetable forms it passes successively through the cycle of worlds, the whole being still a circle of necessity (as no responsibility can yet have accrued to an unconscious individuality, and therefore it cannot at any stage of its progress do anything to select one or other of divergent paths). Or is there something in the life even of a vegetable which, though not responsibility, may lead it up or down at this critical stage of its progress?

Having completed the whole cycle as a vegetable the growing individuality expands on the next circuit into an animal form.

(4) The evolution of the worlds cannot be considered apart from the evolution of everything created or having being on these worlds. Your accepted conceptions of cosmogony—whether from the theological or scientific standpoints—do not enable you to solve a single anthropological, or even ethnical problem and they stand in your way whenever you attempt to solve the problem of the races on this planet. When a man begins to talk about creation and the origin of man, he is butting against the facts incessantly. Go on saying: " Our planet and man were created "—and you will be fighting against *hard facts* for ever, analyzing and losing time over trifling details—unable to ever grasp the whole. But once admit that our planet and ourselves are no more *creations* than the iceberg now before me (in our K. H.'s home) but that both planet and man are—*states* for a given time; that their present appearance—geological and anthropological—is transitory and but a condition concomitant of that stage of evolution at which they have arrived in the descending cycle —and all will become plain. You will easily understand what is meant by the " one and only " element or principle in the universe

and that *androgynous*; the seven-headed serpent *Ananta* of Vishnu, the *Nag* around Buddha—the great dragon eternity biting with its *active* head its *passive* tail, from the emanations of which spring worlds, beings and things.   You will comprehend the reason why the first philosopher proclaimed ALL—Maya—but that one principle which rests during the *maha*-pralayas only—the " nights of Brahm."   . . .

Now think: the *Nag* awakes.   He heaves a heavy breath and the latter is sent like an electric shock all along the wire encircling *Space*.   Go to your pianoforte and execute upon the lower register of keys the *seven* notes of the lower octave—up and down.   Begin *pianissimo, crescendo* from the first key, and having struck *fortissimo* on the last *lower* note go back *diminuendo*, getting out of your last note a hardly perceptible sound—" morendo pianissimo " (as I luckily for my illustration find it printed in one of the musick pieces in K. H.'s old portmanteau).   The first and the last notes will represent to you the first and last spheres in the cycle of evolution —the highest! the one you strike *once* is our planet.   Remember you have to reverse the order on the pianoforte: begin with the seventh note, not with the first.   The seven vowels chanted by the Egyptian priests to the seven rays of the rising sun to which Memnon responded, meant but that.   The one *Life-principle* when in action runs in *circuits* even as known in physical science.   It runs the round in human body, where the head represents and is to the Micro-cosmos (the physical world of matter) what the summit of the cycle is to the Macrocosmos (the world of universal spiritual Forces); and so with the formation of worlds and the great descending and ascend-ing " circle of necessity."   All is one Law.   Man has his seven principles, the germs of which he brings with him at his birth.   So has a planet or a world.   From first to last every sphere has its world of effects, the passing through which will afford a place of final rest to each of the human principles—the seventh principle excepted. The world No. A is born; and with it, clinging like barnacles to the bottom of a ship in motion, evolute from its first breath of life the living beings of its atmosphere, from the germs hitherto inert, now awakening to life with the first motion of the sphere.   With sphere A begins the mineral kingdom and runs the round of mineral evolution. By the time it is completed sphere B comes into objectivity and draws to itself the *life* which has completed its round on sphere A, and has become a *surplus*, (the fount of life being inexhaustible, for it is the true Arachne doomed to spin out its web eternally—save the periods of *pralaya*).   Then comes vegetable life on sphere A, and the same process takes place.   On its downward course " life " becomes with every state coarser, more material; on its upward more shadowy. No—there is [not], nor can there be any responsibility until the time when matter and spirit are properly equilibrized.   Up to *man* " life " has no responsibility in whatever form; no more than has the foetus who in his mother's womb passes through all the forms of life—as a mineral, a vegetable, an animal to become finally *Man*.

(5) Where does it get the animal soul, its fifth principle, from? Has the potentiality of this resided from the first in the original magnetic impulse which constituted the mineral, or at every transition from the last world on the ascending side to sphere I does it, so to speak, pass through an ocean of spirit and assimilate some new principle?

(5) Thus you see his *fifth* principle is evolved from *within himself*, man having as you well say " the potentiality " of all the seven principles as a germ, from the very instant he appears in the first world of causes as a shadowy breath, which coagulates with, and is hardened together with the parent sphere.

Spirit or LIFE is indivisible. And when we speak of the seventh principle it is neither quality nor quantity nor yet form that are meant, but rather the *space* occupied in that *ocean* of spirit by the results or effects—(beneficent as are all those of a co-worker with nature)—impressed thereon.

(6) From the highest animal (non-human) form in sphere I— how does it get to sphere II? It is inconceivable that it can descend to the lowest animal form there, but otherwise how can it go through the whole circle of life on each planet in turn?

If it runs its cycle in a spiral (*i.e.*, from form 1 of sphere I to form 1 of sphere II, etc.—then to form 2 of sphere I, II, III, etc., and then to form 3 of sphere. . . . n^{th}) then it seems to me that the same rule must apply to the mineral and vegetable individualities if they have such, and yet some things I have been told seem to militate against that. **(State them and they will be answered and explained.)**

For the moment I must work on that hypothesis, however.

(Having swept through the cycle in the highest animal form the animal soul in its next plunge into the ocean of spirit acquires the seventh principle which endows it with a sixth. This determines its future on Earth, and at the close of the earth life has sufficient vitality to keep an attraction of its own for the seventh principle, or loses this and ceases to exist as a separate entity. **All this misconceived.**)

Seventh principle always there as a latent force in every one of the principles—even body. As the macrocosmic *Whole* it is present even in the *lower* sphere, but there is nothing there to assimilate it to itself.

(6) Why, " inconceivable? " The highest animal form in sphere I or A being *irresponsible*, there is no degradation for it to merge

into sphere II or B as the most infinitesimal of that sphere. While on its upward course, as you were told, man finds even the lowest animal form *there*—higher than he was himself on earth. How do you know that men and animals and even life in its incipient stage is not a thousand times higher there, than it is here? Besides which, every kingdom (and we have seven—while you have but three) is subdivided into *seven* degrees or classes. Man (physically) is a compound of all the kingdoms, and spiritually—his individuality is no worse for being shut up within the casing of an ant than it is for being inside a king. It is not the *outward* or physical shape that dishonours and pollutes the five principles—but the *mental* perversity. Then it is but at his fourth round, when arrived at the full possession of his *Kama*-energy and completely matured, that man becomes *fully responsible*, as at the *sixth* he may become a *Buddha* and at the seventh before the Pralaya—a " Dhyan Chohan." Mineral, vegetable, animal-man, all of these have to run their *seven* rounds during the period of earth's activity—the *Maha Yug*. I will not enter here on the details of mineral and vegetable evolution, but I will notice only man—or—*animal-man*. He starts downward as a simply spiritual entity—an unconscious seventh principle (a *Parabrahm* in contradistinction to *Para-parabrahm*)—with the germs of the other six principles lying latent and dormant in him. Gathering solidity at every sphere—his six pr. when passing through the worlds of effects, and his outward form in the worlds of causes (for these worlds or stages on the descending side we have other names), when he touches our planet he is but a glorious bunch of light upon a sphere itself yet pure and undefiled (for mankind and every living thing on it increase in their materiality with the planet). At that stage our globe is like the head of a newly born babe—soft, and with undefined features, and man—an *Adam* before the *breath of life was breathed into his nostrils* (to quote your own bungled up Scriptures for your better comprehension). For man and (our planet's) nature—it is day—*the first* (see distorted tradition in your Bible). Man No. 1 makes his appearance at the apex of the circle of the spheres on sphere No. 1, after the completion of the seven rounds or periods of the two kingdoms (known to you) and thus he is said to be created on the eighth day (see Bible Chapter II; note verses 5 and 6 and think what is meant there by " *mist* "—and verse 7 wherein LAW the Universal great fashioner is termed " God " by Christians and Jews, and understood as *Evolution* by Kabbalists). During this first round " animal-man " runs, as you say, his cycle in a spiral. On the descending arc—whence *he starts after the completion of the seventh round of animal life* on his own individual *seven* rounds—he has to enter every sphere not as a *lower animal* as you understand it but as a *lower man*, since during the cycle which preceded his round as a man he performed it as the highest type of animal. Your " Lord

God," says Bible, chapter I, verses 25 and 26—after having made *all* said: " Let us make man in our image," etc., and creates man— an *androgyne ape!* (extinct on our planet) the highest in intelligence in the animal kingdom and whose descendants you find in the anthropoids of to-day. Will you deny the possibility of the highest anthropoid in the next sphere being higher in intelligence than some men down here—savages for instance, the African dwarf-race and our own Veddhas of Ceylon? But man has no such " degradation " to go through as soon as he has reached the fourth stage of his cyclic rounds. Like the lower *lives* and beings during his first, second and third round and while he is an irresponsible compound of *pure* matter and *pure* spirit (none of them as yet defiled by the consciousness of their possible purposes and applications) from sphere I, where he has performed his *local* sevenfold round of evolutionary process from the lowest class of the *highest* species of—say—anthropoids up to rudimentary man [he] certainly enters No. 2 as an *ape* (the last word being used for your better comprehension). At this round or stage his individuality is as dormant in him as that of a foetus during his period of gestation. He has no consciousness, no sense, for he begins as a rudimentary astral man and lands on our planet as a primitive physical man. So far it is a mere passing on of mechanical motion. Volition and consciousness are at the same time self-determining and determined by causes, and the volition of man, his intelligence and consciousness will awake but when his fourth principle *Kama* is matured and completed by its (*seriatim*) contact with the *Kamas* or energizing forces of all the forms man has passed through in his previous three rounds. The present mankind is at its *fourth* round (mankind as a genus or a kind, not a RACE *nota bene*) of the *post-pralayan* cycle of evolution; and as its various races, so the individual entities in them are unconsciously to themselves performing their *local* earthly sevenfold cycles—hence the vast difference in the degrees of their intelligence, energy and so on. Now every individuality will be followed on its ascending arc by the Law of retribution—Karma and death accordingly. The perfect man or the entity which reached full perfection, (each of his seven principles being matured) will not be reborn here. His local terrestrial cycle is completed and he has to either proceed onward or—be annihilated as an individuality. (The incomplete entities have to be reborn or reincarnated).[1] On their fifth round after a partial Nirvana when the zenith of the grand cycle is reached, they will be held responsible henceforth in their descents from sphere to sphere, as they will have to appear on this earth as a still more perfect and intellectual race. This downward course has not yet begun but will soon. Only how many—oh, how many will be destroyed on their way!

[1] By-the-bye, I'll re-write for you pages 345 to 357, Vol. I., of *Isis*—much jumbled, and confused by Olcott, who thought he was improving it!

The above said *is the rule*. The Buddhas and *Avatars* form the exception, as verily we have *yet some Avatars* left to us on earth.

(7) The animal soul having in successive passages round the cycle lost, so to speak, the momentum which previously carried it past the divergent path downward which strikes off here, falls into the lower world, in the relatively brief cycle in which its individuality is dissipated.

But this would only be the case with the animal soul which had not, in its union with spirit, developed a durable sixth principle. If it had done this, and if the sixth principle, drawing to itself the individuality of the complete man, had withered the inferior fifth principle by so doing—as the aloe's flower, when thrown up, withers its leaves—then the animal soul would not have cohesion enough to enter on another existence in a lower world and would be soon dissipated in the sphere of this earth's attraction.

(7) Reforming your conceptions on what I gave you above you will understand now better.

The whole individuality is centred in the three middle or 3rd, 4th and 5th principles.   During earthly life it is all in the fourth, the centre of energy, volition—will.   Mr. Hume has perfectly defined the difference between personality and individuality.   The former hardly survives—the latter, to run successfully its seven-fold downward and upward course, has to assimilate to itself the eternal life-power residing but in the seventh and then blend the three (fourth, fifth and seventh) into one—the sixth.   Those who succeed in doing so become Buddhas, Dhyan Chohans, etc.   The chief object of our struggles and *initiations* is to achieve this union while yet on this earth.   Those who will be successful have nothing to fear during the fifth, sixth and seventh rounds.   But this is a mystery.   Our beloved K. H. is on his way to the goal—the highest of all beyond as on this sphere.

I have to thank you for all you have done for our two friends. *It is a debt of gratitude we owe* you.

M.

For some short time you will not hear of, or from me— PREPARE.

LETTER No. 14 [1]

Letter from K. H.   Answering Queries.   Received by A.O.H., July 9th, 1882.

(1) We understand that the man-bearing cycle of necessity of our solar system consists of thirteen objective globes, of which ours is the lowest, six above it in the ascending, and six in the

[1] Transcribed from a copy in Mr. Sinnett's handwriting.—ED.

descending cycle with a fourteenth world lower still than ours. Is this correct?

(1) The number is not quite correct. There are seven objective and seven subjective globes (I have been just permitted for the first time to give you the right figure), the worlds of causes and of effects. The former have our earth occupying the lower turning point where spirit-matter equilibrates. But do not trouble yourself to go into calculations even on this correct basis for it will only puzzle you, since the infinite ramifications of the number seven (which is one of our greatest mysteries) being so closely allied and interdependent with the seven principles of Nature and man—this figure is the only one I am permitted (so far) to give you. What I can reveal I do so in a letter I am just finishing.

(2) We understand that below man you reckon not three kingdoms as we do (mineral, vegetable and animal) but seven. Please enumerate and explain these.

(2) Below man there are three in the objective and three in the subjective region, with man a septenary. Two of the three former none but an initiate could conceive of; the third is the Inner kingdom— below the crust of the earth—which we could name but would feel embarrassed to describe. These seven kingdoms are preceded by other and numerous septenary stages and combinations.

(3) We understand that the monad, starting in the highest world of the descending series, appears there in a mineral encasement, and there goes through a series of seven encasements representing the seven classes into which the mineral kingdom is divided, and that this done it passes to the next planet and does likewise (I purposely say nothing of the worlds of results, where it takes on the development the result of what it has gone through in the last world and the necessary preparation for the next) and so on right through the thirteen spheres, making altogether 91 mineral existences. (*a*) Is this correct? (*b*) If so, what are the classes we are to reckon in the mineral kingdom? Also (*c*) How does the monad get out of one encasement into another; in the case of inherbations and incarnations, the plant and animal dies, but so far as we know the mineral does not die, so how does the monad in the first round get out of one into another inmetalliation? (*d*) And has every separate molecule of the mineral a monad or only those groups of molecules where definite structure is observable such as crystals?

(3) Yes; in our string of worlds it starts at globe " A " of the descending series and passing through all the preliminary evolutions and combinations of the first three kingdoms it finds itself encased in its first mineral form (in what I call race when speaking of man)

and what we may call class in general)—of class I—there. Only it
passes through *seven* instead of " through the thirteen spheres "
even omitting the intermediate " worlds of results."   Having passed
through its seven great classes of inmetalliation (a good word this)
with their septenary ramifications—the monad gives birth to the
vegetable kingdom and moves on to the next planet " B. "

(a) As you now see, except as to the numbers.   (b) Your geologists
divide, I believe, stones into three great groups—of sandstone, granite
and chalk; or the sedimentary, igneous, and organic, following their
physical characteristics just as the psychologists and spiritualists
divide man into the trinity of body, soul, and spirit.   Our method is
totally different. We divide minerals (also the other kingdoms)
according to their occult properties, *i.e.*, according to the relative
proportion of the seven universal principles which they contain.
I am sorry to refuse you, but I cannot, am not permitted to answer
your question. To facilitate for you a question of simple nomenclature, however, I would advise you to study perfectly the seven
principles in man, and thus[1] to divide the seven great classes of the
minerals correspondentially. For instance, the group of the sedimentary would answer to the compound (chemically speaking) body
of man or his first principle; the organic to the second (some call it
third) principle or jiva, etc., etc. You must exercise your own intuitions in that. Thus you might also intuit certain truths even as to
their properties. I am more than willing to help you but things have
to be divulged *gradually*.   (c) By occult *osmosis*. The plant and
animal leave their carcases behind when life is extinct. So does the
mineral only at longer intervals, as its rocky body is more lasting.
It dies at the end of every *manwantaric* cycle, or at the close of one
" Round " as you would call it. It is explained in the letter I am
preparing for you.   (d) Every molecule is part of the Universal Life.
Man's soul (his fourth and fifth principle) is but a compound of the
progressed entities of the lower kingdom. The superabundance or
preponderance of one over another compound will often determine
the instincts and passions of a man, unless these are checked by the
soothing and spiritualizing influence of his sixth principle.

(4) Please note, we call the Grand Cycle that the monad has
performed in the mineral kingdom a " round " which we understand to contain thirteen (seven) stations, or objective, more or
less material worlds. At each of these stations it performs what
we call a " world ring," which includes seven inmetalliations, one
in each of the seven classes of that kingdom. Is this accepted
for nomenclature and correct?

(4) I believe it will lead to a further confusion. A Round we are
agreed to call the passage of a monad from globe " A " to globe

[1] Query ' then '.—EDS.

" Z " (or " G ") through the encasement in all and each of the four kingdoms, viz., as a mineral, a vegetable, an animal and man or the Deva kingdom. The " world ring " is correct. M. advised Mr. Sinnett strongly to agree upon a nomenclature before going any further. A few stray facts were given to you *par contrebande* and on the smuggling principle hitherto. But now since you seem really and seriously determined to study and utilize our philosophy—it is time we should begin to work seriously. Because we are constrained to deny to our friends an insight into the higher Mathematics it is no reason why we should refuse to teach them arithmetic. The monad performs not only " world rings " or seven major inmetallia-tions, inherbations, zoonisations (?) and incarnations—but an infini-tude of sub-rings or subordinate whirls all in series of sevens. As the geologist divides the crust of the earth into great divisions, sub-divisions, minor compartments and zones; and the botanist his plants into orders, classes and species, and the zoologist his subjects into classes, orders and families, so we have our arbitrary classifications and our nomenclature. But besides all this being incomprehensible to you, volumes upon volumes out of the Books of Kiu-te and others would have to be written. Their commentaries are worse still. They are filled with the most abstruse mathematical calculations the keys to most of which are in the hands of our highest adepts only, since showing as they do the infinitude of the phenomenal manifesta-tions in the side projections of the *one* Force they are again secret. Therefore I doubt whether I will be allowed to give you for the present anything beyond the mere unitary or root idea. Anyhow I will do my best.

(5) We understand that in *each* of your other six kingdoms, a monad similarly performs a complete round, in each round stop-ping in each of the thirteen stations, and there performing in each a world ring of seven lives, one in each of the seven classes into which each of the 6 said kingdoms are divided. Is this correct, and, if so, will you give us the seven classes of these six kingdoms?

(5) If by kingdoms the seven kingdoms or regions of the earth are meant—and I do not see how it can mean anything else—then the query is answered in my reply to your Question (2) and if so then the five out of the seven are already enumerated. The first two are related, as well as the third, to the evolution of the elementals and of the Inner kingdom.

(6) If we are right then the total existences prior to the man-period is 637. Is this correct? Or are there seven existences in each class of each kingdom, 4,459? Or what are the total numbers and how divided? One point more. In these lower

kingdoms is the number of lives, so to speak, invariable, or does it vary, and, if so, how, why, and within what limits?

(6) Not being permitted to give you the whole truth, or divulge the number of isolated fractions, I am unable to satisfy you by giving you the total number. Rest assured, my dear Brother, that to one who does not seek to become a practical occultist these numbers are immaterial. Even our high chelas are refused these particulars to the moment of their initiation into adeptship. These figures as I have already said are so interwoven with the profoundest psychological mysteries that to divulge the key to such figures would be to put the rod of power within the reach of all the clever men who would read your book. All that I can tell you is that within the Solar Manwantara the number of existences or vital activities of the monad is fixed, but there are local variations in number in *minor* systems, individual worlds, rounds, and world rings, according to circumstances. And in this connexion remember also that human *personalities* are often *blotted out*, while the entities whether single or compound complete all the minor and major circles of necessities[1] under whatsoever form.

(7) So far we hope we are tolerably correct, but when we come to Man we have got muddled.

(7) And no wonder, since you were not given the correct information.

(7*a*) Does the monad as Man (ape-man and upwards) make one or seven rounds as above defined? We gathered the latter.

(7a) As a man-ape he performs just as many rounds and rings as every other race or class; *i.e.*, he performs one Round and in every planet from " A " to " Z " has to go through seven chief races of ape-like man, as many sub-races, etc., etc. (See Supplementary Notes) as the above described race.

(7*b*) At each *round* does his *world circle* consist of seven lives in seven races (49) or of only seven lives in one race? We are not certain how you use the word race, whether there is only one race to each station of each round, *i.e.*, one race to each world circle or whether there are seven races (with their seven branchlets and a life in each in either case) in each world circle? Nay, from your use of the words " and through each of these Man *has* to evolute before he passes on to the next higher race and that *seven times*," we are not sure that there are not seven lives in each branchlet as you call it, *sub-race* we will, if you like, say. So now there may be seven rounds each with seven races, each with seven sub-races, each with seven incarnations$=13 \times 7 \times 7 \times 7 \times 7 = 31,213$ lives, or one round with seven races and seven

[1] Query, cycles of necessity.—EDS.

sub-races and a life in each$=13 \times 7 \times 7=637$ lives or again 4,459 lives. Please set us right here, stating the normal number of lives (the exact numbers will vary owing to idiots, children, etc., not counting) and how divided.

(7b) As the above described race: *i.e.*, at each planet—our earth included—he has to perform seven rings thhrough seven races (one in each) and seven multiplied by seven offshoots. There are seven root-races, and seven sub-races or offshoots. Our doctrine treats anthropology as an absurd empty dream of the religionists and confines itself to ethnology. It is possible that my nomenclature is faulty; you are at liberty in such a case to change it. What I call " race " you would perhaps term " stock " though sub-race expresses better what we mean than the word family or division of the genus homo. However, to set you right so far I will say—one life in each of the seven root-races; seven lives in each of the 49 sub-races—or $7 \times 7 \times 7=343$ and add 7 more. And then a series of lives in offshoot and branchlet races; making the total incarnations of man in each station or planet 777. The principle of acceleration and retardation applies itself in such a way, as to eliminate all the inferior stocks and leave but a single superior one to make the last ring. Not much to divide over some millions of years that man passes on one planet. Let us take but one million of years—suspected and now accepted by your science—to represent man's entire term upon our earth in this Round; and allowing an average of a century for each life, we find that whereas he has passed in all his lives upon our planet (in this Round) but 77,700 years he has been in the subjective spheres 922,300 years. Not much encouragement for the extreme modern re-incarnationists who remember their several previous existences!

Should you indulge in any calculations do not forget that we have computed above only full average lives of consciousness and responsibility. Nothing has been said as to the failures of Nature in abortions, congenital idots, death of children in their first septenary cycles, nor of the *exceptions* of which I cannot speak. No less have you to remember that average human life varies greatly according to the Rounds. Though I am obliged to withhold information about many points yet if you should work out any of the problems by yourself it will be my duty to tell you so. Try to solve the problem of the 777 incarnations.

(8) " M " said all mankind is in the fourth round, the fifth has not yet commenced but soon will. Was this a slip? If not, then collating this with your present remarks we gather that all mankind is on the fourth round (though in another place you seemed to say we are on the fifth round). That the highest people now on earth belong to the first sub-race of the fifth race, the majority to the seventh sub-race of the fourth race but with remnants of the

other sub-races of the fourth race and the seventh sub-race of the third race. Pray set us quite right on this.

(8) " M " knows very little English and *hates* writing. But even I might have used very well the same expression. A few drops of rain do not make a monsoon though they presage it. The fifth round has not commenced on our earth and the races and sub-races of one round must not be confounded with those of another round. The fifth round mankind may be said to have " commenced " when there shall not be left on the planet which precedes ours a single man of that round and on our earth not one of the fourth round. You should know also that the casual fifth round men (and very few and scarce they are) who come in upon us as *avant couriers* do not beget on earth fifth round progeny. Plato and Confucius were fifth round men and our Lord a sixth round man (the mystery of his avatar is spoken of in my forthcoming letter) and not even Gautama Buddha's son was anything but a fourth round man.

Our mystic terms in their clumsy re-translation from the Sanskrit into English are as confusing to us as they are to you—especially to " M ". Unless in writing to you one of us takes his pen *as an adept* and uses it from the first word to the last, in this capacity he is quite as liable to " slips " as any other man. No, we are not in the fifth round, but fifth round men have been coming in for the last few thousand years. But what is such a petty stretch of time in comparison with even one million of the several millions of years embraced in man's occupancy of earth in a single round?

K. H.

Please examine carefully the few additional things I give you on the fly-leaves. Damodar has received orders to send you No. 3 of Terry's letters—a good material for pamphlet No. 3 of Fragments of Occult Truth.

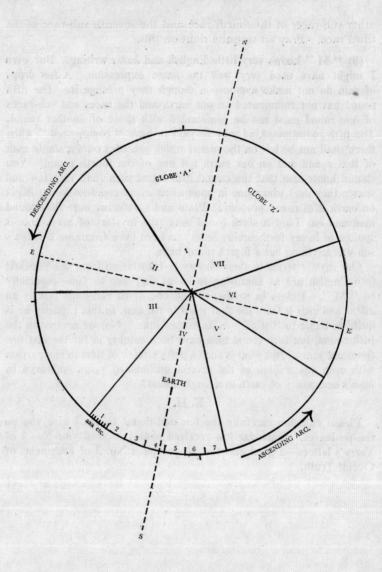

MAN ON A PLANET [1]

This figure roughly represents the development of humanity on a planet—say our earth. Man evolves in seven major or root-races; 49 minor races; and the subordinate races or offshoots, the branchlet races coming from the latter are not shown.

The arrow indicates the direction taken by the evolutionary impulse.

I, II, III, IV, etc., are the seven major or root-races.

1, 2, 3, etc., are the minor races.

a, a, a, are the subordinate or offshoot races.

N, the initial and terminal point of evolution on the planet.

S, the axial point where the development equilibrates or adjusts itself in each race evolution.

E, the equatorial points where in the descending arc intellect overcomes spirituality and in the ascending arc spirituality outstrips intellect.

(N.B.—The above in D.K.'s hand—the rest in K.H.'s.—A.P.S.)

P.S.—In his hurry D. J. K. has made his figure incline somewhat out of the perpendicular but it will serve as a rough memorandum. He drew it to represent development on a single planet; but I have added a word or two to make it apply as well (which it does) to a whole manwantaric chain of worlds.

K. H.

Supplementary Notes

Whenever any question of evolution or development in any Kingdom presents itself to you bear constantly in mind that everything comes under the Septenary rule of series in their correspondences and mutual relation throughout nature.

In the evolution of man there is a topmost point, a bottom point, a descending arc, and an ascending arc. As it is " Spirit " which transforms itself into " matter " and (not " matter " which ascends —but) matter which *resolves once more into spirit*, of course the first race evolution and the last on a planet (as in each round) must be more etherial, more spiritual, the fourth or lowermost one most physical (progressively of course in each round) and at the same time—*as physical intelligence is the masked manifestation of spiritual intelligence*—each evolved race in the downward arc must be more physically intelligent than its predecessor, and each in the upward arc have a more refined form of mentality commingled with spiritual intuitiveness.

The first race (or stock) of the first round after a *solar* manwantara (kindly wait for my forthcoming letter before you allow yourself to be repuzzled or remuddled—it will explain a good deal), would then be a god-man race of an almost impalpable shape, and so it is; but then comes the difficulty to the student to reconcile this fact with the evolution of man from the *animal*—however high his form among the

9

anthropoids. And yet it is reconcilable, for whomsoever will hold religiously to a strict analogy between the works of the two worlds, the visible and the invisible—one world, in fact, as one is working within itself so to say. Now there are—there *must be* " failures " in the etherial races of the many classes of Dhyan Chohans or Devas as well as among men. But still as these failures are too far progressed and spiritualized to be thrown back forcibly from their Dhyan Chohanship into the vortex of a new primordial evolution through the lower kingdoms—this then happens. When a new solar system is to be evolved these Dhyan Chohans are (remember the Hindu allegory of the *Fallen Devas* hurled by Siva into Andarah [1] who are allowed by Parabrahm to consider it as an intermediate state where they may prepare themselves by a series of rebirths in that sphere for a higher state—a new regeneration) borne in by the influx " ahead " of the elementals and remain as a latent or inactive spiritual force in the aura of the nascent world of a new system until the stage of human evolution is reached. Then Karma has reached them and they will have to accept to the last drop in the bitter cup of retribution. Then they become an *active* Force, and commingle with the Elementals, or progressed *entities* of the pure animal kingdom to develop little by little the full type of humanity. In this commingling they lose their high intelligence and spirituality of Devaship to regain them in the end of the seventh ring in the seventh round.

Thus we have:

1st Round.—An ethereal being—*non-intelligent*, but super-spiritual. In each of the subsequent races and sub-races and minor races of evolution he grows more and more into an encased or incarnate being, but still preponderatingly etherial. And like the animal and vegetable he develops monstrous bodies correspondential with his coarse surroundings.

2nd Round.—He is still gigantic and etherial, but growing firmer and more condensed in body—a more physical man, yet still less intelligent than spiritual; for mind is a slower and more difficult evolution than the physical frame, and the mind would not develop as rapidly as the body.

3rd Round.—He has now a perfectly concrete or compacted body; at first the form of a giant ape, and more intelligent (or rather cunning) than spiritual. For in the downward arc he has now reached the point where his primordial spirituality is eclipsed or over-shadowed by nascent mentality. In the last half of this third round his gigantic stature decreases, his body improves in texture (perhaps the microscope might help to demonstrate this) and he becomes a more rational being—though still more an ape than a Deva man.

4th Round.—Intellect has an enormous development in this round. The dumb races will acquire *our* human speech, on our globe, on

[1] Query, should be Antarāla (intermediate state).—EDS.

which from the 4th race language is perfected and knowledge in physical things increases. At this half-way point of the fourth round, Humanity passes the *axial point of the minor manwantaric circle*. (Moreover, at the middle point of every major or *root race* evolution of each round, man passes the equator of his course on that planet, the same rule applying to the whole evolution or the seven rounds of the minor Manwantara—7 rounds ÷ 2 = 3½ rounds). At this point then the world teems with the results of intellectual activity and *spiritual decrease*. In the first half of the fourth race, sciences, arts, literature and philosophy were born, eclipsed in one nation, reborn in another, civilization and intellectual development whirling in septenary cycles as the rest; while it is but in the latter half that the spiritual Ego will begin its real struggle with body and mind to manifest its transcendental powers. Who will help in the forthcoming gigantic struggle? Who? Happy the man who helps a helping hand.

5th Round.—The same relative development, and the same struggle continues.

6th Round.

7th Round.

Of these we need not speak.

LETTER No. 15 [1]

From K.H. to A.O.H. Received July 10th, 1882

(1) Does every mineral form, vegetable, plant, animal, always contain within it that entity which involves the potentiality of development into a planetary spirit? At this present day in this present earth is there such an essence or spirit or soul—the name is immaterial—in every mineral, etc.

(1) Invariably; only rather call it the *germ* of a future entity, which it has been for ages. Take the human foetus. From the moment of its first planting until it completes its seventh month of gestation it repeats in miniature the mineral, vegetable, and animal cycles it passed through in its previous encasements, and only during the last two develops its future human entity. It is completed but towards the child's seventh year. Yet it existed without any *increase* or *decrease* aeons on aeons before it worked its way onward, *through* and *in* the womb of mother nature as it works now in its earthly mother's bosom. Truly said a learned philosopher who trusts more to his intuitions than the dicta of modern science, " The stages of man's intra-uterine existence embody a condensed record of some of the missing pages in Earth's history." Thus you must look back at the animal, vegetable and mineral entities. You must take each

entity at its starting point in the manwantaric course as the primordial cosmic atom already differentiated by the first flutter of the manwantaric life breath. For the potentiality which develops finally in a perfected planetary spirit lurks in, *is* in fact that primordial cosmic atom. Drawn by its "*chemical* affinity" (?) to coalesce with other like atoms, the aggregate sum of such united atoms will in time become a man-bearing globe after the stages of the cloud, the spiral and sphere of fire-mist and of the condensation, consolidation, shrinkage and cooling of the planet have been successively passed through. But mind, not every globe becomes a "*man* bearer". I simply state the fact without dwelling further upon it in this connection. The great difficulty in grasping the idea in the above process lies in the liability to form more or less incomplete mental conceptions of the working of the *one* element, of its inevitable presence in every imponderable atom, and its subsequent ceaseless and almost illimitable multiplication of new centres of activity without affecting in the least its own original quantity. Let us take such an aggregation of atoms destined to form our globe and then follow, throwing a cursory look at the whole, the special work of such atoms. We will call the primordial atom A. This being not a circumscribed centre of activity but the initial point of a manwantaric whirl of evolution, gives birth to new centres which we may term B, C, D, etc., incomputably. Each of these capital points gives birth to minor centres, a, b, c, etc. And the latter in the course of evolution and involution in time develop into A's, B's, C's, etc., and so form the roots or are the developing causes of new genera, species, classes, etc., ad infinitum. Now neither the primordial A and its companion atoms, nor their derived a's, b's, c's, have lost one tittle of their original force or life-essence by the evolution of their derivatives. The force there is not transformed into something else, as I have already shown in my letter, but with each development of a new centre of activity from *within* itself multiplies ad infinitum without ever losing a particle of its nature in quantity or quality. Yet acquiring as it progresses something plus in its differentiation. This "force" so-called, shows itself truly indestructible but does *not* correlate and is *not* convertible in the sense accepted by the Fellows of the R. S., but rather may be said to *grow* and *expand* into "something else" while neither its own potentiality nor being are in the least affected by the transformation. Nor can it well be called *force* since the latter is but the attribute of Yin-sin (Yin-sin or the one "Form of existence," also Adi-Buddhi or Dharmakaya, the mystic, universally diffused essence) when manifesting in the phenomenal world of senses, namely, only your old acquaintance Fohat. See in this connexion Subba Row's article "Aryan Arhat Esoteric Doctrines" on the seven-fold principles in man; his review of your Fragments, pp. 94 and 95. The initiated Brahmin calls it (Yin-sin and Fohat) Brahman and Sakti when manifesting as that force. We will perhaps be near correct to call it *infinite life* and the source of all life visible and invisible, an essence inexhaustible, ever present, in short Swabhavat. (S. in its universal application, Fohat when manifesting throughout our phenomenal world, or rather the visible universe, hence in its limitations.) It is pravritti when active, nirvritti when passive. Call it the Sakti of Parabrahma, if you like, and say with the Adwaitees (Subba Row is one) that Parabrahm plus Maya becomes *Iswar* the creative principle—a power commonly called God which disappears and dies with the rest when pralaya comes. Or you may hold with the northern Buddhist philosophers and call it *Adi-Buddhi*, the all-pervading supreme and absolute intelligence with its periodically manifesting Divinity—" Avalokiteshvara " (a manwantaric intelligent nature crowned with humanity)—the mystic name given by us to the hosts of the Dhyan Chohans (N.B., the solar Dhyan Chohans or the host of only our solar system) taken collectively, which host represents the mother source, the aggregate amount of all the intelligences that were, are or ever will be, whether on our string of man-bearing planets or on any part or portion of our solar system. And this will bring you by analogy to see that in its turn Adi-Buddhi (as its very name translated literally implies) is the aggregate intelligence of the universal intelligences including that of the Dhyan Chohans even of the highest order. That is all I dare now to tell you on this special subject, as I fear I have already transcended the limit. Therefore whenever I speak of humanity without specifying it you must understand that I mean not humanity of our fourth round as we see it on this speck of mud in space but the whole host already evoluted.

Yes, as described in my letter—there is but one element and it is impossible to comprehend our system before a correct conception of it is firmly fixed in one's mind. You must therefore pardon me if I dwell on the subject longer than really seems necessary. But unless this great primary fact is firmly grasped the rest will appear unintelligible. This element then is the—to speak metaphysically—one sub-stratum or permanent cause of all manifestations in the phenomenal universe. The ancients speak of the five cognizable elements of ether, air, water, fire, earth, and of the one incognizable element (to the uninitiates) the 6th principle of the universe—call it Purush Sakti, while to speak of the seventh outside the sanctuary was punishable with death. But these five are but the differentiated aspects of the one. As man is a seven-fold being so is the universe—the septenary microcosm being to the septenary macrocosm but as the drop of rainwater is to the cloud from whence it dropped and whither in the course of time it will return. In that one are embraced or included so many tendencies for the evolution of air, water, fire, etc. (from the purely abstract down to their concrete condition) and when those latter are called elements it is to indicate their productive

potentialities for numberless form changes or evolution of being.
Let us represent the unknown quantity as X; that quantity is the
one eternal immutable principle—and A, B, C, D, E, five of the six
minor principles or components of the same; *viz.*, the principles of
earth, water, air, fire and ether (*akasa*) following the order of their
spirituality and beginning with the lowest.   There is a sixth principle
answering to the sixth principle *Buddhi*, in man (to avoid confusion
remember that in viewing the question from the side of the descending
scale the abstract All or eternal principle would be numerically desig-
nated as the first, and the phenomenal universe as the seventh, and
whether belonging to man or to the universe—viewed from the other
side the numerical order would be exactly reversed) but we are not
permitted to name it except among the initiates.   I may however
hint that it is connected with the process of the highest intellection.
Let us call it N.   And besides these, there is under all the activities
of the phenomenal universe an energizing impulse from X, call this
Y.   Algebraically stated, our equation would therefore read $A+B+C+D+E+N+Y=X$.   Each of these six letters represents, so to
speak, the spirit or abstraction of what you call elements (your
meagre English gives me no other word).   This spirit controls the
entire line of evolution, around the whole manwantaric cycle in its
own department.   The informing, vivifying, impelling, evolving *cause*,
behind the countless phenomenal manifestations in that department of
Nature.   Let us work out the idea with a single example.   Take fire.
D—the primal igneous principle resident in X—is the ultimate cause
of every phenomenal manifestation of fire on all the globes of the
chain.   The proximate causes are the evolved secondary igneous
agencies which severally control the *seven* descents of fire on each
planet, (every element having its seven principles and every principle
its seven sub-principles and these secondary agencies before doing so,
having in turn become primary causes.)   D is a septenary compound
of which the highest fraction is pure spirit.   As we see it on our
globe it is in its coarsest, most material condition, as gross in its
way as is man in his physical encasement.   In the next preceding
globe to ours fire was less gross than here: on the one before that less
still.   And so the body of flame was more and more pure and spiritual,
less and less gross and material on each antecedent planet.   On the
first of all in the manwantaric chain, it appeared as an almost pure
objective shining—the Maha Buddhi, sixth principle of the *eternal
light* Our globe being at the bottom of the arc where matter
exhibits itself in its grossest form along with spirit—when the fire
element manifests itself on the globe next succeeding ours in the
ascending arc it will be less dense than as we see it.   Its spiritual
quality will be identical with that which fire had on the globe preceding
ours in the descending scale; the second globe of the ascending scale
will correspond in quality with that of the second anterior globe to

ours in the descending scale, etc.   On each globe of the chain there are seven manifestations of fire of which the first in order will compare as to spiritual quality with the last manifestation on the next preceding planet: the process being reversed, as you will infer, with the opposite arc.   The myriad specific manifestations of these six universal elements are in their turn but the offshoots, branches or branchlets of the one single primordial " Tree of Life."

Take Darwin's genealogical tree of life of the human race and others, and bearing ever in mind the wise old adage, " As below so above "—that is, the universal system of correspondences—try to understand by analogy.   Thus will you see that in this day on this present earth in every mineral, etc., there is such a spirit.   I will say more.   Every grain of sand, every boulder or crag of granite, *is* that spirit crystallized or petrified.   You hesitate.   Take a primer of geology and see what science affirms there about the formation and growth of minerals.   What is the origin of all the rocks, whether sedimentary or igneous.   Take a piece of granite or sandstone and you find one composed of crystals, the other of grains of various stones (organic rocks or stones formed out of the remains of once living plants and animals, will not serve our present purpose; they are the relics of subsequent evolutions while we are concerned but with the primordial ones).   Now sedimentary and igneous rocks are composed, the former of sand, gravel and mud, the latter of lava. We have then but to trace the origin of the two.   What do we find? We find that one was compounded of three elements or more accurately three several manifestations of the *one* element,—earth, water and fire, and that the other was similarly compounded (though under different physical conditions) out of cosmic matter—the imaginary *materia prima* itself one of the manifestations (6th principle) of the one element.   How then can we doubt that a mineral contains in it a spark of the *One* as everything else in this objective nature does?

(2) When the pralaya commences what becomes of the Spirit that has not worked its way up to man?

(2) . . . The period necessary for the completion of the seven local or earthly—or shall we call it—globe-rings (not to speak of the seven Rounds in the minor manwantaras followed by their seven minor pralayas)—the completion of the so-called mineral cycle is immeasurably longer than that of any other kingdom.   As you may infer by analogy every globe before it reaches its adult period, has to pass through a formation period—also septenary.   Law in Nature is uniform and the conception, formation, birth, progress and develop- ment of the child differs from those of the globe only in magnitude. The globe has two periods of teething and of capillature—its first rocks which it also sheds to make room for new—and its ferns and mosses before it gets forest.   As the atoms in the body change

[every] seven years so does the globe renew its strata every seven cycles. A section of a part of Cape Breton coalfields shows seven ancient soils with remains of as many forests, and could one dig as deep once more seven other sections would be found following. . . .

There are three kinds of pralayas and manwantara:—

1. The universal or Maha pralaya and manwantara.
2. The solar pralaya and manwantara.
3. The minor pralaya and manwantara.

When the pralaya No. 1 is finished the universal manwantara begins. Then the whole universe must be re-evoluted *de novo*. When the pralaya of a solar system comes it affects that solar system only. A solar pralaya = 7 minor pralayas. The minor pralayas of No. 3 concern but our little string of globes, whether man-bearing or not. To such a string our Earth belongs.

Besides this within a minor pralaya there is a condition of planetary *rest* or as the astronomers say " death," like that of our present moon—in which the rocky body of the planet survives but the life impulse has passed out. For example, let us imagine that our earth is one of a group of seven planets or man-bearing worlds more or less elliptically arranged. Our earth being at the exact lower central point of the orbit of evolution, *viz.*, half way round—we will call the first globe A, the last Z. After each solar pralaya there is a *complete* destruction of our system and after each solar p. begins the absolute objective reformation of our system and each time everything is more perfect than before.

Now the life impulse reaches " A " or rather that which is destined to become " A " and which so far is but cosmic dust. A centre is formed in the nebulous matter of the condensation of the solar dust disseminated through space and a series of three evolutions invisible to the eye of flesh occur in succession, *viz.*, three kingdoms of elementals or nature forces are evoluted: in other words the animal soul of the future globe is formed; or as a Kabalist will express it, the gnomes, the salamanders, and the undines are created. The correspondence between a mother-globe and her child-man may be thus worked out. Both have their seven principles. In the Globe, the elementals (of which there are in all seven species) form (a) a gross body, (b) her fluidic double (linga sariram), (c) her life principle (jiva); (d) her fourth principle kama rupa is formed by her creative impulse working from centre to circumference; (e) her fifth principle (animal soul or Manas, physical intelligence) is embodied in the vegetable (in germ) and animal kingdoms; (f) her sixth principle (or spiritual soul, Buddhi) is man (g) and her seventh principle (Atma) is in a film of spiritualized akasa that surrounds her. The three evolutions completed, palpable globe begins to form. The mineral kingdom, fourth in the whole series, but first in this stage leads the way. Its deposits are at first vaporous, soft and plastic, only becoming hard and concrete in the seventh ring. When this ring is completed it projects its essence to globe B—which is already passing through the preliminary stages of formation, and mineral evolution begins on that globe. At this juncture the evolution of the vegetable kingdom commences on globe A. When the latter has made its seventh ring its essence passes on to globe B. At that time the mineral essence moves to globe C and the germs of the animal kingdom enter A. When the animal has seven rings there, its life principle goes to globe B, and the essences of vegetable and mineral move on. Then comes man on A, an ethereal foreshadowing of the compact being he is destined to become on our earth. Evolving seven parent races with many offshoots of sub-races, he, like the preceding kingdoms completes his seven rings and is then transferred successively to each of the globes onward to Z. From the first man has all the seven principles included in him in germ but none are developed. If we compare him to a baby we will be right; no one has ever, in the thousands of ghost stories current, seen the ghost of an infant, though the imagination of a loving mother may have suggested to her the picture of her lost babe in dreams. And this is very suggestive. In each of the rounds he makes one of the principles develop fully. In the first round his consciousness on our earth is dull and but feeble and shadowy, something like that of an infant. When he reaches our earth in the second round he has become responsible in a degree, in the third he becomes so entirely. At every stage and every round his development keeps pace with the globe on which he is. The descending arc from A to our earth is called the shadowy, the ascending to Z the " luminous.". . . We men of the fourth round are already reaching the latter half of the fifth race of our fourth round humanity, while the men (the few earlier comers) of the fifth round, though only in their first race (or rather class), are yet immeasurably higher than we are—spiritually if not intellectually; since with the completion or full development of this fifth principle (intellectual soul) they have come nearer than we have, are closer in contact with their sixth principle Buddhi. Of course many are the differentiated individuals even in the fourth r. as germs of principles are not equally developed in all, but such is the rule.

. . . Man comes on globe " A " after the other kingdoms have gone on. (Dividing our kingdoms into seven, the last four are what exoteric science divides into three. To this we add the kingdom of man or the Deva kingdom. The respective entities of these we divide into germinal, instinctive, semi-conscious, and fully conscious). . . . When all kingdoms have reached globe Z they will not move forward to re-enter A in precedence of man, but under a law of retardation operative from the central point—or earth—to Z and which equilibrates a principle of acceleration in the descending arc—they will have just finished their respective evolution of genera and species when man reaches his highest development on globe Z—in this or any round. The reason for it is found in the enormously greater time required by them to develop their infinite varieties as compared with man; the relative speed of development *in the rings* therefore naturally increases as we go up the scale from the mineral. But these different rates are so adjusted by man stopping longer in the inter-planetary spheres of rest, for weal or woe—that all kingdoms finish their work simultaneously on the planet Z. For example, on our globe we see the equilibrating law manifesting. From the first appearance of man whether speechless or not to his present one as a fourth and the coming fifth round being, the structural intention of his organization has not radically changed, ethnological characteristics, however varied, affecting in no way man as a *human being*. The fossil of man or his skeleton, whether of the period of that mammalian branch of which he forms the crown, whether cyclop or dwarf can be still recognized at a glance as a relic of man. Plants and animals meanwhile have become more and more unlike what they were. . . . The scheme with its septenary details would be incomprehensible to man had he not the power, as the higher Adepts have proved, of prematurely developing his 6th and 7th senses—those which will be the natural endowment of all in the corresponding rounds. Our Lord Buddha—a 6th r. man—would not have appeared in our epoch, great as were his accumulated merits in previous rebirths, but for a *mystery*. . . . Individuals cannot outstrip the humanity of their round any further than by one remove, for it is mathematically impossible —you say (in effect): if the fountain of life flows ceaselessly there should be men of all rounds on the earth at all times, etc. The hint about planetary rest may dispel the misconception on this head.

When man is perfected *qua* a given round on Globe A he disappears thence (as had certain vegetables and animals). By degrees this Globe loses its vitality and finally reaches the moon stage, *i.e.*, death, and so remains while man is making his seven rings on Z and passing his inter-cyclic period before starting on his next round. So with each Globe in turn.

And now as man when completing his seventh ring upon A has but begun his first on Z and as A dies when he leaves it for B, etc., and as he must also remain in the inter-cyclic sphere after Z, as he has between every two planets, until the impulse again thrills the chain, clearly no one can be more than one round ahead of his kind. And Buddha only forms an exception by virtue of the *mystery*. We have fifth round men among us because we are in the latter half of our septenary earth ring. In the first half this could not have happened. The countless myriads of our fourth round humanity who have outrun us and completed their seven rings on Z, have had time to pass their inter-cyclic period [and] begin their new round and work on to globe D (ours). But how can there be men of the 1st, 2nd, 3rd, 6th and

7th rounds? We represent the first three, and the sixth can only come at rare intervals and prematurely like Buddhas (only under prepared conditions) and the last-named the seventh are not yet evolved! We have traced man out of a round into the Nirvanic state between Z and A. A was left in the last round dead. As the new round begins it catches the new influx of life, reawakens to vitality and begets all its kingdoms of a superior order to the last. After this has been repeated seven times comes a minor pralaya; the chain of globes are not destroyed by disintegration and dispersion of their particles but pass *in abscondito*. From this they will re-emerge in their turn during the next septenary period. Within one solar period (of a p. and m.) occur seven such minor periods, in an ascending scale of progressive development. To recapitulate, there are in the round seven planetary or earth rings for each kingdom and one obscuration of each planet. The minor manwantara is composed of seven rounds, 49 rings and 7 obscurations, the solar period of 49 rounds, etc.

The periods with pralaya and manwantara are called by Dikshita " Surya manwantaras and pralayas." Thought is baffled in speculating how many of our solar pralayas must come before the great Cosmic night—but that will come.

. . . In the minor pralayas there is no starting *de novo*—only resumption of arrested activity. The vegetable and animal kingdoms which at the end of the minor manwantara had reached only a partial development are not destroyed. Their life or vital entities, call some of them *nati* if you will—find also their corresponding night and rest —they also have a Nirvana of their own. And why should they not, these foetal and infant entities? They are all like ourselves begotten of the one element. . . . As we have our Dhyan Chohans so have they in their several kingdoms elemental guardians and are as well taken care of in the mass as is humanity in the mass. The one element not only fills space and *is* space, but interpenetrates every atom of cosmic matter.

When strikes the hour of the solar pralaya—though the process of man's advance on his last seventh round is precisely the same, each planet instead of merely passing out of the visible into the invisible as he quits it in turn is annihilated. With the beginning of the seventh Round of the seventh minor manwantara, every kingdom having now reached its last cycle, there remains on each planet after the exit of man but the maya of once living and existing forms. With every step he takes on the descending and ascending arcs as he moves on from Globe to Globe the planet left behind becomes an empty chrysaloidal case. At his departure there is an outflow from every kingdom of its entities. Waiting to pass into higher forms in due time they are nevertheless liberated: for to the day of that evolution they will rest in their lethargic sleep in space until again energized into life in the new solar manwantara. The old elementals will rest until they are called to become in their turn the bodies of mineral, vegetable and animal entities (on another and a higher string of globes) on their way to become human entities (see *Isis*) while the germinal entities of the lowest forms—and in that time of general perfection there will remain but few of such—will hang in space like drops of water suddenly turned to icicles. They will thaw at the first hot breath of a solar manwantara and form the soul of the future globes. . . . The slow development of the vegetable kingdom provided for by the longer inter-planetary rest of man. . . . When the solar pralaya comes the whole purified humanity merges into Nirvana and from that inter-solar Nirvana will be reborn in higher systems. The string of worlds is destroyed and vanishes like a shadow from the wall in the extinguishment of light. We have every indication that at this very moment such a solar pralaya is taking place while there are two minor ones ending somewhere.

At the beginning of the solar manwantara the hitherto subjective elements of the material world now scattered in cosmic dust—receiving their impulse from the new Dhyan Chohans of the new solar system (the highest of the old ones having gone higher)—will form into primordial ripples of life, and separating into differentiating centres of activity combine in a graduated scale of seven stages of evolution. Like every other orb of space our Earth has, before obtaining its ultimate materiality—and nothing now in this world can give you an idea of what this state of matter is—to pass through a gamut of seven stages of density. I say gamut advisedly since the diatonic scale best affords an illustration of the perpetual rythmic motion of the descending and ascending cycle of Swabhavat—graduated as it is by tones and semi-tones.

You have among the learned members of your society one Theosophist who, without familiarity with our occult doctrine, has yet intuitively grasped from scientific data the idea of a solar pralaya and its manwantara in their beginnings. I mean the celebrated French astronomer Flammarion—" La Resurrection et la Fin des Mondes " (Chapter 4 res.). He speaks like a true seer. The facts are as he surmises with slight modifications. In consequence of the secular refrigeration (old age rather and loss of vital power), solidification and desiccation of the globes, the earth arrives at a point when it begins to be a relaxed conglomerate. The period of child-bearing is gone by. The progeny are all nurtured, its term of life is finished. Hence " its constituent masses cease to obey those laws of cohesion and aggregation which held them together." And becoming like a cadaver which, abandoned to the work of destruction, would leave each molecule composing it free to separate itself from the body for ever, to obey in future the sway of new influences, the attraction of the moon (would that he could know the full extent of its pernicious influence) would itself undertake the task of demolition by producing a tidal wave of earth particles instead of an aqueous tide.

His mistake is that he believes a long time must be devoted to the ruin of the solar system: we are told that it occurs in the twinkling of an eye but not without many preliminary warnings. Another error is the supposition that the earth will fall into the sun. The sun itself is first to disintegrate at the solar pralaya.

. . . Fathom the nature and essence of the sixth principle of the universe and man and you will have fathomed the greatest mystery in this our world—and why not—are you not surrounded by it? What are its familiar manifestations, mesmerism, Od force, etc.—all different aspects of one force capable of good and evil applications.

The degrees of an Adept's initiation mark the seven stages at which he discovers the secret of the sevenfold principles in nature and man and awakens his dormant powers.

LETTER No. 16 [1]

(1) The remarks appended to a letter in the last *Theosophist*, page 226, col. 1, strike me as very important and as qualifying —I do not say contradicting—a good deal of what we have hitherto been told *in re* Spiritualism.

We had heard already of a spiritual condition of life in which the redeveloped Ego enjoyed a conscious existence for a time before reincarnation in another world; but that branch of the subject has hitherto been slurred over. Now some explicit statements are made about it; and these suggest further enquiries.

In the *Devachan* (I have lent my *Theosophist* to a friend; and have not got it at hand to refer to but that, if I remember rightly is the name given to the state of spiritul beatitude described) the new Ego retains complete recollection of his life on earth, apparently. Is that so or is there any misunderstanding on that point on my part?

(1) The Devachan, or land of " Sukhavati," is *allegorically* **described by our Lord Buddha himself. What he said may be found in the** *Shan-Mun-yih-Tung.* **Says Tathāgata:—**

" Many thousand myriads of systems of worlds beyond this (ours) there is a region of Bliss called *Sukhavati.* **. . . This region is encircled with** *seven* **rows of railings,** *seven* **rows of vast curtains,** *seven* **rows of waving trees; this holy abode of Árahats is governed by the Tathāgatas (Dhyan Chohans) and is possessed by the Bodhisatwas. It hath** *seven* **precious lakes, in the midst of which flow crystaline waters having '** *seven and one* **' properties, or distinctive**

---

[1] K .H.'s replies to Mr. Sinnett's queries are printed in bold type.—Eds.

qualities (the 7 princip'es emanating from the ONE). This, O Sariputra is the ' Devachan.' Its divine Udumbara flower casts a root *in the shadow of every earth*, and blossoms for all those who reach it. Those born in the blessed region are truly felicitous, there are no more griefs or sorrows *in that cycle* for them. . . . Myriads of Spirits *(Lha)* resort there for rest and then *return to their own regions*.[1] Again, O, Sariputra, in that land of joy many who are born in it are *Avaivartyas* . . ." [2] etc., etc.

(2) Now except in the fact that the duration of existence in the *Devachan* is limited, there is a very close resemblance between that condition and the Heaven of ordinary religion (omitting anthropomorphic ideas of God).

(2) Certainly the new *Ego*, once it is reborn, retains for a certain time—proportionate to its Earth-life, a " complete recollection of his life on earth." [3] (See your preceding query). But it can *never* return on earth, from the Devachan, nor has the latter—even omitting all " anthropomorphic ideas of God "—any resemblance to the paradise or heaven of any religion, and it is H.P.B.'s literary fancy that suggested to her the wonderful comparison.

(3) Now the question of importance is who goes to Heaven—or Devachan? Is this condition only attained by the few who are very good, or by the many who are not very bad,—after the lapse in their case of a longer unconscious incubation or gestation?

(3) " Who goes to Devachan? " The personal Ego of course, but beatified, purified, holy. Every Ego—the combination of the sixth and seventh principles—which, after the period of unconscious gestation is reborn into the Devachan, is of necessity as innocent and pure as a new-born babe. The fact of his being reborn at all, shows the preponderance of good over evil in his old personality. And while the Karma (of evil) steps aside for the time being to follow him in his future earth-reincarnation, he brings along with him but the Karma of his good deeds, words, and thoughts into this Devachan. " Bad " is a relative term for us—as you were told more than once before,—and the Law of Retribution is the only law that never errs. Hence all those who have not slipped down into the mire of unredeemable sin and bestiality—go to the Devachan. They will have to pay for their sins, voluntary and involuntary, later on. Meanwhile, they are rewarded; receive the *effects* of the *causes* produced by them. Of course it is *a state*, one, so to say, of *intense selfishness*, during which an *Ego* reaps the reward of his *unselfishness* on earth. He is completely engrossed in the bliss of all his personal earthly affections,

---

[1] Those who have not ended their earth rings.

[2] Literally—those who will never return—the seventh round men, etc.

[3] See back—(1) of your questions.

preferences and thoughts, and gathers in the fruit of his meritorious actions. No pain, no grief nor even the shadow of a sorrow comes to darken the bright horizon of his unalloyed happiness: for, *it is a state of perpetual " Maya."* . . . Since the conscious perception of one's *personality* on earth is but an evanescent dream, that sense will be equally that of a dream in the Devachan—only a hundred fold intensified. So much so, indeed, that the happy Ego is unable to see through the veil the evils, sorrows and woes to which those it loved on earth may be subjected. It lives in that sweet dream with its loved ones—whether gone before, or yet remaining on earth; it has them near itself, as happy, as blissful and as innocent as the disembodied dreamer himself; and yet, apart from rare visions, the denizens of our gross planet feel it not. It is in this, during *such* a condition of complete *Maya* that the Souls or astral Egos of pure, loving sensitives, labouring under the same illusion, think their loved ones come down to them on earth, while it is their own Spirits that are raised towards those in the Devachan. Many of the *subjective* spiritual communications—most of them when the sensitives are pure minded—are real; but it is most difficult for the *uninitiated* medium to fix in his mind the true and correct pictures of what he sees and hears. Some of the phenomena called psychography (though more rarely) are also real. The spirit of the sensitive getting odylised, so to say, by the aura of the Spirit in the Devachan, becomes for a few minutes *that departed personality*, and writes in the hand writing of the latter, in his language and in his thoughts, as they were during his life time. The two spirits become blended in one; and, the preponderance of one over the other during such phenomena determines the preponderance of *personality* in the characteristics exhibited in such writings, and " trance speaking." What you call " rapport " is in plain fact an identity of molecular vibration between the astral part of the incarnate medium and the astral part of the disincarnate personality. I have just noticed an article *on smell* by some English Professor (which I will cause to be reviewed in the *Theosophist* and say a few words), and find in it something that applies to our case. As, in music, two different sounds may be in accord and separately distinguishable, and this harmony or discord depends upon the synchronous vibrations and complementary periods; so there is *rapport* between medium and " control " when their astral molecules move in accord. And the question whether the communication shall reflect more of the one personal idiosyncracy, or the other, is determined by the relative intensity of the two sets of vibrations in the compound wave of *Akasa*. The less identical the vibratory impulses the more mediumistic and less spiritual will be the message. So then, measure your medium's moral state by that of the alleged " controlling " Intelligence, and your tests of genuineness leave nothing to be desired.

(4) Or are there great varieties of condition within the limits, so to speak, of Devachan, so that an appropriate state is dropped into by all, from which they will be born into lower and higher conditions in the next world of causes? It is no use multiplying hypotheses. We want some information to go upon.

(4) Yes; there are great varieties in the Devachan states, and, it is all as you say. As many varieties of bliss, as on earth there are shades of perception and of capability to appreciate such reward. It is an ideated paradise, in each case of the Ego's own making, and by him filled with the scenery, crowded with the incidents, and thronged with the people he would expect to find in such a sphere of compensative bliss. And it is that variety which guides the temporary personal *Ego* into the current which will lead him to be reborn in a lower or higher condition in the next world of causes. Everything is so harmoniously adjusted in nature—especially in the subjective world, that no mistake can be ever committed by the Tathāgatas—or Dhyan Chohans—who guide the impulses.

(5) On the face of the idea, a purely spiritual state would only be enjoyable to the entities highly spiritualized in this life. But there are myriads of very good people (morally) who are not spiritualized at all. How can they be fitted to pass, with their recollections of this life from a material to a spiritual condition of existence?

(5) It is " a spiritual condition " only as contrasted with our own grossly " material condition," and, as already stated—it is such degrees of spirituality that constitute and determine the great " varieties " of conditions within the limits of Devachan. A mother from a savage tribe is not less happy than a mother from a regal palace, with her lost child in her arms; and although as actual Egos, children prematurely dying before the perfection of their septenary Entity do not find their way to Devachan, yet all the same the mother's loving fancy finds her children there, without one missing that her heart yearns for. Say—it is but a dream, but after all what is objective life itself but a panorama of vivid unrealities? The pleasures realized by a Red Indian in his " happy hunting grounds " in that Land of Dreams is not less intense than the ecstasy felt by a *connoisseur* who passes aeons in the wrapt delight of listening to divine Symphonies by imaginary angelic choirs and orchestras. As it is no fault of the former, if born a " savage " with an instinct to kill—though it caused the death of many an innocent animal—why, if with it all, he was a loving father, son, husband, why should he not also enjoy *his* share of reward? The case would be quite different if the same cruel acts had been done by an educated and civilized person, from a mere love of sport. The savage in being reborn would simply

take a low place in the scale, by reason of his imperfect moral
development; while the *Karma* of the other would be tainted with
moral delinquency. . . .

Every one but that ego which, attracted by its gross magnetism,
falls into the current that will draw it into the " planet of Death "
—the mental as well as physical satellite of our earth—*is* fitted to
pass into a relative " spiritual " condition adjusted to his previous
condition in life and mode of thought.   To my kowledge and recollection H.P.B. explained to Mr. Hume that man's sixth principle,
as something purely spiritual could not exist, or have *conscious* being
in the Devachan, unless it assimilated some of the more abstract and
pure of the mental attributes of the fifth principle or animal Soul,
its *manas* (mind) and memory.   When man dies his second and third
principles die with him; the lower triad disappears, and the fourth,
fifth, sixth and seventh principles form the surviving *Quaternary*.
(Read again page 6 in *Fragments of O.T.*)[1]   Thenceforth it is a
" death " struggle between the Upper and Lower dualities.   If the
upper wins, the sixth, having attracted to itself the quintessence of
Good from the fifth—its nobler affections, its saintly (though they be
earthly) aspirations, and the most Spiritualised portions of its mind
—follows its divine *elder* (the 7th) into the " Gestation " State; and
the fifth and fourth remain in association as an empty *shell*—(the
expression is quite correct)—to roam in the earth's atmosphere,
with half the personal memory gone, and the more brutal instinct
fully alive for a certain period—an " Elementary " in short.   This
is the " angel guide " of the average medium.   If, on the other
hand, it is the Upper *Duality* which is defeated, then it is the fifth
principle that assimilates all that there may be left of *personal*
recollection and perceptions of its personal individuality in the sixth.
But, with all this additional stock, it will not remain in *Kama-Loka*
—" the world of Desire " or our Earth's atmosphere.   In a very
short time like a straw floating within the attraction of the vortices
and pits of the Maelstrom, it is caught up and drawn into the great
whirlpool of human Egos; while the sixth and seventh—now a purely
spiritual, *individual* MONAD, with nothing left in it of the late personality, having no regular " gestation " period to pass through
(since there is no purified *personal* Ego to be reborn), after a more
or less prolonged period of unconscious Rest in the boundless Space
—will find itself reborn in another personality on the next planet.
When arrives the period of " Full Individual Consciousness "—
which precedes that of *Absolute* Consciousness in the *Pari-Nirvana*
—this lost *personal* life becomes as a torn out page in the great
Book of Lives, without even a disconnected word left to mark its
absence.   The purified monad will neither perceive nor remember it
in the series of its past rebirths—which it would had it gone to the

---

[1] " *Fragments of Occult Truth* " appeared in *The Theosophist*, 1881-1883.—EDS.

" World of Forms " (*rupa-loka*)—and its retrospective glance will
not perceive even the slightest sign to indicate that it had been.
The light of *Sammā-Sambuddh*—

> ". . . that light which shines beyond our mortal ken
> The light of all the lives in all the worlds "—

throws no ray upon that *personal* life in the series of lives foregone.

To the credit of mankind, I must say, that such an utter oblitera-
tion of an existence from the tablets of Universal Being does not
occur often enough to make a great percentage. In fact, like the
much mentioned " congenital idiot " such a thing is a *lusus naturae*
—an exception, not the rule.

(6) And how is a spiritual existence in which everything has
merged into the sixth principle, compatible with that consciousness of individual and personal material life which must be
attibuted to the Ego in Devachan if he retains his earthly consciousness as stated in the *Theosophist* Note?

(6) The question is now sufficiently explained, I believe: the sixth
and seventh principles apart from the rest constitute the eternal,
imperishable, but also unconscious " Monad." To awaken in it to
life the latent consciousness, especially that of *personal* individuality,
requires the monad plus the highest attributes of the fifth—the
" animal Soul "; and it is that which makes the ethereal *Ego* that
lives and enjoys bliss in the Devachan. Spirit, or the unalloyed
emanations of the ONE—the latter forming with the seventh and sixth
principles the highest triad—neither of the two emanations are
capable of assimilating but that which is good, pure and holy; hence,
no sensual, material or unholy recollection can follow the purified
memory of the *Ego* to the region of Bliss. The Karma for these
recollections of evil deeds and thought will reach the Ego when it
changes its *personality* in the following world of causes. The *Monad*,
or the " Spiritual Individuality," remains untainted *in all cases*.
" No sorrow or Pain for those born there (in the *Rupa-Loka* of
Devachan); for this is the Pure-land. All the regions in Space
possess such lands (*Sakwala*), but this land of Bliss is the most pure."
In the *Jnāna Prasthāna Shastra*, it is said, " By personal purity and
earnest meditation, we overleap the limits of the World of Desire,
and enter in the World of Forms."

(7) The period of gestation between Death and Devachan
has hitherto been conceived by me at all events as very long.
Now it is said to be in some cases only a few days, in no cases
(it is implied) more than a few years. This seems plainly stated,
but I ask if it can be explicitly confirmed because it is a point on
which so much turns.

(7) Another fine example of the habitual disorder in which Mrs. H.P.B.'s mental furniture is kept. She talks of "Bardo" and does not even say to her readers what it means! As in her writing-room confusion is ten times confounded, so in her mind are crowded ideas piled in such a chaos that when she wants to express them the tail peeps out before the head. "Bardo" has nothing to do with the duration of time in the case you are referring to. "Bardo" is the period between death and rebirth—and may last from a few years to a kalpa. It is divided into three sub-periods (1) when the *Ego* delivered of its mortal coil enters into *Kama-Loka*[1] (the abode of Elementaries); (2) when it enters into its "Gestation State"; (3) when it is reborn in the *Rupa-Loka* of Devachan. Sub-period (1) may last from a few minutes to a *number* of years—the phrase "a few years" becoming puzzling and utterly worthless without a more complete explanation; Sub-period (2) is "very long", as you say, longer sometimes than you may even imagine, yet proportionate to the *Ego's* spiritual stamina; Sub-period (3) lasts in proportion to the good KARMA, after which the *monad* is againr eincarnated. The *Agama Sutra* saying:—"In all these *Rupa-Lokas*, the Devas (Spirits) are equally subjected to birth, decay, old age, and death," means only that an Ego is borne thither, then begins fading out and finally "dies," *i.e.*, falls into that unconscious condition which precedes rebirth; and ends the Sloka with these words: "As the devas emerge from these heavens, they enter the lower world again;" *i.e.*, they leave a world of bliss to be reborn in a world of causes.

(8) In that case, and assuming that Devachan is not solely the heritage of adepts and persons almost as elevated, there *is* a condition of existence tantamount to Heaven actually going on, from which the life of Earth may be watched by an immense number of those who have gone before! (9) And for how long? Does this state of spiritual beatitude endure for years? for decades? for centuries?

(8) Most emphatically "the Devachan *is not* solely the heritage of adepts," and most decidedly there is a "heaven"—if you *must* use this astro-geographical Christian term—for "an immense number of those who have gone before." But "the life of Earth" can be *watched* by none of these, for reasons of the Law of Bliss plus *Maya*, already given.

(9) For years, decades, centuries and milleniums, oftentimes-multi-plied by something more. It all depends upon the duration of Karma. Fill with oil Den's little cup, and a city reservoir of water, and lighting both see which burns the longer. The *Ego* is the wick and Karma the oil, the difference in the quantity of the latter (in the cup and the reservoir) suggesting to you the great difference in the

[1] Tibetan: Yuh-Kai.

duration of various *Karmas*. Every effect must be proportionate to the cause. And, as man's terms of incarnate existence bear but a small proportion to his periods of inter-natal existence in the manvantaric cycle, so the good thoughts, words, and deeds of any one of these "lives" on a globe are causative of effects, the working out of which requires far more time than the evolution of the causes occupied. Therefore, when you read in the Jāts and other *fabulous* stories of the Buddhist Scriptures that this or the other good action was rewarded by Kalpas of several figures of bliss, do not smile at the absurd exaggeration, but bear in mind what I have said. From a small seed, you know, sprung a tree whose life endures now for 22 centuries; I mean the Anuradha-pura *Bo* tree. Nor must you laugh, if ever you come across *Pinda-Dana* or any other Buddhist *Sutra* and read: "Between the *Kama-Loka* and the *Rupa-Loka* there is a locality, the dwelling of 'Mara' (Death). This Mara filled with passion and lust, destroys all virtuous principles, as a stone grinds corn.[1] His palace is 7000 yojanas square, and is surrounded by a *seven-fold* wall," for you will feel now more prepared to understand the allegory. Also, when Beal, or Burnouf, or Rhys Davids in the innocence of their Christian and materialistic souls indulge in such translations as they generally do, we do not bear them malice for their commentaries, since they cannot know any better. But what can the following mean:—"The names of the Heavens" (a mistranslation; *lokas* are not *heavens* but localities or abodes) of Desire, Kama-Loka—so called, because the beings who occupy them are subject to desires of eating, drinking, sleeping and love. They are otherwise called the abodes of the *five* (?) orders of sentient creatures —Devas, men, asuras, beasts, demons " (*Lautan Sutra*, trans. by S. Beal). They mean simply that, had the reverend translator been acquainted with the true doctrine a little better—he would have (1) divided the Devas into two classes—and called them the " *Rupa-*devas " and the " *Arupa-*devas " (the " *form* " or objective, and the "*formless* " or subjective *Dhyan Chohans*) and (2)—would have done the same for his class of " men," since there are *shells*, and " Mara-rupas "—*i.e.*, bodies doomed to annihilation. All these are:

(1) " *Rupa-devas* "—*Dhyan Chohans*,[2] having forms; ⎫
(2) " *Arupa-devas* "   ,,   ,, having *no* forms; ⎬ Ex-men.
(3) " *Pisachas* "—(two-principled) ghosts. ⎭
(4) " *Mara-rupa* "—Doomed to *death* (3 principled).

[1] This Mara, as you may well think, is the allegorical image of the sphere called the "Planet of Death"—the *whirlpool* whither disappear the *lives* doomed to destruction. It is between *Kama* and *Rupa*-Lokas that the struggle takes pace.

[2] The Planetary Spirits of our Earth are not of the highest, as you may well imagine—since, as Subba Row says in his criticism upon Oxley's work that no Eastern Adept would like to be compared with an angel or a *Dêva*.

(5) *Asuras*—Elementals—having human form ⎫
(6) *Beasts*—   „   2nd class—animal Elementals ⎬ Future men.
(7) *Rakshasas* (Demons) Souls or Astral Forms of sorcerers; men who have reached the apex of knowledge in the forbidden art. Dead or alive they have, so to say *cheated* nature; but it is only temporary—until our planet goes into *obscuration*, after which they have *nolens volens* to be *annihilated*.

It is these *seven* groups that form the principal divisions of the Dwellers of the subjective world around us. It is in stock No. 1 that are the *intelligent* Rulers of this world of Matter, and who, with all this intelligence are but the blindly obedient instruments of the ONE; the active agents of a Passive Principle.

And thus are misinterpreted and mistranslated nearly all our Sutras; yet even under that confused jumble of doctrines and words, for one who knows even superficially the *true* doctrine there is firm ground to stand upon. Thus, for instance, in enumerating the seven lokas of the " Kama-Loka " the *Avatamsaka Sutra* gives as the *seventh*, the " Territory of Doubt." I will ask you to remember the name as we will have to speak of it hereafter. Every such " world " within the Sphere of Effects has a Tathāgata, or " Dhyan Chohan "—to protect and watch over, not to interfere with it. Of course, of all men, spiritualists will be the first to reject and throw off our doctrines to " the limbo of exploded superstitions." Were we to assure them that every one of their " Summerland₀ " had seven boarding houses in it, with the same number of " Spirit Guides " to " boss " *in them*, and call these " angels," Saint Peters, Johns, and St. Ernests, they would welcome us with open arms. But whoever heard of Tathagats and Dhyan Chohans, Asuras and Elementals? Preposterous! Still, we are happily allowed—by our friends (Mr. Eglinton, at least)—to be possessed " of a certain knowledge of Occult Sciences " *(Vide Light)*. And thus, even this mite of " Knowledge " is at your service, and is now helping me to answer your following question:

Is there any intermediate condition between the spiritual beatitude of Devachan, and the forlorn shadow life of the only half conscious elementary *reliquiae* of human beings who have lost their sixth principle? Because if so that might give a *locus standi* in imagination to the Ernests and Joeys of the spiritual mediums —the better sort of controlling "spirits." If so surely that must be a very populous world, from which any amount of "spiritual " communications might come?

Alas, no; my friend; not that I know of. From " Sukhavati " down to the " Territory of Doubt " there is a variety of Spiritual States; but I am not aware of any such " intermediate condition." I have told you of the Sakwalas (though I cannot be enumerating them since it would be useless); and even of *Avitchi*—the " Hell " from which there is no return [1], and I have no more to tell about. " The forlorn shadow " has to do the best it can. As soon as it has stepped outside the *Kama-Loka*, and crossed the " Golden Bridge " leading to the " Seven Golden Mountains " the *Ego* can confabulate no more with easy-going mediums. No " Ernest " or " Joey " has ever returned from the *Rupa Loka*—let alone the *Arupa*-Loka—to hold sweet intercourse with mortals.

Of course there is a " better sort " of *reliquiae*; and the " shells " or the " earth-walkers " as they are here called, are not necessarily *all* bad. But even those that are good are made bad for the time being by mediums. The " shells " may well not care, since they have nothing to lose, anyhow. But there is another kind of " Spirits," we have lost sight of, the *suicides* and those *killed by accident*. Both kinds can communicate, and both have to pay dearly for such visits. And now I have again to explain what I mean. Well, this class is the one that the French Spiritists call—"*les Esprits Souffrants.*" They are an exception to the rule, as they have to remain within the earth's attraction, and in its atmosphere—the *Kama-Loka*—till the very last moment of what would have been the natural duration of their lives. In other words, that particular wave of life-evolution must run on to its shore. But it is a sin and cruelty to revive their memory and intensify their suffering by giving them a chance of living an artificial life; a chance to *overload their Karma,* by tempting them into open doors, *viz.*, mediums and sensitives, for they will have to pay roundly for every such pleasure. I will explain. The *suicides*, who, foolishly hoping to escape life, found themselves still alive,—have suffering enough in store for them from that very life. Their punishment is in the intensity of the latter. Having lost by the rash act their seventh and sixth principles, though not for ever, as they can regain both—instead of accepting their punishment, and taking their chances of redemption, they are often made *to regret life* and tempted to regain a hold upon it by sinful means. In the *Kama-Loka*, the land of intense desires, they can gratify their earthly yearnings but through a *living* proxy; and by so doing, at the expiration of the natural term, they generally lose their *monad* for ever. As to the victims of accident—these fare still worse. Unless they were so good and pure, as to be drawn immediately within the Akasic *Samadhi*, *i.e.* to fall into a state of quiet slumber, a sleep full of rosy dreams, during which they have no recollection of the accident, but move and live among their familiar friends and scenes, until their natural life-term is finished, when they find themselves born in the

---

[1] In *Abhidharma* Shastra (Metaphysics) we read:—" Buddha taught that on the *outskirts of all the Sakwalas* there is a black interval, *without Sun or moonlight* for him who falls into it. There is *no re-birth* from it. It is the *cold* Hell, the great *Naraka* ". This is Avitchi.

Devachan—a gloomy fate is theirs. Unhappy shades, if sinful and sensual they wander about—(not *shells*, for their connection with their two higher principles is not quite broken)—until their death-hour comes. Cut off in the full flush of earthly passions which bind them to familiar scenes, they are enticed by the opportunities which mediums afford to gratify them vicariously. They are the *Pisachas*, the *Incubi*, and *Succubi* of mediaeval times. The demons of thirst, gluttony, lust and avarice, elementaries of intensified craft, wickedness and cruelty, provoking their victims to horrid crimes, and revelling in their commission! They not only ruin their victims, but these psychic vampires, borne along by the torrent of their hellish impulses, at last, at the fixed close of their natural period of life—they are carried out of the earth's aura into regions where for ages they endure exquisite suffering and end with entire destruction.

But if the victim of accident or violence be neither very good, nor very bad—an average person—then this may happen to him. A medium who attracts him will create for him the most undesirable of things; a new combination of *Skandhas* and a new and evil *Karma*. But let me give you a clearer idea of what I mean by *Karma* in this case.

In connection with this, let me tell you before, that since you seem so interested with the subject you can do nothing better than to study the two doctrines—of *Karma* and Nirvana—as profoundly as you can. Unless you are thoroughly well acquainted with the two tenets—the double key to the metaphysics of Abhidharma—you will always find yourself at sea in trying to comprehend the rest. We have several sorts of Karma and Nirvana in their various applications—to the Universe, the world, Devas, Buddhas, Bodhisatwas, men and animals —the second including its seven kingdoms. Karma and Nirvana are but two of the seven great MYSTERIES of Buddhist metaphysics; and but four of the seven are known to the best orientalists, and that very imperfectly.

If you ask a learned Buddhist priest, what is Karma?—he will tell you that Karma is what a Christian might call Providence (in a certain sense only) and a Mahomedan—*Kismet*, fate or destiny (again in one sense). That it is that cardinal tenet which teaches that, as soon as any conscious or sentient being, whether man, deva, or animal dies, a new being is produced and he or it reappears in another birth, on the same or another planet, under conditions of his or its own antecedent making. Or, in other words that *Karma* is the guiding power, and *Trishna* (in Pali *Tanha*) the thirst or desire to sentiently live—the proximate force or energy, the resultant of human (or animal) action, which, out of the old *Skandhas* [1]

---

[1] I remark that in the second as well as in the first editon of your *Occult World* the same misprint appears, and that the word *Skandha* is spelt *Shandba*—on page 130. As it now stands I am made to express myself in a very original way for a *supposed* Adept.

produces the new group that form the new being and control the nature of the birth itself. Or to make it still clearer, the *new* being is rewarded and punished for the meritorious acts and misdeeds of the *old* one; Karma representing an Entry Book, in which all the acts of man, good, bad, or indifferent, are carefully recorded to his debit and credit—by himself, so to say, or rather by these very actions of his. There, where Christian poetical fiction created and sees a " Recording " Guardian Angel, stern and realistic Buddhist logic, perceiving the necessity that every cause should have its effect— shows its real presence. The opponents of Buddhism have laid great stress upon the alleged injustice that the doer should escape and an innocent victim be made to suffer,—since the doer and the sufferer are different beings. The fact is, that while in one sense they may be so considered, yet in another *they are identical*. The " old being " is the sole parent—father and mother at once—of the " new being." It is the former who is the creator and fashioner of the latter, in reality; and far more so in plain truth than any father in flesh. And once that you have well mastered the meaning of *Skandhas* you will see what I mean.

It is the group of Skandhas that form and constitute the physical and mental individuality we call man (or any being). This group consists (in the exoteric teaching) of five Skandhas, namely: *Rupa*— the material properties or attributes; *Vedana*—sensations; *Sanna*— abstract ideas; *Samkara*—tendencies both physical and mental; and *Vinnana*—mental powers, an amplification of the fourth—meaning the mental, physical and moral predispositions. We add to them two more, the nature and names of which you may learn hereafter. Suffice for the present to let you know that they are connected with, and productive of *Sakkayaditthi*, the " heresy or delusion of individuality " and of *Attavada* " the doctrine of Self," both of which (in the case of the fifth principle, the soul) lead to the *maya* of heresy and belief in the efficacy of vain rites and ceremonies, in prayers and intercession.

Now, returning to the question of identity between the *old* and the *new* " Ego." I may remind you once more, that even your Science has accepted the old, very old fact distinctly taught by our Lord,[1] *viz.*—that a man of any given age, while sentiently the same, is yet physically not the same as he was a few years earlier (we say *seven* years and are prepared to maintain and prove it): Buddhistically speaking, his *Skandhas* have changed. At the same time they are

[1] See the *Abhidharma Kosha Vyakhya*, the *Sutta Pitaka*, any Northern Buddhist book, all of which show Gautama Buddha saying that none of these Skandhas is the soul; since the body is constantly changing, and that neither man, animal nor plant is ever the same for two consecutive days or even minutes. "Mendicants! remember that there is within man *no abiding principle* whatever, and that only the *learned* disciple who acquires wisdom, in saying ' I am '—knows what he is saying."

ever and ceaselessly at work in preparing the abstract mould, the
" privation " of the future *new* being. Well, then, if it is just that
a man of 40 should enjoy or suffer for the actions of the man of 20,
so it is equally just that the being of the new birth, who is essentially
identical with the previous being—since he is its outcome and creation
—should feel the consequences of that begetting Self or personality.
Your Western law which punishes the innocent son of a guilty father
by depriving him of his parent, rights and property; your civilized
Society which brands with infamy the guiltless daughter of an
immoral, criminal mother; your Christian Church and Scriptures
which teach that the " Lord God visits the sins of the fathers upon
the children unto the third and fourth generation," are not all these
far more unjust and cruel than anything done by Karma? Instead of
punishing the innocent together with the culprit, the Karma *avenges
and rewards the former*, which neither of your three western poten-
tates above mentioned ever thought of doing. But perhaps, to our
physiological remark the objectors may reply that it is only the body
that changes, there is only a molecular transformation, which has
nothing to do with the mental evolution; and that the *Skandhas*
represent not only a material but also a set of mental and moral
qualities. But is there, I ask, either a sensation, an abstract idea, a
tendency of mind, or a mental power, that one could call an absolutely
non-molecular phenomenon? Can even a sensation or the most abstract
of thoughts which is *something*, come out of *nothing*, or be nothing?

Now, the causes producing the " new being " and determining
the nature of *Karma* are, as already said—Trishna (or " Tanha ")
—thirst, desire for sentient existence and *Upadana*—which is the
realization or consummation of *Trishna* or that desire. And both of
these the medium helps to awaken and to develop *nec plus ultra* in
an Elementary, be he a suicide or a victim.[1] The rule is, that a
person who dies a natural death will remain from " a few hours to
several short years " within the earth's attraction, *i.e.*, in the *Kama-
Loka*. But exceptions are, in the case of suicides and those who die
a violent death in general. Hence, one of such Egos, for instance,
who was destined to live, say, 80 or 90 years, but who either killed
himself or was killed by some accident, let us suppose at the age of
20—would have to pass in the *Kama Loka* not " a few years," but
in his case 60 or 70 years, as an Elementary, or rather an " earth-
walker "; since he is not, unfortunately for him, even a " *shell*."
Happy, thrice happy, in comparison, are those disembodied entities
who sleep their long slumber and live in dream in the bosom of Space!
And woe to those whose *Trishna* will attract them to mediums, and
woe to the latter, who tempt them with such an easy *Upadana*. For
in grasping them, and satisfying their thirst for life, the medium

---

[1] Alone the Shells and the *Elementals* are left unhurt, though the morality
of the sensitives can by no means be improved by the intercourse.

helps to develop in them—is in fact the cause of—a new set of
Skandhas, a new body, with far worse tendencies and passions than
was the one they lost. All the future of this new body will be determined thus, not only by the *Karma* of demerit of the previous set or
group but also by that of the new set of the future being. Were the
mediums and Spiritualists but to know, as I said, that with every new
" angel guide " they welcome with rapture, they entice the latter
into an *Upadana* which will be productive of a series of untold evils
for the new Ego that will be born under its nefarious shadow, and
that with every séance—especially for materialization—they multiply
the causes for misery, causes that will make the unfortunate Ego
fail in his spiritual birth, or be reborn into a worse existence than
ever—they would, perhaps, be less lavish in their hospitality.

And now, you may understand why we oppose so strongly Spiritualism and mediumship. And, you will also see why, to satisfy Mr.
Hume,—at least in one direction,—I got myself into *a scrape* with
the Chohan, and *mirabile dictu!*—with both the sahibs, " the young
men by the name of "—Scott and Banon. To amuse you I will
ask H. P. B. to send you with this a page of the " Banon papyrus,"
an article of his that he winds up with a severe literary thrashing of
my humble self. Shadows of the Asuras, in what a passion she flew
upon reading this rather disrespectful criticism! I am sorry she does
not print it, upon considerations of " family honour," as the
" Disinherited " expressed it. As to the Chohan, the matter is
more serious, and he was far from satisfied that I should have allowed
Eglinton to believe it was *myself*. He had permitted this proof of
the power in *living man* to be given to the Spiritualists through a
medium of theirs, but had left the programme and its details to ourselves; hence his displeasure at some trifling consequences. I tell
you, my dear friend, that I am far less free to do as I like than you
are in the matter of the *Pioneer*. None of us but the highest
Chutuktus are their full masters. But I digress.

And now that you have been told much and had explained a good
deal, you may as well read this letter to our irrepressible friend—
Mrs. Gordon. The reasons given *may* throw some cold water on
her Spiritualistic zeal, though I have my reasons to doubt it. Anyhow it may show her that it is not against *true* Spiritualism that we
set ourselves, but only against indiscriminate mediumship and physical
manifestations,—materializations and trance-*possessions* especially.
Could the Spiritualists be only made to understand the difference
between *individuality* and *personality*, between *individual* and *personal*
immortality and some other truths, they would be more easily persuaded that Occultists may be fully convinced of the *monad's*
immortality, and yet deny that of the soul—the vehicle of the *personal*
Ego; that they can firmly believe in, and themselves practise spiritual
communications and intercourse with the *disembodied* Egos of the

Rupa-Loka, and yet laugh at the insane idea of "shaking hands" with a " Spirit "!; that finally, as the matter stands, it is the Occultists and the Theosophists who are true Spiritualists, while the modern sect of that name is composed simply of *materialistic* phenomenalists.

And once that we are discussing " individuality " and " personality," it is curious that H. P. B., when subjecting poor Mr. Hume's brain to torture with her muddled explanations, never thought —until receiving the explanation from himself of the difference that exists between individuality and personality—that it was the very same doctrine she had been taught: that of *Pacceka-Yana*, and of *Amata-Yana*. The two terms as above given by him are the correct and literal translation of the Pali, Sanskrit, and even of the Chino-Tibetan technical names for the many *personal entities* blended in one *Individuality*—the long string of lives emanating from the same Immortal MONAD. You will have to remember them:—

(1) The *Pacceka Yana*—(in Sanskrit " Pratyeka ") means literally the " personal vehicle " or personal *Ego*, a combination of the five lower principles. While—

(2) The *Amata-Yana*—(in Sanskrit " Amrita ") is translated " the immortal vehicle," or the *Individuality*, the Spiritual Soul, or the Immortal *monad*—a combination of the fifth, sixth and seventh.[1]

It appears to me that one of our great difficulties in trying to understand the progress of affairs turns on our ignorance so far of the *divisions* of the seven principles. Each has in turn its seven elements we are told: can we be told something more concerning the seven-fold constitution of the fourth and fifth principles especially? It is evidently in the divisibility of these that the secret of the future and of many psychic phenomena here during life, resides.

Quite right. But I must be permitted to doubt whether with the desired explanations the difficulty will be removed, and you will become able to penetrate " the secret of psychic phenomena." You, my good friend, whom I had once or twice the pleasure of hearing playing on your piano in the quiet intervals between dress-coating and a beef-and-claret dinner—tell me, could you favour me as readily as with one of your easy *waltzes*—with one of Beethoven's Grand Sonatas? Pray, pray have patience! Yet, I would not refuse you by any means. You will find the fourth and the fifth principles, divided into roots and Branches on a fly-sheet herein enclosed, if I find time.[2] And now, how long do you propose to abstain from interrogation marks?

Faithfully,

K. H.

---

[1] To avoid a fresh surprise and confusion at the news of the fifth keeping company with the sixth and seventh, please turn to page 3, *et seq.* [p. 101.—ED.]

[2] I did *not* find time. Will send it a day or two later.

P.S.—I hope I have now removed all cause for reproaches—my delay in answering your queries notwithstanding,—and that my character is re-established. Yourself and Mr. Hume have received now more information about the A. E. Philosophy than was ever given out to *non-initiates* within my knowledge. Your sagacity, my kind friend, will have suggested long ago, that it is not so much because of your combined personal virtues—though Mr. Hume I must confess, has run up a large claim since his *conversion*—or my personal preferences for either of you, as for other and very apparent reasons. Of all our semi-chelas you two are the most likely to utilise for the general good the facts given you. You must regard them received in trust for the benefit of the whole Society; to be turned over, and employed and re-employed in many ways and in all ways that are good. If you (Mr. Sinnett) would give pleasure to your trans-Himalayan friend, do not suffer any month to pass without writing a *Fragment*, long or short, for the magazine, and then, issuing it as a pamphlet—since you so call it. You may sign them as " A Lay-Chela of K. H.," or in any way you choose. I dare not ask the same favour of Mr. Hume, who has already done more than his share in another direction.

I will not answer your query about your *Pioneer* connection just now: something may be said on both sides. But at least take no rash decision. We are at the end of *the* cycle, and you are connected with the T.S.

Under favour of my Karma—I mean to answer to-morrow Mr. Hume's long and kind personal letter. The abundance of MSS. from me of late shows that I have found a little leisure; their blotched, patchy and mended appearance also proves that my leisure has come by snatches, by constant interruptions, and that my writing has been done in odd places here and there, with such materials as I could pick up. But for the RULE that forbids our using one minim of power until every ordinary means has been tried and failed, I might, of course, have given you a lovely " precipitation " as regards chirography and composition. I console myself for the miserable appearance of my letters with the thought that, perhaps, you may not value them the less for these marks of my personal subjection to the way-side annoyances which you English so ingeniously reduce to a *minimum* with your appliances of sorts. As your lady once kindly remarked, they take away most effectually the flavour of miracle, and make us as human beings, more thinkable entities,—a wise reflection for which I thank her.

H. P. B. is in despair: the Chohan refused permission to M. to let her come this year further than the Black Rock, and M. very coolly made her unpack her trunks. Try to console her, if you can. Besides, she is really wanted more at Bombay than Penlor. Olcott is on his way to Lanka and Damodar packed up to Poona for a month, his foolish austerities and hard work having broken down his physical constitution. I will have to look after him, and perhaps to take him away, if it comes to the worst.

Just now I am able to give you a bit of information, which bears upon the so often discussed question of our allowing phenomena. The Egyptian operations of your blessed countrymen involve such local consequences to the body of Occultists still remaining there and to what they are guarding, that two of our adepts are already there, having joined some Druze brethren, and three more on their way. I was offered the agreeable privilege of becoming an eye-witness to the human butchery, but—declined with thanks. For such great emergency is our Force stored up, and hence—we dare not waste it on fashionable tamasha.

In about a week—new religious ceremonies, new glittering bubbles to amuse the babes with, and once more I will be busy night and day, morning, noon, and evening. At times I feel a passing regret that the Chohans should not evolute the happy idea of allowing us also a " sumptuary allowance " in the shape of a little spare time. Oh, for the final Rest! for that Nirvana where—" to be one with Life, yet—to live not." Alas, alas! having personally realized that:—

> "   .   .   .   the soul of Things is sweet,
> The Heart of Being is celestial Rest,"

one does long for—eternal REST!

Yours,

K. H.

LETTER No. 17 [1]

Received Simla, June, 1882.

(1) Some fifth round men have already begun to appear on earth. In what way are they distinguishable from fourth round men of the seventh earthly incarnation? I suppose they are in the first incarnation of the fifth round and that a tremendous advance will be achieved when the fifth round people get to their seventh incarnation.

(1) The natural-born Seers and clairvoyants of Mrs. A. Kingsford's and Mr. Maitland's types; the great adepts of whatsoever country; the geniuses—whether in arts, politics or religious reform. No great physical distinction yet; too early and will come later on.
Quite so.   If you turn to Appendix No. I [2] you will find it explained.

---

[1] K.H.'s Replies to Mr. Sinnett's queries are printed in bold type.—ED.
[2] See Letter No. 18.—ED.

(2) But if a 1st-5th round man devoted himself to occultism and became an adept, would he escape further earthly incarnations?

(2) No; if we except Buddha—a sixth round being, as he had run so successfully the race in his previous incarnations as to outrun even his predecessors. But then such a man is to be found in a *billion* of human creatures. He differed from other men as much in his physical appearance as in spirituality and knowledge. Yet even he escaped further reincarnations but on this earth; and, when the last of the sixth round men of the third ring is gone out of this earth, the Great Teacher will have to get reincarnated on the next planet. Only, and since He sacrificed Nirvanic bliss and Rest for the salvation of his fellow creatures He will be re-born in the highest —the *seventh* ring of the upper planet. Till then He will *overshadow* every decimillenium (let us rather say and add " *has* overshadowed already ") a chosen individual who generally overturned the destinies of nations. See *Isis*, Vol. I, pp. 34 and 35, last and first para. on the pages.

(3) Is there any essential spiritual difference between a man and a woman, or is sex a mere accident of each birth—the ultimate future of the individual furnishing the same opportunities?

(3) A mere accident—as you say. Generally a chance work yet guided by individual Karma,—moral aptitudes, characteristics and deeds of a previous birth.

(4) The majority of the superior classes of civilized countries on earth now, I understand to be seventh " ring " people (*i.e.*, of the seventh earthly incarnation) of the fourth round. The Australian aborigines I understand to be of a low ring? which? and are the lower and inferior classes of civilized countries of various rings or of the ring just below the seventh? And are all seventh ring people born in the superior classes or may not some be found among the poor?

(4) Not necessarily. Refinement, polishedness, and brilliant education, in *your* sense of these words have very little to do with the course of higher Nature's Law. Take a seventh ring African or a fifth ring Mongolian and you can educate him—if taken from the cradle—save his physical appearance, and transform him into the most brilliant and accomplished English lord. Yet, he will still remain but an *outwardly* intellectual parrot. (See Appendix No. II).

(5) The Old Lady told me that the bulk of the inhabitants of this country are in some respects less advanced than Europeans though more spiritual. Are they on a lower ring of the same round

——or does the difference refer to some principle of national cycles which has nothing to do with individual progress?

(5) Most of the peoples of India belong to the oldest or the earliest branchlet of the fifth human Race. I have desired M. to end his letter to you with a short summary of the last scientific theory of your learned Ethnographers and Naturalists, to save myself work. Read what he writes and then turn to No. III of my Appendix.

What is the explanation of " Ernest " and Eglinton's other guide? Are they elementaries drawing their conscious vitality from him or elementals masquerading? When " Ernest " took that sheet of " Pioneer " notepaper how did he contrive to get it without mediumship at this end?

I can assure you it is not worth your while *now* to study the true natures of the " Ernests " and " Joeys " and " other guides " as unless you become acquainted with the evolution of the *corruptions* of elemental dross, and those of the seven principles in man—you would ever find yourself at a loss to understand what they *really* are; there are no written statutes for them, and they can hardly be expected to pay their friends and admirers the compliment of truth, silence or forbearing. If some are related to them as some *soulless* physical mediums are—they shall meet. If not—better leave them alone. They gravitate but to their likes—the mediums; and their relation is not made but *forced* by foolish and sinful phenomena-mongers. They are both elementaries and elementals—at best a low, mischievous, degrading jangle. You want to embrace too much knowledge at once, my dear friend; you cannot attain at a bound all the mysteries. See however Appendix—which is in reality a letter.

I do not know Subba Rao—who is a pupil of M. At least—he knows very little of me. Yet I know, he will *never* consent to come to Simla. But if ordered by Morya will teach from Madras, *i.e.*, correct the MSS. as M. did, comment upon them, answer questions, and be very, *very* useful. He has a perfect reverence and adoration for—H. P. B.

K. H.

LETTER No. 18

Received Simla, June, 1882.

APPENDIX

(I) Every Spiritual Individuality has a gigantic evolutionary journey to perform, a tremendous gyratory progress to accomplish. First—at the very beginning of the great Mahamanvantaric rotation, from first to last of the man-bearing planets, as on each of them, the monad has to pass through seven successive races of man. From the dumb offshoot of the ape (the latter strongly differentiating from the now known specimens) up to the present *fifth* race, or rather variety, and through two more races, before he has done with this earth only; and then on to the next, higher and higher still. . . . But we will confine our attention but to this one. Each of the seven races send seven ramifying branchlets from the Parent Branch: and through each of these in turn man *has* to evolute before he passes on to the next higher race; and that— *seven times*. Well may you open wide your eyes, good friend, and feel puzzled—it is so. The branchlets typify varying specimens of humanity—physically and spiritually—and no one of us can miss one single rung of the ladder. With all that there is *no* reincarnation as taught by the London Seeress—Mrs. A. K., as the intervals between the *re-births* are too immeasurably long to permit of any such fantastic ideas. Please, bear in mind, that when I say " man," I mean a human being of our type. There are other and innumerable manvantaric chains of globes bearing intelligent beings—both in and out of our solar system—the crowns or apexes of evolutionary being in their respective chains, some— physically and intellectually—lower, others immeasurably higher than the man of our chain. But beyond mentioning them we will not speak of these at present.

Through every race, then, man has to pass making seven successive entrances and exits and developing intellect to degrees from the lowest to the highest in succession. In short, his earth-cycle with its rings and *sub*-rings is the exact counterpart of the Great Cycle—only in miniature. Bear in mind again, that the intervals even between these special " race re-incarnations " are enormous, as even the dullest of the African Bushmen has to reap the reward of his Karma, equally with his brother Bushman who may be six times more intelligent.

Your ethnographers and anthropologists would do well to ever keep in their minds this unvarying septenary law which runs throughout the works of nature. From Cuvier—the late grand master of Protestant Theology—whose Bible-stuffed brain made him divide mankind into but three distinct varieties of races— down to Blumenbach who divided them into five—they were all wrong. Alone Pritchard, who prophetically suggested *seven* comes near the right mark. I read in the *Pioneer* of June 12th forwarded to me by H.P.B. a letter on the *Ape Theory* by A.P.W.[1] which contains a most excellent exposition of the Darwinian hypothesis. The last paragraph page 6 column 1 would be regarded—barring a few errors—as a *revelation* in a millenium or so, were it to be preserved. Reading the nine lines from line 21

---

[1] A relevant extract from this Letter appears in *The Early Teachings of the Masters*. Ed. Jinarajadasa, at p. 19—.Eds.

(counting from the bottom) you have a *fact* of which few naturalists are yet prepared to accept the proof. The fifth, sixth and seventh races of the *Fifth* Round—each succeeding race evoluting with and keeping pace, so to say with the " Great Cycle " rounds—and the fifth race of the fifth round, having to exhibit a perceptible physical and intellectual as well as moral differentiation towards its fourth " race " or " earthly incarnation " you are right in saying that a " tremendous advance will be achieved when the fifth round people get to their seventh incarnation."

(II) Nor has wealth nor poverty, high or low birth any influence upon it, for this is all a result of their Karma. Neither has—what you call—civilization much to do with the progress. It is the *inner* man, the spirituality, the illumination of the physical brain by the light of the spiritual or divine intelligence that is *the* test. The Australian, the Esquimaux, the Bushmen, the Veddahs, etc., are all side-shooting branchlets of that Branch which you call " cave-men "—the *third* race (according to your Science—the *second*) that evoluted on the globe. They are the remnants of the seventh ring cave-men, remnants " that have ceased to grow and are the arrested forms of life doomed to eventual decay in the struggle of existence " in the words of *your correspondent*?

See " Isis " Chapter I,—". . . . . the Divine Essence (Purusha) like a luminous arc " proceeds to form a circle—the mahamanvantaric chain; and having attained the highest (or its first starting point) bends back again and returns to earth (the first globe) bringing a higher type of humanity in its vortex— " thus seven times. Approaching our earth it grows more and more shadowy until upon touching ground it becomes as black as night—" *i.e.* it is matter *outwardly*, the Spirit or Purusha being concealed under a quintuple armour of the first five principles. Now see underlined three lines on page 5; for the word " mankind " read *human races*, and for that of " civilization " read *Spiritual evolution of that particular race* and you have the truth which had to be concealed at that incipient tentative stage of the Theosophical Society.

See again pp. 13 last paragraph and 14 first paragraph, and note the underlined lines about Plato. Then see p. 32, remembering the difference between the *Manvantaras* as therein calculated and the MAHAMANVANTARAS (complete seven rounds between two Pralayas,—the four Yugas returning *seven* times, *once for each race*. Having done so far take your pen and calculate. This will make you swear—but this will not hurt your Karma much: lip-profanity finds it deaf. Read attentively in this connection (not with the swearing process but with that of evolution) pp. 301 last line " and now comes a mystery . . ." and continue on to p. 304.

"" Isis " was *not* unveiled but rents sufficiently large were made to afford flitting glances to be completed by the student's own intuition. In this curry of quotations from various philosophic and esoteric truths purposely veiled, behold our doctrine, which is now being partially taught to Europeans for the first time.

(III) As said in my answer on your notes, most of the peoples of India—with the exception of the *Semitic* (?) Moguls—belong to the oldest branchlet of the present *fifth* Human race, which was evoluted in Central Asia more than one million of years ago. Western Science finding good reasons for the theory of human beings having inhabited Europe 400,000 years before your era—this cannot so shock you as to prevent your drinking wine to-night at your dinner. Yet Asia has, as well as Australia, Africa, America and the most northward regions, its remnants—of the fourth— even of the third race (cave-men and Iberians).   At the same time, we have more of the seventh ring men of the fourth race than Europe and more of the first ring of the fifth round, as, older than the European branchlets, our men have naturally come in earlier.   Their being " less advanced " in civilization and refinement trouble their spirituality but very little, Karma being an animal which remains indifferent to pumps and white kid gloves. Neither your knives nor forks, operas and drawing-rooms will any more follow you in your onward progress than will the dead-leaf coloured robes of the British Esthetics prevent the proprietors thereof and wearers from having been born among the ranks of those, who will be regarded—do what they may—by the forth-coming sixth and seventh round men as flesh-eating and liquor-drinking " savages " of the " Royal Society Period." It depends on you, to so immortalize your name as to force the future higher races to divide our age and call the sub-division—the " Pleisto-Sinnettic Period " but this can never be so long as you labour under the impression that " the purposes we have now in view would be met by *reasonable* temperance and self-restraint." Occult Science is a jealous mistress and allows not a shadow of self-indulgence; and it *is* " fatal " not only to the ordinary course of married life but even to flesh and *wine* drinking.   I am afraid that the archæologists of the seventh round, when digging out and unearth-ing the future Pompeii of Punjab—Simla, one day, instead of finding the precious relics of the Theosophical " Eclectic," will fish out but some petrified or vitreous remains of the " Sumptuary allowance."   Such is the latest prophecy current at Shigatse.[1]

And now to the last question. Well, as I say, the " guides " are both elementals and elementaries and not even a decent " half and half " but the very froth in the mug of the mediumistic beer.

---

[1] The Masters spell this town in many ways. We have substituted the modern spelling.—EDS.

The several " privations " of such sheets of notepaper were evoluted during E's stay in Calcutta in Mrs. G.'s atmosphere—since
she frequently received letters from you.   It was then an easy
matter for the creatures in following E's unconscious desire to
attract other disintegrated particles from your box, so as to form
a double.   He is a strong medium, and were it not for an inherent
good nature and other good qualities, strongly counteracted by
vanity, sloth, selfishness, greediness for money and with other
qualities of modern civilization a total absence of *will*, he would
make a superb *Dugpa*, yet, as I said, he is " a good fellow " every
inch of him; *naturally* truthful, under control—the reverse.   I would
if I could save him from . . . .

Note.—In the First and Second Editions appears an Editorial Note to the
effect that the   rest of this Letter is missing.   A student has now pointed out
the missing portion is clearly Letter 95, on pp. 423-424.—Eds.

LETTER No. 19 [1]

Attached to Proofs of Letter on Theosophy.   Received August 12th, 1882.

Yes; verily *known* and as confidently *affirmed* by the adepts from
whom—

> " No curtain hides the spheres Elysian,
> Nor these poor shells of half transparent dust;
> For all that blinds the spirit's vision
> Is pride and hate and lust. . . ."
> (*Not for publication*)

Exceptional cases, my friend.   Suicides *can* and generally do,
but not so with the others.   The good and pure sleep a quiet
blissful sleep, full of happy visions of earth-life, and have no consciousness of being already for ever beyond that life.   Those who
were neither good nor bad, will sleep a dreamless, still a quiet
sleep; while the wicked will in proportion to their grossness suffer
the pangs of a nightmare lasting years: their thoughts become
living things, their wicked passions—real substance, and they
receive back on their heads all the misery they have heaped upon
others.   Reality and *fact* if described would yield a far more
terrible *Inferno* than even Dante had imagined!

[1] Fragments in K.H.'s writing.—Ed.

LETTER No. 20A [1]

Received   August   1882.

10 [X]

My dear Master,

In speaking of Fragments No. III of which you will receive proofs soon, I said it was far from satisfactory though I had done my best.

It was necessary to advance the doctrine of the Society another stage, so as gradually to open the .eyes of the spiritualists—so I introduced as the most pressing matter the Suicide etc., view given in your last letter to S.

Well it is *this that seems to me most unsatisfactory and it will lead to a number of questions that I shall feel puzzled to reply to.*

Our first doctrine is that the majority of objective phenomena were due to shells. $1\frac{1}{2}$ and $2\frac{1}{2}$ principled shells, *i.e.*, principles entirely separated from their sixth and seventh principles.

But as a further (1) development we admit that there are *some spirits*, i.e., 5th and 4th principles not wholly dissevered from their sixth and seventh which also may be potent in the seance room. These are the spirits of suicides and the victims of accident or violence. Here the doctrine is that each particular wave of life must run on to its appointed shore and, with the exception of the *very good*, that all spirits prematurely divorced from the lower principles must remain on earth, until the foredestined hour of what would have been the natural death strikes.

Now this is all very well, but this being so it is clear that in *opposition to our former doctrine, shells will be few and spirits many (2).*

For what difference can there be, to take the case of suicides, whether these be conscious or unconscious, whether the man blows his brains out, or only drinks or womanizes himself to death, or kills himself by over-study? In each case equally the normal natural hour of death is anticipated and a spirit and not a shell the result—or again what difference does it make whether a man is hung for murder, killed in battle, in a railway train or a powder explosion, or drowned or burnt to death, or knocked over by cholera or plague, or jungle fever or any of the other thousand and one epidemic diseases of which the seeds were not ab initio in his constitution, but were introduced therein in consequence of his happening to visit a particular locality or undergo a given experience, both of which he might have avoided? Equally in

---

[1] The original letter of A.O.H. to K.H. has some passages numbered and underlined with blue pencil by K.H. These are printed in bold type italics. The numbers refer to K.H.'s replies, for which see *post* Letter No.20c.—ED.

all cases the normal death hour is anticipated and a spirit instead of a shell the result.

In England it is calculated that not 15% of the population reach their normal death period—and what with fevers and famines and their *sequelae*, I fear the percentage is not much larger here even—where the people are mostly vegetarian and as a rule live under less unfavourable sanitary conditions.

So then the great bulk of all the physical phenomena of spiritualists ought apparently to be due to these spirits and not to shells. I should be glad to have further information on this point.

There is a second point (**3**); very often, as I understand, the spirits of very fair average good people dying *natural* deaths, remain some time in the earth's atmosphere—from a few days to a few years—why cannot such as these communicate? And if they can this is a most important point that should not have been over-looked.

(**4**) And thirdly it is a fact that thousands of spirits do appear in pure circles and teach the highest morality and moreover tell very closely the truths as to the unseen world (witness Alan Kardec's books, pages and pages of which are identical with what you yourself teach) and it is unreasonable to suppose that such are either shells or bad spirits. But you have not given us any opening for any large number of pure high spirits—and until the whole theory is properly set forth and due place made for these which seem to me a thoroughly well established fact, you will never win over the spiritualists. I dare say it is the old story—only *part* of the truth being told to us and the rest reserved—if so it is merely cutting the Society's throat. Better tell the *outside* world *nothing* —than to tell them half truths the incompleteness of which they detect at once, the result being a contemptuous rejection of what *is* truth and though [1] they cannot accept it in this fragmentary state.

Yours affectionately,

A. O. HUME

LETTER No. 20B [2]

Received August, 1882.

Simla, *July 25th*.

My Dear Old Lady,

I began to try to answer N.D.K.'s letter at once so that if K.H. really meant the note to appear in this immediately " next "

---

[1] Query, for ' and though ' substitute ' because '.—Eds.

[2] Letter from Mr. Sinnett to H.P.B. on the backs of the pages of which is part of a long letter from K.H. (No.20c) requeries of Hume's. The passages in bold type italics have been underlined in blue by K.H.—Ed.

appearing Theosophist for August it might just be in time. But I soon got into a tangle. Of course we have received no information that distinctly covers the question now raised, though I suppose we ought to be able to combine bits into an answer. The difficulty turns on giving the real explanation of Eliphas Levi's enigma in your note in the October Theosophist.

If he refers to the fate of this, at present existing race of mankind his statement that the intermediate majority of Egos are ejected from nature or annihilated, would be in direct conflict with K.H.'s teaching. [1] They do not die without remembrance, if they retain remembrance in Devachan and again recover remembrance (even of past personalities as of a book's pages) at the period of full individual consciousness preceding that of absolute consciousness in Pari-Nirvana.

But it occurred to me that E.L. may have been dealing with humanity as a whole, not merely *with the fourth round men. Great numbers of fifth round personalities are destined to perish I understand, and these might be his intermediate useless portion of mankind.* But then the individual spiritual monads, as I understand the matter, do not perish whatever happens, and if a monad reaches the fifth round with all his previous personalities preserved in the page of his book awaiting future perusal, *he* would not be ejected and annihilated because some of his fifth-round pages were " unfit for publication." So again there is a difficulty in reconciling the two statements.

X. But again is it conceivable that a spiritual monad though surviving the rejection of its third and fourth round pages, cannot survive the rejection of fifth and sixth round pages. That failure to lead good lives in these rounds means the annihilation of the whole individual who will never then get to the seventh round at all?

But on the other hand if that were so the Eliphas Levi case would not be met by such a hypothesis, for long before *then the individuals who had become co-workers with nature for evil would have been themselves annihilated by the obscuration of the planet* X between the fifth and sixth rounds—if not by the obscuration between the fourth and the fifth, for to every round there is one obscuration we are told. (5) There is another difficulty here because some fifth rounders being here already it is not clear when the obscuration comes on. Will it be behind the *avant couriers* of the fifth round, who will not count as commencing the fifth, that epoch only really beginning after the existing race has totally decayed out—but this idea will not work.

Having got so far in my reflections yesterday, I went up to Hume to see if he could make out the puzzle and so enable me to write what was wanted for this post. But on looking into it

[1] See over, Letter No.20c.—EDS.

and looking back to the October Theosophist we came to the conclusion that the only possible explanation was that the October Theosophist note was utterly wrong and totally at variance with all our later teaching. Is that really the solution? I do not think so or K.H. would not have set me to reconcile the two.

But you will see that at present, with the best will in the world I am utterly unable to do the job set me, and if my dear Guardian and Master will kindly look at these remarks he will see the dilemma in which I am placed.

And then in the way which will be the least trouble to himself either through you or directly he will perhaps indicate the line which the required explanation ought to take. Manifestly it cannot be done for the August number, but I am inclined to believe he never intended this as the time is now so short.

We all feel so sorry for you, over-worked amid the heat and the flies. When you have got the August number off your hands you might perhaps be able to take flight for here, and get a little rest amongst us. You know how glad at any time we should be to see you. Meanwhile my own individual plans are a little uncertain. I may have to return to Allahabad, in order to leave Hensman free to go as special correspondent to Egypt. I am fighting my proprietors tooth and nail to avert this result—but for a few days still the issue of the struggle will be uncertain.

Ever Yours,

A. P. S.

P.S.—As you may want to print the letter in this number, I return it herewith, but hope that this may *not* be the case and that you will send it me back again so that I may duly perform my little task with the help of a few words as to the line to be followed.

LETTER No. 20c

Received August, 1882.

‡ Except in so far that he constantly uses the terms " God " and " Christ " which taken in their esoteric sense simply mean " Good "—in its dual aspect of the abstract and the *concrete* and nothing more dogmatic—Eliphas Levi is not in any *direct* conflict with our teachings. It is again a straw blown out of a hay-stack and accused by the wind of belonging to a hay-rick. *Most* of those, whom you may call, if you like, candidates for *Devachan*—die and are reborn in the Kama-Loka " without remembrance "; though (and just because) they do get some of it back in the Devachan. Nor can we call it a full, but only a *partial* remembrance. You would hardly call " remembrance " a dream of yours; some particular scene or scenes, within whose narrow limits you would

find enclosed a few persons—those whom you loved best, with an undying love, that holy feeling that alone survives, and—not the slightest recollection of any other events or scenes? *Love* and *Hatred* are the only *immortal* feelings, the only survivors from the wreck of *Ye-dhamma*, or the phenomenal world. Imagine yourself then, in Devachan with those you may have loved with such immortal love; with the familiar, shadowy scenes connected with them for a background and—a perfect blank for everything else relating to your interior, social, political, literary and social life. And then, in the face of that spiritual, purely cogitative existence, of that unalloyed felicity which, in proportion with the intensity of the feelings that *created* it, lasts from a few to several thousand years,—call it the " personal remembrance of A. P. Sinnett "—if you can. Dreadfully monotonous!—you may think.—Not in the least—I answer. Have you experienced monotony during—say—that moment which you considered *then* and *now* so consider it— as the moment of the highest bliss you have ever felt? Of course not. Well, no more will you experience it there, in that passage through Eternity in which a million of years is no longer than a second. There, where there is no consciousness of an external world there can be no discernment to mark differences, hence no perception of contrasts of monotony or variety; nothing in short, outside that immortal feeling of love and sympathetic attraction whose seeds are planted in the fifth, whose plants blossom luxuriantly in and around the fourth, but whose roots have to penetrate deep into the sixth principle, if it would survive the lower groups. (And now I propose to kill two birds with one stone—to answer your and Mr. Hume's questions at the same time) —remember, both, that we *create* ourselves our *devachan* as our *avitchi* while yet on earth, and mostly during the latter days and even moments of our intellectual, sentient lives. That feeling which is the strongest in us at that supreme hour; when, as in a dream, the events of a long life, to their minutest details, are marshalled in the greatest order in a few seconds in our vision,[1] —that feeling will become the fashioner of our bliss or woe, the *life principle* of our future existence. In the latter we have no substantial being, but only a present and momentary existence— whose duration has no bearing upon, as no effect, or relation to its being—which as every other effect of a transitory cause will be as fleeting, and in its turn will vanish and cease to be. The real full remembrance of our lives will come but at the end of the minor cycle—not before. In Karma Loka those who retain their remembrance will not enjoy it at the supreme hour of recollection. Those who *know* they are dead in their physical bodies can

[1] That vision takes place when a person is already proclaimed dead. The brain is the last organ that dies.

only be either adepts or—sorcerers; and these two are the exceptions to the *general rule*. Both having been " co-workers with nature," the former for *good*, the latter—for *bad*, in her work of creation and in that of destruction, they are the only ones who may be called *immortal*—in the Kabalistic and the esoteric sense of course. Complete or true immortality,—which means an unlimited *sentient* existence, can have no breaks and stoppages, no arrest of *Self*-consciousness. And even the *shells* of those good men whose page will not be found missing in the great Book of Lives at the threshold of the Great Nirvana, even they will regain their remembrance and an appearance of Self-consciousness, only after the sixth and seventh principles with the essence of the 5th (the latter having to furnish the material for even that partial recollection of personality which is necessary for the object in Devachan)—have gone to their gestation period, *not before*. Even in the case of suicides and those who have perished by violent death, even in their case, consciousness requires à certain time to establish its new centre of gravity, and evolve, as Sir W. Hamilton would have it—its " perception proper ", henceforth to remain distinct from " sensation proper." Thus, when man dies, his " Soul " (fifth prin.) becomes unconscious and loses all remembrance of things internal as well as external. Whether his stay in Kama Loka has to last but a few moments, hours, days, weeks, months or years; whether he died a natural or a violent death; whether it occurred in his young or old age, and, whether the Ego was good, bad, or indifferent,—his consciousness leaves him as suddenly as the flame leaves the wick, when blown out. When life has retired from the last particle in the brain matter, his perceptive faculties become extinct forever, his spiritual powers of cogitation and volition—(all those faculties in short, which are neither inherent in, nor acquirable by organic matter)—for the time being. His *Mayavi rupa* may be often thrown into objectivity, as in the cases of apparitions after death; but, unless it is projected with the knowledge of[1] (whether latent or potential), or, owing to the intensity of the desire to see or appear to someone, shooting through the dying brain, the apparition will be simply—automatical; it will not be due to any sympathetic attraction, or to any act of volition, and no more than the reflection of a person passing unconsciously near a mirror is due to the desire of the latter.

Having thus explained the position, I will sum up and ask again why it should be maintained that what is given by Eliphas Levi and expounded by H. P. B. is " in direct conflict " with my teaching? E. L. is an Occultist, and a Kabalist, and writing for those who are supposed to know the rudiments of the Kabalistic tenets, uses the peculiar phraseology of his doctrine, and H. P. B. follows

[1] Query, insert, the projector.—EDS.

suit. The only omission she was guilty of, was not to add the word " Western " between the two words " Occult " and doctrine (see third line of *Editor's note*). She is a fanatic in her way, and is unable to write with anything like system and calmness, or to remember that the general public needs all the lucid explanations that to her may seem superfluous. And, as you are sure to remark—" but this is also *our* case; and you too seem to forget it," —I will give you a few more explanations. As remarked on the margin of the October *Theosophist*—the word " immortality " has for the initiates and occultists quite a different meaning. We call " immortal " but the one Life in its universal collectivity and entire or Absolute Abstraction; that which has neither beginning nor end, nor any break in its continuity. Does the term apply to anything else? Certainly it does not. Therefore the earliest Chaldeans had several prefixes to the word " immortality," one of which is the Greek, rarely-used term—*panaeonic* immortality, *i.e.*, beginning with the *manvàntara* and ending with the *pralaya* of our Solar Universe. It lasts the aeon, or " period " of our *pan* or " *all* nature." Immortal then is he, in the *panaeonic* immortality whose distinct consciousness and perception of *Self under whatever form* undergoes no disjunction at any time, not for one second, during the period of his *Egoship*. Those periods are several in number, each having its distinct name in the secret doctrines of the Chaldeans, Greeks, Egyptians and Aryans, and were they but amenable to translation—which they are not, at least so long as the idea involved remains inconceivable to the Western mind—I could give them to you. Suffice for you for the present to know that a man, an *Ego* like yours or mine, may be immortal from one to the other Round. Let us say I begin my immortality at the present fourth Round, *i.e.*, having become a *full adept* (which unhappily I am not) I arrest the hand of Death at will, and when finally obliged to submit to it, my knowledge of the secrets of nature puts me in a position to retain my consciousness and distinct perception of Self as an object to my own reflective consciousness and cognition; and thus avoiding all such dismemberments of principles, that as *a rule* take place after the physical death of average humanity, I remain as Koothoomi in my *Ego* throughout the whole series of births and lives across the seven worlds and *Arupa-lokas* until finally I land again on this earth among the fifth race men of the full fifth Round beings. I would have been, in such a case—" immortal " for an inconceivable (to you) long period, embracing many milliards of years. And yet am " I " *truly* immortal for all that? Unless I make the same efforts as I do now, to secure for myself another such furlough from Nature's Law, Koothoomi will vanish and may become a Mr. Smith or an innocent Babu, when his leave expires. There are men who become such mighty beings, there are men among us who may become immortal during the remainder of the Rounds, and then take their appointed place among the highest Chohans, the Planetary *conscious* " Ego-Spirits." Of course the Monad " never perishes whatever happens," but Eliphas speaks of the *personal* not of the Spiritual Egos, and you have fallen into the same mistake (and very naturally too) as C.C.M.; though I must confess the passage in *Isis* was very clumsily expressed, as I had already remarked to you about this same paragraph in one of my letters long ago. I had to " exercise my ingenuity " over it—as the Yankees express it, but succeeded in mending the hole, I believe, as I will have to many times more, I am afraid, before we have done with *Isis*. It really ought to be *re-written* for the sake of the family honour.

X It is certainly *inconceivable*; therefore, there is no mortal use to discuss the subject.

X You misconceived the teaching, because you were not aware of what you are now told: (*a*) who are the true *co-workers* with nature; and (*b*) that it is by no means *all* the evil co-workers who drop into the eighth sphere and are annihilated.[1]

The potency for *evil* is as great in man—aye—greater—than the potentiality for *good*. An exception to the rule of nature, that exception, which in the case of adepts and sorcerers becomes in its turn a *rule*, has again its own exceptions. Read carefully the passage that C.C.M. left unquoted—on pp. 352-353, *Isis*, Volume 1, para. 3. Again she omits to distinctly state that the case mentioned relates but to those powerful sorcerers whose co-partnership with nature for evil affords to them the means of forcing her hand, and thus accord them also panaeonic immortality. But oh, what kind of immortality, and how preferable is annihilation to their lives! Don't you see that everything you find in *Isis* is delineated, hardly sketched—nothing completed or fully revealed. Well the time has come, but where are the workers for such a tremendous task?

Says Mr. Hume (see affixed letter [2] marked passages—**10 [X]** and **1, 2, 3**). And now when you have read the objections to that most *unsatisfactory* doctrine—as Mr. Hume calls it—a doctrine which you had to learn first as a whole, before proceeding to study it in parts,—at the risk of satisfying you no better, I will proceed to explain the latter.

(1) Although not " wholly dissevered from their sixth and seventh principles " and quite " potent " in the seance room, nevertheless to the day when they would have died a natural

---

[1] Annihilated *suddenly* as *human Egos* and *personlities*, lasting in that world of pure matter under various material forms an inconceivable length of time before they can return to primeval matter.

[2] See ante Letter No. 21A.—ED.

death, they are separated from the higher principles by a gulf. The sixth and seventh remain passive and negative, whereas, in cases of *accidental death* the higher and the lower groups mutually attract each other. In cases of good and innocent Egos, moreover, the latter gravitates irresistibly toward the sixth and seventh, and thus—either slumbers surrounded by happy dreams, or, sleeps a dreamless profound sleep until the hour strikes. With a little reflection, and an eye to eternal justice and fitness of things, you will see why. The victim whether good or bad is *irresponsible* for his death, even if his death were due to some action in a previous life or an antecedent birth; was an act, in short, of the Law of Retribution, still, it was not the *direct* result of an act deliberately committed by the *personal* Ego of that life during which he happened to be killed. Had he been allowed to live longer he might have atoned for his antecedent sins still more effectually: and even now, the Ego having been made to pay off the debt of his maker (the previous Ego) is free from the blows of retributive justice. The Dhyan Chohans, who have no hand in the guidance of the *living* human Ego, protect the helpless victim when it is violently thrust out of its element into a new one, before it is matured and made fit and ready for it. We tell you what we know, *for we are made to learn it through personal experience*. You know what I mean and I CAN SAY NO MORE! Yes; the victims whether good or bad sleep, to awake but *at the hour of the last Judgment*, which is that hour of the supreme struggle between the sixth and seventh, and the fifth and fourth at the threshold of the gestation state. And even after that, when the sixth and seventh carrying off a portion of the fifth have gone into their Akasic Samadhi, even then it may happen that the spiritual spoil from the fifth will prove too weak to be reborn in Devachan; in which case it will there and then reclothe itself in a new body, the subjective " Being " created from the Karma of the victim (or no-victim, as the case may be) and enter upon a new earth-existence whether upon this or any other planet. In no case then, with the exception of suicides and shells, is there any possibility for any other to be attracted to a seance room. And it is *clear* that " this teaching is *not* in opposition to our former doctrine " and that while " shells " will be many, Spirits *very* few.

(2) There is a great difference in our humble opinion. We, who look at it from a stand-point which would prove very unacceptable to Life Insurance Companies, say that there are very few if any of the men who indulge in the above enumerated vices, who feel perfectly sure that such a course of action will lead them eventually to premature death. Such is the penalty of *Maya*. The " vices " will not escape their punishment; but it is

the *cause* not the *effect* that will be punished, especially an unforeseen though probable effect. As well call a *suicide* a man who meets his death in a storm at sea, as one who kills himself with "over-study." Water is liable to drown a man, and too much brain-work to produce a softening of the brain which may carry him away. In such a case no one ought to cross the *Kalapani* nor even to take a bath for fear of getting faint in it and drowned (for we all know of such cases); nor should a man do his duty, least of all sacrifice himself for even a laudable and highly-beneficent cause, as many of us—(H. P. B. for one)—do. Would Mr. Hume call her a *suicide* were she to drop down dead over her present work? *Motive* is everything and man is punished in a case of *direct* responsibility, never otherwise. In the victim's case the natural hour of death was anticipated *accidentally*, while in that of the suicide, death is brought on voluntarily and with a full and deliberate knowledge of its immediate consequences. Thus a man who causes his death in a fit of temporary insanity is *not* a *felo de se*, to the great grief and often trouble of the Life Insurance Companies. Nor is he left a prey to the temptations of the Kama Loka but falls *asleep* like any other victim. A Guiteau will not remain in the earth's atmosphere with his higher principles over him—inactive and paralysed, *still* there. Guiteau is gone into a state during the period of which he will be *ever firing at his President*, thereby tossing into confusion and shuffling the destinies of millions of persons; where he will be *ever tried* and *ever hung*. Bathing in the reflections of his deeds and thoughts— especially those he indulged in on the scaffold,[1] . . . .

. . . .

. . . . . his fate. As for those who were "knocked over by cholera, or plague, or jungle fever" they could not have succumbed had they not the germs for the development of such diseases in them from birth.

"So then, the great bulk of the physical phenomena of Spiritualists" my dear brother, are *not* "due to these Spirits" but indeed—to "shells."

(3) "The Spirits of very fair average good people dying natural deaths remain . . . in the earth's atmosphere from a few days to a few years," the period depending on their readiness to meet their —*creature* not their creator; a very abstruse subject you will learn later on, when you too are more prepared. But why should they "communicate"? Do those you love communicate with you during their sleep objectively? Your Spirits, in hours of danger, or intense sympathy, vibrating on the same current of thought— which in such cases creates a kind of telegraphic spiritual wire between your two bodies—may meet and mutually impress your

[1] Two lines in original have been deleted here.—ED.

memories; but then you are *living*, not *dead* bodies. But how can an *unconscious* 5th principle (see supra) impress or communicate with a living organism, unless it has already become a *shell*? If, for certain reasons they remain in such a state of lethargy for several years, the spirits of the living may ascend to them, as you were already told; and this may take place still easier than in Devachan, where the *Spirit* is too much engrossed in his personal bliss to pay much attention to an intruding element. I say— they *cannot*.

(4) I am sorry to contradict your statement. I know of no " thousands of spirits " who do appear in circles—and moreover positively do not know of one " perfectly *pure* circle "—and " teach the highest morality." I hope I may not be classed with slanderers in addition to other names lately bestowed upon me, but truth compels me to declare that Allan Kardec was not quite immaculate during his lifetime, nor has become a *very pure Spirit* since. As to teaching the " highest morality," we have a Dugpa-Shammar not far from where I am residing. Quite a remarkable man. Not very powerful as a sorcerer but excessively so as a drunkard, a thief, a liar, and—an orator. In this latter *role* he could give points to and beat Messrs. Gladstone, Bradlaugh, and even the Rev. H. W. Beecher—than whom there is no more eloquent preacher of morality, and no greater breaker of his Lord's Commandments in the U.S.A. This Shapa-tung Lama, when thirsty, can make an enormous audience of " yellow-cap " laymen weep all their yearly supply of tears with the narrative of his repentance and suffering in the morning, and then get drunk in the evening and rob the whole village by mesmerising them into a dead sleep. Preaching and teaching morality with an end in view proves very little. Read " J.P.T.'s " article in *Light* and what I say will be corroborated.

(To A.P.S. (5).) The " obscuration " comes on only when the last man of whatever Round has passed into the sphere of effects. Nature is too well, too mathematically adjusted to cause mistakes to happen in the exercise of her functions. The obscuration of the planet on which are now evoluting the races of the fifth Round men—will, of course " be behind the few *avant couriers* " who are now here. But before that time comes we will have to part, to meet no more, as the Editor of the *Pioneer* and his humble correspondent.

And now having shewn that the *October* Number of the *Theosophist* was not *utterly wrong*, nor was it at " variance with the later teaching," may K.H. set you to " reconcile the two "?

To reconcile you still more with Eliphas, I will send you a number of his *MSS*. that have never been published, in a large, clear, beautiful handwriting with my comments all through.

Nothing better than that can give you a key to Kabalistic puzzles.

I have to write to Mr. Hume this week; to give him consolation, and to show, that unless he has a strong desire to live, he
need not trouble himself about *Devachan*. Unless a man *loves*
well or *hates* as well, he will be neither in Devachan nor in Avitchi.
" Nature spews the luke-warm out of her mouth " means only
that she annihilates their *personal* Egos (not the shells, nor yet the
sixth principle) in the Kama Loka and the Devachan. This
does not prevent them from being immediately reborn—and, if
their lives were not very *very* bad, there is no reason why the
eternal Monad should not find the page of that life intact in the
Book of Life.

K. H.

LETTER No. 21 [1]

Received back 22.8.82

August 12th.

My dear Guardian,

I am afraid the present letters on Theosophy are not worth
much, for I have worked on too literal an acceptance of some
passages in your long letter about Devachan. The bearing of
that seemed to be that the " accidents " as well as the suicides
were in danger from the attraction of the séance room. You
wrote:—

" But there is another kind of spirit we have lost sight of,—
the suicides and those killed by accidents. Both kinds can communicate and both have to pay dearly for such visits. . . ."
Correct.

And later on after speaking of the case of the suicides in detail
you say:—

" As to the victims of accident these fare still worse . . .
unhappy shades . . . cut off in the full flush of earthly
passions . . . they are the pisachas etc. . . . They not
only ruin their victims etc. . . ." **Again correct. Bear in
mind that the exceptions enforce the rule.**

And if they are neither very good nor very bad the " victims of
accident or violence," derive a new set of skandhas from the
medium who attracts them. **I have explained the situation on
the margin of proofs. See note.**

It was on this text that I have been working.

If this is not to be maintained or if in some way that as yet I
cannot understand the words bear a different signification from

---

[1] Letter from Mr. Sinnett to K.H. With K.H.'s Comments printed in bold
type.—ED.

that which seems to belong to them, it might be better to cancel these two letters altogether or hold them over for complete alteration. The warning is delivered in too solemn a tone and the danger is made too much of if it is merely to apply to suicides, and in the last slip of the proof the elimination of " the accidents and " makes the rest rather ridiculous because then we are dividing *suicides only* into the *very pure and elevated!* and the medium people etc.

It seems to me that it would hardly do to let even letter (1) stand alone,—though it does not include the mistake, for it would have no *raison d'être* unless followed up by letter (2).

Both letters have gone home to Stainton Moses for transmission to *Light*—the first by the mail from here of July 21, the second by last mail—yesterday. Now if you decide that it is better to stop and cancel them I shall just be in time to telegraph home to Stainton Moses to that effect, and will do this directly I receive a telegram from you or from the Old Lady to that effect.

If nothing is done they will appear in *Light* as written—i.e., as the MSS. sent with the present proof stood barring a few little mistakes which I see my wife has made in copying them out.

It is altogether a very awkward tangle. I was precipitate apparently in sending them home, but I thought I had followed the statements of your long devachan letter so faithfully. Awaiting orders,

Ever your devoted

A. P. S.

On margin I said " rarely " but I have not pronounced the word " *never*." Accidents occur under the most various circumstances; and men are not only killed *accidentally*, or die as *suicides* but are also *murdered*—something we have not even touched upon. I can well understand your perplexity but can hardly help you. Bear always in mind that there are exceptions to every rule, and to these again and other side exceptions, and be always prepared to learn something new. I can easily understand we are accused of *contradictions* and *inconsistencies*—aye, even to writing one thing to-day and denying it to-morrow. What you were taught is the RULE. *Good and pure* " accidents " sleep in the Akasa, ignorant of their change; very wicked and impure—suffer all the tortures of a horrible nightmare. The majority—neither very good nor very bad, the victims of accident *or violence* (including murder)—some *sleep*, others become *Nature pisachas*, while a small minority may fall *victims* to mediums and derive a new set of skandhas from the medium who attracts them. Small as their number may be, their fate is to be the most deplored. What I said in my notes on your MSS., was in

reply to Mr. Hume's statistical calculations which led him to infer
that " there were more Spirits than shells in the seance rooms " in
such a case.

You have much to learn—and we have much to teach nor do we
refuse to go to the very end.   But we must really beg that you should
not jump at hasty conclusions.   I do not blame you, my dear faithful
friend, I would rather blame myself, were anyone here to be blamed
except our respective modes of thought and habits so diametrically
opposed to each other.   Accustomed as we are to teach chelas who
know enough to find themselves beyond the necessity of " *if's* " and
" *but's* " during the lessons—I am but too apt to forget that I am
doing the work with you generally entrusted to these chelas.   Henceforth, I will take more time in answering your questions.   Your
letters to London can do no harm, and are sure, on the contrary to
do good.   They are admirably written and the *exceptions* may be
mentioned and the whole ground covered in one of the future letters.

I have no objection to your making extracts for Colonel Chesney
—except one—*he is not a Theosophist*.   Only be careful, and do not
forget your details and exceptions whenever you explain your rules.
Remember still even in the case of suicides there are many who will
never allow themselves to be drawn into the vortex of mediumship,
and pray do not accuse me of " inconsistency " or *contradiction*
when we come to that point.   Could you but know *how* I write my
letters and the time I am enabled to give to them, perchance you
would feel less critical if not exacting.   Well, and how do you like
Djual Khool's *idea* and *art*? I have not caught a glimpse of Simla
for the last ten days.

Affectionately yours,

K. H.

LETTER No. 22 [1]

Extract from Letter by K. H. to Hume.   Received for my perusal towards
the end of season 1882.   (A.P.S.)

Did it ever strike you,—and now from the standpoint of your
Western science and the suggestion of your own Ego which has
already seized up the essentials of every truth, prepare to deride
the erroneous idea—did you ever suspect that Universal, like
finite, human mind might have two attributes, or a dual power—
one the voluntary and conscious, and the other the involuntary and
unconscious or the mechanical power? To reconcile the difficulty
of many theistic and anti-theistic propositions, both these powers
are a philosophical necessity.   The possibility of the first or the
voluntary and conscious attribute in reference to the infinite mind,

[1] Transcribed from a copy in Mr. Sinnett's handwriting.—Ed.

notwithstanding the assertions of all the Egos throughout the
living world—will remain for ever a mere hypothesis, whereas in
the finite mind it is a scientific and demonstrate fact.   The highest
Planetary Spirit is as ignorant of the first as we are, and the
hypothesis will remain one even in Nirvana, as it is a mere
inferential possibility, whether there or here.

Take the human mind in connexion with the body.   Man has
two distinct physical brains; the cerebrum with its two hemi-
spheres at the frontal part of the head—the source of the voluntary
nerves; and the cerebellum, situated at the back portion of the
skull—the fountain of the involuntary nerves which are the agents
of the unconscious or mechanical powers of the mind to act
through.   And weak and uncertain as may be the control of man
over his involuntary [? functions], such as the blood circulation,
the throbbings of the heart and respiration, especially during sleep
—yet how far more powerful, how much more potential appears
man as master and ruler over the blind molecular motion—the
laws which govern his body (a proof of this being afforded by the
phenomenal powers of the Adept and even the common Yogi)
than that which you *will* call God, shows over the immutable laws
of Nature.   Contrary in that to the finite, the " infinite mind,"
which we name so but for agreement sake, for we call it the infinite
FORCE—exhibits but the functions of its cerebellum, the existence
of its supposed cerebrum being admitted as above stated, but on
the inferential hypothesis deduced from the Kabalistic theory
(correct in every other relation) of the Macrocosm being the prototype of the Microcosm.   So far as *we* know the corroboration of
it by modern science receiving but little consideration—so far as
the highest Planetary Spirits have ascertained (who, remember well
have the same relations with the trans-cosmical world, penetrating
behind the primitive veil of cosmic matter as we have to go behind
the veil of this, our brute physical world—) the infinite mind dis-
plays to them as to us no more than the regular unconscious
throbbings of the eternal and universal pulse of Nature, throughout
the myriads of worlds within as without the primitive veil of our
solar system.

So far—WE KNOW.   *Within* and to the utmost limit, to the very
edge of the cosmic veil we know the fact to be correct—owing to
personal experience; for the information gathered as to what takes
place beyond we are indebted to the Planetary Spirits, to our
blessed Lord Buddha.   This of course may be regarded as secondhand information.   There are those who, rather than yield to
the evidence of fact will prefer regarding even the planetary gods
as " erring " disembodied philosophers if not actually liars.   Be it
so.   " Everyone is master of his own wisdom "—says a Tibetan
proverb, and he is at liberty either to honour or degrade his slave.

However, I will go on for the benefit of those who may yet seize my explanation of the problem and understand the nature of the solution.

It is the peculiar faculty of the involuntary power of the infinite mind—which no one could ever think of calling God—to be eternally evolving subjective matter into objective atoms (you will please remember that the two adjectives are used but in a relative sense) or cosmic matter to be later on developed into form. And it is likewise that same involuntary mechanical power that we see so intensely active in all the fixed laws of nature—which governs and controls what is called the Universe or the Cosmos. There are some modern philosophers who would prove the existence of a Creator from motion. We say and affirm that that motion—the universal perpetual motion which never ceases, never slackens nor increases its speed, not even during the interludes between the pralayas, or " nights of Brahma ", but goes on like a mill set in motion whether it has anything to grind or not (for the pralaya means the temporary loss of every form, but by no means the destruction of cosmic matter which is eternal)—we say this perpetual motion is the only eternal and uncreated Deity we are able to recognise. To regard God as an intelligent spirit, and accept at the same time his absolute immateriality is to conceive of a nonentity, a blank void; to regard God as a Being, an Ego and to place his intelligence under a bushel for some mysterious reasons —is most consummate nonsense; to endow him with intelligence in the face of blind brutal Evil is to make of him a fiend—a most rascally God. A Being however gigantic, occupying space and having length breadth and thickness is most certainly the Mosaic deity; " No-being " and a mere principle lands you directly in the Buddhistic atheism, or the Vedantic primitive *Acosmism*. What lies beyond and outside the worlds of form, and being, in worlds and spheres in their most spiritualized state—(and you will perhaps oblige us by telling us where that beyond can be, since the Universe is infinite and limitless) is useless for anyone to search after, since even Planetary Spirits have no knowledge or perception of it. If our greatest adepts and Bodhisattvas have never penetrated themselves beyond our solar system,—and the idea seems to suit your preconceived theistic theory wonderfully, my respected Brother—they still know of the existence of other such solar systems, with as mathematical a certainty as any western astronomer knows of the existence of invisible stars which he can never approach or explore. But of that which lies within the worlds and systems, not in the trans-infinitude—(a queer expression to use)—but in the cis-infinitude rather, in the state of the purest and inconceivable immateriality, no one ever knew or will ever tell, hence it is something non-existent for the universe. You are at liberty to place in this eternal vacuum the intellectual or voluntary powers of your deity—if you can conceive of such a thing.

Meanwhile we may say that it is motion that governs the laws of nature; and that it governs them as the mechanical impulse given to running water which will propel them either in a direct line or along hundreds of side furrows they may happen to meet on their way and whether those furrows are natural grooves or channels prepared artificially by the hand of man. And we maintain that wherever there is life and being, and in however much spiritualized a form, there is no room for moral government, much less for a moral Governor—a Being which at the same time has no form nor occupies space! Verily if light shineth in darkness, and darkness comprehends it not, it is because such is the natural law, but how more suggestive and pregnant with meaning *for one who knows*, to say that light can still less comprehend darkness, nor ever know it since it kills wherever it penetrates and annihilates it instantly. A pure yet volitional Spirit is an absurdity for volitional mind. The result of organism cannot exist independently of an organized brain, and an organized brain made out of nihil is a still greater fallacy. If you ask me " Whence then the immutable laws?—laws cannot make themselves "—then in my turn I will ask you—and whence their supposed Creator?—a creator cannot create or make himself. If the brain did not make itself, for this would be affirming that brain acted before it existed, how could intelligence, the result of an organized brain, act before its creator was made?

All this reminds one of wrangling for seniority. If our doctrines clash too much with your theories then we can easily give up the subject and talk of something else. Study the laws and doctrines of the Nepaulese Swabhavikas, the principal Buddhist philosophical school in India, and you will find them the most learned as the most scientifically logical wranglers in the world. Their plastic, invisible, eternal, omnipresent and unconscious Swabhavat is Force or *Motion* ever generating its electricity which is life.

Yes; there is a force as limitless as thought, as potent as boundless will, as subtle as the essence of life, so inconceivably awful in its rending force as to convulse the universe to its centre were it but used as a lever, but this Force is not *God*, since there are men who have learned the secret of subjecting it to their will when necessary. Look around you and see the myriad manifestations of life, so infinitely multiform; of life, of motion, of change. What caused these? From what inexhaustible source came they, by what agency? Out of the invisible and subjective they have entered our little area of the visible and objective. Children of Akasa, concrete evolutions from the ether, it was Force which brought them into perceptibility and Force will in time remove them from the sight of man. Why should this plant in your garden to the right have been produced with such a shape, and that other one to the left with one totally dissimilar? Are these not the result of varying action of Force—unlike correlations? Given a perfect monotony of activities throughout the world, and we would have a complete identity of forms, colours, shapes and properties throughout all the kingdoms of nature. It is *motion* with its resulting conflict, neutralization, equilibration, correlation, to which is due the infinite variety which prevails. You speak of an intelligent and good—(the attribute is rather unfortunately chosen)—Father, a moral guide and governor of the universe and man. A certain condition of things exists around us which we call normal. Under this nothing can occur which transcends our every-day experience, " God's immutable laws." But suppose we change this condition and have the best of him without whom even a hair of your head will not fall, as they tell you in the West. A current of air brings [1] to me from the lake near which, with my fingers half frozen I now write to you this letter. I change by a certain combination of electrical, magnetic, odyllic or other influences the current of air which benumbs my fingers into a warmer breeze; I have thwarted the intention of the Almighty, and dethroned him at my will! I can do that, or when I do not want Nature to produce strange and too visible phenomena, I force my nature-seeing, nature-influencing self within me to suddenly awake to new perceptions and feelings and thus am my own Creator and ruler.

But do you think that you are right when saying that " the laws arise?" Immutable laws cannot arise, since they are eternal and uncreated, propelled in the Eternity, and that God himself, if such a thing existed, could never have the power of stopping them. And when did I say that these laws were fortuitous *per se*? I meant their blind correlations, never the laws, or rather the law—since we recognise but one law in the Universe, the law of harmony, of *perfect* EQUILIBRIUM. Then for a man endowed with so subtle a logic, and such a fine comprehension of the value of ideas in general and that of words especially—for a man so accurate as you generally are to make tirades upon an " all wise, powerful and love-ful God " seems to say at least strange. I do not protest at all as you seem to think against your theism, or a belief in an abstract ideal of some kind, but I cannot help asking you, how do you or how can you know that your God is all wise, omnipotent and love-ful, when everything in nature, physical and moral, proves such a being, if he does exist, to be quite the reverse of all

[1] Query ' comes ' or ' brings cold.'—EDS.

you say of him? Strange delusion and one which seems to overpower your very intellect.

The difficulty of explaining the fact that " unintelligent Forces can give rise to highly intelligent beings like ourselves," is covered by the eternal progression of cycles, and the process of evolution ever perfecting its work as it goes along. Not believing in cycles, it is unnecessary for you to learn that which will create but a new pretext for you, my dear Brother, to combat the theory and argue upon it *ad infinitum.* Nor did I ever become guilty of the heresy I am accused of in reference to spirit and matter. The conception of matter and spirit as entirely distinct, and both eternal, could certainly never have entered my head, however little I may know of them, for it is one of the elementary and fundamental doctrines of Occultism that the two are one, and are distinct but in their respective manifestations, and only in the limited perceptions of the world of senses. Far from " lacking philosophical breadth " then, our doctrines show but one principle in nature—spirit-matter or matter-spirit, the third the ultimate Absolute or the quintessence of the two—if I may be allowed to use an erroneous term in the present application—losing itself beyond the view and spiritual perceptions of even the " Gods " or Planetary Spirits. This third principle, say the Vedantic Philosophers—is the only reality, everything else being Maya, as none of the Protean manifestations of spirit-matter or Purusha and Prakriti have ever been regarded in any other light than that of temporary delusions of the senses. Even in the hardly outlined philosophy of *Isis* this idea is clearly carried out. In the book of Kiu-te, Spirit is called the ultimate sublimation of matter, and matter the crystallization of spirit. And no better illustration could be afforded than in the very simple phenomenon of ice, water, vapour and the final dispersion of the latter, the phenomenon being reversed in its consecutive manifestations and called the Spirit falling into generation or matter. This trinity resolving itself into unity—a doctrine as old as the world of thought—was seized upon by some early Christians, who had it in the schools of Alexandria, and made [it] up into the Father, or generative spirit; the Son or matter—man; and into the Holy Ghost, the immaterial essence, or the apex of the equilateral triangle, an idea found to this day in the pyramids of Egypt. Thus once more it is proved that you misunderstand my meaning entirely, whenever for the sake of brevity I use a phraseology habitual with the Western people. But in my turn I have to remark that your idea that matter is but the temporary allotropic form of spirit, differing from it as charcoal does from diamond, is as unphilosophical as it is unscientific from both the Eastern and the Western points of view, charcoal being but a form of residue of matter, while matter *per se* is indestructible, and, as I maintain, coeval with spirit—that spirit which we know and can conceive of. Bereaved of Prakriti, Purusha (Spirit) is unable to manifest itself, hence ceases to exist —becomes *nihil*. Without spirit or Force, even that which Science styles as " not living " matter, the so-called mineral ingredients which feed plants, could never have been called into form. There is a moment in the existence of every molecule and atom of matter when, for one cause or another, the last spark of spirit or motion or life (call it by whatever name) is withdrawn, and in the same instant, with the swiftness which surpasses that of the lightning glance of thought, the atom or molecule or an aggregation of molecules is annihilated to return to its pristine purity of intra-cosmic matter. It is drawn to the mother fount with the velocity of a globule of quicksilver to the central mass. Matter, force, and motion are the trinity of physical objective nature, as the trinitarian unity of spirit-matter is that of the spiritual or subjective nature. Motion is eternal because spirit is eternal. But no modes of motion can ever be conceived unless they be in connection with matter.

And now to your extraordinary hypothesis that Evil with its attendant train of sin and suffering is not the result of matter, but may be perchance the wise scheme of the moral Governor of the Universe. Conceivable as the idea may seem to you, trained in the pernicious fallacy of the Christian,—" the ways of the Lord are inscrutable "—it is utterly inconceivable for me. Must I repeat again that the best Adepts have searched the Universe during milleniums and found nowhere the slightest trace of such a Machiavellian schemer—but throughout, the same immutable, inexorable law. You must excuse me therefore if I positively decline to lose my time over such childish speculations. It is not " the ways of the Lord " but rather those of some extremely intelligent men in everything but some particular hobby, that are to me incomprehensible.

As you say this need " make no difference between us "—personally. But it does make a world of difference if you propose to learn and offer me to teach. For the life of me I cannot make out how I could ever impart to you that which I know since the very A.B.C. of what I know, the rock upon which the secrets of the occult universe, whether on this or that side of the veil, are encrusted, is contradicted by you invariably and *a priori*. My very dear Brother, either we know something or we do not know anything. In the first case what is the use of your learning, since you think you know better? In the second case why should you lose your time? You say it matters nothing whether these laws are the expression of the will of an intelligent conscious God, as you think, or constitute the inevitable attributes of an unintelligent, unconscious " God," as I hold. I say, it matters everything, and since you earnestly believe that these fundamental questions (of spirit and matter—of God or no God) " are admittedly beyond both of us "—in other words that neither I nor yet our greatest adepts can know any more than you do, then what is there on earth that I could teach you? You know that in order to enable you to read you have first to learn your letters—yet you want to know the course of events before and after the Pralayas, of every event here on this globe on the opening of a new cycle, namely a mystery imparted at one of the last initiations, as Mr. Sinnett was told,—for my letter to him upon the Planetary Spirits was simply incidental—brought out by a question of his. And now you will say I am evading the direct issue. I have discoursed upon colla-teral points, but have not explained to you all you want to know and asked me to tell you. I " dodge " as I always do. Pardon me for contradicting you, but it is nothing of the kind. There are a thousand questions I will never be permitted to answer, and it would be dodging were I to answer you otherwise than I do. I tell you plainly you are unfit to learn, for your mind is too full, and there is not a corner vacant from whence a previous occupant would not arise, to struggle with and drive away the newcomer. Therefore I do not evade, I only give you time to reflect and deduce and first learn well what was already given you before you seize on something else. The world of force is the world of Occultism and the only one whither the highest initiate goes to probe the secrets of being. Hence no-one but such an initiate can know anything of these secrets. Guided by his Guru the chela first discovers this world, then its laws, then their centrifugal evolutions into the world of matter. To become a perfect adept takes him long years, but at last he becomes the master. The hidden things have become patent, and mystery and miracle have fled from his sight forever. He sees how to guide force in this direction or that—to produce desirable effects. The secret chem-ical, electric or odic properties of plants, herbs, roots, minerals, animal tissue, are as familiar to him as the feathers of your birds are to you. No change in the etheric vibrations can escape him. He applies his knowledge, and behold a miracle! And he who started with the repudiation of the very idea that miracle is possible, is straightway classed as a miracle worker and either worshipped by the fools as a demi-god or repudiated by still greater fools as a charlatan! And to show you how exact a science is occultism let me tell you that the means we avail ourselves of are all laid down for us in a code as old as humanity to the minutest detail, but everyone of us has to begin from the beginning, not from the end. Our laws are as immutable as those of Nature, and they were known to man an eternity before this strutting game-cock, modern

science, was hatched.   If I have not given you the *modus operandi*
or begun by the wrong end, I have at least shown you that we
build our philosophy upon experiment and deduction—unless you
choose to question and dispute this fact equally with all others.
Learn first our laws and educate your perceptions, dear Brother.
Control your involuntary powers and develop in the right direction
your will and you will become a teacher instead of a learner.   I
would not refuse what I have a right to teach.   Only I had to
study for fifteen years before I came to the doctrines of cycles and
had to learn simpler things at first.   But do what we may, and
whatever happens I trust we will have no more arguing which is
as profitless as it is painful.

LETTER No. 23a [1]

Received at Simla: Oct. 1882.

Herewith—apologizing for their number, I send a few notes of
interrogation.   Perhaps you will be so kind as to take them up
from time to time and answer them by ones and twos as leisure
and time allow.

Memo—At convenience to send A.P.S. those unpublished notes
of Eliphas Levi's with annotations by K.H.

Sent long ago to our " Jako " friend.

I

(1) There is a very interesting allusion in your last; when speaking of Hume you speak of certain characteristics he brought back
with him *from his last incarnation.*

(2) Have you the power of looking back to the former lives of
persons now living, and identifying them?

(3) In that case would it be improper personal curiosity—to ask
for any particulars of my own?

I

**(1) All of us, we bring some characteristics from our previous
incarnations.   It is *unavoidable*.**

**(2) Unfortunately, some of us have.   I, for one do not like to
exercise it.**

**(3) " Man know thyself," saith the Delphian oracle.   There is
nothing " improper "—certainly in such a curiosity.   Only would it
not be still more proper to study our own present personality before
attempting to learn anything of its *creator*, predecessor, and fashioner**

—the man *that was*? Well, some day I may treat you to a little story —no time now—only I promise no details; a simple sketch, and a hint or two to test your intuitional powers.

II[1]

(1) Is there any way of accounting for what seems the curious rush of human progress within the last two thousand years, as compared with the relatively stagnant condition of the fourth round people up to the beginning of modern progress?

(2) Or has there been at any former period during the habitation of the earth by fourth round men, civilizations as great as our own in regard to intellectual development that have utterly passed away?

(3) Even the fifth race (own) of the fourth round began in Asia a million years ago. What was it about for the 998,000 years preceding the last 2,000? During *that* period have greater civilizations than our own risen and decayed?

(4) To what epoch did the existence of the Continent of Atlantis belong, and did the cataclysmical change which produced its extinction come into any appointed place in the evolution of the round,—corresponding to the place occupied in the whole manvantaric evolution by obscurations?

(5) I find that the most common question asked about occult philosophy by fairly intelligent people who begin to enquire about it is " Does it give any explanation of the origin of evil? " That is a point on which you have formerly promised to touch, and which it might be worth while to take up before long.

(6) Closely allied to this question would be another often put. " What is the good of the whole cyclic process if spirit only emerges at the end of all things pure and impersonal as it was at first before its descent into matter? " **(And the portions taken away from the fifth?)** My answer is that I am not at present engaged in excusing, but in investigating the operations of Nature. But perhaps there may be a better answer available.

(7) Can you, *i.e.*, is it permitted ever to answer any questions relating to matters of physical science? If so—here are some points that I should greatly like dealt with.

(8) Have magnetic conditions anything to do with the precipitation of rain, or is that due entirely to atmospheric currents at different temperatures encountering other currents of different humidities, the whole set of motions being established by pressures, expansions, etc., due in the first instance to solar energy? If magnetic conditions are engaged, how do they operate and how could they be tested?

---

[1] For K.H.'s replies to these queries see *post* Letter 23B.—ED.

(9) Is the sun's corona an atmosphere? of any known gases? and why does it assume the rayed shape always observed in eclipses?

(10) Is the photometric value of light emitted by stars a safe guide to their magnitude,[1] and is it true as astronomy assumes *faute de mieux* in the way of a theory, that per square mile the sun's surface emits as much light as can be emitted from any body?

(11) Is Jupiter a hot and still partially luminous body, and to what cause, as solar energy has probably nothing to do with the matter, are the violent disturbances of Jupiter's atmosphere due?

(12) Is there any truth in the new Siemens theory of solar combustion,—*i.e.*, that the sun in its passage through space gathers in at the poles combustible gas (which is diffused through all space in a highly attenuated condition), and throws it off again at the equator after the intense heat of that region has again dispersed the elements which combustion temporarily united?

(13) Could any clue be given to the causes of magnetic variations,—the daily changes at given places, and the apparently capricious curvature of the isogonic lines which show equal declinations? For example—why is there a region in Eastern Asia where the needle shows no variation from the true north, though variations are recorded all round that space? (Have your Lordships anything to do with this peculiar condition of things?)

(14) Could any other planets besides those known to modern astronomy (I do not mean mere planetoids) be discovered by physical instruments if properly directed?

(15) When you wrote " Have you experienced monotony during that moment which you considered then and now so consider it,— as the moment of the highest bliss you have ever felt? "

Did you refer to any specific moment and any specific event in my life, or were you merely referring to an X quantity—the happiest moment whatever it might have been?

(16) You say:—" Remember we create ourselves, our Devachan and our Avitchi, and mostly during the latter days and even moments of our sentient lives."

(17) But do the thoughts on which the mind may be engaged at the last moment *necessarily* hinge on to the predominant character of its past life? Otherwise it would seem as if the character of a person's Devachan or Avitchi might be capriciously and unjustly determined by the chance which brought some special thought uppermost at last?

(18) " The full remembrance of our lives will come but at the end of the *minor cycle*."

[1] Considered of course in connection with distance as guessed by parallax.

Does " minor cycle " here mean one round, or the whole Man-vantara of our planetary chain?

That is, do we remember our past lives in the Devachan of world Z at the end of each round, or only at the end of the seventh round?

(19) You say: " And even the shells of those good men whose pages will not be found missing in the great book of lives—even they will regain their remembrance and an appearance of self-consciousness only after the sixth and seventh principles with the essence of the fifth have gone to their gestation period."

(20) A little later on:—" Whether the personal Ego was good, bad or indifferent, his consciousness leaves him as suddenly as the flame leaves the wick—*his perceptive faculties* become extinct for ever." **(Well? can a physical brain *once dead* retain its perceptive faculties: that which will perceive in the *shell* is something that perceives with a borrowed or reflected light.   See notes.)**

Then what is the nature of the remembrance and self-conscious-ness of the shell? This touches on a matter I have often thought about—wishing for further explanation—the extent of personal identity in elementaries.

(21) The spiritual Ego goes circling through the worlds, retain-ing what it possesses of identity and self-consciousness, always neither more nor less. (*a*) But it is continually evolving personal-ities, in which at all events the sense of identity while it remains united with them is very complete. (*b*) Now these personalities I understand to be absolutely new evolutions in each case. A. P. Sinnett is, for what it is worth,—absolutely a new invention. Now it will leave a shell behind which will survive for a time (*c*) assuming that the spiritual monad temporarily engaged in this incarnation will find enough decent material in the fifth to lay hold of. (*d*) That shell will have no consciousness directly after death, because " it requires a certain time to establish its new centre of gravity and evolve its perception proper." (*e*) But how much consciousness will it have when it has done this? (*f*) Will it still *be* A. P. Sinnett of which the spiritual Ego will think, even at the last, as of a person it had known—or will it be conscious that the individuality is gone? Will it be able to reason about itself at all, and to remember anything of its once higher interests. Will it remember the name it bore? (*g*) Or is it only inflated with recol-lections of this sort in mediumistic presence, remaining asleep at other times? (*h*) And is it conscious of losing anything that feels like life as it gradually disintegrates?

(22) What is the nature of the life that goes on in the " Planet of Death? " Is it a physical reincarnation with remembrance of past personality, or an astral existence as in Kama Loka? Is it an existence with birth, maturity and decay, or a uniform

prolongation of the old personality of this earth under penal conditions?

(23) What other planets of those known to ordinary science, besides Mercury, belong to our system of worlds?

Are the more spiritual planets—(A, B & Y, Z)—visible bodies in the sky or are all those known to astronomy of the more material sort?

(24) Is the Sun (*a*) as Allan Kardec says:—a habitation of highly spiritualized beings? (*b*) Is it the vertex of our Manvantaric chain? and of all the other chains in this solar system also?

(25) You say:—It may happen " that the spiritual spoil from the fifth will prove too weak to be reborn in Devachan, in which case *its* sixth will then and there reclothe itself in a new body—and enter upon a new earth existence, whether upon this or any other planet."

(26) This seems to want further elucidation. Are these exceptional cases in which two earth lives of the same spiritual monad may occur closer together than the thousand years indicated by some previous letters as the almost inevitable limit of such successive lives?

(27) The reference to the case of Guiteau is puzzling. I can understand his being in a state in which the crime he committed is ever present to his imagination, but how does he " toss into confusion and shuffle the destinies of millions of persons? "

(28) Obscurations are a subject at present wrapped in obscurity. They take place after the last man of any given round has passed on to the next planet. But I want to make out how the next superior round forms are evolved. When the fifth round spiritual monads arrive what fleshly habitations are ready for them? Going back to the only former letter in which you have dealt with obscurations I find:—(*a*) " We have traced man out of a round into the Nirvanic state between Z and A. " A " was left in the last round dead. (See note.) As the new round begins it catches the new influx of life, reawakens to vitality, and begets all its kingdoms of a superior order to the last."

(29) But has it to begin at the beginning again between each round, and evolve human forms from animal, these last from vegetable, etc. If so to what round do the first imperfectly evolved men belong? Ex hypothesi to the fifth; but the fifth should be a more perfect race in all respects.

LETTER No. 23B [1]

II

(1) [This answers Question **II** (1) on page 142. Eds.]. The latter end of a very important cycle. Each Round, each ring, as

[1] K.H.'s Replies to the Queries in Letter 23A II.—Ed.

every race has its great and its smaller cycles, on every planet that mankind passes through.

Our fourth Round Humanity has its one great cycle, and so have her races and sub-races. The " curious rush " is due to the double effect of the former—the beginning of its downward course;—and of the latter (the small cycle of your " sub-race ") running on to its apex. Remember, you belong to the fifth Race, yet you are but a *Western sub*-race. Notwithstanding your efforts, what you call civilization is confined only to the latter and its off-shoots in America. Radiating around, its deceptive light may seem to throw its rays a greater distance than it does in reality. There is no " rush " in China, and of Japan you make but a caricature.

A student of occultism ought not to speak of the " stagnant condition of the fourth Race people " since *history* knows next to nothing of that condition " up to the beginning of modern progress " of other nations but the Western. What do you know of America, for instance, before the invasion of that country by the Spaniards? Less than two centuries prior to the arrival of Cortex there was as great a "rush" towards progress among the *sub-races* of Peru and Mexico as there is now in Europe and the U.S.A. Their sub-race ended in nearly total annihilation through causes generated by itself; so will yours at the end of its cycle. We may speak only of the " stagnant conditions " into which, following the law of development, growth, maturity and decline every race and sub-race falls into during its transition periods. It is that latter condition your *Universal* History is acquainted with, while it remains superbly ignorant of the condition even India was in, some ten centuries back. Your sub-races are now running toward the apex of their respective cycles, and that History goes no further back than the periods of decline of a few other sub-races belonging most of them to the preceding fourth Race. And what is the area and the period of time embraced by its *Universal* eye?—At the utmost stretch a few, miserable dozens of centuries. A mighty horizon, indeed! Beyond—all is darkness for it, nothing but hypotheses. . . . .

(2) [For Question see p. 142. Eds.]. No doubt there was. Egyptian and Aryan records and especially our Zodiacal tables furnish us with every proof of it besides our *inner* knowledge. Civilization is an inheritance, a patrimony that passes from race to race along the ascending and descending paths of cycles. During the minority of a sub-race, it is preserved for it by its predecessor, which disappears, dies out generally, when the former " comes of age." At first, most of them squander and mismanage their property, or leave it untouched in the ancestral coffers. They reject contemptuously the advice of their elders and prefer,

boy-like, playing in the streets to studying and making the most of the untouched wealth stored up for them in the records of the Past. Thus during your transition period—the middle ages—Europe rejected the testimony of Antiquity, calling such sages as Herodotus and other learned Greeks—the Father of Lies, until she knew better and changed the appellation into that of "Father of History." Instead of neglecting, you now accumulate and add to your wealth. As every other race you had your ups and downs, your periods of honour and dishonour, your dark midnight and—you are now approaching your brilliant noon. The youngest of the fifth race family you were for long ages the unloved and the uncared for, the Cendrillon in your home. And now, when so many of your sisters have died, and others still are dying, while the few of the old survivors, now in their second infancy, wait but for their Messiah—the sixth race—to resurrect to a new life and start anew with the coming stronger along the path of a new cycle—now that the Western Cendrillon has suddenly developed into a proud wealthy Princess, the *beauty* we all see and admire—how does she act? Less kind hearted than the Princess in the tale, instead of offering to her elder and less favoured sister, the oldest now, in fact since she is nearly "a million years old" and the *only* one who has never treated her unkindly, though she may have ignored her,—instead of offering her, I say, the "Kiss of peace" she applies to her the *lex talionis* with a vengeance that does not enhance her natural beauty. This, my good friend, and brother, is not a far stretched allegory but—*history*.

(3) [For Question see p. 142. EDS.]. Yes; the fifth race—ours —began in Asia a million years ago. What was it about for the 998,000 years preceding the last 2,000? A pertinent question; offered moreover in quite a Christian spirit that refuses to believe that any good could ever have come out from anywhere *before* and *save* Nazareth. What was it about? Well, it was occupying itself pretty well in the same way as it does now—craving Mr. Grant Allen's pardon, who would place our primitive ancestor the "hedgehoggy" man, in the early part of the Eocene Age! Forsooth, your scientific writers bestride their hypothesis most fearlessly, I see. It will really be a pity to find their fiery steed kicking and breaking their heads some day; something that is unavoidably in store for them. In the Eocene Age—even in its "very first part"—the great cycle of the fourth Race men, the Atlanteans, had already reached its highest point, and the great continent, the father of nearly all the present continents, showed the first symptoms of sinking—a process that occupied it down to 11,446 years ago, when its last island, that, translating its vernacular name, we may call with propriety *Poseidonis*, went down with a crash. By the bye, *whoever* wrote the Review of Donnelly's *Atlantis*

is right: Lemuria can no more be confounded with the Atlantic Continent than Europe with America. Both sunk and were drowned with their high civilizations and " gods," yet between the two catastrophes a short period of about 700,000 years elapsed; " Lemuria " flourishing and ending her career just at about that trifling lapse of time before the early part of the Eocene Age, since its race was the *third*. Behold, the relics of that once great nation in some of the flat-headed aborigines of your Australia! No less right is the review in rejecting the kind attempt of the author to people India and Egypt with the refuse of Atlantis. No doubt your geologists are very learned; but why not bear in mind that, under the continents explored and fathomed by them, in the bowels of which they have found the " Eocene Age " and forced it to deliver them its secrets, there may be, hidden deep in the fathomless, or rather *unfathomed* ocean beds, other, and far older continents whose stratums have never been geologically explored; and that they may some day upset entirely their present theories, thus illustrating the simplicity and sublimity of truth as connected with inductive " generalization " in opposition to their visionary conjectures. Why not admit—true, no one of them has ever thought of it—that our *present* continents have, like " Lemuria " and " Atlantis," been *several times already* submerged and had the time to reappear again, and bear their new groups of mankind and civilization; and that, at the first great geological upheaval, at the next cataclysm—in the series of preiodical cataclysms that occur from the beginning to the end of every Round, —our already *autopsized* continents will go down, and the Lemurias and Atlantises come up again. Think of the future geologists of the sixth and seventh races. Imagine them digging deep in the bowels of what was Ceylon and Simla, and finding implements of the Veddahs, or of the remote ancestor of the *civilized* Pahari— every object of the civilized portions of humanity that inhabited those regions having been pulverized to dust by the great masses of travelling glaciers during the next glacial period—imagine him finding only such rude implements as now found among those savage tribes; and forthwith declaring that during that period *primitive* man climbed and slept on the trees, and sucked the marrow out of animal bones after breaking them—as civilized Europeans, no less than the Veddahs will often do—hence jumping to the conclusion that in the year 1882 A.D. mankind was composed of " man-like animals," black-faced, and whiskered, " with prominent prognathous and large pointed canine teeth." True, a Grant Allen of the sixth race may be not so far from fact and truth in his conjecture that during the " Simla period " these teeth *were* used in the combats of the " males " for grass widows—but then metaphora has very little to do with

anthropology and geology. Such is *your* Science. To return to
your questions.

Of course the 4th race had its periods of the highest civilization.
Greek and Roman and even Egyptian civilization are nothing
compared to the civilizations that began with the 3rd race. Those
of the second were *not* savages but they could not be called civilized.
And now, reading one of my first letters on the races (a question
first touched by M.) pray, do not accuse either him or myself of
some new contradiction. Read it over and see, that it leaves out
the question of civilizations altogether and mentions but the
degenerate remnants of the fourth and third races, and gives you
as a corroboration the latest conclusions of your own Science.
Do not regard an unavoidable *incompleteness* as inconsistency. You
now ask me a direct question, and, I answer it. Greeks and
Romans were small *sub-races*, and Egyptians part and parcel of
our own " Caucasian " stock. Look at the latter and at India.
Having reached the highest civilization and, what is more, *learning*
—both went down. Egypt as a distinct sub-race disappearing
entirely (her Copts are a hybrid remnant). India—as one of the
first and most powerful off-shoots of the mother Race, and composed of a number of sub-races—lasting to these times, and struggling to take once more her place in history some day. That
History catches but a few stray, hazy glimpses of Egypt, some
12,000 years back; when, having already reached the apex of its
cycle thousands of years before, the latter had begun going down.
What does, or *can* it know of India 5,000 years ago, or of the
Chaldees—whom it confounds most charmingly with the Assyrians,
making of them one day " Akkadians," at another Turanians
and what not? We say then, that *your* History is entirely
at sea.

We are refused by the *Journal of Science*—words repeated and
quoted by M.A. (Oxon) with a rapture worthy of a great medium
—any claim whatever for " higher knowledge." Says the reviewer :
" Suppose the Brothers were to say ' point your telescope to such
and such a spot in heavens, and you will find a planet yet unknown
to you; or dig into the earth, . . . etc., and you will find a mineral,'
etc." Very fine, indeed, and suppose that was done, what would
be the result? Why a charge of plagiarism—since everything
of that kind, every " planet and mineral " that exists in space or
inside the earth, is known and recorded in our books thousands
of years ago; more; many a true hypothesis was timidly brought
forward by their own scientific men and as constantly rejected by
the majority with whose preconceptions it interfered. *Your intention* is laudable but nothing that I may give you in answer will
ever be accepted from us. Whenever discovered that " it is verily
so," the discovery will be attributed to him who corroborated the

13

evidence—as in the case of Copernicus and Galileo, the latter having availed himself but of the Pythagorean MSS.

But to return to " civilizations." Do you know that the Chaldees were at the apex of their Occult fame *before* what you term as the " bronze Age "? That the " Sons of Ad " or the children of the Fire Mist preceded by hundreds of centuries the Age of Iron, which was an old age already when what you now call the Historical Period—probably because what is known of it is generally no history but fiction—had hardly begun. We hold—but then what warrant can you give the world that we are right?—that far " greater civilizations than our own have risen and decayed." It is not enough to say as some of your modern writers do—that an extinct civilization existed before Rome and Athens were founded. We affirm that *a series* of civilizations existed *before*, as well as after the Glacial Period, that they existed upon various points of the globe, reached the apex of glory and—died. Every trace and memory had been lost of the Assyrian and Phoenicean civilizations until discoveries began to be made a few years ago. And now they open a new, though not by far one of the earliest pages in the history of mankind. And yet how far back do those civilizations go in comparison with the oldest?—and even them, history is shy to accept. Archaeology has sufficiently demonstrated that the memory of man runs back vastly further than history has been willing to accept, and the sacred records of once mighty nations preserved by their heirs are still more worthy of trust. We speak of civilizations of the ante-glacial period; and (not only in the minds of the vulgar and the profane but even in the opinion of the highly learned geologist) the claim sounds preposterous. What would you say then to our affirmation that the Chinese—I now speak of the inland, the true Chinaman, not of the hybrid mixture between the fourth and the fifth Races now occupying the throne—the aborigines, who belong in their unallied nationality wholly to the highest and last branch of the fourth Race, reached their highest civilization when the fifth had hardly appeared in Asia, and that its first off-shoot was yet a thing of the future. When was it? Calculate. You cannot think that we, who have such tremendous odds against the acceptance of our doctrine would deliberately go on *inventing* Races and sub-races (in the opinion of Mr. Hume) were not they a matter of undeniable fact. The group of islands off the Siberian coast discovered by Nordenskjold of the " Vega " was found strewn with fossils of horses, sheep, oxen, etc., among gigantic bones of elephants, mammoths, rhinoceroses and other monsters belonging to periods when man—says your science—had not yet made his appearance on earth. How came horses and sheep to be found in company with the huge " ante-diluvians "? The horse, we are taught in schools—is

quite a modern invention of nature, and *no man* ever saw its pedactyl
ancestor.   The group of the Siberian islands may give the lie to
the comfortable theory.   The region now locked in the fetters of
eternal winter uninhabited by man—that most fragile of animals,
—will be very soon proved to have had not only a tropical climate
—something your science knows and does not dispute,—but having
been likewise the seat of one of the most ancient civilizations of
that fourth race, whose highest relics now we find in the degenerated
Chinaman, and whose lowest are hopelessly (for the profane
scientist) intermixed with the remnants of the third.   I told you
before now, that the highest people now on earth (spiritually)
belong to the first sub-race of the fifth *root* Race, and those are the
Aryan Asiatics; the highest race (physical intellectuality) is the last
sub-race of the fifth—yourselves the white conquerors.   The
majority of mankind belongs to the seventh sub-race of the fourth
Root race,—the above mentioned Chinamen and their off-shoots
and branchlets (Malayans, Mongolians, Tibetans, Javanese, etc.,
etc., etc.), and remnants of other sub-races of the fourth—and the
seventh sub-race of the third race.   All these, fallen, degraded
semblances of humanity are the direct lineal descendants of highly
civilized nations neither the names nor memory of which have
survived except in such books as *Popul Vuh* and a few others
unknown to Science.

(4) [For Question See page 142. Eds.].   To the Miocene times.
Everything comes in its appointed time and place in the evolution
of Rounds, otherwise it would be impossible for the best seer to
calculate the exact hour and year when such cataclysms great and
small have to occur.   All an adept could do would be to predict
an *approximate* time; whereas now events that result in great geological changes may be predicted with as mathematical a certainty
as eclipses and other revolutions in space.   The sinking of Atlantis
(the group of continents and isles) began during the Miocene period
—as certain of *your* continents are now observed to be gradually
sinking—and it culminated—*first,* in the final disappearance of the
largest continent, an event coincident with the elevation of the
Alps; and *second* with that of the last of the fair Islands mentioned
by Plato.   The Egyptian priests of Sais told his ancestor Solon,
that Atlantis (*i.e.* the only remaining large island) had perished
9,000 years before their time.   This was not a fancy date, since
they had for milleniums preserved most carefully their records.
But then, as I say, they spoke but of the " Poseidonis " and would
not reveal even to the great Greek legislator their secret chronology.
As there are no geological reasons for doubting, but on the contrary, a mass of evidence for accepting the tradition, Science has
finally accepted the existence of the great continent and Archi-
pelago and thus vindicated the truth of one more " fable."   It

now teaches, as you know, that Atlantis, or the remnants of it lingered down to post-tertiary times, its final submergence occurring within the palaeozoic ages of American history! Well, truth and fact ought to feel thankful even for such small favours in the previous absence of any, for so many centuries. The deep sea explorations—especially those of the Challenger, *have* fully confirmed the reports of geology and palaeontology. The great event —the triumph of our " Sons of the *Fire Mist*," the inhabitants of " Shamballah " (when yet an island in the Central Asian Sea) over the selfish but not entirely wicked *magicians* of Poseidonis occurred just 11,446 ago. Read in this connection the incomplete and partially veiled tradition in *Isis*, Volume I, p. 588-94, and some things may become still plainer to you. The corroboration of tradition and history brought forward by Donnelly I find in the main correct; but you will find all this and much more in *Isis*.

(5) [For Question See p. 142 Eds.]. It certainly does, and I have touched upon the subject long ago. In my notes on Mr. Hume's MSS., " On God "—that he kindly adds to our Philosophy, something the latter had never contemplated before—the subject is mentioned abundantly. Has he refused you a look into it? For you—I may enlarge my explanations, but not before you have read what I say of the origin of good and evil on those margins. Quite enough was said by me for our present purposes. Strangely enough I found a European author—the greatest materialist of his times, Baron d'Holbach—whose views coincide entirely with the views of our philosophy. When reading his *Système de la Nature*, I might have imagined I had our book of Kiu-te before me. As a matter of course and of temperament our Universal Pundit will try to catch at those views and pull every argument to pieces. So far he only threatens me to alter his *Preface* and not to publish the philosophy under his own name. *Cuneus cuneum tradit*: I begged him not to publish his essays at all.

M. thinks that *for your purposes* I better give you a few more details upon Atlantis since it is greatly connected with *evil* if not with its origin. In the forthcoming *Theosophist* you will find a note or two appended to Hume's translation of Eliphas Levi's *Preface* [1] in connection with the lost continent. And now, since I am determined to make of the present *answers* a volume—bear your cross with Christian fortitude and then, perhaps, after reading the whole you will ask for no more for some time to come. But what can I add to that already told? I am unable to give you purely scientific information since we can never agree entirely with Western conclusions; and that ours will be rejected as " unscientific." Yet both geology and palaeontology bear witness to much we have to say. Of course your Science is right in many

[1] See *The Theosophist*, November, 1882.—EDS.

of her generalities, but her premises are wrong, or at any rate—very faulty. For instance she is right in saying that while the new America was forming the ancient Atlantis was sinking, and gradually washing away; but she is neither right in her given epochs nor in the calculations of the duration of that sinking. The latter—is the future fate of your British Islands, the first on the list of victims that have to be destroyed by fire (submarine volcanos) and water; France and other lands will follow suit. When they reappear again, the last seventh Sub-race of the sixth Root race of present mankind will be flourishing on " Lemuria " and " Atlantis " both of which will have reappeared also (their reappearance following immediately the disappearance of the present isles and continents), and very few seas and *great waters* will be found then on our globe, waters as well as land appearing and disappearing and shifting periodically and each in turn.

Trembling at the prospect of fresh charges of " contradictions " at some future incomplete statement I [would] rather explain what I mean by this. The approach of every new " obscuration " is always signalled by cataclysms—of either fire or water. But, apart from this, every " Ring " or Root Race has to be cut in two, so to say, by either one or the other. Thus, having reached the apex of its development and glory the fourth Race—the Atlanteans were destroyed *by water*; you find now but their degenerated, fallen remnants, whose sub-races, nevertheless, aye—each of them, had its palmy days of glory and relative greatness. What they are now—you will be some day the law of cycles being one and immutable. When your race—the fifth—will have reached its zenith of *physical* intellectuality, and developed the highest civilization (remember the difference we make between *material* and *spiritual* civilizations), unable to go any higher in its own cycle its progress towards *absolute* evil will be arrested (as its predecessors the Lemurians and Atlanteans, the men of the third and fourth races were arrested in their progress towards the same) by one of such cataclysmic changes; its great civilization destroyed, and all the sub-races of *that* race will be found going down their respective cycles, after a short period of glory and learning. See the remnants of the Atlanteans,—the old Greeks and Romans (the modern belong all to the fifth Race); see how great and how short, how evanescent were their days of fame and glory! For, they were but sub-races of the seven off-shoots of the " root race." No mother Race, any more than her sub-races and off-shoots, is allowed by the one Reigning Law to trespass upon the prerogatives of the Race or Sub-race that will follow it; least of all—to encroach upon the knowledge and powers in store for its successor. " Thou shalt not eat of the fruit of Knowledge of Good and Evil of the tree that is growing for thy heirs " we may say with more right than would be willingly conceded us by the Humes of your sub-race. This " tree " is in our safe-keeping, entrusted to us by the Dhyan Chohans, the protectors of our Race and the Trustees for those that are coming. Try to understand the allegory, and to never lose sight of the hint given you in my letter upon the Planetaries.[1] At the beginning of each *Round*, when humanity reappears under quite different conditions than those afforded for the birth of each new race and its sub-races, a " Planetary " has to mix with these primitive men, and to refresh their memories, and reveal to them the truths they knew during the preceding Round. Hence the confused traditions about Jehovahs, Ormazds, Osirises, Brahms, and the *tutti quanti*. But that happens only for the benefit of the *first* Race. It is the duty of the latter to choose the fit recipients among its sons, who are " set apart " to use a Biblical phrase—as the vessels to contain *the whole stock of knowledge* to be divided among the future races and generations until the close of that Round. Why should I say more since you *must* understand my whole meaning; and that I *dare* not reveal it in full. Every race had its adepts; and with every new race, we are allowed to give them out as much of our knowledge as the men of that race deserve. The last seventh Race will have its Buddha as every one of its predecessors had; but, its adepts will be far higher than any of the present race, for among them will abide the future Planetary, the Dhyan Chohan whose duty it will be to instruct or " refresh the memory " of the first race of the fifth Round men after this planet's future obscuration.

En passant, to show to you that not only were not the " races " *invented* by us, but that they are a cardinal dogma with the Lama Buddhists and with all who study our esoteric doctrine, I send you an explanation on a page or two in Rhys Davids' *Buddhism*,—otherwise incomprehensible, meaningless and absurd. It is written with the special permission of the Chohan (*my* Master) and—for your benefit. No Orientalist has ever suspected the truths contained in it, and—you are the first Western man (outside Tibet) to whom it is now explained.

(6) [For Question see p. 142. Eds.]. What emerges at the end of all things is not only " pure and impersonal spirit," but the collective " personal " remembrances skimmed off every new fifth principle in the long series of being. And, if at the end of all things—say in some million of millions years hence, Spirit will have to rest in its pure, *impersonal non*-existence, as the ONE or the Absolute, still there must be " *some* good " in the cyclic process, since every purified *Ego* has the chance in the long *interims* between objective being upon the planets to *exist* as a Dhyan Chohan—

[1] The letter in answer to yours, I believe, where you question me about C.C.M., S.M. and Mrs. K.

from the lowest " Devachanee " to the highest Planetary—enjoying the fruits of its collective lives.

But what is " Spirit " pure and impersonal *per se*? Is it possible that you should not have realized yet our meaning? why, such a *Spirit* is a nonentity, a pure abstraction, an absolute blank to our senses—even to the most spiritual.   It becomes *something* only in union with matter—hence it is always *something* since matter is infinite and indestructible and *non-existent* without Spirit which, in matter is *Life*.   Separated from matter it becomes the absolute negation of life and *being*, whereas matter is inseparable from it. Ask those who offer the objection, whether they know anything of " life " and " consciousness " beyond what they now feel on earth. What conception can they have—unless natural born seers—of the state and consciousness of one's individuality after it has separated itself from gross earthly body? *What is the good* of the whole process of life on earth—you may ask them in your turn—if we are as good as " pure " *unconscious* entities before birth, during sleep, and, at the end of our career? Is not death, according to the teachings of Science, followed by the same state of unconsciousness as the one before *birth*? Does not life when it quits our body become as *impersonal* as it was before it animated the foetus? Life, after all, the greatest problem within the ken of human conception, is a mystery that the greatest of your men of Science will never solve. In order to be correctly comprehended, it has to be studied in the entire series of its manifestations, otherwise it can never be, not only fathomed, but even comprehended in its easiest form—life, as a state of *being* on this earth.   It can never be grasped so long as it is studied separately and apart from universal life.   To solve the great problem one has to become an occultist; to analyze and experience with it personally in all its phases, as life on earth, life beyond the limit of physical death, mineral, vegetable, animal and spiritual life; life in conjunction with concrete matter as well as life present in the imponderable atom.   Let them try and examine or analyze life apart from organism, and what remains of it? Simply a mode of motion; which, unless our doctrine of the all-pervading, infinite, omnipresent Life is accepted—though it be accepted on no better terms than a hypothesis only a little more reasonable than their *scientific* hypotheses which are all absurd— has to remain unsolved.   Will they object? Well, we will answer them by using their own weapons.   We will say that it is, and will remain for ever demonstrated that since motion is all-pervading and absolute rest inconceivable, that under whatever form or *mask* motion may appear, whether as light, heat, magnetism, chemical affinity or electricity—all these must be but phases of One and the same universal omnipotent Force, a Proteus they bow to as the Great " Unknown " (See Herbert Spencer) and we,

simply call the " One Life," the " One Law " and the " One
Element." The greatest, the most scientific minds on earth have
been keenly pressing forward toward a solution of the mystery,
leaving no bye-path unexplored, no thread loose or weak in this
darkest of labyrinths for them, and all had to come to the same
conclusion—that of the Occultists when given only partially—
namely, that life in its concrete manifestations is the legitimate
result and consequence of chemical affinity; as to life in its abstract
sense, life pure and simple—well, they know no more of it to-day
than they knew in the incipient stage of their Royal Society.
They only know that organisms in certain solutions previously
free from life will spring up spontaneously (Pasteur and his biblical
piety notwithstanding)—owing to certain chemical compositions of
such substances. If, as I hope, in a few years, I am entirely my
own master, I may have the pleasure of demonstrating to you on
your own writing table that life *as life* is not only transformable
into other aspects or phases of the all-pervading Force, but that
it can be actually infused into an artificial man. Frankenstein is
a myth only so far as he is the hero of a mystic tale; in nature—he
is a possibility; and the physicists and physicians of the last sub-
race of the sixth Race will inoculate life and revive corpses as they
now inoculate small-pox, and often less comely diseases. Spirit,
life and matter, are not natural principles existing independently
of each other, but the effects of combinations produced by eternal
motion in Space; and they better learn it.

(7) [For Question see p. 142. Eds.]. Most undoubtedly I am
so permitted. But then comes the most important point; how
far satisfactory will my answers appear—even to you? That not
every new law brought to light is regarded as adding a link to the
chain of human knowledge is shown by the ill-grace with which
every fact unwelcome for some reason to science, is received by its
professors. Nevertheless, *whenever* I *can* answer you—I will try to
do so, only hoping that you will not send it as a contribution from
my pen to the *Journal of Science*.

(8) [For Question see p. 142. Eds.]. Most assuredly they have.
Rain can be brought on in a small area of space—artificially and
without any claim to miracle or superhuman powers, though its
secret is no property of mine that I should divulge it. I am now
trying to obtain permission to do so. We know of no phenomenon
in nature entirely unconnected with either magnetism or electricity
—since, where there are motion, heat, friction, light, there magnetism and its *alter ego* (according to *our* humble opinion) electricity
will always appear, as either cause or effect—or rather both if we
but fathom the manifestation to its origin. All the phenomena of
earth currents, terrestrial magnetism and atmospheric electricity
are due to the fact that the earth is an electrified conductor, whose

potential is ever changing owing to its rotation and its annual orbital motion, the successive cooling and heating of the air, the formation of clouds and rain, storms and winds, etc. This you may perhaps, find in some text book. But then Science would be unwilling to admit that all these changes are due to *akasic* magnetism incessantly generating electric currents which tend to restore the disturbed equilibrium. By directing the most powerful of electric batteries, the human frame electrified by a certain process, you can *stop* rain on some given point by making " a hole in the rain cloud," as the occultists term it. By using other strongly magnetized implements within, so to say, an insulated area, rain can be produced artificially. I regret my inability to explain to you the process more clearly. You know the effects produced by trees and plants on rain clouds; and how their strong magnetic nature attracts and even feeds those clouds over the tops of the trees. Science explains it otherwise, maybe. Well, I cannot help it, for such is our knowledge and the fruits of milleniums of observations and experience. Were the present to fall into the hands of Hume, he would be sure to remark that I am vindicating the charge publicly brought by him against us: " Whenever unable to answer your arguments (?) they (we) calmly reply that their (our) rules do not admit of this or that." Charge notwithstanding, I am compelled to answer that since the secret is not mine I cannot make of it a marketable commodity. Let some physicists calculate the amount of heat required to vaporize a certain quantity of water. Then let them compute the quantity of rain needed to cover an area—say, of one square mile to a depth of *one* inch. For this amount of vaporization they will require, of course, an amount of heat that would be equal to at least five million [1] tons of coal. Now the amount of energy of which this consumption of heat would be the equivalent corresponds (as any mathematician could tell you)—to that which would be required to raise a weight of upwards of ten million tons, one mile high. How can *one man* generate such amount of heat and energy? Preposterous, absurd! —we are all lunatics, and you who listen to us will be placed in the same category if you ever venture to repeat this proposition. Yet I say that *one man alone can do it*, and very easily if he is but acquainted with a certain " physico-*spiritual* " lever in himself, far more powerful than that of Archimedes. Even simple muscular contraction is always accompanied with electric and magnetic phenomena, and there is the strongest connection between the magnetism of the earth, the changes of weather and *man*, who is the best barometer living, if he but knew [how] to decipher it properly; again, the state of the sky can always be ascertained by the variations shown by magnetic instruments. It is now several

[1] It would seem this should be ' thousand '.—EDS.

years since I had an opportunity of reading the deductions of science upon this subject; therefore, unless I go to the trouble of catching up what I may have remained ignorant of, I do not know the latest conclusions of Science. But with us, it is an established fact that it is the earth's magnetism that produces wind, storms, and rain. What science seems to know of it is but secondary symptoms always induced by that magnetism and she may very soon find out her present errors. Earth's magnetic attraction of meteoric dust, and the direct influence of the latter upon the sudden changes of temperature, especially in the matter of heat and cold, is not a settled question to the present day, I believe.[1] It was doubted whether the fact of our earth passing through a region of space in which there are more or less of meteoric masses has any bearing upon the height of our atmosphere being increased or decreased, or even upon the state of weather. But we think we could easily prove it; and since they accept the fact that the relative distribution and proportion of land and water on our globe *may be due* to the great accumulation upon it of meteoric dust, snow—especially in our northern regions—being full of meteoric iron and magnetic particles; and deposits of the latter being found even at the bottom of seas and oceans, I wonder how Science has not hitherto understood that every atmospheric change and disturbance was due to the combined magnetism of the two great masses between which our atmosphere is compressed! I call this meteoric dust a " mass " for it is really one. High above our earth's surface the air is impregnated and space *filled* with magnetic, or meteoric dust, which does not even belong to our solar system. Science having luckily discovered that, as our earth with all the other planets is carried along through space, it receives a greater proportion of that dust matter on its northern than on its southern hemisphere, knows that to this are due the preponderating number of the continents in the former hemisphere, and the greater abundance of snow and moisture. Millions of such meteors and even of the finest particles reach us yearly and daily, and all our temple knives are made of this " heavenly " iron, which reaches us without having undergone any change—the magnetism of the earth keeping them in cohesion. Gaseous matter is continually added to our atmosphere from the never ceasing fall of meteoric strongly magnetic matter, and yet it seems with them still an open question whether magnetic conditions *have* anything to do with the precipitation of rain or not! I do not know of any " set of motions established by pressures, expansions, etc., *due in the first instance to solar energy.*" Science makes too much and too little at the same time of " solar energy " and even of the Sun itself; and the Sun

[1] Dr. Phipson in 1867 and Cowper Ranyard in 1879 both urged the theory but it was rejected then.

has nothing to do whatever with rain and very little with heat.
I was under the impression that science was aware that the glacial
periods as well as those periods when temperature is "like that
of the carboniferous age," are due to the decrease and increase
or rather to the expansion of our atmosphere, which expansion is
itself due to the same meteoric presence? At any rate, we *all know*,
that the heat that the earth receives by radiation from the sun is
at the utmost *one third* if not less of the amount received by her
directly from the meteors.

(9) [For Question See p. 143. EDS.].   Call it a chromosphere or
atmosphere, it can be called neither; for it is simply the magnetic
and ever present aura of the sun, seen by astronomers *only* for a
brief few moments during the eclipse, and by some of our chelas
whenever they like—of course while in a certain induced state.
A counterpart of what the astronomers call the red flames in the
" corona " may be seen in Reichenbach's crystals or in any other
strongly magnetic body.   The head of a man in a strong ecstatic
condition, when all the electricity of his system is centred around
the brain, will represent—especially in darkness—a perfect simile
of the Sun during such periods.   The first artist who drew the
aureoles about the heads of his God and Saints was not inspired,
but represented it on the authority of temple pictures and traditions of the sanctuary and the chambers of initiation where such
phenomena took place.   The closer to the head or to the aura-
emitting body, the stronger and the more effulgent the emanation
(due to hydrogen, science tells us, in the case of the flames); hence
the irregular red flames around the Sun or the " *inner* corona."
The fact that these are not always present in equal quantity shows
only the constant fluctuation of the magnetic matter and its energy,
upon which also depend the variety and number of spots.   During
periods of magnetic inertia the spots disappear, or rather remain
invisible.   The further the emanation shoots out the more it loses
in intensity, until gradually subsiding it fades out; hence the
" outer corona," its rayed shape being due entirely to the latter
phenomenon whose effulgence proceeds from the magnetic nature
of the matter and the electric energy and not at all from intensely
hot particles, as asserted by some astronomers.   All this is terribly
unscientific, nevertheless a *fact*, to which I may add another by
reminding you that the Sun we see is not at all the central planet
of our little Universe, but only its veil or its *reflection*.   Science
has tremendous odds against studying that planet which luckily
for us we have not; foremost of all—the constant tremors of our
atmosphere which prevent them from judging correctly the little
they do see.   This impediment was never in the way of the
ancient Chaldee and Egyptian astronomers; nor is it an obstacle
to us, for we have means of arresting, or counteracting such

tremors—acquainted as we are with all the *akasic* conditions. No more than the *rain* secret would this secret—supposing we do divulge it—be of any practical use to your men of Science unless they become Occultists and sacrifice long years to the acquirement of powers. Only fancy a Huxley or a Tyndall studying *Yog-vidya*! Hence the many mistakes into which they fall and the conflicting hypotheses of your best authorities. For instance; the Sun is full of iron vapours—a fact that was demonstrated by the spectroscope, showing that the light of the corona consisted largely of a line in the green part of the spectrum, very nearly coinciding with an iron line. Yet Professors Young and Lockyer rejected that, under the witty pretext, if I remember, that if the corona were composed of minute particles like a dust cloud (and it is this that we call " magnetic matter") these particles would (1) fall upon the sun's body, (2) comets were known to pass through this vapour without any visible effect on them, (3) Professor Young's spectroscope showed that the coronal line was not identical with the iron one, etc. Why they should call those objections " scientific " is more than we can tell.

(1) The reason why the particles—since they call them so—*do not* fall upon the sun's body is self-evident. There are forces co-existent with gravitation of which they know nothing, besides that other fact that there is no gravitation properly speaking, only attraction and repulsion. (2) How could comets be affected by the said passage since their " passing through " is simply an optical illusion; they could not pass within the area of attraction without being immediately annihilated by that force of which no *vril* can give an adequate idea, since there can be nothing on earth that could be compared with it. Passing as the comets do through a " reflection " no wonder that the said *vapour* has " no visible effect on these light bodies." (3) The coronal line may not *seem* identical through the best " grating spectroscope," nevertheless, the *corona* contains iron as well as other vapours. To tell you of what it does consist is idle, since I am unable to translate the words we use for it, and that no such matter exists (not in our planetary system, at any rate)—but in the sun. The fact is, that what you call the Sun is simply the reflection of the huge " storehouse " of our System wherein ALL its forces are generated and preserved; the Sun being the heart and brain of our pigmy Universe, we might compare its *faculae*—those millions of small, intensely brilliant bodies of which the Sun's surface away from the spots is made up—with the blood corpuscles of that luminary, though some of them as correctly conjectured by Science are as large as Europe. Those blood corpuscles are the electric and magnetic matter in its sixth and seventh state. What are those long white filaments twisted like so many ropes, of which the

penumbra of the Sun is made up? What the central part that is seen like a huge flame ending in fiery spires, and the transparent clouds, or rather vapours formed of delicate threads of silvery light, that hangs over those flames—what—but magneto-electric aura—the *phlogiston* of the Sun? Science may go on speculating for ever, yet so long as she does not renounce two or three of her cardinal errors she will find herself groping for ever in the dark. Some of her greatest misconceptions are found in her limited notions on the law of gravitation; her denial that matter may be *imponderable*; her newly invented term " force " and the absurd and tacitly accepted idea that force is capable of existing *per se*, or of acting any more than life, *outside*, independent of, or in any other wise than *through* matter; in other words that *force is anything but matter* in one of her highest *states*, the last three on the ascending scale being denied because only science knows nothing of them; and her utter ignorance of the universal Proteus, its functions and importance in the economy of nature—magnetism and electricity. Tell Science that even in those days of the decline of the Roman Empire, when the tattooed Britisher used to offer to the Emperor Claudius his *nazzur* [1] of " electron " in the shape of a string of amber beads—that even then there were yet men remaining aloof from the immoral masses, who knew more of electricity and magnetism than they, the men of science, do now, and science will laugh at you as bitterly as she now does over your kind dedication to me. Verily, when your astronomers, speaking of *sun-matter*, term those lights and flames " clouds of vapour " and " gases unknown to science " (rather!) chased by mighty whirlwinds and cyclones—whereas we know it to be simply magnetic matter in its usual state of activity—we feel inclined to smile at the expressions. Can one imagine the " Sun's fires fed with *purely mineral* matter "—with meteorites highly charged with hydrogen giving the " Sun a far-reaching atmosphere of ignited gas "? We *know* that the *invisible* Sun is composed of *that* which has neither name, nor can it be compared to anything known by your science—on earth; and that its " reflection " contains still less of anything like " gases," mineral matter, or *fire*, though even we when treating of it in your civilized tongue are compelled to use such expressions as " vapour " and " magnetic matter." To close the subject, the coronal changes have no effect upon the earth's climate, though *spots* have—and Professor N. Lockyer is mostly wrong in his deductions. The Sun is neither a *solid* nor a *liquid*, nor yet a gaseous glow; but a gigantic ball of electro-magnetic Forces, the store-house of universal *life* and *motion*, from which the latter pulsate in all directions, feeding the smallest

[1] Tributary offering.—Eds.

atom as the greatest genius with the same material unto the end of the *Maha Yug*.

(10) [For Question see p. 143. EDS.]. I believe not. The stars are distant from us at least 500,000 times as far as the Sun and some as many times more. The strong accumulation of meteoric matter and the atmospheric tremors are always in the way. If your astronomers could climb on the height of that meteoric *dust*, with their telescopes and *havanas* they might trust more than they can now in their photometers. How can they? Neither can the real degree of intensity of that light be known on earth—hence no trustworthy basis for calculating magnitudes and distances can be had—nor have they hitherto made sure in a single instance (except in the matter of one star in Cassiopeia) which stars shine by reflected and which by their own light. The working of the best double star photometers is deceptive. Of this I have made sure, so far back as in the spring of 1878 while watching the observations made through a Pickering photometer. The discrepancy in the observations upon a star (near Gamma Ceti) amounted at times to half a magnitude. No planets but one have hitherto been discovered outside of the solar system, with all their photometers, while we know with the sole help of our spiritual *naked* eye a number of them; every *completely matured* Sun-star having, like in our own system, several companion planets in fact. The famous "polarization of light" test is about as trustworthy as all others. Of course, the mere fact of their starting from a false premise cannot vitiate either their conclusions or astronomical prophecies, since both are mathematically correct in their mutual relations, and that it answers the given object. [Neither] the Chaldees nor yet our old Rishis had either your telescopes or photometers; and yet their astronomical predictions were faultless, the mistakes, very slight ones in truth—fathered upon them by their modern rivals—proceeding from the mistakes of the latter.

You must not complain of my too long answers to your very short questions, since I answer you for your instruction as a student of occultism, my " lay " chela, and not at all with a view of answering the *Journal of Science*. I am no man of science with regard to, or in connection with modern learning. My knowledge of your Western Sciences is *very* limited in fact; and you will please bear in mind that all my answers are based upon, and derived from, our Eastern occult doctrines, regardless of their agreement or disagreement with those of exact science. Hence I say:—

" The Sun's surface emits per square mile as much light (*in proportion*) as can be emitted from any body." But what can you mean in this case by " light "? The latter is not an independent principle, and I rejoiced at the introduction, with a view to facilitate means of observation of the " diffraction spectrum; " since by abolishing all these imaginary independent existences, such as heat, actinism, light, etc., it rendered to Occult Science the greatest service, by vindicating in the eyes of her modern sister our very ancient theory that every phenomenon being but the effect of the diversified motions of what we call Akasa (not *your* ether) there was, in fact, but one element, the causative principle of all. But since your question is asked with a view to settling a disputed point in modern science I will try to answer it in the clearest way I can. I say then, *no*, and will give you my reasons why. They cannot know it, for the simple reason that heretofore they have in reality found no sure means of measuring the velocity of light. The experiments made by Fizeau and Cornu, known as the two best investigators of light in the world of science, notwithstanding the general satisfaction at the results obtained, are not trustworthy data either in respect to the velocity with which sunlight travels or to its quantity. The methods adopted by both these French-men are yielding correct results (at any rate *approximately* correct, since there is a variation of 227 miles per second between the result of the observations of both experimenters, albeit made with the same apparatus)—only as regards the velocity of light between our earth and the upper regions of its atmosphere. Their toothed wheel, revolving *at a known* velocity records, of course, the strong ray of light which passes through one of the niches of the wheel, and then has its point of light obscured whenever a tooth passes—accurately enough. The instrument is very ingenious and can hardly fail to give splendid results on a journey of a few thousand meters there and back; there being between the Paris observatory and its fortifications no atmosphere, no meteoric masses to impede the ray's progress; and that ray finding quite a different quality of a medium to travel upon than the ether of Space, the ether between the Sun and the meteoric *continent* above our heads, the velocity of light will of course show some 185,000 and odd miles per second, and your physicists shout " Eureka "! Nor do any of the other devices contrived by science to measure that velocity since 1878 answer any better. All they can say is that their calculations are *so far* correct. Could they measure light *above* our atmosphere they would soon find that they were wrong.

(11) [For Question see p. 143. EDs.]. It is—so far; but is fast changing. Your science has a theory, I believe, that if the earth were suddenly placed in extremely cold regions—for instance where it would exchange places with Jupiter—all our seas and rivers would be suddenly transformed into solid mountains; the air,—or rather a portion of the aeriform substances which compose it—would be metamorphosed from their state of invisible fluid owing to the absence of heat into liquids (which now exist on

Jupiter, but of which men have no idea on earth). Realize, or try to imagine the *reverse* condition, and it will be that of Jupiter at the present moment.

The whole of our system is imperceptibly shifting its position in space. The relative distance between planets remaining ever the same, and being in no wise affected by the displacement of the whole system; and the distance between the latter and the stars and other suns being so incommensurable as to produce but little if any perceptible change for centuries and milleniums to come, no astronomer will perceive it *telescopically*, until Jupiter and some other planets, whose little luminous points hide now from our sight millions upon millions of stars (all but some 5000 or 6000)— will suddenly let us have a peep at a few of the *Raja-Suns* they are now hiding. There is such a king-star right behind Jupiter, that no mortal physical eye has ever seen during this, our Round. Could it be so perceived it would appear, through the best telescope with a power of multiplying its diameter ten thousand times, still a small dimensionless point, thrown into the shadow by the brightness of any planet; nevertheless—this world is thousands of times larger than Jupiter. The violent disturbance of its atmosphere and even its red spot that so intrigues science lately, are due—(1) to that shifting and (2) to the influence of that Raja-Star. In its present position in space, imperceptibly small though it be, the metallic substances of which it is mainly composed are expanding and gradually transforming themselves into aeriform fluids—the state of our own earth and its six sister globes before the first Round— and becoming part of its atmosphere. Draw your inferences and deductions from this, my dear " :ay " chela, but beware lest in doing so you sacrifice your humble instructor and the occult doctrine itself on the altar of your wrathful Goddess—*modern science*.

(12) [For Question see p. 143. EDs.] I am afraid not much, since our Sun is but a reflection. The only great truth uttered by Siemens is that inter-stellar space is filled with highly attenuated matter, such as may be put in air vacuum tubes, and which stretches from planet to planet and from star to star. But this truth has no bearing upon his main facts. The sun gives *all* and takes back *nothing* from its system. The sun gathers nothing " at the poles " —which are always free even from the famous " red flames " at all times, not only during the eclipses. How is it that with their powerful telescopes they have failed to perceive any such " gathering " since their glasses show them even the " superlatively fleecy clouds " on the photosphere? Nothing can reach the sun from *without* the boundaries of its own system in the shape of such *gross* matter as " attenuated gases." Every bit of matter in all its *seven* states is necessary to the vitality of the various and

numberless systems—worlds in formation, suns awakening anew to life, etc., and they have none to spare even for their best neighbours and next of kin.   They are mothers, not stepmothers, and would not take away one crumb from the nutrition of their children. The latest theory of radiant energy which shows that there is no such thing in nature, properly speaking, as chemical light, or heat ray is the only approximately correct one.   For indeed, there is but one thing—radiant energy which is *inexhaustible* and knows neither increase nor decrease and will go on with its self-generating work to the end of the Solar manvantara.   The absorption of Solar Forces by the earth is tremendous; yet it is, or may be demonstrated that the latter receives hardly 25 per cent. of the chemical power of its rays, for these are despoiled of 75 per cent. during their vertical passage through the atmosphere at the moment they reach the outer boundary " of the aerial ocean."   And even those rays lose about 20 per cent. in illuminating and caloric power, we are told.   What, with such a *waste* must then be the recuperative power of our Father-Mother Sun?   Yes; call it " Radiant Energy " if you will; we call it Life—all-pervading, omnipresent life, ever at work in its great laboratory—the SUN.

(13) [For Question see p. 143. EDS.].   None can ever be given by your men of Science, whose " bumptiousness " makes them declare that only to those for whom the word magnetism is a mysterious agent can the supposition that the Sun is a huge magnet account for the production by that body of light, heat and the causes of magnetic variations as perceived on our earth.   They are determined to ignore and thus reject the theory suggested to them by Jenkins of the R.A.S. of the existence of strong magnetic poles *above* the surface of the earth.   But the theory is the correct one nevertheless, and one of these poles revolves around the north pole in a periodical cycle of several hundred years.   Halley and Flamsteed—besides Jenkins—were the only scientific men that ever suspected it.   Your question is again answered by reminding you of another *exploded* supposition.   Jenkins did his best some three years ago to prove that it is the north end of the compass needle that is the true north pole, and not the reverse as the current scientific theory maintains.   He was informed that the locality in Boothia where Sir James Ross located the earth's north magnetic pole was purely imaginary; *it is not there*.   If he (and *we*) are wrong, then the magnetic theory that like poles repel and unlike poles attract must also be declared a fallacy; since if the north end of the dipping needle *is a south pole* then its pointing to the ground in Boothia—as you call it—*must be due to attraction*?   And if there is anything there to attract it, why is it that the needle in London is attracted neither to the ground in Boothia nor to the earth's centre?   As very correctly argued, if the north pole

of the needle pointed almost perpendicularly to the ground in Boothia, it is simply because it was repelled by the true north magnetic pole, when Sir J. Ross was there about half a century ago.

No; our " Lordships " have nothing to do with the inertia of the needle. It is due to the presence of certain metals in fusion in that locality. Increase of temperature diminishes magnetic attraction, and a sufficiently high temperature destroys it often altogether. The temperature I am speaking of is, in the present case rather an aura, an emanation, than anything science knows of. Of course, this explanation will *never* hold water with the present knowledge of science. But we can wait and see. Study magnetism with the help of occult doctrines, and then that which now will appear incomprehensible, *absurd* in the light of physical science, will become all clear.

(14) [For Question see p. 143. EDS.]. They must be. Not all of the Intra-Mercurial planets, nor yet those in the orbit of Neptune are yet discovered, though they are strongly suspected. We know that such exist and *where* they exist; and that there are innumerable planets " burnt out " they say,—in *obscuration*, we say;—planets in formation and not yet luminous, etc. But then " we know " is of little use to science, when the Spiritualists will not admit our knowledge. Edison's tasimeter adjusted to its utmost degree of sensitiveness and attached to a large telescope may be of great use when perfected. When so attached, the " tasimeter " will afford the possibility not only to measure the heat of the remotest of visible stars, but to detect by their invisible radiations stars that are unseen and otherwise undetectable, hence planets also. The discoverer,[1] an F.T.S., a good deal protected by M., thinks that if at any point in a blank space of heavens—a space that appears blank even through a telescope of the highest power—the *tasimeter* indicates an accession of temperature and does so invariably, this will be a regular proof that the instrument is in range with the stellar body either non-luminous or so distant as to be beyond the reach of telescopic vision. His *tasimeter*, he says, " is affected by a wider range of etheric undulations than the eye can take cognizance of." Science will *hear* sounds from certain planets before she *sees* them. This is a *prophecy*. Unfortunately I am not a Planet,—not even a " planetary." Otherwise I would advise you to get a *tasimeter* from him and thus avoid me the trouble of writing to you. I would manage then to find myself " in range " with you.

(15) [For Question see p. 143. EDS.]. No, good friend; I am not as indiscreet as all that, I left you simply to your own reminiscences. Every mortal creature, even the less favoured by Fortune,

[1] Edison, who was an Hon. F.T.S.—EDS.

has such moments of relative happiness at some time of his life.
Why shouldn't you?

Yes, it was an X quantity I referred to.

(16) [For Question see p. 143. EDS.]. It is a widely spread
belief among all the Hindus that a person's future pre-natal state
and birth are moulded by the last desire he may have at the time
of death. But this last desire, they say, necessarily hinges on to
the shape which the person may have given to his desires, passions,
etc., during his past life. It is for this very reason, *viz.*—that our
last desire may not be unfavourable to our future progress—that
we have to watch our actions and control our passions and desires
throughout our whole earthly career.

(17) [For Question see p. 143. EDS.]. It *cannot* be otherwise.
The experience of dying men—by drowning and other accidents
—brought back to life, has corroborated our doctrine in almost
every case. Such thoughts are *involuntary* and we have no more
control over them than we would over the eye's retina to prevent
it perceiving that colour which affects it most. At the last moment,
the whole life is reflected in our memory and emerges from all the
forgotten nooks and corners picture after picture, one event after
the other. The dying brain dislodges memory with a strong
supreme impulse, and memory restores faithfully every impression
entrusted to it during the period of the brain's activity. That
impression and thought which was the strongest naturally becomes
the most vivid and survives so to say all the rest which now vanish
and disappear for ever, to reappear but in Devachan.[1] No man
dies insane or unconscious—as some physiologists assert. Even a
madman, or one in a fit of *delirium tremens* will have his instant of
perfect lucidity at the moment of death, though unable to say so
to those present. The man may often appear dead. Yet from
the last pulsation, from and between the last throbbing of his heart
and the moment when the last spark of animal heat leaves the
body—the *brain thinks* and the *Ego* lives over in those few brief
seconds his whole life over again. Speak in whispers, ye, who
assist at a death-bed and find yourselves in the solemn presence
of Death. Especially have you to keep quiet just after Death has
laid her clammy hand upon the body. Speak in whispers, I say,
lest you disturb the quiet ripple of thought, and hinder the busy
work of the Past casting its reflection upon the Veil of the Future.

(18) [For Question see p. 143-4. EDS.]. Yes; the " full " remembrance of our lives (*collective* lives) will return back at the end of
all the seven Rounds, at the threshold of the long, long Nirvana that
awaits us after we leave Globe Z. At the end of isolated Rounds,
we remember but the sum total of our last impressions, those we

---

[1] Good gracious! had I forgotten in my hurry to add the last *five words*, would
not I have caught it as a charge of *flat* contradiction!

had selected, or that have rather *forced* themselves upon us and
followed us in *Devachan*. Those are all " probationary " lives with
large indulgences and new trials afforded us with every new life.
But at the close of the minor cycle, after the completion of all the
seven Rounds, there awaits *us no other* mercy but the cup of good
deeds, of *merit*, outweighing that of *evil* deeds and *demerit* in the
scales of Retributive Justice. Bad, irretrievably bad must be that
Ego that yields no mite from its fifth Principle, and *has* to be
annihilated, to disappear in the *Eighth Sphere*. A mite, as I say,
collected from the Personal Ego suffices to save him from the
dreary Fate. Not so after the completion of the great cycle:
either a long Nirvana of Bliss (unconscious though it be in, and
according to, your crude conceptions); after which—life as a
Dhyan Chohan for a whole Manvantara, or else " *Avitchi Nirvana* "
and a Manvantara of misery and Horror as a——you *must not*
hear the word nor I—pronounce or write it. But " those " have
nought to do with the mortals who pass through the seven spheres.
The *collective* Karma of a future Planetary is as lovely as the collective
Karma of a——is terrible. Enough. I have said too much
already.

(19) [For Question see p. 144. EDS.]. Verily so. Until the
struggle between the higher and middle duad begins—(*with the
exception of suicides who are not dead but have only killed their physical
triad, and whose Elemental parasites, therefore, are not naturally separated
from the Ego as in real death*)—until that struggle, I say, has begun
and ended, no shell can realize its position. When the sixth and
seventh principles are gone, carrying off with them the finer,
spiritual portions of that whlch once was the *personal* consciousness
of the fifth, then only does the shell gradually develop a kind of
hazy consciousness of its own from what remains in the shadow
of personality. No contradiction here, my dear friend,—only
haziness in your own perceptions.

(20) [For Question see p. 144. EDS.]. All that which pertains
to the materio-psychological attributes and sensations of the five
lower skandhas; all that which will be thrown off as refuse by the
newly born Ego in the Devachan, as unworthy of, and not sufficiently related to the *purely* spiritual perceptions, emotions and
feelings of the sixth, strengthened, and so to say, *cemented* by a
portion of the fifth, that portion which is necessary in the Devachan
for the retention of a divine spiritualized notion of the " I " in the
Monad—which would otherwise have no consciousness in relation
to object and subject at all—all this " becomes *extinct for ever*,"
namely at the moment of physical death, to return once more,
marshalling before the eye of the new Ego at the threshold of
Devachan and to be rejected by It. It will return for the *third*
time *fully* at the end of the minor cycle, after the completion of the

seven Rounds when the *sum total* of collective existences is weighed
—" merit " in one cup, " demerit " in the other cup of the scales.
But in that individual, in the Ego—" good, bad, or indifferent "
in the isolated *personality*,—consciousness leaves as suddenly as
" the flame leaves the wick." Blow out your candle, good friend.
The flame has left *that* candle " for ever "; but are the particles
that moved, their motion producing the *objective* flame annihilated
or dispersed for all that? *Never.* Relight the candle and the same
particles drawn by mutual affinity will return to the wick. Place
a long row of candles on your table. Light one and blow it out;
then light the other and do the same; a third and fourth, and so
on. The same matter, the same gaseous particles—representing
in our case the *Karma* of the personality—will be called forth by
the conditions given them by your match, to produce a new
luminosity; but can we say that candle No. 1 has not had its flame
extinct for ever? Not even in the case of the " failures of nature,"
of the *immediate* reincarnation of children and congenital idiots,
etc., that so provoked the wrath of C.C.M., can we call them the
identical ex-personalities; *though the whole of the same life-principle and
identically the same* MANAS (fifth principle) *re-enters a new body* and
may be truly called a " reincarnation of the *personality* "—whereas,
in the rebirth of the Egos from *devachans* and *avitchis* into Karmic
life it is only the spiritual attributes of the Monad and its Buddhi
that are reborn. All we can say of the reincarnated " failures "
is, that they are the reincarnated *Manas*, the fifth principle of Mr.
Smith or Miss Grey, but certainly not that these are the reincarnations of Mr. S. and Miss G. Therefore, the explanation, clear
and concise (though perhaps less literary than you might make it)
given to C.C.M. in the *Theosophist* in answer to his spiteful hit in
Light, is not only correct but *candid* also; and both yourself and
C.C.M. were unjust to Upasika and even to myself who told her
what to write; since even *you* mistook my wail and lament at the
confused and tortured explanations in *Isis* (for its *incompleteness* no
one but we, her inspirers are responsible) and my complaint of
having had to exercise all my " ingenuity " to make the thing
plain, for an avowal of *ingeniousness* in the sense of cunning and
craft, whereas *ingenuousness*—a sincere desire (though very difficult
of realization) to mend and clear up the misconception—was
meant by me. I do not know of anything since the very beginning
of our correspondence that displeased *the Chohan* so much as that.
But we must not return to the subject again.

But what is then " the nature of the remembrance and self-
consciousness of the shell? " you ask. As I said in your note—
no better than a reflected or borrowed light. " Memory " is one
thing, and " perceptive faculties " quite another. A madman
may remember very clearly some portions of his past life; yet he

is unable to perceive anything in its true light for the higher portion
of his *Manas* and his *Buddhi* are paralysed in him, have left him.
Could an animal—a dog, for instance—speak, he would prove [to]
you that his memory in direct relation to his canine personality is
as fresh as yours; nevertheless his memory and instinct cannot be
called " perceptive faculties." A dog remembers that his master
thrashed him when the latter gets hold of his stick—at all other
times he has no remembrance of it. Thus with a shell; once in
the aura of a medium, all he perceives through the borrowed organs
of the medium and of those in magnetic sympathy with the latter,
he will perceive very clearly—but *not further* than what the shell
can find in the perceptive faculties and memories of *circle* and
medium—hence often the rational and at times highly intelligent
answers; hence also a complete oblivion of things known to all
but that medium and circle. The shell of a highly intelligent,
learned, but utterly unspiritual man who died a natural death,
will last longer, and the *shadow* of his own memory helping—that
shadow which is the refuse of the sixth principle left in the fifth—he
may deliver discourses through trance speakers and repeat parrot-
like that which he knew of and thought much over it, during his
life-time. But find me *one single* instance in the annals of Spiritualism where a returning shell of a Faraday or a Brewster (for even
they were made to fall into the trap of mediumistic attraction)
said one word more than it knew during its life-time. Where is
that scientific shell, that ever gave evidence of that which is
claimed on behalf of the " disembodied *Spirit* "—namely, that a
free Soul, the Spirit disenthralled from its body's fetters perceives
and sees that which is concealed from living mortal eyes? Challenge
the Spiritualists fearlessly, I say! Defy the best, the most reliable
of mediums—Stainton Moses for one—to give you through that
high disembodied shell, that he mistakes for the " Imperator " of
the early days of his mediumship, to tell you what you will have
hidden in your box, if S.M. does not know it; or to repeat to you
a line from a Sanskrit manuscript unknown to his medium, or
anything of that kind. Pro pudore! *Spirits* they call them? Spirits
with *personal* remembrances? As well call personal remembrances
the sentences screeched out by a parrot. Why don't you ask
C.C.M. to test + ? Why not settle his and your mind at rest by
suggesting to him to ask a friend or an acquaintance *unknown* to
S.M. to select an object the nature of which will remain in its
turn unknown to C.C.M., and then see whether + will be able to
name that object—something possible even to a good clairvoyant.
Let the " Spirit " of Zöllner—now that he is in the " fourth
dimension of space," and has put up an appearance already with
several mediums—tell them the last word of his discovery, complete his astro-physical philosophy. No; Zöllner when lecturing

through an intelligent medium, surrounded with persons who read his works, are interested in them—will repeat on various tones that which is known to others (not even that which *he alone* knew, most probably), the credulous, ignorant public confounding the *post-hoc* with the *propter-hoc* and firmly convinced of the *Spirit's* identity. Indeed, it will be worth your while to stimulate investigation in this direction. Yes; personal consciousness does leave everyone at death; and when even the centre of memory is re-established in the shell, it will remember and speak out its recollections but through the brain of some *living* human being. Hence—

(21) [For Question see p. 144. Eds.].   A more or less complete, still dim recollection of its personality, and of its purely *physical* life.   As in the cases of complete insanity the final severance of the two higher duads (7th 6th and 5th 4th) at the moment of the former going into gestation, digs an impassable gulf between the two.   It is not even a portion of the fifth that is carried away— least of all $2\frac{1}{2}$ principles as Mr. Hume crudely puts it in his *Fragments*—that go into Devachan leaving but $1\frac{1}{2}$ principles behind. The *Manas* shorn of its finest attributes, becomes like a flower from which all the aroma has suddenly departed, a rose crushed, and having been made to yield all its oil for the *attar* manufacture purposes; what is left behind is but the smell of decaying grass, earth and rottenness.

(*a*) Question the second is sufficiently answered, I believe. (Your second para.)   The Spiritual *Ego* goes on evolving personalities, in which " the sense of identity " is *very complete* while living.   After their separation from the *physical* Ego, that sense returns very dim, and belongs wholly to the recollections of the *physical* man.   The shell may be a perfect Sinnett when wholly engrossed in a game of cards at his club, and when either losing or winning a large sum of money—or a Babu Smut Murky Dass trying to cheat his principal out of a sum of rupees.   In both cases—ex-editor and Babu will, as shells, remind anyone who will have the privilege of enjoying an hour's chat with the illustrious dis-embodied angels, more of the inmates of a lunatic asylum made to play parts in private theatricals as means of hygienic recreation, than of the Caesars and Hamlets they would represent. The slightest shock will throw them off the track and send them off raving.

(*b*) An error.   A. P. Sinnett is *not* " an absolutely *new* invention." He is the child and creation of his antecedent personal self; the *Karmic* progeny, for all he knows, of Nonius Asprenas, Consul of the Emperor Domitian—(94 A.D.) together with Arricinius Clemens,[1] and friend of the *Flamen Dialis* of that day (the high

[1] Should be Clemens Arretinus.—Eds.

priest of Jupiter and chief of the *Flaminis*) or of that *Flamen* himself —which would account for A. P. Sinnett's suddenly developed love for mysticism.   A. P. S.—the friend and brother of K. H. will go to *Devachan*; and A. P. S., the Editor and the lawn-tennis man, the Don Juan, in a *mild* way, in the palmy days of " Saints, Sinners and Sceneries," identifying himself by mentioning a usually covered mole or scar,—will, perhaps, be abusing the Babus through a medium to some old friend in California or London.

(*c*) It *will* find " enough decent material " and to spare.   A few years of Theosophy will furnish it.

(*d*) Perfectly correctly defined.

(*e*) As much as there is of the *personality*—in A. P. S.'s reflection in the looking glass—of the real, living A. P. S.

(*f*) The Spiritual Ego will not think of the A. P. S. *the shell*, any more than it will think of the last suit of clothes it wore; nor will it be conscious that the individuality is gone, since the only *individuality* and *Spiritual personality* it will then behold [will be] in itself alone. *Nosce te ipsum* is a direct command of the oracle to the *Spiritual monad* in *Devachan*; and the " heresy of Individuality " is a doctrine propounded by *Tathagata* with an eye to the Shell. The latter, whose bumptiousness is as proverbial as that of the medium when reminded that it *is* A. P. S.—will echo out: " Of course, no doubt, hand me over some preserved peaches I devoured with such an appetite for breakfast, and a glass of claret! "—and who after this who knew A. P. S. at Allahabad, will dare doubt his identity?   And, when left alone for one short instant by some disturbance in the circle, or the thought of the medium wandering for a moment to some other person—that shell will begin to hesitate in its *thoughts* whether it is A. P. S., S. Wheeler, or Ratigan; and end by assuring itself it is Julius Caesar.   (*g*)—and by finally " remaining asleep."

(*h*) No; it is not conscious of this loss of cohesion.   Besides, such a feeling in a shell being quite useless for nature's purposes, it could hardly realize something that could be never even dreamed by a medium or its affinities.   It is dimly conscious of its own physical death—after a prolonged period of time though—that's all.   The few exceptions to this rule—cases of half successful sorcerers, of very wicked persons passionately attached to Self— offer a real danger to the living.   These very material shells, whose last dying thought was Self,—Self,—Self—and to live, to live! will often feel it instinctively.   So do some suicides—though not all.   What happens then is terrible for it becomes a case of *post mortem* lycanthropy.   The shell will cling so tenaciously to its semblance of life that it will seek refuge in a new organism in any beast—in a dog, a hyæna, a bird when no human organism is close at hand—rather than submit to annihilation.

(22) [For Question see pp. 144-5. Eds.]   A question I have no right to answer.

(23) [For Question see p. 145. Eds.].   Mars and four other planets of which astronomy knows yet nothing.   Neither A, B, nor Y, Z, are known; nor can they be seen through physical means however perfected.

(24) [For Question see p. 145. Eds.].   Most decidedly not.   Not even a Dhyan Chohan of the lower orders could approach it without having its *body* consumed, or rather annihilated.   Only the highest " Planetary " can scan it.   (*b*) Not unless we call it the vertex of an angle.   But it is the vertex of all the " chains " collectively.   All of us dwellers of the chains—we will have to evolute, live and run the up and down scale in that highest and last of the septenary chains (on the scale of perfection) before the Solar Pralaya snuffs out our little system.

(25 & 26) [For Question see p. 145. Eds.].   . . .   " in which case *it* "—the " it " relates to the sixth and seventh principles, not to the fifth, for the *manas* will have to remain a shell in each case; only in the one in hand it will have no time to visit mediums : for it begins sinking down to the eighth sphere almost immediately. " Then and there " in the eternity may be a mighty long period. It means only that the monad having no *Karmic* body to guide its rebirth falls into *non-being* for a certain period and then reincarnates—certainly not earlier than a thousand or two thousand years. No, it is not an " exceptional case."   Save a few exceptional cases in the case of the initiated such as our Teshu-Lamas and the Bodhisatwas and a few others, no monad ever gets reincarnated before its appointed cycle.

(27) [For Question see p. 145. Eds.].   " How does he toss into confusion." . . . If instead of doing to-day something you have to do you put it off till the next day—does not even this—invisibly and imperceptibly at first, yet as forcibly—throw into confusion many a thing, and in some cases even shuffle the destinies of millions of persons, for good, for evil, or simply in connection with a change,—may be unimportant in itself—still a *change*? And do you mean to say that such an unexpected, horrid murder has not influenced the destinies of millions ?

(28) [For Question see p. 145. Eds.].   Here we are, again. Verily ever since I had the folly of touching upon this subject—*i.e.* of harnessing the cart before the horse—my nights are bereft of their hitherto innocent sleep! For Heaven's sake take into consideration the following facts and put them together, if you can. (1) The individual units of mankind remain 100 times longer in the transitory spheres of *effects* than on the globes; (2) The few men of the fifth Round do not beget children of the fifth but of your fourth Round.   (3) That the "obscurations" are not *Pralayas*,

and that they last in a proportion of *1* to *10*, *i.e.*, if a Ring or whatever we call it, the period during which the seven Root races have to develop and reach their last appearance upon a globe during *that* Round—lasts say 10 millions of years, (of course it lasts far longer) then the " obscuration " will last no longer than *one* million. When our globe having got rid of its last fourth Round men and a few, very few of the fifth, goes to sleep, during the period of its rest the fifth Round men will be resting in their devachans and Spiritual lokas—far longer at any rate than the fourth Round " angels " in theirs since they are *far more perfect*. A contradiction, and a " *lapsus calami* of M."—says Hume; because M. wrote something quite correct though he is no more infallible than I am and might have expressed himself, more than once, very carelessly.

" I want to make out how the next superior Round forms are evolved." My friend, try to understand that you are putting me questions pertaining to the highest initiations. That I can give you a *general* view, but that I dare not nor will I enter upon details —though I would if I could satisfy you. Do not you feel that it is one of the *highest mysteries* than which there is no higher one?

(*a*) " Dead " but to resurrect in greater glory. Is not what I say, plain?

(29) [For Question see p. 145. EDs.]. Of course not, since it is *not* destroyed, but remains crystallized, so to say—in *statu quo*. At each Round there are less and less animals—the latter themselves evoluting into higher forms. During the first Round it is *they* that were the " kings of *creation*." During the seventh men will have become *Gods*, and animals—intelligent beings. Draw your inferences. Beginning with the second Round, already evolution proceeds on quite a different plan. Everything is evolved and has but to proceed on its cyclic journey and get perfected. It is only [on] the first Round that man becomes from a human being on Globe B, a mineral, a plant, an animal on Planet *C*. The method changes entirely from the second Round; but— I have learned prudence with you; and *will say nothing* before the time for saying it has come. And now, you [have] had a volume; when will you digest it? Of how many contradictions will I have to be suspected before you understand the whole correctly?

Yours nevertheless, and very sincerely,

K. H.

LETTER No. 24A [1]

THE FAMOUS " CONTRADICTIONS "

Received Autumn 1882.

I hope you will give me great credit for obedience in having laboriously and against my inclination endeavoured to compile a case for the plaintiff *in re* the alleged contradictions. As I have said elsewhere these appear to me not much worth worrying about; though for the present they leave me cloudy in my ideas about Devachan and the victims of accident. *It is because they do not fret me that I have never hitherto acted on your suggestion that I should make notes of them.*

(1)

Hume has been inclined to trace contradictions in some letters referring to the evolution of man, but in conversation with him I have always contended that these are not contradictions at all,— merely due to a confusion about rounds and races—a matter of language. Then he has pretended to think that you have built up the philosophy as you have gone on, and got out of the difficulty by inventing a great many more races than were contemplated at first, which hypothesis I have always ridiculed as absurd.

(2)

I have not re-copied here the passages about victims of accident quoted in my letter of the 12th August and in apparent conflict with the corrections on the proof of my *Letter on Theosophy.* You have already said apropos to these quotations, on back of mine dated August 12th:—

(3)

" I can easily understand we are accused of contradictions and inconsistencies aye even to writing one thing to-day and denying it to-morrow. Could you but know how I write my letters and the time I am enabled to give to them perchance you would feel less critical if not exacting——"

(4)

This passage it was which led me to think it might be that some of the earlier letters had been perhaps the " victim of accident " itself.

But to go on with the case for the plaintiff:—

---

[1] The numbers in brackets refer to K.H.'s replies, for which see Letter 24B. page 182 et seq.—ED.

(5)

" Most of those whom you may call, if you like, candidates for Devachan die and are reborn in the Kama loka without remembrance. . . . You can hardly call remembrance a dream of yours, some particular scene or scenes within whose narrow limits you would find enclosed a few persons . . . etc., call it the personal remembrance of A. P. Sinnett if you can." *Notes on back of mine* to Old Lady.

(6)

" Certainly, the new Ego, once that it is reborn in the Devachan retains for a certain time proportionate to its Earth life, a ' complete recollection of his spiritual life on Earth.' " *Long Devachan letter.*

(7)

"All those who have not slipped down into the mire of un- redeemable sin and bestiality—go to the Devachan," *ibid.*

(8)

" It (Devachan) is an idealised paradise in each case of the Ego's own making and by him filled with the scenery crowded with the incidents and thronged with the people he would expect to find in such a sphere of compensative bliss." *Ibid.*

(9)

"Nor can we call it a full but only a partial remembrance. X. Love and hatred are the only immortal feelings, the only survivors from the wreck of the Ye-dhamma or phenomenal world. Imagine yourself in Devachan then, with those you may have loved with such immortal love, with the familiar shadowy scenes connected with them for a background, and a perfect blank for everything else relating to your interior social political and literary life—" *Former letter: i.e., Notes.*

(10)

" Since the conscious perception of one's personality on Earth is but an evanescent dream, that sense will be equally that of a dream in the Devachan—*only a hundred fold intensified.*" *Long Devachan letter.*

(11)

". . . . a connoisseur who passes aeons in the rapt delight of listening to divine symphonies by imaginary angelic choirs and orchestras." *Long letter. See* (9) X *ante.* **See my notes 10 and 11 about Wagner etc.**

You say:

(12A)

" In no case then, with the exception of suicides and shells is there any possibility for any other to be attracted to a seance room." *Notes*.

(12B)

" On margin I said rarely but I have not pronounced the word *never*." *Appended to mine of 12th Aug*.

LETTER No. 24B

[A]

At this stage of our correspondence, misunderstood as we generally seem to be, even by yourself, my faithful friend, it may be worth our while and useful for both, that you should be posted on certain facts—and very important facts—connected with adept-ship. Bear in mind then, the following points.

(1) An adept—the highest as the lowest—is one *only during the exercise of his occult powers*.

(2) Whenever these powers are needed, the sovereign will unlocks the door to the *inner* man (the adept,) who can emerge and act freely but on condition that his jailor—the *outer* man— will be either completely or partially paralyzed as the case may require; *viz*.: either (*a*) mentally and physically; (*b*) mentally,— but not physically; (*c*) physically but not entirely mentally; (*d*) neither,—but with an akasic film interposed between the *outer* and the *inner* man.

(3) The smallest exercise of occult powers then, as you will now see, requires an effort. We may compare it to the inner muscular effort of an athlete preparing to use his physical strength. As no athlete is likely to be always amusing himself at swelling his veins in anticipation of having to lift a weight, so no adept can be supposed to keep his will in constant tension and the *inner* man in full function, when there is no immediate necessity for it. When the *inner* man rests the adept becomes an ordinary man, limited to his physical senses and the functions of his physical brain. Habit sharpens the intuition of the latter, yet is unable to make them supersensuous. The inner adept is ever ready, ever on the alert, and that suffices for our purposes. At moments of rest then, his faculties are at rest also. When I sit at my meals, or when I am dressing, reading or otherwise occupied I am not thinking even of those near me; and Djual Khool can easily break his nose to blood, by running in the dark against a beam, as he did the other night—(just because instead of throwing a " film "

he had foolishly paralyzed all his outer senses while talking to and with a distant friend)—and I remained placidly ignorant of the fact. *I was not thinking of him*—hence my ignorance.

From the aforesaid, you may well infer that an adept is an ordinary mortal at all the moments of his daily life but those—when the *inner* man is acting.

Couple this with the unpleasant fact that we are forbidden to use one particle of our powers in connexion with the *Eclectics* (for which you have to thank your President and *him alone*—) and that the little that is done is, so to say, smuggled in—and then syllogize *thusly*:—

K. H. when writing to us *is not an adept.*

A *non-*adept—is fallible.

Therefore, K. H. may very easily commit mistakes;—

Mistakes of punctuation—that will often change entirely the whole sense of a sentence; idiomatic mistakes—very likely to occur, especially when writing as hurriedly as I do; mistakes arising from occasional confusion of terms that *I had to learn from you*—since it is *you* who are the author of " rounds "—" rings "—" earthly rings "—etc., etc.   Now with all this, I beg leave to say, that after having carefully read over and over our " Famous Contradictions " myself; after giving them to be read to M.; and then to *a high adept* whose powers are *not* in the Chohan's chancery sequestered by Him to prevent him from squandering them upon the unworthy objects of his personal predilections; after doing all this I was told by the latter the following: " It is all perfectly correct.   Knowing what you mean, no more than any other person acquainted with the doctrine can I find in these detached fragments anything that would really conflict with each other.   But, since many sentences are incomplete, and the subjects scattered about without any order, I do not wonder that your " lay chelas " should find fault with them.   Yes; they do require a more explicit and clear exposition."

Such is the decree of *an adept*—and I abide by it; I will try to complete the information for your sake.

In one and *only* case—marked on your pages and my answers (12A) and (12B), the last—is the " plaintiff " entitled to a hearing, but *not to a farthing even—for damages*; since, as in law, no one—either plaintiff or defendant—has a right to plead ignorance of that law, so in Occult Sciences, the lay chelas ought to be forced to give the benefit of the doubt to their gurus in cases in which, owing to their great ignorance of that science they are likely to misinterpret the meaning—instead of accusing them point blank of *contradiction*! Now I beg to state, that, with regard to the two sentences—marked respectively 12A and 12B—there is a *plain* contradiction but for those who are *not* acquainted with that tenet;

you were not, and therefore I plead " guilty " of an omission, but " not guilty " of a contradiction.   And even as regards the former, that *omission* is so small that, like the girl accused of infanticide, who when brought before the Judge said in her excuse that the baby was so very very little that it was not worth his while calling it a " baby " at all—I could plead the same for my omission, had I not before my eyes your terrible definition of my " exercising ingenuity."   Well, read the explanation given in my " Notes and Answers " and judge.

By the bye, my good Brother, I have not hitherto suspected in you such a capacity for defending and excusing the *inexcusable* as exhibited by you in *my defence*, of the now famous " exercise of ingenuity."   If the article (reply to C. C. Massey) has been written in the spirit you attribute to me in your letter; and if I, or any one of us has " an inclination to tolerate *subtler* and *more tricksy* ways of pursuing an end " than generally admitted as honourable by the *truth-loving*, *straight-forward* European (is Mr. Hume included in this category?)—indeed you have no right to excuse such a mode of dealing, even *in me*; nor to view it " merely in the nature of spots in the sun," since a spot is a *spot* whether found in the bright luminary or upon a brass candlestick.   But you are mistaken, my dear friend.   There was no *subtle*, no *tricky* mode of dealing, to get her out of the difficulty created by her ambiguous style and ignorance of English, *not her ignorance of the subject*—which is not the same thing and alters entirely the question. Nor was I ignorant of the fact that M. had written to you previously upon the subject, since it was in one of his letters (the last but one before I took the business off his hands) in which he touched upon the subject of " races " for the first [time] and spoke of reincarnations.   If M. told you to beware trusting *Isis* too implicitly, it was because he was *teaching you truth and fact*— and that at the time the passage was written we had not yet decided upon teaching the public indiscriminately.   He gave you several such instances—if you will but re-read his letter—adding that were such and such sentences written in such a way they woulde explain facts now merely hinted upon, far better.

Of course " to C. C. M." the passage must seem wrong and contradictory for it *is* " misleading " as M. said.   Many are the subjects treated upon in *Isis* that even H. P. B. was not allowed to become thoroughly acquainted with; yet they are not contradictory if—" misleading."   To make her say—as she was made by me to say—that the passage criticized was " incomplete, chaotic, vague . . . clumsy as many more passages in that work " was a sufficiently " frank admission " I should think, to satisfy the most crotchetty critic.   To admit " that the passage was wrong," on the other hand, would have amounted to a useless falsehood, for

I maintain that it is *not* wrong; since if it conceals the *whole* truth, it does not distort it in the fragments of that truth as given in *Isis*. The point in C. C. M.'s complaining criticism was not that the whole truth had not been given, but that the truth and facts of 1877 were represented as errors and contradicted in 1882; and it was that point—damaging for the whole Society, its " lay " and inner chelas, and for our doctrine—that had to be shown under its true colours; namely that of an entire misconception due to the fact that the " septenary " doctrine had not yet been divulged to the world at the time when *Isis* was written. And thus it *was* shown. I am sorry you do not find *her* answer written under my direct inspiration " very satisfactory," for it proves to me only that up to this you have not yet grasped very firmly the difference between the sixth and seventh and the fifth, or the *immortal* and the *astral* or *personal* " Monads=Egos." The suspicion is corroborated by what H—X gives in *his* criticism of my explanation at the end of his " letter " in the September number; your letter before me completing the evidence thereupon. No doubt the " *real Ego* inheres in the higher principles which are reincarnated " periodically every one, two, or three or more thousands of years. But the *immortal* Ego the " Individual Monad," is not the *personal* monad which is the 5th; and the passage in *Isis* did not answer Eastern reincarnationists, who maintain in that same *Isis*—had you but read the whole of it—that the *individuality* or the immortal " *Ego* " *has to* re-appear *in every cycle*—but the Western, especially the French reincarnationists, who teach that it is the *personal*, or *astral* monad, the " *moi fluidique* " the *manas*, or the intellectual mind, the 5th principle in short, that is reincarnated each time. Thus, if you read once more C. C. M.'s quoted passage from *Isis* against the " Reviewer of the Perfect Way," you will perhaps find that H. P. B. and myself were perfectly right in maintaining that in the above passage only the " astral monad " was meant. And there is a far more " unsatisfactory shock," *to my mind*, upon finding that you refuse to recognise in the astral monad the *personal Ego*—whereas, all of us call it most undoubtedly by that name, and have so called it for millenniums—than there could ever be in yours when meeting with that monad under its proper name in E. Levi's Fragment on Death!

The " astral monad " *is* the " personal Ego," and therefore, it *never* reincarnates, as the French Spirites will have it, but under " exceptional circumstances; " in which case, reincarnating, *it does not become a shell* but, if successful in its *second* reincarnation will become one, and then gradually lose its personality, after being so to say *emptied* of its best and highest spiritual attributes by the immortal monad or the " *Spiritual Ego*," during the last and supreme struggle. The " jar of feeling " then ought to be on *my* side, as indeed it only " *seemed* to be another illustration of the difference between eastern and western methods," but was *not*— not in this case at any rate. I can readily understand, my dear friend, that in the chilly condition you find yourself (mentally) in, you are prepared to *bask* even in the rays of a funeral pile upon which a living *sutti* is being performed; but why, *why* call it a—Sun, and excuse its spot—the corpse?

The letter addressed to me, which your delicacy would not permit you to read, was *for your perusal* and sent for that purpose. I wanted you to read it.

Your suggestion concerning G. K.'s next trial in art is clever, but not sufficiently as to conceal the white threads of the Jesuitically black insinuation.   G. K. was however caught at it: " *Nous verrons, nous verrons* "! says the French song.

G. Khool says—presenting his most humble salaams—that *you have* " *incorrectly* described the course of events as regards the first portrait." What he says is this: (1) " the day she came " she *did not* ask you " to give her a piece of " etc. (page 300) but after you had begun speaking to her of my portrait, which she doubted much whether you could have.   It is but after half-an-hour's talk over it in the front drawing room—you two forming the two upper points of the triangle, near your office door, and your lady the lower one (he was there he says) that she told you she would try.   It was then that she asked you for " a piece of *thick* white paper " and that you gave her a piece of a *thin* letter paper, which had been touched by some very anti-magnetic person.   However he did, he says, the best he could.   On the day following, as Mrs. S. had looked at it just 27 *minutes* before he did it, he accomplished his task.   It was not " an hour or two before " as you say for he had told the " O. L." to let her see it *just before breakfast*. After breakfast, she asked you for a piece of Bristol board, and you gave her *two* pieces, both marked and not one as you say.   The first time she brought it out it was a *failure*, he says, " with the eyebrow like a leech," and it was finished only during the evening, while you were at the Club, at a dinner at which the old *Upasika* would not go.   And it was *he* again, G. K. " great artist " who had to make away with the " leech," and to correct *cap* and features, and who made it " look like *Master* " (he will insist giving me that name though he is no longer my chela in reality), since M. after spoiling it would not go to the trouble of correcting it but preferred going to sleep instead.   And finally, he tells me, my making fun of the portrait notwithstanding, the likeness is good but would have been better had M. sahib not interfered with it, and he, G. K. [been] allowed to have his own " artistic " ways. Such is his tale, and he therefore, is not satisfied with your description and so he said to *Upasika* who told you something quite different.   Now to my notes.

(1) [1]

Nor do they fret me—particularly.   But as they furnish our mutual friend with a good handle against us, which he is likely to use any day in that nasty way, so pre-eminently his own, I [would] rather explain them once more—with your kind permission.

(2)

Of course, of course; it is our usual way of getting out of difficulties.   Having been " invented " ourselves, we repay the inventors by inventing imaginary races.   There are a good many things more we are charged with having invented.   Well, well, well; there's one thing, at any rate, we can never be accused of inventing; and that is *Mr. Hume himself*.   To invent his like transcends the highest *Siddhi* powers we know of.

And now good friend, before we proceed any further, pray read the appended No. [A].   It is time you should know us *as we are*.   Only, to prove *to you*, if not to him, that we have not *invented* those races, I will give out for your benefit that which has never been given out before.   I will explain to you a whole chapter out of Rhys Davids work on Buddhism, or rather on Lamaism, which, in his natural ignorance he regards as a *corruption* of Buddhism!   Since those gentlemen—the Orientalists—presume to give to the world their *soi-disant* translations and commentaries on our sacred books, let the theosophists show the great ignorance of those " world " pundits, by giving the public the right doctrines and explanations of what they would regard as an absurd, fancy theory.

(3)

And because I admit the superficial or apparent inconsistency —and even that in the case only of one who is so thoroughly unacquainted with our doctrines as you are—is that a reason why they should be regarded as conflicting in reality? Suppose I had written in a previous letter—" the moon *has no* atmosphere " and then went on talking of other things; and told you in another letter " for the moon has an atmosphere of its own " etc. no doubt but that I should stand under the charge of saying to-day *black* and to-morrow *white*.   But where could a Kabalist see in the two sentences a contradiction? I can assure you that he would

[1] K.H.'s replies to the " Famous Contradictions "; the numbers correspond to those which appear in the text of Mr. Sinnett's Queries. See *ante* Letter 24A at pp. 175-77.—ED.

not. For a Kabalist *who knows* that the moon has no atmosphere answering in any respect to that of our earth, but one *of its own*, entirely different from that your men of science would call one, knows also that like the Westerns we Easterns, and Occultists especially, have our own ways of expressing thought as plain to us in their implied meaning as yours are to yourselves. Take for instance into your head to teach your Bearer astronomy. Tell him to-day—" see, how gloriously the sun is setting—see how rapidly *it moves*, how it rises and sets etc.; " and to-morrow try to impress him with the fact that the sun is comparatively motionless and that it is but our earth that loses and then again catches sight of the sun in her diurnal motion; and ten to one, if your pupil has any brains in his head, he will accuse you of flatly contradicting yourself. Would this be a proof of your ignorance of the helio-centric system? And could you be accused with anything like justice of " writing one thing to-day and denying it to-morrow," though your sense of fairness should prompt you to admit that you " can easily understand " the accusation.

Writing my letters, then, as I do, a few lines now and a few words two hours later; having to catch up the thread of the same subject, perhaps with a dozen or more interruptions between the beginning and the end, I cannot promise you anything like western accuracy. *Ergo*—the only " victim of accident " in this case is myself. The innocent cross examination to which I am subjected by you—and that I do not object to—and the positively pre-determined purpose of catching me tripping whenever he can, on Mr. Hume's part,—a proceeding regarded as highly legal and honest in western law, but to which we, Asiatic savages, *object* most emphatically—has given my colleagues and Brothers a high opinion of my proclivities to martyrdom. In their sight I have become a kind of Indo-Tibetan Simeon Stylites. Caught by the lower hook of the Simla interrogation mark and impaled on it, I see myself doomed to equilibrize upon the apex of the semicircle for fear of slipping down at every uncertain motion either back-ward or forward.—Such is the present position of your humble friend. Ever since I undertook the extraordinary task of teaching two grown up pupils with brains in which the methods of western science had crystallized for years; one of whom is willing enough to make room for the new iconoclastic teaching, but who, never-theless, requires a careful handling, while the other will receive nothing but on condition of grouping the subjects as *he wants them to group*, not in their natural order—I have been regarded by all our Chohans as a lunatic. I am seriously asked whether my early association with Western " Pelings " had not made of me a half-Peling and turned me also into a " dzing-dzing " visionary. All this had been expected. I do not complain; I narrate a fact, and humbly demand credit for the same, only hoping it will not be mistaken again for a *subtle and tricky* way of getting out of a new difficulty.

(5)

Every just disembodied *four-fold* entity—whether it died a natural or violent death, from suicide or accident, mentally sane or insane, young or old, good, bad, or indifferent—loses at the instant of death all recollection, it is mentally—*annihilated*; it sleeps it's akasic sleep in the Kama-loka. This state lasts from a few hours, (rarely less) days, weeks, months—sometimes to several years. All this according to the entity, to its mental status at the moment of death, to the character of its death, etc. That remembrance will return slowly and gradually toward the end of the gestation (to the entity or Ego), still more slowly but far more imperfectly and *incompletely* to the *shell*, and *fully* to the Ego at the moment of its entrance into the Devachan. And now, the latter being a state determined and brought by its past life, the Ego does not fall headlong but sinks into it gradually and by easy stages. With the first dawn of that state appears that life (or rather *is once more lived over* by the Ego) from its first day of consciousness to its last. From the most important down to the most trifling event, all are marshalled before the spiritual eye of the Ego; only, unlike the events of real life, those of them remain only that are chosen by the new *liver* (pardon the word) clinging to certain scenes and actors, these remain *permanently*—while all the others fade away to disappear for ever, or to return to their creator—*the shell*. Now try to understand this highly important, because so highly just and retributive law, in its effects. Out of the resurrected Past *nothing* remains but what the Ego has felt *spiritually*—that was evolved by and through, and lived over by his spiritual faculties —be they *love* or *hatred*. All that I am now trying to describe is in truth—indescribable. As no two men, not even two photographs of the same person, nor yet two leaves resemble line for line each other, so no two states in Devachan are like. Unless he be an adept, who can realize such a state in his *periodical* Devachan— how can one be expected to form a correct picture of the same?

(6)

Therefore, there is no contradiction in saying that the ego, once reborn in the Devachan, " retains for a certain time proportionate to its earth life a *complete recollection* of his (Spiritual) life on earth." Here again the omission of the word " Spiritual " alone produced a misunderstanding!

(7)

All those that do not slip down into the 8th sphere—*go to the Devachan.* Where's the point made or the contradiction?

(8)

The Devachan *State*, I repeat, can be as little described or explained, by giving a however minute and graphic description of the state of one ego taken at random, as all the human lives collectively could be described by the " Life of Napoleon " or that of any other man.   There are millions of various states of happiness and misery, *emotional* states having their source in the *physical* as well as the *spiritual* faculties and senses, and only the latter surviving.   An honest labourer will feel differently from an honest *millionaire*.   Miss Nightingale's *state* will differ considerably from that of a young bride who dies before the consummation of what she regards as happiness.   The two former love their families; the philanthropist—humanity; the girl centres the whole world in her future husband; the *melomaniac* knows of no *higher* state of bliss and happiness than music—the most divine and *spiritual* of arts.   The Devachan merges from its highest into its lowest degree—by insensible gradations; while from the last step of *Devachan*, the Ego will often find itself in *Avitchi's* faintest state, which, towards the end of the " spiritual selection " of events may become a *bona fide* " Avitchi."   Remember, every feeling is relative.   There is neither *good* nor *evil*, *happiness* nor *misery per se*. *The transcendent, evanescent bliss of an adulterer*, who by his act murders the happiness of a husband, is no less *spiritually* born for its criminal nature.   If a remorse of conscience (the latter *proceeding always from the Sixth Principle*) has only once been felt during the period of bliss and really spiritual love, born in the sixth and fifth, however polluted by the desires of the fourth, or *Kamarupa*—then this remorse *must* survive and *will accompany incessantly the scenes of pure love*.   I need not enter into details, since a physiological expert, as I take you to be, need hardly have his imagination and intuitions prompted by a psychological observer of my sort.   Search in the depths of your conscience and memory, and try to see what are the scenes that are likely to take their firm hold upon you, when once more in their presence you find yourself *living them over* again; and that, ensnared, you will have forgotten all the rest—this letter among other things, since in the course of events it will come far later on in the panorama of your resurrected life.   I have *no right* to look into your *past* life.   Whenever I may have caught glimpses of it, I have invariably turned my eyes away, for I have to deal with the *present* A. P. Sinnett—(also and by far more " a new invention " than the ex-A. P. S.)—not with the ancient man.

Yes; *Love* and *Hatred* are the only immortal feelings; but the gradations of tones along the seven by seven scales of the whole key-board of life, are numberless.   And, since it is those two feelings—(or, to be correct, shall I risk being misunderstood again

and say those two poles of man's " Soul " which is a unity?)—
that mould the future state of man, whether for *Devachan* or *Avitchi*
then the variety of such states must also be inexhaustible. And
this brings us to your complaint or charge, number—

(9)

—for, having eliminated from your past life the Ratigans and
Reeds who with you have never transcended beyond the boundaries
of the lower portion of your fifth principle with its vehicle—the
kama—what is it but the " partial remembrance " of a life? The
lines marked with your *reddest* pencil are also disposed of. For
how can you dispute the fact that music and harmony are for a
Wagner, a Paganini, the King of Bavaria and so many other *true*
artists and melomanes, an object of the profoundest spiritual love
and veneration? With your permission I will not change one word
in clause 9.

(10)

Pity you have not followed your quotations with personal commentaries. I fail to comprehend in what respect you object to
the word " dream "? Of course both bliss and misery are but a
dream; and as they are purely spiritual they are " intensified."

(11)

Answered.

(12A & 12B)

Had I but written,—when answering Mr. Hume's objections,
who after statistical calculations made with the evident intention
of *crushing* our teaching, maintained that after all spiritualists were
right and the majority of séance rooms spooks *were* " Spirits "—
" In no case then, with the exception of suicides and shells "—
and those accidents who die full of some engrossing earthly passion—" is
there any possibility for any other, etc., etc." I would have been
perfectly right and *pukka* as a " professor "? To think that, eager
as you are to accept doctrines that contradict in some most
important points physical science from first to last—you should
have consented to Mr. Hume's suggestion to split hairs over a
simple omission! My dear friend, permit me to remark that simple
common sense ought to have whispered you that one who says
one day: " *in no case* then etc.: " and a few days later denies having
ever pronounced the word *never*—is not only *no adept* but must be
either suffering from softening of the brain or some other
" accident." " On margin I said rarely but I have not pronounced the word *never* "—refers to the *margin* of the proof of your
letter N. II; that margin—or rather to avoid a fresh accusation—
the piece of paper upon which I had written some remarks referring

to the subject and glued to the margin of your proof—you have cut out as well as the four lines of poetry. Why you have done so is known better to yourself. But the word *never* refers to that margin.

To one sin though I *do* plead " guilty." That sin was a very acute feeling of irritation against Mr. Hume upon receiving his triumphant statistical letter; the answer to which you found incorporated in yours when I wrote for you the materials for your answer to Mr. Khandalawala's letter that you had sent back to H. P. B. Had I not been irritated I would not have become guilty of the omission, perhaps. This now is *my* Karma. I had no business to feel irritated, or lose my temper; but that letter of his was I believe the seventh or the eighth of that kind received by me during that fortnight. And I must say, that our friend has the most knavish way of using his intellect in raising the most unexpected sophisms to tickle people's nerves with, that I have ever known! Under the pretext of strict logical reasoning, he will perform feigned thrusts at his antagonist—whenever unable to find a vulnerable spot, and then, caught and exposed, he will answer in the most innocent way: " Why, it is for your own good, and you ought to feel grateful! If I were an adept I would always know what my correspondent *really* meant," etc., etc. Being an " adept " in some small matters I *do* know what he really means; and that his meaning amounts to this: were we to divulge to him the whole of our philosophy, leaving no *inconsistency* unexplained, it would still do no good, whatever. For, as in the observation embodied in the Hudibrasian couplet:

> " These fleas have other fleas to bite 'em,
> And these—*their* fleas *ad infinitum.* . . ."

—so with his objections and arguments. Explain him one, and he will find a flaw in the explanation; satisfy him by showing that the latter was after all correct, and he will fly at the opponent for speaking too slow or too rapidly. It is an IMPOSSIBLE task—and I give it up. Let it last until the whole breaks under its own weight. He says " I can kiss no Pope's toe," forgetting that no one has ever asked him to do so; " I can love, but I cannot worship " he tells me. *Gush*—he can love no one, and *nobody* but A. O. Hume, and never has. And that really one could almost exclaim " Oh Hume,—gush is thy name! "—is shown in the following that I transcribe from one of his letters: " If for no other reason, I should love M. for his entire devotion to you—*and you I have always loved* (!). Even when most cross with you—as one always is most sensitive with those one cares most about—*even when I was fully persuaded you were a myth, for even then my heart yearned to you as it often does to an avowedly fictitious character.*"   A sentimental

Becky Sharp writing to an imaginary lover, could hardly express her feelings better!

I will see to your scientific questions next week. I am not at home at present, but quite near to Darjeeling, in the Lamasery, the object of poor H. P. B.'s longings. I thought of leaving by the end of September but find it rather difficult on account of Nobin's boy. Most probably, also, I will have to interview in my own skin the Old Lady if M. brings her here. And he has to bring her—or lose her for ever—at least, as far as the physical triad is concerned. And now good-bye. I ask you again—do not frighten my little man; he may prove useful to you some day—only do not forget—*he is but an appearance.*

Yours,

K. H.

LETTER No. 25

Devachan Notes Latest Additions.　Received Feb. 2nd, 1883.

ANSWERS TO QUERIES

(1) Why should it be supposed that *Devachan* is a monotonous condition only because some one moment of earthly sensation is indefinitely perpetuated—stretched, so to say, throughout aeons? It is not, it *cannot* be so. This would be contrary to all analogies and antagonistic to the law of effects under which results are proportioned to antecedent energies. To make it clear you must keep in mind that there are two fields of causal manifestation, to wit: the objective and subjective. So the grosser energies, those which operate in the heavier or denser conditions of matter manifest objectively in physical life, their outcome being the new personality of each birth included within the grand cycle of the evoluting individuality. The moral and spiritual activities find their sphere of effects in " Devachan." For example: the vices, physical attractions, etc.—say, of a philosopher may result in the birth of a new philosopher, a king, a merchant, a rich Epicurean, or any other personality whose make-up was inevitable from the preponderating proclivities of the being in the next preceding birth. Bacon, for inst.: whom a poet called—

" The wisest, greatest, *meanest* of mankind "—

might reappear in his next incarnation as a greedy money-getter, with extraordinary intellectual capacities. But the moral and spiritual qualities of the previous Bacon would also have to find a field in which their energies could expand themselves. Devachan is such field. Hence—all the great plans of moral reform, of

intellectual and spiritual research into abstract principles of nature,
all the divine aspirations, would, in Devachan come to fruition,
and the abstract entity previously known as the great Chancellor
would occupy itself in this inner world of its own preparation,
living, if not quite what one would call a *conscious* existence, at
least a dream of such realistic vividness that none of the life-
realities could ever match it. And this " dream " lasts until
Karma is satisfied in that direction, the ripple of force reaches
the edge of its cyclic basin, and the being moves into the next
area of causes. This, it may find in the same world as before,
or another, according to his or her stage of progression through
the necessary rings and rounds of human development.

Then—how can you think that " but one moment of earthly
sensation *only* is selected for perpetuation "? Very true, that
" moment " lasts from the first to last; but then it lasts but as
the key-note of the whole harmony, a definite tone of appreciable
pitch, around which cluster and develop in progressive variations
of melody and as endless variations on a theme, all the aspirations,
desires, hopes, dreams, which, in connection with that particular
" moment " had ever crossed the *dreamer's* brain during his life-
time, without having ever found their realization on earth, and
which he now finds fully realized in all their vividness in Devachan, without ever suspecting that all that blissful reality is but
the progeny begotten by his own fancy, the effects of the mental
causes produced by himself. That particular one *moment* which
will be most intense and uppermost in the thoughts of his dying
brain at the time of dissolution will of course regulate all the other
" moments "; still the latter—minor and less vivid though they
be—will be there also, having their appointed place in this
phantasmagoric marshalling of past dreams, and must give variety
to the whole. No man on earth but has some decided predilection if not a domineering passion; no person, however humble
and poor—and often because of all that—but indulges in dreams
and desires unsatisfied though these be. Is this monotony? Would
you call such variations *ad infinitum* on the one theme, and that
theme modelling itself on, and taking colour and its definite shape
from, that group of desires which was the most intense during life
" a blank destitution of all knowledge in the devachanic mind "—
seeming " in a measure *ignoble* "? Then verily, either you have
failed, as you say, to take in my meaning, or it is I who am to
blame. I must have sorely failed to convey the right meaning,
and have to confess my inability to describe the—*indescribable*.
The latter is a difficult task, good friend. Unless the intuitive
perceptions of a trained chela come to the rescue, no amount of
description—however graphic—will help. Indeed, no adequate
words to express the difference between a state of mind on earth,

and one outside of its sphere of action; no English terms in existence,. equivalent to ours; *nothing*—but unavoidable (as due to early Western education) preconceptions, hence—lines of thought in a. wrong direction in the learner's mind, to help us in this inoculation of entirely new thoughts! You are right. Not only " ordinary people "—your readers—but even such idealists and highly intellectual units as Mr. C. C. M. will fail, I am afraid, to seize the true idea, will *never* fathom it to its very depths. Perhaps, you may some day realize better than you do now, one of the chief reasons for our unwillingness to impart *our* Knowledge to European candidates. Only read Mr. Roden Noel's disquisitions and diatribes in *Light*! Indeed, indeed, you ought to have answered them as advised by me through H. P. B. Your silence is a brief triumph to the pious gentleman, and seems like a *desertion* of poor Mr. Massey.

" A man in the way to learn something of the mysteries of nature seems in a higher state of existence to begin with on earth than that which nature apparently provides for him as a reward for his best deeds."

Perhaps " apparently "—not so in *reality*, when the *modus operandi* of nature is correctly understood. Then that other misconception: " The more merit, the longer period of Devachan. But then in Devachan . . . all sense of the lapse of time is lost; a minute is as a thousand years . . . *á quoi bon* then, etc."

This remark and such ways of looking at things might as well apply to the whole of Eternity, to Nirvāna, Pralaya, and what not. Say at once that the whole system of being, of existence separate and collective, of nature objective and subjective are but idiotic, aimless facts, a gigantic fraud of that nature which, meeting with little sympathy with Western philosophy, has, moreover, the cruel disapprobation of the best " lay-chela." *A quoi bon*, in such a case, this preaching of our doctrines, all this uphill work and swimming in *adversum flumen*? Why should the West be so anxious then to learn anything from the East, since it is evidently unable to digest that which can never meet the requirements of the special tastes of its Esthetics. Sorry outlook for us, since even *you* fail to take in the whole magnitude of our philosophy, or to even embrace at one scope a small corner—the Devachan—of those sublime and infinite horizons of " after life." I do not want to discourage you. I would only draw your attention to the formidable difficulties encountered by us in every attempt we make to explain our metaphysics to Western minds, even among the most intelligent. Alas, my friend, you seem as unable to assimilate our mode of thinking, as to digest our food, or enjoy our melodies!

No; there are no clocks, no timepieces in Devachan, my esteemed chela, though the whole Cosmos is a gigantic chronometer in one sense. Nor do we, mortals,—*ici bas même*—take much, if any, cognizance of *time* during periods of happiness and bliss, and find them ever too short; a fact that does not in the least prevent us from enjoying that happiness all the same—when it does come. Have you ever given a thought to this little possibility that, perhaps, it is because their cup of bliss is full to its brim, that the " devachanee " loses " all sense of the lapse of time "; and that it is something that those who land in *Avitchi* do not, though as much as the *devachanee*, the *Avitchee* has no cognizance of time—*i.e.*, of our earthly calculations of periods of time? I may also remind you in this connection that *time is something created entirely by ourselves;* that while one short second of intense agony may appear, even on earth, as an eternity to one man, to another, more fortunate, hours, days, and sometimes whole years may seem to flit like one brief moment; and that finally, of all the sentient and conscious beings on earth, man is the only animal that takes any cognizance of time, although it makes him neither happier nor wiser. How then, can I explain to you that which *cannot* feel, since you seem unable to comprehend it? Finite similes are unfit to express the abstract and the infinite; nor can the objective ever mirror the subjective. To realize the bliss in *Devachan*, or the woes in *Avitchi*, you have to assimilate them—as we do. Western critical idealism (as shown in Mr. Roden Noel's attacks) has still to learn the difference that exists between the *real being* of super-sensible objects and the shadowy subjectivity of the ideas it has reduced them to. *Time* is not a predicate conception and can, therefore, neither be proved nor analysed, according to the methods of superficial philosophy. And, unless we learn to counteract the negative results of that method of drawing our conclusions agreeably to the teachings of the so-called " system of pure reason," and to distinguish between the matter and the form of our knowledge of sensible objects, we can never arrive at correct, definite conclusions. The case in hand, as defended by me against your (very natural) misconception is a good proof of the shallowness and even fallacy of that " system of pure (materialistic) reason." Space and time may be—as Kant has it—not the product but the regulators of the sensations, but only so far as our sensations on *earth* are concerned, not those in *Devachan*. There we do not find the *a priori* ideas of this " space and time " controlling the perceptions of the denizen of *Devachan* in respect to the objects of *his* sense; but, on the contrary, we discover that it is the *devachanee* himself who absolutely creates both and annihilates them at the same time. Thus, the " after states," so called, can never be correctly judged by practical reason since the latter can have active being only in the sphere of *final* causes or ends, and can hardly be regarded with Kant (with whom it means on one page reason and on the next—will) as the highest spiritual power in man, having for its sphere that WILL. The above is not dragged in—as you may think—for the sake of an (too far stretched, perhaps) argument, but with an eye to a future discussion " at home," as you express it, with students and admirers of Kant and Plato that you will have to encounter.

In a plainer language, I will now tell you the following, and it will be no fault of mine if you still fail to comprehend its full meaning. As physical existence has its cumulative intensity from infancy to prime, and its diminishing energy thenceforward to dotage and death, so the dream-life of Devachan is lived correspondentially. Hence you are right in saying that the " Soul " can never awake to its mistake and find itself " cheated by nature "— the more so as, strictly speaking, the whole of the human life and its boasted realities are no better than such " cheating." But you are wrong in pandering to the prejudices and preconceptions of the Western readers (no Asiatic will ever agree with you upon this point) when you add that " there is a sense of *unreality* about the whole affair which is painful to the mind," since you are the first one to feel that it is no doubt due much more to " an imperfect grasp of the nature of the existence " in Devachan—than to any defect in our system. Hence—my orders to a chela to reproduce in an Appendix to your article extracts from this letter and explanations calculated to disabuse the reader, and to obliterate, as far as possible, the painful impression this confession of yours is sure to produce on him. The whole paragraph is dangerous. I do not feel myself justified in crossing it out, since it is evidently the expression of your real feelings, kindly, though—pardon me for saying so—a little clumsily white-washed with an apparent defence of this (to your mind) *weak* point of the system. But it is not so, believe me. Nature cheats no more the *devachanee* than she does the living, physical man. Nature provides for him far more *real* bliss and happiness *there* than she does *here*, where all the conditions of evil and chance are against him, and his inherent helplessness —that of a straw violently blown hither and thither by every remorseless wind—has made unalloyed happiness on this earth an utter impossibility for the human being, whatever his chances and condition may be. Rather call this life an ugly, horrid nightmare, and you will be right. To call the Devachan existence a " dream " in any other sense but that of a conventional term, well suited to [y]our languages all full of misnomers—is to renounce for ever the knowledge of the esoteric doctrine—the sole custodian of truth. Let me then try once more to explain to you a few of the many states in Devachan and—Avitchi.

As in actual earth-life, so there is for the Ego in Devachan—the first flutter of psychic life, the attainment of prime, the gradual exhaustion of force passing into semi-unconsciousness, gradual oblivion and lethargy, total oblivion and—not death but birth: birth into another personality, and the resumption of action which daily begets new congeries of causes, that must be worked out in another term of Devachan, and still another physical rebirth as a new personality. What the lives in *Devachan* and upon Earth shall be respectively in each instance is determined by Karma. And this weary round of birth upon birth must be ever and ever run through, until the being reaches the end of the seventh round, or—attains in the interim the wisdom of an Arhat, then that of a Buddha and thus gets relieved for a round or two,—having learned how to burst through the vicious circles—and to pass periodically into the Paranirvana.

But suppose it is not a question of a Bacon, a Gœthe, a Shelley, a Howard, but of some hum-drum person, some colourless, planless personality, who never impinged upon the world enough to make himself felt: what then? Simply that his devachanic state is as colourless and feeble as was his personality. How could it be otherwise since cause and effect are equal? But suppose a case of a monster of wickedness, sensuality, ambition, avarice, pride, deceit, etc., but who nevertheless has a germ or germs of something better, flashes of a more divine nature—where is he to go? The said spark smouldering under a heap of dirt will counteract, nevertheless, the attraction of the eighth sphere, whither fall but absolute *nonentities*; " failures of nature " to be remodelled entirely, whose divine monad separated itself from the five principles during their life-time, (whether in the next preceding or several preceding births, since such cases are also on our records), and who have lived as *soulless* human beings.[1] These persons whose sixth principle has left them (while the seventh having lost its *vahan* (or vehicle) can exist *independently* no longer) their fifth or animal Soul of course goes down " the bottomless pit." This will perhaps make Eliphas Levi's hints still more clear to you, if you read over what he says, and my remarks on the margin, thereon (see *Theosophist*, October, 1881, Article " Death ") and reflect upon the words used, such as *drones*, etc. Well, the first named entity then, cannot, with all its wickedness go to the eighth sphere—since his wickedness *is of a too spiritual, refined nature*. He is a *monster*—not a mere *Soulless* brute. He must not be simply *annihilated* but PUNISHED; for, annihilation, *i.e.* total oblivion, and the fact of being *snuffed* out of conscious existence, constitutes *per se* no punishment, and as Voltaire expressed it: " *le néant* ne laisse pas d'avoir du bon."

---

[1] See *Isis*, Vol. 2, pp. 368 and 369—the word *Soul* standing there for " Spiritual " Soul, of course, which, whenever it leaves a person " Soul-less " becomes the cause of the fifth principle (Animal Soul) sliding down into the eighth sphere.

Here is no taper-glimmer to be puffed out by a zephyr, but a strong, positive, maleficent energy, fed and developed by circumstances, some of which may have really been beyond his control. There must be for such a nature a state corresponding to Devachan, and this is found in *Avitchi*—the perfect antithesis of *Devachan* —vulgarized by the Western nations into Hell and Heaven, and which you have entirely lost sight of in your "Fragment." Remember: "To be immortal in good one must identify himself with Good (or God); to be immortal in evil—with evil (or Satan)." Misconceptions of the true value of such terms as "Spirit," "Soul," "individuality," "personality," and "immortality" (especially) —provoke wordy wars between a great number of idealistic debaters, besides Messrs. C. C. M. and Roden Noel. And, to complete your Fragment without risking to fall again under the mangling tooth of the latter honourable gentleman's criticism—I found it necessary to add to Devachan—Avitchi as its complement and applying to it the same laws as to the former. This is done, with your permission, in the *Appendix*.[1]

Having explained the situation sufficiently I may now answer your query No. 1 directly. Yes, certainly there *is* "a change of occupation," a continual change in Devachan, just as much—and far more—as there is in the life of any man or woman who happens to follow his or *her whole life* one sole occupation whatever it may be; with that difference, that to the *Devachanee* his special occupation is always pleasant and fills *his* life with rapture. Change then there must be, for that dream-life is but the fruition, the harvest-time of those psychic seed-germs dropped from the tree of physical existence in our moments of dreams and hopes, fancy-glimpses of bliss and happiness stifled in an ungrateful social soil, blooming in the rosy dawn of Devachan, and ripening under its ever fructifying sky. No failures *there*, no disappointments! If man had but *one* single moment of ideal happiness and experience during his life—as you think—even then, if Devachan exists, it could not be as you erroneously suppose, the indefinite prolongation of that "single moment," but the infinite developments, the various incidents and events, based upon, and outflowing from, that one "single moment" or moments, as the case may be; all in short that would suggest itself to the "dreamer's" fancy. That one note, as I said, struck from the lyre of life, would form but the Key-note of the being's subjective state, and work out into numberless harmonic tones and semi-tones of psychic phantasmagoria. There—all unrealized hopes, aspirations, dreams, become fully realized, and the *dreams* of the objective become the *realities* of the subjective existence. And there behind the curtain of Maya its vapours and deceptive appearances are perceived by the adept,

[1] This Appendix will be found in *The Theosophist*, March, 1883, p. 137.—EDS.

who has learnt the great secret how to penetrate thus deeply into the Arcana of being.

Doubtless my question whether you had experienced monotony during what you consider the happiest moment of your life has entirely misled you. This letter, thus, is the just penance for my laziness to amplify the explanation.

Query (2) What cycle is meant?

The " minor cycle " meant is, of course, the completion of the seventh *Round*, as decided upon and explained. Besides that at the end of each of the seven rounds comes a *less* " full " remembrance; only of the devachanic experiences taking place between the numerous births at the end of each *personal* life. But the *complete* recollection of all the lives—(earthly and devachanic) *omniscience*—in short—comes but at the great end of the full seven Rounds (unless one had become in the interim a Bodhisatwa, an Arhat)—the " threshold " of Nirvana meaning an indefinite period. Naturally a man, a *Seventh-rounder* (who completes his earthly migrations at the beginning of the last race and ring) will have to wait longer at that threshold than one of the very last of those Rounds. That *Life* of the Elect between the minor Pralaya and Nirvana—or rather *before* the Pralaya is the *Great* Reward, the grandest, in fact, since it makes of the Ego (though he may never have been an adept, but simply a worthy virtuous man in *most* of his existences)—virtually a God, an omniscient, conscious being, a candidate—for eternities of aeons—for a Dhyan Chohan. . . . Enough—I am betraying the mysteries of initiation. But what has NIRVANA to do with the recollections of objective existences? That is a state still higher and in which all things objective are forgotten. It is a State of absolute Rest and assimilation with Parabrahm—it is Parabrahm itself. Oh, for the sad ignorance of our philosophical truths in the West, and for the inability of your greatest intellects to seize the true spirit of those teachings. What shall we—what can we do!

Query (3) You postulate an intercourse of entities in Devachan which applies only to the mutual relationship of physical existence. Two sympathetic souls will each work out its own devachanic sensations, making the other a sharer in its subjective bliss, but yet each i⁻ dissociated from the other as regards actual mutual intercourse. For what companionship could there be between two subjective entities which are not even as material as that ethereal body-shadow—the *Mayavi-rupa*?

Query (4) Devachan is a state, not a locality. Kama-Loka, Rupa-Loka and Arupa-Loka, are the three spheres of ascending spirituality in which the several groups of subjective entities find

their attractions.   In the Kama-Loka (semi-physical sphere) dwell
the shells, the victims and suicides; and this sphere is divided into
innumerable regions and sub-regions corresponding to the mental
states of the comers at their hour of death.   This is the glorious
" Summer-land " of the Spiritualists, to whose horizons is limited
the vision of their best seers—vision imeprfect and deceptive because
untrained and non-guided by *Alaya Vijnāna* (hidden knowledge).
Who in the West knows anything of true *Sahalokadhatu*, the mysterious Chiliocosm out of the many regions of which but three
can be given out to the outside world, the *Tribhuvana* (three
worlds) namely: Kama, Rupa, and Arupa-Lokas.   Yet see the
sad mess produced in the Western minds by the mention of even
those three! See " Light " of January 6th!

Behold your friend (M. A. Oxon) notifying the world of his
readers that on your assumption in your " Secret doctrine "—
" no graver indictment could be brought against any man by his
bitterest foe " than the one you bring against us—" these mysterious unknown."   It is not such bitter criticisms that are likely
to draw out more of our knowledge, or to make the " unknown "
more known.   And then, the pleasure of teaching a public one of
whose great authorities (Roden Noel) says a few pages further on,
that theosophists are endowing " shells " with *simulated* consciousness.   See the difference one word will make.   If the word
" assimilated " instead of ' simulated " had been written the true
idea would have been conveyed that the shells' consciousness is
assimilated from the medium and living persons present, whereas
now——! But of course, it is not our European critics, but our
Asiatic chelas' expositions that " seem absolutely Protean in their
ever shifting variety."   The man has to be answered and set right
anyhow, whether by yourself or Mr. Massey.   But alas! the latter
knows but little, and you,—you look at our conception of Devachan
with more than " discomfort "! But to resume.

From Kama Loka, then, in the great Chiliocosm, once awakened
from their post-mortem torpor the newly translated " Souls "
go all (*but the shells*) according to their attractions, either to Devachan or Avitchi.   And those two *states* are again differentiating *ad
infinitum*—their ascending degrees of spirituality deriving their
names from the lokas in which they are induced.   For instance:
the sensations, perceptions and ideation of a *devachanee* in *Rupa*-
Loka, will, of course, be of a less subjective nature than they would
be in Arupa-Loka, in both of which the Devachanic experiences
will vary in their presentation to the subject-entity, not only as
regards form, colour, and substance, but also in their formative
potentialities.   But not even the most exalted experience of a
monad in the highest Devachanic state in *Arupa*-Loka (the last of
the seven states)—is comparable to that perfectly subjective

condition of pure spirituality from which the monad emerged to
" descend into matter," and to which at the completion of the
grand cycle it must return.   Nor is Nirvana itself comparable to
Para-Nirvana.

Query (5) Reviving consciousness begins after the struggle in
Kama-Loka at the door of Devachan, and only *after* the " gestation
period."   Please turn to my responses upon the subject in your
" Famous contradictions."

Query (6) Your deductions as to the indefinite prolongation in
Devachan of some one moment of earthly bliss having been
unwarranted, your question in the last paragraph of this interro-
gatory need not be considered.   The stay in Devachan is proportioned to the unfinished psychic impulses originating in earth-life:
those persons whose attractions were preponderatingly material
will sooner be drawn back into rebirth by the force of *Tanha*.   As
our London opponent truly remarks, these subjects (metaphysical)
are only partly for understanding.   A higher faculty belonging to
the higher life must see, and it is truly impossible to force it upon
one's understanding—merely in words.   One must see with his
spiritual eye, hear with his Dharmakayic ear, feel with the sensations of his *Ashta-vijnāna* (spiritual " I ") before he can comprehend
this doctrine fully; otherwise it may but increase one's " discomfort,"
and add to his knowledge very little.

Query (7) The " reward provided by nature for men who are
benevolent in a large, systematic way " and who have not focussed
their affections upon an individual or speciality, is that—if pure—
they pass the quicker for that through the Kama and Rupa Lokas
into the higher sphere of *Tribhuvana*, since it is one where the
formulation of abstract ideas and the consideration of general
principles fill the thought of its occupants.   Personality is the
synonym for limitation, and the more contracted the person's
ideas, the closer will he cling to the lower spheres of being, the
longer loiter on the plane of selfish social intercourse.   The social
status of a being is, of course, a result of Karma; the law being
that " like attracts like."   The renascent being is drawn into the
gestative current with which the preponderating attractions coming
over from the last birth make him assimilate.   Thus one who died
a ryot may be reborn a king, and the dead sovereign may next see
the light in a coolie's tent.   This law of attraction asserts itself in
a thousand " accidents of birth "—than which there could be no
more flagrant misnomer.   When you realize at least the following
—that the *skandhas* are the elements of limited existence, then will
you have realized also one of the conditions of Devachan which
has now such a profoundly unsatisfactory outlook for you.   Nor

16

are your inferences (as regards the well-being and enjoyment of the upper classes being due to a better Karma) quite correct in their general application. They have a eudæ-monistic ring about them which is hardly reconcilable with Karmic Law, since those " well-being and enjoyment " are oftener the causes of a new and overloaded Karma than the production or effects of the latter. Even as a " broad rule " poverty and humble condition in life are less a cause of sorrow than wealth and high birth, but of that—later on. My answers are once more assuming the shape of a volume rather than the decent aspect of a letter. " Writing a new book, or for the *Theosophist*? " Well do you not think that (since your desire is to reach not merely the *most* but also the *most receptive* minds) you had better write the former, as well as *for* the latter? You might put into *Esoteric Buddhism*—an excellent title bye the bye—such matter as would be a sequel to, or amplification of what has appeared in the *Theosophist*, a systematic, thoughtful exposition of what was and will be given in the Journal in snatched out brief Fragments. I am specially anxious—on M.'s account— that the Journal should be made as much as possible a success; should be circulated more than it is now in England. Your new book drawing, as it is sure to, the attention of the most educated, thoughtful portion of the Western public to the organ of " Esoteric Buddhism " *par excellence*—would thus do it a world of good, and both would prove of mutual assistance. Do not lose sight of Lillie's *Buddha and Early Buddhism* when you write it. With its host of fallacies, unwarranted assumptions and distortion of facts and even Sanskrit and Pali words, this snobbish volume had nevertheless the greatest success with Spiritualists and even mystically inclined Christians. I will have it slightly reviewed by Subba Row or H. P. B., furnishing them with notes myself, but of this more in some future letter. You have ample materials to work upon in my notes and papers. You have given but a few of the many points touched by me and amplified and re-amplified in heaps of letters, as I do now. You could work out of them any number of new articles and Fragments for the magazine, and have enough and to spare—left over for the book. And these in their turn may be followed up in a third volume later on. It may be well to always keep this plan in mind.

Your " wild scheme " with Darjeeling, good friend, as its objective point, is *not wild*, but simply impracticable. The time has not yet come. But the drift of your energies is carrying you slowly yet steadily in the direction of personal intercourse. I will not say that I desire it as much as you do, for seeing you nearly every day of my life I care very little for *objective* intercourse; but for your sake I would if I could, precipitate that interview. However——? Meanwhile, be happy in knowing that you have done more real good to your kind within the two past years than in many previous years. And—to yourself also.

I am quite sure that you do not sympathize with the selfish feeling that prompts the London Branch to wish to withhold even their small proportion of pecuniary support—amounting to a few guineas a year—from the Parent Society. Who of the members would ever think of refusing, or trying to avoid payment of fees to any other Society, Club, or Scientific Association he may happen to belong to? It is this indifference and selfishness that have permitted them to stand by idle and calm from the first, and see the two in India giving their last rupee (and the Upasika actually selling her jewellery—for the honour of the Society)—though many of the British members are far better able to afford the necessary sacrifices than they. Mr. Olcott's sister is actually starving in America, and the poor man, loving her dearly as he does, would not nevertheless spare Rs. 100 from the Society's, or rather the *Theosophist's* fund to relieve her with six small children had not H. P. B. insisted upon, and M. given a small sum for it.

However, I have told Mr. Olcott to send you the necessary official authority to compound the fees or make any other business agreement at London that you may think best. But remember, my very valued brother, that if poor Hindu clerks on Rs. 20 or 30 salaries are expected to help pay the Society's expenses with that fee, it is sheer injustice to totally exempt the far richer London members. Do *justice*, " though the heavens fall." Yet, if concessions are required to *local* prejudices, you are certainly better qualified than we, to see, and hence to negotiate according to the fitness of things. By all means put " the money relations on a better footing " than at present, if the financial wind has to be tempered for the shorn Peling-lamb. I have faith in *your* wisdom my friend, though you would have a certain right to be fast losing yours in mine, considering how tight the negotiations for the *Phoenix*-capital prove. You must have understood that I am still, and notwithstanding the Chohan's approval of my " Lay-Chela " —under last year's restrictions, and cannot bring to bear on the parties concerned all the psychic powers that I otherwise could. Besides, our laws and restrictions with regard to money or any financial operations whether within or outside our Association, are extremely severe—inexorable on some points. We have to proceed very cautiously; hence—the delay. But I do hope that you yourself think that something has already been done in that direction.

Yes; " K. H. did " mean that the review of " Mr. Isaacs should appear in the *Theosophist*," and " By the Author of the Occult World," so do send it before you go. And, for the sake of old

" Sam Ward " I would like to see it *noticed* in the " Pioneer."
But that does not matter much, now that you leave it.

Thereupon—Salam, and best wishes. I am extremely busy
with preparations of initiation. Several of my chelas—Djual-
khool among others—are striving to reach " the other shore."

Yours faithfully,

K. H.

SECTION III

PROBATION AND CHELASHIP

LETTER No. 26

K.H.'s Confidential Memo about Old Lady. Received Simla, Autumn, 1881.

I am painfully aware of the fact that the habitual incoherence of her statements—especially when excited—and her strange ways make her in your opinion a very undesirable transmitter of our messages. Nevertheless, kind Brothers, once that you have learned the truth; once told, that this unbalanced mind, the seeming incongruity of her speeches and ideas, her nervous excitement, all that in short which is so calculated to upset the feelings of sober minded people, whose notions of reserve and manners are shocked by such strange outbursts of what they regard as her temper, and which so revolt you,—once that *you know* that nothing of it is due to any fault of hers, you may, perchance, be led to regard her in quite a different light. Notwithstanding that the time is not quite ripe to let you entirely into the secret; and that you are hardly yet prepared to understand the great Mystery, even if told of it, owing to the great injustice and wrong done, I am empowered to allow you a glimpse behind the veil. This state of hers is intimately connected with her occult training in Tibet, and due to her being sent out alone into the world to gradually prepare the way for others. After nearly a century of fruitless search, our chiefs had to avail themselves of the only opportunity to send out a European *body* upon European soil to serve as a connecting link between that country and our own. You do not understand? Of course not. Please then, remember, what she tried to explain, and what you gathered tolerably well from her, namely the fact of the *seven* principles in the *complete* human being. Now, no man or woman, unless he be an initiate of the " fifth circle," can leave the precincts of *Bod-Lhas* and return back into the world in his integral whole—if I may use the expression. *One* at least of his seven satellites has to remain behind for two reasons; the first to form the necessary connecting link, the wire of transmission—the second as the safest warranter that certain things will never be divulged. She is no exception to the rule, and you have seen another exemplar—a highly intellectual man—who had to leave one of his skins behind; hence, is considered highly eccentric. The bearing and status of the remaining *six* depend upon the inherent qualities, the psycho-physiological peculiarities of the person, especially upon the idiosyncracies transmitted by what modern science calls " atavism." Acting in accordance with my wishes, my brother M. made to you through her a certain offer, if you remember. You had but to accept it, and at any time you liked you would have had for an hour or more the real *baitchooly* to converse with, instead of the psychological cripple you generally have to deal with now. Yesterday it was his mistake. He ought not to have sent her to deliver the message to Mr. Sinnett in the state she was in. But to hold her responsible for her purely physiological excitement, and to let her see your contemptuous smiles—was positively *sinful*. Pardon me, my Brothers and good Sirs, my plain talk. I act but in accord with what was asked from me by yourself in your letter. I took the trouble to " ascertain the spirit and meaning " with which everything in Mr. Sinnett's room was said and done; and though having no right to " condemn " you—since you were ignorant of the true state of things—I cannot otherwise but strongly disapprove of that which, however much polished outwardly, would have been even under quite ordinary circumstances—CRUELTY still. *Buss*! [1]

LETTER No. 27

Received Simla, Autumn, 1881.

I foresaw that which now happens. In my Bombay letter I advised you to be prudent as to what you allowed S.M. to learn of + and his own mediumship, suggesting that he should be told merely the substance of what I said. When, watching you at Allahabad I saw you making instead copious extracts for him from my letter, I again saw the danger but did not interfere for several reasons. One of them is, that I believe the time fully come when social and moral safety demands that someone of the Theos. Soc. should speak the truth though the Himalaya fall on him. The unveiling of the ugly truth has to be done with the greatest discretion and caution, though; and I see that instead of getting friends and supporters in the camp of the Philistines—whether on that or this side of the Oceans—many of you—yourself with the rest—breed but enemies by making too much of me and my personal opinions. On that side, the irritation is great and you will soon find flashes of it in *Light* and elsewhere; and you " *shall* lose S.M.* " The copious extracts have done their work for they were—much too copious. No powers whether human or superhuman can ever open the eyes of S.M.—it was useless to *tear*

[1] Enough (for now).—EDS.

them open. On this side—it is still worse. The good people at
Simla are not very metaphorically inclined, and allegory will no
more stick to their epidermis than would water to the feathers of
a goose. Besides, no one likes to be told that he " smells bad, "
and the *joke* extracted from a remark but too full of deep psychological meaning has produced incalculable harm in quarters where,
otherwise, the S.E.T.S. might have recruited more than one convert. . . . I must return once more to the letter.

The strongest basis of complaint against me is the fact that my
statement implies (*a*) a kind of challenge to S.M. to prove + a
" Spirit "—(*b*) I am severely denounced by our friend for making
out + *a liar*. Now, I mean to be explanatory but not apologetic.
I most certainly meant both; only I meant it *for you*, who had
asked me for the information, by no means for *him*. He has not
proved his case, nor did I expect he would, even if he thought
he could, as the claim rests entirely upon his own personal assertion due to his unwavering faith in his own impressions. It would
be easy for me, on the other hand, to prove + no disembodied
Spirit at all, had I not very good reasons for not doing so at
present. I had worded my letter very carefully, so that, while
letting you have a glimpse of the truth, I showed you most clearly
that I had no right to divulge the " secret of a *Brother*." But,
my very good friend, I had never told you in so many words who
and what *he* was. I might, perhaps, have advised you to judge
+ by his alleged writings, for more fortunate in that than Job, our
" enemies " all " write books." They are very fond of dictating
" inspirational " gospels and so—get caught in the glue of their
own rhetoric. And who of the most intellectual Spirit[ts.] who
have read the complete works fathered upon + would dare maintain that with the exception of a few extremely remarkable pages
the rest is not below what S.M. could have himself written, and
far better? Rest assured that no intelligent, clever and truthful
medium needs " inspiration " from a disembodied " Spirit."
Truth will stand without inspiration from Gods or Spirits, and
better still—will stand in spite of them all; " angels " whispering
generally but falsehoods and adding to the stock of superstition.

It is in view of such little unpleasantnesses that I have to abstain
from satisfying C. C. Massey. I will not avail myself of his
" authority," nor fulfil his " desire," and I refuse most decidedly
to " communicate his secret " as it is of a nature which stands in
his way for the attainment of adeptship, but has nothing whatever
to do with his private character. This information again was
meant for you, as an answer to your surprised query whether
there could be any impediments for my communicating with him
and *guiding* him to the Light, but it was never intended for his

ears. He may have a page or two in his life's history which he would rather see obliterated; but, his loyal and faithful instincts will always give him precedence and place him far above many a man who remained chaste and virtuous only because he never knew what temptation was. I will abstain, then, with your kind permission. In the future, my very dear friend, we will have to limit ourselves entirely to philosophy and avoid—family gossip. Skeletons in family closets are, at times, more dangerous to meddle with than even—dirty turbans, my illustrious and dear friend. And let not your too sensitive heart be troubled, or your imagination lead you to suppose that one single word of what I have now said is meant to convey a reproach. We, half savage Asiatics judge a man by his motives, and yours were all that is sincere and good. But you have to remember that you are at a hard school, and dealing now with a world entirely distinct from your own. Especially have you to bear in mind that the slightest *cause* produced, however unconsciously, and with whatever motive, cannot be unmade, or its effects crossed in their progress—by millions of gods, demons, and men combined. Therefore, you must not think me too hypercritical when I say that all of you have been more or less imprudent, when not indiscreet, the latter word applying—so far—but to one of the members. Hence—you will perhaps see that the mistakes and blunders of H. Steel Olcott are of a lighter hue than they at first appear, since even Englishmen, far more intelligent and versed in the world's ways than he is, are as liable to err. For you have erred, individually and collectively, as will be made apparent in a very near future; and the management and success of the Society will prove as a result far more difficult in your case, since none of you is as ready to admit that he has done so, nor are you as prepared as he is, to follow any advice offered you, though in each case it is based on *foresight* of impending events, even when foretold in a phraseology which may not always come " up to the mark " of the adept—*as he should be* in accordance with your own views.

You may tell Massey what I now say of him, and the reasons given. You may—though I would not advise you—read this letter to Mr. Hume. But I would strongly urge upon you the necessity of a greater caution than ever. Notwithstanding the purity of motives, the Chohan might one day consider but the results, and these may threaten to become too disastrous for him to overlook. There should be a constant pressure brought to bear upon the members of the S.E.S. to keep their tongues and enthusiasm at bay. And yet there is an increasing concern in the public mind in regard to your Society, and you may soon be called upon to define your position more clearly. Very soon I will have to leave you to yourselves for the period of three months.

Whether it will begin in October or January will depend on the impulse given to the Society and its progress.

I would feel personally obliged to you were you to kindly consent to examine a poem written by Padshah, and give your opinion on its merits. I believe it too long for the Theosophical Journal, nor do its literary merits warrant exactly or justify the claim. However, I leave it to your better judgment. I am anxious that the Journal should be more successful this year than it has heretofore been. The suggestion to translate the *Grand Inquisitor* is mine; for its author, on whom the hand of Death was already pressing when writing it, gave the most forcible and true description of the Society of Jesus than was ever given before. There is a mighty lesson contained in it for many and even you may profit by it.

My dear friend, you must not feel surprised if I tell you that I really feel weary and disheartened at the prospect I have before me. I am afraid you never will have the patience to wait for the day when I am permitted to satisfy you. Ages ago our people began to make certain rules, according to which they intended to live. All these rules have now become LAW. Our predecessors had to learn everything they know by themselves, only the foundation was laid for them. We offer to lay for you such a foundation but you will accept nothing short of the complete edifice, ready for you to take possession of. Do not accuse me of indifference or neglect when not receiving for days any reply from me. Very often I have nothing to say, for you ask questions which I have no right to answer.

But I must conclude here, as my time is limited and I have some other work to do.

Yours sincerely,

K. H.

The brandy atmosphere in the house *is* dreadful.

LETTER No. 28

K.H. to A.O. Hume written towards final break-off. (1881?)

My dear Sir,

If no other good ever came of our correspondence than that of showing us once more how essentially opposed are our two antagonistic elements—the English and the Hindu, our few letters will not have been exchanged in vain. Sooner can oil and water mingle their particles than an Englishman—however intelligent, noble-minded and sincere, be made to assimilate even the exoteric Hindu thought, let alone its esoteric spirit. This will, of course provoke you to a smile. You will say—" I expected this." So be it. But if so, it shows no more than the perspicacity of a man of thought and observation who intuitively anticipated an event which his own attitude must precipitate. . . .

You will pardon me if I have to speak frankly and sincerely of your long letter. However cogent its logic, noble some of its ideas, ardent its aspiration, it yet lies here before me a very mirror of that spirit of this age, against which we have fought during our whole lives! At best it is the unsuccessful endeavour of an acute intellect trained in the ways of an exoteric world, to throw light on, and judge of the modes of life and thought in which it is unversed, for they belong to quite a different world from that it deals with. You are no man of petty vanities. To you it is safe to say: " My dear friend, apart from all this, study your letter impartially; weigh some of its sentences, and on the whole you will not feel proud of it." Whether or not you will ever fully appreciate my motives, or misconceive the true causes which make me decline for the present any further correspondence, I yet am confident that some day you will confess that this last letter of yours under the garb of a noble humility, of confessions of " weaknesses and failings, shortcomings and follies " was yet— no doubt quite unconsciously to yourself—a monument of pride, the loud echo of that haughty and imperative spirit which lurks at the bottom of every Englishman's heart. In your present state of mind, very likely even after reading this answer, you will hardly perceive, that not only have you entirely failed to understand the spirit in which my last letter was written to you, but even, in some instances to catch its evident sense. You were preoccupied by one single, all-absorbing idea: and, failing to detect any direct reply to it in my answer, before taking time to think it over, and see its general, not personal applicability, you sat down and accused me right away of giving you a stone when you asked for bread! No need of being " a lawyer " in this or any previous existence to state simple facts. No need to " make the bad appear the better cause " when truth is so very simple and so easily told. My remark—" you take up the position that unless a proficient in arcane knowledge will waste upon your embryonic Society an energy . . ." etc.:—you applied to yourself, whereas it was never so meant. It related to the expectations of *all those* who might desire to join the Society under certain conditions exacted before-hand and that were firmly insisted upon, by yourself and Mr. Sinnett. The letter as a whole was meant for you two, and this special sentence applied to all in general.

You say that I have " to a certain extent mistaken " your " position," and that I " clearly misunderstand " you. This is so evidently incorrect that it will suffice for me to quote a single paragraph from your letter to show that it is *you* who have entirely

" mistaken *my* position " and " clearly misunderstood me." What
else do you do but labour under an erroneous impression, when,
in your eagerness to repudiate the idea of having ever dreamt of
originating a " school " you say of the proposed " Anglo-Indian
Branch "—" it is no Society of mine. . . . I understood it to be
the wish of yourself and chiefs that the Society should be started
and that I should assume a leading position in it." To this I
replied that if it has been constantly our wish to spread on the
Western Continent among the foremost educated classes
" Branches " of the T.S. as the harbingers of a *Universal Brotherhood*
it was not so in your case. We (the Chiefs and I) entirely repudiate
the idea that such was our hope (however we might wish it) in
regard to the projected A.I. Society. The aspiration for brotherhood between our races met no response—nay, it was pooh-poohed
from the first—and so, was abandoned even before I had received
Mr. Sinnett's first letter. On his part and from the start, the
idea was solely to promote the formation of a kind of club or
" school of magic." It was then no " proposal " of *ours*, nor were
we the " designers of the scheme." Why then such efforts to
show us in the wrong? It was Mad. B.—not *we*, who originated
the idea; and it was Mr. Sinnett who took it up. Notwithstanding
his frank and honest admission to the effect that being unable to
grasp the basic idea of *Universal Brotherhood* of the Parent Society,
his aim was but to cultivate the study of occult Sciences, an admission which ought to have stopped at once every further importunity
on her part, she first succeeded in getting the consent—a very
reluctant one I must say—of her own direct chief, and then my
promise of co-operation—as far as I could go. Finally, through
my mediation, she got that of our highest CHIEF, to whom I
submitted the first letter you honoured me with. But, this consent,
you will please bear in mind, was obtained solely under the *express
and unalterable condition* that the new Society should be founded as
a Branch of the *Universal Brotherhood*, and among its members, a
few elect men would—*if they chose to submit to our conditions*, instead
of *dictating theirs*—be allowed to BEGIN the study of the occult
sciences under the written directions of a " Brother." But a
" hot-bed of magick " we never dreamt of. Such an organization
as mapped out by Mr. Sinnett and yourself is unthinkable among
Europeans; and it has become next to impossible even in India—
unless you are prepared to climb to a height of 18,000 to 20,000
amidst the glaciers of the Himalayas. The greatest as well as
most promising of such schools in Europe, the last attempt in this
direction,—failed most signally some 20 years ago in London. It
was the secret school for the practical teaching of magick, founded
under the name of a club, by a dozen of enthusiasts under the
leadership of Lord Lytton's father. He had collected together for

the purpose the most ardent and enterprising as well as some of the most advanced scholars in mesmerism and " ceremonial magick," such as Eliphas Levi, Regazzoni, and the Copt Zergvan Bey. And yet in the pestilent London atmosphere the " Club " came to an untimely end. I visited it about half a dozen of times, and perceived from the first that there was and could be nothing in it. And this is also the reason why the British T.S. does not progress one step practically. They are of the Universal Brotherhood *but in name*, and gravitate at best towards *Quietism*—that utter paralysis of the Soul. They are intensely selfish in their aspirations and will get but the reward of their selfishness.

Nor did *we* begin the correspondence upon this subject. It was Mr. Sinnett who of his own motion addressed to a " Brother " two long letters, even before Mad. B. had obtained either permission or promise from any of us to answer him, or knew to whom of us to deliver his letter. Her own chief having refused point blank to correspond, it was to me that she applied. Moved by regard for her, I consented, even telling her she might give you all my Thibetan mystic name, and—I answered our friend's letter. Then came yours—as unexpectedly. You did not even know my name! But your first letter was so sincere, its spirit so promising, the possibilities it opened for doing general good seemed so great, that if I did not shout *Eureka* after reading it, and throw my Diogenes' lantern into the bushes at once, it was only because I knew too well human and—you must excuse me—Western nature. Unable, nevertheless, to undervalue the importance of this letter I carried it to our venerable Chief. All I could obtain from Him, though, was the permission to temporarily correspond, and let you speak your whole mind, before giving any definite promise. We are not gods, and even they, our chiefs—they *hope*. Human nature is unfathomable, and yours is, perhaps, more intensely so than any other man I know of. Your last favour was certainly if not quite a world of revelation, at least, a very profitable addition to my store of observation of the Western character, especially that of the modern, highly intellectual Anglo-Saxon. But it would be a revelation, indeed, to Mad. B. who did not see it, (and for various reasons had better *not*) for it might knock off much of her presumption and faith in her own powers of observation. I might prove to her among other things that she was as much mistaken in relation to Mr. Sinnett's attitude in this matter as your own; and—that I, who had never had the privilege of your personal acquaintance as she had, knew you far better than she did. I had positively foretold to her your letter. Rather than have no Society at all, she was willing to have it upon any terms at first, and then take her chances afterwards. I had warned her that you were not a man to submit to any conditions but your own;

or even take one step towards the foundation of an organization—
however noble and great—unless you received first such proofs as
we generally give but to those who, by a trial of years have proved
themselves thoroughly trustworthy. She rebelled against the
notion and assured [me] that were I but to give you one unimpeachable test of occult powers you would be satisfied, whereas
Mr. Sinnett never would. And now, that both of you have had
such proofs what are the results? While Mr. Sinnett believes—and
will never repent of it, you have allowed your mind to become
gradually filled with odious doubts and most insulting suspicions.
If you will kindly remember my first short note from Jhelum you
will see to what I then referred in saying that you would find your
mind poisoned. You misunderstood me then as you have ever
since; for in it, I did not refer to C. Olcott's letter in the *Bombay
Gazette* but to your own state of mind. Was I wrong? You not
only doubt the " brooch phenomenon "—you positively *disbelieve*
it. You say to Mad. B. that she may be one of those who believe
that bad means are justified by good ends and—instead of crushing her with all the scorn such an action is sure to awaken in a
man of your high principles—you assure her of your unalterable
friendship. Even your letter to me is full of the same suspicious
spirit, and that which you would never forgive in yourself—the
crime of deception—you try to make yourself believe you can
forgive in another person. My dear Sir, these are strange contradictions! Having favoured me with such a series of priceless
moral reflexions, advice, and truly noble sentiments, you may
perhaps, allow me in my turn to give you the ideas of an humble
apostle of Truth, an obscure Hindu, upon that point. As man
is a creature born with a free will and endowed with reason,
whence spring all his notions of right and wrong, he does not
per se represent any definite moral ideal. The conception of
morality in general relates first of all to the object or motive, and
only then to the means or modes of action. Hence, if we do not
and would never call a moral man him who, following the rule
of a famous religious schemer uses bad means for a good object,
how much less would we call him moral who uses seemingly good
and noble means to achieve a decidedly wicked or contemptible
object? And according to your logic, and once that you confess
to such suspicions, Mad. B. would have to be placed in the first
of these categories, and I in the second. For, while giving her
to a certain extent the benefit of the doubt, with myself you use
no such superfluous precautions, and you accuse me unequivocally
of setting up a system of deceit. The argument used in my
letter, in regard to " the approbation of the Home Government "
you term as " such very *low* motives "; and you add to it the
following crushing and direct accusation: " You do not want this

Branch (the Anglo-Indian) for work. . . . You merely want it *as a lure to your native* brethren. *You know it will be a sham,* but it will look sufficiently like the real thing," etc., etc. This is a direct and positive accusation. I am shown guilty of the pursuit of a wicked, mean object through low and contemptible means, i.e., *false pretences.* . . .

In penning these accusations did you stop to think, that as the projected organization had something grander, nobler and far more important in view than the mere gratification of the desires of one solitary person—however worthy—namely, in case of success to promote the security and welfare of a whole conquered nation—it is just barely possible that that which to your individual pride may appear a " low motive " is after all but the anxious search for means which would be the salvation of a whole country ever distrusted and suspected, the protection by the conqueror of the conquered! You pride yourself upon *not* being a " patriot "— *I do not*; for, in learning to love one's country one but learns to love humanity the more. The lack of that you term " *low motives* " in 1857 caused my country-men to be blown by yours from the mouths of their guns. Why then should I not fancy that a real philanthropist would regard the aspiration for a better under- standing between the Govt. and people of India as a most commendable instead of an ignoble one? " A fig " say you " for the knowledge and the philosophy on which it is based," if— " it would not be of any good to mankind," would not " enable me to be more useful to my generation," etc., etc. But when you are offered the means of doing such good you turn away in scorn and taunt us with a " lure " and a " sham "! Truly wonderful are the contradictions contained in your remarkable letter. . . . And then, you laugh so heartily at the idea of a " reward " or the " approval " of your fellow-creatures. " The reward to which I shall look will be," you say—" in earning *my own self-approval.*" " Self-approval " which cares so little for the corroborative verdict of the better part of the world at large, to which the good and noble deeds of one serve as high ideals and the most powerful stimulants to emulation, is little else than proud and arrogant egotism. It is HIMSELF against all criticism; " aprés moi—le déluge "!—exclaims the Frenchman with his usual flippancy. " Before Jehovah *was*, I AM "! says *Man*—the ideal of every modern intellectual Englishman. Gratified as I feel at the idea of being the means of affording you so much merriment, namely in asking you to draft a general plan for the formation of the A.I. Branch, I yet am bound to say again that your laugh was prema- ture in as much [as] you once more misunderstood entirely my meaning. Had I asked for your help in the organization of a system for teaching the occult sciences, or a plan for a " school of magic " the instance brought by you of an ignorant boy asked to work out " an abstruse problem regarding the motion of a fluid inside another fluid " might be a happy one. As it is, your comparison falls short of the mark and the bit of irony hits no one; for my mentioning the subject related merely to the general plan and outward administration of the projected Society and not in the least to its esoteric studies; to the Branch of the *Universal Brotherhood*, not to the " School of Magick "—the formation of the former being the *sine qua non* for the latter. Most assuredly in such matter as this one—the organization of an A.I. Branch, to be composed of Englishmen and meant to serve as a link between the British and the natives—(the condition being that they who want to share in the secret knowledge, the inheritance of the children of the soil, must be prepared to accord at least some privileges hitherto refused to these natives)—you English people are far more competent than we to draft a general plan. You know the conditions you would be likely to accept or reject as we might not. I asked for a skeleton plan, and you imagined I clamoured for co-operation in the instructions to be given in spiritual sciences! Most unfortunate *quid pro quo*—and yet Mr. Sinnett seems to have understood my wish at a glance.

Again you seem to show an unfamiliarity with the Hindu mind when you say: " not one in ten thousand native minds is as well prepared to realize and assimilate transcendental truths as mine." However much you may be right in thinking that " amongst English men of Science there are not *half a dozen* even whose minds are more capable of receiving these rudiments (of occult knowledge) than mine " (yours)—you are mistaken as to the natives. The Hindu mind is pre-eminently open to the quick and clear perception of the most transcendental, the most abstruse metaphysical truths. Some of the most unlettered ones will seize at a glance that which would often escape the best Western metaphysician. You may be, and most assuredly are our superiors in every branch of physical knowledge; in spiritual sciences we were, are and always will be your—MASTERS.

But let me ask you, what can I, a half civilized native,—think of the charity, modesty and kindness of one belonging to a superior race; one, whom I know as a noble minded, just, and kind hearted man in most circumstances of his life, when, with an ill-disguised scorn he exclaims: " if you want men to rush on blind-fold, heedless of ulterior results [1]—*stick to your Olcotts*—if you want men of a HIGHER CLASS, *whose brains are to work effectually* in your cause, remember   . . ." etc. My dear sir, we neither want men to rush on blind-fold, nor are we prepared to abandon tried friends —*who rather pass for fools* than reveal what they may have learnt

—————
[1] *I never said—I did!*

under a solemn pledge of never revealing it unless permitted—even for the chance of getting men of the very *highest* class,—nor are we especially anxious to have anyone work for us except with entire spontaneity. We want true and unselfish hearts; fearless and confiding souls, and are quite willing to leave the men of the " higher class " and far higher intellects to grope their own way to the light. Such will only look upon us as subordinates.

I believe that these few quotations from your letter and the frank answers they have called forth, are sufficient to show how far we are from anything like an *entente cordiale*. You show a spirit of fierce combativeness and a desire—pardon me—to fight shadows evoked by your own imagination. I had the honour of receiving three long letters from you even before I had barely time to answer in general terms your first one. I had never *positively* refused to comply with your wishes, never had answered as yet one single question of yours. How did you know what Future held in store for you, had you but waited one week? You invite me to a conference only, as it would seem, that you may show me the defects and weaknesses in our modes of action, and the causes for our supposed failure to convert humanity from their evil ways. And in your letter you show plainly that you are the beginning, the middle and the end of the law to yourself. Then why trouble yourself to write to me at all? Even that which you call a " Parthian arrow " was never meant as such. It is not I, who, unable to get the *absolute* will depreciate or undervalue the relative good. Your " little birds " have, no doubt, since you so believe, done much good in their way and I certainly never dreamt of giving offence by my remark that the human race and its welfare were at least as noble a study, and the latter as desirable an occupation, as ornithology. But, I am not quite sure that your parting remark as to our not being *invulnerable* as a body is quite free of that spirit which animated the retreating Parthians. Be it as it may, we are content to live as we do—unknown and undisturbed by a civilization which rests so exclusively upon intellect. Nor do we feel in any way concerned about the revival of our ancient arts and high civilization, for these are as sure to come back in their time, and in a higher form as the Plesiosaurus and the Megatherium in theirs. We have the weakness to believe in ever recurrent cycles and hope to *quicken* the resurrection of what is past and gone. We *could not* impede it even if we would. The " new civilization " will be but the child of the old one, and we have but to leave the eternal law to take its own course to have our dead ones come out of their graves; yet, we are certainly anxious to hasten the welcome event. Fear not; although we do " cling superstitiously to the relics of the Past " our knowledge will not pass away from the sight of man. It is the " gift of the

gods " and the most precious relic of all. The keepers of the
sacred Light did not safely cross so many ages but to find themselves wrecked on the rocks of modern scepticism. Our pilots
are too experienced sailors to allow us [to] fear any such disaster.
We will always find volunteers to replace the tired sentries, and
the world, bad as it is in its present state of transitory period, can
yet furnish us with a few men now and then. You " do not
propose moving further in the matter " unless we make " some
further sign "? My dear sir, we have done our duty: we have
responded to your appeal, and now propose to take no further
step. We, who have studied a little Kant's moral teachings,
analyzed them somewhat carefully, have come to the conclusion
that even this great thinker's views on that form of duty (*das
Sollen*) which defines the methods of moral action—notwithstanding his one-sided affirmation to the contrary—falls short of a full
definition of an unconditional absolute principle of morality—as we
understand it. And this Kantian note sounds throughout your
letter. You so love mankind, you say, that were not your generation to benefit by it, you would reject " Knowledge " itself. And
yet, this philanthropic feeling does not even seem to inspire you
with charity towards those you regard as of an inferior intelligence. Why? Simply because the philanthropy you Western
thinkers boast of, having no character of universality; *i.e.* never
having been established on the firm footing of a moral, universal
principle; never having risen higher than theoretical talk; and
that chiefly among the ubiquitous Protestant preachers, it is but a
mere accidental manifestation but no recognised LAW. The most
superficial analysis will show that, no more than any other
empirical phenomenon in human nature, can it be taken as an
absolute standard of moral activity; *i.e.* one productive of efficient
action. Since, in its empirical nature this kind of philanthropy
is like love, but something accidental, exceptional, and like that
has its selfish preferences and affinities, it is necessarily unable to
warm all mankind with its beneficent rays. This, I think, is the
secret of the spiritual failure and unconscious egotism of this age.
And you, otherwise a good and a wise man, being unconsciously
to yourself the type of its spirit, are unable to understand our ideas
upon the Society as a *Universal Brotherhood*, and hence—turn away
your face from it.

Your conscience revolts, you say, to be made " a stalking horse;
the puppet of a score or more of hidden wire-pullers." What do
you know of us since you cannot see us; what do you know of
our aims and objects; of us, of whom you cannot judge? . . . you
ask. Strange arguments. And do you really suppose you would
" know " us, or penetrate any better our " aims and objects "
were you to see me personally? I am afraid, that with no past

experience of this kind, even *your* natural powers of observation—however acute—would have to be confessed more than useless. Why, my dear Sir, even our *Bahuroopias* [1] can prove a match any day for the acutest political Resident; and never yet one was detected or even recognized; and their mesmeric powers are not of the *highest* order. However suspicious you might ever feel about the details of the " brooch " there is one prime feature in the case which your astuteness has already told you can only be accounted for on the theory of a stronger will influencing Mrs. Hume to think after that particular object and no other. And if Mad. B., a sickly woman, must be credited with such powers, are you quite sure that you yourself would not also be made to succumb to a trained will, ten times stronger than hers? I could come to you to-morrow, and installing myself in your house—as invited—get an entire domination over your whole mind and body in 24 hours, and you never aware of it for one moment. I may be a good man, but so I may, for all you know, as easily be a wicked, plotting schemer, hating profoundly your white race which subjugated and daily humiliates mine, and—take revenge on you—one of the best representatives of that race. If the power of exoteric mesmerism alone were employed—a power acquired with equal ease by the bad as by the good man—even then you could hardly escape the snares laid out for you, were the man you invited but a good mesmeriser, for you are a remarkably easy subject—from the physical stand-point. " But my *conscience*, my intuition! " you may argue. Poor help in such a case as mine. *Your* intuition would make you feel but that which *really was*—for the time being; and as to your conscience—you then accept Kant's definition of it? You, perhaps, believe with him that under all circumstances, and even with the full absence of definite religious notions, and occasionally even with no firm notions about right and wrong at all, MAN has ever a sure guide in his own inner moral perceptions or —*conscience*? The greatest of mistakes! With all the formidable importance of this moral factor, it has one radical defect. Conscience, as it was already remarked may be well compared to that demon whose dictates were so zealously listened to and so promptly obeyed by Socrates. Like that demon, conscience may perchance tell us what we must *not* do; yet it never guides us as to what we ought to perform, nor gives any definite object to our activity. And—nothing can be more easily lulled to sleep and even completely paralyzed, than this same conscience by a trained will stronger than that of its possessor. Your conscience will NEVER show you whether the mesmeriser is a true adept or a very clever juggler, if he once has passed your threshold and got control of the aura surrounding your person. You speak of abstaining from

[1] Lit. man of many forms; an actor who plays many parts.—EDS.

any but an *innocent* work like bird-collecting, lest there be danger of creating another Frankenstein's monster. . . . Imagination as well as will—creates. Suspicion is the most powerful provocative agent of imagination. . . . Beware! You have already begotten in you the germ of a future hideous monster, and instead of the realization of your purest and highest ideals you may one day evoke a phantom, which, barring every passage of light will leave you in worse darkness than before, and will harass you to the end of your days.

Again expressing the hope that my candour may not give offence, I am, dear Sir, as ever,

Your most obedient Servant,
KOOT' HOOMI LAL SINGH.

A. O. Hume, Esq.

LETTER No. 29

In answer to yours I will have to reply by a rather lengthy letter. To begin with I can say the following: Mr. Hume thinks and speaks of me in a way which need only be noticed so far as it affects the frame of mind in which he proposes to apply to me for philosophical instruction. For his respect I care as little as he for my displeasure. But passing over his superficial disagreeableness I recognize fully his goodness of motive, his abilities, his potential usefulness. We had better get to work again without further parley, and while he perseveres, he will find me ready to help—but not to flatter, nor to dispute.

So utterly has he misunderstood the spirit in which both the Memo and P.S. were written, that had he not placed me during the three last days under a debt of profound gratitude for what he is doing for my poor old chela, I would have never gone to the trouble of doing what might seem as an excuse, or an explanation, or both. However that may be, that debt of gratitude is so sacred, that I now do for her sake what I might have refused doing even for the Society: I crave the Sahibs' permission to acquaint them with some facts. With our Indo-Tibetan ways the most sagacious English official is not yet acquainted. The information now offered may be found useful in our future transactions. I will have to be sincere and outspoken and Mr. Hume will have to excuse me. If I once am forced to speak I must say ALL, or say—nothing.

I am not a fine scholar, Sahibs, like my blessed Brother; but nevertheless, I believe I understand the value of words. And if I do, then am I at a loss to understand, what in my P.S. could have so provoked the ironical displeasure against me of Mr. Hume? We of the Indo-Tibetan hovels never quarrel (this in answer to some expressed thoughts in relation to the subject). Quarrels and even discussions we leave to those who, unable to take in a situation at a glance are thereby forced before making up their final decision to anything to analyse and weigh one by one, and over and over again every detail. Whenever we—at least those of us who are *dikshita*—seem, therefore to an European not " quite sure of our facts " it may be often due to the following peculiarity. That which is regarded by most men as a " fact " to us may seem but a simple RESULT, an fter thought unworthy of our attention, generally attracted but to *primary facts*. Life, esteemed Sahibs, when even indefinitely prolonged, is too short to burden our brains with flitting details—mere shadows. When watching the progress of a storm we fix our gaze upon the producing Cause and leave the clouds to the whims of the breeze which shapes them. Having always the means on hand—whenever absolutely needed—of bringing to our knowledge minor details we concern ourselves but with the main facts. Hence we can hardly be *absolutely wrong*—as we are often accused by you, for our conclusions are never drawn from secondary data but from the situation as a whole.

On the other hand, the average man—even among the most intellectual—giving all their attention to the testimony of appearance and outward form, and disabled as they are from penetrating *a priori* to the core of things, are but too apt to misjudge of the whole situation [and are] left to find out their mistake but when too late. Owing to complicated politics, to debates and what you term, if I mistake not, social talk and drawing-room controversies and discussions, sophistry has now become in Europe (hence among the Anglo-Indians) " the logical exercise of the intellectual faculties," while with us it has never outgrown its pristine stage of " fallacious reasoning," the shaky, insecure premises from which most of the conclusions and opinions are drawn, formed and forthwith jumped at. Again, we ignorant Asiatics of Tibet, accustomed to rather follow the thought of our interlocutor or correspondent than the words he clothes it in —concern ourselves generally but little with the accuracy of his expressions. Now this preface will seem as unintelligible as useless to you, and you may well ask what is he driving at. Patience, pray, for I have something more to say before our final explanation.

A few days before leaving us, Koot'hoomi speaking of you said to me as follows: " I feel tired and weary of these never ending disputations. The more I try to explain to both of them the circumstances that control us and that interpose between us so many obstacles to free intercourse, the less they understand me! Under the most favourable aspects this correspondence must always be unsatisfactory, even exasperatingly so, at times; for nothing short of personal interviews, at which there could be discussion and the instant solution of intellectual difficulties as they arise, would satisfy them fully. It is as though we were hallooing to each other across an impassable ravine and only one of us seeing his interlocutor. In point of fact, there is nowhere in physical nature a mountain abyss so hopelessly impassable and obstructive to the traveller as that spiritual one, which keeps them back from me."

Two days later when his " retreat " was decided upon, in parting he asked me: " Will you watch over my work, will you see it falls not into ruins? " I promised. What is there I would not have promised him at that hour! At a certain spot not to be mentioned to outsiders, there is a chasm spanned by a frail bridge of woven grasses and with a raging torrent beneath. The bravest member of your Alpine clubs would scarcely dare to venture the passage, for it hangs like a spider's web and *seems* to be rotten and impassable. Yet it is not; and he who dares the trial and succeeds—as he will if it is right that he should be permitted—comes into a gorge of surpassing beauty of scenery—to one of *our* places and to some of *our* people, of which and whom there is no note or minute among European geographers. At a stone's throw from the old Lamasery stands the old tower, within whose bosom have gestated generations of Bodhisatwas. It is there, where now rests your lifeless friend—my brother, the light of my soul, to whom I made a faithful promise to watch during his absence over *his* work. And is it likely, I ask you, that but two days after his retirement I, his faithful friend and brother would have gratuitously shown disrespect to his European friends? What reason was there, and what could have caused such an idea in Mr. Hume's and even in your mind? Why, a word or two entirely misunderstood and misapplied by him. I'll prove it.

Don't you think that had the expression used " coming to hate the sut-phana " been changed into and made to read " coming to feel again flashes of dislike " or of temporary irritation this sentence alone would have wonderfully changed the *results*? Had it been *so* phrased Mr. Hume would hardly have found an opportunity for *denying the fact* as vigorously as he did. For there he is right and the WORD is wrong. It is a perfectly correct statement when saying that such a feeling as *hatred* has never existed in him. Whether he will be as able to protest against the statement in general remains to be seen. He confessed to the fact that he was " irritated," and to a " feeling of distrust " created by H.P.B. That " irritation," as he will no longer deny, lasted for several days. Where does he then find the *misstatement*? Let us moreover admit, that the word to use *was* an incorrect one. Then, since he is so particular in the choice of words, so desirous that they should always convey the correct meaning, why not apply the same rule of action to himself? What might be well excused in an Asiatic ignorant of English and one, moreover, who never was in the habit of choosing his expressions, for reasons given above, and because among *his* people he *cannot* be misunderstood, ought to become *inexcusable* in an educated, highly literary Englishman. In his letter to Olcott he writes: " He (I) or she (H.P.B.), or both between them, so muddled and misunderstood a letter written by Sinnett and myself as to lead to our receiving a message wholly inapplicable to the circumstances and such as necessarily *to create distrust*." Humbly soliciting permission to put a question—when did either *I*, or *she* or both of us, see, read and hence " muddled and misunderstood " the letter in question? How could she, or I, have muddled *that* which *she had never seen*, and I, having neither inclination nor right to look into and mix myself in an affair concerning but the Chohan and K.H. —never paid the slightest attention to? Did she inform you on the day in question, that it was in consequence of that letter of yours that I had sent her into Mr. Sinnett's room with the message? I was there, respected Sahibs, and can repeat to you every word she said: " What is it? . . . What have you been doing, or saying to K.H."—she shouted in her usual excited nervous way to Mr. Sinnett who was alone in the room—" that M., (naming me) that he should be so angry—should tell me to prepare to go and settle our headquarters at Ceylon? " were the first words she said, thus showing that *she knew nothing certain*, was *told still less*, and simply surmised from what I had told her. And what I had told her, was simply that she had better prepare for the worst and depart to settle in Ceylon than make a fool of herself, trembling so over every letter given to her to forward to K.H.; that unless she learned to control herself better than she did, I would put a stop to that *dak* business. These words were said by me to her not because I had anything to do with *your* or *any* letter, nor in consequence of any letter sent, but because I happened to see the aura all around the new *Eclectic* and herself, black and pregnant with future mischief, and I sent her to say so to Mr. Sinnett, *not* to Mr. Hume. My remark and message upsetting her (owing to that unfortunate disposition and shattered nerves) in the most ridiculous way, the well known scene ensued. Is it because of the phantoms of theosophical ruin evoked by her unbalanced brain that she is now accused—in my company—to have muddled and misunderstood a letter she had never seen? Whether there is in Mr. Hume's statement one single word that might be called correct—the term " correct " being now applied by me to the actual meaning of the whole sentence, not merely to isolated words—I leave to the judgment of minds superior to those of Asiatics. And if I am permitted to question the correctness of opinion in one, so vastly superior to myself in education, intelligence and acuteness in the perception of the eternal fitness of things—in view of the above explanation, why should I be held as " absolutely wrong " for the following statement: " I have also seen the growing up of a sudden dislike (say irritation) *begotten of distrust* (Mr. Hume confessing to, and using the identical expression in his answer to Olcott—please compare quotation from his letter as given above) on the day I sent her with a message to Mr. Sinnett's room." Is this incorrect? And further: " they know how excitable and ill balanced she is, and this hostile feeling on his part was almost cruel. *For days he barely looked at her* let alone speaking to her—and inflicted upon her supersensitive nature severe and unnecessary pain! *And when told of it by Mr. Sinnett he denied the fact? . . .*" This last sentence, continued on page 7 with *many other like truths*, I tore out with the rest (as upon enquiry you can ascertain from Olcott, who will tell you that originally there were 12 pages, not 10, and that he had sent the letter with far more details than you now find in it, for he is unaware of what I have done, and *why* it was done. Unwilling to remind Mr. Hume of details long forgotten by him and irre- levant to the case in hand, I tore out the page and obliterated much of the rest. His feelings had already changed and I was satisfied.)

Now the question is not whether Mr. Hume " cares a twopence " if his feelings *are pleasing to me or not*, but rather whether he was warranted by *facts* to write to Olcott as he did, *i.e.*, that I had *entirely misunderstood* his real feelings. I say *he was not*. He can no more prevent me from being " displeased," than I can go to the trouble of making him feel otherwise than what he now feels, namely, that he does " not care a twopence whether his feelings are pleasing to me or not." All this is childishness; and he who is desirous to learn how to benefit humanity, and believes himself able to read the characters of other people, must begin first of all, *to learn to know himself*, to appreciate his own character at its true value. And this, I venture to say, he has never learned yet. And he has also to learn in what particular cases *results* may in their turn become important and primary *causes*, when the result becomes a *Kyen*. Had he *hated* her with the most bitter hatred, he could not have tortured her foolishly sensitive nerves more effectually than he has, while " still loving the dear old woman." He has done so with those he loved best, and, unconsciously to himself, he will do so more than once in the hereafter; and yet his first impulse will be always to deny it, for he is indeed fully *unconscious* of the fact, the extreme kindness of his heart being in such cases entirely blinded and paralyzed by another feeling, which, if told of, he will also deny. Undismayed by his epithets of " goose " and " Don Qui- chote," true to my promise to my Blessed Brother, I will tell him of it whether he likes it or not; for now that he has openly given expression to his feelings, we have either to understand each other or break off. This is " no half veiled threat " as he expresses it for " a threat in a man is like the bark in a dog "—it means nothing. I say, that unless he understands how utterly inapplicable to us is the standard according to which he is accustomed to judge Western people of his own society, it would simply be a loss of time for me or K.H. to teach and for him to learn. We never regard a friendly warning as a " threat," nor do we feel irritated when it is offered to us. He says that personally he does not care in the least, " were the Brothers to break with him to-morrow; " the more reason then that we should come to an understanding. Mr. Hume prides himself in the thought that he never had " a spirit of veneration " for anything but his own abstract ideals. We are perfectly aware of it. Nor could he possibly have any veneration for anyone or anything, as all the veneration his nature is capable of is—*concentrated upon himself*. This is a fact and the cause of all his life-troubles. When his numerous official " friends " and his own family say that it is *conceit*—they misstate and say a very foolish thing. He is too highly intellectual to be conceited: he is simply and unconsciously to himself *the embodiment of pride*. He would have no veneration for even his *God*, were not that God—*of his own creation and making*; and that is why he could neither be made amenable to any established doctrine, nor would he ever submit to a philosophy that did not come all armed, like the Grecian *Saraswati* or Minerva, out of his own—her father's—brain. This may throw light upon the fact why I refused giving him during the short period of my instruction—anything but half problems, hints and puzzles to solve for himself. For only then would he believe, when his own extraordinary capacity for grasping at the nature of things would clearly show him that it must be so, since it dovetails with what HE conceives to be mathematically correct. If he accused—and so unjustly!—K.H. whom he really affections—of feeling " huffish " at his lack of reverence for him—it is because he built his ideal of my brother in his own image—Mr. Hume accuses us of treating him *de haut en bas*! If he but knew that in our sight an honest boot-black was as good as an honest king, and an *immoral* sweeper far higher and more excusable than an *immoral* Emperor—he would have never uttered such a fallacy. Mr. Hume complains (thousand pardons—" laughs " is the correct term) that we show a desire of *sitting upon him*. I venture to suggest most respectfully that it is absolutely *vice versa*. It is Mr. Hume who (again unconsciously and yielding but to a life-long habit) tried that most uncomfortable posture with my brother in every letter he wrote to Koothoomi. And when certain expressions denoting a fierce spirit of self-approbation and confidence which reached the apex of human pride, were noticed and mildly contradicted by my brother, Mr. Hume forthwith gave them another meaning and, accusing K.H. of having misunderstood them, called him to himself puffed up and " huffish." Do I accuse *him* then, of unfairness, injustice or worse? Most decidedly *not*. A more honest, sincere or a kinder man never breathed on the Himalayas.   I know actions of his of which his own family and lady are utterly ignorant—so noble, so kind and grand, that even his own pride remains blind to their full worth. So that anything he might do or say, is unable to diminish my respect for him; but with all this, I am *forced* to tell him the truth: and while that side of his character has all my admiration, his pride will never win my approbation,—for which once more, Mr. Hume will not care one twopence, but that matters very little, indeed.   The most sincere and outspoken man in India, Mr. Hume is unable to tolerate a contradiction; and, be that person *Dev* or mortal, he *cannot* appreciate or even permit without protest the same qualities of sincerity in any other than himself.   Nor can he be brought to confess that anyone in this world can know better than himself anything that HE has studied and formed *his* opinion thereupon.   " They will not set about the joint work in what seems to ME the best way," he complains of us in his letter to Olcott, and that sentence alone gives to us the key to his whole character; it gives us the clearest insight into the working of his inner feelings. Having a right—he thinks—to regard himself as slighted and wrongly, in consequence of such an " ungenerous," " selfish " refusal to work under *his* guidance, he cannot help thinking himself at the bottom of his heart, as a most *forgiving, generous* man, who, instead of resenting our refusal is nevertheless " willing to go on in their (our) way."   And this irreverence of ours for *his* opinions cannot be pleasing to him; and thus the feeling of this great wrong we do him rises, and becomes proportional to the magnitude of our " selfishness " and " huffishness."   Hence his disenchantment, and the sincere pain he feels at finding the Lodge and all of us so much below the mark of *his* ideal.   He laughs, for my defending H.P.B.; and giving way to a feeling unworthy of his nature, very unfortunately forgets that his is just the disposition to warrant friends and foes calling him " protector of the poor " and like names, and that his enemies, among others, never fail to apply such epithets to himself; and yet, far from falling upon him as an insult, that chivalrous feeling which has ever prompted him to take the defence of the weak and the oppressed and to redress the wrongs done by his colleagues—as in the last instance of the Simla municipality row—covers him with a garment of undying glory spun out of the gratitude and affection for him of the people he so fearlessly defends.   Both of you labour under the strange impression that *we can*, and even *do* care for anything that may be said or thought of us.   Disabuse your minds, and remember that the first requisite in even a simple fakir, is that he should have trained himself to remain as indifferent to moral pain as to physical suffering. Nothing can give US *personal* pain or pleasure.   And what I now say is, rather to bring you to understand US than *yourselves* which is the most difficult science to learn. That Mr. Hume's intention —prompted by a feeling as transient as it was hasty, and due to a sense of growing irritation against me whom he accused of a desire " to sit upon him "—was to revenge himself by an ironical, hence (to the European mind) an insulting fling at me—is as certain as that he missed the mark. Ignorant, or rather forgetful of the fact that we Asiatics are utterly devoid of that sense of the ridiculous which prompts the Western mind to caricature the best, the noblest aspirations of mankind—could I yet feel offended or flattered by the world's opinion I would have felt rather complimented than otherwise. My Rajput blood will never permit me to see a woman hurt in her feelings—though she be a " visionary," and the now called " imaginary " wrong but another of her " fancies "—without defending her; and Mr. Hume knows enough of our traditions and customs to be sufficiently aware of that remnant of chivalrous feeling for our women in our otherwise degenerated race. Therefore do I say, that whether hoping that the satirical epithets would reach and hurt me, or aware of the fact that he was apostrophizing a granite pillar—the feeling that prompted him was unworthy of his nobler and better nature, as in the first case it was to be regarded as a petty feeling of revenge, and in the second as *childishness*. Then in his letter to O. he complains of or denounces (you must forgive the limited number of English words I have at my command) the attitude of " half threat " to break with you that he imagines he finds in our letters. Nothing could be more erroneous. We have no more the intention of breaking with him, than an orthodox Hindu has of leaving the house he is visiting until told that his company is no more wanted. But when the latter is hinted to him he leaves. So with us. Mr. Hume quite prides himself at repeating that personally he has no desire to see us, no curiosity to meet us; that our philosophy and teaching cannot benefit *him* in the least, *him* who has learnt and knows all that can be learnt; that he cares not a snap whether we break with him or not, nor is he in the least concerned whether we are pleased with him or not. *Cui bono* then? Between the (by him) imagined reverence we expect from him, and that uncalled for combativeness, which may degenerate at any day with him, into unexpressed yet real hostility, there is an abyss and no middle ground that even the Chohan can see. Though he cannot now be accused of not making, as in the past, any allowance for circumstances and our own peculiar rules and laws, yet he is always hurrying towards that black border-land of amity, where trust is obscured and dark suspicions and erroneous impressions cloud the whole horizon. I, am as I was; and, as I was and am, so am I likely always to be— the slave of my duty to the Lodge and mankind; not only taught, but desirous to subordinate every preference for individuals to a love for the human race. It is gratuitous, therefore, to accuse me or any one of us of selfishness, and desire to regard or treat you as " paltry Pelingis " and to " ride donkeys," only because we are unable to find convenient horses. Neither the Chohan, nor K.H., nor myself ever under-valued Mr. Hume's worth. He has done invaluable service to the Th. Soc. and to H.P.B. and is alone capable of making the Society an efficient agent for good. When the spiritual soul is left to guide him, no purer, no better, nor kinder man can be found. But, when his *fifth* principle rises in irrepressible pride, we will always confront and challenge it. Unmoved by his excellent worldly counsel as to how you should be armed with proofs of our reality, or how you should set about the joint work in the way that seems the best to HIM, I will remain so unmoved, till I receive contrary orders. Referring to your last letter (Mr. Sinnett's) clothe your ideas as you may, in the pleasantest of phrases, you are nevertheless surprised and as regards Mr. Sinnett disappointed, that I should neither accord permission for phenomena nor yet any of us make one step towards you. I cannot help it, and whatever the consequences there will be no change in my attitude until my Brother's return among the living. You know both of us love our country and our race; that we regard the Theos. Society as a great potentiality for their good in proper hands; that he has joyfully welcomed Mr. Hume's identification with the cause and that I have placed a high—but only a proper —value upon it. And so you ought to realize that whatever we *could* do to bind you and him closer to us we would do with all our heart. But still if the choice lies between our disobeying the lightest injunction of our Chohan as to when we may see either of you, or what we may write, or how, or where, and the loss of your good opinion, even the feeling of your strong animosity and the disruption of the Society, we should not hesitate a single instant. It may be considered unreasonable, selfish, huffish and ridiculous, denounced as jesuitical and the blame all laid at our door, but law is LAW with us, and no power can make us abate one jot or tittle of our duty. We have given you a chance to obtain all you desired by improving your magnetism, by pointing you to a nobler ideal to work up to, and Mr. Hume has been shown what he already knew, how he may benefit immensely some millions of his fellow men. Choose according to your best light. Your choice is made I know—but Mr. Hume may yet change his ideas more than once; I shall be the same to my group and promise, whatever he may determine. Nor, do we fail to appreciate the great concessions made already by him; concessions the more great in our sight, as he becomes less interested in our existence, and makes a violence to his feelings solely in the hope of benefitting humanity. No one in his place would have accommodated himself to his situation with such a good grace as he has, or stood more strictly upon the declaration "of primary objects" at the meeting of 21st Aug.; while "proving to the native community that members of the ruling class" also are desirous of promoting the commendable projects of the T.S., he bides his time, for even the obtaining of our metaphysical truths. He has already done an immense good and has yet received nothing in return. Nor does he expect anything. Reminding you that the present is an answer to *all* your letters, and to all your objections and suggestions, I may add that you are right and that in spite of all "your earthiness" my blessed Brother certainly entertains a real regard for you, and Mr. Hume, who I am happy to find has some good feeling for him, though he is not like you and really *is* "too proud to look for his reward in our protection." Only where you are and will be ever wrong, my dear sir, it is in entertaining the idea that phenomena can ever become "a powerful engine" to shake the foundations of erroneous beliefs in the Western mind. None but those who see for themselves will ever believe, do what you may. "Satisfy us and then we will satisfy the world," you once said. You were satisfied and what are the results? And I wish I could impress upon your minds the deep conviction that we do not wish Mr. Hume or you to prove conclusively to the public that we really exist. Please realize the fact that so long as men doubt there will be curiosity and enquiry, and that enquiry stimulates reflection which begets effort; but let our secret be once thoroughly vulgarized and not only will sceptical society derive no great good but our privacy would be constantly endangered and have to be continually guarded at an unreasonable cost of power. Have patience, friend of my friend. It took Mr. Hume years to kill enough birds to make up his book; and he did not command them to leave their leafy retreats, but had to wait for them to come and let him stuff and label them: so must you be patient with us. Ah, Sahibs, Sahibs! if you could only catalogue and label *us* and set us up in the British Museum, then indeed might your *world* have the absolute, the dessicated truth.

And so it all comes around again as usual to the starting point. You have been chasing us around your own shadows, just catching a vanishing glimpse of us now and again, but never coming near enough to escape the gaunt skeleton of suspicion that is at your heel and stares you in the future. So I fear [it] may be to the end of the chapter, as you have not the patience to read the volume to its end. For you are trying to penetrate the things of the spirit with the eyes of the flesh, to bend the inflexible to your own crude model of what should be, and finding it will not bend, you are as likely as not to break that model and—bid good-bye for ever to the dream.

And now for a few parting words of explanation. O's *memo*, which produced such disastrous results and a most unique *quid pro quo*, was written on the 27th. On the night of the 25th, my beloved Brother told me, that having heard Mr. Hume say in H.P.B.'s room that he had never himself heard O. state to him that, he, O., had personally seen us, and also had heard added that were Olcott to tell him so, he had confidence enough in the man to believe in what he said,—he, K.H. thought of asking me to go and tell O. to do so; believing it might please Mr. Hume to learn some of the details. K.H. wishes are—law to me. And that is why Mr. Hume received that letter from O., at a time when his doubts were already settled. At the same time as I delivered my message to O., I satisfied his curiosity as to your Society and told what I thought of it. O. asked my permission to send to you these notes which I accorded. Now, that is the *whole* secret. For reasons of my own I desired you should know what I thought of the situation, a few hours after my beloved Brother went out of this world. When the letter reached you my feelings were somewhat changed and I altered, as said before, the memo a good deal. As O's style had made me laugh, I added my *postcriptum* which related solely to Olcott, but was nevertheless applied wholly by Mr. Hume to himself?

Let us drop it. I close the longest letter I have ever written in my life; but as I do it for K.H.—I am satisfied. Though Mr. Hume may not think it, the " mark of the adept " is kept at ————not at Simla, and I try to keep up to it, however poor I may be as a writer and a correspondent.

M.

LETTER No. 30 [1]

Private.

My dear Brother.

Perhaps, a week ago, I would have hardly failed to embrace this available opportunity and say that your letter concerning Mr. Fern is as complete a misrepresentation of the spirit, and above all, of the attitude of M. towards the said young gentleman, as your complete ignorance of the aim he is pursuing could produce— and I would have said no more. But now, things have changed; and though you have " come to *know* " that we "did not really possess the power of reading minds " as *had been pretended*, never- theless, we know enough of the spirit in which my last letters were received, and of the dissatisfaction produced,—to suspect, if not to know that unwelcome as truth may often come, yet the time has arrived for me to speak frankly and openly with you. Lying

[1] The portion of A. O. Hume's letter quoted by K.H. pp. 226-7, is a fac- simile precipitation of A.O.H.'s own writing, and the passages in italics in it have been underlined by K.H.—ED.

is a refuge to the weak, and we are sufficiently strong, even with
all the shortcomings you are pleased to discover in us, to dread
truth very little; nor are we likely to *lie*, only because it is to our
interest to appear wise concerning matters of which we are
ignorant. Thus, perchance it might have been more prudent to
remark that you knew that we did not really possess the power
of reading minds, unless we brought ourselves *thoroughly en rapport*
with, and concentrated an undivided attention on, the person
whose thoughts we wanted to know—since that would be an
undeniable *fact*, instead of a gratuitous assumption as it now
stands in your letter. However it may be, I now find but two
ways before us, with not the smallest path for compromise. Henceforth, if your desire is that we should work together, we must
do so on a footing of perfect understanding. You will be at
perfect liberty to tell us—since you seem, or rather have brought
yourself to sincerely believe it—that most of us, owing to the
mystery that enshrouds us, live by getting credit for knowing
what we really *do not* know; while I, for instance, will be as entitled
as you are, to let you know what I may think of you, yourself
meanwhile promising that you will not laugh at it *outwardly*, and
bear a grudge for it *inwardly* (something that notwithstanding
your efforts you can rarely help) but that, in case I am mistaken
you will prove it by some demonstration weightier than a mere
denial. Unless you bind yourself by such a promise, it is utterly
useless for any of us to be losing our time in controversies and correspondence. Better shake hands astrally, across space, and wait until
either you have acquired the gift of discerning truth from falsehood
to a greater degree than you now have it; or, that we are shown to
be no better than impostors (or still worse—lying spooks); or finally,
that some one of us is in a position to demonstrate our existence
to yourself or Mr. Sinnett—not astrally, for that might only
strengthen the " Spirit " theory but—by visiting you personally.

Since it becomes quite hopeless to convince you that even *we*
occasionally *do* read other people's thoughts, may I hope that you
will credit us, at least, with a sufficient knowledge of the English
language not to have entirely misunderstood your very plain letter?
And, to believe me, when I say, that having perfectly understood
it, I answer you as plainly, " My dearest Brother, you are egre-
giously mistaken from first to last! " Your whole letter is based
upon a *misconception*, an entire ignorance of " missing links," which
alone may have given you a true key to the whole situation. What
can you mean by the following?

My dear Master,
    Amongst you you are utterly spoiling Fern—it is a thousand pities—
for he is really a good fellow at heart and he has an intense

desire for occult knowledge—and strong will and a great capacity for self-mortification—he would I am sure he useful for
your purposes; but his self-conceit is growing intolerable and he
is becoming a confirmed fabricator of fiction and *this is due to
you all. He has thoroughly humbugged Morya!!* from the first—
and he has gone persistently lying to Sinnett to keep up the
delusion he *has got Morya to entrust him with secrets* and to accept
him as a chela and he now thinks himself a match for anyone.
. . . *Morya replies quite falling into the trap . . . this fraud no doubt
commenced in (y)our interests . . . etc. etc. etc.*

It is unnecessary for me to repeat once more what I have said
before; namely, that up to receiving your first letter concerning
Mr. Fern, I had never given him *one* moment's attention. Who
then, amongst *us*—spoils that young gentleman? Is it Morya?
Well, it is easy to see that you know still less of him than he
knows, in your conceptions, of what you have in your mind.
" He has thoroughly *humbugged* Morya." Has he? I am sorry
to be obliged to confess that, in accordance with your Western
code it would look rather the reverse; that it was my beloved
Brother who " humbugged " Mr. Fern—had not the ill-sounding
term another meaning with us, as also another name. The latter
of course, may appear to you still more " revolting," since even
Mr. Sinnett, who is but the echo in that of every English Society
man, regards it as thoroughly revolting to the feelings of the
average Englishman. That other name is—PROBATION; something
every chela who does not want to remain simply ornamental, has
nolens volens to undergo for a more or less prolonged period;
something that—for this very reason that it is undoubtedly based
upon what you Westerns would ever view as a system of *humbug*
or deception—that I, who knew European ideas better than Morya,
have always refused to accept or even to regard any of you two
as—*chelas*. Thus, what you have now mistaken for " humbug "
as coming from Mr. Fern, you would have charged M. with it,
had you only known a little more than you do of our policy;
whereas the truth is, that one is utterly irresponsible for much he
is now doing, and that the other is carrying out that of which he
has honestly warned Mr. Fern beforehand; that, which,—if you
have read, as you say, the correspondence—you must have learned
from H.P.B.'s letter to Fern from Madras, that in her jealousy
for M.'s favours, she wrote to him to Simla, hoping she would
thereby frighten him off. A chela under probation is allowed to
think and do whatever he likes. He is warned and told beforehand:
"You will be tempted and deceived by appearances; two paths will be
open before you, both leading to the goal you are trying to attain;
one easy, and that will lead you more rapidly to the fulfilment

of orders you may receive; the other—more arduous, more long; a path full of stones and thorns that will make you stumble more than once on your way; and, at the end of which you may, perhaps, find failure after all and be unable to carry out the orders given for some particular small work,—but, whereas the latter will cause the hardships you have undergone on it to be all carried to the side of your credit in the long run, the former, the easy path, can offer you but a momentary gratification, an easy fulfilment of the task." The chela is at perfect liberty, *and often quite justified from the standpoint of appearances*—to suspect his Guru of being " a fraud " as the elegant word stands. More than that: the greater, the sincerer his indignation—whether expressed in words or boiling in his heart—the more fit he is, the better qualified to become an *adept*. He is free to [? use], and will not be held to account for using the most abusive words and expressions regarding his guru's actions and orders, provided he comes out victorious from the fiery ordeal; provided he resists all and every temptation; rejects every allurement, and proves that nothing, not even the promise of that which he holds dearer than life, of that most precious boon, his future adeptship—is able to make him deviate from the path of truth and honesty, or force him to become a *deceiver*. My dear Sir, we will hardly ever agree in our ideas of things, and even of the value of words. You have once upon a time called us *Jesuits*; and, viewing things as you do, perhaps, you were right to a certain extent in so regarding us, since *apparently* our systems of training do not differ much. But it is only externally. As I once said before, *they* know that what they teach *is a lie*; and *we* know that what we impart is truth, the only truth and nothing but the truth. *They* work for the greater power and glory (!) of *their order*; we—for the power and final glory of individuals, of isolated units, of humanity in general, and we are content, nay *forced*—to leave *our* Order and its chiefs entirely in the shade. They work, and toil, and *deceive*, for the sake of worldly power in *this life*; we work and toil, and allow our chelas *to be temporarily deceived*, to afford them means never to be deceived hereafter, and to see the whole evil of falsity and untruth, not alone in this but in many of their after lives. *They*—the Jesuits sacrifice the inner principle, the Spiritual brain of the ego, to feed and develop the better the physical brain of the personal evanescent man, sacrificing the whole humanity to offer it as a holocaust to their Society—the insatiable monster feeding on the brain and marrow of humanity, and developing an incurable cancer on every spot of healthy flesh it touches. We—the criticized and misunderstood Brothers—we seek to bring men to sacrifice their personality —a passing flash—for the welfare of the whole humanity, hence for their own *immortal* Egos, a part of the latter, as humanity is a fraction of the integral whole, that it will one day become. *They* are trained to deceive; we—to *undeceive*; they do the scavenger's work themselves—barring a few poor sincere tools of theirs—*con amore*, and for selfish ends; we—leave it to our menials—the *dugpas* at our service, by giving them *carte blanche* for the time being, and with the sole object of drawing out the whole *inner* nature of the chela, most of the nooks and corners of which would remain dark and concealed for ever, were not an opportunity afforded to test each of these corners in turn. Whether the chela wins or loses the prize—depends solely on himself. Only, you have to remember that our Eastern ideas about " motives " and " truthfulness " and " honesty " differ considerably from your ideas in the West. We both believe that it is moral to tell the truth and immoral to lie; but here every analogy stops and our notions diverge in a very remarkable degree. For instance it would be a most difficult thing for you to tell me, how it is that your civilized Western Society, Church and State, politics and commerce have ever come to assume a virtue that it is quite impossible for either a man of education, a statesman, a trader, or anyone else living in the world —to practice in an unrestricted sense? Can any one of the above mentioned classes—the flower of England's chivalry, her proudest peers and most distinguished commoners, her most virtuous and truth speaking ladies—can any of them speak the truth, I ask, whether at home, or in Society, during their public functions or in the family circle? What would you think of a gentleman, or a lady, whose affable politeness of manner and suavity of language would cover no falsehood; who, in meeting you would tell you plainly and abruptly what he thinks of you, or of anyone else? And where can you find that pearl of honest tradesmen or that god-fearing patriot, or politician, or a simple casual visitor of yours, but *conceals* his thoughts the whole while, and is obliged under the penalty of being regarded as a *brute*, a madman—*to lie* deliberately, and with a bold face, no sooner he is forced to tell you what he thinks of you; unless for a wonder his real feelings demand no concealment? *All is lie, all falsehood*, around and in us, my brother; and that is why you seem so surprised, if not affected, whenever you find a person who will tell you bluntly truth to your face; and also why it seems impossible for you to realize that a man may have *no* ill feelings against you, nay even like and respect you for some things, and yet tell you to your face what he honestly and sincerely thinks of you. In noticing M's opinion of yourself expressed in some of his letters—(you must not feel altogether so sure that because they are in *his* handwriting, they are written by him, though of course every word is sanctioned by him to serve certain ends)—you say he has " a peculiar mode of expressing himself to say the least." Now, that " way " is simply the bare

18

truth, which he is ready to write to yourself, or even say and repeat to your face, without the least concealment or change—(unless he has purposely allowed the expressions to be exaggerated for the same purposes as mentioned above); and he is—of all the men I know just the one to do it without the least hesitation! And for this, you call him " an imperious sort of chap very angry if he is opposed," but add, that you " bear him for it no malice, and like him none the less for that." Now THIS IS NOT SO, my brother, and YOU KNOW IT. However, I am prepared to concede the definition in a limited sense, and to admit and repeat with you (and himself at my elbow) that he is *a very imperious* sort of chap, and certainly very apt *sometimes* to become angry, especially if he is opposed in what he knows to be right. Would you think more of him, were he to *conceal* his anger; to *lie* to himself and the outsiders, and so permit them to credit him with a virtue he has not? If it is a meritorious act to extirpate with the roots all feelings of anger, so as to never feel the slightest paroxysm of a passion we all consider sinful, it is a still greater sin with us *to pretend* that it is so extirpated. Please read over the " Elixir of Life " No. 2 (April, p. 169 col. 1, paras. 2, 3, 4, 5, and 6). And yet in the ideas of the West, everything is brought down to *appearances* even in religion. A confessor does not inquire of his penitent whether he *felt* anger, but whether he has *shown* anger to anyone. " Thou shalt in lying, stealing, killing, etc., *avoid being detected* "—seems to be the chief commandment of the Lord gods of civilization—Society and Public opinion. That is the sole reason why you, who belong to it, will hardly if ever be able to appreciate such characters as Morya's: a man as stern for himself, as severe for his own shortcomings, as he is indulgent for the defects of other people, not *in words* but in the innermost feelings of his heart; or, while ever ready to tell you to your face anything he may think of you, he yet was ever a stauncher friend to you than myself, who may often hesitate to hurt anyone's feelings, even in speaking the strictest truth. Thus, were M. one to ever descend to an explanation he could have told you: " My Brother, in my opinion you are intensely egotistical and haughty. In your appreciation and self-adulation you generally lose sight of the rest of mankind, and I verily believe that you regard the whole universe created for man, and that *man*—yourself. If I cannot bear to be opposed when I know I am right, you can bear contradiction still less, even when your conscience plainly tells you that you are wrong. You are unable to *forget*—though I admit that you are one to *forgive*—the smallest slight. And, sincerely believing yourself to have been so slighted, by me (*sat upon*—as you once expressed it) to this day the supposed offence exercises a silent influence over all your thoughts in connexion with my humble individual.

And through your great intellect will ever prevent any vindictive feelings from asserting themselves and thus over-ruling your better nature, yet they are not without a certain influence even over your reasoning faculties, since you find pleasure (though you will hardly admit it to yourself)—in devising means to catch me tripping to the length of representing me in your imagination a *fool*, a credulous ignoramus capable of falling into the traps of a—Fern! Let us reason, my Brother. Let us put entirely aside the fact of my being an initiate, an adept—and reason out the position your imaginative faculties have created for me, like two common mortals with a certain dose of common sense in mine, and a great dose of the same in your head. If you are prepared to concede me even so little, I am prepared to prove to you that it is absurd to think that I could have been *taken in* in the meshes of so poor a scheme! You write that in order to *test* me, Fern wanted to know ' if Morya wished it (his vision) published—and Morya replies quite falling into the trap that he did wish it.' Now, to credit the last assertion is rather hard; and it needs a man of but moderate good sense and reasoning powers to perceive that there are two insuperable difficulties in the way of reconciling your foregoing opinion of myself and the belief that I was actually *caught in the trap*. 1st: The substance and text of the vision. In that vision there are three mysterious beings—the ' guru '—the ' Mighty one ' and the ' Father ';—the latter one being your humble servant. Now it is hard to believe—unless I am credited with faculties of a *hallucinated medium*—that I, knowing well that I had never approached, until then, the young gentleman from within a mile's distance, nor had I ever visited him in his dreams—that I should believe the reality of the vision described, or that, at least, my suspicions should not have been aroused by such a strange assertion.

" 2nd. The difficulty of reconciling the double fact of my being ' an imperious chap ' who gets very *angry when opposed*, and, my quiet submission to the disobedience, the *rebellion* of a chela under probation, who upon learning that ' Morya *did wish it* '—*i.e.* to have his vision published—and had actually promised to rewrite it, never thought of obeying the wish after that, nor had the poor fatuous *guru* and ' Father ' thought any more of the matter. Now the whole of the foregoing would be made quite plain even to a man of an average intellect. The reverse having happened, and a man of undoubtedly great intellectual and still greater *reasoning* powers, having been caught in the poorest cobweb of falsehoods ever imagined—the conclusion is imperative and no other can be formed: that man allowed, unknown to himself, to have his little vindictive feeling gratified at the expense of his logic and good sense. *Buss*, and we will talk no more of it. With all that, and while openly expressing my dislike for your haughtiness and selfishness in many things, I frankly recognise and express my admiration for your many other admirable qualities, for your sterling merits, and good sense in everything unconnected directly with yourself,—in which cases you become as imperious as myself, only far more impatient—and heartily hope you will pardon me for my blunt—and according to your western code of manners— *rude* talk. At the same time, like yourself, I will say, that not only do I not bear you malice, and like you none the less for that—but that what I say is a strict reality, the expression of my genuine feelings, not merely words written to satisfy a sense of assumed duty."

And now, that I have made myself the spokesman unto you for Morya, I may, perhaps [be] permitted to say a few words for myself. I will begin by reminding you, that at different times, especially during the last two months, you have repeatedly offered yourself as a *chela*, and the first duty of one is to hear without anger or malice anything the guru may say. How can we ever *teach* or you *learn* if we have to maintain an attitude utterly foreign to us and our methods:—that of two Society men? If you really want to be a *chela* i.e. to become the recipient of our mysteries, *you* have to adapt yourself to *our* ways, not we to *yours*. Until you do so, it is useless for you to expect any more than we can give under ordinary circumstances. You wanted to teach Morya, and you may find out, (and *will* if I am allowed by M. to have my own way) that he has taught you one [thing], which will either make us friends and brothers for ever, or—if there is more of the Western *gentleman* in you than of the Eastern chela and future adept—you will break with us in disgust and perhaps proclaim it all over the world. For this we are all prepared and are trying to hurry on the crisis one way or the other. November is fast approaching and by that time everything has to be settled. The second question: do not you think good Brother, that the uncivilized, *imperious* chap who would tell you his mind, honestly and for your own good, and, at the same time would be carefully though unseen—protecting yourself, family and reputation from any possible harm—aye, brother, to the length of watching for nights and days a ruffian Mussulman menial bent upon having his revenge of you, and actually destroying his evil plans—do not you think him worth ten times his weight in gold, a British Resident, a *gentleman*, who tears down your reputation to shreds behind your back and will smile upon and heartily shake hands with you whenever he meets you? Do not you think that it is far nobler to say what one thinks, and having said that which even you will naturally regard as an impertinence—and then render to the person so treated all manner of services of which he is never likely to hear, not only [? not] to find them out—than to do what the highly civilized Colonel or General Watson and especially his lady have done, when upon

seeing for the first time in their lives the two strangers in their
house—Olcott and a native judge in Baroda—took a pretext to
disparage the Society—*because you were in it*! I will not repeat to
you the *lies* they were guilty of, the exaggerations and slanders
directed against you by Mrs. Watson, and corroborated by her
husband—the gallant soldier, so struck and unruffled was poor
Olcott, by the unexpected attack—he who feels so proud of your
belonging to the Society that he appealed in his dismay to M.
Had you heard what was told by the latter of you, how much he
appreciated your present work and frame of mind, you would have
willingly conceded him the right of being occasionally *apparently*
rude. He forbade him telling any more than what he had already
told to H.P.B. and which—woman-like—she immediately imparted
to Mr. Sinnett—though angry as she was with you at the time
even she resented the insult and offence done to you deeply—and
went actually to the trouble of looking back into that past when as
Mrs. Watson said you were receiving the hospitality at their house.
Such is, then, the difference between alleged well wishers and
friends of Western superior origin, and the as alleged—ill-wishers
of the Eastern *inferior* race. Apart from this I concede to you
the right of feeling angry with M.; for he has done something
that though it is in strict accordance with our rules and methods,
will, when known be deeply resented by a Western mind, and,
had I known it in time to stop it, I would have certainly prevented
it from being done. It is certainly very kind of Mr. Fern to
express his intention " to catch " us—" not of course to expose
the Old Lady," for what has the poor " Old Lady " to do with
all this? But he is quite welcome to *catch* us and even to *expose* us,
not only for his and your protection but for that of the whole
world if it can in any way console him for his failure. And
fail he *will*, that's certain, if he goes on in that way playing a
double game. The option of receiving him or not as a regular
chela—remains with the Chohan. M. has simply to have him
tested, tempted and examined by all and every means, so as to
have his real nature drawn out. This is a rule with us as inexorable
as it is disgusting in your Western sight, and I could not prevent it
even if I would. It is not enough to know thoroughly what the
chela is capable of doing or not doing at the time and under the
circumstances during the period of probation. We have to know
of what he *may* become capable under different and every kind of
opportunities. Our precautions are all taken. None of our
Upasika or *Yu-posah*,[1] neither H.P.B. nor O., nor even Damodar,
nor any of them can be incriminated. He is welcome to show
every letter in his possession, and to divulge that, which was
offered to him to do, (the choice between *the two paths* being left

[1] Query, should be Upasaka, the male form of Upasika.—Eds.

at his option) and that *which he has actually done*, or rather *not* done. When the time comes—if it ever comes to his misfortune—we have the means to show how much of it is true, and how much wrong and invented by him. In the meanwhile, I have an advice to offer. *Watch* and do not say a word. He was, is, and will be *tempted* to do all manner of wrong things. As I say, I knew nothing of what was going on till the other day; when learning that even my name was indirectly mixed in the *probation*, I warned whom I had to warn, and forbid strictly my own business being mixed up with it. Yet, he is a magnificent subject for clairvoyance, and not at all as bad as you think him. He is conceited—but who is not? Who of us is entirely free from this defect? He may imagine and say what he likes, but that *you* should allow yourself to be so carried away with a prejudice the existence of which you are not even prepared to admit, is surpassingly strange! Your sincerely crediting the statement that M. was *humbugged* and caught *into the trap* by Mr. Fern is something really too ludicrous, when even O., not only the "Old Lady" never believed in it, since they knew he was to be under probation, and also knew what the thing meant. M. took pains a few days ago, to prove to you that he was never *taken* in, as you hoped, and that he laughed at the very idea; and most certainly Olcott will give you a good proof of it, albeit he is in the interior of Ceylon at this moment, where no letters let alone telegrams can reach. Nor was this "fraud"—if you will call it so, ever *commenced in our interests*, for the simple reason that we have no interest in it—but in that of Mr. Fern and the Society, in the ideas of H.P.B. But why call it *fraud*? He asked her advice, he worried and supplicated her, and she told him—"Work for the cause; try to enquire and search and so to obtain every evidence you can of the existence of the Brothers. You see they will not come this year, but there are plenty of Lamas descending every year to Simla and the neighbourhood, and so, get all the evidence you can for yourself and Mr. Hume, etc." Is there anything wrong in this? When she received the MSS. containing his vision, she asked M., and he who is called in it "the mighty One" and the "Father" and what not, *told her the truth* and then ordered her to ask Mr. Fern whether he would publish it, telling her and O. beforehand that he *would not*. What Morya knows of this and other visions, *he alone knows* and even I will never interfere in his ways of training, however distasteful they may be to me personally. The "Old Lady" since you ask me, will of course know nothing. But you must know that since she went to Baroda, she has a worse opinion of Fern than even yourself. She learned there certain things of him and of Brookes, and heard others from the latter, he being as you know the Baroda *Mejnour* of Fern's. She is a woman though she be an *Upā-si-ka* (female disciple) and except on occult matters can hardly hold her tongue. I believe we had enough of this. Whatever has or will yet happen it will affect but Fern—no one else.

I hear of the projected grand theosophical *Conversazione*—and if at that time *you are still theosophists*, of course it is better that it should be in your house. And now, I would like to say to you a few parting words. Notwithstanding the painful knowledge I have of your chief and almost one defect—one that you have yourself confessed to in your letter to me, I wish you to believe me, my dearest Brother, when I say that my regard and respect for you in all other things is great and very sincere. Nor am I likely to forget, whatever happens, that for many months past, without expecting or asking for any reward or advantage for yourself you have worked and toiled, day after day, for the good of the Society and of humanity at large in the only hope of doing good. And, I pray you, good Brother, not to regard as " reproaches " any simple remarks of mine. If I have argued with you, it was because I was forced to do so, since the Chohan regarded them (your *suggestions*) as something quite unprecedented; claims, in his position, not to be listened to for one moment. Though you may now regard the arguments directed against you in the light of " undeserved reproaches," yet you may recognise some day, that you were really " wanting unreasonable concessions." The fact that, your pressing proposals, that *you*—(not anyone else)— should, if possible be allowed to acquire some phenomenal gift, which would be used in convincing others,—though it may be accepted as standing simply, in *its dead letter* sense " as a suggestion for (my) consideration " and that it, " *in no way constituted a claim* " —yet for anyone who could read beneath the surface of the lines, it appeared as a definite claim, indeed. I have all your letters, and there is hardly one that does not breathe the spirit of a deter- mined claim, a *deserved* request, *i.e.*, a demand of that which is *due* and the rejection of which gives you a right to feel yourself wronged. I doubt not, that such was *not* your intention in penning them. But such was your secret thought and that innermost feeling was always detected by the Chohan, whose name you several times used, and who took note of it. You undervalue what you got so far on the ground of *inconsistency* and incompleteness? I have asked you: take notes of the former, beginning with the inconsistencies— as you regard them—in our first arguments *pro* and *con* the existence of God and ending with the supposed contradictions in respect to " accidents " and " suicides." Send then to me and I will prove to you that there is not one for him who knows well the whole doctrine. It is strange to accuse one in the full possession of his brains that on Wednesday he wrote one thing, and on Saturday or Sunday next had forgotten all about it and contradicted himself point blank! I do not think even our H.P.B. with her ridiculously impaired memory could be guilty of such a complete oblivion. In your opinion " it is not worth while to be working merely for the second class minds," and you propose following out the line of such an argument, either to get *all*, or leave off the work entirely if you cannot get out *immediately* " a scheme of philosophy, which will bear the scrutiny and criticism of such men as Herbert Spencer." To this I reply that you sin against the multitudes. It is not among the Herbert Spencers and Darwins or the John Stuart Mills that the millions of Spiritualists now going intellectually to the dogs are to be found, but it is they who form the majority of the " second class minds." If you had but patience, you would have received all that you would like to get out of our *speculative* philosophy—meaning by " speculative " that it would have to remain such, of course, to all but adepts. But really, my dear brother, you are not overloaded with that virtue. However I still fail to see why you should be disheartened with the situation.

Whatever happens, I hope you may not resent the friendly truths you have heard from us. Why should you? Would you resent the voice of your conscience whispering to you that you are at times unreasonably impatient, and not at all as forbearing as you yourself should like to be? True, you have been labouring for the cause without remission for many months and in many directions; but you must not think that because *we have never shown any knowledge of what you have been doing*, nor that, because we have never acknowledged or thanked you for it in our letters—that we are either ungrateful for, or ignore purposely or otherwise what you have done, for it is really not so. For, though no one ought to be expecting thanks, for doing his duty by humanity and the cause of truth,—since, after all, he who labours for others, labours but for himself—nevertheless, my Brother I feel deeply grateful to you for what you have done. I am not very demonstrative by nature but I do hope to prove to you some day, that I am not an ingrate, as you think. And you yourself, though you have been, indeed, forbearing in your letters to me, in not complaining about what you call the flaws and inconsistencies in our letters, yet you have not carried so far that forbearance, as to leave to time and further explanations the task of deciding whether such flaws were real or only apparently so upon their surface. You have always complained to Sinnett and even, in the beginning, to Fern. If you but consented for five minutes or so to fancy yourself in the position of a native *guru* and a European *chela*, you would soon perceive how monstrous must appear any such relations as ours to a native mind; and you would blame no one for disrespect. Now, pray, understand me; *I* do not complain; but the bare fact of your addressing me as " Master " in your letters—makes me the laughing-stock of all our *Tchutuktus* who know anything of our mutual relations. I would never have mentioned this fact, but that I am in a position to demonstrate to you by enclosing here a letter from Subba Row to myself—full of *excuses*, and another to H.P.B.—as full of *sincere truths*,—since they are both chelas, or rather disciples. I hope I am not committing an indiscretion—in the Western sense. You will please return to me both after reading them and noting what they say. This is sent to you in strict confidence and only for your personal instructions. You will perceive therein, how much you English have to *undo* in India, before you can hope to *do* anything good in the country. Meanwhile, I must close, reiterating to you once more the assurance of my sincere regards and esteem.

Yours,

K. H.

Believe me you are too severe upon and—*unjust* to Fern.

LETTER No. 31

Received London, March 26th, 1881.

It is from the depths of an unknown valley, amid the steep crags and glaciers of Terich-Mir—a vale never trodden by European foot since the day its parent mount was itself breathed out from within our Mother Earth's bosom—that your friend sends you these lines. For, it is there K.H. received your " Affectionate homages," and there he intends passing his " summer vacations." A letter " from the abodes of eternal snow and purity " sent to and received—" At the abodes of vice "! . . . Queer, *n'est-ce pas*? Would, or rather could I be with you at those " abodes "? No; but I was at several different times, elsewhere, though neither in " astral " nor in any other tangible form, but simply in thought. Does not satisfy you? Well, well, you know the limitations I am subjected to in your case, and you must have patience.

Your future book [1] is a little jewel; and, small and tiny as it is, it may, one day, be found to soar as high as Mount Everest over your Simla hills. Among all other works of that class, in the wild jungle of Spiritualistic literature, it shall undoubtedly prove the Redeemer, offered as a sacrifice for the sin of the world of Spiritualists. They will begin by rejecting—nay—vilifying it; but, it will find its faithful twelve and—the seed thrown by your hand into the soil of speculation will not grow up as a weed. So far may be promised. You are oft too cautious. You remind too often the reader of your ignorance; and presenting but as a modest theory that which at the bottom of your heart you know and feel to be an axiom, a primary *truth*—instead of helping, you but perplex him and—create doubt. But it is a spirited and

[1] The *Occult World*.—EDS.

discriminative little memoir, and as a critical estimate of the
phenomena witnessed by you personally, far more useful than
Mr. Wallace's work.   It is at this sort of spring that Spiritualists
ought to be compelled to slake their thirst for phenomena and
mystic knowledge instead of being left to swallow the idiotic gush
they find in the *Banners of Light* and others.   The world—meaning that of individual existences—is full of those latent meanings
and deep purposes which underlie all the phenomena of the
Universe, and Occult Sciences—*i.e.*, *reason* elevated to supersensuous Wisdom—can alone furnish the key wherewith to unlock
them to the intellect.   Believe me, there comes a moment in the
life of an adept, when the hardships he has passed through are
a thousandfold rewarded.   In order to acquire further knowledge,
he has no more to go through a minute and slow process of investigation and comparison of various objects, but is accorded an
instantaneous, implicit insight into every first truth.   Having
passed that stage of philosophy which maintains that all fundamental truths have sprung from a blind impulse—it is the philosophy of your Sensationalists or Positivists; and left far behind
him that other class of thinkers—the Intellectualists or Skeptics—
who hold that fundamental truths are derived from the intellect
alone, and that we, ourselves, are their only originating causes,
the adept sees and feels and lives in the very source of all fundamental truths—the Universal Spiritual Essence of Nature, SHIVA
the Creator, the Destroyer, and the Regenerator.   As Spiritualists
of to-day have degraded " Spirit," so have the Hindus degraded
Nature by their anthropomorphic conceptions of it.   Nature alone
can incarnate the Spirit of limitless contemplation.   " Absorbed in
the absolute self-unconsciousness of *physical Self*, plunged in the
depths of true Being, which is no being but eternal, universal
Life," his whole form as immoveable and white as the eternal
summits of snow in Kailasa where he sits, above care, above sorrow,
above sin and worldliness, a mendicant, a sage, a healer, the King
of Kings, the Yogi of Yogis, such is the ideal Shiva of *Yoga Shastras*,
the culmination of *Spiritual Wisdom*. . . . Oh, ye Max Mullers and
Monier Williamses, what have ye done with our Philosophy!

   But you can hardly be expected to enjoy or even understand the
above *phanerosis* [1] of our teachings.   Pardon me.   I write but seldom
letters; and whenever compelled to do so follow rather my own
thoughts than strictly hold to the subject I ought to have in view.
I have laboured for more than a quarter of a century night and
day to keep my place within the ranks of that invisible but ever
busy army which labours and prepares for a task which can bring
no reward but the consciousness that we are doing our duty to
humanity; and, meeting you on my way I have tried to—do not

---

[1] Presumably means a making visible.—EDS.

fear,—not to enroll you, for that would be impossible, but to simply draw your attention, excite your curiosity if not your better feelings to the one and only truth. You proved faithful and true, and have done your best. If your efforts will teach the world but one single letter from the alphabet of Truth—that Truth which once pervaded the whole world—your reward will not miss you. And now that you have met the " mystics " of Paris and London what do you think of them? . . .

Yours,

K. H.

P.S.—Our hapless " Old Lady " is sick. Liver, kidneys, head, brain, legs, every organ and limb shows fight and snaps its fingers at her efforts to ignore them. One of us will have to "*fix* her " as our worthy Mr. Olcott says, or it will fare badly with her.

LETTER No. 32

I am sorry for all that has happened, but it was to be expected. Mr. Hume has put his foot in a hornet's nest and must not complain. If my *confession* has not altered *your* feelings—I am determined not to influence you and therefore will not look your way to find out how the matter stands with you, my friend—and if you are not entirely disgusted with our system and ways; if in short it is still your desire to carry on a correspondence and learn, something must be done to check the irresponsible " Benefactor." I prevented her sending to Hume a worse letter than she wrote to yourself. I *cannot* force her to transmit his letters to me nor mine to him; and since it is no longer possible for me to trust Fern, and that G.K. can hardly be sacrificed with any sense of justice, to a man who is utterly unable to appreciate any service rendered except his own,—what shall we do about it? Since we have mixed ourselves with the outside world, we have no right to suppress the personal opinion of its individual members, nor eschew their criticism, however unfavourable to us—hence the positive order to H.P.B. to publish Mr. Hume's article. Only, as we would have the world see both sides of the question, we have also allowed the joint protest of Deb, Subba Row, Damodar and a few other chelas—to follow his criticism of ourselves and our System in the Theosophist.

I gave you but hints of what at some other time I will write more at length. Think in the meantime of the difficulties that lie naturally in our way, and let us not, if your friendship for me is sincere,—by struggling with our chains, make them straiter and heavier. For my part I will run willingly the hazard of being thought a self-contradicting ignoramus, and criticized in unmeasured terms by Mr. Hume in print, provided you really profit by the tuition, and share from time to time your knowledge with the world. But to give you my thoughts without disguise I am never like to risk myself again with any other European but yourself. As you now see, connection with the outside world can bring but sorrow to those who so faithfully serve us, and discredit to our Brotherhood. No Asiatic is ever likely to be affected by Mr. Hume's egotistical thrusts against us (the result of my last letter, and of the promise exacted that he will write to me more rarely and less than he has done) but these thrusts and criticisms that the European readers will accept as a revelation and a confession, without ever suspecting from whence they have arisen and by what a deeply egotistical feeling they have been generated —these thrusts are calculated to do a great harm—in a direction you have not hitherto dreamt of. Resolved not to lose so useful a tool (useful in one direction, of course) the Chohan permitted himself to be over-persuaded by us into giving sanction to my intercourse with Mr. Hume. I had pledged my word to him that he had repented,—was a changed man. And now how shall I ever face my Great Master, who is laughed at, made the object of Mr. Hume's wit, called Rameses the Great, and such like indecent remarks? And he used terms in his letters, the brutal grossness of which prevents me from repeating them, which have revolted my soul when I read them; words so filthy as to pollute the very air that touched them, and that I hastened to send to you with the letter that contained it, so as not to have those pages in my house, full of young and innocent chelas, that I would prevent from ever hearing such terms.

Then you yourself, my friend, influenced in this by him more than you know or suspect—you yourself deduce but too readily from *incompleteness* " contradiction." The novelty or inexplicable aspect of any asserted fact in our science is not a sufficient reason for setting it immediately down as a contradiction, and proclaim as Hume does in his article that he could teach in one week that which he succeeded in drawing out of us in eighteen months, for your knowledge is as yet so limited that it would be difficult for him to say how much we do or do not know.

But I have lingered too long over this irrational, unphilosophical and illogical attack upon ourselves and System. One day we will show the invalidity of the objections preferred by Mr. H. He may be regarded as a sapient councillor in the municipality, but he could hardly be regarded in such a light by us. He accuses me of giving through him " false ideas and facts " to the world; and adds that he would willingly keep aloof from—break with us but for his desire of benefitting the world! Verily a most easy method of burking all the sciences, for there is not one in which

" false facts " and wild theories do not abound.   Only while the Western Sciences make confusion still more confused our Science explains all the seeming discrepancies and reconciles the wildest theories.

However, if you do not bring him to his senses there will be soon an end to all—this time irrevocable.   I need not assure you of my sincere regard for you and our gratitude for what you have [done] for the Society here—indirectly for us two.   Whatever happens, I am at your service.   I would, could I but see my way, do all that can be done for your friend Colonel Chesney.   For *your* sake, if the crisis is avoided and the black cloud blows off—I will instruct him as far as I can.   But—may it not be too late?

Yours in good faith,

K. H.

LETTER No. 33
K.H. Letter received through M. shown to A.B.

I am sincerely afraid that you may have been perplexed by the apparent contradiction between the notes received by you from my Brother M.—and myself.   Know my friend that in our world though we may differ in methods we can never be opposed in *principles of action*, and the broadest and most practical application of the idea of the Brotherhood of Humanity is not incompatible with your dream of establishing a nucleus of honest scientific enquirers of good repute, who would give weight to the T.S. organization in the eyes of the multitude, and serve as a shield against the ferocious and idiotic attack of sceptics and materialists.

There are—even among English men of Science—those who are already prepared to find our teachings in harmony with the results and progress of their own researches, and who are not indifferent to their application to the spiritual needs of humanity at large. Amongst these it may be your task to throw the seeds of Truth and point out the path.   Yet as my brother reminded you, not one of those who have only tried to help on the work of the Society, however imperfect and faulty their ways and means, will have done so in vain.   The situation will be more fully explained to you by and by.

Meanwhile use every effort to develop such relations with A. Besant that your work may run on parallel lines and in full sympathy; an easier request than some of mine with wh'ch you have ever loyally complied.   You may, if you see fit—show this note to her, *only*.   In travelling your own thorny path I say again *courage* and *hope*.   This is *not* an answer to your letter.

Yours ever truly,

K. H.

LETTER No. 34

It is positively distressing to find oneself so systematically misunderstood, one's intentions misconceived, and the whole plan imperilled by this endless hurrying on. Are we never then to be granted any credit for knowing what we are about, or allowed the benefit of the doubt in the absence of any reasonable proof whatever that we have determined to " bar the progress " of the Theos.: Society? Mr. Hume maintains that he does not say— " K.H. or any other brother *is wrong* "—withal every line of his numerous letters to myself and H.P.B. breathes the spirit of *complaint* and bitter accusation. I tell you, my good friend, he will *never* be satisfied do what we may! And as we cannot consent to over-flood the world at the risk of drowning them, with a doctrine that has to be cautiously given out, and bit by bit like a too powerful tonic which can kill as well as cure—the result will be a reaction in that insatiable craving of his, and then—well you yourself know the consequences. Enclosed two letters written and addressed to her with an eye to myself. Well, we can do no better for the present. The Society will never perish as an institution, although branches and individuals in it may. I have done to *humour* him lately more than I have ever done for you; and you may judge of the situation in the chaotic but on the whole reasonable remarks that H.P.B. addresses to-day to Mr. H.

We must be left to judge for ourselves and be permitted to be the best judges. Everything will be explained and given out, in good time if we are but allowed our own ways. Otherwise, rather give up the *Eclectic*. I had volumes from him during the past week! I send you a few notes through her. Keep *this* confidential.

Yours,

K. H.

LETTER No. 35

Letter from K. H. Received Allahabad, March 18th, 1882.

You did not quite apprehend the meaning of my note, good friend, of March 11th. I said it was easy to produce phenomena, when the necessary conditions were given, but not that even the presence of Olcott and Mallapura at your house brought such an accession of force as would suffice for the tests you propose.

These latter were reasonable enough from your point of view, I do not at all blame you for asking them. I, myself, would perhaps wish you to have them—for your personal gratifications, not that of the public for, as you know, conviction in these cases must be reached by individual experience. Secondhand testimony never really satisfied any but a credulous (or rather non-sceptical) mind.

No Spiritualist who should read in your second edition even a
narrative of the very tests you have named to me, would for one
moment ascribe the facts to aught but mediumship; and your lady
and yourself would probably be included by them in the sum of
the mediumistic factors. Fancy that! No—bide your time; you
are slowly gathering together the materials for what we here call,
as you know, real dgiü,[1] make the best of it. It is not *physical*
phenomena that will ever bring conviction to the hearts of the
unbelievers in the " Brotherhood " but rather phenomena of
intellectuality, *philosophy* and logic, if I may so express it. See
" Spirit teachings " by + as given out by Oxon—the most intellectual as the best educated of all mediums. Read and—*pity*!
Do you not see then *where we are* " driving at " as O. says? Do you
not realize that were it not for your exceptional intellect and the
help to be derived therefrom the Chohan would have long ago
closed every door of communication between us? Yes, read and
study, my friend; for there is an object. You seemed annoyed,
disappointed, when reading the words, " Impossible: no power
here, will write through Bombay." Those eight words will have
cost me eight days recuperative work—in the state I am in at
present. But *you know not* what I mean; you are absolved.

You will not diguise from yourself the difficulties of working out
your scheme of " Degrees." I wanted you to develop it at your
leisure, " as the spirit moved you." For even though you should
not quite succeed in forming a scheme that would fit the needs of
Asia and Europe, you might hit upon something that would be
good for either the one or the other, and another hand might then
supply the lacking portion. Asiatics are so poor, as a rule, and
books are so inaccessible to them in these degenerate days, that you
can see plainly how different a plan of intellectual culture—in
preparation for practical experiments to unfold psychic power in
themselves—must be thought. In the olden time, this want was
supplied by the Guru, who guided the chela through the difficulties
of childhood and youth, and afforded him in oral teaching as much
as, or more than through books the food for mental and psychic
growth. The want of such a " guide, philosopher and friend,"
(and who so well deserves the tripartite title?) can never be supplied, try as you may. All you can do is to prepare the intellect:
the impulse toward " soul-culture " must be furnished by the
individual. Thrice fortunate they who can break through the
vicious circle of modern influence and come up above the vapours!

To recur to your Degrees: Are you not drawing the lines too
vaguely between the first three or four groups? What test do you
apply to decide their respective mental states? How guard against
mere " cramming? and copying? and substitute writing? " Many

---

[1] True knowledge, as distinct from knowledge of the ephemeral.—Eds.

clever Jesuits might pass all your Degrees, even up to the 6th and 7th: would you, then, admit him into the second section? Remember the lessons of the past and Carter Blake. It is quite possible—as Moorad Ali Beg said and Olcott confirmed to you—for one who had passed the first five stages to acquire " occult faculties " in the 6th. Nay, it can be done without the help of either—by adopting either the method of the Arhats, the Dasturs, the Yogis, or the Sufis; among each of which groups of mystics there have been many who did not even read or write. If the psychic idiosyncracy is lacking, no culture will supply it. And the highest theoretical as also practical school of this kind is that one in which we associates—your *interested correspondents*—were taught.

All that precedes has been said not for your discouragement but as a stimulus. If you are a true Anglo-Saxon, no obstacle will daunt your zeal; and unless my Eye has been dimmed this is your character—*au fond*. We have one word for all aspirants: TRY.

And now, to your laugh in September last as to the imaginary dangers to him who produces phenomena, dangers growing in size in proportion to the magnitude of the phenomena so produced, and the impossibility to refute them. Remember the proposed test of the *Times* to be brought here. My good friend, if the trifling phenomena (for they are trifling in comparison with what could and might be done) shown by Eglinton provoked such bitter hatred, evoking before him scenes of imprisonment owing to *false witnesses*, what would not be the fate of the poor " Old Lady "! You are yet barbarians with all your boasted civilization.

And now to Morya. (This *strictly between us and you must not breathe it even to Mrs. Gordon*). Eglinton was preparing to depart leaving on poor Mrs. G.'s mind the fear that she had been deceived; that there were *no* " Brothers " since Eglinton had *denied their existence* and that the " Spirits " were silent as to that problem. Last week then M., stalking in, into the motley crowd took the spooks by the skin of their throats and,—the result was the unexpected admission of the Brothers, the actual existence and the honour claimed of a personal acquaintance with the " Illustrious." The lesson for you and others, derived from the above, may be useful in future—events having to grow and to develop.

Yours faithfully,

K. H.

LETTER No. 36

Received about January, 1882.

My impatient friend—allow me, as one having some authority in your theosophical *mella*, to empower you to " ignore the rules " for a short time. Make them fill up the forms and initiate the candidates

right away. Only whatever you do, do it without delay.
Remember, you are the only one now. Mr. Hume is fully
engrossed in his *index* and expects *me* to write to him and make
puja first. I am rather too tall for him to reach so easily to my
head—if he has any intention to cover it with the ashes of contri-
tion. Nor will I put [on] a sack-cloth to show repentance for
what I have done. If he writes and puts questions all well and
good, I'll answer them, if not—I will keep my lectures for someone
else. Time is no object with me.

Had your letter. I know your difficulties. Will see to them.
Great will be the disappointment of K.H. if upon returning to us
he finds so little progress done. You—you are sincere, others—
put their pride above all. Then those Prayag theosophists—the
Pundits and Babus! They do *naught* and expect us to correspond
with them. Fools and arrogant men.

M.

LETTER No. 37

Received at Allahabad, January, 1882.

Private.

Honoured Sir,

The Master has awaked and bids me write. To his great regret
for certain reasons He will not be able until a fixed period has
passed to expose Himself to the thought currents inflowing so
strongly from beyond the Himavat. I am therefore commanded
to be the hand to indite His message. I am to tell you that He
is " quite as friendly to you as heretofore and well satisfied with
both your good intentions and even their execution so far as it lay
in your power. You have proved your affection and sincerity by
your zeal. The impulse you have personally given to the Cause
we love, will not be checked; therefore the fruits of it (the word
" reward " is avoided being used but for the " goody-goody ")
will not be withheld when your balance of causes and effects—your
Karma is adjusted. In unselfishly and at personal risk labouring
for your neighbour, you have most effectually worked for yourself.
One year has wrought a great change in your heart. The man
of 1880 would scarcely recognise the man of 1881 were they confronted. Compare them, then, good friend and Brother, that you
may fully realize what time has done, or rather what you have
done with time. To do this meditate—alone, with the magic
mirror of memory to gaze into. Thus shall you not only see the
lights and shadows of the Past, but the possible brightness of the
Future, as well. Thus, in time, will you come to see the Ego of
aforetime in its naked reality. And thus also you shall hear from

me *direct* at the earliest, practicable opportunity, " for we are not ungrateful and even Nirvana cannot obliterate GOOD."

These are the Master's words, as with His help I am enabled to frame them in your language, honoured Sir. I am personally permitted, at the same time to thank you very warmly for the genuine sympathy which you felt for me at the time when a slight accident due to my forgetfulness laid me on my bed of sickness.

Though you may have read in the modern works on mesmerism how that which we call " Will-Essence "—and you " fluid "—is transmitted from the operator to his objective point, you perhaps scarcely realize how everyone is practically, albeit unconsciously, demonstrating this law every day and every moment. Nor, can you quite realize how the training for adeptship increases both one's capacity to emit and to feel this form of force. I assure you that I, though but a humble chela as yet, felt your good wishes flowing to me as the convalescent in the cold mountains feels from the gentle breeze that blows upon him from the plains below.

I am also to tell you that in a certain Mr. Bennett of America who will shortly arrive at Bombay, you may recognise one, who, in spite of his national provincialism, that you so detest, and his too infidelistic bias, is one of our agents (unknown to himself) to carry out the scheme for the enfranchisement of Western thoughts from superstitious creeds. If you can see your way towards giving him a correct idea of the actual present and potential future state of Asiatic but more particularly of Indian thought, it will be gratifying to my Master. He desires me to let you know, at the same time, that you should not feel such an exaggerated delicacy about taking out the work left undone from Mr. Hume's hands. That gentleman chooses to do but what suits his personal fancy without any regard whatever to the feelings of other people. His present work also—a pyramid of intellectual energy misspent —his objections and reasons, are all calculated but to exonerate himself only. Master regrets to find in him the same spirit of utter, unconscious, selfishness with no view to the good of the Cause he represents. If he seems interested in it at all, it is because he is opposed and finds himself roused to combativeness. Thus the answer to Mr. Terry's letter sent to him from Bombay ought to have been published in the January number. Will you kindly see to it—Master asks? Master thinks you can do it as well as Mr. Hume if you but tried, as the metaphysical faculty in you is only dormant but would fully develop were you but to awake it to its full action by constant use. As to our reverenced M:, he desires me to assure you that the secret of Mr. Hume's professed love for Humanity lies in, and is based upon, the chance

presence in that word of the first syllable; as for " mankind "—he
has no sympathy for it.

Since Master will not be able to write to you himself for a month
or two longer (though you will always hear of him)—He begs you
to proceed for his sake with your metaphysical studies; and not
to be giving up the task in despair whenever you meet with
incomprehensible ideas in M. Sahib's notes, the more so, as M.
Sahib's only hatred in his life is for writing. In conclusion Master
sends you His best wishes and praying you may not forget Him,
orders me to sign myself, your obedient servant,

The " Disinherited."

P.S. Should you desire to write to Him, though unable to
answer Himself Master will receive your letters with pleasure; you
can do so through D. K. Mavalankar.

Dd.

LETTER No. 38

Received Allahabad. About February, 1882.

Your " illustrious " friend did not mean to be " satirical,"
whatever other construction might be put on his words. Your
" illustrious " friend was simply feeling sad at the thought of
the great disappointment K.H. is sure to experience when he
returns among us. The first retrospective glance at the work he
has so much at heart, will show him such samples of mutual feeling exchanged as the two herein enclosed. The undignified,
bitter, sarcastic tone of one will give him as little cause to rejoice
as the undignified, foolish and childish tone of the other. I would
have left the subject untouched had you not so misunderstood the
feeling that dictated my last. It is better I should be frank with
you. The term " Highness " to which I am not in the least
entitled is far more suggestive of *satire* than anything I have
hitherto said. Yet as " no epithet will hang to the shirt-collar of
a Bod-pa " I heed it not, advising you to do the same and see no
satire where none is meant and which is but frankness in speech,
and the correct definition of the general state of your feelings
toward the natives.

Your solicitor knows better—of course. If the paragraph in
question is not *libellous* then all I can say is, that a complete recodi-
fication of your libel law is very much needed.

You will certainly have trouble with her about the " female
branch." Her scorn for the *sex*—has no bounds and she can
hardly be persuaded that any good can ever come from that
quarter. I will be frank with you again. Neither myself nor
any of us—K.H. being entirely left out of the question—would

consent to become the founders, let alone the conductors of a *female* branch—we all having had enough of our *anis*.[1] Yet we confess that a great good may result of such a movement, the females having such an influence over their children and the men in the houses, you being such an old and experienced hand in that direction could with Mr. Hume's help be of immense use to K.H., from within the area of whose " loveable nature," with the exception of his sister, females were always excluded and love for his country and humanity reigned alone. He knows nothing of the creatures—you do. He always felt the need of enrolling women —yet would never meddle with them. There's a chance for you to help him.

On the other hand we claim to know more of the secret cause of events than you men of the world do. I say then that it is the vilification and abuse of the founders, the general misconception of the aims and objects of the Society that paralyses its progress— nothing else. There's no want of definitiveness in these objects were they but properly explained. The members would have plenty to do were they to pursue reality with half the fervour they do *mirage*. I am sorry to find you comparing Theosophy to a painted house on the stage whereas in the hands of true philan- thropists and theosophists it might become as strong as an impregnable fort. The situation is this: men who join the Society with the one selfish object of reaching power, making occult science their only or even chief aim may as well not join it—they are doomed to disappointment as much as those who commit the mistake of letting them believe that the Society is nothing else. It is just because they preach too much " the Brothers " and too little if at all *Brotherhood* that they fail. How many times had we to repeat, that he who joins the Society with the sole object of coming in contact with us and if not of acquiring at least of assuring himself of the reality of such powers and of our objective existence —was pursuing a mirage? I say again then. It is he alone who has the love of humanity at heart, who is capable of grasping thoroughly the idea of a regenerating practical Brotherhood who is entitled to the possession of our secrets. He alone, such a man —will never misuse his powers, as there will be no fear that he should turn them to selfish ends. A man who places not the good of mankind above his own good is not worthy of becoming our *chela*—he is not worthy of becoming higher in knowledge than his neighbour. If he craves for phenomena let him be satisfied with the pranks of spiritualism. Such is the real state of things. There was a time, when from sea to sea, from the mountains and deserts of the north to the grand woods and downs of Ceylon, there was but one faith, one rallying cry—to save humanity from the miseries

[1] Nuns.—EDS.

of ignorance in the name of Him who taught first the solidarity of all men. How is it now? Where is the grandeur of our people and of the one Truth? These, you may say, are beautiful visions which were once realities on earth, but had flitted away like the light of a summer's evening. Yes; and now we are in the midst of a conflicting people, of an obstinate, ignorant people seeking to know the truth yet not able to find it, for each seeks it only for his own private benefit and gratification, without giving one thought to others. Will you, or rather they, never see the true meaning and explanation of that great wreck and desolation which has come to our land and threatens all lands—yours first of all? It is *selfishness* and *exclusiveness* that killed ours, and it [is] selfishness and exclusiveness that will kill yours—which has in addition some other defects which I will not name. The world has clouded the light of true knowledge, and *selfishness* will not allow its resurrection, for it excludes and will not recognise the whole fellowship of all those who were born under the same immutable natural law.

You are mistaken again. I may blame your " curiosity " when I know it to be profitless. I am unable to regard as an " impertinence " that which is but the free use of intellectual capacities for reasoning. You may see things in a false light and you do often so see them. But you do not concentrate all the light *in yourself* as some do, and that's one superior quality you possess over other Europeans we know. Your affection for K.H. is sincere and warm and that is your redeeming quality in my eyes. Why should you then await my reply with any " nervousness " at all. Whatever happens we two will ever remain your friends, as we would not blame *sincerity* even when it is manifested under the somewhat objectionable form of trampling upon a prostrated enemy—the hapless Babu.

Yours,

M.

LETTER No. 39

Received Allahabad, about December, 1881.

If my advice is sought and asked, then first of all the real and *true* situation has to be defined. My " *Arhat* " vows are pronounced, and I can neither seek revenge nor help others to obtain it. I can help her with cash only when I know that not a *mace*, not a fraction of a *tael* will be spent upon any unholy purpose: and revenge *is* unholy. But we have *defence* and she has a right to it. Defence and *full vindication she* must have, and that is why I telegraphed to offer option before proceeding to file a suit. Demand retraction and *threaten* with a law suit she has a right;

and she can also institute proceedings—for *he will* retract. For that reason have I laid a stress upon the necessity of an article touching upon no other subject but that of the alleged " debt." This alone will prove sufficient to frighten the traducer for it will reveal him before the public as a " slanderer " and show to himself that he was in the wrong box. The mistake is due to the very illegible and ugly handwriting of Macauliffe (a calligrapher and scribe of my kind) who sent in the information to *Statesman.* This *was* a lucky mistake for on that may be built the whole vindication if you act wisely. But the most has to be made of it now—or you will lose the opportunity. So, if you condescend once more to take my advice—since you have opened the first shot in *Pioneer,* seek out the accounts in *Theosophist* and on that data and the Tuesday article write for her a nice pungent letter signed with her name and Olcott's. This can be published first in the *Pioneer* or, if you object to it, in some other paper—but at all events they will have to print it in the form of a circular letter and send it to every paper in the land. Demand retraction in it from *Statesman* and threaten with law suit. If you do that I promise success.

The Odessa Old Lady—the *Nadyejda*—is quite anxious for your autograph—that of " a great and celebrated writer "; she says she was very undisposed to part with your letter to the General but had to send you a proof of her own identity. Tell her I—the " *Khosyayin* "[1] (her niece's *Khosyayin* she called me as I went to see her thrice) gossiped the thing to you advising you to write to her, furnishing her thus with your autograph—also send back through H.P.B. her portraits as soon as shown to your lady, for she at Odessa is very anxious to have them back especially the young face. . . . That's her, as I knew her first " the lovely maiden."

I'm a little busy just now—but will furnish you with explanatory appendix as soon as at leisure—say in two three days. The " Illustrious " will look to all that needs watching. What about Mr. Hume's superb address? Can't you have it ready for your January Number? *Ditto* your editorial answer to *Spiritualist's* editorial. Hope y'll not accuse me of any desire to *sit upon you*— nor will you view my humble request in any other light than the true one. My object is twofold—to develop your metaphysical intuitions and help the journal by infusing into it a few drops of real literary good blood. Your three articles are certainly praiseworthy, the points well taken and as far as I can judge—calculated to arrest the attention of every scholar and metaphysician especially the 1st. Later on you will learn more about creation.

Meanwhile I have to create my dinner—you would scarcely like it—I'm afraid.

M.

---

[1] Russian for manager or boss.—EDS

Your young friend the Disinherited is on his legs again. Would you really care for his writing to you? In such case, better ventilate in *Pioneer* the question as to the advisability of coming to terms with China in regard to the establishment of a regular postal service between Prayag and Shigatse.

LETTER No. 40

Received about February, 1882.

To your first—there's little to answer: " Can you do anything to help on the Society? " Want me to speak frankly? Well I say No; neither yourself nor the Lord Sang-gias Himself—so long as the equivocal position of the Founders is not perfectly and undeniably proved due to fiendish malice and a systematic intrigue —could help it on.   That's the situation as I found it, as ordered by the chiefs.   Watch the papers—all except two or three; the " dear old lady " ridiculed when not positively libelled, Olcott attacked by all the hell-hounds of the press and missions.   A pamphlet headed " Theosophy " printed and circulated by the Christians at Tinevelly October 23rd on the day of O.'s arrival there with the Buddhist delegates—a pamphlet containing the *Saturday Review* article and another *filthy*, heavy attack by an American paper.   The *C.* and *M.* of Lahore hardly missing a day without having some attack and other papers reprinting them, etc., etc.   You English have your notions—we have *our own* upon the subject.   If you keep the clean kerchief in your pocket and throw but the soiled one into the crowd—who will pick it up? Enough.   We must have patience and do what, meanwhile, we can.   My opinion is, that if your Rattigan is not quite a scoundrel, one of his papers having thrown and throwing daily dishonour upon an innocent woman, he would be the first to suggest [to] you the idea of translating and publishing her uncle's letters (to you and herself) in the *Pioneer*; with a few words in a leader, to say that a still more substantial *official* proof is shortly expected from the Prince D. which will settle the vexed question as to her identity for ever at rest.   But you know best.   This idea may have struck *you*; but will it ever be seen in such a light by others?

Suby Ram—a truly good man—yet a devotee of another error. Not his guru's voice—*his own*.   The voice of a pure, unselfish, earnest soul, absorbed in misguided, misdirected mysticism.   Add to it a chronic disorder in that portion of the brain which responds to clear vision and the secret is soon told: that disorder was developed by *forced* visions; by *hatha* yog and prolonged asceticism. S. Ram is the chief *medium* and at same time the principal magnetic factor, who spreads his disease by infection—unconsciously to himself; who innoculates with his vision all the other disciples. There is one general law of vision (physical and mental or spiritual) but there is a qualifying special law proving that all vision must be determined by the quality or grade of man's spirit and soul, and also by the ability to translate diverse qualities of waves of astral light into consciousness. There is but one general law of life, but innumerable laws qualify and determine the myriads of forms perceived and of sounds heard. There are those who are willingly and others who are *unwillingly*—blind. Mediums belong to the former, sensitives to the latter. Unless regularly initiated and trained—concerning the spiritual insight of things and the supposed revelations made unto man in all ages from Socrates down to Swedenborg and " Fern "—no self-tutored seer or clairaudient ever saw or heard *quite* correctly.

No harm and much instruction may come to you by joining his Society. Go on *until he demands what you will be obliged to refuse.* Learn and study. You are right: they say and affirm that *the one* and only God of the Universe was incarnated in their guru, and were such an individual to exist he would certainly be higher than any " planetary." But they are idolators, my friend. Their guru was no initiate, only a man of extraordinary purity of life and powers of endurance. He had never consented to give up his notions of a personal god and even gods though offered more than once. He was born an orthodox Hindu and died a *self-reformed* Hindu, something like Keshub Chunder Sen but higher, purer and with no ambition to taint his bright soul. Many of us have regretted his self-delusion but he was too good to be forcibly interfered with. Join them and learn—but remember your sacred promise to K.H. Two months more and he will be with us. I think of sending her to you. I believe you could persuade her for I do not wish to use my authority in this case.

M.

LETTER No. 41

Received about February, 1882.

I believe verily I am unfit to express my ideas clearly in your language. I never thought of giving any importance to the *circular letter*—I had asked you to draft for them—appearing in the *Pioneer*, or ever meant to imply that it *should* so appear. I had asked you to compose it for them, send your drafted copy to Bombay and make them issue it as a *circular letter*; which, once out, and on its round in India might be copied in your journal as other papers would be sure to copy it. Her letter B.G. *was* foolish, childish and silly. I have overlooked it. But you must not so labour under the impression that it will *undo* all the good yours has done. There are a few sensitive persons on whose nerves it will jar, but the rest will never appreciate its true spirit; nor is it in any way libellous—only vulgar and foolish. I will force her to stop.

At the same time I must say she suffers acutely and I am unable to help her, for all this is effect from causes which *cannot* be *undone* —occultism in theosophy. She has now to either conquer or die. When the hour comes she will be taken back to Tibet. Do not blame the poor woman, blame me. She is but a "shell" at times and I, often careless in watching her. If the laugh is not turned on the *Statesman* the ball will be caught up by other papers and flung at her again.

Do not feel despondent. Courage my good friend and remember you are working off by helping her your own law of retribution, for more than one cruel fling she receives is due to K.H.'s friendship for you, for his using her as the means of communication. But—Courage.

I saw the lawyer's papers and perceive he is averse to taking up the case. But for the little he is needed for, he will do. No law suit will help—but publicity in the matter of vindication as much as in the question of accusation—10,000 *circular letters* sent throughout to prove accusations false.

Yours till the morrow.

M.

LETTER No. 42 [1]

Received about February, 1882.

I say again what you like me not to say, namely that *no regular* instruction, no regular communication is possible between us before our mutual path is cleared of its many impediments, the greatest being the public misconception about the Founders. For your impatience you cannot nor will you be blamed. But if you fail to make a profitable use of your newly-acquired privileges, you would indeed be unworthy, friend. Three, four weeks more —and I will retire to give room with you all to him to whom that room belongs, and whose place I could but very inadequately occupy, for I am neither a scribe nor a Western scholar. Whether the Chohan finds yourself and Mr. Hume more qualified than he did before to receive instructions through us—is another question. But you ought to prepare for it. For much remains yet to break forth. You perceived, hitherto but the light of a new day—you may, if you try, see with K.H.'s help the sun of full noon-day when it reaches its meridian. But you have to work for it, work

---

[1] This letter is unsigned but is in M.'s handwriting.—ED.

for the shedding of light upon other minds through yours. How, will you say? Hitherto of you two, Mr. H. was positively antagonistic to our advice, you—passively resisting it at times, often yielding against what you conceived your better judgment—such is my answer. The results were—what they had to be expected. No good or very little came out of a kind of spasmodic defence—the solitary defence of *a friend* presumably prejudiced in favour of those whose champion he had come out and a member of the Society. Mr. Hume would never listen to K.H.'s suggestion of a lecture in his house during which he might have well disabused the public mind of a part of the prejudice at least, if not entirely. You thought it was unnecessary to publish and spread among the readers *as to who* she was. Think ye, Primrose and Rattigan are likely to spread the knowledge and give out reports of what they know to be the case? And so on. *Hints* are all sufficient to an intelligence like yours. I tell you this for I know how profound and sincere is your feeling for K.H. I know how bad y'll feel, if when among us again you find that communication between you has not improved. And its sure to pass when the Chohan finds no progress since he made *him* have you. See what the *Fragments*—the most superb of articles—has done; how little effect it will produce unless the opposition is stirred up, discussion provoked and spiritualists forced to defend their foolish claims. Read editorial in *Spiritualist* November 18, " Speculation-Spinning "—she cannot answer it as either he or you might and the result will be that the most precious hints will fail to reach the minds of those craving for truth, for a solitary pearl is soon outshone in the midst of a heap of false diamonds, when *there's no jeweller to point* out its worth. So on again. What can we do! I hear already K.H. exclaiming.

It is so, friend. The pathway through earth-life leads through many conflicts and trials, but he who does naught to conquer them can expect no triumph. Let then the anticipation of a fuller introduction into our mysteries under more congenial circumstances, the creation of which depends *entirely upon yourself* inspire you with patience to wait for, perseverance to press on to, and full preparation to receive the blissful consummation of all your desires. And for that you have to remember that when K.H. shall say to you, Come up hither—you should be ready. Otherwise the all powerful hand of our Chohan will appear once more between you and *Him.*

Send both portraits sent to you from Odessa back to H.P.B., the O.L. when you [have] done with them. Write a few lines to the old *Generaless* to Odessa—for she sorely wants *your autograph*—I know. Remind her that both [of] you belong to one Society and are—*Brothers*, and promise help for her niece.

LETTER No. 43

Received Allahabad, February, 1882.

Before another line passes between us we must come to an agreement, my impulsive friend. You will have first to promise me faithfully never to judge of either of us, nor of the situation, nor of anything else bearing any relation to the " mythical Brothers " —tall or short—thick or thin—by your worldly experience or you will never come at the truth. By doing so until now you have only disturbed the solemn quiet of my evening meals several nights running and made my snake-like signature what with your writing it and thinking about it to haunt me even in my sleep—as by sympathy I felt it being pulled by the tail at the other side of the hills. Why will you be so impatient? You have a life time before you for our correspondence; though while the dark clouds of the *Deva-Lok* " Eclectic " are lowering on the horizon of the " Parent " it has to be a spasmodic and an uncertain one. It may even suddenly break off owing to the tension given it by our too intellectual friend. Oy-hai, Ram Ram! To think that our very mild criticism upon the pamphlet, a criticism reported by you to Hume Sahib—should have brought the latter to kill us at a blow! to destroy, without giving us one moment to call a Padri in or even time to repent; to find ourselves alive, and yet to cruelly deprived of our existence is truly sad, tho' not quite unexpected. But it is all our own fault. Had we instead prudently sent a laudatory hymn to his address we might now have been alive and well, waxing in health and strength—if not in wisdom—for long years to come and finding in him our Ved-Vyasa to sing the occult prowess of the Krishna and Arjuna on the desolate shores of Tsam-pa. Now that we are dead and desiccated tho', I may as well occupy a few minutes of my time to write as a *bhut* to you, in the best English I find lying idle in my friend's brain; where also I find in the cells of memory the phosphorsecent thought of a short letter to be sent by himself to the Editor of the Pioneer to soothe his English impatience. My friend's friend—K.H. has not forgotten you; K.H. does not intend breaking off with you—unless Hume Sahib should spoil the situation beyond mending. And why should he? You have done all you could, and that is as much as we ever intend asking of any one. And now we will talk.

You must thoroughly put aside the personal element if you would get on with occult study and—for a certain time—even with himself. Realize, my friend, that the social affections have little, if any, control over any true adept in the performance of his duty. In proportion as he rises towards perfect adeptship the fancies and antipathies of his former self are weakened: (as K.H. in substance explained to you) he takes all mankind into his heart and regards them in the mass. Your case is an exceptional one. You have *forced* yourself upon him, and stormed the position, by the very violence and intensity of your feeling for him—and once he accepted he has to bear the consequences in the future. Yet it cannot be a question with him what the visible Sinnett may be—what his impulses, his failures or successes in his world, his diminished or undiminished regard for him. With the " visible " one we have nothing to do. He is to us only a veil that hides from profane eyes that other *ego* with whose evolution we are concerned. In the external *rupa* do what you like, think what you like: only when the effects of that voluntary action are seen on the body of our correspondent—is it incumbent upon us to notice it.

We are neither pleased nor displeased because you did not attend the Bombay meeting. If you *had* gone, it would have been better for your " merit "; as you did not go you lost that little point. I could [not] and had no right to influence you any way—precisely because you are no *chela*. It was a trial, a very little one, tho' it seemed important enough to you to make you think of " wife and child's interests." You will have many such; for though you should never be a *chela*, still we do not give confidences even to correspondents and "*protégés*" whose discretion and moral pluck have not been well tested. You are the victim of *maya*. It will be a long struggle for you to tear away the " cataracts " and see things as they are. Hume Sahib is a *maya* to you as great as any. You see only his mounds of flesh and bones, his official personality, his intellect and influences. What are these, pray, to his true self that you *cannot* see, do what you may? What has his ability to shine in a *Durbar* or as the leader of a scientific society to do with his fitness for occult research, or his trustworthiness to keep our secrets? If we wanted anything about our lives and work to be known is not the *Theosophist* columns open to us? Why should we dribble facts thro' him, to be dressed for the public meal with a currie of nauseous doubts and biting sarcasm fit to throw the public stomach into confusion? To him there is nothing sacred, either within, or without occultism. His is a bird-killing and a faith-killing temperament; he would sacrifice his own flesh and blood as remorselessly as a singing bulbul; and would desiccate [1] yourself and us, K.H. and the " dear Old Lady " and make us all bleed to death under his scalpel—if he could—with as much ease as he would an owl, to put us away in his " museum " with appropriate labels outside and then recount our necrologies in " Stray Feathers " to the amateurs. No Sahib; the *outside* Hume is as different (and superior) from the *inside* Hume, as the outside Sinnett is different (and inferior) to the nascent inside " protégé."

[1] Query, the word meant was dissect.—EDS.

Learn that and set the latter to watching the editor, lest he play him a bad trick some day.   Our greatest trouble is to teach pupils not to be befooled by appearances.

As you have already been notified by Damodar thro' the D—, I did not call you a chela—examine your letter to assure yourself of it—I but jokingly asked O. the question whether he recognised in you the stuff of which chelas are made.   You saw only that Bennett had unwashed hands, uncleaned nails and used coarse language and had—to you—a generally unsavoury aspect.   But if *that* sort of thing is your criterion of moral excellence or potential power, how many adepts or wonder-producing *lamas* would pass your muster? This is part of your blindness.   Were he to die this minute—and I'll use a Christian phraseology to make you comprehend me the better—few hotter tears would drop from the eye of the recording Angel to Death over other such ill-used men, than the tear Bennett would receive for his share.   Few men have suffered—and unjustly suffered—as he has; and as few have a more kind, unselfish and truthful a heart.   That's all; and the unwashed Bennett is *morally* as far superior to the gentlemanly Hume as you are superior to your *Bearer*.

What H.P.B. repeated to you is correct: " the natives do not see Bennett's coarseness and K.H. is also a native."   What did I mean? Why simply that our Buddha-like friend *can see thro' the varnish* the grain of the wood beneath, and inside the slimy, stinking oyster—the " priceless pearl within! " B—is an honest man and of a sincere heart, besides being one of tremendous moral courage and a martyr to boot.   Such our K.H. loves—whereas he would have only scorn for a Chesterfield and a Grandison.   I suppose that the stooping of the finished " gentleman " K.H., to the coarse-fibred infidel Bennett is no more surprising than the alleged stooping of the " gentleman " Jesus to the prostitute Magdalene. There's a moral smell as well as a physical one, good friend.   See how well K.H. read your character when he would not send the Lahore youth to talk with you without a change of dress.   The sweet pulp of the orange is *inside* the skin—Sahib: try to look insides boxes for jewels and do not trust to those lying in the lid. I say again: the man is an *honest* man and a very earnest one; not exactly an angel—they must be hunted for in fashionable churches, parties at aristocratical mansions, theatres and clubs and such other *sanctums*—but as angels are outside our cosmogony we are glad of the help of even honest and plucky tho' dirty men.

All this I say to you without any malice or bitterness, as you erroneously imagine.   You have made progress during the past year—and therefore nearer to us—hence I talk with you as with a friend whom I hope of finally converting to some of our ways of thinking.   Your enthusiasm for our study has a tinge of selfishness in it; even your feeling for K.H. has a mixed character: still *you are nearer*. Only you trusted Hume too much, and mistrusted him too late, and now his bad karma reacts upon yours, to your detriment. Your friendly indiscretions as to things confided to you alone by H.P.B.—the cause—produces his rash publicities—the effect. This I am afraid must count against you. Be wiser hereafter. If our rule is to be chary of confidences it is because we are taught from the first that each man is personally responsible to the Law of Compensation for every word of his voluntary production. Mr. Hume would of couse call it *jesuitry*.

Also try to break thro' that great *maya* against which occult students, the world over, have always been warned by their teachers—the hankering after phenomena. Like the thirst for drink and opium, it grows with gratification. The Spiritualists are drunken with it; they are thaumaturgic sots. If you cannot be happy without phenomena you will never learn our philosophy. If you want healthy, philosophic thought, and can be satisfied with such—let us correspond. I tell you a profound truth in saying that if you (like your fabled Shloma) but choose wisdom all other things will be added unto it—in time. It adds no force to our metaphysical truths that our letters are dropped from space on to your lap or come under your pillow. If our philosophy is wrong a *wonder* will not set it right. Put that conviction into your consciousness and let us talk like sensible men. Why should we play with Jack-in-the-box; are not *our* beards grown?

And now it is time to put a stop to my abominable penmanship and so relieve you from the task. Yes—your " cosmogony "! Well, good friend, your cosmology is—between the leaves of my *Khuddaka Patha*—(my family Bible)—and making a supreme effort I will try to answer it as soon as I am relieved, for just now I am on duty. It is a life long task you have chosen, and somehow instead of generalizing you manage always to rest upon those details that prove the most difficult to a beginner. Take warning, my good Sahib. The task *is* difficult and K.H. in remembrance of old times, when he loved to quote poetry, asks me to close my letter with the following to your address:

> " Does the road wind up-hill all the way? "
> " Yes to the very end."
> " Will the day's journey take the whole long day? "
> " From morn to night, my friend."

Knowledge for the mind, like food for the body, is intended to feed and help to growth, but it requires to be well digested and the more thoroughly and slowly the process is carried out the better both for body and mind.

I saw Olcott and instructed him what to say to our Simla Sage. If the O.L. rushes into epistolary explanations with him, stop her

—as O. covered all the ground. I have no time to look after her, but I made her promise never to write to him without showing her letter first to you.

Namaskar.[1]

Yours M.

LETTER No. 44

Received Allahabad, February, 1882.

Your letter was addressed to me, as you were not aware that K.H. had again put himself in relations with you. Nevertheless, as I am addressed I will answer. " Do so; by all means: go ahead." The result may be disastrous to Spiritualism, though the reality of the phenomena be proved; hence beneficial to Theosophy. It does seem cruel to allow the poor sensitive lad to risk himself inside the lion's den; but as the acceptance or rejection of the kind invitation is with the medium under the counsel and inspiration of his mighty and far-seeing " Ernest " why should others worry themselves!

As we are not likely, worthy sir, to correspond very often now— I will tell you something you should know, and may derive profit from. On the 17th of November next the Septenary term of trial given the Society at its foundation in which to discreetly " preach us " will expire. One or two of us hoped that the world had so far advanced intellectually, if not intuitionally, that the Occult doctrine might gain an intellectual acceptance, and the impulse given for a new cycle of occult research. Others—wiser as it would now seem—held differently, but consent was given for the trial. It was stipulated, however, that the experiment should be made independently of our personal management; that there should be no abnormal interference by ourselves. So casting about we found in America the man to stand as leader—a man of great moral courage, unselfish, and having other good qualities. He was far from being the best, but (as Mr. Hume speaks in H.P.B.'s case)—he was the best one available. With him we associated a woman of most exceptional and wonderful endowments. Combined with them she had strong personal defects, but just as she was, there was no second to her living fit for this work. We sent her to America, brought them together—and the trial began. From the first both she and he were given to clearly understand that the issue lay entirely with themselves. And both offered themselves for the trial for certain remuneration in the far distant future as—as K.H. would say—soldiers volunteer

[1] (I do) homage.—EDS.

for a Forlorn Hope. For the 6½ years they have been struggling against such odds as would have driven off any one who was not working with the desperation of one who stakes life and all the prizes on some desperate supreme effort. Their success has not equalled the hopes of their original backers, phenomenal as it has been in certain directions. In a few more months the term of probation will end. If by that time the status of the Society as regards ourselves—the question of the " Brothers " be not definitely settled (either dropped out of the Society's programme or accepted on our own terms) that will be the last of the "—Brothers " of all shapes and colours, sizes or degrees. We will subside out of public view like a vapour into the ocean. Only those who have proved faithful to themselves and to Truth through everything, will be allowed further intercourse with us. And not even they, unless, from the President downward they bind themselves by the most solemn pledges of honour to keep an inviolable silence thenceforth about us, the Lodge, [and] Tibetan affairs, not even answering questions of their nearest friends, though silence might seem likely to throw the appearance of "humbug" upon all that has transpired. In such a case effort would be suspended until the beginning of another septenary cycle when, if circumstances should be more auspicious, another attempt might be made, under the same or another direction.

My own humble impression is that Hume Sahib's present pamphlet, highly intellectual as it is, *might* be improved so as to help enormously in giving the needed turn to Society affairs. And if he would trust more to his personal intuitions—which when he heeds them are strong—and less to the voice of one who neither represents entirely—as you seem to think—public opinion nor *would he believe though he were to have a 1000 proofs*—the pamphlet would be converted into one of the most powerful works that this modern movement has evolved.

Your cosmological questions will be attended to when I am not harassed with mightier business. Health and prosperity.

M.

LETTER No. 45

First received after revival in February, 1882.

My Brother—I have been on a long journey after supreme knowledge, I took a long time to rest. Then, upon coming back, I had to give all my time to duty, and all my thoughts to the Great Problem. It is all over now: the New Year's festivities are at an end and I am " Self" once more. But what is *Self*? Only a passing guest, whose concerns are all like a mirage of the great desert. . . .

Anyhow—this is my first moment of leisure. I offer it to you, whose inner Self reconciles me to the outer man who but too often forgets that great man is he who is strongest in the exercise of patience.   Look around you, my friend: see the " three poisons " raging within the heart of man—anger, greed, delusion, and the five obscurities [1]—envy, passion, vacillation, sloth, and unbelief— ever preventing them seeing truth.   They will never get rid of the pollution of their vain, wicked hearts, nor perceive the spiritual portion of themselves. Will you not try—for the sake of shorten- ing the distance between us—to disentangle yourself from the net of life and death in which they are all caught, to cherish less—lust and desire? Young Portman is seriously meditating to leave all, to come over to us, and " become a Tibetan monk " as he puts it. His ideas are singularly mixed upon the two entirely different characteristics and qualifications of the " Monk " or *Lama* and the living " Lha," or *Brother*: but let him try by all means.

Aye—I am only now able to correspond with you. At the same time let me tell you that it is more difficult than before to exchange letters with you, though my regard for you has sensibly increased, instead of being lessened—as you feared—and will not diminish unless—but as the consequence of your own acts. That you will try to avoid in raising any such obstacle, I know well; but man, after all, is the victim of his surroundings while he lives in the atmosphere of society. We may be anxious to befriend such as we have an interest in, and yet be as helpless to do so, as is one who sees a friend engulfed in a stormy sea when no boat is near to be launched and his personal strength is paralysed by a stronger hand that keeps him back. Yes, I see your thought . . . but you are wrong. Blame not the holy man for strictly doing his duty by humanity. Had it not been for the Chohan and his restraining influence you would not be reading now again a letter from your trans-Himalayan correspondent. The world of the Plains is antagonistic to that of the mountains, that you know; but what you do not know is the great harm produced by your own unconscious indiscretions. Shall I give you an instance? Remember the wrath produced in Stainton Moses by your too imprudent letter quoting *ad libitum*, and with a freedom pregnant with the most disastrous results, from my letter to you about him. . . . The cause generated at that time has now developed its results: not only has S.M. completely estranged himself from the Society some of whose members believe in us, but he has determined in his heart the utter annihilation of the British Branch. A *psychic* Society is being founded and he has succeeded in bringing over to it Wyld, Massey and others. Shall I also tell you the future of

[1] Query obstructions.—EDS.

20

that new body? It will grow and develop and expand and finally the Theos. Soc. of London will be swamped in it, and lose first its influence then—its name, until Theosophy in its very name becomes a thing of the Past. It is you alone, the simple action of your swift pen which will have produced the *nidana* and the ten-del, the " cause " and its " effect " and thus the work of seven years, the constant untiring efforts of the builders of the Theos. Society will perish—killed by the wounded vanity of a medium.

This simple act on your part is silently digging out a chasm between us. The evil may yet be averted—let the Society exist but in name till the day it can get members with whom we can work *de facto*—and by the creation of another counteracting cause we may save the situation. The hand of the Chohan alone can bridge it, but it must be *yours* that places the first stone for the work. How will you do it? How can you do it? Think of it well, if you care for further intercourse. They want something new. A *Ritual* to amuse them. Consult with Subba Row, with Sankariah, the Dewan Naib of Cochin, read attentively his pamphlet, extracts from which you will find in the last *Theosophist* (see, " A Flash of Light upon Occult Free Masonry." Page 135). I can come nearer to you, but you must draw me by a purified heart and a gradually developing will. Like the needle the adept follows his attractions. Is this not the law of the disembodied Principles? Why then not of the living also? As the social ties of the carnal man are too weak to call back the " Soul " of the deceased except where there is a mutual affinity which survives as a force in the region within the terrestrial region, so the calls of mere friendship or even enthusiastic regard are too feeble to draw the " Lha " who has passed on a stage of the journey to him he has left behind, unless a parallel development goes on. M. spoke well and truthfully when saying that a love of collective humanity is his increasing inspiration; and if any one individual should wish to divert his regards to himself, he must overpower the diffusive tendency by a stronger force.

All this I say, not because its substance has not been told you before, but because I read your heart and detect in it a shade of sadness, not to say disappointment, that hovers there. You have had other correspondents but are not perfectly satisfied. To gratify, I write you therefore with some effort to bid you keep a cheerful frame of mind. Your strivings, perplexities and forebodings are equally noticed, good and faithful friend. In the imperishable RECORD of the Masters *you have written them all*. There are registered your every deed and thought; for, though not a chela, as you say to my Brother Morya, nor even a " protégé "—as you understand the term—still, you have stepped within the circle of our work, you have crossed the mystic line which separates your world from ours, and now whether you persevere or not; whether we become later on, in your sight, still more living *real* entities or vanish out of your mind like so many dream fictions—perchance an ugly night-mare—you are virtually OURS. Your hidden *Self* has mirrored itself in *our* Akasa; your nature is—yours, your essence is—ours. The flame is distinct from the log of wood which serves it temporarily as fuel; at the end of your apparitional birth—and whether we two meet face to face in our grosser *rupas*—you cannot avoid meeting us in *Real Existence.* Yea, verily good friend your *Karma* is ours, for you imprinted it daily and hourly upon the pages of that book where the minutest particulars of the individuals stepping inside our circle—are preserved; and that your *Karma* is your *only* personality to be when you step beyond. In thought and deed, by day, in soul-struggles by nights, you have been writing the story of your desires and your spiritual development. This, every one does who approaches us with any earnestness of desire to become our co-worker; he himself " precipitates " the written entries by the identical process used by us when we write inside your closed letters and uncut pages of books and pamphlets in transit. (See pp. 32, 35 *Report* sent by Olcott, once more.) I tell you this for your private information and it must not figure in the next pamphlet from Simla. During the past few months, especially, when your weary brain was plunged in the torpor of sleep, your eager soul has often been searching after me, and the current of your thought been beating against my protecting barriers of Akàs as the lapping wavelets against a rocky shore. What that " inner Self," impatient, anxious—has longed to bind itself to, the carnal man, the worldlings' master has not ratified; the ties of life are still as strong as chains of steel. Sacred, indeed, some of them are, and no one would ask you to rupture them. There below, lies your long-cherished field of enterprise and usefulness. Ours can never be more than a bright phantom-world to the man of thorough " practical sense "; and if your case be in some degree exceptional, it is because your nature has deeper inspirations than those of others, who are still more "business-like" and the fountain-head of whose eloquence is in the brain not in the heart, which never was in contact with the mysteriously effulgent, and pure heart of Tathāgata.

If you hear seldom from me, never feel disappointed, my Brother, but say—" It is *my* fault." Nature has linked all parts of her Empire together by subtle threads of magnetic sympathy, and, there is a mutual correlation even between a star and a man; thought runs swifter than the electric fluid, and your thought *will find me* if projected by a pure impulse, as mine will find, has found, and often impressed your mind. We may move in cycles of activity divided—not entirely separated from each other. Like the light in the sombre valley seen by the mountaineer from his peaks, every bright thought in your mind, my Brother, will sparkle and attract the attention of your distant friend and correspondent. If thus we discover our natural Allies in the *Shadow*-world—your world and ours outside the precincts—and it is our law to approach every such an one if even there be but the feeblest glimmer of the true "Tathāgata" light within him—then how far easier for you to attract us. Understand this and the admission into the Society of persons often distasteful to you will no longer amaze you. "They that be whole need not the physician, but they that be sick"—is an axiom, whoever may have spoken it.

And now, let me bid you farewell for the present until the next. Indulge not in apprehensions of what evil might happen if things should not go as your worldly wisdom thinks they ought; doubt not, for this complexion of doubt unnerves and pushes back one's progress. To have cheerful confidence and hope is quite another thing from giving way to the fool's blind optimism: the wise man never fights misfortune in advance. A cloud does lower over your path—it gathers about the hill of Jakko. He whom you made your confidant—I advised you to become but his co-worker, not to divulge things to him that you should have kept locked within your bosom—is under a baneful influence, and may become your enemy. You do right to try to rescue him from it, for it bodes ill to him, to you and to the Society. His greater mind fumed by vanity and charmed by the pipings of a weaker but more cunning one, is for the time under a spell of fascination. You will easily detect the *malign power* that stands behind *both* and *uses them as tools* for the execution of its own nefarious plans. The intended catastrophe can be averted by redoubled vigilance and increased fervour of pure will on the part of the friends of S.B.L. Work then, if you still will, to turn the blow aside; for if it falls you will not escape unhurt however great my Brothers' efforts. The cause will never be ruined though albeit the Sisyphus' rock may crush a good many toes. Farewell, again, my friend—for longer or shorter, as you may determine. I am called to duty.

Yours faithfully,

K. H.

LETTER No. 46

Received Simla, 1882.

I will thank you, my dear Sinnett Sahib, for a personal favour. Since K.H. is too much of a *perfect* Yogi-Arhat, to stop the hand that undaunted by failure keeps on trying to catch the Tibetan yak by the neck to bend it under its yoke, then all that remains for me to do is to make once more my appearance on the *nataka-shala* to put a stop to a performance that threatens to become monotonous even to us—well trained in patience. I cannot avail myself of your kind advice to write to Mr. Hume in *my brightest red* since it would be opening a new door for an endless correspondence, an honour I would rather decline. But I write to you instead, and send you a telegram and answer on back on't, for your perusal. What talk of his is this? Reverence may not be in his nature, nor does any one claim or care for it any way! But I should have thought that his head, that is capacious enough to hold anything, had a corner in it for some common sense. And that sense might have told him that either we are what we claim, or we are not. That in the former case, however exaggerated the claims made on behalf of *our powers* still, if our knowledge and foresight do not transcend his, then we are no better than *shams and impostors* and the quicker he parts company with us—the better for him. But if we are in any degree what we claim to be, then he acts like a wild ass. Let him remember, that we are not Indian Rajahs in need of and compelled to accept political *Ayahs*, and nurses to lead us on by the string. That the Society was founded, went on and will go on *with or without him*—let him suit himself as to the latter.

So far his help, that he thrusts on us, much after the fashion of Spanish mendicant *hidalgos*, who offer their sword to protect the traveller with one hand and clutch him by the throat with the other, has not—as far as I can find [been] very beneficial to the Society so far. Not to one of its founders, at any rate, whom he has nigh killed last year at Simla and whom he now harasses, sticking to her like grim death, turning her blood into water and eating her liver out.

Therefore I expect you to impress upon his mind that all we should " give thanks for," would be to see him take care of his *Eclectic* and to leave the Parent Society to take care of itself. His advice and help to the editor of the *Theosophist* has no doubt been advantageous to the editor, and she does feel grateful to him for it after deducting the large share she owes to yourself. But we beg leave to state, that some line ought to be drawn somewhere— between said editor and ourselves; for we are not quite the Tibetan triplets he takes us to be. Therefore, whether we be the ignorant savages and Orientals of his making—every wolf being master in his own den—we claim the right to know our own business best, and respectfully decline his services as a captain to steer our Theosophical ship even on " the ocean of *worldly life* " as he metaphorizes in his *sloka*. We have allowed him, under the good pretext of saving the situation with the British theosophists, to ventilate his animosity against us in the organ of our own Society and to draw our portrait-likenesses, with a brush dipped in haughty bile—what more does he want? As I ordered the old woman to telegraph him back—he is not the only skilful navigator in the world; he seeks to avoid Western breakers, and we to steer our canoe clear off Eastern sandbanks. Does he mean in addition to this to dictate from the Chohan down to [D] juala Khool and Deb what we shall and what we shall not do? Ram, Ram and the holy Nagas! is it after centuries of independent existence that we have to fall under a foreign influence, to become the puppets of a Simla Nawab? Are we school boys, or what, in his fancy to submit to the rod of a Peling schoolmaster. . . .

Notwithstanding his sulks I beg you will tell him that you heard *from me*—and that I have asked you to let him know my *ultimatum*: if he would not break with the whole shop altogether, and *for ever*, I will not suffer him to interfere with his wisdom between our ignorance and the Parent Society. Nor shall he ease his bad humour on one who is not responsible for anything we may do or say—a woman so sick that as in 1877 I am again forced to carry her away—when she is so needed where she now is, at Headquarters—for fear she will fall to pieces. And that this state of hers was brought on lately by him owing to constant anxiety for the Society, and partially if not wholly by his behaviour at Simla—you can take my word for it. The whole situation and future of the *Eclectic* hangs on Koothumi if you will not help him. If notwithstanding my advice and the Chohan's evident displeasure he will persist making a fool of himself, sacrificing himself for a man who is the evil genius of the Society in one direction —well it's his own business, only I will have nothing to do with it. *Your true friend* I will ever remain though you turn against me one of these days. Fern was tested and found a thorough *Dugpa* in his moral nature. We will see, we will see; but very little hope left notwithstanding his splendid capacities. Had I hinted to him to deceive his own father and mother he would have thrown in *their* fathers and mothers in the bargain. Vile, vile nature—yet irresponsible. Oh ye Westerns, who boast of your morality! May the bright Chohans keep you and all yours from the approaching harm is the sincere wish of your friend.

M.

LETTER No. 47

Received Allahabad, 3rd March, 1882.

Reply to my remonstrance against treatment of Europe.
(Through Damodar.)

Well, say I am an *ignoramus* in your English ways, and I'll say you are one in our Tibetan customs and we will split the difference and shake our astral hands over *Barnaway* and square the discussion.

The old woman? Of course she will be *frantic*—but who cares? It's kept from her however secret. No use making her more miserable than what she is. Cook is a *pump of filth*, with perpetually working pistons, and the sooner he screws them up—the better for him. Your last letter to me is less a "petition" than a protest, my respected Sahib. Its voice is that of the war *sankh* of my Rajput ancestors, rather than the cooing of a friend. And I like it all the more, I promise you. It has the right ring of honest frankness. So let us talk—for sharp as your voice may be, your heart is warm and you end by saying "Whether you decree that what seems to me right be done or not" you are ever ours faithfully etc. Europe is a large place but the world is bigger yet. The sun of Theosophy must shine for all, not for a part. There is more of this movement than you have yet had an inkling of, and the work of the T.S. is linked in with similar work that is secretly going on in all parts of the world. Even in the T.S. there is a division, managed by a Greek Brother about which not a person in the Society has a suspicion excepting the old woman and Olcott; and even he only knows it is progressing, and occasionally executes an order I send him in connection with it. The cycle I spoke of refers to the whole movement. Europe will not be overlooked, never fear; but perhaps you even may not anticipate *how* the light will be shed there. Ask your *Seraph*—K.H. to let you have details thereof. You speak of Massey and Crookes; do you not recollect that Massey was offered 4 years ago the chance to head the English movement and—*declined*? In his place was set up that old grim idol of the Jewish Sinai—Wyld, who with his Christian rant and fanatical rot *shut us out* of the movement altogether. Our Chohan forbade us absolutely to take any part in it. Massey has to thank but *himself* for it, and you may tell him so. You ought to have learned by this time our ways. We *advise*—and never *order*. But we *do* influence individuals. Ransack the Spiritualistic literature if you will till the year 1877.[1] Search and find in it—if you can, one single word about occult philosophy,

[1] When *Isis Unveiled* was published.—EDS.

or esotericism or anything of that element now so largely infused in the spiritual movement. Ask and enquire whether the very word of " occultism " was not so completely *unknown* in America, that we find Cora of the 7 husbands, the Tappan woman and talking medium *inspired* in her lectures to say that the word was *one just coined* by the Theosophists—then dawning—; that no one ever heard of elementary spirits and " astral " light—save the *petroleum* manufacturers and so on and on. Well ascertain this and compare. *This* was the first war cry, and the battle kept raging hot and fierce to the very day of the departure for India. To say and point out to Edison and Crookes and Massey—would sound much like boasting of that which can never be *proven*. And Crookes—has he not brought science within our hail in his " radiant matter " discovery? What but occult research was it that *led* him first to that. You know K.H. and me—buss! know you anything of the *whole* Brotherhood and its ramifications? The Old Woman is accused of *untruthfulness, inaccuracy* in her statements. " Ask no questions and you will receive *no lies.*" *She is forbidden* to say what she knows. You may cut her to pieces and she will not tell. Nay—she is ordered *in cases of need* to *mislead people*; and, were she more of a natural born *liar*— she might be happier and won her day long since by this time. But that's just where the shoe pinches, Sahib. She is *too truthful, too outspoken, too incapable* of *dissimulation*: and now she is being daily crucified for it. Try not to be hasty, respected Sir. The world was not made in a day; nor has the tail of the yak developed in one year. Let evolution take its course naturally—lest we make it deviate and produce monsters by presuming to guide it. Massey talks of coming to India—does he not? And supposing that after coming here and doing what is right and spending the needed time for disciplinary training he should be sent back with a message? And supposing that Crookes and Edison and others have other things to discover? So I say, " WAIT." Who knows what may be the situation in November? You might think it such as to justify us in carrying out our " threat " to " lock the door," while it might seem very different to us. Let us all do our best. There are cycles of 7, 11, 21, 77, 107, 700, 11,000, 21,000 etc.; so many cycles will make a major and so on. Bide your time, the *record book is well kept*. Only, look out sharp; the *Dugpas* and the *Gelukpas* are not fighting but in Tibet alone; see their vile work in England among the " Occultists and *seers* "! Hear your acquaintance Wallace preaching like a true " Hierophant " of the " left hand " the marriage of " soul with the spirit " and getting the true definition topsy-turvy, seeking to prove that every *practising Hierophant* must at least be *spiritually* married—if for some reasons he cannot do so *physically*—there being otherwise a great danger of Adulteration of God and Devil! I tell you the Shammars are there already and their pernicious work is everywhere in our way. Do not regard this as metaphorical but as a real fact, which may be demonstrated to you some day.

It's quite useless to say anything more about Olcott's eccentricity and the inferiority of America to England; all that is *real* in your point we recognise and knew long ago; but you do not know how much that is mere superficial prejudice glares in your eyes like the reflection of a thin taper on deep water. Take care lest we should some day take you at your thought and put *you* in Olcott's place, after taking him to our own, as he has longed to have us do these several years. Martyrdom is pleasant to look at and criticise, but harder to suffer. There never was a woman more unjustly abused than H.B. See the infamous insulting letters she was sent from England for publication against herself and us and the Society. You may find them undignified perhaps. But the " Answers to Correspondents " *in Supplement* are written by *myself*. So do not blame her. I'm curious to know your frank opinion on them. Perchance you might think she might have done better herself.

M.

LETTER No. 48

Received Allahabad, March 3rd, 1882.

Good friend, I " know "—of course. And *knowing*, without your telling me I would, were I but authorized to influence you in any one direction—answer most gladly: " that knowledge thou shalt share with me some day." When, or how—" is not for me to say, nor for myself to know," as you, aye, *you alone*, have to weave your destiny. Perhaps soon and perchance—never: but why feel " despairing," or even doubting? Believe me: we may yet walk along the arduous path together. We may yet meet: but if at all, it has to be along and *on*—those " adamantine rocks with which our occult rules surround us "—never *outside* them, however bitterly we may complain. No, *never* can we pursue our further journey—*if* hand in hand—along that high-way, crowded thoroughfare, which encircles them, and on which Spiritualists and mystics, prophets and seers elbow each other now-a-day. Yea, verily, the motley crowd of candidates may shout for an eternity to come, for the *Sesame* to open. It never will, so long as they keep outside those rules. Vainly do your modern seers and their prophetesses, creep into every cleft and crevice without outlet or continuity they chance to see; and still more vainly, when once within do they lift up their voices and loudly cry: " *Eureka*! We have gotten a Revelation from the Lord! "—for verily have they nothing of the kind. They have disturbed but bats, less blind than their intruders; who, feeling them flying about, mistake them as often for angels—as they too have wings! Doubt not, my friend: it is but from the very top of those " adamantine rocks " of ours, not at their foot, that one is ever enabled to perceive the *whole* Truth, by embracing the whole limitless horizon. And though they may seem to you to be standing in your way, it is simply because you have hitherto failed to discover or even so much as suspect the reason and the operation of those laws; hence they appear so cold and merciless and selfish in your sight; although yourself have intuitionally recognised in them the outcome of ages of wisdom. Nevertheless, were one but to obediently follow them out, they could be made to gradually yield to one's desire and give to him *all* he asks of them. But no one could ever violently break them, without becoming the first victim to his guilt; yea, to the extent of risking to lose his own, his hard won share of immortality, *here* and *there*. Remember: too anxious expectation is not only tedious, but dangerous too. Each warmer and quicker throb of the heart wears so much of life away. The passions, the affections are not to be indulged in by him who seeks TO KNOW; for they " wear out the earthly body with their own secret power; and he, who would gain his aim—*must be cold.*" He must not even desire too earnestly or too passionately the object he would reach: else, the very wish will prevent the possibility of its fulfilment, at best—retard and throw it back. . . .

You will find in the forth-coming number, two articles which you must read, I need not tell you why, as I leave it with your intuitions. As usual, it is an indiscretion, which however, I have allowed to remain as there are few, if any, who will understand the hint contained—but you. There are more than one such hint though; hence your attention is asked to the " Elixir of Life " and W. Oxley's " Philosophy of Spirit." The former contains references and explanations, the haziness of which may remind you of a man who stealthily approaching one gives him a hit upon his back, and then runs away; as they most undeniably belong to the genus of those " Fortunes " that come to one like the thief by night and during one's sleep, and go back, finding no one to respond to the offer—of which you complain in your letter to Brother. This time, you are warned, good friend, so complain no more. Article No. 2, is penned by the Manchester Seer—Oxley. Having received no reply to his summons to K.H., he criticises—mildly so far—the utterances of that " Internal Power "—for which new title I feel rather obliged to him. At the sight of the gentle rebuke, our blunderbuss Editor failed not to explode. Nor would she be soothed, until Djual-Khul, with whom the famous review was concocted—(one by-the-bye, which

seen by, ought to have never been permitted to see the day by
you)—was authorized, under the safe *nom-de-plume* of " Reviewer "
to answer (by correcting some of his blunders) the Seer, in a few
innocent foot-notes. Yet, I must say, that of all the present
English " prophets," W. Oxley is *the only one* who has an inkling
of truth; hence the only one calculated to effectually help our
movement. The man runs constantly in and out of the straight
road, deviating from it every time he thinks he perceives a new
path; but finding himself in a *cul-de-sac* as invariably returns to
the right direction. I must admit, there is much sound philosophy here and there in what he writes; and, though his story of
" Busiris " in its anthropomorphic presentation is ridiculous nonsense, and his rendering of Sanskrit names is mostly wrong; and
though he seems to have but very hazy notions about what he
calls the " astro-masonic basis of *Bhagavad Gita* " and *Mahabharata*
to both of which he evidently attributes the same author—yet he
is positively and absolutely the only one whose general comprehension of *Spirit*, and its capabilities and functions after the first
separation, we call *death*, are on the whole if not quite correct,
at least approximating very nearly Truth. Read it, when it
comes out, especially Par. 3, Col. I, page 152 *et seq*, where you
will find them. You may then understand, why, instead of
answering your direct question I go into a subject, so far, perfectly
indifferent to you. Follow, for instance his definition of the term
" Angel " (it will be on line 30,) and try to follow and comprehend
his thought, so clumsily yet withal so correctly expressed and then,
compare it with the Tibetan teaching. Poor, poor Humanity,
when shalt thou have the whole and unadulterated Truth!
Behold, each of the " privileged " ones saying: " I alone am right!
There is no lacuna. . . ." No; none:—not on that one special page
opened before him, and which he alone is reading in the endless
volume of " Spirit Revelation," called *Seership*. But why such
stubborn oblivion of the important fact that there are other and
innumerable pages before and after that one solitary page that
each of the " Seers " has so far hardly learnt to decipher? Why
is it, that every one of those " Seers " believes himself the Alpha
and the Omega of Truth? Thus—S.M. is taught that there are
no such " Beings " as *Brothers*, and to reject the doctrine of frequent
annihilation and that of the Elementary and of the *non*-human
Spirits. Maitland and Mrs. K. have *revealed* to them—by *Jesus*
and GOD themselves (that alone would beat +) that many of the
supposed " Spirits " which control mediums and converse with
visitors—Spiritualists, are no " disembodied " spirits at all, but
only " flames," and the *reliquiae* of dogs, cats and pigs, helped to
communicate with mortals by the spirits of " trees," vegetables
and minerals. Though more hazy than the human, *cautious*

discourses of the alleged + those teachings are nearer to the mark
than anything uttered so far by the mediums, and I will tell you
why.   When the " Seeress " is made to reveal that " immortality
is by no means a matter of course for all " . . . that " souls shrink
away and expire," it being " the nature of them to *burn out* and
expend themselves " . . . etc., she is delivering herself of *actual*,
incontrovertible *facts*.   And why? Because both Maitland and
herself as well as *their circle*—are *strict vegetarians*, while S.M. is a
flesh-eater and a wine and liquor drinker.   Never will the Spiritualists find reliable, trustworthy mediums and Seers (not even to
a degree) so long as the latter and their " circle " will saturate
themselves with animal blood, and the millions of *infusoria* of the
fermented fluids.   Since my return I found it *impossible* for me to
breathe—even in the atmosphere of the *Headquarters*! M. had to
interfere, and to force the whole household to give up meat; and
they had, all of them, to be purified and thoroughly cleansed with
various disinfecting drugs before I could even help myself to my
letters.   And I am not, as you may imagine, half as sensitive to the
loathsome emanations as a tolerably respectable disembodied *shell*
would be,—leaving out of question a real PRESENCE, though but a
" projecting " one.   In a year or so, perchance earlier, I may find
myself *hardened* again. At present I find it *impossible*—do what I may.
      And now, with such a *Preface* instead of answering I will put
you a question. You know S. Moses, and you know Maitland
and Mrs. K. personally.   And, you have heard of and read about
a good many Seers, in the past and present centuries, such as
Swedenborg, Boehme, and others.   Not one among the number
but thoroughly *honest, sincere*, and as intelligent, as well educated;
aye, even learned.   Each of them in addition to these qualities,
has or had an + of his own; a " Guardian " and a *Revelator*—
under whatever " mystery " and " mystic name "—whose mission
it is—or has been to spin out to his spiritual ward—a new system
embracing all the details of the world of Spirit. Tell me, my
friend, do you know of two that agree? And why, since truth is
one, and that putting entirely the question of discrepancies in
details aside—we do not find them agreeing even upon the most
vital problems—those that have either " *to be*, or *not* to be "—and
of which there can be *no two* solutions? Summed up, it comes to
the following:—All the " *Rosicrucians*," all the *mediaeval mystics*,
Swedenborg, P. B. Randolf, Oxley, etc., etc.: " there are secret
Brotherhoods of *Initiates* in the East, especially in Tibet and Tar-
tary; there only can the LOST WORD (which is *no* Word) be found ";
and, there are Spirits of the Elements, and Spirit-Flames, that were
never incarnated (in this cycle), and immortality *is conditional*.
      Mediums and *clairvoyants*, (of the type of S. Moses) [? say] there
are no Brothers in Tibet or India, and the ' Lost Word ' is in the

sole keeping of my ' Guardian ' who knows *the* word but knows of *no* Brothers. And immortality is for all and *unconditional*, there being no Spirits but the human and the disembodied, etc., etc."—a system of radical denial of the first one and in complete antagonism with it. While Oxley and Mrs. H. Billing are in direct communication with the " Brothers," S.M. rejects the very idea of one. While " Busiris " is an " angel " *au pluriel*, or the Spirit of a congeries of Spirits (Dhyan Chohans) the + is the soul of a disembodied Sage *solo*. His teachings are *authoritative*, yet we always find a ring of uncertainty and hesitation in them: " *We* are not able to say now " . . " It is doubtful " . . " We do not understand whether it is pretended " . . it " seems that " . . " we do not feel sure," etc. Thus speaketh a *man* conditioned and limited in his means of obtaining absolute knowledge; but why should a " Soul within the Universal Soul " a " Spirit Sage " use such a cautious, uncertain phraseology if the truth is known to him? Why not, in answer to her direct, fearless, and challenging remark: " You want objective proof of the Lodge? Have you not + ? and can you not ask him whether I speak the truth? "—why not answer—(if it is + who answers)—either one way or the other, and say:—" the poor wench is *hallucinated* "; or, (as there cannot be another or a third alternative *if* S.M. is right) " she *lies* intentionally, with such and such an object, *beware of her*! " Why so hazy?—Aye, verily, because " he (+) *knows*," and " his name be blessed,"—but he (S.M.) knoweth not; for, as his " spirits," + he thinks—repeatedly remind him: " You do not appear to have gathered rightly what *we* said . . ." controversy stirs up your mind and feeling, and in place of a transparent medium gives us one that is turbid . . . . we require a *passive* mind, and cannot act without it " . . . (see *Light* February 4th).

As *we* do not " require a *passive* mind " but on the contrary are seeking for those most active, which can put two and two together once that they are on the right scent, *we* will, if you please, drop the subject. Let your mind work out the problem for itself.

Yes; I am indeed satisfied with your last article, though it will satisfy no Spiritualist. Yet there is more philosophy and sound logic in it than in a dozen of their most pretentious publications. *Facts*—will come later on. Thus, little by little, the now incomprehensible will become the self-evident; and many a sentence of mystic meaning will shine yet out before your Soul-eye, like a transparency, illuminating the darkness of your mind. Such is the course of gradual progress; a year or two back you might have written a more brilliant, never a more profound article. Neglect then, not, my good Brother, the humble, the derided Journal of your Society, and mind not either its quaint, pretentious cover, nor the " heaps of manure " contained in it—to repeat the charitable, and to yourself the too familiar remark used often at Simla. But let your attention be rather drawn to the few pearls of wisdom and *occult truths* to be occasionally discovered under that " manure." Our own ways and manners are, perchance, as quaint and as uncouth—nay more so. Subba Rao is right; he who knows aught of the ways of the *Siddhas* shall concur with the views expressed on the third page of his incomplete letter: many of us would be mistaken for *Madmen*, by you English gentlemen. But he who would become a son of Wisdom can always see beneath the rugged surface. So, with the poor old Journal. Behold, its mystically bumptious clothing!, its numerous blemishes and literary defects, and with all that cover the most perfect symbol of its contents: the main portion of its original ground, thickly veiled, all smutty and as black as night, through which peep out grey dots, and lines, and words, and even—sentences. To the truly wise those breaks of grey may suggest an allegory full of meaning, such as the streaks of twilight, upon the Eastern sky, at morning's early dawn, after a night of intense darkness; the aurora of a more " spiritually intellectual " cycle. And who knows, how many of those, who, undismayed by its unprepossessing appearance, the hideous intricacies of its style, and the other many failures of the unpopular *magazine*, will keep on tearing its pages, who may find themselves rewarded some day for their perseverance! Illuminated sentences may gleam out upon them, at some time or other, shedding a bright light upon some old puzzling problems. Yourself, some fine morning, while poring over its crooked columns with the sharpened wits of a well rested brain, peering into what you now view as hazy, impalpable speculations, having only the consistency of vapour,—yourself you may, perchance, perceive in them the unexpected solution of an old, blurred, forgotten " dream " of yours, which once *recalled* will impress itself in an indelible image upon your *outer* from your inner memory, to never fade out from it again. All this is possible and *may* happen; for our ways *are* the ways of " Madmen " . . .

Then why feel " unhappy " and " disappointed "? My good, my *faithful* friend, remember that hope deferred is not hope lost. " Conditions " may change for the better—for we too—spook-like need *our* conditions, and can hardly work without them; and then, the vague depression of Spirit, which is now settling down upon you like a heavy cloud on a landscape may be blown away at the first favourable breeze. Bhavani Shanker is with O., and he is stronger and fitter in many a way more than Damodar or even our mutual " female " friend.

No; you will not be snatched away from your study before you have thoroughly mastered the alphabet, so as to learn to read by yourself; and, it depends but on you alone to *nail* for ever " the

too attractive vision " which seems to you now to be fading
away. . . . .
. . . .[1] whole situation. That I am not a " Seraph "
yet, is shown in the fact of my writing to you this endless letter.
When it is proved that you have not misunderstood my meaning,
I may say more. Morya, to enable you as he says to confront
your enemies, the believers in the materialisation of " individual
souls," wanted me to acquaint you with the totality of the sub-
tile bodies and their collective aggregate, as well as with the
distributive aggregate or the *sheaths*. I believe it is premature.
Before the world can be made to understand the difference between
the " Sutratma " (thread-soul) and " Taijasa," (the brilliant or
the luminous) they have to be taught the nature of the grosser
elements. What I blame him for, is that he allowed you to begin
from the wrong end—the most difficult unless one has thoroughly
mastered the preparatory ground. I have looked over you(r)
MS. to him; and more than once have I detected on the white
margin the shadow of your face, with its earnest, enquiring gaze
in the eyes: your thought having projected your image on the
spot you had on your mind, and which you longed to receive back
filled—" thirsting " as you say—for more notes and information.
Well, if his laziness overcomes his good intentions much longer,
I will have to do it myself, though my time *is* limited. At all
events to write for you is no ungrateful task, as you make the best
use of the little you may pick up here and there. Indeed, when
you complain of being unable to comprehend the meaning of
Eliphas Levi, it is only because you fail like so many other readers
to find the key to their way of writing. On close observation,
you will find that it was never the intention of the Occultists really
to conceal what they had been writing from the earnest determined
students, but rather to lock up their information for safety-sake,
in a secure safe-box, the key to which is—intuition. The degree
of diligence and zeal with which the hidden meaning is sought by
the student, is generally the test—how far he is entitled to the
possession of the so buried treasure. And certainly if you are
able to make out that which was concealed under the red ink of
M.—you need despair of nothing. I believe it is time now to
bid you farewell, hoping you will find less trouble to read the blue
than the red hieroglyphics. O. will be with you shortly, and you
ought to make the best of this opportunity which may be the last
for both. And now, need I remind you that this letter is STRICTLY
private?

Yours, whatever may come of it,

K. H.

---

[1] One whole page of the original letter is missing here.—ED.

LETTER No. 49

From K.H. Received at Umballa on the way to Simla, August 5, 1881.

Just home. Received more letters than I care to answer—yours excepted. Having nothing particular to say, I will simply attend to your questions; a task which may seem an easy one, but is not so, in reality, if we but remember that similar in that to the deity described in *Upanishad* " Sokāmayata bahuh syām prajāye yeti " —they " love to be many and to multiply." At any rate, thirst for knowledge was never regarded as a sin and you will always find me prompt to answer such queries—that can be answered.

Certainly I am of opinion that since our correspondence was established for the good of the many it would prove very little profitable to the world at large unless you do recast the teachings and ideas contained therein " in the form of an essay," not only on the occult philosophical view of creation but upon every other question. The sooner you begin your " future book " the better; for who can answer for unexpected incidents? Our correspondence may break off suddenly, the obstacle coming from those who *know best*. THEIR mind—as you know, is a sealed book for many of us, and which no amount of " art magic " can break open. Further " aids to reflection " will however come in good time; and the little I am permitted to explain may, I hope, prove more comprehensive than Eliphas Levi's *Haute Magie*. No wonder you find it cloudy, for it was never meant for the uninitiated reader. Eliphas studied from the Rosicrucian MSS. (now reduced to three copies in Europe). These expound our eastern doctrines from the teachings of Rosencreuz, who, upon his return from Asia dressed them up in a semi-Christian garb intended as a shield for his pupils, against clerical revenge. One must have the key to it and that key is a science *per se*. Rosencreuz taught orally. Saint Germain recorded the good doctrines in figures, and his only cyphered MS. remained with his staunch friend and patron the benevolent German Prince from whose house and in whose presence he made his last exit—HOME. Failure, dead failure! Speaking of " figures " and " numbers " Eliphas addresses those who know something of the Pythagorean doctrines. Yes; some of them do sum up all philosophy and include all doctrines. Isaac Newton understood them well; but withheld his knowledge very prudently for his own reputation, and very unfortunately for the writers of *Saturday Review* and its contemporaries. You seem to admire it—I do not. However talented from the literary point of view, a paper which gives vent to such unprogressive and dogmatic ideas as the one I came across in it, lately, ought to lose caste among its more liberal confrères. Scientific men, it

thinks—" do not make at all good observers " at exhibitions of
modern magic, spiritism and other " nine days wonders." This
is certainly not as it should be, it adds: for, " *knowing as well as they
do the limits of the natural* (? ! !) they should begin by assuming that
what they see, or what they think they see, *cannot be done*, and should
next look for the fallacy " etc. etc. Circulation of the blood,
electric telegraph, railway and steamer argument all over again.
They know " the limits of the natural "!! Oh, century of conceit
and mental obscuration! And we are invited to London, among
these academical rags whose predecessors persecuted Mesmer and
branded St. Germain as an impostor! All is *secret* for them as yet
in nature. Of *man*—they know but the skeleton and form; hardly
are they able to outline the paths through which the invisible
messengers they call " senses " pass on their way to man's perceptions; their school science is a hot-bed of doubts and conjectures;
it teaches but for its own sophistry, infects with its emasculation,
its scorn for truth, its false morality and dogmatism, and its
representatives would boast knowing " *the limits of the natural.*"
Bus—my good friend; I would forget you belonged to this generation, and are an admirer of your " modern Science." Her behests
and oracular verdicts are on a level with the papal—*non possumus*.
Yes; the *Saturday Review* has let us off easily enough to be sure.
Not so the *Spiritualist.* Poor perplexed, wee paper! You gave it a
tremendous blow. Losing its footing on mediumistic ground, it
fights its death struggle for supremacy of English adeptship over
Eastern knowledge. I almost hear its *sub rosa* cry: " If we Spiritualists are shown to be in the wrong box so are you—theosophists."
The great " Adept," the formidable J.K. is certainly a dangerous
enemy; and I am afraid our Bodhisatwas will have to confess
some day their profound ignorance before his mighty learning.
" Real Adepts like Gautama Buddha or Jesus Christ did not
shroud themselves in mystery, but came and talked openly,"
quoth our oracle. If they did it's news to us—the humble followers
of the former. Gautama is qualified the " Divine Teacher " and
at the same time " *God's* messenger "!! (See *Spt.*, July, 8th, p. 21.
para 2.) Buddha has now become the messenger of one, whom
He, Shakya K'houtchoo, the precious wisdom, has dethroned
2,500 years back, by unveiling the Tabernacle and showing its
emptiness. Where did that cockney adept learn his Buddhism,
I wonder? You really ought to advise your friend Mr. C. C. Massey
to study with that London Jewel who so despises Indian occult
knowledge " *The Lotus of the Good Law*," and " *Atma Bodha* "—in
the light of Jewish Kabalism.

I, " annoyed at newspaper ribald notices? " Certainly not.
But I do feel a little wrathful at the sacrilegious utterances of J.K.;
that I confess. I felt like answering the conceited fool—but

" so far shalt thou go and no further "—again. The Khobilgan to whom I showed the passage laughed till the tears streamed down his old cheeks. I wish I could. When the " Old Lady " reads it, there will be a cedar or two damaged at Simla. Thanks indeed for your kind offer to let me have possession of the Review scraps; but I [would] rather you should preserve them yourself, as these notices may prove unexpectedly valuable to you in a few years hence.

To your offer to give a solemn pledge never to divulge anything without permission, I can give no answer, at present. Neither its acceptance nor rejection depends on me, to tell you the truth, since it would be quite an unprecedented event to pledge an outsider to our own particular form of oath or promise, and that no other would hold good in my Superior's opinion. Unfortunately for both of us, once—or rather *twice*—upon a time you made use of an expression which was recorded, and but three days ago, when pleading for some privileges for you, it was brought out before me very unexpectedly, I must say. Upon hearing it repeated and seeing it recorded, I had but to turn, as gently as I could, the other cheek to still more unexpected buffets of fortune dealt out by the respected hand of him whom I so revere. Cruel as the reminder seemed to me it was just, for you have pronounced these words at Simla: " I am *a member* of the Theosophical Society but in no way a *Theosophist*," you said. I am not breaking confidence in revealing this result of my *plaidoyer* to you, as I am even advised to do so. We have to travel then, at the same slow rate at which we have hitherto gone, or—halt at once and write *Finis* at the bottom of our letters. I hope you will give preference to the former.

Once we are upon the topic, I wish you would impress upon your London friends some wholesome truths that they are but too apt to forget, even when they have been told of them over and over again. The Occult Science is *not* one in which secrets can be communicated of a sudden, by a written or even verbal communication. If so, all the " Brothers " would have to do, would be to publish a *Hand-book* of the art which might be taught in schools as grammar is. It is the common mistake of people that we willingly wrap ourselves and our powers in mystery—that we wish to keep our knowledge to ourselves, and of our own will refuse—" wantonly and deliberately " to communicate it. The truth is that till the neophyte attains to the condition necessary for that degree of Illumination to which, and for which, he is entitled and fitted, most *if not all* of the Secrets are *incommunicable*. The receptivity must be equal to the desire to instruct. The illumination *must come from within*. Till then no hocus pocus of incantations, or mummery of appliances, no metaphysical lectures or discussions, no self-imposed penance can give it. All these are but means to an end, and all we can do is to direct the use of such means as have been empirically found by the experience of ages to conduce to the required object. And this was and has been *no secret* for thousands of years. Fasting, meditation, chastity of thought, word, and deed; silence for certain periods of time to enable nature herself to speak to him who comes to her for information; government of the animal passions and impulses; utter unselfishness of intention, the use of certain incense and fumigations for physiological purposes, have been published as the means since the days of Plato and Iamblichus in the West and since the far earlier times of our Indian *Rishis*. How these must be complied with to suit each individual temperament is of course a matter for his own experiment and the watchful care of his tutor or *Guru*. Such is in fact part of his course of discipline, and his Guru or initiator can but assist him with his experience and will power but can do no more *until the last and Supreme initiation*. I am also of opinion that few candidates imagine the degree of inconvenience—nay suffering and harm to himself—the said initiator submits to for the sake of his pupil. The peculiar physical, moral, and intellectual conditions of neophytes and Adepts alike vary much, as anyone will easily understand; thus, in each case, the instructor has to adapt his conditions to those of the pupil, and the strain is terrible, for to achieve success we have to bring ourselves into a *full* rapport with the subject under training. And as the greater the powers of the Adept the less he is in sympathy with the natures of the profane who often come to him saturated with the emanations of the outside world, those animal emanations of the selfish, brutal, crowd that we so dread—the longer he was separated from that world and the purer he has himself become, the more difficult the self-imposed task. Then— knowledge can only be communicated gradually; and some of the highest secrets—if actually formulated even in your well prepared ear—might sound to you as insane gibberish, notwithstanding all the sincerity of your present assurance that " absolute trust defies misunderstanding." This is the real cause of our reticence. This is why people so often complain with a plausible show of reason that no new knowledge is communicated to them, though they have toiled for it for two, three or more years. Let those who really desire to learn *abandon all* and come to us, instead of asking or expecting us to go to them. But how is this to be done in your world, and atmosphere? " Woke up sad on the morning of the 18th." Did you? Well, well, patience, my good brother, patience. Something *has* occurred, though you have preserved no consciousness of the event; but let this rest. Only what more can I do? How am I to give expression to ideas for which you have as yet no language? The finer and more susceptible heads get, like yourself, more than others do, and even when *they* get a little extra dose it is lost for want of words and images to fix the floating ideas. Perhaps, and undoubtedly you know not to what I now refer. You *will* know it one day—Patience. To give more knowledge to a man than he is yet fitted to receive is a dangerous experiment; and furthermore, other considerations go to restrain me. The sudden communication of facts, so transcending the ordinary, is in many instances fatal not only to the neophyte but to those directly about him. It is like delivering an infernal machine or a cocked and loaded revolver into the hands of one who had never seen such a thing. Our case is exactly analogous. We feel that the time is approaching, and that we are bound to choose between the triumph of Truth or the Reign of Error and—Terror. We have to let in a few chosen ones into the great secret, or—allow the infamous *Shammars* to lead Europe's best minds into the most insane and fatal of superstitions—Spiritualism; and we *do* feel as if we were delivering a whole cargo of dynamite into the hands of those we are anxious to see defending themselves against the Red Capped Brothers of the Shadow. You are curious to know where I am travelling about; to learn more of my great work and mission? Were I to tell you, you could hardly make anything of it. To test your knowledge and patience, I may answer you though —this once. I now come from *Sakya-Jong*. To you the name will remain meaningless. Repeat it before the "Old Lady" and—observe the result. But to return. Having then, to deliver with one hand the much needed yet dangerous weapon to the world, and with the other to keep off the Shammars (the havoc produced by them already being immense) do you not think we have a right to hesitate, to pause and feel the necessity of caution, as we never did before? To sum up: the misuse of knowledge by the pupil always reacts upon the initiator; nor do I believe you know yet, that in sharing his secrets with another the Adept, by an immutable Law, is delaying his own progress to the Eternal Rest. Perhaps, what I now tell you may help you to a truer conception of things, and to appreciate our mutual position the better. Loitering on the way does not conduce to a speedy arrival at the journey's end. And, it must strike you as a truism that a *Price* must be paid for everything and every truth by *somebody*, and in this case—WE pay it. Fear not; I am willing to pay my share, and I told so those who put me the question. I will not desert you; nor will I show myself less self-sacrificing than the poor, worn-out mortality we know as the "Old Lady." The above must remain between us two. I expect you to regard this letter as strictly confidential for it is neither for publication nor your friends. I want you alone to know it. Only, if all this was more generally known to candidates

for initiation, I feel certain they would be both more thankful
and more patient as well as less inclined to be irritated at what
they consider our reticence and vacillations. Few possess your
discretion; fewer still know [how] to appreciate at their true value
the results obtained. . . . Your two letters to S.M. will lead to no
result whatever. He will remain as immovable and your trouble
will have been taken in vain. You will receive a letter from him
full of suspicion and with no few unkind remarks. You cannot
persuade him that + is a living Brother for that was tried and—
failed; unless, indeed, you convert him to popular *exoteric* Lamaism,
which regards our " Byang-chubs " and " Tchang-chubs "—the
Brothers who pass from the body of one great Lama to that of
another—as *Lhas* or *disembodied* Spirits. Remember what I said in
my last of Planetary Spirits. The *Tchang-chub* (an adept who has,
by the power of his knowledge and soul enlightenment, become
exempt from the curse of UNCONSCIOUS transmigration)—may, at
his will and desire, and instead of reincarnating himself only after
bodily death, do so, and repeatedly—during his life if he chooses.
He holds the power of choosing for himself new bodies—whether
on this or any other planet—while in possession of his old form,
that he generally preserves for purposes of his own. Read the
book of Kiu-te and you will find in it these laws. She might
translate for you some *paras*, as she knows them by rote. To her
you may read the present.

Do I often laugh at " the helpless way in which you grope in
the dark? " Most decidedly not. That would be as unkind and
about as foolish for me to do as for you to laugh at a Hindu for
his pidgin English, in a district where your Government *will not*
teach people English. Whence such a thought? And whence
that other to have my portrait? Never had but one taken, in my
whole life; a poor ferrotype produced in the days of the
" Gaudeamus " by a travelling female artist—(some relative, I
suppose, of the Munich beer hall beauties that you have inter-
viewed of late)—and from whose hands I had to rescue it. The
ferrotype is there, but the image itself has vanished: the nose
peeled off and one of the eyes gone. No other to offer. I dare
not promise for I never break my word. Yet—I may try—some
day to get you one.

Quotations from Tennyson? Really cannot say. Some stray
lines picked up in the astral light or in somebody's brain and
remembered. I never forget what I once see or read. A bad
habit. So much so, that often and unconsciously to myself I string
together sentences of stray words and phrases before my eyes, and
which may have been used a hundred years ago or will be hundred
years hence, in relation to quite a different subject. Laziness and
real lack of time. The " Old Lady " called me a " brain pirate "

and a plagiarist the other day for using a whole sentence of five lines which, she is firmly convinced, I must have *pilfered* from Dr. Wilder's brain, as three months later he reproduced it in an essay of his on prophetic intuition. Never had a look into the old philosopher's brain cells. Got it somewhere in a northern current—don't know. Write this for your information as something new for you, I suppose. Thus a child may be born bearing the greatest resemblance and features to another person, thousands of miles off, no connexion to the mother, never seen by her, but whose floating image was impressed upon her soul-memory, during sleep or even waking hours, and reproduced upon the sensitized plate of living flesh she carries in her. Yet, I believe, the lines quoted were written by Tennyson years ago, and they are published. I hope these disjointed reflections and explanations may be pardoned in one who remained for over nine days in his stirrups without dismounting. From Ghalaring-Tcho Lamasery (where your *Occult World* was discussed and commented upon—Heaven save the mark! will you think), I crossed to the Horpa Pa La territory, " the unexplored regions of Turki tribes " say your maps, ignorant of the fact that there are no tribes there at all—and thence—home. Yes; I am tired, and therefore will close.

Yours faithfully,

K. H.

In October I will be in Bhutan. I have a favour to ask of you: try and make friends with Ross Scott. *I need him.*

LETTER No. 50

Received August, 1882.

My dear friend,

I feel terribly *pulled down* (mentally) with this unceasing attitude of unavoidable oppositions, and as continual attacks on our strongholds! During the whole of my quiet, contemplative life, I have never met with a man more tenacious and unreasonable! I cannot go on like that, passing my life in useless protest; and if you cannot bring to bear upon him your friendly influence, we will have all of us to part company, at some not distant day. I was with the Chohan when I received the letter I now enclose, and the Chohan was perfectly disgusted, and called the whole thing the Tibetan name for " comedy." It is not that he is anxious to " do good " or " help the progress of the T.S." It is simply, believe me or not—*insatiable pride* in him; a ferocious, intense desire to feel and show to others that he is the " one elect," that he *knows* that which all others are barely allowed to suspect. Do not protest for it is useless. *We know*, and you do not. The Chohan heard the other day the idiotic but painfully sincere lamentations of the " wife " and—took note of them.   Such is not a man who aims at becoming a " perfect soul," and he who would write of a brother Theosophist what he has written to me of Fern—is no theosophist.   Let this be *strictly private*, and do not let him know but what he will read himself in my letter.   I want you to read the two letters before you take them to him, and I beg of you to be present *when he reads them*.

I will see what can be done for Colonel Chesney and I believe Djual Khool is after him.   For the first time during my life I think I feel *really disheartened*.   Yet for the sake of the Society, I would not lose him.   Well I will do *all* I can, but I am seriously afraid that he will spoil the broth himself some day.

Yours with sincere affection,

K. H.

LETTER No. 51

Received 22—8—82.

Private.

My good friend,

Remember that in the phenomenon intended for Colonel Chesney there *was, is, and will be* but one real phenomenal thing, or rather —*an act of occultism*—the likeness of your humble servant, the best of the two productions of D. Khool, I am sorry to say—for you. The rest of the performance is, notwithstanding its mysterious character, something but too natural, and of which I do not at all approve.   But I have no right to go against the traditional policy however much I would like to avoid its practical application.

Keep this strictly within your own friendly heart until the day comes to let several persons know that *you were warned of it*.   I dare not say more.   The probations are hard all round and are sure not to meet your European notions of truthfulness and sincerity.   But reluctant as I do feel to use such means or even to permit them to be used in connection with *my chelas*, yet I must say that the deception, the lack of good faith, and the *traps* (!!) intended to inveigle the Brothers, have multiplied so much of late; and there is so little time left to that day that will decide the selection of the *chelas*, that I cannot help thinking that our chiefs and especially M. may be after all right.   With an enemy one has to use either equal or better weapons.   But do not be deceived by appearance.   Would that I could be as frank with Mr. Hume whom I as sincerely respect for some of his genuine, sterling, qualities as I cannot help blaming for some others.   When will any of you know and understand what we *really* are, instead of indulging in a world of fiction!

In case Col. Chesney speaks to you of certain things tell him not to trust to appearances. He is a gentleman, and ought not to be allowed to labour under a deception *never meant for him* but only as a test for those who would impose themselves upon us with an *unclean* heart. The crisis is near at hand. Who will win the day!

K. H.

LETTER No. 52

Received Simla, Autumn, 1882.

There is nothing " below the surface," my faithful friend— absolutely *nothing*. Hume is simply furiously jealous of anyone who received, or is likely to receive any information, favours (?) attention, or anything of the sort, emanating from us. The word " jealous " is ridiculous, but correct unless we call it *envious*, which is still worse. He believes himself *wronged*, because he fails to become our sole centre of attraction; he attitudinises before himself and feels maddened to fury in finding no one who would admire him; writes out a Hebrew passage which means in Eliphas Levi's book as I have rendered it, and failing to catch me in a new contradiction, for the purpose of which he went to the trouble of quoting it, he impresses himself with the illusion that he is " far more of an *Adwaitee* " than either M. or myself ever were (an easy thing to prove since we never were *Adwaitees*), and writes an abusive letter directed against our system and ourselves to the O.L. by way of soothing his feelings.

Are you really so generous as not to have suspected long ago the whole truth? Did I not warn you; and is it possible that you should not have perceived that he will never allow *even an adept* to know more or better than himself!; that his was a *false* humility; that he is an actor, who enacts a part for his own benefit, regardless of the pleasure or displeasure of his audience, though when the latter is manifested to the slightest degree, he turns round, concealing admirably his rage and hisses and spits *internally*. Every time I contradict and prove him wrong,—whether in a question of Tibetan terms, or in any other trifle, the record he keeps against me swells, and he comes out with some new accusation. It is idle, my dear brother, to be always repeating that there are [not], nor can there be any contradictions in what was given to you. There may be inaccuracy of expression, or incompleteness of detail; but to accuse us of blundering is really too funny. I have asked you several times to make notes and to send them to me, but neither

Mr. Hume nor you have thought of doing it; and indeed, I have very little time to explore back letters, compare notes, look into your heads, etc.

I confess my ignorance, in one thing at any rate. I am perfectly at a loss to understand why the expression used by me with regard to H.P.B.'s answer to C.C.M. should have so shocked you; and why you should object to my " exercising my ingenuity "? If, perchance, you give it another meaning than I do, then we are again both at sea—*faute de s'entendre*. Put yourself for a moment in my place, and see whether you would not have to exercise all the ingenuity you had at your command, in a case like that between C.C.M. and H.P.B. In *reality*, there is no contradiction between that passage in *Isis* and our later teaching; to anyone who never heard of the *seven* principles—constantly referred to in *Isis* as a trinity, without any more explanation—there certainly appeared to be as good a contradiction as could be. " You will write so and so, give *so far*, and no more "—she was constantly told by us, when writing her book. It was at the very beginning of a new cycle, in days when neither Christians nor Spiritualists ever thought of, let alone mentioned, more than two principles in man—*body* and *Soul*, which they called Spirit. If you had time to refer to the spiritualistic literature of that day, you would find that with the phenomenalists as with the Christians, *Soul* and *Spirit* were synonymous. It was H.P.B., who, acting under the orders of Atrya (one whom you do not know) was the first to explain in the *Spiritualist* the difference there was between *psyche* and *nous*, *nefesh* and *ruach*—Soul and Spirit. She had to bring the whole arsenal of proofs with her, quotations from Paul and Plato, from Plutarch and *James*, etc., before the Spiritualists admitted that the theosophists were right. It was then that she was ordered to write *Isis*—just a year after the Society had been founded. And, as there happened such a war over it, endless polemics and objections to the effect that *there could not be in man two souls*—we thought it was premature to give the public more than they could possibly assimilate, and before they had digested the " two souls ";—and thus, the further sub-division of the trinity into 7 principles was left unmentioned in *Isis*. And is it because she obeyed our orders, and wrote, purposely *veiling* some of her facts—that now, when we think the time has arrived to give most of, if not the *whole* truth —that she has to be left in the lurch? Would I, or any of us, ever leave her as a target for the Spiritualists to shoot at, and laugh at the contradictions when these were entirely apparent, and proceeded but from their own ignorance of the whole truth; a truth they would not listen to, nor will they accept it even now, except under protest and with the greatest reservations? Certainly not. And when I use the word " ingenuity "—that may be an American slang expression for all I know, and that I suspect has with the English another meaning—I meant neither " cunning " nor anything like a " dodge," but simply to show the difficulty I had to labour under, to explain the right meaning with an endless and clumsy paragraph before me, that insisted upon *non*-reincarnation without inserting one word in it to show that the latter had reference but to the *animal* soul, not Spirit, to the astral, not the Spiritual monad.

Will you kindly explain to me at the first opportunity what you mean by referring to my expression as " an unhappy phrase "? If you asked a friend to draw for the *Pioneer* a cow, and that friend, starting with the intention of reproducing a cow should, owing to his inability in drawing sketch instead an ox or a buffalo, and the engraving should so appear—perhaps because you were crowded with other work, and had no time to perceive the shortcomings—would you not " exercise *your* ingenuity " and try your best to set the readers right, to prove to them that in truth a cow was meant by the artist: and confessing your friend's inability, do whatever you could, at the same time, to screen him from unmerited humiliation? Yes, you are right. H. has neither delicacy of perception and feelings, nor any real, genuine kindness of heart. He is one to sacrifice his own family, those nearest and dearest to him (if there are such for him, something I doubt)—for any whim of his own; and he would be the first to allow a hecatomb of victims if he needed one drop of blood; to insist upon the advisability of *Suttee* if it were the only thing that would keep him warm, help his benumbed fingers to do their work, and he diligently writing a treatise upon some philanthropic subject during that time, and sing sincerely " *Hosanna* " to himself in his own thought. Exaggeration, you think? Not so; for you have no conception of the potential selfishness there is in him; of the cruel, remorseless egotism he brought back with him from his last incarnation—a selfishness and egotism which remained latent only owing to the uncongenial soil of the sphere he is in, of his social status and education—and *we have*. Can you believe he wrote his famous article in the *Theosophist* simply for the reason he gives you—to help break the *unavoidable* fall? to save the situation, and by answering Davidson and C.C.M., etc. to make the work—of answering in the future and reconciling the contradictions in the past—easier? Not at all. If he sacrifices in it remorselessly H.P.B., and the author of the Review of the " Perfect Way," and shows the " Brothers " as *inferior in intelligence* to the " educated European gentlemen," and devoid of any correct notions about honesty or right and wrong—in the European sense—*selfish* and cold, stubborn and domineering—it is not at all because he cares one button for either of you, least of all for the Society; but simply because in

view of certain possible events, that he is too highly intelligent
not to have fore-shadowed in his mind—he wants *to screen himself*;
to be the only one to come out unscarred if not immaculate in
case of a crash, and to dance, if need be, the " death dance " of
the Maccabeans over the prostrate body of the T.S. rather than
risk one little finger of the great Simla " I am " to be sneered at.
Knowing him as we do, we say that Mr. Hume is at perfect
liberty to quote the " unhappy phrase " as many times a day as
his breath will allow him to, if it can in any way soothe his ruffled
feelings.   And, it is just because Morya saw through him as plainly
as I see my writing before me, that he allowed the " sell " as you
call it.   Nay more; for the things are so prepared, that in case
the " *Eclectic* " has to sink—*he will be the only one to go down with it*;
the only one laughed at, and thus his selfishness and carefully
prepared plans will prove of no avail.   Believing he knew better
than I did, he was kind and considerate enough to add his explanations to mine in H.P.B.'s answer to C.C.M.—and with the exception of *Karma*—that he explained correctly enough—made a mess
of the rest.   And now, the first time I contradict what he says in
his article, he will turn round in fury and express his disgust at
what he will call *my* (not his) contradictions.   I am sorry to have
to—what will appear to you—denounce him.   But I must draw
your attention to the fact, that nine times out of ten, when he
accuses me of having entirely *misconceived his meaning*—he says,
what anyone has a right to regard as a deliberate falsehood.   The
instance of E. Levi's אהיה אשר אהיה [1] is a good instance.   In
order to prove *me* at fault, he had to become an *Adwaitee* and deny
his " moral Governor and Ruler of the Universe," by throwing
him overboard "for the last 20 years."   This is *not honest*, my
friend, and I do not see any help for it.   For who can prove—
when he says that the arguments embodied in his letters to me
were not the expressions of his own personal belief and opinions,
but brought forward simply to answer the probable objections of
a *theistic* public—that it is no better than *cheating*?   With such an
intellectual acrobat, ever ready to perform the " grand trapeze,"
whether in reference to what he states verbally, or—puts on paper,
even *we* have to appear beaten.   For the latter we care very little
personally.   But then he is ever ready to crow victory in his
private letters, and even in print.   He is willing *that we should
exist*—he is too clever to risk at this hour being caught in a want
of sagacity, since he knows through correspondents who are dead
against the " Founders " of the *actual existence* of our Brotherhood
—but, he will never submit to the recognition of such powers or
knowledge in us, as would render his unasked advice and interference as ridiculous as they are useless;—and he works on that line.

[1] " I am that I am."—EDS.

I had no right to suppress the " offensive " article—as you call it, for several reasons. Having allowed our name to be connected with the T.S. and ourselves dragged into publicity, we have to suffer (the verb, a simple figure of speech if you please)—as Olcott would put it " the penalty of our greatness." We must permit the expression of every opinion whether benevolent or malevolent; to feel ourselves picked to pieces—one day; " preached "—on the following, worshipped—on the next; and—trampled down in the mud—on the fourth. Reason No. 2—the Chohan *has so ordained it.* And with him this means fresh developments, unexpected results, and DANGER, I am afraid. The two names that you find heading the signatures of the 12 chelas who protest, belong to the confidential *chelas* of the Chohan himself. In this direction there is no more hope for Mr. Hume—*consummatum est.* He has overdone the thing, and I will never have any more opportunities of pronouncing his name before our venerable chief. On the other hand, the *denunciation* has done good. The Chohan gave orders that the young Jyotirmoy—a lad of 14, the son of Babu Nobin Banerjee whom you know—should be accepted as a pupil in one of our lamaseries near Chamto-Dong about 100 miles off *Shigatse,* and his sister, a virgin Yoginee of 18, at the female monastery of Palli. Thus, the Founders will have two witnesses in good time, and will not depend upon the caprice of Mr. Hume to kill and resurrect us at pleasure. As to proving whether we do, or do not know more of the mysteries of nature than your men of Science and your theologians do, *it rests with you* and those you will select to help you in the important task.

I hope, my dear friend, that you will undertake to impress upon Mr. Hume the following facts:—Though the work done by him for the Society would become ultimately most important, and that it might have borne the most useful fruits, yet his denunciatory article has nigh upset the labour done by him. People will now regard him more than ever a *lunatic*—Hindu members will blame him for years, and our chelas can never be made to look upon him but in the light of an iconoclast, a haughty intruder, incapable of any gratitude, hence—unfit to be one of them. This you must give out as your *personal* opinion—of course not unless it meets your own views, and may be given as the expression of your real feelings in the matter—for I, personally am ordered not to break with him until the day of the crisis comes. If he desires to retain his official position in the Eclectic, help him to do so. If not, I beg you most urgently to accept the position of President yourself. But I leave all this to your tact and discretion. Let him also know that the *Protest* of the Chelas is no work of ours, but the result of a positive order emanating from the Chohan. The *Protest* was received at the Headquarters, two hours before the postman brought the famous article, and telegrams were received from several chelas in India on the same day. Together with the foot-note sent by Djual Khool to be appended to W. Oxley's article, the September Number is calculated to create a certain sensation among the mystics of England and America, not only among our Hindus. The " Brothers " question is kept up pretty alive, and may bear its fruit. Mr. Hume's graphic pen spurts, under the mask of philanthropy, the bitterest gall, assailing us with weapons which, for being represented or rather imagined as lawful and legitimate, and used for *the most honest* of purposes—wield by turns ridicule and abuse. And yet he has so preserved the semblance of a sincere belief in our knowledge, that we are more than likely to be thenceforth remembered as he has painted us, and not as in reality we are. What I once said of him, I maintain. He may, outwardly, sometimes sincerely forgive, he can never *forget*. He is that which Johnson is said to have much admired, " a good hater."

Oh, my friend, with all your faults, and your rather too lively past, how much, how immeasureably much higher you stand in our sight than our " I am," with all his high " splendid mental capacity," and *outwardly* pathetic nature concealing the inward absence of anything like real feeling and heart!

M. wants me to tell you that he refuses most decidedly to take any precaution of the nature you suggest. He despises H. thoroughly; yet in a case of any real danger would be the first to protect him for the pains and labour given by him for the T.S. He says that in case H. comes to know of his ridiculous blunder, he will be ready to prove to others the existence of occult powers, but *will not leave* H. one leg to stand upon. His punishment must be allowed to be *complete* or else it will have no effect upon him, and he will only retaliate upon innocent victims. H. has shown us to the world as dishonest and lying, before he ever had one single *undeniable* proof that we were that, and that he was justified in his denunciation by even an appearance, a semblance of dishonesty. If H. chooses to-morrow to represent us as murderers M. will try to *raise a maya* to make the words good, and then destroy it, and show him a calumniator. I am afraid he is right, from the standpoint of our rules and customs. They are *anti-European*, I confess. With the exception of the telegram, M. never wrote Fern but one letter, the five or six other letters in his handwriting emanating from the *Dugpa* who has charge of Fern. He hopes that you will not *spoil his work*, and that you will ever remain a loyal and true friend to him, as he will be one to you. Fern will *never repeat* any experiment *à la* napkin, for the simple reason that he will be trusted with no more letters.

I have received a letter from Colonel Chesney and will answer it in a few days with a young chela who will deliver it *to your care*

with my respectful greeting. Do not frighten the boy. He is
ordered to answer all the questions *he can answer*, but no more.
From Simla he will proceed to Buddha Gaya and Bombay, on
business, and will be back home about November.

With sincere friendship,

Yours,

K. H.

LETTER No. 53

Strictly private and confidential

My patient—friend:—Yesterday, I had a short note posted to
you, and it accompanied a long letter to Hume—I had it registered somewhere in Central P. by a happy, *free* friend; to-day, it
is a long letter to yourself, and it is intended to be accompanied
by a tolling of *jeremiads*, a doleful story of a discomfiture, which
may or may not make you laugh as it does that bulky Brother of
mine—but which makes me feel like the poet who could not sleep
aright,

" For his soul kept up too much light
Under his eyelids for the night."

I hear you uttering under breath: " Now what in the world *does*
he mean! " Patience, my best Anglo-Indian friend, patience; and
when you have heard of the disreputable conduct of my wicked,
more than ever laughing Brother, you will plainly see why I come
to regret, that instead of tasting in Europe of the fruit of the Tree
of the Knowledge of Good and Evil—I have not remained in Asia,
in all the *sancta simplicitas* of ignorance of *your* ways and manners,
for then—I would be now grinning too!

I wonder what *you* will say when you will have learned the
dreadful secret! I long to know it, to be delivered of a nightmare.
Were you to meet me now, for the first time, in the shadowy alleys
of your Simla, and demanded of me the *whole* truth, you would
hear me tell it to you, most unfavourably for myself. My answer to
you would remind the world—if you were cruel enough to repeat
it—of the famous answer given by Warren Hastings to " dog
Jennings " on his first meeting with the ex-governor after his return
from India! " My dear Hastings "—asked Jennings—" is it possible
you are the great rascal Burke says, and the whole world is inclined
to believe? "—" I can assure you, Jennings," was the sad and mild
reply, " that though sometimes obliged to appear rascal for the
Company, I was never one for myself." I am the W.H. for the
sins of the Brotherhood. But to facts.

Of course you know—the " O.L." told you I think—that when
we take *candidates* for chelas, they take the vow of secrecy and silence
respecting every order they may receive.   One has to prove himself
fit for *chelaship*, before he can find out whether he is fit for *adeptship*.
Fern is under such a probation; and a nice mess they have prepared
for me between the two! As you already know from my letter to
Hume, he did not interest me, I knew nothing of him, beyond his
remarkable faculties, his powers for clairaudience and clairvoyance,
and his still more remarkable tenacity of purpose, strong will, and
other etcs.   A loose, immoral character for years,—a tavern Pericles
with a sweet smile for every street Aspasia, he had entirely and
suddenly reformed after joining the Theosoph: Society, and " M."
took him seriously in hand.   It is no business of mine to tell even
yourself, how much of his visions is truth and how much hallucination, or even perchance—fiction.   That he bamboozled our
friend Hume considerably, must be so, since Mr. Hume tells me
the most marvellous yarns of him.   But the worst of all this business
is the following.   He *bamboozled* him so well, indeed, that whereas
H. did not believe one word when Fern was speaking *the truth*,
nearly every lie uttered by F. was accepted by our respected Prest.
of the *Eclectic*—as gospel truth.

Now you will readily understand, that it is impossible for me to
try and set him (H) right, since F. is M.'s chela, and that I have
no right whatever—either legal, or social, according to *our* code—to
interfere between the two.   Of the several grievances, however, it
is the smallest.   Another of our customs, when corresponding with
the outside world, is to entrust a chela with the task of delivering
the letter or any other message; and if not absolutely necessary—to
never give it a thought.   Very often our very letters—unless
something very important and secret—are written in our handwritings by our chelas.   Thus, last year, some of my letters to you
were *precipitated*, and when sweet and easy precipitation was stopped
—well I had but to compose my mind, assume an easy position, and
—think, and my faithful " Disinherited " had but to copy my
thoughts, making only occasionally a blunder.   Ah, my friend, I
had an easy life of it unto the very day when the *Eclectic* sprung into
its checkered existence. . . . Anyhow, this year, for reasons we need
not mention, I have to do my own work—the whole of it, and I
have a hard time of it sometimes, and get impatient over it.   As
Jean Paul Richter says somewhere, the most painful part of our
bodily pain is that which is bodiless or immaterial, namely our impatience, and the delusion that it will last for ever. . . Having one
day permitted myself to act as though I were labouring under such
a delusion, in the innocence of my unsophisticated soul, I trusted
the sacredness of my correspondence into the hands of that *alter ego*
of mine, the wicked and " imperious " chap, your " Illustrious,"

who took undue advantage of my confidence in him and —placed me in the position I am now in! The wretch laughs since yesterday, and to confess the truth I feel inclined to do the same. But as an Englishman, I am afraid you will be terror-struck at the enormity of his crime. You know, that notwithstanding his faults Mr. Hume is *absolutely* necessary, so far, to the T.S. I grow sometimes very irritated at his petty feelings and spirit of vindictiveness; yet withal, I have to put up with his weaknesses, which lead him at one moment to vex himself that it is *not yet*—and at another that it is *already* mid-day. But our " Illustrious " is not precisely of that opinion. Mr. Hume's pride and self-opinion— he argues—wish as our saying goes—that all mankind had only two bent knees, to make *puja* to him; and he M. is not going to humour him. He will do nothing, of course, to harm or even to vex him purposely; on the contrary, he means to always protect him as he has done until now; but—he will not lift his little finger to disabuse him.

The substance and pith of his argument are summed up in the following:

" Hume laughed and chuckled at *real*, *genuine* phenomena (the production of which have brought us well nigh into the Chohan's disgrace)—only and solely because the manifestations were not sketched by himself, nor were they produced in his honour or for his sole benefit. And now let him feel happy and proud over mysterious manifestations of his own making and creation. Let him taunt Sinnett in the depths of his own proud heart, and even by throwing out hints to others—that even he, Sinnett, was hardly so favoured. No one has ever attempted a *deliberate* deception, nor would anyone be permitted to attempt anything of the sort. Everything was made to follow its natural, ordinary course. Fern is in the hands of two clever—' dwellers of the threshold ' as Bulwer would call them—two *dugpas* kept by us to do our scavengers' work, and to draw out the latent vices—if there be any—from the candidates; and Fern has shown himself on the whole, far better and more moral than he was supposed to be. Fern has done but what he was ordered to do; and he holds his tongue because it is his first duty. As to his posing with Hume, and attitudinizing before himself and others as a seer, since he has brought himself to believe it, and that it is but certain details that can be really called a fiction, or to put it less mildly *fibs*—there is no real harm done but to himself. Hume's jealousy and pride will ever be in the way. to prevent him swallowing *truth* as much as ornamental *fiction*; and Sinnett is shrewd enough to sift very easily Fern's realities and dreams. . . . Why then, should I, or you or any one else " concludes M.—" offer advice to one who is sure not to accept it, or, which will be still worse, in case he learns for a certainty that he has been permitted to make a fool of himself—is still more sure to become an *irreconcilable enemy* to the Society, the Cause, the much suffering Founders and all.   Let him, then, strictly alone. . . . He will not be thankful for undeceiving him.   On the contrary.   He will forget that no one is to be blamed but himself; that no one had ever whispered him one word that could have led him into his extra delusions; but will turn more fiercely than ever on those *chaps*—the adepts—and he will call them publicly *impostors, jesuits* and *pretenders*.   You (I) gave him one genuine *pukka* phenomenon —and that ought to satisfy him as to the possibility of everything else."

Such is M.'s reasoning; and were I not indirectly mixed in the *quid pro quo*—it would be also mine.   But now, owing to the *plants* of that little double-dealing monkey—Fern, I am compelled to disturb you for a friendly advice, since *our* ways are not *your* ways— and *vice versa.*

But now see what happened.   Hume has lately received a good many letters from me; and I hope you will kindly follow with me the fate and various fortunes of three of them, ever since he began to receive them in a direct way.   Try also, to well understand the situation and to thus realize *my* position.   Since we had three chelas at Simla,—two regular ones and one an irregular one—the candidate Fern, I conceived the unfortunate idea of *saving power*, of economizing as though I had a " Savings bank."   To tell truth, I sought to separate as much as it was possible under the circumstances the suspected " Headquarters " from every phenomenon produced at Simla; hence from the correspondence that passed between Mr. Hume and myself.   Unless H.P.B., Domodar, and Deb—were entirely *disconnected*, there was no saying what might, or might not, happen.   The first letter—the one found in the conservatory—I gave to M. to have it left at Mr. H.'s house by one of the two regular chelas.   He gave it to Subba Row—for he had to see him on that day; S.R. passed it in the ordinary way (posted it) to Fern, with instructions to either leave it at Mr. Hume's house, or to send it to him through post, in case he were afraid that Mr. H. should ask him—since Fern *could not*, had not the right to answer him and thus would be led to telling an untruth.   Several times D.Kh. had tried to penetrate into Rothney Castle, but suffered each time so acutely that I told him to give it up.   (He is preparing for initiation and might easily fail as a consequence).   Well, Fern did *not* post it but sent a friend—his dugpa—to leave it at the house and the latter placed it in the conservatory about 2 a.m.   This was *half* of a phenomenon but H. took it for an entire thing, and got very mad when M. refused as he thought to take up his answer in the same way.   Then I wrote to console him, and told him as plainly as I could say, without breaking M.'s confidence in relation to Fern

22

that D.K. could do nothing for him, at present, and that it was one of Morya's chelas that had placed the letter there, etc., etc. I believe the hint was quite broad enough and no *deception* practised? The second letter, I think, was thrown on his table by Dj. Khool (the spelling of whose name is Gjual, but not so phonetically) and, as it was done by himself it was a *pukka* orthodox phenomenon and Hume has no need to complain. Several were sent to him in various ways—and he may be sure of one thing: however ordinary the means by which the letters reached him, they could not be but phenomenal in reaching India from Tibet. But this does not seem to be taken into any consideration by him. And now we come to the really *bad* part of it, a part for which I blame entirely M. for permitting it and exonerate Fern, *who could not help it.*

Of course you understand that I write you this in *strict confidence*, relying upon your *honour* that whatever happens you will not betray Fern. Indeed (and I have looked most attentively into the thing) the boy was led to become guilty of a deliberate *jesuitical* deception rather through Hume's constant insults, suspicious attitude and deliberate slights at meals, and during the hours of work, than from any motives in consequence of his loose notions of morals. Then M.'s letters (the production of the amiable dug-pa, in reality *ex*-dugpa, whose past sins will never permit him to fully atone for his misdeeds) distinctly say:—" do, either so and so, or in such a way "; they *tempt* him, and lead him to imagine that in doing no injury to any human being and when *the motive* is good every action becomes legal!! *I* was thus tempted in my youth, and had nearly succumbed twice to the temptation, but was saved by my uncle from falling into the monstrous snare; and so was the *Illustrious*—who is a *pukka* orthodox Occultist and holds religiously to the old traditions and methods; and so would be any one of you had I consented to accept you for chelas. But as I was aware from the first of what you have confessed to, in a letter to H.P.B., namely that there was something supremely revolting to the better class of European minds in that idea of being tested, of being under probation—I therefore had always avoided the acceptance of Mr. Hume's often expressed offer to become a chela. This may, per- haps, give you the key to the whole situation. However, this is what happened. Fern had received a letter of mine through a chela, with the injunction of causing it to reach its destination *immediately*. They were going to take breakfast, and there was no time to lose. Fern had thrown the letter on a table and ought to have left it there, since there would have been no occasion for him then, to *lie*. But he was vexed with H., and he devised another dodge. He placed the letter in the folds of Mr. H.'s napkin, who at breakfast took it up and accidentally shook out the letter on to the floor; it appears, to the terrible fright of " Moggy " and the contented surprise of Hume. But, his old suspicion returning to him, (a suspicion he had always harboured since I wrote to him that my first letter was brought into the conservatory by one of M.'s chelas, and that *my* chela could do little, though he had visited invisibly every part of the house before)—Hume looks at Fern full and asks him—whether it was *he who* had placed it there. Now I have the entire picture before me of F.'s brain at that moment. There's the rapid flash in it—" this saves me . . . for I can swear I never put it *there* " (meaning the spot on the floor—where it had fallen)—No —he boldly answers.—" I have never put it THERE "—he adds mentally. Then a vision of M. and a feeling of intense satisfaction and relief for not having been guilty of a direct lie. Confused pictures of some *Jesuits* he had known, of his little child—a disconnected thought of his room and beams in Mr. H.'s garden, etc. —not a thought of *self*-deception! Truly then, our friend was *taken* in but once, but I would pay any price could I but *recall* the event and replace my letter with somebody else's message. But you see how *I am* situated. M. tells me he gives me *carte blanche* to tell anything I like *to you*, he will not have me say a word to Hume; nor would he ever forgive you—he says, were you to interfere between the punishment of Hume's pride, and—*fate*. Fern is not really to be blamed, for thinking that so long as the result is accomplished the details are of no account, since he was brought [up] at such a school, and that he really has the welfare of the Cause at heart, whereas, with Hume—it is really *bona fide* Selfishness, egotism —the chief and only motive power. " Egotistic philanthropist " is a word which paints his portrait at full length.

Now for Col. Chesney. Since he really and sincerely was kind enough, it appears, to discern *something* in the outlines of your poor, humble friend's face; an impression drawn, most probably, from the depths of his imagination rather than from any real presence of such an expression as you say, in Dj. Khool's or M.'s production—the former felt quite proud and begged my permission to *precipitate* another such likeness, for Col. Chesney. Of course, the permission was granted, though I laughed at the idea, and M. told D.K. that the Col. would also laugh at what he will suspect as my conceit. But D.K. *would* try and then went and begged permission to present it himself to Col. Chesney; a permission which was, as a matter of course, refused by the Chohan and he himself reprimanded. But the picture was ready three minutes after I had consented to it, and D.K. seemed enormously proud of it. He says—and he is right, I think, that this likeness is the best of the three. Well, it went the usual way, *via* Djual Khool, Deb and Fern—the H.P.B. and Damodar being both at Poona at that time. M. was training and testing Fern for a phenomenon— of course a *genuine* one—so that a pukka manifestation could be produced in Col. Chesney's house by Fern; but, while Fern swore he needed but three months' preparation, M. knew he would never be ready for this season—nor do I think he will be ready next year. Anyhow, he entrusted the new picture to Fern, telling him again to better send it by post, for were the Colonel to ever learn that Fern was concerned in it, he would disbelieve even in its precipitated production. But D.K. wanted it delivered immediately, and while the Col. as he said—" had Master *hot* in his head still "—and Fern, the conceited young fool, answers—" No; before I do anything in connection with the ' packet ' I must study him (Col. Chesney) more fully (!!) I want, this time, to obtain the highest possible results at the first onset. From what I have seen of the author of the ' Battle of Dorking ' I have not been able to satisfy myself about him. . . . Father told me to be his ' eyes ' and ' ears '—he not having always the time—I must find out the character *we have to deal with* "!!

In the interval, I, fearing that Master Fern may, perhaps, place the portrait in the folds of Col. Chesney's " napkin," and produce some " *spiritual* manifestation with his foot "—I wrote to you from Poona through Damodar, giving you a very broad hint I believe, which, of course, you did not understand but will now. Meanwhile, yester morning D.K. came and told me that Fern still had his picture and that he feared that some trick had or would be played. Then I immediately aroused my too indifferent Brother from his apathy. I showed to him how dangerous was the situation left in the unscrupulous hands of a boy, whose sense of morality was still more blunted by the " probation " tests and deceit which he regarded nigh as legal and permissible and—aroused him finally into action. A telegram was sent to Fern in M.'s *own* handwriting, this time, from the Central Provinces—(Bussawal, I believe—where lives a *chela*) ordering Fern to send on immediately the packet he had for the Colonel to his address by post—and Fern, as I see, received it yesterday, in the forenoon by our time (Tuesday, 22). And thus when you hear of it, you will know the *whole* truth.

I have strictly forbidden my letters or anything connected with my business to ever be given to Fern. Thus Mr. H. and yourself or anyone else at Simla may take my *word of honour* that Fern will have nothing more to do with *my* business. But, my dearest friend, you must promise me faithfully, and for my sake, never to breathe one word of what I told you to anyone—least of all *to Hume* or Fern; unless Fern *forces you* by his fibs to stop him, in which case you may use what you think proper of it, to force him to *shut up*, yet, without ever allowing him to know how, and from whom you have learnt it. Apart from this, use of the knowledge at your discretion. Read my letter, registered and sent to your name from Bussawal yesterday—or rather my letter to Hume—carefully and think well over before sending it to him; for this letter may provoke him to a fit of madness and hurt pride and make him quit the Society at once. Better keep it, as means for future emergency to prove to him that at least I am one who will not permit even my enemies to be won over by *unfair* means. At least, I so regard the means that Mr. Fern seems but too ready to use. But above all, good and faithful friend, do not allow your self to misconceive the real position of our Great Brotherhood. Dark and tortuous as may seem to your Western mind the paths trodden, and the ways by which our candidates are brought to the great Light—you will be the first to approve of them when you know *all*. Do not judge on appearances—for you may thereby do a great wrong, and lose your own personal chances to learn more. Only be vigilant and— watch. If Mr. Hume but consents to wait he will have more, and far more extraordinary phenomena to silence the critics than he hitherto had. Exercise your influence with him. Remember in November comes the great crisis, and September will be full of dangers. Save at least our personal relations from the great wreck. Fern is the queerest psychological subject I have ever met. The pearl is inside, and truly profoundly hidden by the unattractive oyster-shell. We cannot break it at once; nor can we afford to lose such subjects. While *protecting yourself—protect him from Hume.* Generally I never trust a woman, any more than I would an echo; both are of the female gender because the goddess Echo—like woman —will always have the last word. But with your lady it is otherwise, and I firmly believe that you can trust her with the above—if you think proper. But beware of poor Mrs. Gordon. An excellent lady but would talk Death herself *to death*. And now I have done.

Yours ever faithfully,

K.H.

Please do not regard it as a compliment—but believe me when I say that your two *Letters* and especially " The Evolution of Man " is simply SUPERB. Do not fear any contradictions or inconsistencies.

I say again—make notes of them and send them to me and you will see.[1]

I pray you, kind sir, to lock the foolish letter sent on yesterday to Hume-Sahib into your trunk and leave it there to roost until in demand. I tell you it will create *mischief* and no better. K.H. is too sensitive by far—he is becoming in your Western Society a regular Miss.

Yours,

M.

[1] These two paragraphs are still in the handwriting of Master K.H. The last paragraph alone is in the handwriting of Master M.—Eds.

LETTER No. 54

Received Simla, October, 1882.

My dear friend:—the deposition and abdication of our great
" I am " is one of the most agreeable events of the season for your
humble servant.   *Mea culpa!*—I exclaim, and willingly place my
guilty head under a shower of ashes—from the Simla cigars if you
like—for it was my doing! Some good has come of it in the shape
of excellent literary work—(though, indeed, I prefer your style)
—for the Parent body, but none whatever for the hapless
" Eclectic." What has he done for it? He complains in a letter to
Shishir Koomar Gosh (of the A.B. *Patrika*) that owing to *his* (?)
Hume's incessant efforts, *he* had nearly " converted Chesney to
Theosophy " when the great anti-Christian spirit of the *Theosophist*
threw the Colonel violently back. This is what we may call—
tampering with historical facts. I send you his last letter to me, in
which you will find him entirely under the influence of his new
guru—" the good Vedantin Swami " (who offers to teach him the
Adwaita philosophy with a god in it by way of improvement)—
and of the Sandaram Spirit. His argument is, as you will find, that
with the " good old Swami " he will at any rate learn *something*,
while with us, it is impossible for him to " ever learn *anything*." I
—" never gave him the assurance that all the letters were not
evolved out of the Old Lady's fertile brain." Even now, he adds,
when he has obtained subjective *certainty* that we are distinct
entities from Mad. B—" I cannot tell what you are—you might be
Djual Kool, or a spirit of the high Eastern plane "—etc. in like
strain. In the letter enclosed he says—we " may be *tantrikists* "
(better ascertain the value of the compliment paid)—and, he is
preparing, nay—all prepared—to plunge from extreme *Adwaitism*
into transcendental *theism*, once more. Amen. I hand him over to
the Salvation Army.

I would not like to see him sever his connection with the Society
altogether, though; first for his own intrinsic literary worth, and
then—because you would be sure to have an indefatigable though
a *secret* enemy, who would pass his time in writing out his ink dry
against theosophy, denouncing all and everyone in the Society to
all and everyone outside of it, and making himself disagreeable in a
thousand ways. As I once said before, he may seem to forgive, and
he is just the man to bamboozle himself before his own reflection in
the looking-glass into magnanimous forgiveness, but in reality he
neither forgives nor ever forgets. It was pleasant news for M. and
all of us to hear how unanimously and quietly you were elected
President, and we all—" masters " and chelas—greet fraternally
and warmly your ascension to the office; an accomplished fact

which reconciles us even with the sad and humiliating tidings that Mr. Hume expressed his utter indifference to *chelas* and even to their *masters*, adding that he cared very little to meet either. But enough of him who may better be described in the words of the Tibetan proverb:

". . . Like the bird of night: by day a graceful cat, in darkness an ugly rat."

One word of advice—an earnest warning from both of us: *trust not little Fern—beware of him.* His placid serenity and smiles when talking to you of the " mild scolding tempered with mercy," and that it is better to be scolded than cast off—are all *assumed.* His letter of penitence and remorse to M—which he sends you to keep —is not sincere. If you do not watch him closely, he will mix the cards for you in a way that may lead the Society to ruin, for he swore a great oath to himself that the Society will either *fall* or *rise* with himself. If he fails next year again—and with all his great gifts, how can such an incurable little jesuit and liar help failing?— he will do his best to pull down the Society with him—as regards belief in the " Brothers " at least. Try to save him, if possible, my dearest friend; do your best to convert him to truth and unselfishness. It is real pity that such gifts should be drowned in a mire of vice—so strongly engrafted upon him by his early tutors. Meanwhile, beware of ever allowing him to see any of my letters.

And now to C.C. Massey and your letters. Both answer and your reply are excellent. Doubtless a more sincere, truthful or a more noble minded man (S. Moses *not* excepted) could hardly be found among the British theosophists. His only and chief fault is —*weakness.* Were he to learn some day how deeply he has wronged H.P.B. in thought—no man would feel more miserable over it than himself. But of this anon. If you remember in my letter to H. upon the subject I " forbade all arrangements " for the simple reason that the Bsh. Theos. Soc. had collapsed, and virtually was no more. But, if I remember right I added—that if they reestablished it on a firm basis with such members as Mrs. K. and her scribe—that we would have no objection to teach them through you—or words to that effect. I certainly objected having my letters printed and circulated like those of Paul in the bazaars of Ephesus—for the benefit (or perchance derision and criticism) of isolated members who hardly believed in our existence. But I have no objection, in case of an arrangement as proposed by C.C.M. Only let them first organize, leaving such bigots as Wyld —strictly out in the cold. He refused to admit Mr. Hume's sister Mrs. B. because, having never seen any mesmeric phenomena she disbelieved in mesmerism; and refused to admit Crookes, recommended by C.C.M., as I was told. I will never refuse my help and co-operation to a group of men sincere and ardent to learn; but if again such men as Mr. Hume are to be admitted, men who generally delight in playing in every organized system they get into the parts played by Typhon and Ahriman in the Egyptian and Zoroastrian systems—then the plan had better be left aside. I dread the appearance in print of our philosophy as expounded by Mr. H. I read his three essays or chapters on God (?) cosmogony and glimpses of the origin of things in general, and had to cross out nearly all. He makes of us *Agnostics*! ! *We* do not believe in God because so far *we have no proof*, etc. This is preposterously ridiculous: if he publishes what I read, I will have H.P.B. or Djual Khool deny the whole thing; as I cannot permit our sacred philosophy to be so disfigured. He says that people will not accept the whole truth; that unless we humour them with a hope that there may be a " loving Father and creator of all in heaven " our philosophy will be rejected *a priori*. In such a case the less such idiots hear of our doctrines the better for both. If they do not want the whole truth and nothing but the truth, they are welcome. But never will they find *us*—(at any rate)—compromising with, and pandering to public prejudices. Do you call *this* " candid " and—*honest* " from *a European standpoint* "? Read his letter and judge. The truth is, my dear friend, that notwithstanding the great tidal wave of mysticism that is now sweeping over a portion of the intellectual classes of Europe, the Western people have as yet scarcely learned to recognise that which we term *wisdom* in its loftiest sense. As yet, he only is esteemed truly wise in his world who can most cleverly conduct the business of life, so that it may yield the largest amount of material profit—honours or money. The quality of wisdom ever was, and will be yet for a long time—to the very close of the fifth race—denied to him who seeks the wealth of the mind for its own sake, and for its own enjoyment and result without the secondary purpose of turning it to account in the attainment of material benefits. By most of your gold worshipping countrymen our facts and theorems would be denominated fancy-flights, the dreams of madmen. Let the *Fragments* and even your own magnificent letters now published in *Light*, fall into the hands and be read by the general public—whether materialists or theists or Christians; and ten to one every average reader will curl his lip with a sneer; and with the remark—" all this may be very profound and learned but of what *use* is it in practical life? "— dismiss letters and *Fragments* from his thoughts for ever.

But now your position with C.C.M. seems changing, and you are gradually bringing him round. He longs sincerely to give Occultism another trial and—is " open to conviction "; we must not disappoint him. But, I cannot undertake to furnish either them or even yourself with *new* facts until all I have already given is put into shape from the beginning, (*vide* Mr. Hume's *Essays*) and taught to them systematically, and by them learned and digested. I am now answering your numerous series of questions —scientific and psychological—and you will have material enough for a year or two. Of course I will be always ready with further explanations, hence unavoidably, additions—but I positively refuse to teach any further before you have understood and learned all that is already given. Nor do I want you to print anything from my letters unless previously *edited* by you, and put into shape and form. I have no time for writing regular " papers," nor does my literary ability extend so far as that.

Only how about C.C.M.'s mind so prejudiced against the author of *Isis* and ourselves, who have dared an attempt to introduce Eglinton into the sacred precincts of the B.T.S. and to denominate + a " Brother "? Shall not our joint sins and transgressions " from a European standpoint "—be sorely in the way of mutual confidence; and will they not lead to endless suspicions and misconceptions? I am not prepared just now to afford the British Theosophists the proof of our existence in flesh and bones, or that I am not altogether H.P.B.'s " confederate "; for all this is a question of time and—*Karma*. But, even supposing it very easy to prove the former, it would be far less easy to disprove the latter. A " K.H.," *i.e.* a mortal of very ordinary appearance and acquainted tolerably well with the English, Vedanta and Buddhist philosophy, and with even a bit of drawing-room *juggling*—is easily found and furnished, so as to demonstrate his objective existence beyond doubt or cavil. But how about giving the positive, moral certitude that the individual, who may thus make his appearance is not a *bogus* K.H., a " confederate " of H.P.B.? Were not St. Germain, and Cagliostro, both gentlemen of the highest education and achievements—and presumably *Europeans*— not " niggers " of my sort—regarded at the time, and still so regarded by posterity—as impostors, confederates, jugglers and what not? Yet I am morally bound to set his mind at rest— through your kind agency—with regard to H.P.B. *deceiving* and *imposing* upon him. He seems to think he has obtained proofs of it absolutely *unimpeachable*. I say *he has not*. What he has obtained is simply proof of the villainy of some men, and ex-theosophists such as Hurrychund Chintamon of Bombay, now of Manchester and elsewhere; the man who robbed the Founders and Dayanand of Rs. 4,000, deceived and imposed upon them from the first (so far back as New York), and then, exposed and expelled from the Society ran away to England and is ever since seeking and thirsting for his revenge. And such other as Dr. Billing, the husband of that good, honest woman, the only *really* and thoroughly reliable and *honest* medium I know of—Mrs. M. Hollis-Billing; whom he married for her few thousands pounds, ruined her during the first year of his married life, went into concubinage with another medium; and when vehemently reproached by H.P.B. and Olcott, —left his wife and Society and turned with bitter hatred against both women; and since then is ever seeking to secretly poison the minds of the British Theosophists and Spiritualists against his wife and H.P.B. Let C.C.M. put all those facts together; fathom the mystery and trace the connection between his *informants* and the two traducers of the two innocent women. Let him investigate thoroughly and patiently, before he believes in certain reports— and even *proofs* brought forward—lest he overloads his Karma with a heavier sin than any. There is not a stone these two men leave unturned in order to succeed in their evil design. While Hurrychund Chintamon never failed once during the last three years to take into his confidence every theosophist he met, pouring into his ears pretended news from Bombay about the duplicity of the Founders; and to spread reports among the spiritualists about Mad. B's *pretended* phenomena, showing them all as simply " impudent tricks "—since she has no real idea of the Yoga powers; or again showing letters from her, received by him while she was in America; and in which she is made to advise him to *pretend*—he is a " Brother " and thus deceive the British theosophists the better; while H.C. is doing all this and much more, Billing is " working " the London mystics. He attitudinizes before them as a *victim* of his over confidence in a wife whom he found out as a false tricky medium, helped and supported in this by H.P.B. and H.S.O.; he complains of his cruel fate and swears on *his honour* (!) he left her only because he had found her an impostor, his *honesty* revolting at such a union. Thus, it is on the strength and authority of the reports of such men, and the too confiding persons who, believing in them help them that C.C.M. gradually came to disown and repudiate the disgusting and deformed change-ling which was imposed upon him under the guise of H.P.B. Believe me—it is not so. If he tells you be was shown *documentary* proof—answer him that a letter in his own handwriting and over his own signature, which, if placed in the hands of law would send him in 24 hours on the bench of criminals, may be forged as easily as any other document. A man who was capable of forging on a bogus will the signature of the testator and then, getting hold of the hand of the already dead man, put a pen into it and guide it over the ready signature, to afford the witnesses a chance of taking their oath that they had seen the man sign it—is ready to do more serious work than simply slandering an unpopular foreigner.

When, smarting under the exposure and bent upon revenge H. Ch. arrived three years ago from Bombay, C.C.M. would neither receive nor see him, nor would he listen to his justification, for Dayanand—whom he recognised and accepted at that time as his spiritual chief—had sent him word to hold no communication with the thief and traitor. Then it was that the latter and C. Carter Blake, the jesuit expelled from the Society for slandering in the *Pall Mall Gazette* both Swami and Hurrychund—became fast friends. Carter Blake had for over two years moved heaven and earth to get readmitted into the Society but H.P.B. had proved a Chinese Wall against such readmission. Both the *ex-fellows* made peace, put their heads together and worked since then in a most charming accord. This made secret enemy—No. 3. C.C.M.'s devotion was in their way—they went to work to break the object of that devotion—H.P.B.—by shaking his confidence in her. Billing, who could never hope to achieve success in that direction —for C.C.M. knew him too well, having legally defended his ruined and forsaken wife—succeeded to arouse his suspicions against Mrs. Billing *as a medium* and against her friend H.P.B. who had defended and supported her against him. Thus was the ground well prepared for sowing in it any kind of weed. Then came— like a thunderbolt—Swami's unexpected attack upon the Founders and proved the death blow to C.C.M.'s friendship. Because Swami had been represented by her to them as a high chela, an initiate, he imagined *he had never been one*, and that in her misguided zeal to advance the cause H.P.B. had deceived them all! After the April row, his and her enemies made an easy prey of him. Take *Light*; compare dates and the various cautious and covered attacks. Behold C.C.M.'s hesitation, and then his sudden pouncing upon her. Cannot you read between the lines, friend?

But what of S. Moses? Ah—he at least is never the man to utter a deliberate falsehood, much less repeat a slanderous report. He, at least, as well as C.C.M., *is* a gentleman every inch of him, and an *honest* man. Well; and what of that? You forget his profound, sincere irritation with us and H.P.B., as a Spiritualist the chosen vessel of election of *Imperator*? C.C.M. is ignorant of the laws and mysteries of mediumship and he is his staunch friend. Take again *Light* and see how plainly his irritation grows and becomes louder in his *Notes By The Way*. He has entirely mis-conceived your meaning, or rather quotations (followed by no *explanations*) from a letter of mine to yourself, who, in your turn have never correctly understood the situation. What I then said I now repeat:—There is an abyss between the highest and lowest degrees of Planetaries (this to your query—Is + a Planetary Spirit?) and then my assertion that—"+ *is* a Brother." But what is a " Brother," in reality—do you know? For what H.P.B. has added out of the depths of her own consciousness, perhaps, I do not hold myself responsible; for *she knows nothing for a dead certainty* about +, and often " dreaming dreams " she draws her own original conclu-sions therefrom. *Result*: S.M. regards us as *impostors* and *liars*, unless

we be but a *fiction*; in which case the compliment returns
to H.P.B.

Now what are the *facts* and what the accusations against H.P.B.?
Many are the shadowy points against her in C.C.M.'s mind, and
with every day they become blacker and uglier. I will give you
an instance. While in London, at the Billings, Jan. 1879, H.P.B.
who had produced a china pot from under the table, was asked
by C.C.M. to give him some phenomenally produced object too.
Consenting, she caused a small card-case, as carved in Bombay to
appear in the pocket of his overcoat hung in the hall. Inside—
whether then or later in the evening, was found a slip of paper,
with the *facsimile* of Hurrychund C's signature on it. At the time,
no suspicion entered his mind, since there really was no ground
for any. But now you see, he believes it—if not all a *trick*, at any
rate a half-deception. Why? Because at that time he believed
H.C. *a chela*, all but a great adept, as allowed and led to suppose
by H.P.B.; and now he *knows* that H.C. was *never* a chela—since
he *himself* denies it; that, he never had any *powers*, denies any
knowledge of, or belief in such; and tells to everyone that even
Dayanand has never been a *Yogi* but is simply " an ambitious
impostor " like Mohamet. In short, so many lies brought and
left at the Founders' door. And then her *letters*, and the reports
by trustworthy witnesses of her confederacy with Mrs. Billing.
Hence—confederacy between her and Eglinton. She is proved,
at any rate, an arch plotter, a deceiver, a crafty character; either
that—or a visionary lunatic, an obsessed medium! European,
western logic. Letters? Very easy to alter words, hence the whole
meaning of a sentence in letters. So has the Swami letters from
her, which he freely translates, quotes from and comments upon
in the face of the July *Supplement*. Now pray, oblige me by
carefully reading over again the " Defence." Note the bare-faced
lies of India's " great Reformer." Remember what was admitted
to you and then denied. And if *my* word of honour has any
weight with you, then know that D. Swami *was* an initiated Yogi,
a very high chela at Badrinath, endowed some years back with
great powers and a knowledge he has since forfeited, and that
H.P.B. told you but the truth, as also that H.C. was a chela of his,
who preferred to follow the " left path." And now see what has
become of this truly great man, whom we all knew and placed
our hopes in him. There he is—a moral wreck, ruined by his
ambition and panting for breath in his last struggle for supremacy,
which *he knows* we will *not* leave in his hands. And now, if this
man—ten times greater morally and intellectually than Hurrychund—could fall *so* low, and resort to such a mean course, of
what may his ex-friend and pupil Hurrychund not be capable to
satisfy *his* thirst for revenge! The former has at least an excuse—

his ferocious ambition that he mistakes for patriotism; his once *alter ego* has no excuse but his desire to harm those who exposed him. And, to achieve such results he is prepared *to do anything*. But you will perhaps enquire, why *we* have not interfered? Why *we*, the natural protectors of the Founders, if not of the Society, have not put a stop to the shameful conspiracies? A pertinent question; only I doubt whether my answer with all its sincerity will be clearly understood. You are thoroughly unacquainted with our system, and could I succeed in making it clear to you, ten to one your " better feelings "—the feelings of a European— would be ruffled, if not worse, with such a " shocking " discipline. The fact is, that to the last and supreme initiation every chela— (and even some adepts)—is left to his own device and counsel. We have to fight our own battles, and the familiar adage—" the adept *becomes*, he is not *made* " is true to the letter. Since every one of us is the *creator* and producer of the *causes* that lead to such or some other *results*, we have to reap but what we have sown. *Our chelas are helped but when they are innocent of the causes that lead them into trouble*; when such causes are generated by foreign, outside influences. Life and the struggle for adeptship would be too easy, had we all scavengers behind us to sweep away the *effects* we have generated through our own rashness and presumption. Before they are allowed to go into the world they—the chelas— are everyone of them endowed with more or less clairvoyant powers; and, with the exception of that faculty that, unless paralyzed and watched would lead them perchance to divulge certain secrets that must not be revealed—they are left in the full exercise of their powers—whatever these may be:—why don't they exercise them? Thus, step by step, and after a series of punishments, is the chela taught by bitter experience to suppress and guide his impulses; he loses his rashness, his self-sufficiency and never falls into the same errors. All that now happens is brought on by H.P.B. herself; and to you, my friend and brother, I will reveal her short- comings, for you were tested and tried, and you alone have not hitherto failed—at any rate not in one direction—that of discretion and silence. But before I reveal her one great fault to you—(a fault, indeed, in its disastrous results, yet withal a virtue) I must remind you of that which you so heartily hate; namely, that no one comes in contact with us, no one shows a desire to know more of us, but has to submit to being tested and put by us on probation. Thus, C.C.M. could no more than any other escape his fate. He has been tempted and allowed to be deceived by appearances, and to fall but too easily a prey to his weakness—suspicion and lack of self-confidence. In short, he is found wanting in the first element of success in a candidate—*unshaken faith*, once that his conviction rests upon, and has taken root in knowledge, not simple belief in certain facts. Now C.C.M. *knows* that certain phenomena of hers are undeniably genuine; his position with regard to that being precisely the position of yourself and your lady, in reference to the yellow ring-stone. Thinking you had reasons to believe the stone in question was simply *brought* (like the doll), not *doubled* —as she asserted, and disliking in the depths of your soul such a useless *deception*—as you always thought—on her part, you have not repudiated her for all that, nor exposed or complained of her in the papers as he has. In short, even when refusing her the benefit of the doubt in your own hearts, you have not doubted the phenomenon but only her accuracy in explaining it; and *while being utterly wrong*, you were undeniably right in acting with such a discretion in that matter. Not so, in his case. After entertaining during the period of three years *a blind faith* in her, amounting almost to a feeling of veneration, at the first breath of successful calumny, he, a staunch friend and an excellent *lawyer* falls a victim to a wicked plot, and his regard for her is changed into positive contempt and *a conviction* of her guilt! Instead of acting as you would have acted in such a case, namely either never mentioning the fact to her or else, asking her for an explanation, giving the accused the opportunity of defending herself, and thus acting consistently with his honest nature, he preferred giving vent to his feelings in public print, and to satisfy his rancour against herself and *us* by adopting an indirect means of attacking her statements in *Isis*. By the bye, and begging your pardon for this digression, he does not, it seems regard her answer in the *Theosophist*— " candid "! Funny logic, when coming from such an acute logician. Had he proclaimed in all the papers and at the top of his voice that the author or authors of *Isis* have not been *candid* while writing the book; that they often and purposely mislead the reader by withholding the necessary explanations and have given but portions of the truth; had he even declared, as Mr. Hume does—that the work teems with " practical errors " and deliberate misstatements —he would have been gloriously acquitted, because he would have been right—" from a European standpoint," and heartily excused by *us*—again because of his European way of judging—something innate in him and that *he cannot help*. But to call a correct and truthful explanation *not* " candid " is something I can hardly realize, though I am quite aware that his view is shared even by yourself. Alas, my friends, I am very much afraid that our respective standards of right and wrong will never agree together, since *motive* is everything for us, and that you will never go beyond appearances. However, to return to the main question.

Thus C.C.M. *knows*; he is too intelligent, too acute an observer of human nature to have remained ignorant of that most important of facts, namely that the woman *has no possible motive* for deception.

There is a sentence in his letter which, framed in a little kinder spirit, would go far to show how well he could appreciate and recognise the *real motives*, had not his mind been poisoned by prejudice, due, perhaps, more to S. Moses' irritation than to the efforts of her three above enumerated enemies. He remarks *en passant*—that the system of deception may be due to her *zeal*, but regards it as a *dishonest* zeal. And now, do you want to know how far she is guilty? Know then, that if she ever became guilty of real, *deliberate* deception, owing to that " zeal," it was when in the presence of phenomena produced she kept constantly denying —except in the matter of such trifles as bells and raps—that she had anything to do with their production *personally*. From your " European standpoint " it is downright deception, a big thunder-ing *lie*; from our *Asiatic* standpoint, though an imprudent, blamable zeal, an untruthful exaggeration, or what a Yankee would call " a blazing cock-a-hoop " meant for the benefit of the " Brothers," —yet withal, if we look into the motive—a sublime, self-denying, noble and meritorious—not *dishonest*—zeal. Yes; in that, and in that alone, she became constantly guilty of *deceiving* her friends. She could never be made to realize the utter uselessness, the danger of such a zeal; and how mistaken she was in her notions that she was adding to our glory, whereas, by attributing to us very often phenomena of the most childish nature, she but lowered us in the public estimation and sanctioned the claim of her enemies that she was " but a medium "! But it was of no use. In accordance with our rules, M. was not permitted to forbid her such a course, in so many words. She had to be allowed full and entire freedom of action, the liberty of *creating causes* that became in due course of time her scourge, her public pillory. He could at best forbid her producing phenomena, and to this last extremity he resorted as often as he could, to her friends' and theosophists' great dis-satisfaction. Was, or rather is it lack of intellectual perceptions in her? Certainly not. It is a psychological disease, over which she has little if any control at all. Her impulsive nature—as you have correctly inferred in your reply—is always ready to carry her beyond the boundaries of truth, into the regions of exaggera-tion; nevertheless without a shadow of suspicion that she is thereby deceiving her friends, or abusing their great trust in her. The stereotyped phrase: " It is *not I*; I can do nothing by myself . . it is all they—the Brothers. . . I am but their humble and devoted slave and instrument " is a downright *fib*. She can and did pro-duce phenomena, owing to her natural powers combined with several long years of regular training, and her phenomena are sometimes better, more wonderful and far more perfect than those of some high, initiated chelas, whom she surpasses in artistic taste and purely Western appreciation of art—as for instance in the

instantaneous production of pictures: witness her portrait of the
" fakir " Tiravalla mentioned in *Hints*, and compared with my
portrait by Djual Khool. Notwithstanding all the superiority of
his powers, as compared to hers; his youth as contrasted with her
old age; and the undeniable and important advantage he possesses
of having never brought his pure unalloyed magnetism in direct
contact with the great impurity of your world and society—yet do
what he may, he will never be able to produce *such* a picture,
simply because he is unable to conceive it in his mind and Tibetan
thought. Thus, while fathering upon us all manner of foolish,
often clumsy and *suspected* phenomena, she has most undeniably
been *helping* us in many instances, saving us sometimes as much
as two-thirds of the power used, and when [we] remonstrated—for
often we are unable to prevent her doing it on her end of the line
—answering that she had no need of it, and that her only joy was
to be of some use to us. And thus she kept on killing herself inch
by inch, ready to give—for our benefit and glory, as she thought
—her life-blood drop by drop, and yet invariably denying before
witnesses that she had anything to do with it. Would you call
this sublime, albeit foolish self-abnegation—" dishonest "? We do
not; nor shall we ever consent to regard it in such a light. To
come to the point: moved by that feeling, and firmly believing at
the time (because allowed to) that Hurrychund was a worthy
chela [1] of the Yogee Dayanand, she allowed C.C.M. and all those
who were present to labour under the impression that it was
Hurrychund who had produced the phenomena; and then went
on rattling for a fortnight of Swami's great powers and of the
virtues of Hurrychund, his prophet. How terribly she was punished,
every one in Bombay (as you yourself)—well knows. First—the
" chela " turning a traitor to his Master and his allies, and—a
common thief; then the " great Yogin," the " Luther of India "
sacrificing her and H.S.O. to his insatiable ambition. Very
naturally, while Hurrychund's treason—shocking as it appeared at
the time to C.C.M. and other theosophists—left her unscarred,
for Swami himself having been robbed took the defence of the
" Founders " in hand, the treachery of the " Supreme Chief of
the Theosophists of the Arya Samaj " was not regarded in its true
light; it was not *he* that had played false, but the whole blame fell
upon the unfortunate and too devoted woman, who, after extolling
him to the sky, was compelled in self-defence to expose his *mala
fides* and true motives in the *Theosophist*.

Such is the true history and *facts* with regard to her " deception " or, at best—" *dishonest* zeal." No doubt she has merited a
portion of the blame; most undeniably she is given to exaggeration

[1] The latter he certainly was, though never very " worthy," for he had always
been a selfish, plotting rascal, in the secret pay of the late Gaekwar.

in general, and when it becomes a question of " puffing up " those she is devoted to, her enthusiasm knows no limits. Thus she has made of M. an Apollo of Belvedere, the glowing description of whose physical beauty made him more than once start in anger, and break his pipe while swearing like a true—Christian; and thus, under her eloquent phraseology, I myself had the pleasure of hearing myself metamorphosed into an " angel of purity and light "—shorn of his wings. We cannot help feeling at times angry with, oftener—laughing at, her. Yet the feeling that dictates all this ridiculous effusion is too ardent, too sincere and true, not to be respected or even treated with indifference. I do not believe I was ever so profoundly touched by anything I witnessed in all my life, as I was with the poor old creature's ecstatic rapture, when meeting us recently both in our natural bodies, one—after three years, the other—nearly two years absence and separation in flesh. Even our phlegmatic M. was thrown off his balance by such an exhibition—of which he was chief hero. He had to use his *power*, and plunge her into a profound sleep, otherwise she would have burst some blood-vessel including kidneys, liver and her " interiors "—to use our friend Oxley's favourite expression—in her delirious attempts to flatten her nose against his riding mantle besmeared with the Sikkim mud! We both laughed; yet could we feel otherwise but touched? Of course, she is utterly unfit for a *true adept*: her nature is too passionately affectionate and we have no right to indulge in *personal* attachments and feelings. You can never know her as we do, therefore—none of you will ever be able to judge her impartially or correctly. You see the surface of things; and what you would term " virtue," holding but to appearances, we—judge but after having fathomed the object to its profoundest depth, and generally leave the appearances to take care of themselves. In your opinion H.P.B. is, at best, for those who like her despite herself—a quaint, strange woman, a psychological riddle; impulsive and kindhearted, yet not free from the vice of untruth. We, on the other hand, under the garb of eccentricity and folly—we find a profounder wisdom in her *inner* Self than you will ever find yourselves able to perceive. In the superficial details of her homely, hard-working, commonplace daily life and affairs, you discern but unpracticality, womanly impulses, often absurdity and folly; we, on the contrary, light daily upon traits of her inner nature the most delicate and refined, and which would cost an uninitiated psychologist years of constant and keen observation, and many an hour of close analysis and efforts to draw out of the depth of that most subtle of mysteries —human mind—and one of her most complicated machines, —H.P.B.'s mind—and thus learn to know her true *inner* Self.

23

All this you are at liberty to tell C.C.M. I have closely watched him, and feel pretty certain that what you will tell him will have far more effect upon him than what a dozen " K.H.'s " might tell him personally. " Imperator " stands between us two, and will, I am afraid, stand thus for ever. His loyalty to, and faith in the assertions of a European *living* friend can never be shaken by the assurances to the contrary, made by Asiatics, who to him—if not mere figments, are unscrupulous " confederates." But I would, if possible, show *to you* his great injustice, and the wrong done by him to an innocent woman—at any rate—*comparatively* innocent. However crazy an enthusiast, I pledge to you my word of honour, she was never *a deceiver*; nor has she ever wilfully uttered an untruth, though her position often becomes untenable, and that she has to conceal a number of things, as pledged to by her solemn vows. And now I have done with the question.

I am now going to approach once more a subject, good friend, I know is very repulsive to your mind, for you have told and written so repeatedly. And yet, in order to make some things clear to you, I am compelled to speak of it. You have often put the question, " why should the Brothers refuse turning their attention to such worthy, sincere theosophists as C.C.M. and Hood, or such a precious *subject* as S. Moses? " Well, I now answer you very clearly, that we have done so—ever since the said gentleman came into contact and communication with H.P.B. They were all tried and tested in various ways, and not one of them came up [to] the desired mark. M. gave a special attention to " C.C.M." for reasons I will now explain, and, with results as at present known to you. You may say that such a secret way of testing people is *dishonest*; that we ought to have warned him, etc. Well, all I can say is, that it may be so from your European standpoint, but that, being Asiatics, we cannot depart from our rules. A man's character, his true inner nature can never be thoroughly drawn out if he believes himself watched, or strives for an object. Besides, Col. O. had never made a secret of that way of ours, and all the Bsh. theosophists *ought* to—if they did not—know that their body was, since we had sanctioned it, under a regular probation. As for C.C.M.—of all the theosophists he was the one selected by M. and with a definite purpose, owing to H.P.B.'s importunities and his special promise. " He will turn back on you some day, *pumo*! " [1] M. repeatedly told her, in answer to her prayers to accept him as a regular chela with Olcott—" That he never, *never* will! " she exclaimed in answer. " C.C.M. is the best, most noble, etc., etc., etc."—a string of laudatory and admiring adjectives. Two years later, she said the same of Ross Scott. " Such two staunch, devoted friends—I never had! " she assured her " Boss "

[1] Query, *bu-mo*, daughter or young woman. (Tib.).—EDS.

—who only laughed in his beard, and bid me arrange the
" theosophical " marriage. Well; one was tested and tried for
three years, the other for three months, with what results I hardly
need remind you.   Not only NO temptations were ever put in the
way of either, but the latter was furnished with a wife amply
sufficient for his happiness, and connections that will prove beneficent to him some day.   C.C.M. had but objective, undoubted
phenomena to stand upon; R. Scott had, moreover, a visit in
astral shape from M.   In the case of one—the revenge of three
unprincipled men; in the case of the other—the jealousy of a
petty-minded fool made short work of the boasted friendship, and
showed the " O.L." what it was worth.   Oh, the poor, trusting,
credulous nature! Take away from her her clairvoyant powers;
plug up in a certain direction her intuitions—as in duty bound
was done by M.—and what remains? A helpless, broken-hearted
woman!

Take another case, that of Fern.   His development, as occurring
under your eye, affords you a useful study and a hint as to even
more serious methods adopted in individual cases to thoroughly
test the latent moral qualities of the man.   Every human being
contains within himself vast potentialities, and it is the duty of
the adepts to surround the would-be chela with circumstances
which shall enable him to take the " right-hand path,"—if he
have the ability in him.   We are no more at liberty to withhold
the chance from a postulant than we are to guide and direct him
into the proper course.   At best, we can only show him—after his
probation period was successfully terminated—that if he does this
he will go right; if the other, wrong.   But until he has passed that
period, we leave him to fight out his battles as best he may; and
have to do so occasionally with higher and *initiated* chelas such as
H.P.B., once they are allowed to work in the world, that all of us
more or less avoid.   More than that—and you better learn it at
once, if my previous letters to you about Fern have not sufficiently
opened your eyes—we allow our candidates *to be tempted* in a
thousand various ways, so as to draw out the whole of their inner
nature and allow it the chance of remaining conqueror either one
way or the other.   What has happened to Fern has befallen every
one else who has preceded, will befall with various results every
one who succeeds him.   We were all so tested; and while a
Moorad Ali—*failed*—I, succeeded.   The victor's crown is only for
him who proves himself worthy to wear it; for him who attacks
Mara single handed and conquers the demon of lust and earthly
passions; and not *we* but he himself puts it on his brow.   It was
not a meaningless phrase of the Tathagata that " he who masters
Self is greater than he who conquers thousands in battle ": there
is no such other difficult struggle.   If it were not so, adeptship

would be but a cheap acquirement. So, my good brother, be
not surprised, and blame us not as readily as you have already
done, at any development of our policy towards the aspirants
past, present or future. Only those who can look ahead at the
far remote consequences of things are in a position to judge as to
the expediency of our own actions, or those we permit in others.
What may seem present bad faith may in the end prove the truest,
most benevolent loyalty. Let time show who was right and who
faithless. One who is true and approved to-day, may to-morrow
prove, under a new concatenation of circumstances a traitor, an
ingrate, a coward, an imbecile. The reed, bent beyond its limit
of flexibility, will have snapped in twain. Shall we accuse it?
No; but because we can, and *do* pity it, we cannot select it as part
of those reeds that have been tried and found strong, hence fit to
be accepted as material for the indestructible fane we are so
carefully building.

And now—to other matters.

We have a reform in head, and I look to you to help me. Mr.
H.'s annoying and indiscreet interference with the Parent Society,
and his passion of domineering all and everything, have made us
come to the conclusion that it would be worth our while to attempt
the following. Let it be made known " to all concerned " through
the *Theosophist* and circulars issued to every Branch, that hitherto
they have looked too often and too unnecessarily to the Parent
Body for guidance and as an exemplar to follow. This is quite
impracticable. Besides the fact that the Founders have to show
themselves and try earnestly to be *all* to everyone and all things
—since there is such a great variety of creeds, opinions and expectations to satisfy, they cannot possibly and at the same time satisfy
all as they would like to. They try to be impartial, and never to
refuse one what they may have accorded to another party. Thus
they have repeatedly published criticisms upon Vedantism, Buddhism and Hinduism in its various branches, upon the *Veda Bashya*
of Swami Dayanand—their staunchest and at that time most
valued ally; but, because such criticisms were all directed against
non-Christian faiths, no one ever paid the slightest attention to it.
For over a year and more, the journal came out regularly with
an advertisement inimical to that of the *Veda Bashya* and was
printed side by side with it to satisfy the Benares Vedantin. And
now Mr. Hume comes out with his public castigation of the
Founders and seeks to prohibit the advertisement of anti-Christian
pamphlets. I want you, therefore, to please bear this in mind,
and point out these facts to Col. Chesney, who seems to imagine
that theosophy is *hostile* but to Christianity; whereas it is but
impartial, and whatever the personal views of the two Founders,
the journal of the Society has nothing to do with them, and *will*

publish as willingly criticism directed against Lamaism as against Christianism. At all events, willing as we both are, that H.P.B. should always and gratefully accept your advice in the matter, it was *I* who advised her to " kick " as she says against Mr. H.'s attempts at authority, and you are at liberty to inform him of the fact.

Now in view to mending matters, what do you think of the idea of placing the Branches on quite a different footing? Even Christendom, with its *divine* pretensions to a Universal Brotherhood has its thousand and one sects, which, united as they all may be under one banner of the Cross are yet essentially inimical to each other, and the authority of the Pope is set to naught by the Protestants, while the decrees of the Synods of the latter are laughed at by the Roman Catholics. Of course, I would never contemplate, even in the worst of cases such a state of things among the theosophical bodies. What I want, is simply a paper on the advisability of remodelling the present formation of Branches and their privileges. Let them be all chartered and initiated as heretofore by the Parent Society, and depend on it nominally. At the same time, let every Branch before it is chartered, choose some one object to work for, an object, naturally, in sympathy with the general principle of the T.S.—yet a distinct and definite object of its own, whether in the religious, educational or philosophical line. This would allow the Society a broader margin for its general operations; more real, useful work would be done; and, as every Branch would be so to say, independent in its *modus operandi*, there would remain less room for complaint and *par consequence*—for interference. At any rate, this hazy sketch, I hope, will find an excellent soil to germinate and thrive in, in your business-like head; and if you could, meanwhile, write a paper based on the aforesaid explanations of the *Theosophist's* true position, giving all the reasons as above-mentioned and many more for the December, if not for the November number you would, indeed, oblige M. and myself. It is impossible, and dangerous, to entrust with such a subject, which requires the most delicate handling—either one or the other of our Editors. H.P.B. would never fail to break the *padris*' heads on such a good opportunity, or H.S.O. to turn a neat extra compliment or two to the Founders address, which would be useless, for I strive to show the two entities of Editor and Founder quite distinct and apart from each other, blended though they be in one and same person. I am no practical business man and therefore, I feel utterly unable for the task. Will you help me, friend? It would be better, of course, if the " feeler " would be made to appear in the *November*, as though in answer to Mr. Hume's very impolite letter, which, of course, I will not permit to be published. But you could take it for your ground-work and basis to frame your editorial answer upon. To return to the reform of Branches, this question will have of course to be seriously considered and weighed before it is finally settled. There must be no more disappointment in members once they have joined. Each Branch has to choose its well-defined mission to work for, and the greatest care should be taken in the selection of Presidents. Had the " Eclectic " been placed from the first on such a footing of distinct independence, it might have fared better. Solidarity of thought and action within the broad outline of the chief and general principles of the Society there must always be between the Parent and Branch bodies; yet the latter must be allowed each their own independent action in everything that does not clash with those principles. Thus a Branch composed of *mild* Christians sympathizing with the *objects* of the Society might remain neutral in the question of every other religion, and utterly indifferent to and unconcerned with the private beliefs of the " Founders," the *Theosophist* making room as willingly for hymns on the Lamb, as for slokas on the sacredness of the cow. Could you but work out this idea, I would submit it to our venerable Chohan, who now gently smiles from the corner of an eye, instead of frowning as usual—ever since he saw you become President. Had I not, last year, owing to the *ex*-President's truculence, been " sent to bed " earlier than at first contemplated, I was going to propose it. I have a letter of lofty reproach, dated October 8th, from the " I am." In it, he sends for you on the 5th and explains his " unwillingness to continue to hold office " and his " great desire " that you should take his place. He condemns " altogether the system and policy," of our order. It seems to him " quite wrong." He winds up by: " Of course I shall ask you to get the O.L. to refrain from proposing me for the council of the Society." No fear, no fear of this; he may sleep soundly and undisturbed and see himself in dream the Dalai Lama of the Theosophists. But I must hasten to enter my indignant and emphatic protest against his definition of our " faulty " system. Because he succeeds in catching but a few stray sparks of the principles of our Order, and could not be allowed to examine and *remodel* the whole, we must all need be—what he would represent us! If we could hold such doctrines as he would impose upon us; if we in aught resembled the picture he has drawn; if we could submit for a single hour to stand silently under the load of such imputations as he has thrown upon us in his *September* letter; verily we should deserve to lose all credit with the Theosophists! We ought to be dismissed and hunted out of the Society and people's thoughts as charlatans and impostors—wolves in sheep's clothing, who come to steal away men's hearts with mystic promises, entertaining all the while the most despotic intentions, seeking to *enslave* our confiding chelas and turn the

masses away from truth and the " divine revelation of nature's
voice " to blank and " dreary atheism ";—*i.e.* a thorough disbelief in the " kind, merciful Father and Creator of all " (evil and
misery, we must suppose?) who lolls from the eternity, reclining
with his backbone supported on a bed of incandescent meteors,
and picks his teeth with a lightning fork. . . .

Indeed, indeed, we have enough of this incessant jingle on the
Jew's harp of Christian revelation!

M. thinks that the *Supplement* ought to be enlarged if necessary,
and made to furnish room for the expression of thought of every
Branch, however diametrically opposed these may be. The *Theosophist* ought to be made to assume a distinct colour and become
a unique specimen of its own. We are ready to furnish the
necessary extra sums for it. I *know* you will catch my idea however
hazily expressed. I leave our plan entirely in your own hands.
Success in this will counteract the effects of the cyclic crisis. You ask
what you can do? Nothing better or more efficient than the
proposed plan.

I cannot close without telling you of an incident which, however
ludicrous, has led to something that makes me thank my stars for
it, and will please you also. Your letter, enclosing that of C.C.M.
was received by me on the morning following the date you had
handed it over to the " little man." I was then in the neighbourhood of Phari-Jong, at the gom-pa of a friend, and was very busy
with important affairs. When I received intimation of its arrival,
I was just crossing the large inner courtyard of the monastery.
Bent upon listening to the voice of Lama Töndhüb Gyatcho, I had
no time to read the contents. So, after mechanically opening the
thick packet, I merely glanced at it, and put it, as I thought, into
the travelling bag I wear across the shoulder. In reality though,
it had dropped on the ground; and since I had broken the envelope
and emptied it of its contents, the latter were scattered in their fall.
There was no one near me at the time, and my attention being
wholly absorbed with the conversation, I had already reached the
staircase leading to the library door, when I heard the voice of a
young *gelong* calling out from a window, and expostulating with
someone at a distance. Turning round I understood the situation
at a glance; otherwise your letter would have never been read by
me for I saw a venerable old goat in the act of making a morning
meal of it. The creature had already devoured part of C.C.M.'s
letter, and was thoughtfully preparing to have a bite at yours,
more delicate and easy for chewing with his old teeth than the
tough envelope and paper of your correspondent's epistle. To
rescue what remained of it took me but one short instant, disgust
and opposition of the animal notwithstanding—but there remained
mighty little of it! The envelope with your crest on had nearly

disappeared, the contents of the letters made illegible—in short I was perplexed at the sight of the disaster. Now you know *why* I felt embarrassed: *I had no right to restore it*, the letters coming from the " Eclectic " and connected directly with the hapless " Pelings " on all sides. What could I do to restore the missing parts! I had already resolved to humbly crave permission from the Chohan to be allowed an exceptional privilege in this dire necessity, when I saw his holy face before me, with his eye twinkling in quite an unusual manner, and heard his voice: " Why break the rule? I will do it myself." These simple words *Kam mi ts'har* —" I'll do it," contain a world of hope for me. He has restored the missing parts and done it quite neatly too, as you see, and even transformed a crumpled broken envelope, very much damaged, into a new one—crest and all. Now I know what great power had to be used for such a restoration, and this leads me to hope for a relaxation of severity one of these days. Hence I thanked the goat heartily; and since he does not belong to the ostracised Peling race, to show my gratitude I strengthened what remained of teeth in his mouth, and set the dilapidated remains firmly in their sockets, so that he may chew food harder than English letters for several years yet to come.

And now a few words about the chela. Of course you must have suspected that since the Master was prohibited the slightest *tamasha* exhibition, so was the disciple. Why should you have expected then, or " felt a little disappointed " with his refusing to forward to me your letters *via* Space—in your presence? The little man is a promising chap, far older in years than he looks, but young in European wisdom and manners and hence committing his several indiscretions, which, as I told you, put me to the blush and made me feel foolish for the two savages. The idea of coming to you for money was absurd in the extreme! Any other Englishman but you would have regarded them after that as two travelling charlatans. I hope you have received by this time the loan I returned with many thanks.

Nath is right about the phonetic (vulgar) pronunciation of the word " Kiu-te "; people usually pronounce it as *Kiu-to*, but it is *not* correct; and he is wrong in his view about Planetary Spirits. He does not know the word, and thought you meant the " devas " —the servants of the Dhyan-Chohans. It is the latter who are the " Planetary, " and of course it is *illogical* to say that Adepts are greater than they, since we all strive to become Dhyan-Chohans in *the end*. Still, there have been adepts " greater " than the *lower* degrees of the Planetary. Thus your views are *not* against our doctrines, as he told you, but would be had you meant the " devas " or *angels*, " little gods." Occultism is certainly not necessary for a good, pure Ego to become an " Angel " or Spirit

in or out of the *Devachan* since Angelhood *is* the result of Karma.
I believe you will not complain of my letter being too short. It is
going to be soon followed by another voluminous correspondence,
" Answers to your many Questions." H.P.B. is *mended*, if not
thoroughly at least for some time to come.

With real affectionate regard,

Yours,

K. H.

LETTER No. 55 [1]

And now, friend, you have completed one of your minor cycles;
have suffered, struggled, triumphed. Tempted, you have not
failed, weak you have gained strength, and the hard nature of the
lot and ordeal of every aspirant after occult knowledge is now better
comprehended by you, no doubt. Your flight from London and
from yourself was necessary; as was also your choice of the localities
where you could best shake off the bad influences of your social
" season " and of your own house. It was not best that you should
have come to Elberfeld sooner; it is best that you should have
come now. For you are better able now to bear the strain of the
present situation. The air is full of the pestilence of treachery;
unmerited opprobrium is showing upon the Society, and falsehood
and forgery have been used to overthrow it. Ecclesiastical England
and official Anglo-India have secretly joined hands to have their
worst suspicions *verified* if possible, and at the first plausible pretext
to crush the movement. Every infamous device is to be employed
in the future as it has in the present to discredit *us* as its promoters,
and yourselves as its supporters. For the opposition represents
enormous vested interests, and they have enthusiastic help from the
Dugpas—in Bhootan and the Vatican!

Among the " shining marks " at which the conspirators aim, you
stand. Tenfold greater pains than heretofore will be taken to cover
you with ridicule for your *credulity*, your belief in me—especially,
and to refute your arguments in support of the esoteric teaching.
They may try to shake still more than they already have your confidence with pretended letters alleged to have come from H.P.B.'s
laboratory, and others, or with forged documents showing and
confessing fraud and planning to repeat it. It has ever been thus.
Those who have watched mankind through the centuries of this
cycle, have constantly seen the details of this death-struggle between
Truth and Error repeating themselves. Some of you Theosophists
are now only wounded in your " honour " or your purses, but those

---

[1] The envelope is addressed in K.H.'s writting to "A. P. Sinnett, Esq., c/of
L.C.H."—Ed.

who held the lamp in preceding generations paid the penalty of their lives for their knowledge.

Courage then, you all, who would be warriors of the one divine Verity; keep on boldly and confidently; husband your moral strength, not wasting it upon trifles but keeping it against great occasions like the present one.   I warned you all through Olcott in April last of what was ready to burst at Adyar, and told him not to be surprised when the mine should be fired.   All will come right in time—only you, the great and prominent heads of the movement be steadfast, wary and united.   We have gained our object as regards L.C.H.   She is much improved, and her whole life here-after will be benefited by the training she is passing thro'.   To have stopped with you would have been to her an irreparable psychic loss.   She had this shown her, before I actually consented to interfere at her own passionate prayer, between you; she was ready to fly to America, and but for my intervention would have done so.   Worse than that; her mind was being rapidly unsettled and made useless as an occult instrument.   False teachers were getting her into their power and false revelations misled her and those who consulted her.   Your house, good friend, has a colony of Elementaries quartering in it, and to a sensitive like her it was as dangerous an atmosphere to exist in as would be a fever cemetery to one subject to morbific physical influences.   You should be more than ordinarily careful when you get back not to encourage sensitiveness in your household, not to admit more than can be helped the visits of known mediumistic sensitives.   It would be well also to burn wood-fires in the rooms now and then, and carry about as fumigators open vessels (braziers?) with burning wood. You might also ask Damodar to send you some bundles of incense-sticks for you to use for this purpose.   These are helps, but the best of all means to drive out unwelcome guests of this sort is to live purely in deed and thought.   The talismans you have had given you, will also powerfully aid you *if you keep your confidence in them and in us unbroken.*   (?)

You have heard of the step H.P.B. was permitted to take.   A fearful responsibility is cast upon Mr. Olcott; a still greater— owing to *O.W.*[1] and *Esot: Buddhism*—upon you.   For this step of hers is in *direct* relation with and as a direct result of the appearance of these two works.   *Your* Karma, good friend, this time.   I hope you will understand my meaning rightly.   But if you remain true to and stand faithfully by the T.S. you may count upon our aid and so may all others to the full extent that they shall deserve it.   The original policy of the T.S. must be vindicated, if you would not see it fall into ruin and bury your reputations under it.   I have told you long ago.   For years to come the Soc. will be unable to stand,

---

[1] *The Occult World.*—EDS.

when based upon " Tibetan Brothers " and phenomena alone. All this ought to have been limited to an *inner* and very SECRET circle. There is a hero-worshipping tendency clearly showing itself, and you, my friend, are not quite free from it yourself. I am fully aware of the change that has lately come over you, but this does not change the main question. If you would go on with your occult studies and literary work—then learn to be loyal to the Idea, rather than to my poor self. When something is to be done never think whether I wish it, before acting: I wish *everything* that can, in great or small degree, push on this agitation. But I am far from being perfect hence infallible in all I do; tho' it is not quite as you imagine having now discovered. For you know—or think you know, of *one* K H.—and can know but of one, whereas there are two distinct personages answering to that name *in him* you know. The riddle is only apparent and easy to solve, were you only to know what a real *Mahatma* is. You have seen by the Kiddle incident— perchance allowed to develop to its bitter end for a purpose—that even an " adept " when acting in his body is not beyond mistakes due to human carelessness. You now understand that he is as likely as not to make himself look absurd in the eyes of those who have no right understanding of the phenomena of thought-trans- ference and astral precipitations—and all this, thro' lack of simple caution. There is always that danger if one has neglected to ascertain whether the words and sentences rushing into the mind have come all from *within* or whether some may have been impressed from *without*. I feel sorry to have brought you into such a false position before your many enemies and even your friends. That was *one* of the reasons why I had hesitated to give my consent to print my private letters and specifically excluded a few of the series from the prohibition. I had no time to verify their contents—nor have I now. I have a habit of often quoting, *minus* quotation marks —from the maze of what I get in the countless folios of our Akasic libraries, so to say—with eyes shut. Sometimes I may give out thoughts that will see light years later; at other times what an orator, a Cicero may have pronounced ages earlier, and at others, what was not only pronounced by modern lips but already either written or printed—as in the Kiddle case. All this I do (not being a trained writer for the Press) without the smallest concern as to where the sentences and strings of words may have come from, so long as they serve to express, and fit in with my own thoughts. I have received a lesson now on the European plane on the danger of corresponding with western *literati*! But my " inspirer " Mr. Kiddle is none the less ungrateful, since to me alone he owes the distin- guished honour of having becoming known by name, and having his utterances repeated even by the grave lips of Cambridge " Dons." If fame is sweet to him why will he not be consoled with the thought that the case of the " Kiddle—K.H. *parallel* passages " has now become as much a *cause célèbre* in the department of " who is who ," and " which plagiarized from the other? " as the Bacon-Shakespeare mystery; that in intensity of scientific research if not of *value*, our case is on a par with that of our two great predecessors.

But the situation—however amusing in one way—is more serious for the Society; and the " parallel passages " must yield first place to the " Christian-mission-Coulomb " conspiracy. Turn then to the latter all your thoughts, good friend—*if* friend all notwithstanding. You are very wrong to contemplate absence from London the coming winter. But I shall not urge you, if you do not feel equal to the situation. At any rate, if you desert the " Inner Circle " some other arrangement has to be made: it is out of question for me to be corresponding with, and teaching both. Either you have to be my mouthpiece and secretary in the *Circle*, or I shall have to use somebody else as my delegate, and thus have positively *no time* to correspond with you. They have pledged themselves—(most of them) to me *for life and death*—the copy of the pledge is in the hands of Maha-Chohan—and I am bound to them.

I can now send my occasional instructions and letters with any certainty only thro' Damodar. But before I can do even so much the Soc. especially the H.Q rs. will have to pass first thro' the coming crisis. If you still care to renew the occult teachings save first our post-office. H.P.B.—I say again, is not to be approached any longer without her full consent. She has earned so much, and has to be left alone. She is permitted to retire for three reasons (1) to disconnect the T.S. from *her* phenomena, now tried to be represented all fraudulent; (2) to help it by removing the chief cause of the hatred against it; (3) to try and restore the health of the body, so it may be used for some years longer. And now as to the details consult all of you together: for that I have asked them to send for you. The sky is black now, but forget not the hopeful motto " *Post nubila Phœbus!* " Blessings upon you, and your ever loyal lady.

K.H.

LETTER No. 56
Received January, 1883, Allahabad.

It is my turn, kind friend, to intercede for lenient treatment, especially a very *prudent* one of Mr. Hume, and I ask you to give me a hearing. You must not overlook an element which has much to do with his moral turpitude, one which certainly does not excuse though it mitigates in a degree, his offence. He is pushed on and half maddened by evil powers, which he has attracted to himself and come under subjection to by his innate moral turbulence. Near him lives a fakir who has an animalizing aura about him; the parting curses—I dare not say they were unjust or unprovoked —of Mr. Fern have produced their effect; and while his own self-painted adeptship is entirely imaginary, he has nevertheless, by the injudicious practice of *pranayam*, developed in himself to some extent mediumship—is tainted for life with it. He has opened wide the door to influences from the wrong quarter, and is, henceforth almost impervious to those from the right. So, he must not be sweepingly judged as one who has sinned with thorough and entirely unmixed deliberation. Avoid him, but do not madden him still more, for he is more than dangerous now to one who is unable, like yourself, to fight him with his own weapons. Suffice that you should know him—as he is, and so be forewarned and prudent in future, since for the present he has succeeded in spoiling our plans in the most hopeful quarters. He is now in his days— which will extend for weeks and perhaps months—of the most selfish vanity and combativeness—during which he is capable of doing most desperate things. So, think twice, my good friend before you precipitate a crisis the results of which might thus be very severe.

As regards his connection with Theosophical matters, he is largely your chela, the captive of your spear and bow; but, since you have thus acted under my own instructions—I take the blame upon myself—the *whole blame*, understand me well; and I would not allow a single speck of the present disastrous results to taint *your* Karma. But the latter is a thing of the future, and in the meanwhile he can play the deuce with yourself and Society. It cost you no little trouble to get him in and now you must beware how you prematurely hurl him out. For, you have seen from his correspondence what malice he is capable of, and how industriously he can work to breed suspicion and discontent so as to centre interest and loyalty upon himself. The T.S. has just tided safely through a tempest raised by another vain and ambitious malcontent —Dayanand S.—and if the issue has been favourable it is because D.S. had a short memory and *was made* to forget all about the documents he had issued. It is the prudent part, therefore, to wait, and watch, and lay by the materials for the defence against the time when this new iconoclast shall " charge upon your entrenchments "—if he ever does, which up to this moment is not determined, but which would be almost inevitable if he were suddenly denounced by yourself. I do not ask you to evince friendship for him, (nay, I would strongly advise you not to even write to him yourself for some time to come, and when pressed for an explanation, ask your good lady, *of whom he is afraid* and whom he is forced to respect to tell him bluntly and honestly the truth—

in a way only women are capable of)—but simply to postpone an open breach until the hour comes when longer delay would be unpardonable. Neither of us ought to imperil a cause whose promotion is a duty paramount to considerations of Self.

I must not close my letter with this black image, but tell you that in Madras there are fairer prospects of success than at Calcutta. In a few days you will hear the results of Subba Row's work.

How do you like " Mr. Isaacs "? As you will see (for you must read and review it) the book is the Western echo of the Anglo-Indian " Occult world." The ex-editor of the " Indian Herald " has not quite grown up to the size of the editor of the *Pioneer*, but something is being done in the same direction. The cruel enemy of 1880-1 is turned in quasi an admirer in 1882. I think it rather hard to see people finding K.H. " Lal Singh "—mirrored in " Ram Lal "—the " all-grey " adept, of Mr. Marion Crawford. Had the book been written a year ago, I might have said the author was himself *gris* when making " Ram Lal " talk of eternal love and bliss in the realms of the world of Spirit. But since a certain vision procured for him by the famous " Ski " in whom Mr. C. C. M. does not believe—the man gave up entirely drinking. One man more saved. I forgive him my very " grey " appearance and even Shere-Ali!

Yours affectionately,
K.H.

LETTER No. 57
Received 6-1-83.

My dear friend,

I approach a subject which I have purposely avoided for several months, until furnished with proofs that would appear conclusive even in your sight. We are not—as you know—always of the same way of thinking; nor has that which *to us* is—FACT—any weight in *your* opinion unless it violates in no way the Western methods of judging it. But now the time has come for us to try to have you, at least, understand us better than we hitherto have been even by some of the best and most earnest amongst western Theosophists—such for instance as C. C. Massey. And though I would be the last man living to seek to make you follow in my wake as your " prophet " and " inspirer," I would, nevertheless, feel truly sorry were you ever brought to regard me as a " moral paradox," having to suffer me either as one guilty of a false assumption of powers I never had, or—of misusing them to screen unworthy objects and, as unworthy persons. Mr. Massey's letter explains to you what I mean; that which seems conclusive proof to him and unimpeachable evidence, is neither for me—who know the whole truth. On this last day of your year 1882, his name comes third on the list of failures,—something (I hasten to say for fear of a new misconception) that has nothing to do whatever with the present arrangement regarding the proposed new Branch in London, yet everything with his personal progress. I deeply regret it, but have no right to bind myself so securely to any person or persons by ties of pernal sympathy and esteem that my movements shall be crippled, and I, unable to lead the rest to something grander and nobler than their present faith. Therefore, I choose to leave him in his present errors. The brief meaning of this is the following: Mr. Massey labours under the strangest misconceptions, and (literally) " dreams dreams "—though no medium, as his friend, Mr. S. Moses. With all he is the noblest, purest, in short, one of the best men I know, though occasionally too trusting in wrong directions. But he lacks entirely—correct intuition. It will come to him later on, when neither H.P.B. nor Olcott will be there. Until then—remember, and tell him so: we demand neither allegiance, recognition (whether public or private) nor will we have anything to do with, or say to the British Branch,—*except through you*. Four Europeans were placed on probation twelve months ago; of the four—only one, yourself, was found worthy of our trust. This year it will be *Societies* instead of individuals that will be tested. The result will depend on their collective work, and Mr. Massey errs when hoping that I am prepared to join the motley crowd of Mrs. K.'s " inspirers." Let them remain under their masks of St. John the Baptists and like Biblical aristocrats. Provided the latter teach *our doctrines*—however muddled up with foreign chaff—a great point will be gained. C.C.M. wants *light*— he is welcome to it—*through you*. Since it is all he wants what matters it whether *he* regards the " light-bearer " handing his torch to you—as a man of clean or unclean hands, so long as *light* itself is not affected by it? Only let me give you a warning. An affair now so trivial as to seem but the innocent expression of feminine vanity may, unless at once set aright, produce very evil consequences. In a letter from Mrs. Kingsford to Mr. Massey conditionally accepting the presidentship of the British T.S. she expresses her belief—nay, points it out as an undeniable fact— that before the appearance of " The Perfect Way " no one " knew what the Oriental school really held about Reincarnation "; and adds that " seeing how much has been told in that book the adepts are hastening to unlock their own treasures, so ' grudgingly doled out hitherto ' (as H.X. puts it)." Mr. Massey, thereupon gives in reply a full adherence to this theory, and blossoms into an adroit compliment to the lady that would not discredit a plenipotentiary. " Probably," says he, " it is felt (by the Brothers) that a community among whom such a work as " The Perfect

Way " can be produced and find acceptance is ready for the light! "
Now, let this idea gain currency, and it will tend to convert into a
sect the school of the highly estimable authoress, who, albeit a
fifth rounder, is not exempt from quite a considerable dose of vanity
and despotism, hence—bigotry. Thus, elevate the misconception
into an undue importance; impair thereby her own spiritual
condition by feeding the latent sense of Messiahship; and you will
have obstructed the cause of free and general independent enquiry
which her " Initiators " as well as we would wish promoted.
Write then, good friend, to Mr. Massey the truth. Tell him that
you were possessed of the Oriental views of reincarnation several
months before the work in question had appeared—since it is in
July (18 months ago) that you began being taught the difference
between Reincarnation *à la* Allan Kardec, or personal rebirth—
and of the Spiritual Monad; a difference first pointed out to you
on July 5th at Bombay. And to allay another uneasiness of hers,
say that no allegiance by her to the " Brothers " will be expected,
(nor even accepted *if* offered) in as much as we have no present
intention of making any further experiments *with Europeans* and
will use no other channel than yourself to impart our Arhat
philosophy. The intended experiment with Mr. Hume in 1882
failed most sadly. Better than your Wren are we entitled to the
motto, *festina lente*!

And now, you will please follow me into still deeper waters.
An unsteady, wavering, suspicious candidate at one end of the line;
a declared *unprincipled*, (I say the word and maintain it) vindictive
enemy at the other end; and you will agree that between London
and Simla we are not very likely to appear in either a very attractive
or anything like a true light. Personally such a state of things is
hardly calculated to deprive us of sleep; as regards the future
progress of the British T.S. and a few other Theosophists, the
current of enmity travelling between the two places is sure to
affect all those who will find themselves on its way—even yourself,
in the long run, perchance. Who of you could disbelieve the
explicit statements of two " gentlemen " both noted for their
intellectual eminence, and one of whom, at least, is as incapable of
uttering an untruth as of flying in the air? Thus, end of the cycle
notwithstanding, there is a great personal danger for the B$^{sh.}$ T.S.
as for yourself. No harm can come now to *the* Society; much
mischief is in store for its proposed Branch and its supporters,
unless yourself and Mr. Massey are furnished with some facts and
a key to the true situation. Now, if for certain and very good
reasons, I have to leave C.C.M. to his delusions of guilt, regarding
H.P.B., and my own moral *shakiness*, the time is ripe to show to you
Mr. Hume in his true light, thus making a way with one false
witness against us, while deeply regretting the fact that I am bound

by the rules of our Order and my own sense of honour (however little it may be worth in the eyes of a European) not to divulge at present certain facts that would show C.C.M. at once, how deeply he is in error. I may tell you no news if I say that it was Mr. Hume's attitude when the *Eclectic* was formed that caused our chiefs to bring Mr. Fern and Mr. Hume together. The latter reproached us vehemently for refusing to take in as chelas—himself, and that sweet, handsome, spiritual and truth aspiring boy— Fern. We were daily dictated laws, and as daily taken to task for being unable to realize our own interests. And it will be no news though it may disgust and shock you, to learn that the two were brought into the closest relationship in order to bring out their mutual virtues and defects—each to shine in his own true light. Such are the laws of Eastern *probation*. Fern was a most remarkable psychic subject, naturally very spiritually inclined, but corrupted by Jesuit masters, and with his sixth and seventh Principles completely dormant and paralysed within him. No idea of right and wrong whatever; in short—*irresponsible* for anything but the direct and voluntary actions of the *animal man*. I would not have burdened myself with such a subject knowing beforehand that he was sure to fail. M. consented, for the chiefs have so wished it; and he deemed it useful and good to show to you the moral stamina and worth of him whom you regarded and called a friend. Mr. H.— you think, though lacking the *finer*, better feelings of a gentleman is yet one by his instincts as well as by birth. I do not pretend to be thoroughly well acquainted with the code of honour of Western nations. Yet, I doubt whether a man who, during the absence of the proprietor of certain private letters, avails himself of the key from the pocket of a waistcoat carelessly left on the verandah during work, opens with it the drawer of a writing desk, reads the private letters of that person, takes notes from them and then uses those contents as a weapon to satisfy his hatred and vindictiveness against their writer—I doubt, I say, whether even in the West such a man would be regarded as the ideal of even the average gentleman. And this and much more, *I maintain*, was done by Mr. Hume. Had I told you of it last August *you would have never believed me*. And now I am prepared to prove it over his own signature. Having been caught in the same honest occupation by M. *twice*, my Brother wrote purposely (or rather caused Damodar purposely to write) a certain letter to Fern enclosing a copy of a letter of Mr. H.'s to me. The knowledge of their contents was to bring out to light, when the time came, the true gentlemanly instincts and the honesty of him who sets himself so high above humanity. He is now caught in his own meshes. Hatred, and the irresistible thirst of abusing and vilifying in a letter to Olcott one who is so immeasurably higher than all his detractors,

24

have led Mr. Hume into an imprudent confession. When caught
and cornered—he resorts to a down-right, barefaced LIE.

  I am going, after this preliminary *entrée en matière* and necessary
explanation to make you acquainted with certain extracts from
private letters not intended for your eye, nevertheless, far from
" confidential," since in nearly every one of them Mr. H. begs the
addressee to have them read by other theosophists. I hope this
will not be imputed to me as a mark of " ungentlemanly instincts "
by you. As to every other man, since, now-a-days, a man
universally recognised as a " gentleman " is often a low wretch,
and gentleman-like externals often hide the soul of a villain—he
is welcome to regard me in any light he pleases. These extracts
I give you because it becomes absolutely necessary that you should
be correctly informed of the true nature of him, who now passes
his time in writing letters to the London theosophists and candidates
for membership—with the determined object of setting every
mystic in the West against a Brotherhood of " atheists, hypocrites
and sorcerers." It will help to guide your action in the event of
possible contingencies, and mischief caused by your friend and our
well-wisher, who, while denouncing my Brother, my more than
friend, as a pilferer, coward, liar, and the incarnation of baseness,
insults me with words of pitying praise which he thinks I am traitor
enough to accept and imbecile enough not to weigh at their value.
Remember—such a *friend* is to be guarded against as one takes
precautions against a duellist who wears a corslet beneath his
shirt. His good actions are many, vices far more numerous; the
former have always been largely controlled and promoted by his
inordinate self-love and combativeness; and if it is not yet determined which will finally control the impetus whose outcome will
be his next birth, we may prophesy with a degree of perfect
assurance, that he will never become an adept either in *this* or
his future life. His " Spiritual " aspirations received a full chance
to develop. He was tested, as all have to be—as the poor moth
was, who was scorched in the candle of Rothney Castle and its
associations—but the victor in the struggle for adeptship was ever
Self and Self alone. His cerebral visions have already painted
for him the image of a new Regenerator of Mankind in place of
the " Brothers " whose ignorance and black magical dealings he
has found out. That new Avatar does not live at Almorah but on
Jakko. And so the demon—Vanity—which has ruined Dayanand
is ruining our quondam " friend " and preparing him to make an
assault upon us and the T.S. far more savage than the Swami's.
The future however may take care of itself; I shall only have to
trouble you now with the data above indicated. You will now
realize, perchance, why I was made to collect evidence of his
untruthful, cunning nature, in October last. Nothing, my friend,

—even apparently absurd and reprehensible actions—is done by us without a purpose.

On the 1st of December, Mr. H. writing to Colonel O. said of us: " As for the Brothers, I have a sincere affection for K.H. and always shall have, and as for the others *I have no doubt that they are very good men*, and acting according to their lights. But as to their system, I am, of course, entirely opposed, . . . but that has nothing to do with the exoteric practical aims of the T.S. in which and in their furtherance I can as cordially and cheerfully co-operate with *your good Brothers* as etc. etc."

Eight days *earlier* (22nd November,) he had written to P. Sreenevas Row, Judge S.C.C. at Madras,—" I find the Brotherhood a set of *wicked selfish men*, caring as a body for nothing but their own spiritual development (mind, in this respect K.H. is an exception but *he is I believe the only one*) and their system one of deception and *tainted largely with sorcery* (!) in that they employ spooks, *i.e.* elementals to perform their phenomena. As to deception, once a man has become a chela and bound himself by the vows they exact, *you cannot believe a word he says*; . . . he will lie systematically; as for sorcery, the fact is that until the time of Sonkapa, . . . they were a set of unmitigated, vile sorcerers. . . . Every chela is a slave—a slave of the most abject description—a slave in thought, as well as in word and deed . . .; our Society . . . is an edifice noble in outside show—but built not on the rock of ages, but on the shifting sands of atheism, a whited sepulchre all bright . . . inside full of deceit and the dead bones of a *pernicious, jesuitical system*. . . . You are *at liberty to make what use you please of this letter inside the Society*," etc.

On the 9th of the same month he wrote to Mr. Olcott of the " manifest selfishness of the Brotherhood, intent solely on their spiritual development."

On the 8th of September in a letter to 12 chelas (the very ones he was referring to in the letter to Judge Sreenevas Row of November 22nd—after having received from them an exasperatingly candid joint reply to the aforesaid diplomatic letter—as *liars* and *bound slaves*)—he said, as you know, he " should not have expected any European to read between the lines," of his plot in the HX letter in the *Theosophist*; but " a set of Brahmins . . . the subtlest minds, in the world . . . not ordinary Brahmins, but men *of the highest, noblest training*, etc." (!!). They—" may rest assured that I (he) shall never say or do anything that is not for the advantage of the Brothers, the Society and all its objects." . . . . (Thus it seems the charges of sorcery and dishonesty are to the " advantage " of *Asiatic* adepts). In this same letter, if you remember, he adds that it " is the most efficient weapon for the conversion of the infidels at home yet forged," and that he " of course expected " (by writing this letter in the Theosophist) " *to take our dear old lady in—I could not take her into the plot,*" etc. etc.

With all his cunning and diplomacy he really seems to suffer from a loss of memory. Not only had he taken the " dear old lady " into the plot in a long private letter written to her a few hours after the said " efficient weapon " had been sent for publication, (a letter sent by her to you and which you lost in your packing up at Simla to come down) but he had actually gone out of his way to put a few words of explanation *on the back of the said " Letter.*" It is preserved as every other MSS. by Damodar and the note runs thus . . . " Please print this carefully and without alteration. It answers admirably Davison's and other letters from home." . . . (Extracts from these letters were enclosed in his manuscript). . . . " We can't long, I fear, bolster up—but *hints* like these will help to break the fall " etc. . . .

Having thus himself forged this most efficient weapon for the conversion of the infidels at home, *as to our actual existence*, and unable henceforth to deny it, what better antidote than to add to the *hints* therein contained full and well defined charges of *sorcery*, etc. ?

When accused by the 12 Chelas in their joint answer to his letter to them, of a deliberate falsification of facts with reference to the " dear Old Lady " whom he had, notwithstanding all he could say to the contrary, " taken into the plot " he writes in a letter to Subba Row that *he had never done so.* That his letter to the " Madam " explaining to her the whys and reasons for that " Letter " of his by " H.X."—was written and sent to her long after the said denunciatory Letter " was already *in print.*" To this Subba Row, in his letter to whom he had bitterly abused and vilified M., answered by quoting to him the very words he had written on the back of the manuscript, thus showing to him how useless was any further falsehood. And now you may judge of his love for Subba Row!

And now comes the *bouquet.* Writing on the 1st of December to Mr. Olcott (letter first above referred to), he distinctly claims adept powers. " I am very sorry I cannot join you in the body in Bombay—but—*if allowed I may nevertheless perhaps assist you there* . . ." Yet in Fern's case he says " it is a perfect chaos and *no one can tell what* is really owing and what is not; " and several letters upon the same topic teem with acknowledgment that he had no power to see what was going on " during the past six months." Quite the contrary, it would seem, since in a letter to me within this period he describes himself as " not on a level spiritually with him (Fern) Sinnett " and others. He did not dare brag *to me* of his spiritual clairvoyance; but now, having " broken forever with the Tibetan Sorcerers " his potential adept powers have suddenly developed into monstrous proportions. They must have been from birth marvellously great since he informs Olcott (same letter) that " a certain amount of *Pranayam* for a few months (six weeks in all) was necessary to ensure concentration—at first. . . . *I have passed that stage* and—I AM A YOGI."

The charge preferred now against him is of so grave a character, that I would have never asked you to believe it on my simple assertion. Hence—this long letter, and the following evidence, which, please read with the utmost care and drawing your conclusions *solely* on that evidence.

In his July letter to me he imputes to us the blame for Fern's course *of falsehood*, his *pretended visions* and pretended inspirations from us; and in the letter to Mr. Olcott (December 1st) he charges Morya, my beloved brother, with acting " in a most dishonourable manner," adding that he has " never since looked upon him as a gentleman, for having caused Damodar . . . to send Fern a transcript of my confidential report on him. . . ." This he regards as " a dishonourable breach of confidence " so *gross* that " *Moriar was afraid* (! !) to let even K.H. know how he had stolen and made a bad use of my letter to him. K.H. is a *gentleman* I believe and would scorn so base an act." No doubt I would, had it been done without my knowledge and were it not absolutely necessary—in view of *clearly foreseen events*—to bring Mr. Hume to betray himself and thus counteract the influence and authority of his vindictive nature. The letter so transcribed was *not* marked confidential, and the words " I am ready to say so to Fern's face, at any day "—are there. However—the unmeasured abuse and his truly saintly and *gentlemanly* indignation at M.'s *treachery* are followed by these words of confession; [1] very startling as you will see: ". . . Fern *does not*, let me do him that justice, *know to this day that I knew of this* " i.e. of the letter pilfered by M. and sent to Fern through Damodar. In short, then, Mr. Hume had means of reading the contents of a private letter addressed to Fern *registered*, sent to his (Mr. Hume's) care, kept in a drawer of a table belonging to the house. The proof is complete since it is himself who furnishes it. How then? Of course, either by reading its physical substance with his natural eyes, or, its astral essence by transcendental power. If the latter, then by what brief forcing system was the psychic power of this " yogi," who, in July last, was " not on a level spiritually " with yourself, or even with Fern, suddenly shot out into such full flower and fruitage, whereas it takes even us, trained " sorcerers " ten or fifteen years to acquire it ? Besides, if this and other letters to Fern were presented to him in the " astral light " (as he maintains in his letter in reply to Colonel O.'s query, herein enclosed), how comes it that the

---

[1] Fern was at Bombay and he dreaded the just denial of even a " rascal. "

benevolent Almorah genius (through whose help he suddenly acquired such tremendous powers) could cause him to take note of the contents, to read *word for word and to remember* ONLY such letters as were kept by Fern—*in accordance with M.'s positive orders*—in his desk in Mr. Hume's house? While WE DEFY HIM to repeat one word of other and (for him) far more important letters sent by my Brother to the " probationary chela " in which the latter was forbidden to keep them at Rothney Castle, but had them securely shut up in a locked desk at his own house? These queries arising at M.'s will in Olcott's mind, he flatly put the question to Mr. Hume. As M.'s chela, revering him, of course, as a Father as well as Teacher he very properly put to this *Censor Elegantiarum* the direct question whether he had been himself guilty of the very " dishonourable " breach of *gentlemanlike* conduct of which he was complaining in Morya's case. (And unjustly as you now see; for what he did had my approval, since it was a necessary part of a preconceived plan to bring out—besides Mr. H.'s *true* nature,—of a disgraceful situation, itself developed by the wicked appetites, follies and Karma of sundry weak men—ultimate good, as you will find).

We have no *gentlemen*—now at all events, that would come up to the Simla standard—in Tibet, though many honest and truthful men. To Mr. Olcott's question came a reply so reeking with *deliberate, bare falsehood*, foolish vanity, and so miserable an attempt to explain away the only possible theory that without the owner's knowledge he had read his private correspondence, that I have asked Morya to procure it for me for you to read. After doing this you will kindly return it to me through Dharbagiri Nath who will be at Madras within this week.

I have done an unpleasant and distasteful task, but a great point will be achieved if it helps you to know us better—whether your European standard of right and wrong inclines the scales in your opinion either one way or the other. Perchance, you may find yourself in C.C.M.'s attitude deploring to find yourself obliged to either accept or reject for ever such a " distressing moral paradox " as myself. No one would regret it more deeply than I; but our *Rules* have proved wise and beneficent to the world in the long run, and the world in general and its individual units especially are so terribly wicked that one *has to* fight each one with his or her own weapons.

As the situation stands at present, and though we would not allow too much " procrastination," it does seem desirable that you should go for a few months home—say till June. But unless you go to London and with C.C.M.'s help explain the true situation and establish the Society *yourself*, Mr. Hume's letters will have done too much harm to undo the mischief. Thus your temporary absence will have achieved a dual good purpose: the foundation of a true theosophical occult Society, and the salvation of a few promising individuals for future careers, now jeopardized. Besides, your absence from India will not be an unmixed evil, since the friends of the country will feel your loss, and perhaps be all the more ready for your recall: especially if the " *Pioneer* " changes its tone. Some of your holiday time it might be agreeable to you to utilize in one form or another of theosophical writing. You have now a large store of materials, and if you would contrive to get copies of the didactic papers given to Mr. Hume it would be a timely precaution. He is a prolific letter writer and now that he has disburdened himself of all restraints he will bear close watching. Remember the Chohan's prophesy.

Yours ever sincerely,   K. H.

LETTER No. 58

Received at Madras, March, 1883.

My Dear " Ward,"

We will not, if you please, deal at present with the situation concerning " stars " and *obscurations*—for reasons very plainly told to you this morning by H.P.B. My task becomes with every letter more dangerous. It becomes exceedingly difficult to teach you and hold at the same time strictly to the original programme: " so far shall we go and no further." Yet—hold to it we *must* and *will*.

You have entirely mistaken my meaning in the telegram. The words, " more at Adyar " related to the true explanation of your vision, not by any means to a promise of some further psychological experiments made in that direction by myself. The vision was due to an attempt by D.K. who is extremely interested in your progress. While he succeeded in getting you out of your body, he failed entirely in his effort to open your inner vision, for reasons correctly surmised at the time by yourself. I took no personal active part in the attempt. Hence my answer, " surmises correct—more at Adyar." I am in a very false position just now, and have—in order not to jeopardise the possibilities of the future —to be doubly cautious.

The probable date of your departure? Well—on or about April 7th. If your impatience disagrees with this desire of mine you are free to do as you like. Yet, I would look upon it as a personal favour. I am profoundly disgusted with the apathy of my countrymen in general. More than ever I trust but in the few staunch workers of the luckless and hapless T.S. The Viceroy's letter would be of the greatest help if it could be but judiciously used. But in such matters, I see I am no judge, as I now augur from the impression left on your mind by R. Srinivasa Rao and others.

The incident of February the 7th being explained, your question relating to " earlier restrictions " is already covered.

May I beg of you two more personal and important favours? First—to ever bear in mind that *whenever* and *whatever* is possible will be always done for you unurged; hence *never* to either ask for, or suggest it, yourself—since it will amount to simply avoiding to me the supremely disagreeable task of having to refuse a friend's request without, moreover, being in a position to explain the reason why; and second—to remember that though personally and for *your own sake* I may be prepared to do a great deal I have in no way bound myself to do anything of the sort for the Fellows of the British T.S. I have pledged my word to you to teach them through your kind agency our philosophy, and whether they accept it or not. But I have never undertaken to convince any of them of the extent of our powers nor even of our personal existence. Their belief or disbelief in the latter is a matter of very trifling importance to us indeed. If they are ever to be benefitted by our promise, it must be through you alone, and your own personal efforts. Nor can you ever see me (in flesh),—not even in a clearly defined vision—unless you are prepared to pledge your honour never to reveal the fact to anyone, so long as you live, (save you receive permission to that effect). That the consequence of such a pledge will be a never satisfied as an ever recurring doubt in the minds of your British Fellows—*is just what we want for the present.* Too much, or too little was said and proved of us as M.A. (Oxon) justly remarked. *We are ordered* to set ourselves to work to sweep away the few vestiges—for which fresh policy you are indebted to the incessant *underground* intrigues of our ex-friend Mr. Hume—(now entirely in the hands of the Brothers of the Shadow)—and the more our actual existence be doubted—the better. As to tests and convincing proofs to the Sadducees of Europe generally and those of England especially—this is something to be left entirely out of our future programme. Unless allowed to use our own judgment and means—the course of future events will by no means run smooth. Thus you should never use such phrases as " for the sake of strength with friends at home " as they would be sure to do no good and would simply irritate the more the *other* " powers that be "—to use the ridiculous phrase. It is not always flattering, good friend, to be placed even by those one likes the best—on the same level with *shells* and mediums—for the purpose of *tests.* I thought you had luckily outgrown that stage. Let us hold at present to the simply intellectual aspect of our *intercourse* and busy ourselves but with philosophy and your future paper, and leave the rest to *time* and its *unforeseen developments.*

It is precisely because I follow and perceive the *dual* working of your mind in making such requests that I sign myself invariably.

Your affectionate friend,

K. H.

LETTER No. 59

Received London about July, 1883.

With whatever shortcomings my always indulgent " lay-chela " may have to charge me, he will, it appears, credit me with having given him a new source of enjoyment. For even the sombre prophecy of Sir Charles Turner (a recent *obscuration* of his) that you would fall into Roman Catholicism as the inevitable outcome of your dabbling in Theosophy and believing in the " K.H." *maya* —has not dampened the ardour of your propaganda in the gay world of London. If this zeal should be cited by the Altruist of Rothney, in support of his declaration that your grey vesicles are surcharged with Shigatse *Akāsa*, it will still doubtless be balm to your wounded feelings to know that you are essentially aiding to build the bridge over which the British metaphysicians may come within thinking distance of us!

It is the custom among some good people to glance back at their life's path from the hillocks of time they annually surmount. So, if my hope has not betrayed me you must have been mentally comparing your present " greatest pleasure " and " constant occupation " with that which was so in the olden time, when you threaded the streets of your metropolis, where the houses are as if " painted in Indian ink," and a day's sunshine is an event to remember. You have measured yourself against yourself, and found the Theosophist an " Anak " morally, as compared with the " old man " (the *beau valseur*); is it not so? Well, this is, perhaps, your reward—the beginning of it: the end you will realize in Devachan, when " floating along " in the circumambient ether, instead of the circummuded British Channel—foggy though that state may now appear to your mind's eye. Then only will you " see thyself by thyself" and learn the true meaning of *Atmānam*, *ātmanā pasya*:—

> " To know *itself* e'en as a shinning light
>   Requires no light to make itself perceived. . . ."

of the great Vedanta Philosophy.

Again and once more, an attempt has been made to dispel some of that great mist that I find in Mr. Massey's *Devachan*. It will appear as a contribution to the August number of the *Theosophist*, and to that I shall refer Mr. Massey and yourself. Quite possibly even then the " obscuration " will not be removed and it may be thought that the intended explanation is nothing of the kind; and that, instead of winding the clock, a clumsy hand has but broken out some cogs. This is our misfortune, and I doubt if we shall ever get *quite* free of these obscurities and alleged contradictions; since there is no way to bring the askers and respondents face to face. Still, at the worst it must be conceded that there is *some* satisfaction in the fact that there is now a ford across this river and you are building spans for a royal bridge. It is quite right that you should baptize your new brain-babe with the waters of Hope; and, within the limits of possibility that by it " a further and very sensible impulse will be imparted to the present movement." But, friend, even the " green cheese " of the shining moon is periodically lunched upon by *Rahu*; so do not think yourself altogether above the contingency of popular fickleness, that would put out your light in favour of some new man's " farthing dip." The culture of Society more often inclines to lawn-tennis philosophy than to that of the banned " adepts," whose wider game has worlds for balls, and etheric space for its shaven lawn. The *plāt* of your first book was spiced with phenomena to tickle the spiritualistic palate: this second one is a dish of cold philosophy, and in your " large section of London Society " you will scarcely find enough of the wine of sympathy to wash it down. Many, who now think you mildly mad will buy the book to find out if a commission *De lunatico* should issue to prevent your doing more damage; but of all your readers few are likely to follow your lead towards our *ashram*. Still the theosophist's duty is like that of the husbandman; to turn his furrows and sow his grains as best he can: the issue is with nature, and she, the slave of Law.

I shall waste no condolences upon the poor " lay-chelas " because of the " delicate weapons they can alone work with." A sorry day it would be for mankind if any sharper or deadlier ones were put in their unaccustomed hands! Ah! you would concur with me, my faithful friend, if you could but see the plaint one of them has just made on account of the agonizing results of the poisoned weapons he got the wielding of, in an evil hour, through the help of a sorcerer. Crushed morally, by his own selfish impetuosity; rotting physically from diseases engendered by the animal gratifications he snatched with " demon " help; behind him a black memory of wasted chances and hellish successes; before him a pall of dark despair,—of *avitchi*,—this wretched man turns his impotent rage against our " starry science " and ourselves, and hurls his ineffectual curses at those he vainly besieged for more powers in chelaship, and whom he deserted for a necromantic " Guru " who now leaves the victim to his fate. Be satisfied, friend, with your " delicate weapons "; if not as lethal as the discus of Vishnu, they can break down many barriers if plied with power. The poor wretch in question confesses to a course of "lies, breaches of faith, hatreds, temptings or misleading of others, injustices, calumnies, perjuries, false pretences," etc. The "risk" he "voluntarily took," but he adds, "if *they* (we) had been good and kind as well as wise and powerful, *they* (we) *would have certainly prevented me* from undertaking a task to which they knew I was unequal." In a word, we, who have gained our knowledge, such as it is, by the only practicable method, and who have no right to hinder any fellow man from making the attempt (though we have the right to warn, and we *do* warn every candidate), we are expected to take upon our own heads the penalty of such interference, or try to save ourselves from the same by making incompetents into adepts in spite of themselves! Because *we* did not do this, he is "left to linger out a wretched existence as an animated poison bag, full of mental, moral, and physical corruption." This man has, in despair, turned from a "heathen," an atheist and a free-thinker—[? into] a Christian, or rather a theist, and now humbly "submits" to Him (an extra cosmical God for whom he has even discovered a *local*) and to all delegated by *Him* with lawful authority. And we, poor creatures, are "traitors, Liars, *Devils*, and all my (his) crimes (as enumerated above) are as a shining robe of glory compared to Theirs"—his capitals and underscorings being quoted as well as his words! Now friend, put away that thought that I ought not to compare your case with his, for I do not. I have only given you a glimpse into the hell of this lost soul, to show you what disaster may come upon the "lay-chela" who snatches at forbidden power before his moral nature is developed to the point of fitness for its exercise. You must think well over the article "Chelas and Lay Chelas" which you will find in the *Supplement* of the July *Theosophist*.

So the great Mr. Crookes has placed one foot across the threshold for the sake of reading the Society's papers? Well and wisely done, and really brave of him. Heretofore he was bold enough to take a similar step and loyal enough to truth to disappoint his colleagues by making his facts public. When he was seeing his invaluable paper smothered in the "Sections" and the whole Royal Society trying to cough him down, metaphorically if not actually, as its sister Society in America did to that matryr, Hare—he little thought how perfect a revenge Karma had in store for him. Let him know that its cornucopia is not yet emptied, *and that Western Science has still three additional states of matter to discover*. But he should not wait for us to condense ourselves up to the stethescopic standard as his Katie did; for we men are subject to laws of molecular affinity and polaric attraction which that sweet simulacrum was not hampered with. We have no favourites, break no rules.

If Mr. Crookes would penetrate Arcana beyond the corridors the tools of modern science have already excavated, let him—*Try*. He tried and found the Radiometer; tried again, and found Radiant matter; may try again and find the " Kama-rupa " of matter—its *fifth* state. But to find its *Manas* he would have to pledge himself stronger to secrecy than he seems inclined to. You know our motto, and that its practical application has erased the word " impossible " from the occultist's vocabulary. If he wearies not of trying, he may discover that most noble of all facts, his true SELF. But he will have to penetrate many strata before he comes to *It*. And to begin with let him rid himself of the *maya* that any man living can set up " claims " upon Adepts. He may create irresistible *attractions* and compel their attention, but they will be spiritual, not mental or intellectual. And this bit of advice applies and is directed to several British theosophists, and it may be well for them to know it. Once separated from the common influences of Society, *nothing* draws us to any outsider save his evolving spirituality. He may be a Bacon or an Aristotle in knowledge, and still not even make his current felt a feather's weight by us, if his power is confined to the *Manas*. The supreme energy resides in the *Buddhi*; latent—when wedded to *Atman* alone, active and irresistible when galvanized by the *essence* of " Manas " and when none of the dross of the latter commingles with that pure essence to weigh it down by its finite nature. *Manas*, pure and simple, is of a lower degree, and of the earth earthly: and so your greatest men count but as nonentities in the arena where greatness is measured by the standard of spiritual development. When the ancient founders of your philosophical schools came East, to acquire the lore of our predecessors, they filed no claims, except the single one of a sincere and *unselfish* hunger for the truth. If any now aspire to found new schools of science and philosophy the same plan will win—*if the seekers have in them the elements of success*.

Yes; you are right about the Society for Psychic Research: its work is of a kind to tell upon public opinion by experimentally demonstrating the elementary phases of Occult Science. H. S. Olcott has been trying to convert each of the Indian Branches into such a school of research, but the capacity for sustained independent study for knowledge's sake is lacking, and must be developed. The success of the S.P.R. will greatly aid in this direction and we wish it well.

I also go with you in your views as to the choice of the new President of the B.T.S.; in fact I concurred, I believe, before the choice was made.

There is no reason why you should *not* " attempt mesmeric cures " by the help, not of your locket but the power of your own will. Without this latter in energetic function, no locket will do much good. The hair in it is in itself but an " accumulator " of the energy of him who grew it, and can no more cure of itself than stored electricity can turn a wheel until liberated and conducted to the objective point. Set your will in motion and you at once draw upon the person upon whose head it (the hair not the will) grew, through the psychic current which ever runs between himself and his severed tress. To heal diseases it is not indispensable, however desirable, that the .psychopathist should be absolutely pure; there are many in Europe and elsewhere who are not. If the healing be done under the impulse of perfect benevolence, unmixed with any latent selfishness, the philanthropist sets up a current which runs like a fine thrill through the *sixth* condition of matter, and is felt by him whom you summon to your help, if not at that moment engaged in some work which compels him to be repellent to all extraneous influences. The possession of a lock of any adept's hair is of course a decided advantage, as a better tempered sword is to the soldier in battle; but the measure of its actual help to the psychopathist will be in ratio with the degree of will power he excites in himself, and the degree of psychic purity in his motive. The talisman and his *Buddhi* are in sympathy.

Now that you are at the centre of modern Buddhistic exegesis, in personal relations with some of the clever commentators (from whom the holy Devas deliver us!) I shall draw your attention to a few things which are really as discreditable to the perceptions of even *non*-initiates, as they are misleading to the general public. The more one reads such speculations as those of Messrs. Rhys Davids, Lillie, etc.—the less can one bring himself to believe that the unregenerate Western mind can ever get at the core of our abstruse doctrines. Yet hopeless as their cases may be, it would appear well worth the trouble of testing the intuitions of your London members—of some of them, at any rate—by half expounding through you one or two mysteries and leaving them to complete the chain themselves. Shall we take Mr. Rhys Davids as our first subject, and show that, indirectly as he has done it yet it is himself who strengthened the absurd ideas of Mr. Lillie, who fancies to have proved belief in a personal God in ancient Buddhism. Mr. Rhys Davids' *Buddhism* is full of the sparkle of our most important esotericism; but always, as it would seem, beyond not only his reach but apparently even his powers of intellectual perception. To avoid " absurd metaphysics " and its *inventions*, he creates unnecessary difficulties and falls headlong into inextricable confusion. He is like the Cape Settlers who lived over diamond mines without suspecting it. I shall only instance the definition of " Avalokitesvara " on pp. 202 and 203. There, we find the author saying that which to any occultist seems a palpable absurdity:—

" The name Avalokitesvara, which means ' the Lord who looks down from on high,' is a purely metaphysical invention. The curious use of the past particle passive *avalokita* in an active sense is clearly evident from the translations into Tibetan and Chinese."

Now saying that it means " the Lord who looks down from on high," *or*, as he kindly explains further—" the Spirit of the Buddhas present in the church," is to completely reverse the sense. It is equivalent to saying " Mr. Sinnett looks down from on high (his *Fragments of Occult Truth*) on the British Theos. Society," whereas it is the latter that looks up to Mr. Sinnett, or rather to his *Fragments* as the (in their case only *possible*) expression and culmination of the knowledge sought for. This is no idle simile and defines the exact situation. In short, *Avalokita Isvar* literally interpreted means " the Lord that *is seen*," " Iswara " implying moreover, rather the adjective than the noun, *lordly*, self-existent *lordliness*, *not* Lord. It is, when correctly interpreted, in one sense " the *divine Self* perceived or seen by *Self*," the *Atman* or seventh principle ridded of its *mayavic* distinction from its Universal Source —which becomes the object of perception for, and by the *individuality* centred in *Buddhi*, the sixth principle, something that happens only in the highest state of *Samadhi*. This is applying it to the microcosm. In the other sense Avalokitesvara implies the seventh *Universal* Principle, as the object perceived by the Universal *Buddhi*, " Mind " or Intelligence which is the synthetic aggregation of all the Dhyan Chohans, as of all other intelligences whether great or small, that ever were, are or will be. Nor is it the " Spirit of Buddhas present in the Church," but the Omnipresent Universal Spirit in the temple of nature—in one case; and the seventh Principle—the *Atman* in the temple—man—in the other. Mr. Rhys Davids might have at least remembered the (to him) familiar simile made by the Christian Adept, the Kabalistic Paul: " Know ye not that ye are the temple of God, *and that the Spirit of God dwelleth in you* "—and thus avoided to have made a mess of the name. Though as a grammarian he detected the use of the " past particle passive," yet he shows himself far from an inspired " Panini " in overlooking the true cause and saving his grammar by raising the hue and cry against metaphysics. And yet he quotes Beal's *Catena* as his authority for the invention when, in truth, this work is perhaps the only one in English that gives an *approximately* correct explanation of the word, at any rate, on page 374. " *Self*-manifested "—How? it is asked. " Speech or *Vāch* was regarded as the Son or the manifestation of the *Eternal Self*, and was adored under the name of Avalokitesvara, the manifested God." This shows as clearly as can be that Avalokitesvara is both the *un*-manifested *Father* and the manifested *Son*, the latter proceeding from, and identical with, the other; namely, the *Parabrahm*

and *Jivātman*, the Universal and the individualized seventh
Principle,—the Passive and the Active, the latter the *Word*, Logos,
the Verb.   Call it by whatever name, only let these unfortunate,
deluded Christians know that the real *Christ* of every Christian is
the *Vāch*, the " mystical Voice," while the man *Jeshu* was but a
mortal like any of us, an adept more by his inherent purity and
ignorance of real Evil than by what he had learned with his
initiated Rabbis and the already (at that period) fast degenerating
Egyptian Hierophants and priests.   A great mistake is also made
by Beal who says: " This name (Avalokiteswara) in Chinese took
the form of Kwan-Shai-yin, and the divinity worshipped under
that name (was) generally regarded as a female."   (374) *Kwan-
shai-yin*—or the universally manifested voice is active—*male*; and
must not be confounded with *Kwan-yin*, or *Buddhi* the Spiritual
Soul (the sixth Pr.) and the vehicle of its " Lord."   It is *Kwan-yin*
that is the female principle or the manifested *passive*, manifesting
itself " to every creature in the universe, in order to deliver all
men from the consequences of sin "—as rendered by Beal, this
once quite correctly (383), while *Kwan-shai-yin*, " the Son identical
with his Father " is the *absolute activity*, hence—having no direct
relation to objects of sense—is *Passivity*.

What a common *ruse* it is of your Aristoteleans! With the sleuth
hound's persistence they track an idea to the very verge of the
" impassable chasm," and then, brought to bay, leave the metaphysicians to take up the trail if they can, or let it be lost.   It is
but natural that a Christian theologian, a missionary, should act
upon this line, since—as easily perceived even in the little I gave
out just now—a too correct rendering of our *Avalokitesvara* and
Kwan-Shai-Yin might have very disastrous effects.   It would simply
amount to showing Christendom the true and undeniable origin of
the " awful and *incomprehensible* " mysteries of its Trinity, Tran-
substantiation, Immaculate Conception, as also *whence* their ideas
of the Father, Son, *Spiritus* and—Mother.   It is less easy to shuffle
al piacere [1] the cards of Buddhistic chronology than those of Chrishna
and Christ.   They *cannot* place—however much they would—the
birth of our Lord Sangyas Buddha A.D. as they have contrived to
place that of Chrishna.   But why should an atheist and a materialist
like Mr. Rhys Davids so avoid the correct rendering of our dogmas
—even when he happens to understand them,—which does not
happen every day—is something surpassingly curious! In this instance
the blind and guilty Rhys Davids leads the blind and innocent
Mr. Lillie into the ditch; where the latter, catching at the proffered
straw rejoices in the idea that Buddhism teaches in reality—a
personal God!!

---

[1] As you please.—EDS.

Does your B.T.S.[1] know the meaning of the white and black interlaced triangles, of the Parent Society's seal that it has also adopted? Shall I explain? The double triangle viewed by the Jewish Kabalists as Solomon's Seal is, as many of you doubtless know the *Sri-yantra* of the archaic Aryan Temple, the "mystery of Mysteries," a geometrical synthesis of the whole occult doctrine. The two interlaced triangles are the *Buddhangams* of Creation. They contain the "squaring of the circle," the "philosophers' stone," the great problems of Life and Death, and—the Mystery of Evil. The *chela* who can explain this sign from every one of its aspects—is *virtually an adept*. How is it then, that the only one among you who has come so near to unravelling the mystery is also the only one who got none of her ideas from books? Unconsciously she gives out—to him who has the key—the first syllable of the *Ineffable Name*! Of course you know that the double-triangle —the *Satkona Chakram* of Vishnu—or the six-pointed star, is the perfect seven. In all the old Sanskrit works—*Vedic* and *Tantrik*— you find the number 6 mentioned more often than the 7—this last figure, the central point, being implied, for it is the germ of the six and their matrix. It is then thus . .[2]—the central point standing for seventh, and the circle, the *Mahākāsha* महाकाश— endless space—for the seventh *Universal* Principle. In one sense, both are viewed as *Avalokitesvara*, for they are respectively, the Macrocosm and the microcosm. The interlaced triangles—the upper pointing one is Wisdom concealed, and the downward pointing one Wisdom *revealed* (in the phenomenal world). The circle indicates the bounding, circumscribing quality of the *All*, the Universal Principle which from any given point expands so as to embrace all things, while embodying the potentiality of every action in the Cosmos. As the point, then, is the centre round which the circle is traced they are identical and *one*, though from the standpoint of *Maya* and *Avidya*—(illusion and ignorance)—one is separated from the other by the manifested triangle, the 3 sides of which represent the three *gunas*—finite attributes. In symbology the central point is *Jivātma* (the 7th principle), and hence Avalokitesvara, the *Kwan-Shai-yin*, the manifested "Voice" (or *Logos*), the germ point of manifested activity; hence, in the phraseology of the Christian Kabalists, "the Son of the Father and Mother," and agreeably to ours—"the Self manifested in Self—*Yi-hsin*, the "one form of existence," the child of *Dharmakaya* (the universally diffused Essence), both male and female. Parabrahm or "Adi-Buddha," while acting through that germ point outwardly as an active force, reacts from the circumference inwardly as the Supreme

---

[1] British Theosophical Society.—Eds.

[2] At this point in the original there is a rough drawing of the interlaced triangles inscribed in a circle.—Ed.

but latent Potency. The double triangles symbolize the Great Passive and the Great Active; the male and female; Purusha and Prakriti. Each triangle is a Trinity because presenting a triple aspect. The white represents in its straight lines: *Jnanam*— (Knowledge); *Jnata*—(the Knower); and *Jneyam*—(that which is known). The black—form, colour, and substance, also the *creative*, *preservative*, and *destructive* forces, and [these] are mutually correlating, etc., etc.

Well may you admire and more should you wonder at the marvellous lucidity of that remarkable seeress, who ignorant of Sanskrit or Pali, and thus shut out from their metaphysical treasures, has yet seen a great light shining from behind the dark hills of exoteric religions. How, think you, did the writers of " the Perfect Way " come to know that Adonai was the Son and not the Father; or that the third Person of the Christian Trinity is—female? Verily, in that work they lay their hands several times upon the keystone of Occultism. Only does the lady—who persists using without an explanation the misleading term " God " in her writings—know how nearly she comes up to our doctrine when saying:—" Having for Father Spirit *which is Life* (the endless Circle or Parabrahm) and for Mother the Great Deep, which is Substance (Prakriti in its undifferentiated condition)—Adonai possesses the potency of both and wields the *dual* powers of all things."? We would say *triple*, but in the sense as given this will do. Pythagoras had a reason for never using the finite, useless figure—2, and for altogether discarding it. The ONE, can, when manifesting, become only 3. The unmanifested when a simple duality remains passive and concealed. The dual monad (the 7th and 6th principles) has, in order to manifest itself as a *Logos*, the " Kwan-shai-yin, " to first become a *triad* (7th, 6th and half of the 5th); then, on the bosom of the " Great Deep," attracting within itself the *One Circle*, form out of it the perfect Square, thus " squaring the circle "—the greatest of all the mysteries, friend—and inscribing within the latter the WORD (the Ineffable Name)—otherwise the duality could never tarry as such, and would have to be reabsorbed into the ONE. The " Deep " is *Space*—both male and female. " *Purush* (as Brahma) breathes in the Eternity; when ' he ' *in*-breathes, Prakriti (as manifested Substance) disappears in his bosom; when ' he ' *out*-breathes she reappears as *Maya*," says the sloka. The One reality is *Mulaprakriti* (undifferentiated Substance)—the " Rootless root," the . . But we have to stop, lest there should remain but little to tell for your own intuitions.

Well may the Geometer of the R.S.[1] not know that the apparent absurdity of attempting to square the circle covers a mystery

---

[1] The Royal Society.—EDS.

25

ineffable.   It would hardly be found among the foundation stones
of Mr. Roden Noel's speculations upon the " pneumatical body
. . . of our Lord," nor among the *débris* of Mr. Farmer's " A New
Basis of Belief in Immortality "; and to many such metaphysical
minds it would be worse than useless to divulge the fact that the
Unmanifested Circle—the *Father*, or *Absolute* Life—is non-existent
outside the Triangle and Perfect Square, and is only manifested in
the *Son*; and that it is when reversing the action and returning to
its absolute state of Unity, and the square expands once more into
the Circle, that " the Son returns to the bosom of the Father."
There it remains until called back by his Mother, the " Great
Deep," to remanifest as a *triad*—the *Son* partaking at once of the
Essence of the Father and of that of the Mother—the active
Substance, *Prakriti* in its differentiated condition.   " My Mother
—(Sophia, the manifested Wisdom)—took me," says Jesus in a
Gnostic treatise; and he asks his disciples to tarry *till he comes*. . .
The true " Word " may only be found by tracing the mystery of
the passage inward and outward of the Eternal Life, through the
states typified in these three geometric figures.

The criticism of " A Student of Occultism " (whose wits are
sharpened by the mountain air of his home) and the answer of
" S.T.K. . . . Chary " (June *Theosophist*) upon a part of
your annular and circular expositions need not annoy or disturb
in any way your philosophic calm.   As our Pondichery *chela*
significantly says, neither you nor any other man across the
threshold has had or ever will have the " complete theory " of
Evolution taught him; or get it unless he guesses it for himself.   If
anyone can unravel it from such tangled threads as are given him,
very well; and a fine proof it would indeed be of his or her spiritual
insight.   Some—have come *very near it*.   But yet there is always
with the best of them just enough error,—colouring and misconception; the shadow of *Manas* projecting across the field of *Buddhi*
—to prove the eternal law that only the unshackled Spirit shall
see the things of the Spirit without a veil.   No untaught amateur
could ever rival the proficient in this branch of research; yet the
world's real Revelators have been few, and its pseudo-Saviours
legion; and fortunate it is if their half-glimpses of the light are not,
like Islam, enforced at the sword's point, or like Christian Theology,
amid blazing faggots and in torture chambers.   Your *Fragments*
contain some—still very few—errors, due solely to your two pre-
ceptors of Adyar, one of whom *would not*, and the other *could not*
tell you all.   The rest could not be called mistakes—rather
incomplete explanations.   These are due, partly to your own
imperfect education in your last theme—I mean the everthreaten-
ing *obscurations*—partly to the poor vehicles of language at our
disposal, and in part again, to the reserve imposed upon us by

rule.   Yet, all things considered, they are few and trivial; while as to those noticed by " A Student, etc." (the Marcus Aurelius of Simla) in your No. VII, it will be pleasant for you to know that every one of them, however now seeming to you contradictory, can (and if it should seem necessary *shall*) be easily reconciled with facts.   The trouble is that (*a*) you cannot be given the real figures and difference in the Rounds, and (*b*) that you do not open doors enough for explorers.   The bright Luminary of the B.T.S. and the Intelligences that surround her (embodied I mean) may help you to see the flaws: at all events Try.   "Nothing was every lost by trying."   You share with all beginners the tendency to draw too absolutely strong inferences from partly caught hints, and to dogmatize thereupon as though the last word had been spoken.   You will correct this in due time.   You may misunderstand us, are more than likely to do so, for our language must always be more or less that of parable and suggestion, when treading upon forbidden ground; we have our own peculiar modes of expression and what lies behind the fence of words is even more important than what you read.   But still—TRY.   Perhaps if Mr. S. Moses could know just what was meant by what was said to him, and about his Intelligences, he would find all *strictly true*. As he is a man of interior growth, his day may come and his reconciliation with " the Occultists " be complete.   Who knows? Meanwhile, I shall, with your permission, close this *first* volume.

K. H.

LETTER No. 60

My good friend—Shakespeare said truly that " our doubts are traitors."   Why should you doubt or create in your mind ever growing monsters?   A little more knowledge in occult laws would have set your mind at rest long ago, avoided many a tear to your gentle lady and pang to yourself.   Know, then, that even the chelas of the same guru are often made to separate and keep apart for long months while the process of development is going on— simply on account of the two contrary magnetisms that, attracting each other, prevent mutual and INDIVIDUALIZED development in some one direction.   There is no offence meant or even possible. This ignorance has caused of late immense suffering on all sides. When shall you trust *implicitly*, in my heart if not in my wisdom for which I claim no recognition on your part?   It is extremely painful to see you wandering about in a dark labyrinth created by your own doubts every issue of which, moreover, you close with your own hands.   I believe you are now satisfied with my portrait made by Herr Schmiechen and as dissatisfied with the one you have? Yet all are like in their way. Only while the others are the productions of chelas, the last one was painted with M.'s hand on the artist's head, and often on his arm.

K. H.

Pray remain for the Wednesday meeting—if you *feel you are not to leave the* INNER CIRCLE. Otherwise—go, remembering my friendship had WARNED YOU. Only avoid, if you do, hurting the feelings of those who sin thro' an *excess*, not *lack* of devotion.

LETTER No. 61

Sinnett Sahib is, my respectful salams—informed that his " guardian " is so occupied upon official business that he cannot give even a moment's consideration to the L.L. or its members; nor to write him individually whether by pen or precipitation— the more difficult, not to say costly, method of the two—to our reputations in the West anyhow.

Mohini cannot stop in London indefinitely, nor for any greater length of time as he has duties to perform elsewhere—duties to his family as well as others to the Theosophical Society. Besides being a chela and so not a free man—in the ordinary acceptation of the term—he has numerous mouths to feed at Calcutta, and moreover must earn enough more to repay the friend who advanced him £125 money toward the expenses of his present mission, whatever K.H. may or may not do for him, something he is prohibited counting upon, as every other chela. At the same time let it be known to you that he needs temporary change of climate. He suffered greatly from cold in that high room where there is no fireplace in your house, and K.H. had to surround him with a double shell against a death cold that threatened him. Remember Hindus are exotic plants in your inclement pays[1] and cold, and those who need them have to take care of them. (If when annoying Olcott on Sunday last to tell you this information, I did not make him tell you, and add this, it is because I wanted to spare him in your mind, already prejudiced against him and inclining towards a belief that he spoke out of his head.)

Again, if you need Mohini's help at London the Theosophists at Paris require it even more since their occult education is inferior to yours. It is planned that he should divide his time equally among all the European " centres of spiritual activity," and if he is now required at Paris on the 11th inst. he will also be allowed to come back to London when the Continental movement is fairly inaugurated. In any event you will have Olcott the better part of

---

[1] This might be ' days,' or it may be '*pays*,' French for country or land.—EDS.

the time.   But fear not: if Henry is allowed to prolong his stay in London he will not " worry " either of you by coming down in his extravagant Asiatic undresses—for he will not stop with you but with the Arundale ladies—as ordered before now, the order being reiterated by me when Madame Sahib remarked it was better he should stop where he was after Upasika had left.   Nor is Olcott worse than many others, and though some persons may not concede it there are worse wranglers than he.   I must not close without letting you know that in the Kingsford row justice is no longer on your side.   Though unwilling to confess—you show *spite* Sahib, personal spite.   You have defeated her and you now would mortify and punish her.   This is *not* right.   You ought to learn to dissociate your consciousness from your external self more than you do if ye *would not lose K.H.*   For he is much annoyed at what goes on.   Excuse my remarks but it is for your own benefit. So begging pardon.

M.

LETTER No. 62

Received 18-7-84.

My poor, blind friend—you are entirely unfit for practical occultism! Its laws are immutable; and no one can go back on an order once given.   She can send on no letters to me, and *the* letter ought to have been given to Mohini.   However, I have read it; and I am determined to make one more effort—(the last that I am permitted)—to open your inner intuition.   If my voice, the voice of one who was ever friendly to you in the human principle of his being—fails to reach you as it has often before, then our separation in the present nnd for all times to come—becomes unavoidable.   It pains me for you, whose heart I read so well— every protest and doubt of your purely intellectual nature, of your cold Western reason—notwithstanding.   But my first duty is to *my* Master.   And duty, let me tell you, is for us stronger than any friendship or even love; as without this abiding principle which is the indestructible cement that has held together for so many milleniums, the scattered custodians of nature's grand secrets— our Brotherhood, nay, our doctrine itself—would have crumbled long ago into unrecognisable atoms.   Unfortunately, however great your purely *human* intellect, your spiritual intuitions are dim and hazy, having been never developed.   Hence, whenever you find yourself confronted by an apparent contradiction, by a difficulty, a kind of *inconsistency* of occult nature, one that is caused by our time honoured laws and regulations—(of which you know nothing, for your time has not yet come)—forthwith your doubts are aroused, your suspicions bud out—and one finds that they have made mock at your better nature, which is finally crushed down by all these deceptive appearances of outward things! You have not the faith required to allow your Will to arouse itself in defiance and contempt against your purely worldly intellect, and give you a better understanding of things hidden and laws unknown. You are unable, I see, to force your better aspirations —fed at the stream of a real devotion to the Maya you have made yourself of me—(a feeling in you that has always profoundly touched me)—to lift up the head against cold, *spiritually blind* reason; to allow your heart to pronounce loudly and proclaim that which it has hitherto only been allowed to whisper: " Patience, patience. A great design has never been snatched at once." You were told, however, that the path to Occult Sciences has to be trodden laboriously and crossed at the danger of life; that every new step in it leading to the final goal is surrounded by pit-falls and cruel thorns; that the pilgrim who ventures upon it is made first to confront and *conquer* the thousand and one furies who keep watch over its adamantine gates and entrance—furies called Doubt, Skepticism, Scorn, Ridicule, Envy and finally Temptation —especially the latter; and that he who would see *beyond* had to first destroy this living wall; that he must be possessed of a heart and soul clad in steel, and of an iron, never failing determination and yet be meek and gentle, humble and have shut out from his heart every human passion, that leads to evil. Are you all this? Have you ever begun a course of training which would lead to it? No; you know it as I do. You are not born for it; nor are you in a position,—a family man with wife and child to support, with work to do—fitted in any way for the life of an ascetic, not even of a— Mohini. Then why should you complain that powers are not given you, that even *proof of our own powers* begins to fail you, etc.? True, you have offered several times to give up meat and drink, and I have refused. Since you cannot become a regular *chela* why should you? I thought you had understood all this long ago; that you had resigned yourself, satisfied to wait patiently for future developments and for my personal freedom. You know I was the only one to attempt and persevere in my idea of the necessity of, at least, a small reform, of however slight a relaxation from the extreme rigidity of our regulations if we would see European theo- sophists increase and work for the enlightenment and good of humanity. I failed in my attempt, as you know. All I could obtain was to be allowed to communicate with a few—you, fore- most of all, since I had chosen you as the exponent of our doctrine that we had determined to give out to the world—to some extent at least. Unable on account of work to continue my teaching regularly, I was decided to resume it after my work had been done, and I had a few hours of leisure at my disposal. I was tied hand and foot when I made that attempt to let you have a paper of your own. I was not permitted to use any psychical powers in that matter. You know the results. Yet, I would have succeeded even with the small means of action I had at my disposal had it not been for the Ilbert Bill excitement. Have you ever given a thought, or ever suspected the real reason of my failure? No; for you know nothing of the *ins* and outs of the work of karma—of the " sideblows " of this terrible Law. But you *do know* that there was a time when you felt the profoundest contempt for us all, of the dark races; and had regarded the Hindus as an *inferior* race. I will say no more. If you have any intuition, you will work out *cause* and *effect* and perhaps realize *whence* the failure. Then again you had against you the command of our Supreme Chief—not to interfere with the *natural* growth of the L.L. and the development, psychic and spiritual, of its members—especially *with yours*. You know that even to write to you occasionally has been permitted only as a special favour after the *Phoenix* failure. As to the exhibition of any psychic or occult powers—that was, and still is, entirely out of question. You felt astonished at the *interference* in the quarrel between the L.L. and Kingsford? And you are unable yet to realize *why* we did this and that? Believe me that you will learn some day when you know better—*that it was all brought on* BY YOURSELF.

You also resent the apparent absurdity of entrusting H.S.O. with a mission *you* find him unfit for, in London at any rate—socially and intellectually. Well—some day, perchance, you may also learn that you were equally wrong in this, as in many other things. Coming results may teach you a bitter lesson.

And now to the latest development, to the proof that you were *not* " unjustly treated "—as you complain in your letter—tho' you have treated both H.S.O. and H.P.B. in a very cruel way. Your greatest grievance is caused by your perplexity. It is *agonizing*—you say—to be ever kept in the dark, etc. You feel profoundly hurt at what you choose to call an evident and growing " unfriendliness, the change of tone " and so on. *You are mistaken from first to last.* There was neither " unfriendliness," nor any change of feeling. You simply mistook M.'s natural *brusqueness* whenever he speaks or writes seriously.

As for my short remarks about you to H.P.B., who appealed to me and who *was in her right*—you never thought of the real and true reason; I had no time; I could hardly give a passing thought to yourself or the L.L. As well said by her, " No one has ever thought of accusing you of any *intentional* wrong "—to either ourselves or chelas. As to an *unintentional* one—happily prevented in time by me—there was one certainly: *carelessness.* You never thought of the difference between the constitution of a Bengali and that of an Englishman, the power of endurance of one, and the same power in the other. Mohini was left for days in a very cold room without a fireplace. He never uttered one word of complaint, and I had to protect him from a serious illness, to give him my time and attention, to him I so needed to bring about certain results, to him who had sacrificed everything for me. . . . Hence, M.'s *tone* you complain of. Now you have it *explained*, that you were not " unjustly treated " but simply had to submit to a remark which it was impossible for you to avoid, since the mistake might have happened again. Then you *deny* there ever was any *spite* in you against K. Very well; call it by any other name you like; yet it *was* a feeling that interfered with strict justice, and made O. commit a still worse blunder than he had already committed—*but which was allowed to take its course* for it suited our purposes, and did no great harm except to himself—alone, who was so ungenerously snubbed for it. You accuse him of having done *mischief* to your Society and perhaps, " irretrievably "? Where is the harm done? . . . You are again mistaken. It is your *nerves* that made you write to H.P.B. words I would you had never uttered—for your own sake. Shall I prove to you—at any rate in *one* case—how utterly *unjust* you have been in suspecting either of them, of having either *complained* or told falsehoods to us about you? I trust, however, that you will never repeat what I will tell you: *i.e.* who *it was* (or might have been but *was not*, for she came too late)—my innocent *informer* about Mohini. You are at liberty to verify it one day, but I would not have that most excellent woman feel discomforted or miserable on my account. *It was Mme. Gebhard* whom I had promised to visit subjectively. I saw her one morning, when I was busy with Mohini making him *impermeable* —descending the stairs. She had heard his teeth chatter, as he was also coming down from the floor above. She knew he was still in his little fireless room days after Olcott had gone and when he might have been easily placed in the next room. She had stopped to wait for him and as I looked *into her* I heard the words pronounced mentally: " Well, well . . . if his Master only knew! . . ." and then stopping on the landing she asked him if he would not have some additonal warm clothing and such other kind words. " His master—*knew* " and had already remedied the evil; and knowing also, that it was *unintentional*—felt no " unfriendliness " at the time for he knows Europeans too well to expect from them more than they can give. Nor was it the only *mute* reproach I found addressed to you in Mme. Gebhard's heart, as in the minds of several others of your friends:—and it is but right that you should know it—remembering that like yourself they judge nearly everything *on appearance*.

I will say no more. But, if you would have another look at *Karma* ponder over the above, and remember that it ever works in the most unexpected ways. And now put yourself the question how far you were justified in entertaining suspicions against Olcott who knew nothing of the circumstances whatever, and against H.P.B. who was at Paris and knew still less. Nevertheless, mere suspicion degenerated into *conviction* (!) and became objectivised in written reproaches and very ungenerous expressions which were, moreover, from first to last, *undeserved*. All this notwithstanding, you complained bitterly yesterday to Miss A. of Mme. B.'s answer to you—which was—making every allowance for the peculiar circumstances, and her own temper, surprisingly *mild* when confronted with *your* letter to her. Nor can I approve of your attitude to Olcott—if *my* advice and opinion are wanted. Had you been in his place and *guilty* you would have hardly permitted him to accuse you in such terms of *falsification, slandering, lies, falsehoods* and the most idiotic incompetency for his work. And Olcott is entirely innocent of any such sin! As to his work—we really must be permitted to know better. What we want is *good results* and you will find that we have them.

Verily " suspicion overturns, what confidence builds "! And if, on the one hand, you have some reasons to quote Bacon against us, and say that " there is nothing that makes a man suspect much, more than to know little," on the other hand you ought also to remember that our *Knowledge* and *Science* cannot be pursued altogether on the Baconian methods. We are not permitted—come what may—to offer it as a remedy against, or to cure people from suspicion. They have to earn it for themselves, and he who will not find our truths in his soul and within himself—has poor chances of success in Occultism. It is certainly not suspicion that will mend the situation for it is—

> ". . . a heavy armour, and
> with its own weight *impedes more than it protects*."

With this last remark we may, I think, let this matter drop for ever. You have brought suffering upon yourself, upon your lady and many others—which was quite useless and might have been avoided had you only abstained from creating yourself most of its causes. All that Miss Arundale told you was right and well said. You are yourself ruining that which you have so laboriously erected; but then, the strange idea that we are quite unable to see for ourselves, that our only data is that which we find in our chela's minds, hence—that we are not " the powerful beings " you have represented us, seems to haunt you with every day more. Hume has begun in the same way. I would gladly help you and protect you from his fate, but unless you shake off yourself the ghastly influence that is upon you I can do very little.

You ask me if you can tell Miss Arundale what I told you thro'
Mrs. H. You are quite at liberty to explain to her the situation,
and thereby justify in her eyes your *seeming* disloyalty and rebellion
against us as she thinks. You can do so the more since I have
never bound you to anything thro' Mrs. H.; never communicated
with you or any one else thro' her—nor have any of my, or M.'s
chelas, to my knowledge, except in America, once at Paris and
another time at Mrs. A.'s house. She is an excellent but quite
undeveloped clairvoyante. Had she not been imprudently
meddled with, and had you followed the old woman's and Mohini's
advice indeed, by this time I might have spoken with you thro'
her—and such *was* our intention. It is again your own fault, my
good friend. You have proudly claimed the privilege of exercising
your own, uncontrolled judgment in occult matters you could
know nothing about—and the occult laws you believe you can
defy and play with with impunity have turned round upon you
and have badly hurt you. It is all as it should be. If, throwing
aside every preconceived idea, you could TRY and impress yourself
with this profound truth that intellect is not all powerful by itself;
that to become " a mover of mountains " it has first to receive life
and light from its higher principle—Spirit, and then would fix
your eyes upon everything occult, spiritually trying to develop the
faculty according to the rules, then you would soon read the mystery
right. You need not tell Mrs. H. that she has never seen correctly,
for it is not so. Many a time she saw correctly—when left alone
to herself, never has she left one single statement undisfigured.

And now I have done. You have two roads lying before you;
one leading thro' a very dreary path toward knowledge and truth
—the other . . . but really I must not influence your mind. If
you are not prepared to break with us altogether then I would ask
you—not only to be present at the meeting but also to speak—as
it will otherwise produce a very unfavourable impression. This
I ask you to do *for my sake* and also for your own.

Only whatever you do let me advise you *not to stop midway*: it
may prove disastrous to you.

So far my friendship for you remains the same as ever—for we
never were yet ungrateful for services rendered.

K.H.

LETTER No. 63

Received London, Summer, 1884.

Good friend—

When our first correspondence began, there was no idea then of
any publications being issued on the basis of the replies you might
receive. You went on putting questions at random, and the

answers being given at different times to disjointed queries, and so to say, under a semi-protest, were necessarily imperfect, often from different standpoints. When the publication of some of these were permitted for the *Occult World*, it was hoped that among your readers some might be able, like yourself, to put all the different pieces together and evolve out of them the skeleton, or a shadow of our system, which, although not exactly the original—this would be an impossibility—would be as near an approach to it as could be made by a non-initiate. But the results have proved quasi-disastrous! We had tried an experiment and sadly failed! Now we see that none but those who have passed at least their third initiation are able to write upon those subjects comprehensively. A Herbert Spencer would have made a mess of it under your circumstances. Mohini is certainly not quite right, in some details he is positively wrong, but so are you, my old friend, though the outside reader is none the wiser for it and no one, so far, has noticed the real vital errors in *Esoteric Buddhism* and *Man*; nor are they likely to. We can give no further information on the subject already approached by you and have to leave the facts already communicated to be woven into a consistent and systematic philosophy by the chelas at the Headquarters. The *Secret Doctrine* will explain many things, set to right more than one perplexed student.

Therefore, to put before the world all the crude and complicated materials in your possession in the shape of old letters, in which, I confess, much was purposely made obscure, would only be making confusion worst confounded. Instead of doing any good thereby to yourself and others it would only place you in a still more difficult position, bring criticism upon the heads of the " Masters " and thus have a retarding influence on human progress and the T.S. Hence *I protest* most strongly against your new idea. Leave to the *Secret Doctrine* the task of avenging you. My letters *must not* be published, in the manner you suggest, but on the contrary, if you [would] save Djual K. trouble, copies of some should be sent to the Literary Committee at Adyar—about which Damodar has written to you—so that with the assistance of S.T.K. Charya, Djual K., Subba Row and the Secret Committee (from which H.P.B. was purposely excluded by us to avoid new suspicions and calumnies) they might be able to utilise the information for the realization of the object with which the Committee was started, as explained by Damodar in the letter written by him under orders. It is neither new " Kiddle developments " that I seek to avoid, nor criticism directed against my personality, which indeed can hardly be reached; but I rather try to save yourself and Society from new troubles which would be serious this time. The letters, in short, were not written for publication or public comment upon them, but for private use, and neither M. nor I will ever give our consent to see them thus handled.

As regards your first letter Dj. K. has been instructed to attend to it. In such delicate matters I am still less competent to give advice than to satisfy aspiring " chelas " of the " L.C.H." sort. I am afraid the " poor, dear Mrs. Holloway " is showing her white teeth and would hardly be found now " a charming companion." Under instructions Olcott wrote a letter to Finch—which gives the key to the little problem. It is Fern, Moorad Ali, Bishen Lal and other wrecks, over again. Why will "would-be " *chelas* with such intense self personalities, force themselves within the enchanted and dangerous circle of probation! Pardoning my short letter, I am very busy just now with the coming new year.

K.H.

LETTER No. 64

Received London, Summer, 1884.

Entirely private except for Mohini and F.A.

Good friend—

This is not an answer to your last. The letter to my address sent by you through Mohini was never written by yourslf. Verily it was penned by one, at that time, entirely under the influence of a creature of Attavāda—

> " The sin of Self, who in the Universe
> As in a mirror sees her fond face shown "

—and *only hers*; whose every word he then implicitly trusted; perhaps, (this is to a certain extent a justification) because there came no half expected interference, no word of warning from our quarters. Thus—no response to it, for we rather turn a new page.

Ah, how long shall the mysteries of chelaship overpower and lead astray from the path of truth the wise and perspicacious, as much as the foolish and the credulous! How few of the many pilgrims who have to start without chart or compass on that shoreless Ocean of Occultism reach the wished for land. Believe me, faithful friend, that *nothing* short of full confidence in us, in our good motives if not in our wisdom, in our foresight, if not omniscience—which is not to be found on this earth—can help one to cross over from one's land of dream and fiction to our Truth land, the region of stern reality and fact. Otherwise the ocean will prove shoreless indeed; its waves will carry one no longer on waters of hope, but will turn every ripple into doubt and suspicion; and bitter shall they prove to him who starts on that dismal, tossing sea of the Unknown, with a prejudiced mind!

Nevertheless, feel not too much perplexed. The hour of trial is half over; try rather to understand the " whys and whatfors " of the situation, to study more seriously the laws that govern our " Occult World." I grant you, those laws *do* seem very often unjust, even at times cruel. But this is due to the fact that they were never meant either for the immediate redress of wrongs, or the direct help of those who offer at random their allegiance to the legislators. Still, the seemingly real, the evanescent and quick passing evils they bring about are as necessary to the growth, progress and final establishment of your small Th. Society as those cataclysms in nature, which often decimate whole populations, are necessary to mankind. An earthquake may, for all the world knows, be a bliss and a tidal wave prove salvation to the many at the expense of the few. The " fittest " were seen to survive in the destruction of every old race and made to merge into, and assimilate with, the new, for nature is older than Darwin. Say rather, then, to yourself " whatever happened, there can be no cause for regret "; for it is not so much that new facts should be revealed to the " inner group " as that old puzzles and mysteries should have been explained and made clear to its few entirely staunch members. Even an innocent quotation mark fallen from under my pencil and by you objected to, would have had a world of meaning for one less beclouded than you were in writing your last letter—based entirely on the crafty insinuations of your would-be sibyl. It was absolutely necessary that within the personal experience of those few staunch members (yourself included) the secret working of Karma should take place; that its deeper meaning should be practically illustrated (as also its effects) —on those self-opinionated volunteers and candidates for chelaship who will rush under the dark shadow of her wheels.

As against the above some will say—how then about her great clairvoyance, her chelaship, her selection among the many by the Masters?

Her clairvoyance is a fact, her selection and chelaship, another. However well fitted psychically and physiologically to answer such *selection*, unless possessed of spiritual, as well as of physical unselfishness a chela whether selected or not, must perish, as a chela in the long run. Self personality, vanity and conceit harboured in the *higher* principles are enormously more dangerous than the same defects inherent only in the lower physical nature of man. They are the breakers against which the cause of chelaship, in its probationary stage, is sure to be dashed to pieces unless the would-be disciple carries with him the white shield of perfect confidence and trust in those he would seek out through mount and vale to guide him safely toward the light of Knowledge. The world moves and lives under the shadow of the deadly upas-tree of Evil; yet its dripping is dangerous to, and can reach only those whose higher and middle natures are as much susceptible of infection as their lower one. Its venomous seed can germinate but in a willing, well prepared soil. Bring to your memory the cases of Fern, Moorad Ali and Bishen Lal, good friend, and remember what you have learnt. The mass of human sin and frailty is distributed throughout the life of man who is content to remain an average mortal. It is gathered in and centred, so to say, within one period of the life of a chela—the period of probation. That which is generally accumulating to find its legitimate issue only in the next rebirth of an ordinary man, is quickened and fanned into existence in the chela—especially in the presumptuous and selfish candidate who rushes in without having calculated his forces.

" One who dug so many and deep pit-falls for her friends and brothers fell into them herself "—said M. to H.P.B. on the night of the mutual revelations. I tried to, but could not save her. She had entered, or rather I should say—*forced* herself into the dangerous path, with a double purpose in view:

(1) To upset the whole structure in which *she* had no part, and thus obstruct the path to all others, if she did not find the system and Society at the level of *her* expectations; and

(2) To remain true and work out her chelaship and natural gifts, that are considerable indeed, only if those expectations were *all* answered. It is the intensity of that resolution that first attracted my attention. Led on gradually and gently into the right direction the acquisition of such an individuality would have been invaluable. But there are persons, who, without ever showing any external sign of selfishness, are intensely selfish in their inner spiritual aspirations. These will follow the path once chosen by them with their eyes closed to the interests of all but themselves, and see nothing outside the narrow pathway filled with their own personality. They are so intensely absorbed in the contemplation of their own supposed " righteousness " that nothing can ever appear right to them outside the focus of their own vision distorted by their self-complacent contemplation, and their judgment of the right and wrong. Alas, such an one is our new mutual friend L.C.H. " The right in thee is base, the wrong a curse," was said by our Lord Buddha for such as she; for *right* and *wrong* " cheat such as love themselves," and the others only in proportion to the benefits derived—though these benefits be purely spiritual. Aroused some 18 months ago to spasmodic, hysterical curiosity by the perusal of your *Occult World* and later on by that of *Esoteric Buddhism* to enthusiastic envy, she determined to " find out the truth " as she expressed it. She would either become a chela herself—first and foremost, *to write books*, thus eclipsing her " lay " rival, or upset the whole imposture in which she had no concern. She

decided to go to Europe and seek you out. Her surexcited fancy, putting a mask on every stray spook, created the " Student " and made him serve her purpose and desire. She believed in it sincerely. At this juncture foreseeing the new danger I interfered. Dharb: Nath was despatched and made to impress her thrice in my name. Her thoughts were for a certain period guided, her clairvoyance made to serve a purpose. Had her sincere aspirations conquered the intense personality of her lower self I would have given the T.S. an excellent help and worker. The poor woman is naturally good and moral; but that very purity is of so narrow a kind, of so *presbyterian* a character, if I may use the word, as to be unable to see itself reflected in any other but her own *Self*. She alone is good and pure. All others must and shall be suspected. A great boon was offered her—her wayward spirit would allow her to accept of none that was not shaped in accordance with her own model.

And now she will receive a letter from me which will contain my *ultimatum* and conditions. She will not accept them, but will complain bitterly to several among you, suggesting new hints and insinuations aganist one whom she professed to adore. Prepare. A plank of salvation is offered to her but there is very little hope that she will accept it. However, I will try once more; but I have no right to influence her either way. If you will accept my advice, abstain from any serious correspondence with her until some fresh development. Try to save " Man " by looking it over with Mohini, and by erasing from it the alleged inspirations and dictation by " Student." Having had also " an object and a purpose " in view, I had to leave her under her self-delusion that this new book was written with the view of " correcting the mistakes " of *Esoteric Buddhism* (—*of killing it*—was the true thought); and it was only on the eve of her departure that Upasika was ordered to see that Mohini should carefully expunge from it all the objectionable passages. During her stay in England Mrs. H. would have never permitted you to see her book before the final publication. But I would save five months labour of Mohini and will not permit it to remain unpublished.

Much as remains unexplained, the little you may have gathered from this letter will serve its purpose. It will start your thoughts in a new direction and will have unveiled another corner in the domain of psychological *Isis*.

If you would learn and acquire Occult Knowledge, you have, my friend, to remember that such tuition opens in the stream of chelaship many an unforeseen channel to whose current even a " lay " chela must perforce yield, or else strand upon the shoals; and knowing this to abstain for-ever judging on mere appearance. The ice is broken once more. Profit by it if you may.

K.H.

LETTER No. 65

Received London, Summer, 1885.

My friend:

You ask me " to throw light " upon the " new distressing event " arising from Mr. A. Gebhard's fanciful accusation? For the matter of that, dozens of events of a far more distressing character, each of them calculated to crush the hapless woman chosen as victim, are ripe and ready to burst over her head, wounding as badly the Society. Again, I should have imagined that, after my signal failure to satisfy your rigorous logicians in the " Billing—Massey " and " Kiddle—Light " incidents, my personal opinion and explanations were held in small honour in the West? You seem, however, to think with Whewell that " every failure is a step to success " and your confidence in me must alarm seriously your friends?

With your permission, I have left the explanation of the " distressing incident " to Mad. B. herself. As she wrote to you, however, only simple truth, there is very little chance for her of being believed, save perhaps, by her few immediate friends—if she has any left by the time this reaches you.

You must have understood by this time, my friend, that the centennial attempt made by us to open the eyes of the blind world —has nearly failed: in India—partially, in Europe—with a few exceptions—absolutely. There is but one chance of salvation *for those* who still believe: to rally together and face the storm bravely. Let the eyes of the most intellectual among the public be opened to the foul conspiracy aganist theosophy that is going on in the missionary circles and in one year's time you will have regained your footing. In India it is: " either Christ or the *Founders*(!!) Let us stone them to death! " They have nearly finished killing one—they are now attacking the other victim—Olcott. The padris are as busy as bees. The P.R.S. has given them an excellent opportunity of making capital of their ambassador. Mr. Hodgson fell quite easily a victim to false evidence; and the scientific *a priori* impossibility of such phenomena helping the reality of the phenomena he was sent to investigate and report upon is utterly and totally discredited. He may plead as an excuse the personal disappointment he felt, which made him turn in a fury against the alleged authors of the " gigantic swindle "; but there is no doubt that if the Society collapses it will be due to him. We may add the praiseworthy efforts of our mutual friend of Simla (A. O. Hume) who has not, however, resigned,—and those of Mr. Lane-Fox. What Society could withstand in its integrality the effects of two such tongues as those of Messrs. H.

and L.F.! While the former, taking into his confidence every theosophist of note, assures him that since the beginning of the Society *not one of the letters* alleged to have come from the *Masters* was *genuine*, Mr. L. Fox goes about preaching that he is only carrying out the wishes of the Master (M.) in acquainting the theosophists with all the defects of the T.S. and the mistakes of its Founders whose Karma it is *to betray the* sacred trust they had received from their Gurus.

After this you will, perhaps, blame less our chelas for detesting the Europeans at H.Q., and saying that it is *they* who have ruined the Society.

Thus, my friend, there comes a forcible end to the projected occult instructions. Everything was settled and prepared. The secret Committee, appointed to receive our letters and teachings and to convey them to the Oriental group, was ready, when a few Europeans—for reasons I prefer not mentioning—took upon themselves the authority of reversing the decision of the whole Council. They declined (though the reason they gave was another one)—to receive our instructions through Subba Row and Damodar, the latter of whom is hated by Messrs. L. Fox and Hartmann. Subba R. resigned and Damodar went to Tibet. Are our Hindus to be blamed for this?

And now Hume and Hodgson have goaded Subba Row to fury by telling him, that as a friend and fellow occultist of Madam B.'s he was suspected by the Government of being also *a spy*. It is the history of the " Count St. Germain " and Cagliostro told over again. But I may tell you, who have ever been faithful and true to *me* the fruits of your devotion shall not be allowed to decay and crumble down into dust from the tree of action. And now, may I not say a few words that may prove useful?

It is an old truism that none of you have ever formed an accurate idea of either the " Masters " or the laws of Occultism they are guided by. For instance, I, because I have received a bit of Western education—must needs be fancied as the type of a " gentleman " who strictly conforms his action to the laws of *etiquette*, and regulates his intercourse with Europeans after the regulations of *your* world and Society! Nothing could be more erroneous: the absurd picture of an Indo-Tibetan ascetic playing at Sir C. Grandison need hardly be noticed. Nevertheless, having failed to answer to the said description, I was hung in effigy, and publicly branded and degraded, as Mad. B. would say. What a poor parody! When shall you realize that I am nothing of the kind? That if, to a certain extent, I may be familiar with your (to me) peculiar notions about the propriety of this thing or another, and the obligations of a *Western* gentleman, so are you, to a degree acquainted with the manners and customs of China and Tibet.

For all that, as you would decline to conform yourself to our habits and live according to our customs—so do I, preferring our modes of life to yours, and our ideas to those of the West. I am accused of "*plagiarism.*" We, of Tibet and China, know not what you mean by the word. I do, but this is no reason, perhaps, why I should accept *your* literary laws. Any writer has the privilege of taking out whole sentences from the dictionary of *Pai-Wouen-Yen-Ju* the greatest in the world, full of quotations from every known writer, and containing all the phrases ever used—and to frame them to express his thought. This does not apply to the Kiddle case which happened just as I told you. But you may find, perchance throughout my letters twenty detached sentences which may have been already used in books or MSS. When you write upon some subject you surround yourself with books of references etc.: when we write upon something the Western opinion about which is unknown to us, we surround ourselves with hundreds of paras: upon this particular topic from dozens of different works—impressed upon the Akasa. What wonder then, that not only a chela entrusted with the work and innocent of any knowledge of the meaning of plagiarism, but even myself—should use occasionally a whole sentence already existent, applying it only to another—our own idea? I have told you of this before and it is no fault of mine if your friends and enemies will not remain satisfied with the explanation. When I shall undertake to write an original prize-essay I may be more careful. For the *Kiddle* business it is your own fault. Why have you printed the *Occult World* before sending it to me for revision? I would have never allowed the passage to pass; nor the " Lal Sing " either foolishly invented as half a *nom de plume* by Djual K. and carelessly allowed by me to take root without thinking of the consequences. *We are not infalliable, all-foreseeing " Mahatmas " at every hour of the day*, good friend: none of you have even learned to remember so much. And now for Occultism.

We were expected to allow the Occult forces to be treated in the same manner as their rind—physical forces in nature. We are taken to task for not giving out to every man of learning who had joined the T.S. the fruits of the researches of generations of occultists who had all devoted their lives to it, and who had as often lost them in the great struggle of wrenching her secrets from the heart of Nature. Unless we did that—Occultism could not be recognised: it has to remain within the limbo of magic and superstition, spiritualism—in the sight of some—*fraud* in the opinion of others. Who thought for one instant that an occult law revealed ceased to be occult to become public property, unless it was given to *an Occultist who dies before he betrays the secret*?

What grumblings, what criticism on *Devachan* and kindred subjects for their incompleteness and many a seeming contradiction! Oh blind fools! They forget—or never knew that he who holds the keys to the secrets of *Death* is possessed of the keys of *Life*. That could everyone become a *creative God* in this race, acquiring knowledge so easily that there would be no necessity for a 6th and 7th races? And that we, we should have perverted the programme of BEING, garbled the accounts in the Book of Life, defeated in a word the ETERNAL WILL!

My friend, I have little if anything more to say. I regret deeply my inability to satisfy the honest, sincere aspirations of a few chosen ones among your group—not at least, for the present. Could but your L.L. understand, or so much as suspect, that the present crisis that is shaking the T.S. to its foundations is a question of perdition or salvation to thousands; a question of the progress of the human race or its retrogression, of its glory or dishonour, and for the majority of this race—of *being or not being*, of annihilation, in fact—perchance many of you would look into the very root of evil, and instead of being guided by false appearances and scientific decisions, you would set to work and save the situation by disclosing the dishonourable doings of your missionary world.

Meanwhile—accept my best wishes.

K.H.

I believe I [had] better tell you once more what I would have you remember always. I should be glad if every question could be answered as easily as your query about the " distressing event." Why is it that doubts and foul suspicions seem to beset every aspirant for chelaship? My friend, in the Masonic Lodges of old times the neophyte was subjected to a series of frightful tests of his constancy, courage and presence of mind. By psychological impressions supplemented by machinery and chemicals, he was made to believe himself falling down precipices, crushed by rocks, walking spider-web bridges in mid-air, passing through fire, drowned in water and attacked by wild beasts. This was a reminiscence of and a programme borrowed from the Egyptian Mysteries. The West having lost the secrets of the East, had, as I say, to resort to artifice. But in these days the vulgarization of science has rendered such trifling tests obsolete. The aspirant is now assailed entirely on the psychological side of his nature. His course of testing—in Europe and India—is that of Raj-yog and its result is—as frequently explained—to develop every germ good and bad in him in his temperament. The rule is inflexible, and not one escapes whether he but writes to us a letter, or in the privacy of his own heart's thought formulates a strong desire for occult communication and knowledge. As the shower cannot fructify the rock, so the occult teaching has no effect upon the unreceptive mind; and as the water develops the heat of caustic lime so does the teaching bring into fierce action every unsuspected potentiality latent in him.

Few Europeans have stood *this test*. Suspicion, followed by self-woven conviction of fraud seems to have become the order of the day. I tell you *with a very few exceptions*—we have failed in Europe. Henceforth, the policy of absolute neutrality of the T.S. in occult teachings and phenomena will be rigidly enforced: whatever is imparted will be to individual members from individuals. For inst: if Mad. B. finds the necessary strength to live (and this depends entirely on her *will* and its powers of exertion) and is willing under the guidance of her guru, or even myself, to serve us as an amanuensis for you, (Sinnett, not for the group) she can, if she likes, send you weekly or monthly instructions. Mohini could do the same—but under the pledge that neither our names, nor that of the sender will be ever made public; nor shall the T.S. be made responsible for these teachings. If the Oriental group survives, something could be yet done for it. But never, henceforth, shall the Society in India be allowed to be compromised again by phenomena that are denounced wholesale as fraud. The good ship is sinking, friend, because its precious cargo has been offered to the public at large; because some of its contents have been desecrated by profane handling, and its gold—received as brass. Henceforth, I say, no such profane eye will see its treasures, and its outer decks and rigging must be cleansed of the impurity and dross that was accumulated on them by the indiscretion of its own members. Try to remedy the evil done. Every step made by one in our direction will force us to make one toward him. But it is not by going to Ladakh that one shall find us, as Mr. Lane-Fox imagines.

Once more, accept my blessing and parting greeting *if* they have to be my last.

K.H.

LETTER No. 66

Received London, Oct. 10th, 1884.

For reasons perfectly valid though not necessary for me to enter into in detail, I could neither answer your letter at Elberfeld, nor transmit it to you through L. C. H. Since it has become impossible to utilize the main channel—H.P.B. thro' which I have hitherto reached you, because of your personal and mutual relations with her I employed the common post. Even this required more expenditure of power from a friend, than you can imagine.

It would not be the part of a friend to withhold the truth when the speaking of it can do good, so I must tell you that you ought to put a close watch upon yourself, if you would not put an end for ever to my letters. Insensibly to yourself you are encouraging a tendency to dogmatism and unjust misconception of persons and motives. I am well aware of your ideas upon that which you call the " goody goody " absurdity; and I feel as painfully confident that since in your world no one is allowed to moralize the other and that you are very likely to resent it, these words are probably written in vain. But I also know your sincere desire that our correspondence should not be broken; and knowing this, I point out to your notice that which is certain to have that result.

Beware then, of an uncharitable spirit, for it will rise up like a hungry wolf in your path, and devour the better qualities of your nature which have been springing into life. Broaden instead of narrowing your sympathies; try to identify yourself with your fellows, rather than to contract your circle of affinity. However caused—whether by faults at Adyar, or Allahabad, or by my negligence, or H.P.B.'s viciousness—a crisis is here, and it is a time for the utmost practicable expansion of your moral power. It is not the moment for reproaches or vindictive recriminations, but for united struggle. Whomsoever has sown the seeds of the present tempest, the whirlwind is strong, the whole Society is reaping it and it is rather fanned than weakened from Shigatse. You laugh at *probations*—the word seems ridiculous as applied to you? You forget that he who approaches our precincts even in thought, is drawn into the vortex of probation. At any rate your temple totters, and unless you put your strong shoulders against its wall you may share the fate of Samson. Pride and " dignified contempt " will not help you in the present difficulties. There is such a thing—when understood allegorically—as treasures guarded by faithful gnomes and fiends. The treasure is our occult knowledge that many of you are after—you foremost of all; and it may not be H.P.B. or Olcott or anyone else individually who has awakened the guardians thereof, but yourself, more than they and the Society collectively. Such books as the *Occult World* and *Esoteric Buddhism* do not pass unnoticed under the eyes of those faithful guardians, and it is absolutely necessary that those who would have that knowledge should be *thoroughly* tried and tested. Infer from this what you will; but remember that my Brother and I are the only among the Brotherhood who have at heart the dissemination (to a certain limit) of our doctrines, and H.P.B. was hitherto our sole machinery, our most docile agent. Granting that she is all you describe her—and I have already told you that the ricketty old body becomes sometimes positively dangerous—still it does not excuse in you the smallest relaxation of effort to save the situation and push on the work (and especially protect our correspondence) all the faster. Deem it, what it is, a positive advantage to the rest of you that she should have been what she is, since it has thrown upon you the greater stimulus to accomplish in spite of the difficulties you believe she has created. I do not say we should have preferred her had a more tractable agent been available; still, so far as yourselves are concerned it has been an advantage, yet you have alienated her for a long time if not for ever and thereby thrown tremendous difficulties in my way. Remember what I said to you some two years ago, " were H.P.B. to die before we found a substitute," the powers through which we work in our communications with the outside world may permit the transimssion of two or three letters more, then it would die out and you would have no more letters from me. Well—she is virtually dead; and it is yourself—pardon me this one more truth—who have killed the rude but faithful agent, one moreover who was really devoted to you personally. Let us drop the subject if it is distasteful to you. I have done my best to stop the evil but I have neither jurisdiction or control over her, nor shall I have any better chance with Mrs. H. She is a magnificent subject naturally but so distrustful of herself and others, so apt to take the real for hallucination and *vice versa* that it will require a long time before she becomes thoroughly controllable even by herself. She is far, far from being ready; moreover she understands neither herself nor us. Verily *our* ways are not *your* ways, hence there remains but little hope for us in the West.

Do not, I pray you, attribute the above to any influence from H.P.B. She has doubtless complained bitterly to her Master and says so openly, but this does not alter his opinion nor affect my own attitude towards you in the least. Not alone we two, but even she knows how important to the Society's welfare are your services, and no personal grievances of hers would be allowed to stand in the way of your receiving strict justice; or to prevent our according it to her either. Her Master and I directed her to do and say *all that she did* concerning Mrs. H. Any unpleasantness resulting, was due to the execution of her orders. We had found Mrs. H. in America, we impressed her to prepare for the writing of the book she has produced with the aid of Mohini. Had she consented to stop at Paris, as requested, a few days longer and come over to England with H.P.B. the later complication could have been averted. The effect of her coming to your house has been described to you by her before; and in resenting what Mohini and H.P.B. were saying to you and Mrs. H. you have been simply resenting our *personal* wishes. You will resent my words even now when I tell you that you have been—unconsciously, I agree —in my way, in her development. Yet you would have been the first one to profit thereby. But not understanding our ways and the occult methods you insisted upon knowing the cause and reason for everything done—especially things that did not suit you. You even demanded that the reason why you have been asked to come to Elberfeld should be thoroughly explained to you. This is unreasonable—from the occult point of view, good friend. You either trust in me, or do not. And I must frankly tell you that my friendly regard suffered a shock from the hearing of your " ultimatum " which may be condensed thus:—" Either Mrs. H., passes a week or so at our house, or I (you) leave the L.L. to get on as best it can." It almost meant this; " Masters " or no Masters to the contrary notwithstanding, I must and shall show the L.L. that anything they may have heard about this affair was false, and that the " Masters " would never consent to any action hurtful to my pride: that must be protected in any event." My friend, this is treading upon dangerous ground. In our mountains here, the Dugpas lay at dangerous points, in paths frequented by our Chelas, bits of old rag, and other articles best calculated to attract the attention of the unwary, which have been impregnated with their evil magnetism. If one be stepped upon a tremendous psychic shock may be communicated to the wayfarer, so that he may lose his footing and fall down the precipice before he can recover himself. Friend, beware of Pride and Egoism, two of the worst snares for the feet of him who aspires to climb the high paths of Knowledge and Spirituality. You have opened a joint of your armour for the Dugpas—do not complain if they have found it out and wounded you there. Mrs. H. did not really want to go to your house, for, as she said to you very truthfully, I had told her not to do so for reasons that you must know yourself by this time; you also should have known, that if we were worth anything in our individuality, and not mere powerless puppets, we were not to be influenced by H.P.B., nor driven by threats to do anything contrary to our light and the necessities of Karma. I am sorry that you did not recall these facts before speaking, as this makes my position still more embarrassing before my chief, who, of course has had the " ultimatum " put on record. You deny having ever applied to be accepted as a chela: Ah! my friend, with such feelings smouldering in your heart, you could not be even a " lay chela." But once more I say let us drop the subject. Words will not obliterate deeds, and what is done is done. My brother M. who has more authority than I, has just written the promised letter to the " Inner Circle." Your " honour," good friend, is saved—at what price—read and you shall see.

You do not find certain recent letters and notes of mine—including the one to the treasurer of the L.L., " philosophical " and in my usual style. It could scarcely be helped: I wrote but on the business of the moment—as I am doing now—and had no time for philosophy. With the L.L. and most of the other Western Branches of the T.S. in a deplorable state, philosophy may be invoked to restrain one's impatience, but the chief thing called for at present, is some practicable scheme for dealing with the situation. Some, most unjustly, try to make H.S.O. and H.P.B., solely responsible for the state of things. Those two are, say, far from perfect—in some respects, quite the opposite. But they have that in them (pardon the eternal repetition but it is being as constantly overlooked) which we have but too rarely found elsewhere —UNSELFISHNESS, and an eager readiness for self-sacrifice for the good of others; what a " multitude of sins " does not this cover! It is but a truism, yet I say it, that in adversity alone can we discover the real man. It is a true manhood when one boldly accepts one's share of the collective Karma of the group one works with, and does not permit oneself to be embittered, and to see others in blacker colours than reality, or to throw all blame upon some one " black sheep," a victim, specially selected. Such a true man as that we will ever protect and, despite his shortcomings, assist to develop the good he has in him. Such an one is sublimely *unselfish*; he sinks his personality in his cause, and takes no heed of discomforts or personal obloquy unjustly fastened upon him.

I have done, my good friend, and have nothing more to say. You have too much intelligence not to see clearly, as the Americans would say—the *fix* I am in, and that I, personally can do very little. The present situation, as you will find from M's letter has been gradually created by all of you as much as by the wretched " Founders." Yet without at least one of them we can hardly do, for several years more to come. You have treated the old body too cruelly and it now has its day. You will never agree in this fully with me—but it is *fact*, nevertheless. All I can do for you personally—I will do it, unless you make the situation still worse by not changing your policy. One who would have higher instruction given to him has to be a *true* theosophist in heart and soul, not merely in appearance.

Meanwhile, receive my poor blessings.

K.H.

LETTER No. 67

Written to Colonel Olcott.

You have been ordered home for a rest that you need—so you should decline any further healings until you hear from M. The Maha-Chohan will intimate when you are to go to the Punjab. As the English mail goes to-morrow, you might do well to give

Mr. Sinnett a friendly caution against being surprised if his paper project should have checks upon checks. The state of India is just now almost comparable to a great body of dry matter in which sparks are smouldering. Agitators of both races have been and are doing their best to stir up a great flame. In the mad fanaticism of the hour there is hardly patience enough to think soberly upon any matter, least of all one that appeals like this to conservative men. Capitalists are more ready—like Holkar—to hoard away their rupees than put them into share companies. So—" miracles " being barred from the first as you and Mr. Sinnett know—I see delays, disappointments, trials of patience, but—(as yet) no failure. The lamentable issue of Bishenlal's rapid scramble up the Himalayas as would-be chela has sadly complicated matters. And your eminent Simla correspondent has made matters worse. Tho' unaware of it he has helped precipitate Bishenlal's insanity and (here, consciously) is plotting and scheming in many ways to make us all into a holocaust from out whose vapours may loom the giant spectre of the Jakko. Already he tells you that Sinnett is a credulous imbecile to be led by the nose (pardon, my worthy friend, the bad taste which compelled me to duplicate for my " ward " A. P. Sinnett that last long letter of Mr. H. to yourself which you have at the bottom of your dispatch box and *did not* intend H.P.B. to see in full). I had it neatly copied and for your fiery colleague he has had a deadly mine long prepared. Mr. Sinnett is now able to verify my old warning that he meant to set all your friends in London against the Society. The turn of the Kingsford-Maitland party has come. The diabolical malice which breathes thro' his present letter comes straight from the *Dugpas* who provoke his vanity and blind his reason. When you open M.'s letter of 1881 you will find the key to many mysteries—this included. Intuitive as you naturally are—*chelaship* is yet almost a complete puzzle for you as for my friend Sinnett and the others they have scarcely an inkling of it yet. Why must I even now—(to put your thoughts in the right channel) remind you of the three cases of *insanity* within seven months among " lay chelas," not to mention one's turning a thief? Mr. Sinnett may consider himself lucky that his *lay chelaship* is in " fragments " only, and that I have so uniformly discouraged his desires for a closer relationship as an *accepted* chela. Few men know their inherent capacities—only the ordeal of crude chelaship develops them. (Remember these words: they have a deep meaning.)

M. sends you thro' me these vases as a home greeting.

You had better say plainly to Mr. Sinnett that his quondam friend of Simla has—no matter under what influence—distinctly injured the newspaper project not only with the Maharajah of

Cashmere but with many more in India. All he hints at in his letter to you and *more* he has done or is preparing to do.

This is "a K.H. letter" and you may say to Mr. S. from—

K.H.

LETTER No. 68

I have just taken your note from where it was placed by her as, although I might take cognisance of its contents otherwise, you will prefer that the paper itself should pass into my own hand.— Does it seem to you a small thing that the past year has been spent only in your " family duties "? Nay, but what better cause for reward, what better discipline, than the daily and hourly performance of duty? Believe me my " pupil," the man or woman who is placed by Karma in the midst of small plain duties and sacrifices and loving-kindness, will through these faithfully fulfilled rise to the larger measure of Duty, Sacrifice and Charity to all Humanity—what better path towards the enlightenment you are striving after than the daily conquest of Self, the perseverance in spite of want of visible psychic progress, the bearing of ill-fortune with that serene fortitude which turns it to spiritual advantage— since good and evil are not to be measured by events on the lower or physical plane.—Be not discouraged that your practice falls below your aspirations, yet be not content with *admitting* this, since you clearly recognise that your tendency is too often towards mental and moral indolence, rather inclining to drift with the currents of life, than to steer a direct course of your own. Your spiritual progress is far greater than you know or can realize, and you do well to believe that such development is *in itself* more important than its realization by your physical plane consciousness. I will not now enter into other subjects since this is but a line of sympathetic recognition of your efforts, and of earnest encouragement to hold a calm and brave spirit toward outward events in the present, and a hopeful spirit for the future on *all* planes— truly yours, K.H.

LETTER No. 69

I am sincerely pleased, my " pupil " that you should write to me as agreed—whether you have—or have not—any special question to put to me. It is impossible under your present health conditions that you should bring back to your physical brain the consciousness of higher planes of existence, yet remember, that the sense of magnetic refreshment is no true measure of spiritual benefit, and you may even attain greater spiritual progress whilst your psychic development appears to stand still.

Now to answer your questions.

(1) In esoteric teachings " Brahma," " Pitri," and " Deva " lokas, are states of consciousness belonging to the various ethereal hierarchies or classes of Dhyanis and Pitris (the " creators " and " ancestors " of Humanity) and of Devas—some far higher than man (spiritually), some—among the Deva classes—far behind on the descending arc of evolution, and only destined to reach the human stage in a future Manvantara. Exoterically these lokas represent Nirvana, Devachan and the Astral world. The meaning of the terms Devachan and Deva-loka, is identical; " *chan* " and "*loka*" equally signifying *place* or *abode*. "Deva" is a word too indiscriminately used in Eastern writings, and is at times merely a blind.

(2) You will be right in referring the " Real Knowledge " and " True Cause " of the verse quoted to the highest plane of spiritual enlightenment; the " greater darkness " into which the perfected " Siddha " is finally merged thereby, is that *Absolute Darkness* which is *Absolute Light*. The Real Knowledge here spoken of is not a mental but a spiritual state, implying full union between the Knower and the Known.

I hope that these brief replies may throw all the light you needed upon these points.

With sincere good-will,

Yours truly, K.H.

LETTER No. 70

You will have learned ere now, my friend, that I was not deaf to your appeal to me, altho' I was unable to answer it as you—and I too—could have wished, by lifting for a moment the ever-thinning veil between us—" When? " do you ask me? I can but reply " not yet." Your probation is not ended, patience a little longer. Meanwhile you know the path to travel, it lies plainly before you for the present, tho' the choice of an easier if longer way may await you in the distant future.

Farewell my Brother.

Ever yours in sympathy, K.H.

LETTER No. 71

Very kind Sinnett Sahib—many thanks and salaams for the tobacco-machine. Our frenchified and pelingized Pandit tells me the little short thing has to be *coolooted*—whatever he may mean by this—and so I will proceed to do so. The pipe is short and my nose long, so we will agree very well toge[ther] I hope. Thanks— many thanks.

The situation is more serious than you may imagine and we will want our best forces and hands to work at pushing away bad luck. But our Chohan willing and you helping we will scramble out somehow or another. There are clouds which are below your horizon and K.H. is right—the storm is threatening. Could you but go to Bombay to the Anniversary you would confer upon K.H. and myself a great obligation, a lasting one—but that you know best. This meeting will be either the triumph or the downfall of the Society and a—gulf. You are wrong too about the Peling Sahib—he is as dangerous as a friend as an enemy, very very bad as both—I know him best. Anyhow you Sinnett Sahib reconciled me to a good many things; you are true and true I will be.

Yours always   M.

LETTER No. 72

My good Brother—the little Doctor and the chela Mohini will explain to you the object of their visit and a *serious conference* which I believe necessary. The objections of last year are creeping out also; you have a letter from me in which I explain *why* we never *guide* our chelas (the most advanced even); nor do we forewarn them, leaving the effects produced by causes of their own creation to teach them better experience. Please bear in mind that particular letter. Before the cycle ends every misconception ought to be swept away. I trust in and rely upon you to clear them entirely in the minds of the Prayag Fellows. They are a troublesome lot—especially Adityaram, who influences the whole group. But what they say of last night is right. You were a little bit too much carried away with your enthusiasm for occultism and mixed it up very imprudently with Universal Brotherhood. They will explain to you all.

Yours   K.H.

LETTER No. 73

Mr. Sinnet—you will receive a long letter—posted Sunday at Bombay—from the Brahmin boy. Koot-hoomi went to see him (as he is his *chela*) before going into " Tong-pa-ngi " [1]—the state in which he now is—and left with him certain orders. The boy has a little bungled up the message so be very careful before you show it to Mr. Hume lest he should again misunderstand my Brother's real meaning. I will *not* stand any more nonsense, or bad feeling against him, but retire at once.

We do the best we can.   M.

[1] Tibetan. The ' Void '.—EDS.

LETTER No. 74

If you are so anxious to find out the particular spot where I erased and precipitated instead another sentence last night at post-office I can satisfy your curiosity, Mr. Sinnett, " but that it was the *Chohan's* KNOWLEDGE that neither you nor anyone cared for the real object of the Society, nor had any respect for the BROTHERHOOD but only a personal feeling for a few of the Brothers. So you cared only for K.H. *personally* and *phenomena*; Mr. Hume to get at the secrets of their philosophy and to assure himself that the Tibetan Mahatmas—the Lhas—if at all existing outside of Mme. B.'s imagination—were connected any way with *certain adepts* he had in his mind."

All this is *what K.H. said*, what I had to write and precipitate *instead of that which stood then* written by the boy in a phraseology which would have called out from Mr. Hume a whole torrent of fine words and the word " *ignorance* " applied to my Brother. I would not have even the desert wind listen to a word said at low breath against him who now sleeps. Such is the cause of the *tamasha* produced by me and for no other cause.

Yours

M.

LETTER No. 75

The right is on *her* side. Your accusations are extremely unjust, and coming from *you*—pain me the more. If after this distinct statement you still maintain the same attitude—I shall have to express my deep regret at this new failure of ours—and wish you with all my heart better success with more worthy teachers. She certainly lacks charity, but indeed, you lack—discrimination.

Regretfully yours

K.H.

LETTER No. 76 [1]

X. . . . *Chela* training. Poor Subba Row is " in a fix "—that is why he does not answer you. On one hand he has the indomitable H.P.B. who plagues Morya's life to *reward* you, and M. himself who would if he could gratify your aspirations; on the other he encounters the unpassable Chinese wall of rules and *Law*. Believe me, good friend, learn what you can under the

---

[1] The first part of this letter will be found on p. 453 at the end of a letter of Subba Row to H.P.B. which was written on thin rice paper, whereas the continuation is upon rough parchment-like paper entirely dissimilar.—ED.

circumstances—*viz.*—the *philosophy* of the phenomena and our doctrines on Cosmogony, inner man, etc. This Subba Row will help you to learn, though his terms—he being an initiated Brahmin and holding to the *Brahmanical* esoteric teaching—will be different from those of the "Arhat Buddhist" terminology. But essentially both are the same—*identical* in fact. My heart melts when I read Mr. Hume's sincere noble letter—especially what I perceive between the lines. Yes; to one from his standpoint our policy must seem selfish and *cruel*. I wish I were the Master! In five or six years I hope to become my own "guide" and things will have somewhat to change, then. But even Cæsar in irons cannot shuffle off the irons and transfer them to Hippo or Thraso the turnkey. Let us wait. I cannot think of Mr. Hume without remembering each time an allegory of my own country: the genius of Pride watching over a treasure, an inexhaustible wealth of every human virtue, the divine gift of Brahma to man. The Genius has fallen asleep over its treasure now, and one by one the virtues are peeping out. . . . Will he awake before they are all freed from their life long bonds? That is the question—

K.H.

SECTION IV

THE "PHŒNIX" VENTURE AND THE CONDITION OF INDIA

LETTER No. 77

Received Madras, March, 1883.

Pray, convey to Col. Gordon the expression of my sympathy and friendly esteem. He is indeed a loyal friend and trustworthy ally. Tell him that with every allowance for the motives given and his own quiet modesty I yet believe he may do much good in his own unassuming way. A Howrah Branch is really needed and he alone can create the nucleus. Why not try? He cares not for the Service and is ready at any moment to throw it up. But this is unnecessary so long as it lasts and gives him a strength and authority with some native members which otherwise he would not have. At any rate then he is going to be taken to Simla and will have plenty of " nothing-to-do " time. Why not use his opportunities for putting the *Eclectic* and *Himalayan* in order—of course in his official capacity, as a member of Council and Vice-President of the *Eclectic*. I will have Olcott send him an official paper to that effect and write instructions for him myself. I am anxious to remove the *Anglo-Indian* " Eclectic " to Calcutta, and have its Headquarters (though it be nominal for a while) announced through the journal hitherto as established in the capital—the native members of the Eclectic incorporated in the *Himalayan* and a para: inserted to notify all those who would join the Anglo-Indian Branch that in your absence they would have to address themselves to Col. W. Gordon, Acting President in your place. Some are born for diplomacy and intrigue: I rather think that it is not my particular province. Withal, I believe the arrangement calculated to impede the disastrous effects of Mr. Hume's intrigue and his endeavours to have the Society (Eclectic) dead and buried, thus showing those concerned with it, that he was its Creator and Preserver, and that his retirement was its death-knell. Thanks for Col. G.'s letter.

The 30th is as good as any other day after the 27th. No; a Branch at Madras is not absolutely necessary from the very starting. But it does stand to reason that if it is Madras that is

to furnish the largest share of the funds that it would also have
the preference after Calcutta. So long as the money is not in,
it is useless to fix any dates. Our paper once established I will
never concern myself any more with any worldly enterprise. Yes,
I have worry and annoyance indeed; but then it had to be expected, and no fish undertaking a ramble on the river's bank and
outside its own element need complain of catching lumbago.
We are near the end now, one way or the other, and once I take
my leap back into the crystal wave—few will ever have a chance
of seeing me peeping out again. Mankind are not always what
they seem and I have lost much of my optimism in the late affray.
Mankind was somewhere named the poetry of creation and woman
the poetry of earth. When she is not an angel she must be a
fury. It is in the latter capacity that I have ever met her on my
way when Rajahs and Zemindars were quite ready to disburse
the necessary funds. Well, the affray is still raging and we may
yet win brilliantly the day.

Yours truly,

K. H.

LETTER No. 78

My dear friend, do not accuse me—after having started it myself
—of indifference to, or oblivion of, our little speculation. The
Chohan is not to be consulted every day on such "worldly"
matters, and that is my excuse for the unavoidable delay.

And now, I am permitted by my venerated Chief to convey to
you a memorandum of His views and ideas upon the fortune and
destinies of a certain paper upon which his *foresight* was asked by
your humble friend and his servant. Putting them into business
shape I have noted his views as follows.

I.   The establishment of a new journal of the kind described
is desirable, and very feasible—with proper effort.

II.   That effort must be made by your friends in the world,
and every Hindu theosophist who has the good of his country at
heart, and not very afraid to spend energy and his time. It has
to be made by *outsiders*—i.e. those who do not belong to our Order
irretrievably; as for ourselves—

III.   We can direct and guide their efforts and the movement,
in general. Tho' separated from your world of action we are not
yet entirely severed from it so long as the Theosophical Society
exists. Hence, while we cannot inaugurate it publicly and to the
knowledge of all theosophists and those concerned, we may, and
will so far as practicable, aid the enterprise. In fact, we have
begun already to do so. Moreover, we are permitted to reward
those who will have helped the most effectually to realize this

grand idea (which promises in the end to change the destiny of a whole nation, if conducted by one like yourself).

IV.   In proposing to capitalists, especially to natives, the risk (as they are likely to think) of so large a sum, special inducements should be held out to them.   Therefore, we are of opinion that you should ask no more compensation than you now receive, until your exertions have made the journal a decided success—something that *must* and *shall* happen, if I am good for anything.   For a certain time, then, it is desirable that the affair should be stripped in the eyes of the future shareholders of every objectionable feature. Capital may now be invested in various ways so as to secure moderate interest with little or no risk.   But for the ordinary speculator, there is much risk in founding a new journal of high cost, which is to favour the side of just native interests in those too frequent cases of injustice (which can hardly be proven to you under ordinary circumstances, but that will)—which always occur when a country is held by foreign conquerors.   Cases which, as regards India, tend to multiply with the gradual entrance of officials of a lower social origin under the competitive system of appointment; and increased friction due to a selfish resentment of the admission of natives to Civil Service.   To your capitalists, therefore, you should hold out the inducement that you will unselfishly labour for the same emolument as at your disposal now—to make their venture more than ordinarily profitable, and only claim a share of profits—as delineated by yourself with a slight change—when that point will be reached.   I am ready to offer myself as a guarantee that it speedily will.

V.   My suggestion is therefore, agreeable with the Chohan's opinion, that you should offer to accept the consolidated monthly pay you mention, (with the usual and necessary personal expenses of travel when on business for the journal) until the capital shall be earning 8 per cent.   Of the profits between 8 and 12 per cent you should have one quarter share.   Of all above 12 per cent., one half share.

VI.   You should have certainly entire control over the journal; with some reassuring provisos that that power should not be transferable to a successor without the consent of a majority of the capital represented in the ownership; and that it should cease when it became apparent that the journal was being used against the interests to promote which it was founded.   Without some such reservation, my venerable Chohan, and *we* too, think that deep-seated prejudices and suspicions would cause native capitalists —especially *the* rajahs—to hesitate—not for fear to make the large risks of this undertaking, but owing to doubts as to its success. The whole Anglo-European community now suffers in native opinion for the commercial sins of dishonest houses who have heretofore broken faith with the capitalists; and there are several Rajahs, who now follow in pensive gloom the far distant form of Sir Ashley Eden, who walks off with one pocket full of never fulfilled promises and the other loaded with the remembrance of several lakhs of rupees borrowed from and never returned to his friends—the rajahs. At the same time, these provisos should be so framed *as to protect your interrerests as well.* Some offer on your part, spontaneous of course, inviting the occasional inspection of books and papers at reasonable times for the verification of accounts rendered, should be given, since your personal integrity cannot be guaranteed for all your servants. But this is not to diminish your authority over the management of the journal in all departments.

VII. It is better that the whole capital should be paid in before the journal is begun, as it is always unpleasant and troublesome to call in assessments on top of original losses. But it should be provided that so much as was not immediately needed should be kept at interest; and that a Sinking Fund should be created out of the income of the journal, to provide for any unforeseen exigency. The surplus capital as well as earnings, to be distributed from time to time.

VIII. The usual contracts and co-partnership papers might be executed from the beginning, but deposited in confidential hands mutually agreeable and their nature kept secret until the arrival of a certain specified contingency. This would show good faith on both sides and *inspire confidence.*

IX. No remark upon the other features of your programme seems called for. Therefore—to something else now.

Two or three nights ago, the following conversation, or rather, profession of independent opinion was listened to by myself, and approved, as far as worldly reasoning goes. Olcott was talking with several influential theosophists concerned with, and interested in our future journalistic operations. Your colleague and brother, the good and sincere Norendro Babu of the *Mirror* said wise words to this effect:

" Of the several princes, whom Mr. Sinnett's friends have in view in India, probably not one would be influenced to subscribe the capital from patriotic motives. The Nizam wants the Berars, and is hoping that England will be as generous to him as she is to Cetewayo. Holkar wants cent per cent or as nearly that as possible. Kashmir fears the *G. and M. Gazette* and the cupidity that has long yearned to annex his rich province (to this, my conservative and patriotic friend A.P.S. is sure to demur); Benares is orthodox and would spend freely to abolish *cow-* (not *ox-*) killing. Baroda is a boy, with a colt's restiveness and no clear idea, as yet, about life. With proper agents and discreet negotiations the 5 lakhs *may* (?) be raised, but it cannot be said how soon; (right, there, especially he who has little if any faith in *our* helping them).

H.P.B. forwarded me since then your letter. In case my advice is asked I should counsel—(1) the keeping of your Proprietors in suspense as to your actual chances, so as to give you the option of doing what may develop into the best thing. I, for one, confess to you now that I have two strings to my bow. When the new capital is raised, in case even it is so very soon—it will make no very great difference whether your paper be started next cold weather or the following so long as *you* are at the head of the *Pioneer*. You would be at its helm until November and meanwhile your friends would have time to manage their difficult and delicate negotiations, and provisions might be made for you to receive an equitable proportion of salary while perfecting your arrangements at home, to begin in the cold weather of 1884. On the other hand, if the capital could be secured shortly you could put it at interest, and draw no pay until you leave the *Pioneer*. Of course, without forcing the events—in violation of our laws, save the Chohan's permission—all this is an uncertainty and a dilemma in some sort. Yet I *can* help your friends, and they will find it out very quick no sooner they begin. No: I would *not* promise, if I were you, not to start another paper; for, to begin with, you do not know what might turn up; and then it is always useful to have a sword of Damocles hanging over such heads as Rattigan's and Walker's. *They are frightened to death*—I tell you. They might even make it pleasant and profitable to you to continue directing the *Pioneer*, *with increased editorial powers and salary*, for this they could better afford than to have you compete with them with 5 lakhs at your back. As to the advisability of such a thing—time will show. As advised at present I still hold to the original programme. You must be complete and sole master of a paper devoted to the interests of my benighted countrymen. The " Indo-British nation " is the pulse I go by. More—anon.

I enclose a letter kindly lent to me—without his knowledge tho'—by the Colonel. Our friend foams with rage in the most *unyogi* like manner, and Subba Row is right in his opinions of him. Such letters *and worse* will be received by C. C. M., S.M. and others. And this is the man who swore his word of honour but the other day that he would *never* injure the Society, whatever may be his opinion of us personally! The close of the cycle good friend—the very last efforts. . . . Who will win the day? Of the *Dugpas*, under whose influence he has now placed himself altogether, whom he attracts in every way and manner or——
But that will do!   Yours sincerely,
                                                                    K. H.

LETTER No. 79

Since you did not " deal exhaustively with the case " in your previous note I said only what I did, for I am no business man. One used to mercantile affairs would doubtless have deduced the entire plan from even smaller fragments than you have. But now that you have opened out the question I may say (holding at the same time my amateur opinion in very light esteem) that your scheme appears reasonable and just enough. Mr. Dare, no less than yourself should be substantially rewarded for his valuable and devoted services. Your proposal that the alienated 4-12th's of shares shall not participate in profits until their respective owners have made the remaining 8-12th's yield fair remuneration to capital—is a fair one to both parties.

Whether you shall or shall not eventually issue a duplex, or quadruplex journal, I still think that if practicable, the larger amount of capital should be sought after, for, when you are fully equipped for any emergency you may deliberately adopt such plan as cool judgment and a calculation of all the chances may indicate as best.

And now, before quitting my novel relation of a business adviser, I must repeat that while we will help the enterprise from first to last as fully as possible within our rules, the initiative *must* be taken by your friends and *ought* to be guided and sympathised with by yourself, and I will just tell you why. While the greatest good ought to result from the successful establishment of such a journal, the strict law of justice forbids us to do aught to lessen in the slightest degree the merit to which *he who* shall make the dream a reality will be entitled. Few are those who know their future or what is best for them. No doubt, life on the European continent and in England possesses charms lacked by poor, dull India. But the latter can, on the other hand, offer privileges and attractions undreamt of by the average mystic. I dare not say more; but, you are wrong, friend, *very* wrong in consenting to stop here ONLY for *my* sake. I, at least, do not feel myself selfish enough to accept the sacrifice, had I not known what I do.

For your obliging compliance with our wishes that you should attend the anniversary celebration accept our *best* thanks. The effects of your presence and speech will be greater and better than you can now conceive. And, like all good actions, they will bring abundant reward for yourself—here and—hereafter. Let it be a consolation to you that you helped in a positive degree to neutralize the evil influences which the enemies of Truth had concentrated upon the Society. The dead-point of the revolving cycle is past: a new one begins for the Theosophical Society—on the 17th of December. Watch and see. Ever your friend,

K. H.

LETTER No. 80

M.'s " son's " impression convexing lens being not yet ground to a perfect surface, he puts the matter in a somewhat crooked shape. M. did not want him to say there was anything like a *possibility* of failure, but just the usual possibility of *delay* in every business transaction left with our countrymen alone: plus, the malevolent (or if you prefer eccentric) meddling of the Rothney Swedenborg and other artists in calamity. From all I know of the situation—and I claim to watch it as closely as I am permitted to—the chances are that the money *will* be raised, by the end of March; but Chance being a squinting jade, according to report the time of collection is not yet written in the memorandum book of Fate. Much depends upon contingencies but still more upon the Simla Yogi leaving us for awhile alone. 3 lakhs of rupees have been just as good as lost, owing to a letter written by him to an editor at Calcutta *with a delineation of our true character (Jesuits, sorcerers, a deceitful, selfish set,* etc.) and by that editor shown to a rajah, hitherto well disposed and ready to do the bidding of the " Mahatma Brothers "—of patriotism in this transaction there will be very little if any. I will send you in a day or two, *facts* which will show to you persons in their true light.

Meanwhile if I advise your acting entirely upon your own judgment as to your departure, it is because of the *false* light in which nearly all our actions are viewed by the Europeans who are however indirectly concerned with us. I do not want to be *misjudged* by you even for one moment. But strange and *crooked* as our ways may appear at first sight I hope you will never allow your European mind to get influenced by your Rothney friend. Well more anon,

Yours ever faithfully,

K. H

LETTER No. 81

Received London about July, 1883.

Private but not *very* Confidential.

I have, you observe, left for a separate private letter—in case you should like to read the other to your British " Brethren and Sisters—" and to the last any reference to the proposed new journal, about whose prospects Col. Gordon has written you so encouragingly. I scarcely knew until I had begun to watch the development of this effort to erect a bulwark for Indian interests, how deeply my poor people had sunk. As one who watches the signs of fluttering life beside a dying bed, and counts the feeble breaths to learn if there may still be room for hope, so we Aryan exiles in our snowy retreat have been attentive to this issue. Debarred from using any abnormal powers that might interfere with the nation's *Karma*, yet by all lawful and normal means trying to stimulate the zeal of those who care for our regard, we have seen weeks grow into months without the object having been achieved. Success is nearer than ever before, yet still in doubt. The letter of Govindan Lal, which I shall ask Upasika to send you, shows that there is progress. In a few days a meeting of native capitalists is to be held at Madras, which Mr. Olcott is to attend and from which there may be fruits. He will see the Geikwar at Baroda and Holkar at Indore, and do his best—as he has already at Behar and in Bengal. There was never a time when the help of a man like yourself was more needed by India. We foresaw it, as you know and patriotically tried to make your way easy for a speedy return. But,—alas! that it must be confessed—the word Patriotism has now scarcely any electric power over the Indian heart. The " Cradle Land of Arts and Creeds " swarms with unhappy beings, precariously provided for, and vexed by demagogues who have everything to gain by chicane and impudence. We knew all this in the mass, but not one of us Aryans had sounded the depths of the Indian question as we have of late. If it be permissible to symbolize things subjective by phenomena objective, I should say that to the psychic sight India seems covered with a stifling grey fog—a moral meteor [1]—the odic emanation from her vicious social state. Here and there twinkles a point of light which marks a nature still somewhat spiritual, a person who aspires and struggles after the higher knowledge. If the beacon of Aryan occultism shall ever be kindled again, these scattered sparks must be combined to make its flame. And this is the task of the T.S., this the pleasant part of its work in which we would so gladly assist, were we not impeded and thrown back by the *would-be chelas* themselves. I stepped outside our usual limits to aid your particular project from a conviction of its necessity and its potential usefulness: having begun I shall continue until the result is known. But in this uncongenial experience of meddling in a business affair, I have ventured within the very breath of the world's furnace. I have suffered so much from the enforced insight at short distance into the moral and spiritual condition of my people; and been so shocked by this nearer view of the selfish baseness of human nature (the concomitant, always, of the passage of humanity through our stage of the evolutionary circuit): I have seen so distinctly the certainty that it cannot be helped—that I shall henceforth abstain from any repetition of the unbearable experiment. Whether your paper should succeed or

[1] See reference at p. 158 to meteoric dust.—EDS.

not—and if the latter, it will be due *to yourself* exclusively, to the unfortunate inspiration on the 17th, published in the *Times*—I shall have no more to do with the financial side of these worldly affairs; but confine myself to our prime duty of gaining knowledge and disseminating through all available channels such fragments as mankind in the mass may be ready to assimilate. I shall, of course, be interested in your journalistic career here—if I am able to overcome and soothe the bitter feelings you have just awakened in those who confided in you most,—by that unfortunate and UNTIMELY confession, *honest as its object may have been*—and you may always depend upon my practical sympathy; but the genius of Mr. Dare must preside in your Counting Room as your own in the Editor's office. The great pain you have inflicted upon me, shows clearly that either I understand nothing in the fitness of political duties and therefore, could hardly hope to be a wise business and *political* " control ", or that the man whom I regard as a true friend, however honest and willing, will never rise above English prejudices and the sinful antipathy towards *our race* and colour. " Madame " will tell you more.

Though you do not " ask me to deal with it afresh " yet I will say two words more about Mr. Massey's difficulty as regards the letter from our Brother H——then in Scotland, sent him circuitously through " Ski." Be just and charitable to—a European at least. If Mr. Massey had " declared to the English spiritualists that he was in communication *with the* BROTHERS by Occult means " he would have spoken the simple truth. For not only once but twice had he such occult relationship—once with his Father's glove, sent him by M. through " *Ski*," and again with the note in question, for the delivery of which the same practical agency was employed, though without an equal expenditure of power. His you see, is one more example of the ease with which even a superior intellect may deceive itself in occult matters, by the *maya* of its own engendering. And, as regards the other case, may it not be noted—I am no barrister and therefore speak under reserve—as a mitigating circumstance for the accused that Mr. Massey is not even to this day sure that Dr. Billing did not intercept the Simpson letter to his wife, keep it to use against her at a fortunate time and actually so use it in this instance? Or, even allowing the letter to have been delivered to the addressee, know what was the answer—if any written? Has the idea struck your observant friend that at that very time there was a womanly— worse than that—medium's spite far worse than the *odium theologicum* between the Simpson and Hollis-Billing, concerning their respective claims to the favours shown by Ski? That Mrs. Billing called the Ski of her " friend " Simpson " a *bogus* spook;" that Dr. Billing complained bitterly to Olcott and H.P.B. of the fraud perpetrated by the Simpson who tried to palm off a false *Ski* as the genuine one—the oldest as the most faithful "control" of his wife. The row got even into the papers. Strange, that at the time when she was publicly reproached by Mrs. B. with pretending to be controlled by *her* Ski Mrs. S. should have asked her for such a delicate and dangerous service! I say again—I speak under reserve—I have never looked into the accusation seriously, and know of it by having caught a glimpse of the situation in Olcott's head when reading Mr. C. C. M.'s letter. But the hint may, perchance, be of some service. But this I do know, and say; the long and short of the matter is, that your friend has hastily suspected and *unjustly* condemned the innocent and done himself harm spiritually. He really has no right to accuse even H.P.B. of *deliberate deceit*. I protest most emphatically against the woman being dealt with so uncharitably. She had no intention to deceive —unless withholding a fact be a direct deceit and *lie*, on the theory *suppressio veri, suggestio falsi*—a legal maxim which she knows nothing about. But then on this theory we all (Brothers and Chelas) ought to be regarded *as liars*. She was ordered to see that the letter should be delivered; she had no other means of doing so at that time but through "*Ski*." She had no power of sending it *direct*, as was the glove; M. *would not* help her, for certain reasons of his and very weighty too—as I have found out later—; she knew Mr. C. C. M. distrusted *Ski*, and was foolish enough to believe that Mr. Massey separated the medium from the "spirit" as proved by her letter; she was anxious out of pure and unselfish devotion for him that he should see that he was noticed at last by a real Brother. Hence—she tried to conceal the fact that Ski had a hand in it. Moreover, an hour after having sent her letter to Mrs. B. to be delivered by Ski, a letter *read at the time*, not found *accidentally* as alleged—she forgot all about it as she forgets everything. No idea, no thought of the slightest deceit on her part had ever crossed her mind. Had Mr. Massey asked her to tell him honestly the truth, after the letter had been shown to him she would have probably either sent him to a very hot place, and said nothing, or honestly confessed the truth. She simply thought it best that the intended good effect of the Brother's message should not be cancelled by arousing in Mr. C. C. M's mind a hostile disposition, the fruit of such unwarranted suspicion. We, my dear sirs, always judge men by their motives and the moral effects of their actions: for the world's false standards and prejudice we have no respect.

K. H.

LETTER No. 82

Strictly Confidential

The " quart d'heure de Rabelais " has come. On your answer, consent or refusal—depends the resurrection of the *Phœnix*—prostrated in a death-like *Samadhi*, if not in actual death. If you believe in my word, and, leaving the Ryots to our care are prepared for a somewhat *unclean* work—from the European standpoint though—and consent to oppose our work *apparently*, serving our ends in reality and thus saving our respective countries from a great evil that overhangs both—then consent to the proposal that will be made to you from India.

You may work to all intents and purposes to oppose The Bengal Rent Bill, for do whatever you or others may, you will never be able to impede our work in the opposite direction. Therefore, —one scruple less as one *non*-permitted confidence more. A riddle, verily.

And now good friend, I must explain. Only you have to prepare your European, cultured notions of *right and wrong* to receive a shock. A plan of action of a purely Asiatic character is laid bare before you; and since I may not move one finger—nor would I if I could in this case—to guide your understanding or feelings it may be found *too* Jesuitical, to suit your taste. Alas for all! that you should be so little versed in the knowledge of occult antidotes, as not to be able to perceive the difference between the Jesuitical " tout chemin est bon qui mène à Rome " added to the cunning and crafty—" the end justifies the means "—and necessity of the practical application of these sublime words of our Lord and Master:—" O ye Bhikkhus and Arhats—be friendly to the race of men—our brothers! Know ye all, that he, who sacrifices not his *one* life to save the life of his fellow-being; and he who hesitates to give up more than life—his *fair name and honour* to save the fair name and honour of *the many*, is unworthy of the sin-destroying, immortal, transcendent Nirvana." Well, it cannot be helped.

Allow me to explain to you the situation. It is very complicated; but to him who, without any previous training was able to assimilate so well some of our doctrines as to write *Esoteric Buddhism* —the *inner* springs that we have to use ought to become intelligible.

(1) The Behar Chiefs propose *one and a half* lakhs down for the *Phœnix*; as much when they see you back to India, if the Bengal Rent Bill is opposed by the new paper and you promise to give them your support. Unless the proposition is accepted by you we may prepare for the final incremation of our *Phœnix*—and for good. Exclusive of this sum—Rs. 150,000—we can count but

upon Rs. 45,000 in shares—so far.   But let the Raises [1] put down cash and all will follow.

(2) If you refuse they will secure another editor: were there any danger for the Ryots and the Bill they—the Raises or Zemindars would lose nothing thereby, except in the degree of cleverness of their editor; but they hope and are thoroughly unaware of being *doomed*—in the long run.   The only and real loser in the case of refusal will be—India and your own country—eventually.   *This is prophecy.*

(3) The resistance to, and the intrigues set on foot by the Zemindars against the Bill *are infamous* in their nature, yet very natural.   Those who examine things at the core, perceive the real culprit in Lord Cornwallis and the long line of his successors. However infamous it may be, as I say, there it is and cannot be helped for it is human nature itself; and, there is no more dishonour to support their claims from a legal standpoint on the part of an Editor, who knows them to be doomed, than there is for a Counsel to defend his client—a great criminal sentenced to be hung.   I am now trying to argue from your European standpoint, for fear, and lest you should not be able to see things from our *Asiatic* point of view, or rather in the light we, who are enabled to discern future events—see them.

(4) A conservative Editor whose field of action will be found to *run on parallel lines with that of a conservative* Viceroy, will find himself having lost nothing in fact, for a slight opposition that cannot last long after all.   There are great flaws in the present Bill, examined from its legal, dead-letter aspect.

(5) Owing to the idiotically *untimely* " Ilbert's Bill," and the still more idiotic " Saligram-Surendro " Contempt case, the agitation is carrying the population of India to the verge of self-destruction.   You must not feel as tho' I were exaggerating if I say more: the English and especially Anglo-Indians are running the same course from an opposite direction.   You are at liberty to refuse my *warning*: you will show yourself wise if you do not.   To return to our direct object—

(6) There are several Englishmen of great intellect and ability who feel ready to defend—(and even to ally themselves—with) the Zemindars—and oppose the Bill, against their own principles and feelings—simply because the Raises hate and oppose the man whom the rest of the Hindus profess, for the time being, to adore, and whom they are exalting with all the ardour of simple-minded, short-sighted savages.   Thus the Ryots cannot escape their fate for a few months longer whether you accept the offer or not.   In the latter case, of course the paper scheme is at an end.

---

[1] Landowners.—EDS.

(7) At the same time it is better that you should be prepared to know the unavoidable results: there are ninety-nine chances against one that—if the offer of the Zemindars is rejected—the *Phœnix* will [n]ever come into existence; not so long at any rate as the present agitation is going on. And when it finally fails, as the project is bound to unless we become masters of the situation, then *we will have to part*. In order to obtain from the Chohan permission to defend the teeming millions of the poor and the oppressed in India, bringing on to bear all our knowledge and powers—I had to pledge myself, in case of the Phœnix's failure to interfere no more with such worldly matters and—to bid an eternal farewell to the European element. M. and Djual Khool would have to take my place. On the other hand, should you consent to the offer, your opposition to the Rent Bill would have no more effect on our work *for* the Ryots than a straw to save a vessel from sinking; whereas, if another editor is selected we would have no pretext to exercise our influence on their behalf. Such is the situation. It is a curious medley with no *raison d'être* in your opinion. You can hardly be expected by us to see clearly through it at present, nor is there much likelihood that you will judge it fairly owing to this Egyptian darkness of cross purposes; nor is there any special need you should, if the offer has to fall to the ground. But, if your answer is favourable, I may perhaps as well add a few particulars. Know then, that opposition notwithstanding, and just because of it, you will bring the great national boil to a head sooner than it could be otherwise expected. Thus, while carrying out strictly your programme and promise made to the Raisas you will be helping the events that have to be brought about to save the unfortunate population that has been sat upon ever since 1793—the year of Lord Cornwallis's great political mistake. At the same time you may be doing immense good in every other direction. Recall the past and this will help you to see clearer into our intentions. When you took over Bengal from the native Rulers, there were a number of men who exercised the calling of Tax Collectors under their Government. These men received, as you are aware, a percentage for collecting the rents. The spirit of the letter of the tithe and tribute under the Moossulman Rulers was never understood by the East India Company; least of all the rights of the Ryots to oppose an arbitrary interchange of the Law of *Wuzeefa* and *Mukassimah*. Well, when the Zemindars found that the British did not exactly understand their position they took advantage of it, as the English had taken advantage of their force: they claimed to be Landlords. Weakly enough, you consented to recognise the claim, and admitting it notwithstanding the warning of the Moossulman who understood the real situation and were not bribed as most of the Company

were—you played into the hands of the few against the many, the result being the " Perpetual Settlement " documents. It is this that led to every subsequent evil in Bengal. Seeing how the unfortunate Ryots are regarded by your proud nation in the full progress of the 19th Century, being in your sight of far less value than a horse or cattle, it is not difficult to imagine how they were regarded by your countrymen then—a century ago—when every Englishman was a pious Christian at heart and ordered by the Bible to draw a broad distinction between the descendants of Ham and themselves—the heirs of the chosen people. The agreement drawn between Lord Cornwallis and the *Raises* which stipulated that the " black human cattle " should be treated by the Zemindars kindly and justly, and that they should not raise the rents of the Ryots, etc., was a legal farce. The Chohan was then in India and he was an eye-witness to the beginning of horrors. No sooner had they secured the Perpetual Settlement Agreement than the Raises began to disregard their engagements. Failing to fulfil any of these they brought yearly ruin and starvation on the miserable Ryots. They exacted tribute, sold them up, and trumped up false charges against them under the name of *Abwab*. These " doors " and " openings " led them wherever they wanted and they levied for over 50 years most extraordinary taxes. All this the Zemindars have done and much more and they will be surely made to account for it. Things too horrible to mention were done under the eyes and often with the sanction of the Company's servants, when the Mutiny put a certain impediment by bringing as its result another form of Government. It is to redress the great wrong done, to remedy the now irremediable that Lord Ripon took it into his head to bring forward the new Bill. It was not thought expedient by his Councillors (not those *you* know of) to crush the Zemindary system without securing at the same time popularity among the majority in another direction: hence " Ilbert's Bill " and some other trifles. We say then that to all appearance it is to *redress* the wrongs of the Past, that is the object of the present Bengal Rent Bill. My friend you are a remarkably clever Editor and an astute and observant politician; and no one, perhaps, in all India goes as deep as you do into the inner constitution of the Anglo-Indian *coups d'état*. Still you do not go far enough, and the original primitive layers of the political soil as the *genesis* of some acts of my Lord Ripon were and are *terra incognita* to yourself as to so many others perhaps still older hands in politics than you are. Neither Lord Ripon nor his Councillors (those behind the veil) anticipate any great results during his power in India. They are more *Occultists* than you 'may imagine. Their liberal reforms are not meant for India, to the weal or woes of which they are quite indifferent: they look far off *to future results*

and Press acts, Ilbert's Bills, Bengal Rent Bills and the rest are
aimed at Protestant England which, very soon, *too soon* if Somebody
or *Something* does not interfere, will find itself suffocating in the
invisible coils of the Romish Apophis. Friend and Brother, the
only one of your race whom I regard with a warm, sincere affection, take care! Do not reject too lightly my warning for it is a
solemn one, and but a hint I am permitted to make. Political
skepticism, like every other, scorns and laughs at the observations
of those who do not belong to its factions. It finds out its mistakes when in a ditch. Beware, for it is no more a simple ditch
but an abyss that is being prepared for you!

But let us see on what grounds an honest Englishman can
oppose the Rent Bill. However great the misery of the Ryots
even at present, however just the reprisals that are in store for
the Zemindars, however human and generous, in short, on its
surface the object of the Rent Bill, yet no honest Government
strictly speaking has the right to break at will and its own pleasure
solemn pledges and engagements. Because it is found that the
Raises have not fulfilled their part of the Agreement, it gives no
right to the other party to make away with their signature and
tear in shreds the Perpetual Settlement Agreement. The sins of
the few cannot well be visited upon the many. There are heavy
flaws in the present Rent Bill as there were in the old System;
and there is no clause in the old documents [which] stipulated to
the effect that the Settlement becomes *nil* at the will of the British.
I will not enter upon the defects of the dead-letter meaning in
either the one or other, but will limit myself by telling you that
there *are* such flaws and that, until modified you have a perfect
right to object to them. You are not expected to cause the Bill
to be withdrawn but to simply support the Zemindars' analysis
of its defects. And this you can freely promise. However I
must not seem trying to influence you one way or the other. Some
of the claims of the Raises are infamous and no honest man can
be made to support them; while others are not without a strong
legal foundation in their favour. The Ruling power, for instance,
was never yet and in no case the proprietor of the *Khirajee* land—
not even under the Moossulman laws and sway. You have thus
the Spirit of *Khiraj* and *Ooshr* to work upon, in order to redeem
your promise to the landowners and amuse them for a few months
unto the day of the " almighty smash " that is in store for them.
All that you are asked to do for the benefit of (*your* as well as) *my*
country is, to overlook the ugly frontispiece of the edifice, taking
into consideration only the real nature of the situation and the
future good results, in case you should get over your very natural
squeamishness. In a few days you may receive a formal proposal. Think well over it. Do not allow yourself to be influenced

by any consideration in connection with my desires. If you
honestly believe the offer inconsistent with your European notions
and criterion of truth and honour refuse its acceptance without
any hesitation and let me bid you a sad, though ever grateful and
friendly farewell. I cannot expect to see you looking at things
from my own standpoint. You look *without*, I *see within*. This
is no hour of sentimentalities. The whole future of the " brightest (!) jewel "—oh, what a dark satire in that name!—in the
Crown of England is at stake, and I am bound to devote the whole
of my powers as far as the Chohan will permit me to help my
country at this eleventh hour of her misery. I cannot work except
with those *who will work with us.* Accuse me not, my friend, for you
do not know, you *cannot* know the extent of the limitations I am
placed under. Think not, that I am seeking to place a bait—
an inducement, for you to accept that which [you] would refuse
under other circumstances, for I am not. Having pledged my
solemn word of honour to Him to whom I am indebted for everything I am and know, I am simply helpless in case of your refusal
and—we will have to part. Had not the Rent Bill been
accompanied by the din and clash of the Ilbert Bill and " contempt case " I would have been the first to advise you to refuse.
As the situation stands now, however, and prohibited as I am to
use any but ordinary powers—I am powerless to do both, and
am constrained to choose between helping my hapless mother-
country, and our future intercourse. It is for you to decide. And
if this letter is fated to be my last, I beg you to remember—for
your sake, not mine—the message I sent at Simla to yourself and
Mr. Hume through H.P.B.—" Lord Ripon is not a free agent;
the real Viceroy and ruler of India is not at Simla but at Rome;
and the effective weapon used by the latter is—the Viceroy's
confessor."

Give, pray, my best wishes to your lady and the " Morsel."
Be certain, that with a few undetectable mistakes and omissions
notwithstanding, your *Esoteric Buddhism* is the only right exposition—however incomplete—of our Occult doctrines. You have
made no cardinal, fundamental mistakes; and whatever may be
given to you hereafter will not clash with a single sentence in your
book but on the contrary will explain away any seeming contradiction. How greatly mistaken was Mr. Hume's theory is shown
by the " Chela " in the *Theosophist*. With all that, you may feel
sure that neither M. nor I have contradicted each other in our
respective statements. He was speaking of the *inner*—I, of the
outer Round. There are many things that you have not learned
but may some day; nor will you be able to ever comprehend the
process of the *obscurations* until you have mastered the mathematical progress of the *inner* and the *outer* Rounds and learned

more about the specific difference between the seven.   And thus
according to Mr. Massey's philosophical conclusion *we have no
God*? He is right—since he applies the name to an extracosmic
anomaly, and that we, knowing nothing of the latter, find each
man his *God*—within himself in his own personal, and at the same
time *impersonal* Avalokiteswara.   And now—farewell.   And if it is
so decreed that we should correspond no more, remember me with
the same sincere good feeling as you will ever be remembered by,

K. H.

LETTER No. 83

Received London, Octobet 8th, 1883.

A temporary absence upon imperative business prevented for a
few days my even knowing anything about your affairs, and it
was not until to-day that I had the leisure to give them a thought.
Upon reading your letter, the situation presented itself to me in
such colours that I concluded to have you immediately given your
freedom and so sent you a cable despatch. This was with the
object of removing from your mind any feeling of compulsion,
moral or otherwise, and of leaving you to either take or reject
the further proposals which may come to you from any part of
India, at your option. If any consideration could have prompted
a different course, it would have been entirely removed by the
tone of your letter of August the 16th. The advocacy of the
Bengal measure in the present aspect of affairs you think would
ruin every prospect of the commercial success of the proposed
journal; " *The Phœnix* cannot possibly as now designed prove a
commercial success. And a paper which is a commercial failure
can have very little political weight." To persist then, would as
you see it, be to lead a number of persons to fruitlessly waste a
large sum of money. For " the project thus crippled is pretty
effectually stripped of its grand financial possibilities." Still
despite all this, you are disposed to go on if I wish it, cast the
moral responsibility on me and " swallow the somewhat repulsive pledge."

My friend, you shall do nothing of the sort. The responsibility,
notwithstanding all I could, and am willing to do, would fall upon
you since you have been given plainly the option in my last letter
to you. If henceforth, you have anything more to do with this
unfortunate affair, it must be entirely upon your own judgment
and responsibility. You have ill comprehended the Law of Karma
—(and my letter)—if you could have imagined that I would dare
to provoke its awful retaliations by forcing you or anyone to take

up a line of action with such feelings in his heart. Knowing you, it was easy to foresee your—(nay, the feelings of any honourable man having to face such a situation)—repulsion for the work contemplated. Therefore, had I taken great care to impress upon you in my letter that you were entirely and absolutely free in your choice. I blame myself for but one thing, *viz.*, my having hinted at the probable consequence of your refusal,—as implied in my pledge to the Chohan to thenceforward abstain from collaboration with Europeans until some future and more favourable time. It was that which caused you " to swallow the repulsive pledge " more than anything said. This goes to my Karma. But this aside, by referring to my last letter you will perceive that the necessity for independent, unbiased action on your part was strongly urged. I hoped—even against the disheartening moral condition of my countrymen, and forced myself almost to *believe* it possible to found a journal so obviously necessary at this great crisis, upon a basis thoroughly satisfactory to you and to all who might be concerned. I had forgotten that *external* appearance is everything in your world and that I was simply subjecting you to be regarded with contempt. But rest assured; had the money been collected as first attempted, and no pressure of working in a certain direction had been offered to you; and had you been left entirely your own master in the line of policy pursued; yet at this hour of bitter hatred, of mutual malice and contempt, the mere fact that you were advocating the cause of the despised, and now more than ever hated and crushed down " nigger "—would have stripped The Phœnix of even a shadow of any " grand financial possibility." Still hardly a month ago I was so confident—from seeing the still deep, strong feelings lurking in the national soul— that I allowed you to grow equally and even more confident than myself. Others, whose intuition and foresight had not been blinded by their superiors, thought differently and some would have dissuaded me; yet, the aim being so worthy, and the possibility really existing, I was permitted to watch the project and use natural external means to aid its consummation. If indefinite waiting were practicable for you, the original scheme could be realized; but this is not so, and I must, therefore, withdraw the last appearance of constraint upon your free judgment, and thank you for having so loyally seconded the attempt to do good to India, even at the cost of your feelings and pecuniary interests. I should be most unwilling, apart from the rule of our Order as regards Karma, to draw you into a position where I could recompense you in any way for loss of social prestige or financial disappointments. To do that is beyond my power. I could not look at you, if you were hourly feeling that you were regarded no better than a " blackguard," and had " no political weight with Society

at large on the score of Character." If your lot was to be cast in
with ours, such considerations would not weigh one moment.
To all, whether Chohan or chela, who are obligated workers
among us the first and last consideration is whether we can do
good to our neighbour, no matter how humble he may be; and
we do not permit ourselves to even think of the danger of any
contumely, abuse or injustice visited upon ourselves. We are
ready to be " spat upon and crucified " daily—not once—if real
good to another can come of it. But the case is totally different
with you; you have your path to tread in the more " practical "
world, and *your* standing in it must not be jeopardized.

Again, besides yourself the contributors to capital must be justly
dealt by. Among them are wealthy Zemindars, but there are
also poor patriots, who have made great exertions to subscribe
their small sums from pure reverence to us and love of mother-
land. At least fifty such are waiting the latest turn of events, and
husbanding their resources until the last moment before sending
on their remittances to Calcutta. Devoted Theosophists in various
parts of India have been actively soliciting for subscriptions, upon
the theory of possible profit to capital set forth in Mr. Morgan's
circulars; the project has been warmly advocated by Olcott,
Colonel Gordon, Norendro, and others known and unknown to
you: a financial disaster to The Phœnix of the nature you anticipate
would compromise the personal influence of all. With such prospects, moreover, your late co-adjutor Mr. Dare would not care
to help you even though Mr. Allen should permit him. And,
finally, unless your personal faith in me were so blind as to swallow
up your last instinct of prudence, you would not risk your own
hard-earned capital in a fore-doomed failure, and so could not in
conscience allow anyone else to do it. Except—except you were
allowed to " cast the moral responsibility upon me "; in short, to
make me by miracle—were that possible—force a success. If that
had been permitted, the journal would have been already founded,
and its voice have made itself heard amid the harsh din of contemporary Indian affairs.

I would have phrased my dispatch of to-day even stronger but
that I should, by telling you to abandon the affair, again assume
the responsibility of blocking your free-will. It is best that you
should give the Bengal party the chance to state their conditions
definitely and finally, and thereupon answer " yes " or " no."
To save your time and expense I asked Olcott to cause Norendro
Babu to send *him* the Landholders' proposals, that he may, upon
the instant—knowing your views and character—say whether they
are fit to lay before you or not. And if not, that he will immediately communicate with your Calcutta solicitors, as you
requested.

28

This is the present situation of affairs and very bad it is for India. It is premature as yet to tell you more of the secret influence that has brought it on, but you may hear of it later. Nor may I forecast the future, except so far as to draw more than ever your attention to the black clouds that are gathering over the political sky. You know I told you long ago to expect many and great disturbances of all kinds as one cycle was closing and the other beginning its fateful activites. You already see in the seismological phenomena of late occurrence some of the proof; you will see a great many more and shortly. And if we have to regret the blasting of a humanitarian project, it should at least mitigate the severity of your disappointment to feel that in a bad time like this one has to contend against seen and unseen influences of the most hostile nature.

And now, a pleasanter word before concluding. Your decision to follow my lead into the Phœnix matter even with the, to you, certainty of social degradation and pecuniary loss, had the reward of its Karma already. So I conclude, at any rate, by the results. Though there was *no test*—(so odious to you)—meant, yet you were as good as tested and you have not quailed. The fiat of contingent non-intercourse between us has been partially revoked. The prohibition with regard to *other Europeans* is as strict as ever, but in *your* case it is removed. And *this* consent, I know, has a direct bearing upon *your* consent—the great sacrifice of your personal feelings in the present situation. " This *Peling* " was found to have " really *redeeming qualities!*" But be warned, my friend, that this is not the last of your probations. It is not I who create them, but *yourself*—by your struggle for light and truth against the world's dark influences. Be more careful as to what you say upon forbidden topics. The " eighth sphere " mystery is a very confidential subject, and you are far from understanding even its general aspects. You were repeatedly warned and should not have mentioned it. You have unintentionally brought ridicule upon a solemn matter. I have nought to do with the *Replies* to Mr. Myers, but, you may recognise in them, perhaps, the brusque influence of M.

K. H.

I am advised to request that, for the future, communications intended for me may be sent thro' either Damodar or Henry Olcott. Madam B's discretion is not improving in ratio with her physiological enfeeblement.

SECTION V

THE LONDON LODGE OF THE THEOSOPHICAL SOCIETY

LETTER No. 84

Private

To One of the Vice-Presidents or Councillors of The London
Lodge Theosophical Society, from K.H.

My dear friend—

The enclosure is to be transmitted to the L.L.T.S. through you
in your capacity of Vice-President of the Parent Society and therefore representative of the President Founder, *not as member of the
Branch at London.*

The recent occurrences in which you have borne a part not
altogether pleasant, may be distressing to some and tiresome to
others, yet it is better so than that the old paralytic calm should
have continued. An outbreak of fever in the human body is
nature's evidence that she is trying to expel the seeds of disease
and perhaps death anteriorily absorbed. As things were, the
London Branch was but vegetating and the vast possibilities of
psychic evolution in Britain were completely untried. Karma
evidently required that the repose should be broken by the agency
of the one most responsible for it—C. C. Massey, and so it was he
who brought Mrs. K. to her present position. *She has not accomplished her object, but Karma has its own*: henceforth the London
group aroused, stimulated and warned, have a clear field in which
to exercise their activities. Your own karma my friend, destines
you to play a still more conspicuous part in European theosophical affairs than you have yet. Olcott's forthcoming visit will
result in important developments, in whose out-working you are
to have a hand. My desire is that you should be gathering together all the reserved forces of your being so that you may rise
to the dignity and importance of the crisis. However little you
may seem to achieve—psychically—in this birth, remember that
your interior growth proceeds every instant, and that toward the
end of your life as in your next birth your accumulated merit shall
bring you all you aspire to.

It is not politic that H. S. Olcott should be exclusively your
guest during his whole stay in Britain; his time should be divided
between yourself and others of various opinions—should they
wish to invite him for a short time. He will be accompanied by
Mohini, whom I have chosen as my chela and with whom I sometimes communicate directly. Treat the boy kindly, forgetting he

is a Bengalee, and only remembering *he is now my chela*. Do what you can to dignify Olcott's office; for he represents the entire Society, and by reason of his official position, if for no other, stands, with Upasika, closest to ourselves in the chain of Theosophical work. *Asirvadam*.[1]

K. H.

LETTER No. 85

To One of the Vice-Presidents or Councillors of " The London Lodge," Theosophical Society, from K.H.

To the Members of the " London Lodge," Theosophical Society, —Friends and Opponents,

I have just ordered two telegrams to be sent to Mrs. A. Kingsford and Mr. A. P. Sinnett to notify both that the former should continue to be the President of the " London Lodge " Theos. Society.

This is not the desire alone of either of us two, known to Mr. Sinnett, or of both, but the express wish of the *Chohan* Himself. Mrs. Kingford's election is not a matter of personal feeling between ourselves and that lady but rests entirely on the advisability of having at the head of the Society, in a place like London, a person well suited to the standard and aspirations of the (so far) ignorant (of esoteric truths) and therefore, malicious public. Nor is it a matter of the slightest consequence whether the gifted President of the " London Lodge " Theos. Soc. entertains feelings of reverence or disrespect toward the humble and unknown individuals at the head of the Tibetan Good Law,—or the writer of the present, or any of his Brothers—but rather a question whether the said lady is fitted for the purpose we have all at heart, namely the dissemination of TRUTH through Esoteric doctrines, conveyed by whatever religious channel, and the effacement of crass materialism and blind prejudices and skepticism. As the lady has rightly observed, the Western public should understand the Theosophical Society to be " a Philosophical School constituted on the ancient Hermetic basis "—that public having never heard of the Tibetan, and entertaining very perverted notions of the Esoteric Buddhist System. Therefore, and so far, we agree with the remarks embodied in the letter written by Mrs. K. to Madam B. and which the latter was asked to " submit to K.H."; and, we would remind our members of the " L.L." in this reference, that *Hermetic* Philosophy is universal and unsectarian, while the Tibetan School will ever be regarded by those who know little, if anything of it, as coloured more or less with sectarianism. The former knowing neither caste, nor colour, nor creed, no lover

[1] Blessings.—EDS.

of Esoteric wisdom can have any objection to the name, which otherwise he might feel, were the Society to which he belongs to be placarded with a specific denomination pertaining to a distinct religion. Hermetic Philosophy suits every creed and philosophy and clashes with none. It is the boundless ocean of Truth, the central point wither flows and wherein meet every river, as every stream—whether its source be in the East, West, North, or South. As the course of the river depends upon the nature of its basin, so the channel for communication of Knowledge must conform itself to surrounding circumstances. The Egyptian Hierophant, the Chaldean Mage, the Arhat, and the Rishi, were bound in days of yore on the same voyage of discovery and ultimately arrived at the same goal though by different tracks. There are even at the present moment three centres of the Occult Brotherhood in existence, widely separated geographically, and as widely *exoterically*—the true esoteric doctrine being identical in substance though differing in terms; all aiming at the same grand object, but no two agreeing *seemingly* in the details of procedure. It is an every day occurrence to find students belonging to different schools of occult thought sitting side by side at the feet of the same Guru. *Upasika* (Madam B.) and Subba Row, though pupils of the same Master, have not followed the same Philosophy—the one is Buddhist and the other an Adwaitee. Many prefer to call themselves Buddhists not because the word attaches itself to the ecclesiastical system built upon the basic ideas of our Lord Gautama Buddha's philosophy, but because of the Sanskrit word " Buddhi " —*wisdom*, enlightenment; and as a silent protest to the vain rituals and empty ceremonials which have in too many cases been productive of the greatest calamities. Such also is the origin of the Chaldean term *Mage*.

Thus it is plain that the methods of Occultism, though in the main unchangeable, have yet to conform to altered times and circumstances. The state of the general Society of England—quite different from that of India, where our existence is a matter of common and, so to say, of inherent belief among the population, and in a number of cases of positive knowledge—requires quite a different policy in the presentation of Occult Sciences. The only object to be striven for is the amelioration of the condition of MAN by the spread of truth suited to the various stages of his development and that of the country he inhabits and belongs to. TRUTH has no ear-mark and does not suffer from the name under which it is promulgated—if the said object is attained. The constitution of the " L. Lodge, Theos. Society," affords ground of a hope for the right method being put in operation before long. It is well known that a magnet would cease to be a magnet if its poles cease to be antagonistic. Heat on one side should be met by

frost on the other, and the resulting temperature will be healthy
to all people. Mrs. Kingsford and Mr. Sinnett are both useful,
both needed and appreciated by our revered Chohan and Master,
—just because they are the two poles calculated to keep the
whole body in magnetic harmony, as the judicious disposal of
both will make an excellent middle ground to be attained by no
other means; one correcting and equilibrising the other. The
direction and the good services of both is necessary for the steady
progress of the Theosophical Society in England. But both cannot be Presidents. Mrs. Kingsford's views being at the bottom
(*minus* the details) identical with those of Mr. Sinnett in matters
of Occult philosophy; and, by reason of their association with the
names and symbols familiar to Christian ears and eyes, they falling in better than those of Mr. Sinnett with the actual bent of
English national intelligence and spirit of conservatism, Mrs. K.
is thus more adapted to lead the movement successfully in England. Therefore, if our advice and desire are of any account with
the members of the " London Lodge "—she will have to occupy
the Presidential Chair for the ensuing year, at any rate. Let the
members under her leadership resolutely try to live down the un-
popularity which all esoteric teaching and all reform are sure to
attract at the outset and they *will* succeed. The Society will be
a great help to, and a great power in, the world, as well as a secure
channel for the flow of its President's philanthropy. Her constant and not altogether unsuccessful strife in the cause of anti-
vivisection and her staunch advocacy of vegetarianism are alone
sufficient to entitle her to the consideration of our Chohans as
of all true Buddhists and Adwaitees—hence our Maha-Chohan's
preference in this direction. But, as the services of Mr. Sinnett
in the good cause are great indeed—far greater, so far, than of
any Western Theosophist—therefore, a new arrangement is found
advisable.

It seems necessary for a proper study and correct understanding of our Philosophy and the benefit of those whose inclination
leads them to seek esoteric knowledge from the Northern Buddhist
Source, and in order that such teaching should not be even
virtually imposed or offered to those Theosophists who may differ
from our views, that an exclusive group composed of those members who desire to follow absolutely the teachings of the School
to which we, of the Tibetan Brotherhood, belong, should be
formed under Mr. Sinnett's direction and *within* the " London
Lodge T.S." Such is, in fact, the desire of the Maha Chohan.
Our last year's experience amply shows the danger of so reck-
lessly submitting our sacred doctrines to the unprepared world.
We expect, therefore, and are resolved to urge, if necessary more
caution than ever from our followers in the exposition of our

secret teachings. Consequently many of the latter which Mr.
Sinnett and his fellow-students may from time to time receive
from us, will have to be kept entirely *secret* from the world—if
they would have us give them our help in that direction.

I need hardly point out how the proposed arrangement is calculated to lead to a harmonious progress of the " L.L.T.S." It
is a universally admitted fact that the marvellous success of the
Theosophical Society in India is due entirely to its principle of
wise and respectful toleration of each other's opinions and beliefs.
Not even the President-Founder has the right directly or indirectly to interfere with the freedom of thought of the humblest
member, least of all to seek to influence his personal opinion. It
is only in the absence of this generous consideration, that even
the faintest shadow of difference arms seekers after the same truth,
otherwise earnest and sincere, with the scorpion-whip of hatred
against their brothers, equally sincere and earnest. Deluded
victims of distorted truth, they forget, or never knew, that discord
is the harmony of the Universe. Thus in the Theos. Society,
each part, as in the glorious *fugues* of the immortal Mozart, ceaselessly chases the other in harmonious discord on the paths of
Eternal progress to meet and finally blend at the threshold of
the pursued goal into one harmonious whole, the keynote in
nature सत्. *Absolute Justice* makes no difference between the
many and the few. Therefore, while thanking the majority of
the " L.L." Theosophists for their " loyalty " to us their invisible
teachers, we must at the same time remind them that their
President, Mrs. Kingsford, is *loyal* and *true* also—to that which
she believes to be the Truth. And, as she is thus loyal and true
to her convictions, however small the minority that may side with
her at present, the majority led by Mr. Sinnett, our representative in London, cannot with justice charge her with the guilt,
which—since she has emphatically disclaimed all intention of
breaking the letter or the spirit of Article VI of the *Rules* of the
Parent Theos. Society (which please see and read)—is one only
in the eyes of those who would be rather too severe. Every
Western Theosophist should learn and remember, especially those
of them who would be our followers—that in our Brotherhood all
personalities sink into one idea—abstract right and absolute practical justice for all. And that, though we may not say with the
Christians, " return good for evil "—we repeat with Confucius
" return good for good; for evil—JUSTICE." Thus, the Theosophists of Mrs. K.'s way of thinking,—were they even to oppose
some of us personally to the bitter end,—are entitled to as much
respect and consideration (so long as they are sincere) from us
and their fellow-members of opposite views, as those who are
ready with Mr. Sinnett to follow absolutely but our special teaching.

A dutiful regard for these rules in life will always promote the best interests of all concerned. It is necessary for the parallel progress of the groups under Mrs. K. and Mr. S. that neither should interfere with the beliefs and rights of the other. And it is seriously expected that both of them will be actuated by an earnest and sleepless desire to respect the philosophical independence of each other, while preserving at the same time their unity as a whole—namely the objects of the Parent Theos. Society in their integrity—and those of the London Lodge, in their slight modification. We wish the London Society should preserve its harmony in division like the Indian Branches where the representatives of all the different schools of Hinduism seek to study Esoteric Sciences and the Wisdom of old, without necessarily giving up for it their respective beliefs. Each Branch, often members of the same Branch—Christian converts included in some cases—study esoteric philosophy each in his own way, yet always knitting together brotherly hands for the furtherance of the common objects of the Society. To carry out this programme, it is desirable that the " London Lodge " should be administered by at least *fourteen* Councillors—one half openly inclining towards the Christian Esotericism as represented by Mrs. K., and the other half following Buddhist Esotericism as represented by Mr. S.; all important business to be transacted by majority of votes. We are well aware of and quite alive to the difficulties of such an arrangement. Yet, it seems absolutely necessary in order to re-establish the lost harmony. The constitution of the " London Lodge " has to be amended and can be so amended if the members would but try; and so bring about more strength in such friendly division than in forced unity.

Unless, therefore, both Mrs. Kingsford and Mr. Sinnett agree to *disagree* in details and work in strict unison for the chief objects as laid down in the *Rules* of the Parent Society, we can have no hand in the future development and progress of the *London Lodge*.

K. H.

December 7th, 1883,
    Mysore.

LETTER No. 86

Received January, 1884.

Good, friend, I take you at your word. In one of your recent letters to the " O.L." you express your readiness to follow my advice in almost anything I may ask you. Well—the time has come to prove your willingness. And since, in this particular case, I myself am simply carrying out the wishes of my Chohan, I hope you will not experience too much difficulty in sharing my fate by doing—as I do. "Fascinating" Mrs. K. has to remain President—*jusqu' au nouvel ordre*. Nor can I conscientiously, after reading her apologetic letter to H.P.B.—say that I do not side with her in much she has to say in her excuse. Of course much of it is—after-thought; still her very eagerness to retain her post contains good hope for the future of the London Lodge, especially if you help me by carrying out *the spirit* of my instructions. Thus, the London Theos. Soc. will be no more " *a tail* for her to wag " at her own sweet pleasure and fancy, but she will become herself part and parcel of that " tail "—and, the more she helps to wag it—the better such activity for your Society. Minute explanations would be rather too long and tedious a job. Suffice that you should know that her anti-vivisection struggle ard her strict vegetarian diet have won entirely over to her side our stern Master. He cares less than we do for any outward—or even inward—expression or feeling of disrespect to the " Mahatmas." Let her do her duty by the Society, be true to her principles and all the rest will come in good time. She is very young, and her personal vanity and other womanly short-comings are to be laid at the door of Mr. Maitland and the Greek chorus of her admirers.

The enclosed paper is to be delivered by you *sealed* to one of the Councillors or *Vice*-Presidents of your Society—Mr. C. C. Massey, I believe, would be the best fitted person for the task, as he is the sincere friend of both parties concerned. The choice is left to your own discretion and judgment, however. All that you are asked to insist upon is that it should be read before a general meeting composed of as many theosophists as you can gather, and at the earliest opportunity. It contains and carries within its folds and characters *a certain occult influence* that ought to reach as many theosophists as possible. What it is you may, perhaps, gather hereafter from its direct and indirect effects. Meanwhile—read and seal it; and allow no one to put the indiscreet question whether you have taken note of its contents, for you will have to keep the knowledge secret. In case the condition should appear to you dangerous, as it might necessitate a denial of fact—better leave it alone and unread. Fear not, I am there to watch over your interests. At all events the programme is as follows: the memo written by your humble correspondent must be read to the Theosophists assembled in solemn meeting and preserved in the Society's records. It contains a statement of our views in regard to the questions raised concerning its management and basis of work. Our sympathy with it will depend upon the carrying out of the programme therein contained and laid down after mature thought.

To turn to a few of your philosophical questions—(being on my way, I cannot answer them all). It is difficult to perceive what relations you wish to establish between the different stages of subjectivity in Devachan and the various states of matter. If it be supposed that in Devachan the Ego passes through all these states of matter, then the answer would be that existence in the seventh state of matter is *Nirvana* and not *Devachanic* conditions. Humanity, although in different stages of development, yet belongs to the three dimensional condition of matter. And there is no reason why in Devachan the Ego should be varying its " dimensions."

Molecules occupying a place in infinity is an inconceivable proposition. The confusion arises out of the Western tendency of putting an objective construction upon what is purely subjective. The book of *Kiu-te* teaches us that space is infinity itself. It is formless, immutable and absolute. Like the human mind, which is the exhaustless generator of ideas, the Universal Mind or Space has its ideation which is projected into objectivity at the appointed time; but space itself is not affected thereby. Even your Hamilton has shown that infinity can never be conceived by any series of additions. Whenever you talk of *place* in infinity, you dethrone infinity and degrade its absolute, unconditioned character.

What has the number of incarnations to do with the shrewdness, cleverness, or the stupidity of an individual? A strong craving for physical life may lead an entity through a number of incarnations and yet these may not develop its higher capacities. The Law of Affinity acts through the inherent *Karmic* impulse of the Ego, and governs its future existence. Comprehending Drawin's Law of Heredity for the body, it is not difficult to perceive how the birth-seeking Ego may be attracted at the time of rebirth to a body born in a family which has the same propensities as those of the reincarnating Entity.

You need not regret that my *restriction* should include Mr. C. C. Massey. One point righted and explained would but lead to other still darker points ever arising in his suspicious, restless mind. He is a bit of a misanthrope, you friend. His mind is clouded with black doubt, and his psychological state is pitiable. All the brighter intentions are being stifled, his Buddhic (not Buddhistic) evolution checked. Take care for him, if he will not—of himself! The prey of illusions of his own creation, he is slipping down toward a deeper depth of spiritual misery, and it is *possible* that he may seek asylum from the world and himself within the pale of a theology which he would once have passionately scorned. Every lawful effort has been tried to save him, especially by Olcott, whose warm brotherly love has prompted him to make to his heart the warmest appeals—as you know. Poor, poor, deluded man! My letters are written by H.P.B., and he has no doubt I got

" defrauded Mr. Kiddle's " ideas out of her head! But let him rest as he is.

Our friend, Samuel Ward, regrets his friend Ellis's discomfiture; it should concern *me* and I must see, I suppose, when I return if a pair of horns—the " coveted horns," may not be picked up by some caravan, where dropped naturally by the animal. Unless in this way, " Uncle Sam " could not fairly expect me to help him out; for you would not have me shoulder a rifle and leave " Esoteric Buddhism " behind me at the foot of the chamois-crags!

I am sorry you took the trouble of posting me about Bradlaugh. I know him and his partner well. There is more than one trait in his character I esteem and respect. He is *not* immoral; nor could anything that might be said against or for him by Mrs. K. or even yourself, change or even influence my opinion of both himself and Mrs. Besant. Yet the book published by them—" *The Fruits of Philosophy* " *is* infamous and *highly pernicious* in its effects whatever and however beneficent and philanthropic the objects that led to the publication of the work. I regret—very deeply, my dear friend, to be obliged to differ widely in my views upon the said subject from you. I would rather avoid the unpleasant discussion. As usual, H.P.B. blundered greatly in rendering what she was told to say to Mrs. K., but on the whole she gave it out correctly. I *have not* read the work—nor ever will; but I have its unclean spirit, its brutal aura before me, and I say again in my sight the advices offered in the work are abominable; they are the fruits of Sodom and Gommorah rather than of Philosophy, the very name of which it degrades. The sooner we leave the subject—the better.

And now I have to go. The journey before me is long and tedious and the mission nearly hopeless. Yet *some* good will be done.

Yours ever sincerely,

K. H.

LETTER No. 87 [1]

To the London Lodge, Theosophical Society—Greeting.

Since the telegrams to Mrs. Kingsford and Mr. Sinnett and my letter from Mysore have not been fully understood, I was ordered by the Maha-Chohan to advise the postponement of the annual election, so as to avoid anything like precipitancy, and gain time for the consideration of this letter. After the cold reception given by the members of the L.L.T.S. on December the 16th to the

[1] The words " From Bhola Deva Sarma " are written on the *envelope* of this letter which was posted at Adyar, 16th January, 1884, and received in London, February 7th, 1884. The postscript only is in K.H.'s writing.—ED.

proposal contained on page 29 of the printed and confidential circular of Mrs. Kingsford and Mr. Maitland (in the latter's *Remarks and Propositions*), namely the necessity of forming a distinct body or group within the general group of the L.L.T.S.—which proposition, if not identical in its suggested practical method, is so in substance with that thrown out by me in my letter of December 7th—on the one hand, and certain misconceptions, false hopes and displeasure on the other—the postponement *was found absolutely necessary*.

As implied in my last, at the date of the above communication the burning question was not as to the literal or allegorical character of Mr. Sinnett's latest work but the loyalty or disloyalty of your President and her co-worker towards ourselves, whom many of you have seen fit to choose as your esoteric Teachers. From such a standpoint, and no other complaint having been lodged at that time (October 21st), an imperative necessity arose to maintain, in the wise words of Mrs. Kingsford—themselves but the echo of the Tathagatha's own voice—the policy of dissociating " the authority of names, whether in the past or in the present, from abstract principles." (Inaugural Address of the President, October 21st, 1883.)   The question involved being that of Justice, Mrs. Kingsford's ignorance of our real character, our doctrines and status (underlying as they do all her uncomplimentary remarks in connection with the present writer and his colleagues) made them of not even the weight of a flake of cotton in the matter of her re-election.   This, coupled with her own intrinsic and individual worth and her charity to the poor brutes, as also the fact of her asking Madam H. P. Blavatsky to " submit my (her) letter to Koothoomi " —made the former course the proper one.

And now, the development of events since the despatch of the telegrams in question, will have perhaps suggested to some of you the true reasons for so unusual, not to say arbitrary, an action as an interference with the reserved elective rights of a Branch. Time often neutralizes the gravest evils by hastening a crisis. Moreover, and once more in the language of her address,—(your President referring to a private letter of mine to Mr. Ward, which she had read, wherein I wrote, as she thinks) " in evident ignorance of the facts, and this is not wonderful "—we may be supposed to have been likewise ignorant of the forthcoming printed " Letter, private and confidential " circulated among the members of the L.L.T.S. on December the 16th.   Thus she need hardly be surprised to find that this " Letter " has greatly altered the case. Always on the strength of the principle of impartial justice involved, we find ourselves obliged not to ratify literally our decision as to her re-election but to add to it certain clauses and make it henceforth impossible for the President and members to misconceive our mutual position. Far from our thoughts may it ever be to erect a new hierarchy for the future oppression of a priest-ridden world. As it was our wish *then* to signify to you that one could be both an active and useful member of the Society without inscribing himself our follower or co-religionist, so it is *now*. But it is just because the principle has to work both ways, that (our personal desire for her re-election notwithstanding) we feel and would have it known that we have no right to influence the free will of the members in this or any other matter. Such interference would be in flagrant contradiction to the basic law of esotericism that personal psychic growth accompanies *pari passu* the development of individual effort, and is the evidence of acquired personal merit. Moreover, a great discrepancy is observable in the reports to us *of the effects* produced by the " Kingsford—Sinnett incident " upon the members. In the face of this I find it impossible to accede to Mrs. Kingsford's several desires as expressed in her letters to Madam Blavatsky. If Mr. Massey and Mr. Ward give the lady their " entire approbation and sympathy " a very large majority of members seem to give theirs to Mr. Sinnett. Therefore, were I to act up to Mr. Massey's suggestion as reported by Mrs. Kingsford in her letter of December 20th in which she gives as his opinion that " a word only from Mahatma K.H. would be quite sufficient to reconcile Mr. Sinnett to my (the lady's) view of the matter and to establish between him and the Lodge the most perfect cordiality and understanding "—I would be actually making myself the quasi-Pope she deprecates and an unjust and an arbitrary one besides. I would then truly lay myself and Mr. Sinnett open to just criticism, even more severe than that found in her inaugural address, in the several remarkable utterances wherein she affirms her " mistrust of all appeals to authority." One who has just said: " I look with sorrow and concern on the growing tendency of the Theosophical Society to introduce into its methods . . . the exaggerated veneration for persons and personal authority . . . the veritable outcome of which is a *mere servile hero-worship*. . . . There is far too much talk among us about the Adepts our ' MASTERS ' and the like. . . . Too much capital is made of their sayings and doings, etc. . . ."—should not have asked me for such interference even though sure that my faithful friend, Mr. Sinnett, would not have resented it. Were I to have acceded to the lady's desire to appoint her as the " Apostle of Eastern and Western Esotericism " and try to force her election on even *one* unwilling member, and taking advantage of Mr. Sinnett's never wavering warm regard for myself, influence his future attitude toward herself and the movement, I would then indeed deserve to be taunted as " the oracle of the Theosophists " and classed with " Jo Smith of the Latter-Day-Saints, and Thomas

Lake Harris," the transcendental miscegenist of two worlds. I cannot believe that one who maintained only a few days previously that " our wise and truly theosophical course is not to set up new Popes and proclaim new Lords and Masters "—should now in her own case seek the protection and evoke the aid of an " authority," which could only assert itself upon the hypothesis of a blind surrender of private judgment. And, as I prefer to attribute Mrs. Kingsford's desire to her ignorance of the real feeling of some of her colleagues, the nature of which is perhaps disguised now under the polished insincerities of civilized Western life,—I would recommend her and others interested in the present dispute to appeal to the decision of the ballot, by which all may express their wishes without invidiously exposing themselves to the charge of discourtesy. This would be but to take advantage of the the privilege given to them at the close of Art. 3 of their *Rules*.

And now for another consideration. However little we might care for personal subserviency to us, the accepted leaders of the Founders of the Parent Theosophical Society, we can never approve or tolerate disloyalty in any member of whatsoever Branch *to the fundamental principles represented by the Parent Organization*. The rules of the mother-body must be lived up to by those composing its Branches; provided of course, that they do not transcend the three declared objects of the organization. The experience of the Parent Society proves that the usefulness of a Branch very largely, if not entirely, depends upon the loyalty, discretion and zeal of its President and Secretary; however much their colleagues may do to assist them, the efficient activity of their group develops proportionately with that of those officers.

In conclusion I must repeat that it is to prevent action in the matter of Mrs. Kingsford's re-election until the effacement of any misapprehension produced by my previous communications, that I have advised the annual election of office-bearers of your Lodge to stand over until the arrival of the present letter. Moreover, as the President-Founder—who knows our mind and has our confidence—is expected to be in England in a very short time, we do not see the necessity of taking any hasty steps in the matter. He has been given such a general view of the situation as will enable him to deal impartially with this case and others upon his arrival, as the representative at once of his Master and of the best interests of the Society.

(By order of my Most Venerated
Guru Deva Mahatma K ⟁)
मोलरेव शमां

It would be wise to read this letter to the members—including Mrs. Kingsford—before the new day of election. I would have you prevent, if possible, another " coup de théatre." However natural such sensational surprises may be in politics when parties are composed of devotees whose souls rejoice in party intrigue, they are very painful to witness in an association of persons who profess to give themselves up to the most solemn questions affecting human interest. Let meaner natures wrangle if they will; the wise compound their differences in a mutually forbearing spirit.

K. H.

Mr. Maitland's Remarks and Observations on Esoteric Buddhism are fully answered by Subba Row and another still greater scholar. They will be sent next week in pamphlet form, and Mr. Sinnett asked to distribute them among those members especially who may have been affected by the criticism.

SECTION VI

SPIRITUALISM AND PHENOMENA

LETTER No. 88

Short Note received at Allahabad during stay of Olcott and Bhavani Rao.

My good friend—it is very easy for us to give phenomenal proofs when we have necessary conditions. For instance—Olcott's magnetism after six years of purification is intensely sympathetic with ours—physically and morally is constantly becoming more and more so. Damodar and Bhavani Rao being congenitally sympathetic their auras help—instead of repelling and impeding phenomenal experiments. After a time you may become so— it depends on yourself. To force phenomena in the presence of difficulties magnetic and other is forbidden, as strictly as for a bank cashier to disburse money which is only entrusted to him. Mr. Hume cannot comprehend this, and therefore is "indignant " that the various tests he has secretly prepared for us have all failed. They demanded a tenfold expenditure of power since he surrounded them with an aura not of the purest—that of mistrust, anger, and anticipated mockery. Even to do this much for you so far from the Headquarters would be impossible but for the magnetisms O. and B.R. have brought with them—and I could do no more.

K. H.

P.S.—Perhaps, tho', I could put down for you to-day's date March the 11th, 1882.

LETTER No. 89

Received Allahabad March 24th, 1882.

Private.

Good friend, I will not, in sending forth the letter, reiterate again the many remarks that might be made respecting the various objections which we have the right to raise against Spiritual phenomena and its mediums. We have done our duty; and, because the voice of truth came thro' a channel which few liked, it was pronounced as false, and along with it—Occultism. The time has gone by to argue, and the hour when it will be proved to the world that Occult Science instead of being, in the words of Dr. R. Chambers—" superstition itself," as they may be disposed to think it, will be found the explanation and the extinguisher of all superstitions—is nearby. For reasons that you will appreciate, though at first you will be inclined to consider (in regard to yourself) *unjust*, I am determined to do that, for once, which hitherto I have never done; namely, *to personate myself* under *another form*, and, perhaps—character. Therefore, you need not grudge Eglinton the pleasure *of seeing me* personally to talk with me, and —be " dumbfounded " by me, and with the results of my visit to him, on board " The Vega." This will be done between the 21st and the 22nd of this month and, when you read this letter, will be a " vision of the past,"—if Olcott sends to you the letter to-day.

" All things being are in mystery; we expound mysteries by mysteries "—you may perhaps say. Well, well; to you as to one forewarned it will not be one; since, for several reasons—one more plausible than the other—I take you into my confidence. One of them is,—to save you a feeling of involuntary envy (the word is queer isn't it?) when you hear of it. As he will see somebody quite different from the real K.H., though it *will still be K.H.*, you need not feel like one wronged by your trans-Himalayan friend. Another reason is, to save the poor fellow from the suspicion of boasting; the third and *chiefest*, though neither least nor last, is, that theosophy and its adherents have to be vindicated at last. Eglinton is going home; and were he upon his return to know *nothing* of the Brothers, there would be a sore day of trial for poor old H.P.B. and H.S.O. Mr. Hume twitted us for not appearing to Eglinton. He chuckled and defied us to do it before Fern and others. For reasons which he may or may not be able to appreciate—but that *you will*—we could not or rather *would* not do so, as long as E. was in India. No less had we very good reasons to forbid H.P.B. to either correspond with him, or take too much notice of him in the *Theosophist*. But now that he is gone, and will be on the 22nd hundreds of miles away at sea; and that no suspicion of fraud can be brought against either of them, the time for the *experiment* has come. He thinks of putting *her* to test—he will be tested himself.

Thus, my faithful friend and *supporter*, keep yourself prepared. As I will recommend Eglinton to recommend in his turn to Mrs. Gordon discretion, and that [1] the good lady may feel inclined to carry it on too far and take it *à la lettre*, I furnish you beforehand with a *bull* for her, calculated to unseal her lips.

Now for Mr. Hume. He *has* worked for us, and is certainly entitled to our consideration—so far. I would fain have written

[1] Query ' that ' should be ' as '.—EDS.

to him myself, but that the sight of my familiar characters may produce a diversion in his feelings—for the worse—before he goes to the trouble of reading what I have to say. Will you kindly undertake the delicate task of notifying him of what I now write to you? Tell him that there are persons—*enemies*—who are anxious to catch the " old lady " at CHEATING, to entrap her, so to say, and that for that very reason I am determined to settle the question and have it once for ever at rest. Say to him that profiting by his suggestion and advice I,—K.H., will appear to Eglinton in *propria persona* as *in actu* at sea, between the 21 and 22 of this month; and that, if successful in bringing the rebel who denies the " Brothers " to his senses, Mrs. Gordon and consort will be notified of the fact *immediately*. That's all. We have waited on purpose to produce our experiment until his departure, and now—WE MEAN TO ACT.

Yours ever,

K. H.

Till the 25th of March, Mr. Sinnett is expected to keep hi. lips closed as they will be in death—three score and ten hence. *Not a soul*, but Mrs. S., your good lady, must know one word of this letter. This I expect of your friendship, and now put it to test. To Mr. Hume—you may write just now, so that the letter might be received by him on the 24th, in the afternoon. Your future depends on this, your silence.

K. H.

LETTER No. 90 [1]

University College, London, W.C.,
November 26th,' 81.

My dear Sinnett,

I ought to have answered your letter before this, but deferred doing so till I had had the pleasure of a conversation with Mrs. Sinnett. This I have had, and greatly to my enjoyment. She is, as you led me to expect, thoroughly convinced of the reality of what she has seen and heard. Like me, she does not know what to make of the last departure, I mean in respect of my spirit-experiences. I really do not know what to say about it. There is no way of harmonizing facts with the claim made; and to your belief that ' The Brothers cannot be ignorant . . cannot be mistaken,' I can only reply that *they most undoubtedly are both in respect of me*.[2] This, however, would merely be my opinion, were it not

---

[1] K.H.'s Comments on this letter are written in ink on the original, and are here printed in bold type. Unless there is a footnote to the contrary italics indicate that the passage has been underlined by K.H.—ED.

[2] This passage was underlined by S. Moses.—ED.

that I have an unbroken chain of documentary and other evidence extending in absolute sequence from the first time Imperator appeared down to yesterday. These are all dated communications, notes, and records which speak for themselves, and which in substance can be attested by the knowledge of my friends who have been concerned with me all thro' this matter.

When the old lady first hinted at some connexion between the " Lodge " and me, I entered at once into the thing with Imperator and put the case over and over again. Here is one record which I transcribe. Dec. 24, 1876. " I asked some questions respecting a letter from H.P.B. in which she says in reply to one of mine— ' If you are profoundly certain that I have not understood you, both your intuition and mediumship have failed you. . . . I never said that you had mistaken Imperator for another spirit. He is not to be mistaken, once that he is known. He knows and his name be blessed for ever. You want objective proof of the Lodge. Have you not Imperator and can you not ask him whether I speak the truth? '

To this the answer written was long and precise. Among other things is this:—(The first person plural is always used by I.) **Why?**

" We have already told you that your American friends understand neither your character, nor your training, nor your spiritual experiences . . . So far from your Intuition having failed you, it has protected you. *We are not able to say* how (!) far any with whom your correspondent is in communication CAN give her a correct account of you. It is doubtful, so far as we know: though some have the power *as Magus.* But even he does not understand. (! !) **I will try one more. honest medium—Eglinton, when he is gone; and see what comes of it. I will do so much for the Society.** His work is other than ours and he is not concerned with your inner life. *If any have the power, they have not been willing to exercise it. We do not understand whether it is pretended that we ourselves have given any information.* It SEEMS that the hint is conveyed without direct statement. We may say at once clearly that we have at no time held any intercourse with your friend on the subject. She does not know us in any way, and we know nothing of this Lodge or Brotherhood." . . . .

(As to my mistaking a personating spirit for Imperator, it was said) " Assuredly you would not mistake any other spirit for us. It would be impossible. We are what we have revealed ourselves to you: no other; and our name and presence could not be taken by any other. *We have been permanently your Guardian,* and no other takes our *place.*" **No: the 6th principles cannot be shifted.**

And so on quite unmistakeably. I may say here that Imperator stated when he first came to me, and many times *subsequently that he had been with me all my life, tho' I was not conscious of his presence,* till he revealed it—*NOT at Mt. Athos most surely!?*—but in quite another place and way. The coherent development of my mediumship has been uninterrupted. There is no LACUNA. Now objective mediumship is gone, and my inner spirit-sense is opened. Only yesterday I sought and got from Imper. *who was clearly visible and audible to me* * exact and precise renewal of what he has so often repeated that I am ashamed to seek a repetition of his assurance. Whatever may be the explanation, *rest assured without room for doubt that not only is he not a Brother, but that he knows nothing* whatever of any such beings. **(I)**

Your warning as to my being on the wrong scent if I supposed this were a made up story of the Old Lady's is heeded, one must entertain every sort of theory to account for such a thing: but I should not have been found for years defending her against every kind of calumny if I thought her capable of a mere vulgar fraud.

It will not, however, escape your critical mind that an allegation such as this confronted by such plain and perfect testimony as I bring, must be capable of some sort of proof, if it is to be seriously entertained. It is unfortunately the fact that not only is the claim incompatible with all the facts; but the alleged facts put forward are just those, and only those, made known by me: and the guesses made are so ludicrously wide of truth—as can be shown by evidence not resting on me alone—that it is plain they *are* mere shorts.

That is a destructive criticism from the negative side. Now what positive proof is produced? None. Can any be given? This Brother who cast his eye on me at Mt. Athos and assumed the style and title of Imperator. What did he ever say to me or tell me? When and where did he appear, and what proof can he give of the fact? During a long intercourse such as he claims he can surely produce some positive evidence to rebut the presumption drawn above.

If not, any sane person would know what conclusion to draw.

Pardon me for pursuing this subject at length. I see in fact that I am come to a place where two ways meet: and I sadly fear that Fragments of Occult Truth show that *Spiritualism and Occultism* are incompatible. I should be heartily sorry if you were to waste your time and force over anything that cannot found itself demonstrably on *Truth*. Hence my desire to have this raked out.

Otherwise I should dismiss it with much contempt. As you say of the Old Lady, "just consider the opportunities I have had of forming an opinion."

Hearty good wishes,

Yours ever,
W. STAINTON MOSES.

* See K.H.'s comments in bold type *post*.—ED.

* So was Madme. Lebendorff to the Russian child medium.
. . . So is Jesus and John the Baptist to Edward Maitland; as
true and as *honest* and *sincere* as S.M.; though neither knew the
other John the Baptist having never heard of Jesus who is a spiritual
abstraction and no living man of that epoch. And does not
E. Maitland see Hermes the first and second and Elijah, etc?
Finally does not Mrs. Kingsford feel as sure as S.M. with regard
to + that she *saw* and *conversed* with *God*!! ; and that but a few
evenings after she had talked with, and received a written communication from the Spirit of a dog? Read, read Maitland's *Soul, etc.*,
once more my friend, see pp. 180, 194, 239, 240, and 267-8-9, etc.
And who purer or more truthful than that woman or Maitland!
Mystery, mystery will you exclaim. IGNORANCE we answer: the
creation of that we believe in and *want* to see.

(1) A Brother? Does *he* or even yourself know what is understood by the name of *Brother?* Does he know what we mean by
Dhyan Chohans or Planetary Spirits, by the disembodied and
embodied Lha?, by—but it is and must remain yet for some time a
mere vexation of spirit for you all. My letter is *private*. You may
use the arguments but not my authority or name. It will be all
explained to you *rest assured*. A living *Brother* may show himself
and be *de facto* ignorant of many things. But a Spirit, an omniscient Planetary show himself so completely ignorant of what is going
round him: most extraordinary.

LETTER No. 91A

Received Allahabad, cold weather, 1882-83.

Read the enclosed from C.C.M.; summon to your recollection,
and then tell Sinnett the whole truth about the message which I
gave you in London about the £100 in Mrs. Billing's and
Upasika's presence. Do not forget to state the conditions under
which I spoke. Do not let H.P.B. see C.C.M.'s letter but return
it to Allahabad with your remarks.

                                                         K.H.

LETTER No. 91B

I got out the letters of C.C.M. and yourself and gave the former
to Mr. Olcott to answer. Thus one half of the " damaging "
accusation is disposed of and explained away naturally enough.
Poor woman! Incessantly and intensely engrossed with one ever
working thought—the CAUSE and Society—even her carelessness
and lack of memory, her forgetfulness and distraction are viewed

in the light of criminal acts. I have now again "osmosed" his answer to return it with a few more words of explanation that should come from me.

The deduction of Mr. Massey that "the adept foresight was not available" in sundry noted cases of theosophical failure is but the restatement of the old error that the selections of members and the actions of Founders and Chelas are controlled by us! This has been often denied, and—as I believe—sufficiently explained to you in my Darjeeling letter, but objectors cling to their theory despite all. We have no concern with, nor *do we guide the events generally*: yet take the series of names he quotes and see that each man was a useful factor toward producing the net result. Hurry-chund drew the party to Bombay—although they had prepared to go to Madras, which would have been fatal at that stage of the Theosophical movement; Wimbridge and Miss Bates gave an English complexion to the party and caused from the first much good by causing a bitter journalistic assault upon the Founders which brought on reaction; Dayanand stamped the movement with the impress of Aryan nationality; and lastly Mr. Hume—who is already the secret and may well become the open foe of the cause—has aided it greatly by his influence and will promote it more despite himself, by the ulterior results of his defection. In each instance the individual traitor and enemy was given his chance, and but for his moral obliquity might have derived incalculable good from it to his personal Karma.

Mrs. Billing is—a medium, and when that is said all is said. Except this, that among mediums she is *the most honest* if not the best. Has Mr. Massey seen *her* answer to Mrs. Simpson, the Boston medium that the questions—very compromising no doubt for the New England prophetess and Seer—should be brought forward as evidence of her guilt? Why—if honest, has she not exposed *pro bono publico* all such false mediums?—may be the question asked. She tried to warn her friends repeatedly; result: "friends" fell off and she herself was regarded in the light of a slanderer, a "Judas." She tried to do so, indirectly, in the case of Miss Cook (junior). Ask Mr. Massey to recollect what were *his* feelings in 1879, at the time he was investigating the *materialization* phenomena of that young lady, when told by Mrs. Billing —guardedly, and by H.P.B. bluntly, that he was mistaking a piece of white muslin for a "spirit." In your world of *maya* and kaleidoscopic change of feelings—truth is an article rarely wanted in the market; it has its seasons and very short ones. The woman has more sterling virtues and honesty in her little finger than many of the *never distrusted* mediums put together. She has been a loyal member of the Society from the time she joined it, and her rooms in New York are the rallying centre where our theosophists meet.

Her loyalty, moreover, is one that costs her the regard of many patrons. She also, unless closely watched by " Ski " can *turn a traitor*—precisely because she is a medium, though it is not likely she would do it—withal she is incapable of either a falsehood or deceit in her normal state.

I cannot control a feeling of repugnance to going into particulars about this, that, and the other phenomenon that may have occurred. They are the playthings of the tyro and if we sometimes have gratified the craving for them (as in Mr. Olcott's and in a lesser degree your own case at the beginning, since we knew what good spiritual growth would come of it) we do not feel called upon to be continually explaining away deceptive appearances, due to mixed carelessness and credulity, or blind skepticism, as the case may be. For the present we offer our knowledge— some portions of it at least—to be either accepted or rejected on its own merits independently—entirely so—from the source from which it emanates. In return, we ask neither allegiance, loyalty, nor even simple courtesy—nay, we [would] rather have nothing of the sort offered since we would have to decline the kind offer. We have in view the good of the whole association of earnest British theosophists and care little for individual opinions or the regard of this or that member. Our four year old experience has sufficiently delineated the future of the *best possible* relations between ourselves and Europeans to make us still more prudent and less lavish of *personal* favours. Suffice then for me to say that " Ski " has more than once served as carrier and even mouthpiece for several of us; and that in the case Mr. Massey alludes to, the letter from " a Scotch Brother " was a genuine one to deliver which to him mysteriously we—the " Scotch " Brother included—refused point blank, as, notwithstanding Upasika's passionate prayers to make a few exceptions in favour of C. C. Massey, her " best and dearest friend," *one whom she loved* and trusted so implicitly that she actually offered to accept one year more of her long, dreary exile, and work far way from her final goal would we but consent to gratify him with our presence and teachings—as notwithstanding all this, I say, we were not allowed to waste our powers so ruthlessly. Madame B. was therefore left to send it by post, or if she preferred it, to go by " Ski "—M. having forbidden her to exercise her own occult means. Surely no crime can be imputed to her—unless absolute and frenzied devotion to a great Idea and those whom she regards as her best and truest friends, may now be imputed as an offence. And now, I hope, I may be relieved of the necessity of going into detailed explanation about the famous Massey-Billing letter affair. Let me only point out to you what is the impression made on anyone with a fair unbiassed mind who would happen to read Mr. Massey's letter and the lame evidence contained therein. (1) *No clever medium* bent on carrying out a plan of deception previously concocted would have the idiotic idea of *producing, and placing before* him with her own hands, any article (minute-book in her case) in which the tricky " phenomenon " was to take place. Had she known that " Ski " placed the letter inside that book there are 99 chances out of 100 that she would not have brought it to him herself. It is over twenty years since she made of mediumship her profession. A fraud and an unscrupulous deceiver in one thing, she must have been in many. Among hundreds of enemies and still more skeptics she passed triumphantly and unscathed the most crucial tests, producing the most wonderful mediumistic phenomena. Her husband is the *only one*—he who ruined to now dishonour her—who accuses her with documentary proof in hand of being a trickster. H.P.B. wrote to him the most violent letters of reproach and insisted upon his expulsion from the Society. He hates her. What's the use of seeking for further motives? (2) Mr. Massey is but half a prophet when saying—he supposes " you will be told that these things were occult forgeries (!) " No; the message on the back of Dr. Wyld's letter is in her own handwriting, as also the first portion of the letter copied and now quoted by him for your benefit—the most *damaging* portion in his opinion —and no harm in it as far as I see, and as explained already. She does not want him to know that she used " Ski " whose entity he was known to distrust, the shortcomings and crimes of several other " Skis " having been fathered on the *real* " Ski," and Mr. Massey unable to recognise one from the other. In her loose, careless way she says: " Let him think *what he likes but he must not suspect you have been near him* with Ski at your orders." Thereupon, Mrs. B. the " clever impostor " hardened and " experienced in deceit" does precisely that *which she is plainly asked not to do, i.e.* goes near him and hands to him the very book in which Ski had placed the letter! Very clever; quite so. (3) He argues that, " even if otherwise conceivable (the occult forgery) the later contents of the letter were inconsistent with the supposed object, for it went on to speak of the T.S. and of the adepts with as much apparently genuine devotion etc. etc." Mr. Massey, I see, makes no difference between an " occult " and a *common* forger such as his legal experience may have made him acquainted with. An " occult " forger, a *dugpa* would have *forged* the letter precisely in this tone. He would have never become guilty of being carried away by his personal grudge, so as to deprive his letter of its cleverest feature. The T.S. would not be shown by him " a superstructure upon fraud," and it is " the very opposite impression " that *is* its crown. I say *is* for half of the letter *is* a forgery and a *very occult* one. Mr. Massey may perhaps believe me since it is

not that portion which concerns him that is denied (all with the
exception of the words "mysterious" and (or some other still
more mysterious place ")—but "the later portion," just that one
which "Billing himself reluctantly admitted" as giving "the very
opposite impression." "L.L" is nobody living or dead.   Certainly not "Lord Lindsay," since he was not known to H.P.B.,
nor had she then nor had she ever since the least concern about
his "Lordship."   This portion bears so much the impression of
clumsy fraud upon its face that it could have deceived but one
whose mind was already well prepared to see fraud in Mrs. Billing
and her "Ski."   I have done, and you may show this to your
friend Mr. Massey.   Whatever his personal opinion about myself
and Brothers can in no way influence the promised "teachings"
through your friendly agency.

Yours,

K. H.

LETTER No. 92

23-11-82.

**P.S—It may so happen that for purposes of our own, mediums
and their spooks will be left undisturbed and free not only to personate the "Brothers" but even to *forge our handwriting*. Bear
this in mind and be prepared for it in London. Unless the *message*
or communication or whatever it may be is *preceded* by the triple
words: "Kin-t-an, Na-lan-da, Dha-ra-ni," *know it is not me, nor
from me.***

K.H.

LETTER No. 93

Received in London 1883-84.

My good and faithful friend—the explanation herein contained
would have never been made but that I have of late perceived
how troubled you were during your conversations upon the subject
of "plagiarism" with some friends—C.C.M. particularly.   Now
especially that I have received your last in which you mention so
delicately "this wretched little Kiddle incident," to withhold
truth from you would be cruelty; nevertheless, to give it out to
the world of prejudiced and malignantly disposed Spiritualists,
would be sheer folly.   Therefore, we must compromise: I must
lay both yourself and Mr. Ward, who shares my confidence, *under
a pledge never to explain without special permission from me the facts* here-
inafter stated by me to anyone—not even to M. A. Oxon and

C. C. Massey, included for reasons I will mention presently and that you will readily understand. If pressed by any of them you may simply answer that the " psychological mystery " was cleared up to yourself and some others; and—IF satisfied—you may add, that " the parallel passages " cannot be called *plagiarism* or words to this effect. I give to you *carte blanche* to say anything you like— even the reason why I rather have the real *facts* withheld from the general public and most of the London Fellows—all except the details you alone with a few others will know. As you will perceive, I do not even bind you to defend my reputation— *unless* you feel yourself satisfied beyond any doubt, and have well understood the explanation yourself. And now I may tell you why I prefer being regarded by your friends an " ugly plagiarist."

Having been called repeatedly a " sophist," a " myth," a " Mrs. Harris " and a " lower intelligence " by the enemies, I [would] rather not be regarded as a deliberate artificer and *a liar* by bogus friends—I mean those who would accept me reluctantly even were I to rise to their own ideal in their estimation instead of the reverse—as at present. Personally, I am indifferent, of course, to the issue. But for *your* sake and that of the Society I may make one more effort to clear the horizon of one of its " blackest " clouds. Let us then recapitulate the situation and see what your Western sages say of it. " K.H."—it is settled—is a *plagiarist*—if it be, after all a question of K.H. and not of the " two Occidental Humourists." In the former case, an alleged " adept " unable to evolve out of his " small oriental brain " any idea or words worthy of Plato, turned to that deep tank of profound philosophy, the *Banner of Light,* and drew therefrom the sentences best fitted to express his rather entangled ideas, which had fallen from the inspired lips of Mr. Henry Kiddle! In the other alternative, the case becomes still more difficult to comprehend—save on the theory of the irresponsible mediumship of the pair of Western jokers. However startling and impracticable the theory, that two persons who have been clever enough to carry on undetected the fraud of personating for five years several adepts—not one of whom resembles the other;—two persons, of whom one, at any rate, is a fair master of English and can hardly be suspected of paucity of original ideas, should turn for a bit of plagiarism to a journal as the *Banner*, widely known and read by most English knowing Spiritualists; and above all, pilfer their borrowed sentences from the discourse of a conspicuous new convert, whose public utterances were at the very time being read and welcomed by every *medium* and Spiritualist; however improbable all this and much more, yet any alternative seems more welcome than simple truth. The decree is pronounced; " K.H.," whoever he is, has stolen passages from Mr. Kiddle. Not only this, but as shewn by " a Perplexed Reader " he has omitted inconvenient words and has *so distorted the ideas he has borrowed* as to divert them from their original intention to suit his own very different purpose.

Well, to this, if I had any desire to argue out the question I might answer that of what constitutes plagiarism, being a borrowing of *ideas* rather than of words and sentences, there was none in point of fact, and I stand acquitted by my own accusers. As Milton says—" such kind of borrowing as this, *if it be not bettered* by the borrower is accounted *plagiary*." Having *distorted* the ideas " appropriated," and, as now published—diverted them from their original intention to suit my own " very different purpose," on such grounds my literary *larceny* does not appear very formidable after all? And even, were there no other explanation offered, the most that could be said is, that owing to the poverty of words at the command of Mr. Sinnett's correspondent, and his ignorance of the art of English composition, he has adapted a few of innocent Mr. Kiddle's effusions, some of his excellently constructed sentences—to express his own contrary ideas. The above is the only line of argument I have given to, and permitted to be used in, an editorial by the " gifted editor " of the *Theosophist*, who has been off her head since the accusation. Verily woman—is a dreadful calamity in this fifth race! However, to you and some few, whom you have permission to select among your most trusted theosophists, taking first care to pledge them by *word of honour* to keep the little revelation to themselves, I will now explain the real facts of this " very puzzling " psychological mystery. The solution is so simple, and the circumstances so amusing, that I confess I laughed when my attention was drawn to it, some time since. Nay, it is calculated to make me smile even now, were it not the knowledge of the pain it gives to some true friends.

The letter in question was framed by me while on a journey and on horse-back. It was dictated mentally, in the direction of, and " precipitated " by, a young chela not yet expert at this branch of psychic chemistry, and who had to transcribe it from the hardly visible imprint. Half of it, therefore, was omitted and the other half more or less distorted by the " artist." When asked by him at the time, whether I would look it over and correct I answered, imprudently, I confess—" anyhow will do, my boy—it is of no great importance if you skip a few words." I was physically very tired by a ride of 48 hours consecutively, and (physically again) —half asleep. Besides this I had very important business to attend to *psychically* and therefore little remained of me to devote to that letter. It was doomed, I suppose. When I woke I found it had already been sent on, and, as I was not then anticipating its publication, I never gave it from that time a thought. Now,

I had never evoked spiritual Mr. Kiddle's physiognomy, had never heard of his existence, was not aware of his name. Having —owing to our correspondence and your Simla surroundings and friends—felt interested in the intellectual progress of the Phenomenalists, which progress by the by I found rather moving backward in the case of American Spiritualists—I had directed my attention some two months previous to the great annual camping movement of the latter, in various directions, among others to Lake or Mount Pleasant. Some of the curious ideas and sentences representing the general hopes and aspirations of the American Spiritualists remained impressed on my memory, and I remembered only these ideas and detached sentences quite apart from the personalities of those who harboured or pronounced them. Hence, my entire ignorance of the lecturer whom I have innocently defrauded as it would appear, and who now raises the hue and cry. Yet, had I dictated my letter in the form it now appears in print, it would certainly look suspicious, and, however far from what is generally called plagiarism, yet in the absence of any inverted commas it would lay a foundation for censure. But I did nothing of the kind, as the original impression now before me clearly shows. And before I proceed any further, I must give you some explanation of this mode of *precipitation*. The recent experiments of the Psychic Research Society will help you greatly to comprehend the rationale of this " mental telegraphy." You have observed in the *Journal* of that body how thought transference is cumulatively affected. The image of the geometrical or other figure which the active brain has had impressed upon it, is gradually imprinted upon the recipient brain of the passive subject—as the series of reproductions illustrated in the cuts show. Two factors are needed to produce a perfect and instantaneous mental telegraphy—close concentration in the operator, and complete receptive passivity in the " reader " subject. Given a disturbance of either condition, and the result is proportionately imperfect. The " reader " does not see the image as in the " telegrapher's " brain, but as arising in his own. When the latter's thought wanders, the psychic current becomes broken, the communication disjointed and incoherent. In a case such as mine, the chela had, as it were, to pick up what he could from the current I was sending him and, as above remarked, patch the broken bits together as best he might. Do not you see the same thing in ordinary mesmerism—the *maya* impressed upon the subject's imagination by the operator becoming, now stronger, now feebler, as the latter keeps the intended illusive image more or less steadily before his own fancy? And how often the clairvoyants reproach the magnetiser for taking their thoughts off the subject under consideration? And the mesmeric healer will always bear you witness that if he permits himself to think of anything but the vital current he is pouring into his patient, he is at once compelled to either establish the current afresh or stop the treatment. So I, in this instance, having at the moment more vividly in my mind the psychic diagnosis of current Spiritualistic thought, of which the Lake Pleasant speech was one marked symptom, unwittingly transferred that reminiscence more vividly than my own remarks upon it and deductions therefrom. So to say, the " despoiled victim's "—Mr. Kiddle's—utterances came out as a " high light " and were more sharply photographed (first in the chela's brain and thence on the paper before him, a *double* process and one far more difficult than " thought reading " simply) while the rest, my remarks thereupon and arguments—as I now find, are hardly visible and quite blurred on the original scraps before me. Put into a mesmeric subject's hand a sheet of blank paper, tell him it contains a certain chapter of some book that you have read, concentrate your thoughts upon the words, and see how—*provided that he has himself not read the chapter*, but only takes it from your memory—his reading will reflect your own more or less vivid successive recollections of your author's language. The same as to the precipitation by the chela of the transferred thought upon (or rather, *into*) paper; if the mental picture received be feeble his visible reproduction of it must correspond. And the more so in proportion to the closeness of attention he gives. He might— were he but merely a person of the true mediumistic temperament—be employed by his " Master " as a sort of *psychic printing machine* producing lithographed or psychographed impressions of what the operator had in mind; his nerve-system, the machine, his nerve-aura the printing fluid, the colours drawn from that exhaustless store-house of pigments (as of everything else) the Akasa. But the medium and the chela are diametrically dissimilar and the latter acts consciously, except under exceptional circumstances during development not necessary to dwell upon here.

Well, as soon as I heard of the charge—the commotion among my *defenders* having reached me across the eternal snows—I ordered an investigation into the original scraps of the impression. At the first glance I saw that it was I, the only and most guilty party, the poor little boy having done but that which he was told. Having now restored the characters and the lines—omitted and blurred beyond hope of recognition by anyone but their original *evolver*—to their primitive colour and places, I now find my letter reading quite differently as you will observe. Turning to the *Occult World*—the copy sent by you—to the page cited, (namely p. 149 in the first edition) I was struck, upon carefully reading it, by the great discrepancy between the sentences. A gap, so to say, of ideas between part 1 (from line 1 to line 25) and part 2—the plagiarized portion so-called. There seems no connection at all between the two; for what has, indeed, the determination of our chiefs (to prove to a skeptical world that physical phenomena are as reducible to law as anything else) to do with Plato's ideas which " rule the world " or " practical Brotherhood of Humanity?" I fear that it is your personal friendship alone for the writer that has blinded you to the discrepancy and disconnection of ideas in this abortive " precipitation," *even until now.* Otherwise you could not have failed to perceive that something was wrong on that page; that there was a glaring defect in the connection. Moreover, I have to plead *guilty* to another sin: I have never so much as looked at my letters in print—until the day of the forced investigation. I had read only your own original matter, feeling it a loss of time to go over my hurried bits and scraps of thought. But now, I have to ask you to read the passages as they were originally dictated by me, and make the comparison with the *Occult World* before you.

I transcribe them with my own hand this once, whereas the letter in your possession was written by the chela. I ask you also to compare this hand-writing with that of some of the *earlier letters* you received from me. Bear in mind, also the " O.L.'s " emphatic denial at Simla that my *first* letter had ever been written *by myself.* I felt annoyed at her gossip and remarks *then*; it may serve a good purpose *now.* Alas! by no means are we all " gods "; especially when you remember that since the palmy days of the " impressions " and " precipitations "—" K.H." has been born into a *new* and *higher* light, and even that one, in no wise the most dazzling to be acquired on this earth. Verily the *Light of Omniscience* and infallible Prevision on this earth—that shines only for the highest CHOHAN alone—is yet far away from me!

I enclose the copy *verbatim* from the restored fragments, underlining in red [1] the *omitted* sentences for easier comparison.

(Page 149.—First Edition.)

. . . . . Phenomenal elements previously unthought of, . . . will disclose at last the secrets of their mysterious workings. Plato was right *to readmit every element of speculation which Socrates had discarded. The problems of universal being are not unattainable or worthless if attained. But the latter can be solved only by mastering those elements that are now looming on the horizons of the profane. Even the Spirits with their mistaken, grotesquely perverted views and notions are hazily realizing the new situation. They prophesy and their prophecies are not always without a point of truth in them, of intuitional pre-vision, so to say. Hear some of them reasserting the old, old axiom that* " Ideas rule the world "; and as men's minds receive new ideas, laying aside

---

[1] These passages are printed in italics.—ED.

the old and effete the world (*will*) advance; mighty revolutions (*will*) spring from them; *institutions* (*aye, and even* creeds and powers, *they may add*)—WILL crumble before their onward march crushed by their own *inherent force not the* irresistible force *of the " new ideas " offered by the Spiritualists! Yes; they are both right and wrong.* It will be just as impossible to resist their influence when the time comes as to stay the progress of the tide,—*to be sure. But what the Spiritualists fail to perceive, I see, and their " Spirits " to explain (the latter knowing no more than what they can find in the brains of the former) is, that all this* will come gradually on; and *that* before it comes *they as well as ourselves* have all a duty *to perform, a task* set before us: that of sweeping away as much as possible the dross left to us by our pious forefathers. New ideas have to be planted on clean places, for these ideas touch upon the most momentous subjects. It is not physical phenomena *or the agency called Spiritualism* but these universal ideas that we *have precisely to* study; *the noumenon not the phenomenon,* for, to comprehend the LATTER we have first to understand the FORMER. They *do* touch man's true position in the Universe, to be sure, *but only* in relation to his FUTURE *not* PREVIOUS births. *It is not physical phenomena however wonderful that can ever explain to man* his origin *let alone* his ultimate destiny, *or as one of them expressess it*—the relation of the mortal to the immortal, of the temporary to the eternal, of the finite to the Infinite, *etc., etc. They talk very glibly of what they regard as new ideas* "larger, *more general*, grander, more comprehensive, *and at the same time, they recognise instead* of the eternal reign of immutable law, *the universal reign of law as the expression of a divine will* (*!*). *Forgetful of their earlier beliefs, and that " it repented the Lord that he had made Man "* these would-be *philosophers and reformers would impress upon their hearers that the expression of the said divine Will " is unchanging and unchangeable*—in regard to which there is only an ETERNAL NOW, while to mortals (uninitiated?) time is past or future as related to their finite existence on this material *plane "—of which they know as little as of their spiritual spheres*—a speck of dirt *they have made the latter like our own earth, a future life that the true philosopher would rather avoid than court. But I dream with my eyes open. . . . At all events this is not any privileged teachings of their own. Most of these ideas are taken piece-meal from Plato and the Alexandrian Philosophers.* It is what we *all* study and what many have solved. . . . . etc., etc.

This is the true copy of the original document as now restored —the " Rosetta stone " of the Kiddle incident. And now, if you have understood my explanations about the process as given in a few words further back, you need not ask me how it came to pass that though somewhat disconnected, the sentences transcribed by the chela are mostly those that are now considered as plagiarized while the " missing links " are precisely those phrases that would have shown the passages were simply *reminiscences* if not quotations—the key-note around which came grouping my own reflections on that morning. In those days you were yet hesitating to see in Occultism, or the " O.L.'s " phenomena anything beyond a variety of Spiritualism and mediumship. For the first time in my life I had paid a serious attention to the utterances of the poetical " media," of the so-called " inspirational " oratory of the English and American lecturers, its quality and limitations. I was struck with all this brilliant but empty verbiage, and recognised for the first time fully its pernicious intellectual tendency. M. knew all about them—but since I had never had anything to do with any of them they interested me very little. It was their gross and unsavoury materialism hiding clumsily under its shadowy spiritual veil that attracted my thoughts at the time. While dictating the sentences quoted—a small portion of the many I had been pondering over for some days— it was those ideas that were thrown out *en relief* the most, leaving out my own parenthetical remarks to disappear in the precipitation. Had I looked over the impressed *negative* (?) there would have been one more weapon broken in the enemy's hand. Having neglected this duty, my Karma evolved what the mediums of the future and the *Banner* may call the " Kiddle triumph." The coming ages will divide Society after the manner of your modern Baconians and Shakesperians into two quarrelling camps of partisans, called respectively the " Kiddlites " and the " Koothumites " who will fight over the important literary problem— " which one of the two plagiarized from the other "? I may be told that meanwhile the American and English spiritualists are gloating over the " Sinnett—K.H." *Sedan*? May their great orator and champion and they enjoy their triumph in peace and happiness, for no " adept " will ever cast his Himalayan shadow to obscure their innocent felicity. To you and a few other true friends I feel it may duty to give an explanation. To all others I leave the right to regard Mr. Kiddle—whoever he may be—as the inspirer of your humble servant. I have done, and you may now, in your turn, do what you please with these facts, except the making use of them in print or even speaking of them to the opponents, save in general terms. You must understand my reasons for this. One does not cease entirely, my dear friend to be a *man* nor lose one's dignity for being an *adept*. In the latter capacity, one, no doubt, remains in every case quite indifferent to the opinion of the outside world. The former always draws the line between *ignorant surmise* and—deliberate, *personal insult*. I cannot really be expected to take advantage of the first to be ever hiding the problematic " adept " behind the skirts of the two supposed " humourists " and as *man*, I had too much experience

lately in such above said insults with Messrs. S. Moses and
C. C. Massey to give them any more opportunities to doubt the
word of " K.H.", or see in him a vulgar defendant, a kind of
guilty, tricky Babu before a panel of stern European jurymen and
Judge.

I have no time to answer fully now your last, long business
letter, but will shortly. Nor do I answer Mr. Ward—since it is
useless. I highly approve of *his* coming to India, but disapprove
as highly his fancy of bringing Mr. C. C. Massey here. The result
of the latter would be to injure the cause among Englishmen.
Distrust and prejudice are contagious. His presence in Calcutta
would be as disastrous as Mr. Ward's presence and services to the
cause I live for would be beneficent and fruitful of good effects.
But I would insist upon his passing some time at the Headquarters
before his taking up his proposed labour of love among the officials.

It is certainly most flattering to hear from him that Mrs. K.
" had essayed her best to meet me in one or more of her trances ";
and most sad to learn that " though she had invoked you (me)
with all her spiritual intensity—she could get no response." It
is too bad, really, that this " ladie fair " should have been put to
the trouble of a fruitless ramble through space to find insignificant
me. Evidently we move in different astral " circles," and hers
is not the first instance of persons becoming skeptical as to the
existence of things outside their own *milieu*. There are, you know,
" Alps upon Alps " and from no two peaks does one get the same
view! Nevertheless, it is, as I say flattering to find her evoking me
by name, while preparing for myself and colleagues a disastrous
Waterloo. To tell the truth, I was not aware of the former,
though painfully conscious of the latter. Yet, had not even the
dismal plot ever entered her spiritual mind, to be honest, I do not
think I could have ever responded to her call. As an American
Spiritualist would put it—there seems to be very little *affinity* between our two natures. She is too haughty and imperious, too
self-complacent for me; besides which she is too young and
" fascinating " for a poor mortal like myself. To speak seriously,
Mme. Gebhard is quite another sort of person. Hers is a genuine,
sterling nature; she is a born Occultist in her intuitions and I
have made a few experiments with her—though it is rather M.'s
duty than my own, and that, as you would say, it was not
" originally contemplated " that I should be made to visit all the
sibyls and sirens of the Theosophical establishment. My own
preferences make me keep to the safer side of the two sexes in my
occult dealings with them, though for certain reasons, even such
visits—in my own natural skin—have to be extremely restricted
and limited. I enclose a telegram from Mr. Brown to the " O.L."
This day week I will be at Madras *en route* to Singapore and Ceylon,

30

and Burmah. I will answer you through one of the chelas at the Headquarters.

The poor "O.L." in *disgrace*? Oh dear, no! We have nothing against the old woman with the exception that she is one. To save us from being *insulted* as she calls it, she is ready to give our real addresses and thus lead to a catastrophe. The real reason is that the hapless creature was too much compromised, too bitterly insulted owing to our existence. It all falls upon her and, therefore, it is but right that she should be *screened* in some things.

Yes; I would see *you*, President, if possible. Unless permitted by the Chohan (who forwards you His Blessing) to act on other lines of business—*i.e.*, psychologically, I renounce to trust for the rebirth of *Phoenix* to the good-will of my countrymen. The feeling between the two races is now intensely bitter, and anything undertaken by the natives *now* is sure to be opposed to the bitter end by the Europeans in India. Let us drop it for a while. I'll answer your questions in my next. If you find time to write for the *Theosophist* and can induce someone else, as Mr. Myers, for instance—you will oblige me personally. You are wrong in distrusting Subba Row's writings. He does not write *willingly*, to be sure, but he will never make a false statement. See his last in the November number. His statement concerning the errors of General Cunningham ought to be regarded a whole revelation leading to a revolution in Indian archaeology. Ten to one—it will never receive the attention it deserves. Why? Simply because his statements contain sober *facts*, and that what you Europeans prefer generally is *fiction* so long the latter dovetails with, and answers preconceived theories.

K. H.

The more I think of it, the more reasonable appears to me your plan of a Society within *the* London Society. Try, for something *may* come out of it.

LETTER No. 94

My dear friend—Amid the various and arduous labours it has pleased the venerable Chohan to entrust me with—I had entirely forgotten the "Kiddle incident." You have my explanation. In asking you to keep me the secret I only meant the withholding of certain details that, in their ignorance of the scientific process, your and my opponents would take exception to, make of it a pretext for poking fun at occult sciences and finally charge me with clumsy lies and yourself with credulity, or "hero-worship" as the golden-haired nymph of the Vicarage puts it. But if you are prepared to stand the fire of furious denial and adverse criticism, make of my letter and explanations the best use you can. The several letters and articles in the last numbers of the *Theosophist* given out with my permission—by Gen. Morgan, Subba Row and Dharani Dhar may pave the way for you. I would not have " the propagation of Theosophy " impeded on my account and to save my name from a few extra blows.

Yours in haste,

K. H.

LETTER No. 95 [1]

such a life of infamy. I will try my best to make of him a vegetarian and a teetotaller. *Total* abstinence from flesh and liquor are very wisely prescribed by Mr. Hume, if he would have good results. In good hands E. will do an immense good to the T.S. in India, but for this he has [to go] through a training of purification. M. had to prepare him for six weeks before his departure; otherwise it would have been impossible for me to project into his atmosphere even the *reflection* of my " double." I told you already, my kind friend, that what he saw was *not me.* Nor will I be able to project that reflection for you—unless he is thoroughly purified. Therefore, as the matter now stands I have not a word to say against Mr. Hume's conditions as expressed in his last " official " letter, except in congratulating him with all my heart. For the same reason it is impossible for me to answer him and his questions just now. Let him have patience, pray, in the E. matter. There are dirty conspiracies set on foot, germinating in London, among the spiritualists; and I am not at all sure that E. will resist the tide that threatens to submerge him unless they obtain from him at least a partial recantation. We departed from our policy and the experiment was made with him on the " Vega " solely for the benefit of some Anglo-Indian theosophists. Mr. Hume had expressed his surprise that even E.'s " spirits " should know nothing of us, and that despite the interests of the cause we did not show ourselves even to him. On the other hand, the Calcutta spiritualists and Mrs. Gordon with them were triumphant, and Colonel G. followed suit. The " dear departed ones " were for the short period of his stay at Calcutta in odour of sanctity, and the " Brothers " rather low in public estimation. Many of you thought that our appearing to E. would " save the situation " and force Spiritualism to recognise the claims of Theosophy. Well, we complied with your wishes. M. and I were determined to show to you that there was no ground for such

---

[1] The beginning of this letter will be found on pp. 115-19. See Note on p. 119.—EDS.

hopes. The Bigotry and Blindness of the Spiritualists fed by the selfish motives of professional mediums are rampant and the opponents are now desperate. We must allow the natural course of events to develop, and can only help on the coming crisis by having a hand in the increasing frequency of exposures. It would never do for us to *force* events, as it would be only making " martyrs " and allowing these the pretext for a new craze.

Thus, pray have patience. Mr. Hume—if he only holds on to his resolutions—has a grand and noble work before him—the work of a true Founder of a new social era, of a philosophical and religious Reform. It is so vast and so nobly conceived, that if, as I hope, we will now finally agree, he will have quite enough to do during the interval that is necessary for me to probe and prepare Eglinton. I will write to Mr. Hume and answer his every point in a few days, explaining the situation as I conceive it. Meanwhile you will do well to show him this letter. Your *Review* of the *Perfect Way* is more perfect than its author's conception. I thank you, my friend, for your good services. You are beginning to attract the Chohan's attention. And if you only knew what significance *that* has, you would not be calculating to a nicety what reward you are entitled to for certain recent services mentioned.

Yours affectionately,
K. H.

LETTER No. 96

Received 1883 or '84?

My humble pranams, Sahib. Your memory is not good. Have you forgotten the agreement made at Prayag and the pass-words that have to precede every genuine communication coming from us though a भूत डाक *Bhoot-dak* or medium? How like the *seance* of December the 15th—coroneted card, my letter and all! Very similar —as a Peling pundit would say. Yet, first a loving greeting from old woman to *Lonie* misspelled on card Louis, then to C. C. Massey whose name she now never pronounces, and that greeting coming after supper—when C.C.M. had already left. Then my message in a feigned hand when I am at dead loggerheads with my own; again I am made to date my supposed message from Ladakh December 16th, whereas I swear I was at Ch-in-ki (Lhasa), smoking your pipe. Best of all my asking you to " prepare for our coming as soon as we have won over Mr. Eglinton Sahib!!! " One Saturday and Lord Dunraven having failed why not *try* again. A solemn evening, that Saturday, at Piccadilly over old Sotheran the mouldy bookseller. Knew premises well, felt amused and watched with your leave. Why feel so disgusted? Spooks worked remarkably well nothing abashed by my presence of which neither W.E. nor his bodyguard knew anything. My attention was attracted by their forging H.P.B.'s handwriting. Then I put aside my pipe and watched. Too much light for the creatures coming from a Piccadilly Street though Sotheran emanations helped good deal. I would call your friend Mr. Myers' attention to psychic fact of rotten emanations. Raise a good Bhoot crop. Yes; the room with windows overlooking Piccadilly is a good place for psychic development. Poor entranced wretch.

" We wish to state to prevent any future misunderstanding that whatever phenomena may present themselves to you this evening we are in no way responsible for them and have no hand in their production." This is pure self-abnegation—modesty is no name for it. He paced the room and I followed from a distance. He went to Mr. Ward's writing desk and took a sheet of his monogram paper—and I helped myself to one—just to show you I watched. As for all of you, you did not watch very keenly while he was guided to place paper and envelope between the leaves of a book and when he laid it upon the table, or you would have seen something very interesting for science. The clock's silvery tongue strikes ten-fifteen and K.H.'s form descending a hill on horseback —(he is in the far off woods of Cambodia now)—is supposed to cross the horizon of " Uncle Sam's " vision—and disturbs the activity of the Pisachas. The astral disturbance impedes their dull progress. Their bells are fine—very.

Now Sahib, you must not be too hard upon the wretched young fellow. He was utterly *irresponsible* on that night. Of course his belonging to your L.L.T.S. is pure nonsense, for a paid and suspected medium is no peer for English gentlemen. Yet he is honest in his way, and however much K.H. made fun of him in his card addressed to the Gordons—that all of you took seriously at the time—he is really honest in his way and to be pitied. He is a poor epileptic *subject to fits especially on the days when he is expected to have dinner with you*. I mean to ask K.H. to beg a favour from Mr. Ward; to save the poor wretch from the two elementaries which have fastened on him like two barnacles. It is easy for good " Uncle Sam " to get for him an appointment somewhere and thus save him from a life of infamy which kills him; he will thereby do a meritorious and a Theosophical act of charity. Mr. Ward is wrong. W.E. is not guilty of any *conscious*, deliberate jugglery that night. He got a passionate desire to join the L.L., and as the wish is father to the deed his astral ticks fabricated that letter of *mine* through means of their own. Had he done it himself he would have remembered it was not my handwriting as he is familiar with it through Gordons. Woe to the spiritualists! Their *Karma* is heavy with the ruin of men and women they entice into mediumship, and then throw off to starve like a toothless dog. At any rate ask him for the card of *Upasika* with her alleged writing on it. It is a good thing to keep and show occasionally to the Masseys of the L.L. who believe pure lies and will suspect fraud where none is meant. You are at liberty to regard me as a " nigger " and savage, Sahib. But though I am the first to advise Mrs. K.'s re-election—nevertheless, I would sooner trust W.E.'s clairvoyance than Mrs. K.'s, or rather her *rendering* of her visions. But this will soon stop. Subba Row is vindicating you.—Writing an answer to the Australian convert.

M.

LETTER No. 97

" Common people " are the masses as different from those who are distinguished. Your methods were not abandoned, it was only sought to show a drift of cyclic change no doubt that is helped by you too. Are you not man of the world enough to bear the small defects of young disciples? In their way they also help—and greatly. In you is also concealed a power to help from your side, for the poor Society will even yet need all it can get. It is good that you have seen the work of a noble woman, who has left all for the cause. Other ways and times will appear for your help, for you are a single witness and well knowing the facts that will be challenged by traitors.

We cannot alter Karma my " good friend " or we might lift the present cloud from your path. But we do all that is possible in such material matters. No darkness can stay for ever. Have hope and faith and we may disperse it. There are not many left true to the " original program "! And you have been taught much and have much that is, and will be, useful.

M.

SECTION VII

MISCELLANEOUS LETTERS

LETTER No. 98

* I realized it perfectly. But however sincere, these feelings are too deeply covered by a thick crust of self sufficiency and egoistical stubbornness to awaken in me anything like sympathy.

(1) For centuries we have had in Tibet a moral, pure hearted, simple people, unblest with civilization, hence—untainted by its vices. For ages has been Tibet the last corner of the globe not so entirely corrupted as to preclude the mingling together of the two atmospheres—the physical and the spiritual. And he would have us exchange this for *his* ideal of civilization and Govt.! This is pure self peroration, an intense passion for hearing himself discuss, and for imposing his ideas upon every one.

(2) Now really, Mr. H. ought to be sent by an international Committee of Philanthropists, as a Friend of Perishing Humanity to teach our Dalai Lamas—*wisdom*. Why he does not straightway sit down and frame a plan for something like Plato's Ideal *Republic* with a new scheme for everything under the Sun and moon —passes *my* poor comprehension!

(3) This is indeed benevolent in him to go so far out of his way to teach us. Of course, this is pure kindness, and not a desire to over-top the rest of humanity. It is his latest acquisition of mental evolution, which, let us hope, will not turn in to—dissolution.

(4) Amen! My dear friend, you ought to be held responsible for not starting in his head the glorious idea to offer his services as a General School Master for Tibet, Reformer of ancient superstitions and Saviour of future generations. Of course, were he to read this, he would show immediately that I argue like an " educated monkey."

(5) Now just listen to the man jabbering about what he knows nothing. No men living are freer than we when we have once passed out of the stage of pupilage. Docile and obedient but never slaves during that time we must be; otherwise, and if we passed our time in arguing we never would learn anything at all.

(6) And whoever thought of proposing him as such? My dear fellow can you really blame me for shrinking from closer relations with a man whose life seems to hang upon incessant

* The asterisk and numbers refer to Letter 99 from A.O. Hume on which K.H. comments in this letter.—Ed.

argumentation and philipics? He says that he is no *doctrinaire* when he is the very essence of one! He is worthy of all the respect and even affection of those who know him well. But my stars! in less than 24 hours he would paralyse any one of us who might be unfortunate enough to come within a mile of him, merely by his monotonous piping about his own views. No; a thousand times *no*: such men as he make able statesmen, orators anything you like but—never Adepts. We have not one of that sort among us. And that is perhaps why we never felt the necessity for a house of lunatics. In less than three months he would have driven half of our Tibetan population mad!

I mailed a letter for you the other day at Umballa. I see you did not receive it yet.

Yours ever affectionately,
KOOT HOOMI.

LETTER No. 99 [1]

Simla. 20-11-80.

My Dear Koot Humi,

I have sent Sinnett your letter to me and he has kindly sent me yours to him—I want to make some remarks on this, not by way of cavil, but because I am so anxious that you should understand me. Very likely it is my conceit, but whether or no I have a deep rooted conviction that I *could* work effectually if I only saw my way, and I cannot bear the idea of your throwing me over under any misconception of my views. And yet every letter I see of yours, shows me that you do not yet realize what I think and feel.* To explain this I venture to jot down a few comments on your letter to Sinnett.

You say that if Russia does not succeed in taking Tibet, it will be due to you and herein at least you will deserve our gratitude— I do not agree to this in the sense in which you mean it. (1) If I thought that Russia would on the whole govern Tibet or India in such wise as to make the inhabitants on the whole happier than they are under the existing Governments, I would myself welcome and work for her advent. But so far as I can judge the Russian Government is a corrupt despotism, hostile to individual liberty of action and therefore to real progress . . . etc.

Then about the English-speaking vakil. Was the man so much to blame? You and yours have never taught him that there was anything in " Yog Vidya." The only people who have taken the trouble to educate him at all have in so doing taught him materialism—you are disgusted with him, but who is to blame? . . . I judge perhaps as an outsider, but it does seem to me, that

---

[1] Extracts only are given from this letter. The numbers in brackets refer to the previous letter from K.H. No. 98.—ED.

the impenetrable veil of secrecy by which you surround yourselves, the enormous difficulties which you oppose to the communication of your spiritual knowledge, are the main causes of the rampant materialism which you so much deplore. . . . You alone do possess the means of bringing home to the ordinary run of men, convictions of this nature, but you, apparently bound by ancient rules, so far from zealously disseminating this knowledge, envelope it in such a dense cloud of mystery, that naturally the mass of mankind disbelieve in its existence . . . there can be no justification for not giving clearly to the world the more important features of your philosophy, accompanying the teaching with such a series of demonstrations as should ensure the attention of all sincere minds. That you should hesitate to confer hastily great powers too likely to be abused, I quite understand—but this in no way bars a dogmatic denunciation of the results of your psychical investigations, accompanied by phenomena, sufficiently clear and often repeated to prove that you really did know more of the subjects with which you dealt than Western Science does (2) . . .

Perhaps you will retort " how about Slade's case? " but do not forget that *he* was taking money for what he did; making a living out of it. Very different would be the position of a man, who came forward to teach gratuitously, manifestly at the sacrifice of his own time, comfort and convenience, what he believed it to be for the good of mankind to know. At first no doubt everyone would say the man was mad or an impostor—but then when phenomenon on phenomenon was repeated and repeated, they would have to admit there was something in it, and within three years you would have all the foremost minds in any civilized country intent upon the question, and tens of thousands of anxious enquirers out of whom ten per cent. might prove useful workers, and one in a thousand perhaps develop the necessary qualifications for becoming ultimately an adept. If you desire to react on the native through the European mind that is the way to work it. Of course, I speak under correction and in ignorance of conditions, possibilities, etc., but for this ignorance at any rate *I* am not to blame . . . (3).

Then I come to the passage. " Has it occurred to you that the two Bombay publications if not influenced, may at least have not been prevented by those who might have done so because they saw the necessity for that much agitation to effect the double result of making a needed diversion after the brooch grenade, and perhaps of trying the strength of your personal interest in occultism and theosophy? I do not say it was, I but enquire whether the contingency ever presented itself to your mind." Now of course this was addressed to Sinnett, but still I wish to answer it in my fashion. First I should say, *cui bono* throwing out such a hint? You must know whether it was so or not. If it was not, why set us speculating as to whether it may have been, when you know it was *not*. But if it was so, then I submit that in the first place an idiotic business like this could be no test of any *man's* (there are of course lots of human beings who are only a sort of educated monkey) personal interest in anything. . . . In the second place if the Brothers did deliberately allow the publication of those letters, I can only say that, from my worldly non-initiated standpoint, I think they made a sad mistake . . . and the object of the Brothers being avowedly to make the T.S. respected, they could hardly have selected any worse means, than the publication of these foolish letters. . . . but still when the question is broadly put, did you ever consider whether the Brothers allowed this publication, I cannot avoid replying, if they did not, it is futile wasting consideration on the matter, and if they did, it seems to me that they were unwise in so doing. (4)

Then come your remarks about Colonel Olcott. Dear old Olcott, whom everyone who knows must love. I fully sympathize in all you say in his favour—but I cannot but take exception to the terms in which you praise him, the whole burthen of which is that he never questions but always obeys. This is the Jesuit organization over again—and this renunciation of private judgement, this abnegation of one's own personal responsibility, this accepting the dictates of outside voices as a substitute for one's own conscience, is to my mind a *sin* of no ordinary magnitude. . . . Nay further I feel bound to say that if . . . this doctrine of blind obedience is an essential one in your system, I greatly doubt whether any spiritual light it may confer can compensate mankind for the loss of that private freedom of action, that sense of personal, individual responsibility of which it would deprive them. . . . (5)

. . . But if it be intended that I shall ever get instructions to do this or that, and without understanding the why or the where-fore, without scrutinizing consequences, blind and heedless, straightway go and do it,—then frankly the matter for me is at an end—I am no military machine—I am an avowed enemy of the military organization—a friend and advocate of the industrial or co-operative system, and I will join no Society or no Body which purports to limit or control my right of private judgment. Of course I am not *doctrinaire!,?* and do not desire to ride any principle as a hobby horse. . . .

To return to Olcott—*I* do not think his connection with the proposed Society would be any evil. . . .

In the first place *I* should not object in any way to dear old Olcott's supervision, because I know it would be nominal, as even if he tried to make it otherwise, Sinnett and I are both quite capable of shutting him up if he interfered needlessly. But neither of us could accept him *as our real guide* (6), because we both know that we are intellectually his superiors. This is a brutal way, as the French would say, of putting it, but que voulez vous?. Without perfect frankness there is no coming to an understanding. . . .

Yours sincerely,

A. O. HUME.

LETTER No. 100 [1]

The new "*guide*" has meanwhile a few words to say to you. If you care anything about our *future relations*, then, you better try to make your friend and colleague Mr. Hume give up his insane idea of going to Tibet. Does he really think that *unless we allow it*, he, or an army of Pelings will be enabled to hunt us out, or bring back news, that we are, after all, but a "moon-shine" as she calls it. Madman is that man who imagines that even the British Govt: is strong and rich enough and powerful enough to help him in carrying out his insane plan! Those whom we desire to know us will find us at the very frontiers. Those who have set against themselves the Chohans as he has—would not find us were they to go [to] L'hasa with an army. His carrying out the plan will be the signal for an absolute separation between your world and ours. His idea of applying to the Govt: for permission to go to Tibet is ridiculous. He will encounter dangers at every step and—will not even hear the remotest tidings about ourselves or our whereabouts. Last night a letter was to be carried to him as well as to Mrs. Gordon. The Chohan *forbid* it. You are warned, good friend—act accordingly.

K. H.

LETTER No. 101

Received Simla, 1881.

Your letter received. I believe you had better try and see whether you could not make your ideas less polemical and dry than his. I begin to think there may be some stuff in you, since you are able so to appreciate my beloved friend and brother. I have attended to the Brahmin boy's letter and erased the offensive sentence, replacing it with another. You can now show it to the

---

[1] This communication is written across the lines of a letter of H.P.B.'s to A.P.S.; the subject matter of the 2 letters, however, bear no relation to each other.—ED.

Maha Sahib; him so proud in his *bakbak* [1] humility and so humble in his pride. As for phenomena you will have none—I have written through Olcott. Blessed is he who knows our Koothoomi and blessed is he who appreciates him. What I now mean you will understand some day. As for your A.O.H. I *know him better* than you ever will.

M.

LETTER No. 102

Received Simla, 1881.

My dear young friend, I am sorry to differ from you in your last two points. If he can stand one sentence of rebuke he will stand far more than what you would have me alter. *Ou tout ou rien*—as my frenchified K.H. taught me to say. I have thought your suggestion No. 1—good and have fully adopted it, hoping that you will not refuse some day to give me lessons of English. I had " Benjamin " stick a patch in the page, and made him forge my calligraphy while smoking a pipe on my back. Not having the right to *follow* K.H. I feel very lonely without my boy. Hoping to be excused for writing, and refusal, I trust you will not shrink from telling the truth, if need be, even in the face of the son of " a member of Parliament." You have too many eyes watching you to afford making mistakes *now*.

M.

LETTER No. 103

Received Allahabad, 1880-81.

To accomplish a plan like the one in hand many agencies must be employed, and failure in any one direction jeopardises the results tho' it may not defeat it. We have had various checks and may have more. But observe: *first*—that two points are auspicious —thanks to kind Providence; Allen has become friendly, and a friend of yours (I believe) is Resident at Kashmir. And *second* that until the Maharajah of Kashmir—the prince first on the programme—has been sounded the vital point will not have been touched. He—the first as I say on the programme has been left to the last! Not much was expected from others and thus far each of the others who has been approached has failed to respond. Why do not the *chelas* (?) do *as* they are told? If *chelas* neglect orders, and *strained sense of delicacy interferes*, how without miracle can results be expected! I have telegraphed you to await Olcott's

[1] Babbling.—EDS.

coming because it is best that you should work together at Calcutta to try and set things in motion. One word from you to the Resident would have been sufficient—but you are proud as all your race. Olcott will be at Calcutta about the 20th. Do not listen to the old woman—she becomes weak-headed when left to herself. But M. will take her in hand.

Yours,

K. H.

LETTER No. 104

Received October, 1881. (?) P. p.c. letter written before retirement.

My dear friend: Your note received. What you say in it shows me that you entertain some fears lest I should have been offended by Mr. Hume's remarks. Be at ease, pray, for I never could be. It is not anything contained in his observations that annoyed me, but the persistence with which he was following out a line of argument that I knew was pregnant with future mischief. This *argumentum ad hominem*—renewed and taken up from where we had left it off last year was as little calculated as possible to draw the Chohan from his principles, or force him into some very desirable concessions. I dreaded the consequences and my apprehensions had a very good foundation, I can assure you. Please assure Mr. Hume of my personal sympathy and respect for him and give him my most friendly regards. But I will not have the pleasure of " catching up " any more of his letters or answering them for the next three months. As nothing whatever of the Society's original programme is yet settled upon, nor do I hope of seeing it settled for some time to come, I have to give up my projected voyage to Bhootan, and my Brother M. is to take my place. We are at the end of September and nothing could be done by October 1st that might warrant my insisting to go thither. My chiefs desire me particularly to be present at our New Year's Festivals, February next, and in order to be prepared for it I have to avail myself of the three intervening months. I will, therefore, bid you now good-bye, my good friend, thanking you warmly for all you have done and tried to do for me. January next I hope to be able to let you have news from me; and,—save new difficulties in the way of the Society arise again from " your shore " —you will find me in precisely the same disposition and frame of mind in which I now part with both of you. Whether I will succeed in bringing my beloved but very obstinate Brother M. to my way of thinking is what I am now unable to say. I have tried and will try once more, but I am really afraid Mr. Hume and he would never agree together. He told me he would answer your letter and request through a third party—not Mad. B. Meanwhile she knows quite enough to furnish Mr. Hume with

ten lectures had he but a desire to deliver them, and were he but
to recognise the fact, instead of entertaining such a poor [? idea]
of her in one direction and such a very erroneous conception in
some others. M. promised me, though to refresh her failing
memory and to revive all she has learned with him in as bright
a way as could be desired. Should the arrangement fail to get
Mr. Hume's approbation I will have but to sincerely regret it,
for it is the best I can think of.

I leave orders with my " Disinherited " to watch over *all* as
much as it lies in his weak powers.

And now I must close. I have but a few hours before me, to
prepare for my long, *very* long journey. Hoping we part as good
friends as ever, and that we might meet as better ones still, let me
now " astrally " shake hands with you and assure you of my good
feelings once more.

Yours as ever,

K. H

LETTER No. 105

My dear friend—

Before I give you any definite answer to your business letter
I desire to consult our venerable Chohan. We have, as you say
12 months time before us. For the present I have a little business
on hand that is very important, as it hinges on to a series of other
deliberate untruths, whose real character it is nigh time to prove.
We are called in so many words, or rather in five letters " liars "
(*sic*) and accused of " base ingratitude." The language is strong,
and willing as we should feel to borrow many a good thing from
the English, it is not politeness, I am afraid, that we would feel
inclined to learn from the class of gentlemen represented by Mr.
Hume. Left standing by itself, the business I am now concerned
with you may truly regard as of very little importance; collated
with other facts, unless shown on good and unimpeachable testimony as, to say the least, a perversion of facts—it tends to become
a *cause* which will yield unpleasant effects and ruin the whole
fabric. Do not, therefore, I pray you, stop to argue the utter
unworthiness of the small remembrance, but relying upon our
seeing something of the future which remains hidden to you, pray
answer my question, as a friend and brother. When you have
done that you will learn why this letter is written.

H.P.B. has just quarrelled with Djual Khool, who maintained
that the unpleasant proceeding was *not* entered in the minutes by
Davison, while she affirmed that it was. Of course he was right
and she wrong. Yet if her memory failed her in this particular,
it served her well as to the fact itself. You remember, of course
the event. Meeting of the Eclectics in the Billiard room.

Witnesses—yourself, the Hume pair, the Gordon couple, Davison and H.P.B. Subject: S. K. Chatterji, his letter to Hume expressing contempt for theosophy and suspicious about the good faith of H.P.B. Handing over the letter I had returned her to Mr. Hume, she said that I had given orders through her to the General Council to invite the Babu to resign. Thereupon Mr. Hume proclaimed most emphatically: " In such case your Koot Hoomi *is no gentleman.* The letter is a private letter and under these circumstances no gentleman would ever think of acting as desired by him." Now the letter was not a private one, since it was circulated by Mr. Hume among the members. At the time I paid no attention whatever to the fling. Nor had I come to know of it through H.P.B., but through D. Khool who had heard it himself and has an excellent memory.

Now, will you oblige me by writing for me two lines telling me as *you* remember the event. Were the words " no gentleman " applied to your humble servant or in general? I ask you *as a gentleman*, not as a friend. This has a very important bearing on the future. When done, I will let you see the latest development of the infinite " fertility of resource " at the command of our mutual friend. It may be, that under any other circumstances Mr. H.'s braggadocios about Lord Ripon's high opinion of Hume's theosophy and his " big talk " about his literary, monetary and other services rendered to us might pass unnoticed, for we all know his weaknesses; but in the present case they must be dealt with so as not to leave him a single straw to catch at, because his last letter to me (which you will see)—is not only entirely at variance with all the acknowledged rules of good breeding, but also because unless his own mis-statements are actually proved, he will boast hereafter of having given the direct lie to our Brotherhood, and that no member of the latter could ever permit it. You cannot fail to remark the absurd contrast between his apparent confidence in his wonderful powers and superiority and the soreness he exhibits at the slightest remark passed upon him by myself. He must be made to realize that were he really as great as he asserts, or even if he were himself quite satisfied of his greatness and the infallibility of his power of memory, whatever even the adepts might think, he would remain indifferent to, at any rate, would not be as vulgarly abusive as he is now. His sensitiveness is in itself evidence of the doubts lurking in his mind as to the validity of the claims he so boastfully puts forth; hence his irritability, excited by anything and everything that is likely to disturb his self-delusions.

I hope you will not refuse a direct and clear answer to my direct and clear question.

Yours ever affectionately,

K. H.

LETTER No. 106

I desire to answer your letter carefully and explicitly. I must, therefore, ask you to accord me a few days longer when I will be quite at leisure. We have to take measures for effectually protecting our country and vindicating the spiritual authority of our Priestly King. Perhaps, never, since the invasion of Alexander and his Greek legions have so many Europeans stood together under arms so near to our frontiers *as they do now*. My friend, your correspondents seem to acquaint you with the greatest news but superficially—at best: perhaps, because they do not know it themselves. Never mind, it will all be known some day. However, as soon as I get a few hours leisure, you will find at your service your friend.

K. H.

Try to believe more than you do in the " old lady." She *does* rave betimes; but she *is* truthful and does the best she can for you.

LETTER No. 107

My dear Ambassador—

To quiet the anxiety I see lurking within your mind, and which has even a more definite form than you have expressed, let me say that I will use my best endeavours to calm our highly sensitive —not always sensible old friend, and make her stop at her post. Ill health resulting from natural causes, and mental anxiety have made her nervous to an extreme degree and sadly impaired her usefulness to us. For a fortnight past she has been all but useless, and her emotions have sped along her nerves like electricity thro' a telegraphic wire. All has been chaos. I am sending these few lines by a friend to Olcott so that they may be forwarded without her knowledge.

Consult freely with our friends in Europe and return with a good book in your hand and a good plan in your head. Encourage the sincere brethren at Galle to persevere in their work of education. Some cheering words from you will give them heart. Telegraph to Nicolas Dias Inspector of Police Galle that you, a member of the Council of the T.S. are coming (the date and name of steamer given) and I will cause H.P.B. to do the same to *another* person. Think on the way of your true friend.

K. H. and ——.

LETTER No. 108 [1]

The man sent by me last night was a Ladakhee chela and had nothing to do with you. What you just said about " initiation " is true. Any Fellow who truly and sincerely repents ought to be taken back. As you see I am with you *constantly*.

LETTER No. 109

I cannot make a miracle, or I would have shown myself fully to Mrs. Sinnett at least in spite of the matches [2] of the French woman and to yourself in spite of the physical and psychical conditions. Kindly realize that my sense of justice is so strong that I would not deny you a satisfaction I gave Ramaswami and Scott. If you have not seen me it is simply because it was an impossibility. If you had gratified K.H. by attending the meeting no harm would as a matter of fact have been done to you, for K.H. had foreseen and prepared all, and the very effort you made to be firm, even at supposed personal risk, would have totally changed your condition. Now let us see what the future has in store.

M.

LETTER No. 110

My dear friend—

May I trouble you to hand the enclosed Rs. 50 to Dharbagiri Nath when you see him? The little man is in trouble but has to be remonstrated; and the best punishment for an *accepted* chela is to receive the reproof through a " lay " one. On his way from Ghoom to Bengal through imprudence and indiscretion he lost money, and instead of addressing himself directly to me he tried to dodge the " Master's eye " and called upon a probationary chela upon whom he has not the slightest claim to help him out of his difficulty. So please tell him that Ram S. Gargya has not received his telegram from Burdwan but that it went direct into the hands of the Lama who notified me of it. Let him be more prudent in future. You now see the danger in allowing young chelas out of sight even for a few days. Money losses are nothing, but it is the results involved and the temptation that are terrible. My friend, *I am afraid you too, have been again* IMPRUDENT. I have a

---

[1] This fragment is in M.'s handwriting.—ED. It is on the back of No. 109.—EDS.

[2] Query machinations.—EDS.

31

letter from Colonel Chesney—very polite and quite diplomatic. Several such messages may do for an excellent *refrigerator*.

Yours,

K. H.

P.S.—I am glad to find you reprinting in the *Pioneer* " A Day with my Indian Cousins " by Atettjee Sahibjee, etc., from *Vanity Fair*. Last year I had asked you to give some work to the author of those sketches after the manner of the once famous *Ali Baba* —but was refused. You thought he did not write well enough for the *Pioneer*. You distrusted a " native," and now his articles are accepted in *Vanity Fair*.

I am glad for poor Padshah. He is a madcap, yet of excellent heart and sincerely devoted to Theosophy and—*our* Cause.

I must consult you. Hume writes to H.P.B. (a most *loving* letter!). He sends her two corrected copies of a letter of his in the *Pioneer* of the 20th and remarking that the time has come when, if the native press all over the country will only following this, *his* lead, push the question strongly—material concessions *will* be obtained—he adds "*you will of course reprint this* in the *Theosophist*." How can she do it, without connecting her journal directly with politics? I would have extremely liked to have his letter on *Education* reproduced from your *Pioneer* in the *Theosophist*, but hesitated to tell her to do it, fearing it would give a new colouring to the magazine. Some of his articles are extremely able.

Well, and what are you to do about anniversary of " Eclectic " and *cyclic* conclusion?

She is better and we have left her near Darjeeling. She is not safe in Sikkim. The Dugpa opposition is tremendous and unless we devote the whole of our time to watching her, the " Old Lady " would come to grief since she is now unable to take care of herself. See what happened to the little man—he will tell you. You ought to take her in for October and November.

Yours again,

K. H.

This little wretch forced me to blush before you on account of his indiscretion—" from a European standpoint." I cannot be always looking after my Chelas in their travels—and their knowledge of your ways and usages amounts to *cipher*! It is but to-day that I learned of his borrowing from you Rs. 30—through Djual Khool. He had no business and *no right* to do so; but you must pardon him for he has not the least conception of a difference between a Tibetan and a European chela and acted as unceremoniously with you as he would with Djual Khool. I send you back with thanks the money lent, hoping you will not take us all for savages!

I am writing you a long letter by fits and starts as usual. When that *business* letter will be on its way, I will send another with answers to your questions.

A ludicrous thing happened in connexion with C. C. M.'s letter that I will relate in my next.

Hail and success to the " new President " at last!!

Yours ever fondly,

K. H.

Pardon the unavoidable delay. This letter with the enclosed cannot reach Darjeeling before 4 or 5 days.

LETTER No. 111

My dear friend,

The present will be delivered at your house by Dharbagiri Nath, a young Chela of mine, and his brother Chela, Chandra Cusho. They are forbidden to enter anyone's house without being invited to do so. Therefore, I pray you to pardon our savage customs and, at the same time to humour them by sending them an invitation in your name, either now—if you can receive them privately and without risking their meeting at your place with any stranger; or—at any other time during the evening, or late at night.

I have not the slightest objection to Mrs. S. your lady seeing either of them; but I pray her not to address them, since they are forbidden by our religious laws to speak with any lady—their mothers and sisters excepted—and that she would otherwise greatly embarrass them. I pray her to do so in my name, and for my sake. I trust also to your friendship that *none but you* will speak with them. They have their mission and beyond that they must not go (1) to deliver into your hands my " answers to the famous contradictions " and (2) to interview Mr. Fern. If you have an answer for me, Dharbagiri Nath will come for it whenever you are ready. I also entreat you most earnestly not to inflict upon them Mr. Hume. Do not think of what has happened until everything is explained.

Ever yours,

K. H.

P.S.—They are also forbidden to shake hands with any man or woman *i.e.*, *to touch* anyone; but you can invite my little man to come and talk with you as much as you like provided you are discreet.

LETTER No. 112

My reply to Colonel Chesney in answer to his letter was already written and ready to be forwarded by my little man, when I received yours advising me not to correspond with him. Therefore I forward it to you to be read, and should you think it expedient —to deliver it to its address. It seems rude to leave his letter without any acknowledgement—whether he is or is not in sympathy with the movement.

But good friend I leave this entirely in your hands and pray you to use in the matter your own discretion. You ought to know that decidedly young Fern is a little humbug and worse—a *congenital* though often an irresponsible liar. He tries in his last to bamboozle M. and make him believe he, Fern, is a new Zanoni *en herbe*. He is *testing* us in every way and manner, and constant skirmishes notwithstanding has a certain and very strong influence on Hume, whom he bamboozles with imaginary " powers " whose mission is to supplant the Brothers. He made him believe indirectly he belonged to a Society whose " name is unmentionable " a Society that seeks no one, whose one member knows not who the other is, nor will he know till the real nature of the " Brothers " is made public, though the system on which it works precludes all deception, etc. etc. To M. he writes that he confesses he " ought not to have put temptation " in his (Hume's) way. For having over-estimated his strength, he has " unwittingly caused him to fall."!! This individual is at the bottom of much that has happened. Watch and beware of him. One thing is certain though. These are not times for visiting with severity the offences of the too indiscreet and but half faithful " lay chelas." Now that Mr. Hume alienated the Chohan and M. I remain alone to carry on the difficult work. You read H.'s letter. How do you like that huge shadow of a Yogi with solemnly stretched out hand, and defiant haughty eyes disavowing with contemptuous gesture the intent of hurting the Society

Let me echo your sigh for the poor Society, and before fading away again into the foggy distance between Simla and Phari Jong assure you of my ever friendly feelings for yourself,

K. H.

Mr. W. Oxley wants to join the Eclectic. I'll tell her to send on to you his letter. Kindly write to him to say that he must not feel vexed at my denial. I know he is thoroughly sincere and as incapable of a deception or even exaggeration as you are. But he trusts too much to his subjects. Let him be cautious and very guarded; and, if he joins the Society I may help and even correspond with him through you. He is a valuable man, and indeed, more worthy of sincere respect than any other *Spiritualistic* mystic I know of. And though I have never approached him astrally or conversed with [him] I have often examined him in thought. Do not fail to write to him with the first steamer.

K. H.

LETTER No. 113

Private.

My dearest Friend,

Please pardon me for troubling you with my own business—but though I am *forced* by the Chohan to answer I really do not know whether I am within the limits of your code of politeness or outside of it. I have a long letter to write to you upon something that troubles me and I want you to advise me. I am in a most disagreeable position, placed as I am between the risk of betraying a friend and—your *code of honour* (the friend is not yourself.) I hope I may place entire confidence in your personal friendship and of *course* honour.

Honour! What funny, very funny notions you seem to have about that sacred thing! Do not be frightened for indeed the whole thing is more ludicrous than dangerous. Yet there is a danger in losing Mr. Hume.

To-morrow I will write more fully. Fern is a little ass but he is a clairvoyant and likewise a little hallucinated. But Mr. H. is too severe upon him. The boy hopes that if we are myths or *frauds* he will find us out. Well, where is the harm in such a hallucination? Yet H. *betrays* his confidence and sends me a letter three yards long with advice how to get out of our difficulties! He wants to be our benefactor and place us under an eternal obligation for saving M. from falling once more into Fern's *trap*. I would have sent you on his letter but it is superscribed " private and confidential " and I would be in his eyes no *gentleman* were he [to] find out such a breach of confidence. Well I want you to read this letter at any rate and leave it at your option to be either sent or destroyed. If you do not want him to know you have read it—well put a stamp on it and throw it into the letter-box. I do not think he will take you into his confidence this once. However, I may be mistaken. Soon you will learn more.

Yours affectionately,

K. H.

LETTER No. 114

Received about February, 1882 [1], Allahabad.

The letter forwarded is from a Baboo, your nausea-inspiring Bengalee, from whom, I ask you, for K.H.'s sake—to conceal the feeling of queasiness that may overcome you at his sight—if he comes. Read it with attention. The lines underlined contain the germ in them of the greatest reform, the most beneficent results obtained by the Theosophical movement. Were our friend of Simla less cantankerous, I might have tried to influence him to draft our special rules and a distinct pledge with apps and obligs for the Zenana women of India. Profit by the suggestion and see whether you can prevail upon him to do so. Write to him without delay to Bombay to come and meet the old woman at your house and then pass him on to his countryman and Brother-Fellow the " Prayag " Babu—the young leach of your Society. Then telegraph to her to Meerut to come, *using my name*—otherwise she will not. I already answered him in her name. Do not feel surprised; I have a reason for everything of mine, as you may learn some years hence.

And why should you be so anxious to see my *chits* to other people ? Have you not sufficient trouble to make out my letters addressed to yourself?

M.

LETTER No. 115

Received during brief visit to Bombay in January, 1882.

It was certainly K.H.'s and my great desire that since Scott could not attend the anniversary you should—not to take any part in its proceedings but simply—be present at it. This hapless organization will once more exhibit its representation without one single European of position and influence. But neither of us would force a course of action—against your wish—upon you. Therefore what I say must not be construed into an order or urgent request. We think it good—but you must obey your own cool judgment—the more so as perhaps to-day marks a crisis. One reason for my calling you was K.H.'s wish that you should be brought under certain magnetic and other occult influences that would favourably act upon yourself in future.

I will write more to-morrow for I yet hope you will give us a day or two and so let us have time to see what can be done for you by Khoothoomi.

M.

---

[1] Query, should be November, 1881.—EDS.

LETTER No. 116

A. P. Sinnett.

My dear Friend,

I am tired and disgusted with all this wrangling to death. Please read this before giving it to Mr. Hume. If, as a debt of gratitude, he would exact but a pound of flesh, I would have naught to say—but a pound of useless verbiage is indeed more than even I can stand!

Yours ever,

K. H.

LETTER No. 117

This will introduce to my Chela (lay) No. 1, " lay Chela No. 2 " —Mohini Babu. The experiences of the latter and what he has to say will interest Mr. Sinnett. Mohini Babu is sent by me on a certain mission in reference to the forthcoming and very threatening end of the cycle (theosophical)—and has no time to lose. Please, receive him at once and take his evidence.

Yours,

K. H.

LETTER No. 118

This is a fraudulent intrusion into private correspondence. No time to even answer your queries—will do so to-morrow or next day. For several days I have noticed something like anxiety in your lady's thoughts about " Den." Children's diseases are seldom dangerous even when somewhat neglected, if the child have naturally a strong constitution; the pampered ones falling naturally victims to contagion.

I remarked her fear of carrying the germs of the disease home with her at Mr. Hume's the other day, as my attention was drawn to her by the " Disinherited " who was on the watch. Fear not *in any case.* I hope you will pardon me if I advise you to sew up the enclosed in a small bag—a part of it will do—and hang it on the child's neck.

Unable as I am to carry into your homestead the full magnetism of my physical person I do the next best thing by sending you a lock of hair as a vehicle for the transmission of my aura in a concentrated condition. Do not allow anyone to handle it except

Mrs. Sinnett. You'll do well not to approach Mr. Fern too near for a time.

Yours,

K. H.

Say nothing of this note to anybody.

LETTER No. 119

Give Mr. Sinnett my salams—and ask him to comment upon the slip enclosed. He may know what I mean him to write upon the subject editorially. Tell him also that time is short and precious and ought not to be wasted.

K. H.

The following may lead later on to a curious confirmation of our " obscuration " doctrine which so puzzles my friend—the Editor of the " Phoenix."

Will you kindly and likewise, comment upon it and oblige thereby,

Yours,

K. H.

Newspaper Cutting

Sir John Lubbock's opinion confirms or endorses the conclusion long since put forth by some of the most eminent astronomers, namely, that there are now in the solar system, or firmament, many dark bodies—that is, bodies which now emit no light, or comparatively little. He points out, for example, that in the case of Procyon the existence of an invisible body is demonstrated by the movement of the visible stars. Another illustration which he cites relates to the notable phenomena presented by Algoe, the bright star in the Head of Medusa. This star shines without change for two days and thirteen hours; then, in three hours and a half, dwindles from a star of the second to one of the fourth magnitude; and then, in another three and a half hours, resumes its original brilliancy. According to the view entertained by Professor Lubbock, these changes must be regarded as indicating the presence of an opaque body, which intercepts at regular intervals a part of the light emitted by Algoe.

LETTER No. 120

To Mr. Sinnett's " lady."

Wear the hair enclosed in a *cotton* tape (and if preferred in a metal armlet) a little lower than your *left* armpit below the left shoulder. Follow advice that will be given to you by Henry

Olcott. It is good and we shall not object. Harbour not ill-feelings even against an enemy and one who has wronged you: for hatred acts like an antidote and may damage the effect of even *this hair*.

K. H.

LETTER No. 121

Received at Bombay on return to India, July, 1881.

Thanks. The little things prove very useful, and I gratefully acknowledge them. You ought to go to Simla. TRY. I confess to a weakness on my part to see you do so. We must patiently await the results, as I told you, of *the* Book. The *blanks* are provoking and " tantalizing " but we cannot go against the inevitable. And as it is always good to mend an error I already did so by presenting the *Occult World* to the C—'s notice. Patience, patience.

Yours, ever

K. H.

LETTER No. 122

My good friend; tho' Mr. Eglinton has promised to return by the end of June he cannot do so—after the danger that has threatened him at Calcutta on the very day of his departure—unless he is thoroughly protected against any such disgraceful recurrence. If Mr. Hume is anxious to have him, let him for want of something better offer him the place of his private secretary, for a year or so, now that Mr. Davison is away. If you or Mr. Hume are really anxious to *see me*—(or rather *my astral Self*) there's a chance for you. H.P.B. is too old and not passive enough. Besides she has done too many services to be forced into it. With Mr. Eglinton, and he willing, the thing would become easy. Profit then by the chance offered; in a year more it WILL BE TOO LATE.

Yours,

K. H.

London, April 27.

To Mr. A. P. Sinnett,

   Editor Pioneer, Allahabad.

LETTER No. 123

Do not be impatient—good friend, I will answer to-morrow. When you learn one day the difficulties that are in my way you will see how mistaken you are at times in your notions about my movements.

K. H.

LETTER No. 124

Cannot you manage to pick up for me three pebbles? They must come from the shores of the Adriatic—Venice preferably; as near to the Dogal Palace as they can possibly be found; (under the Bridge of Sighs would be the most desirable but for the mud of the ages). The pebbles must be of three different colours, one red, the other black; the third white (or greyish). If you manage to get them, please keep them apart from every influence and contact but yours, and oblige ever yours,

K. H.

LETTER No. 125

I am commanded by my beloved Master, known in India and the Western lands as Koot Hoomi Lal Singh, to make in his name the following declaration, in answer to a certain statement made by Mr. W. Oxley, and sent by him for publication in the Theosophist. It is claimed by the said gentleman that my Master Koot Hoomi (a) has thrice visited him " by the astral form "; and (b) that he had a conversation with Mr. Oxley when, as alleged he gave the latter certain explanations in reference to astral bodies in general, and the incompetency of his own *Mayavirupa* to preserve its consciousness simultaneously with the body " at both ends of the line ". Therefore my Master declares that:—

1. Whomsoever Mr. Oxley may have seen and conversed with at the time described, it was not with Koot Hoomi, the writer of the letters published in the *Occult World*.

2. Notwithstanding that my Master knows the gentleman in question who once honoured him with an autograph letter, thereby giving him the means of making his (Mr. Oxley's) acquaintance and of sincerely admiring his intuitional powers and *western* learning—yet he has never approached him whether astrally or otherwise: Nor has he ever had any conversation with Mr. Oxley, least of all one of that nature in which both the subject and predicate, the premises and conclusions are all wrong.

3. In consequence of the said claims, the repetition of which is calculated to lead many of our theosophists into error, my Master has determined to issue the following resolution.

Henceforth any medium or seer who will feel disposed to claim either to have been visited by, or to have held conversation with, or to have seen my Master,—will have to substantiate the claim by prefixing his or her statement with THREE SECRET WORDS, which he, my Teacher, will divulge to and leave in the safe keeping of Mr. A. O. Hume and Mr. A. P. Sinnett, the respective President and Vice-President of " The Eclectic Theosophical Society " of Simla. As long as they do not find these three *words* correctly repeated by a medium or heading a statement to that effect, whether verbal or printed, emanating from him or her, or on his or her behalf, the claim shall be regarded as a gratuitous assumption and no notice will be taken of it. To his regret my Master is forced to adopt this step, as unfortunately of late such self-deceptions have become quite frequent, and would demand a speedy check.

The above declaration and statement to be appended as a footnote to Mr. Oxley's published statement.

By order,
DJUAL-KHOOL. M. xxx.

LETTER No. 126

P.S. It is exceedingly difficult to make arrangements for a Punjab address through which to correspond. Both B. and I had counted much upon the young man whose sentimentalism we find unfits him for the useful office of intermediary. Still, I will not cease trying and shall hope to send you the name of a post office either in the Punjab or N.W.P. where one of our friends will be passing and re-passing once or twice a month.

K. H.

LETTER No. 127 [1]

Extracts from Letters of K.H. to A.O.H. and A.P.S. Received by A.P.S. August 13th, 1882.

One of your letters begins with a quotation from one of my own: " Remember that there is within man no abiding principle " —which sentence I find followed by a remark of yours, " How about the sixth and seventh principles? " To this I answer, neither Atma nor Buddhi ever were *within* man,—a little metaphysical

---

[1] The extracts are in Mr. Sinnett's handwriting.—ED.

axiom that you can study with advantage in Plutarch and Anaxagoras. The latter made his νους αυτοχρατης[1] the spirit self-potent, the *nous* that alone recognised *noumena* while the former taught on the authority of Plato and Pythagoras that the *demonium* or this *nous* always remained without the body; that it floated and overshadowed, so to say, the extreme part of man's head, it is only the vulgar who think it is within them. Says Buddha, " you have to get rid entirely of all the subjects of impermanence composing the body that your body should become permanent. The permanent never merges with the impermanent although the two are one. But it is only when all outward appearances are gone that there is left that one principle of life which exists independently of all external phenomena. It is the fire that burns in the eternal light, when the fuel is expended and the flame is extinguished; for that fire is neither in the flame nor in the fuel, nor yet inside either of the two but above beneath and everywhere —(Parinirvana Sutra kuan XXXIX).

. . . You want to acquire gifts. Set to work and try to develop lucidity. The latter is no gift but a universal possibility common to all. As Luke Burke puts it, " idiots and dogs have it, and to a more remarkable degree often than the most intellectual men." It is because neither idiots nor dogs use their reasoning faculties but allow their natural instinctive perceptions to have full play.

. . . You use too much sugar in your food. Take fruit, bread, tea, coffee and milk and use them as freely as you would like to, but no chocolate, fat, pastry and but very little sugar. The fermentation produced by it especially in that climate of yours is very injurious. The methods used for developing lucidity in our chelas may be easily used by you. Every temple has a dark room, the north wall of which is entirely covered with a sheet of mixed metal, chiefly copper, very highly polished with a surface capable of reflecting in it things, as well as a mirror. The chela sits on an insulated stool, a three-legged bench placed in a flat-bottomed vessel of thick glass,—the lama operator likewise, the two forming with the mirror wall a triangle. A magnet with the North Pole up is suspended over the crown of the chela's head without touching it. The operator having started the thing going leaves the chela alone gazing on the wall, and after the third time is no longer required.

---

[1] Nous autokrates.—EDS.

LETTER No. 129 [1]

Class P.   INDIAN TELEGRAPH.   Local No. 48

To		From	
Station	Adyar Madras	Station	Jummoo
To		From	
Person	Madame Blavatsky	Person	Col. Olcott

The	Masters	have
taken	Damodar	return
not	promised	

We will send him back.

Adyar 25-11-83.   Hour 10.15.   **K.H.**

LETTER No. 129

INDIAN TELEGRAPH.

To		From	
Station	Adyar Madras	Station	Jammoo
To		From	
Person	Madame Blavatsky	Person	Colonel Olcott

Editor of the Theosophist.

Damodar left before dawn—at about eight o'clock letters from him and Koothumi found on my table—Don't say whether return or not—Damodar bids us all farewell conditionally and says brother theosophists should all feel encouraged knowing that he has found the blessed masters and been called by them. The dear boys recent developments astonishing. Homey [2] bids me await orders.

Madras 25-11-83.   Hour 17.30.

---

[1] These two letters have been reversed to put them in order of time.—EDS.

[2] Thus in MS. Presumably an official's phonetic rendering of Homi.—EDS.

APPENDIX

LETTER No. 130

Triplicane,
Madras, 7th May, 1882.

To A. P. Sinnett Esq.,
   Editor of the Pioneer, etc. etc. etc.
Dear Sir,

I have been requested by Madame Blavatsky several times within the last three months to give you such practical instruction in our occult Science as I may be permitted to give to one in your position; and I am now ordered by —— to help you to a certain extent in lifting up a portion of the first veil of mystery. I need hardly tell you here that the Mahatmas can hardly be expected to undertake the work of personal instruction and supervision in the case of beginners like you, however sincere and earnest you may be in your belief in their existence and the reality of their science and in your endeavours to investigate the mysteries of that science. When you know more about them and the peculiar life they lead, I am sure you will not be inclined to blame them for not affording to you *personally* the instruction you are so anxious to receive from them.

I beg to inform you that the help hereby promised will be given to you provided you give your consent to the following conditions:—

(1) You must give me your word of Honour that you will never reveal to anybody whether belonging to the Theosophical Society or not, the Secrets communicated to you unless you previously obtain my permission to do so.

(2) You must lead such a life as is quite consistent with the Spirit of the rules already given you for your guidance.

(3) You must reiterate your promise to promote as far as it lies in your power the objects of the Theosophical Association.

(4) You must strictly act up to the directions that will be given to you with the instruction herein promised.

I must also add here that anything like a wavering state of mind as to the reality of Occult Science and the efficacy of the prescribed process is likely to prevent the production of the desired result.

In sending me a reply to this letter I hope you will be good enough to let me know whether you are acquainted with the Sanskrit Alphabet and whether you can pronounce Sanskrit words *correctly and distinctly.*

I beg to remain,

Yours sincerely,

T. SUBBA ROW.

LETTER No. 131

Coconada.

26th June, 1882.

To A. P. Sinnett, Esq., etc. etc. etc.

Dear Sir,

Please kindly excuse me for not having sent you a reply to your letter up to this time. The *qualified* assent which you were pleased to give to the conditions laid down by me necessitated a reference to the Brothers for their opinion and orders. And now I am sorry to inform you that anything like practical instruction in the ritual of Occult Science is impossible under the conditions you propose. So far as my knowledge goes, no student of Occult Philosophy has ever succeeded in developing his psychic powers without leading the life prescribed for such students; and it is not within the power of the teacher to make an exception in the case of any student. The rules laid down by the ancient teachers of Occult Science are inflexible; and it is not left to the discretion of any teacher either to enforce them or not to enforce them according to the nature of the existing circumstances. If you find it impracticable to change the present mode of your life, you cannot but wait for practical instruction until you are in a position to make such sacrifices as Occult Science demands; and for the present you must be satisfied with such theoretical instruction as it may be possible to give you.

It is hardly necessary now to inform you whether the instruction promised you in my first letter under the conditions therein laid down would develop in you such powers as would enable you either to see the Brothers or converse with them clairvoyantly. Occult training, however commenced, will in course of time necessarily develop such powers. You will be taking a very low view of Occult Science if you were to suppose that the mere acquirement of psychic powers is the highest and the only desirable result of occult training. The mere acquisition of wonder-working powers can never secure immortality for the student of Occult Science unless he has learnt the means of shifting gradually his sense of individuality from his corruptible material body to the incorruptible and eternal *Non-Being* represented by his seventh principle. Please consider this as the real aim of Occult Science and see whether the rules you are called upon to obey are necessary or not to bring about this mighty change.

Under the present circumstances, the Brothers have asked me to assure you and Mr. Hume that I would be fully prepared to give you both such theoretical instruction as I may be able to give in the Philosophy of the Ancient Brahminical religion and Esoteric Buddhism.

I am going to leave this place for Madras on the 30th of this month.

I beg to remain your sincerely,

T. Subba Row.

LETTER No. 132 [1]

Extracts I got for your benefit—pitying your impatience—from " Rishi M. " See my note.

It would no doubt cause him considerable inconvenience if he were obliged to change his mode of life completely. You will find from the letters that he is very anxious to know beforehand the nature of the Siddhis or wonder-working powers that he is expected to obtain by the process or ritual I intend prescribing for him.

The power to which he will be introduced by the process in question will no doubt develop wonderful clairvoyant powers both as regards sight and sound in some of its higher correlations; and that the highest of its correlations is intended by our Rishi—M— to lead the candidate through *the first three stages of initiation* if he is properly qualified for it.

But I am not prepared to assure Mr. Sinnett now that I will teach him any of its higher correlations. What I mean to teach him now is a necessary preliminary preparation for studying such correlations. . . . .

. . . .

. . . .

my proposal into consideration.

As I have been wandering here and there since my arrival here I have not been able to complete my second article with reference to Mr. Oxley's book.

---

[1] Parts of this letter are missing. The comments in K.H.'s handwriting are printed in bold type.—Ed.

But I will try my best to finish it as soon as possible.
For the present I beg to remain
Your most obedient servant

T. Subba Row.

To Madam H. P. Blavatsky, etc.   Coconada 3rd June, 1882.

My dear friend, I strongly advise you not to undertake at present a task beyond your strength and means; *for once pledged* were you to break your promise it would cut you off for years, if not for ever from any futher progress.   I said from the first to *Rishi* "M." that his intention was kind but his project *wild*.   How can you in your position undertake any such labour?   Occultism is not to be trifled with.   It demands *all* or nothing. I read your letter to S.R. sent by him to Morya and I see you do not understand the first principles of . . . X.

(*Contd. ante p*. 369-70.)

LETTER No. 133

My dear Mr. Sinnett,

It is very strange that you should be ready *to deceive yourself* so willingly.   I have seen last night whom I had to see, and getting the explanation I wanted I am now settled on points I was not only doubtful about but positively averse to accepting.   And the words in the first line are words I am bound to repeat to you as a warning, and because I regard you, after all, as one of my best *personal* friends.   Now you *have* and *are* deceiving, in vulgar parlance, *bamboozling* yourself about the letter received by me yesterday from the Mahatma.   The *letter is from Him*, whether written through a chela or not; and—perplexing as it may seem to you, contradictory and "absurd," it is the full expression of his feelings and *he maintains* what he said in it.   For me it is surpassingly strange that you should accept as His only that which dovetails with your own feelings, and reject all that contradicts your own notions of the fitness of things.   Olcott has behaved like an ass, utterly devoid of tact; he confesses it, and is ready to confess it and to say *mea culpa* before all the Theosophists—and it is more than any Englishman would be willing to do.   This is perhaps why, with all his lack of tact, and his frequent freaks that justly shock your susceptibilities and mine too, heaven knows! going as he does against every *conventionality*—he is still so liked by the Masters, who care not for the flowers of European civilization.   Had I known last night what I have learnt since—*i.e.* that you imagine, or rather force yourself to imagine that the Mahatma's letter is not wholly orthodox and was written by a chela to please me, or something of the sort, I would not have

32

rushed to you as the only plank of salvation. Things *are* getting dark and hazy. I have managed last night to get the Psychic Research Society rid of its nightmare, Olcott; I may manage to get England rid of its bugbear—Theosophy. If you—the most devoted, the best of all Theosophists—are all ready to fall a victim to your own preconceptions and believe in new gods of your own fancy dethroning the old ones—then, notwithstanding all and everything Theosophy has come too early in this country. Let your L.L.T.S. go on as it does—I cannot help it, and what I mean I will tell you when I see you. But *I* will have nothing to do with the new arrangement and—retire from it altogether unless we agree to disagree no more.

Yours,

H.P.B.

LETTER No. 134

Dehra Dun. Friday. 4th.

Arrived only yesterday, last night late from Saharanpur. The house very good but cold, damp and dreary. Received a whole heap of letters and answer yours first.

Saw at last M. and showed him your last or rather Benemadhab's on which you have scratched a query. It is the latter Morya answers. I wrote this under his dictation and now copy it.

[1] I wrote to Sinnett my opinion on the Allahabad theosophists. (Not through me though?) Adityaram B. wrote a foolish letter to Damodar and Benemadhab writes a foolish request to Mr. Sinnett. Because K.H. chose to correspond with two men who proved of the utmost importance and use to the Society, they all—whether wise or stupid, clever or dull, *possibly* useful or utterly useless—lay their claims to correspond with us directly—too. Tell him (you) that this must be stopped. For ages we never corresponded with anyone, nor do we mean to. What has Benemadhab or any other of the many claimants done to have a right to such a claim? Nothing whatever. They join the Society, and though remaining as stubborn as ever in their old beliefs and superstitions, and having never given up caste or one single of their customs, they, in their selfish exclusiveness, expect to see and converse with us and have our help in all and everything. I will be pleased if Mr. Sinnett says, to everyone of those who may address him with similar pretensions, the following: " The ' Brothers ' desire me to inform one and all of you, *natives*, that unless a man is prepared to become a thorough theosophist *i.e.* to do as D. Mavalankar did,—give up entirely caste, his old superstitions and show himself a true reformer (especially in the case of

---

[1] From here to ' at their tail.' on p. 456 is a quotation from Master M.—Eds.

child marriage) he will remain simply a member of the Society with no hope whatever of ever hearing from us. The Society, acting in this directly in accordance with our orders, *forces no one to become a theosophist of the IId. Section.* It is left with himself and at his choice. It is useless for a member to argue ' I am one of a pure life, I am a teetotaller and an abstainer from meat and vice. All my aspirations are for good etc.' and he, at the same time, building by his acts and deeds an impassable barrier on the road between himself and us. What have we, the disciples of the true *Arhats*, of esoteric Buddhism and of Sang-gyas to do with the *Shastras* and Orthodox Brahmanism? There are 100 of thousands of Fakirs, Sannyasis and Sadhus leading the most pure lives, and yet being as they are, on the path of *error*, never having had an opportunity to meet, see or even hear of us. Their forefathers have driven away the followers of the only true philosophy upon earth from India and now it is not for the latter to come to them but for them to come to us if they want us. Which of them is ready to become a Buddhist, a *Nastika* as they call us? None. Those who have believed and followed us have had their reward. Mr. Sinnett and Hume are exceptions. Their beliefs are no barrier to us for they have *none*. They may have had influences around them, bad magnetic emanations the result of drink, Society and promiscuous physical associations (resulting even from shaking hands with impure men) but all this is physical and material impediments which with a little effort we could counteract and even clear away without much detriment to ourselves. Not so with the magnetism and invisible results proceeding from erroneous and sincere beliefs. Faith in the Gods and God, and other super- stitions attracts millions of foreign influences, living entities and powerful agents around them, with which we would have to use more than ordinary exercise of power to drive them away. We do not choose to do so. We do not find it either necessary or profitable to lose our time waging war on the unprogressed *Planetaries* who delight in personating gods and sometimes well known characters who have lived on earth. There are Dhyan- Chohans and " Chohans of Darkness," not what they term *devils* but imperfect " Intelligences " who have never been born on this or any other earth or sphere, any more than the " Dhyan Chohans " have, and who will never belong to the " builders of the Universe," the pure Planetary Intelligences, who preside at every *Manvantara* while the Dark Chohans preside at the *Pralayas*. Explain this to Mr. Sinnett (I CAN'T)—tell him to read over what I said to them in the few things I have explained to Mr. Hume; and let him remember that as all in this universe is contrast (I cannot translate it better) so the light of the Dhyan Chohans and their pure intelligence is contrasted by the " *Ma-Mo* Chohans "

—and their destructive intelligence. These are the gods the Hindus and Christians and Mahomedans and all others of bigoted religions and sects worship; and so long as *their* influence is upon their devotees we would no more think of associating with or counteracting them in their work than we do the Red-Caps on earth whose evil results we try to palliate but whose work we have no right to meddle with so long as they do not cross *our* path. (You will not understand this, I suppose. But think well over it and you will. M. means here, that they have no right or even power to go against the natural or that work which is prescribed to each class of beings or existing things by the law of nature. The Brothers, for instance could *prolong* life but they could not *destroy* death, not even for themselves. They can to a degree palliate evil and relieve suffering; they could not destroy evil. No more can the Dhyan Chohans impede the work of the Mamo Chohans, for *their* Law is *darkness, ignorance, destruction* etc., as that of the former is Light, knowledge and creation. The Dhyan Chohans answer to *Buddh*, Divine Wisdom and Life in blissful knowledge, and the Ma-mos are the personification in nature of *Shiva*, Jehovah and other invented monsters with Ignorance at their tail).

The last phrase of M.'s I translate is thus. " Tell him (you) then that for the sake of those who desire to learn and have information, I am ready to answer the 2 or 3 enquiries of Benemadhab from the Shastras, but I will enter in no correspondence with him or any other. Let him put their questions clearly and distinctly to (you) Mr. Sinnett, and then I will answer through him (you)."

I send you my uncle's letter just received by me. He says (as my translation of his Russian letter shows) that he wrote to you the same. Whether you received it or not, I know not, but I send you this. If it is identical with yours then send me back mine. I suppose that by this time it is pretty well proved that I am *I*—and not someone else; that my uncle being now adjunct (or asst.) Minister of the Interior, is a personage who by signing his name in full can certainly be trusted, unless, indeed, the *C.* and *M.* and your friend Primrose invent a new version and say that we have *forged* the documents. But my uncle says in his *official* letter to me that the Prince Dondoukoff is going to send me an official document to prove my identity, and so we will wait. His other *private* letter I cannot translate as its phraseology is far from complimentary for Mr. Primrose in particular, and the Anglo-Indians who insult and vilify me in general. I will ask the Prince to write to Lord Ripon, or Gladstone *direct*.

Yours in the love of Jesus

H. P. Blavatsky.

Why the deuce does the " Boss " want me now to go to Allahabad? I can't be spending money there and back for *I have* to go
by Jeypur and Baroda and he knows it. What all this means is
more than I can tell. He made me go to Lahore and now it's
Allahabad!!

LETTER No. 135

My dear Mr. Sinnett,
For fear that you should " trace back " to me a new treachery,
permit me to say that I have never said to Hübbe Schleiden and
Frank Gebhard that the existence of our seven *objective* planets
was an allegory. What I said was, that the objectivity and
actuality of the septenary chain had nothing to do with the *correct*
understanding of the seven rounds. That outside of the *initiates*
no one knew the *mot final* of this mystery. That you could not
understand it thoroughly, nor explain it, because Mahatma K.H.
told you a hundred times that you could not be told the *whole*
doctrine; that you knew Hume had made him questions and cross-
examined Him until his hair became grey. That there were a
hundred *apparent* inconsistencies just because you had not the key
to the x777x and could not be given it. In short that you gave
the truth, but by *far not* the whole truth especially about rounds
and rings which was only at best *allegorical*.
                                        Yours,

                                                    H.P.B.

LETTER No. 136

                                                    March 17th.
My dear Mr. Sinnett,
Your invitation read with surprise.
Not " surprise " at myself being invited, but surprise at *you*
inviting me *again*, just as if you had not had enough of me! Now
what good can I be to any one in this world, except to make some
stare, others to speculate upon my cleverness as an impostor, and
the small minority to eye me with the feeling of wonder generally
in store for " monsters " exhibited in museums or *aquariums*.
This is *fact*; and I had enough proof of it, not to run again my
neck into the halter if I can help it. My coming to stop with you
even for a few days would be only a source of disappointment to
yourself, and one of *torture* to me.
Now, you must not take these words *en mauvaise part*. I am
simply sincere with you. You are and have been, especially Mrs.
Sinnett, for ever so long my best friends here; but it is just because

I consider you as such, that I am forced to rather give a momentary than a prolonged annoyance to you; rather a refusal, than an acceptance of the kind invitation. Besides—as *a medium* of communication between yourself and K.H. (for I suppose you do not invite me *pour mes beaux yeux*, alone?) I am utterly useless now. There is a limit to endurance, there is one to the greatest self-sacrifice. I have worked for them faithfully and unselfishly for years, and the result was that I ruined my health, dishonoured my ancestral name, got reviled by every green-grocer from Oxford Street, and every fishmonger from Hungerford market who had become a C.S. and—finally did no good to them, very little to the Society and none at all to either poor Olcott or myself. Believe me, we are better friends with several hundred miles between us than—a few steps. Besides this, Boss says there's a new development hanging over our heads. He and K.H. put their wise heads together and are preparing *to work* as they tell me. We have but a few months left until November and if things are not entirely whitewashed until then and fresh blood poured into the Brotherhood and Occultism—we may just as well go to bed all of us. Personally for myself it is a matter of very little moment, whether it is so or not. My time is also fast approaching when *my hour of triumph* will strike. Then is it, that I also may prove to those who *speculated* about me, those who believed as those who disbelieved, that none of them approached within 100 miles of the area of truth. I have suffered *hell* on earth, but before I leave it I promise myself *such a triumph* as will make the Ripons and his Roman Catholics, and the Baly's and Bishop Sargeant with their Protestant donkeys—bray as loud as their lungs will bear. Now, do you really think that you know ME, my dear Mr. Sinnett? Do you believe that, because you have fathomed—as you think—my physical crust and brain; that shrewd analyst of *human* nature though you be—you have ever penetrated even beneath the first cuticles of my *Real Self*? You would gravely err, if you did. I am held by all of you as *untruthful* because hitherto I have shown the world only the true *exterior* Mme. Blavatsky. It is just as if you complained of the *falseness* of a moss and weed covered, and *mud*-covered, stony and rugged rock for writing outside "*I* am *not* moss covered and mud-plastered; your eyes deceive you for you are unable to see beneath the crust," etc. You must understand the allegory. It is not *boasting* for I do not say whether *inside* that unprepossessing rock there is a palatial residence or an humble hut. What I say is this: you *do not know* me; for whatever there is *inside* it, is *not what you think* it is; and—to judge of me therefore, as of one *untruthful* is the greatest mistake in the world besides being a flagrant injustice. *I*, (the inner real "I") am in prison and cannot show myself as I am with all the desire I may have to.

Why then, should I, because speaking for myself *as I am* and feel myself to be, why should I be held responsible for the *outward* jail-door and *its* appearance, when I have neither built nor yet decorated it?

But all this will be for you no better than vexation of spirit. "The poor old lady is crazy again—" will you remark. And let me prophesy that the day will come when you will accuse K.H. too of having *deceived* you; for only failing to tell *you* what he has *no right* to tell anyone. Yes; you will blaspheme *even against him*; because you always secretly hope that he may make *an exception in your favour*.

Why, such an extravagant, seemingly useless *tirade* as contained in this letter? Because, the hour is near; and that after having proved what I have to, I will bow myself out from the refined Western Society and—be no more. You may all whistle then for the Brothers.—GOSPEL.

Of course *it was* a joke. No; you *do not hate me*; you only feel a friendly, indulgent, a kind of *benevolent contempt for H.P.B.* You are right there, so far *as you know her* the one who is ready to fall into pieces. Perchance you may find out yet your mistake concerning the other—the well hidden party. I have now with me *Deb*; Deb "Shortridge" as we call him, who looks a boy of 12, though is past 30 and more. An ideal little face with small cut delicate features, pearly teeth, long hair, almond cut eyes and a Chinese-tartar purple cap on the top of his head. He is my "heir of Salvation" and I have work to do with him. I cannot leave him and have no right to, now. I have to make over my work to him. He is my *right* hand (and K.H.'s *left* one)—at imposture and *false pretence*.

And now—God bless you. Better *not be angry* at anything I may do or say; only as a friend, a *real friend*, I say to you, so long as you have not changed your mode of living, expect no *exception*.

Yours truly

H.P.B.

My sincere love to Mrs. Sinnett and a kiss to dear little Dennie.

LETTER No. 137

Clan Drummond: Algiers.
Sunday 8th.

My dear Mr. Sinnett,

You see I am as good as my word. Last night as we were hopelessly tossed about and pitched in our Clan wash-tub Djual K. put in an appearance and asked in his Master's name if I would send you a chit. I said I would. He then asked me to prepare some paper—which I had not. He then said any would do. I then proceeded to ask some from a passenger, not having Mrs. Holloway to furnish me with [it]. Lo! I wish those passengers who quarrel with us every day about the possibility of phenomena could see what was taking place in my cabin on the foot of my berth! How D.K.'s hand, as real as life, was impressing the letter at his Master's dictation which came out in *relief* between the wall and my legs. He told me to read the letter but I am no wiser for it. I understand very well that it was all probation and all for the best; but it is devilish hard for me to understand why it should all be performed over my long suffering back. She is in correspondence with Myers and the Gebhards and many others. You will see what splatters *I* will receive as an effect of the causes produced by that probation business. I wish I had never seen the woman. Such treachery, such a deceit I would never have dreamt of. I was also a chela and guilty of more than one flapdoodle; but I would have thought as soon of murdering physically a man as to murder morally my friends as she has. Had not Master brought about the explanation I would have gone away leaving a nice memory of myself in Mrs. Sinnett's and your hearts. We have on board Mrs. (Major) Burton of Simla. She left it the day before I came and has been always anxious since, to meet me. She wants to join us and is a charming little woman. We have several Anglo Indians and all kindly disposed. The steamer is a rolling wash-tub and the steward an *infamy*. We are all starving, and live upon our own tea and biscuits. Do write a word to Port Said, *poste restante*. We shall remain in Egypt perhaps a fortnight. It all depends on Olcott's letters and news from Adyar. Can't write for the rolling. Love to all.

Yours ever truly

H. P. BLAVATSKY.

LETTER No. 138

Adyar, March 17th.

My dear Mr. Sinnett,

I am very sorry that the Mahatma should have selected me to fight this new battle. But since there must be concealed wisdom even in the act of choosing a half dead individual who just rises from eight weeks of sick bed and can hardly gather her scattered ideas to say that which had better be left unsaid—I obey.

You cannot have forgotten what I told you repeatedly at Simla and what the Master K. H. wrote to you himself, namely, that the T.S. is first of all a universal Brotherhood, not a Society for phenomena and occultism. The latter must be held secret etc. I know that owing to my great zeal for the cause and your assurances that the Society *would never* prosper unless the occult element was introduced into it and the Masters proclaimed I am more guilty than any for having listened to this. Still all of you have now to suffer Karma. Well, the phenomena are now all found, on the evidence of padris, and other enemies, *frauds* (by Mr. Hodgson), from the " brooch " phenomenon downward; and the Masters are dragged before the public and their names desecrated by every rascal in Europe.

The padris have spent thousands for false and other witnesses, and I was not permitted to go to law where at least I could produce my evidence: and now Hodgson, who unto this day seemed most friendly and came nearly daily to us changed front. He went to Bombay and saw Wimbridge and all my enemies. Returning he assured Hume, (who is here, and also coming daily) that in his opinion the evidence of our boys in office and other witnesses is so contradictory that after Bombay he came to the conclusion that all our phenomena were frauds. *Amen.*

And now what is the use in writing to disabuse Mr. Arthur Gebhard's mind? As soon as the P.R.S. oracle will have proclaimed me a wholesale " fraud " and all of you my dupes (as Hume does here laughingly, and with the greatest unconcern)— your L.L. Society is sure to collapse. Can even *you*, the true and the faithful, stand this storm? Happy Damodar! He went to the land of Bliss, to Tibet and must now be far away in the regions of our Masters. No one will ever see him now, I expect.

Well, this is where the accursed phenomena led us to. Olcott is returning from Burma in three days and will find nice things. At first Hume was all friendly. Then came the revelations. Hodgson had *traced* the brooch!!! I had given an *identical* brooch or pin to mend to Servai before going to Simla, he was told, and it was *that* brooch. Does Mrs. Sinnett remember that I spoke at that time of having had a pin very like it with pearls that I sent with another I bought at Simla to my sister's children? I spoke of the likeness even to Mr. Hume. I asked Mr. H. to have his pin sent to the jeweller (unknown but to Servai, Wimbridge's partner and my mortal enemy), who will or will not identify it. Most probably *he will*. Why shouldn't he—for a hundred rupees or so?

Mr. Hume wants *to save* the Society and has found a means. He called yesterday a Council meeting composed of Ragunath Row, Subba Row, Sreenavas Row, Honourable Subramanya Iyer and Rama Iyer. All leaders of Hindus. Then having selected Rag: Row Chairman and the audience being composed of the two Oakleys, Hartmann and the chelas—he gave him a paper. In it he proposed, to save the Society (he imagines and insists that it is falling to pieces after the " revelations," though *not one* fellow has yet resigned); to force Colonel Olcott its life-President, Madame Blavatsky, (ditto) Damodar (absent), Bowaji, Bhavani Row, Ananda, Rama Swami, etc. in all 16 persons *to resign* as they were all *frauds and accomplices*, since many of them asserted they *knew* the Masters independently of me and that the Masters did not exist. The Headquarters must be sold and on its place a new Scientifico-Philosophico-Humanitarian Theosophical society raised. I was not present at the meeting, I am confined to my room. But the Councillors came to me in a body after the proceedings. Instead of accepting the proposal though, and proclaiming the phenomena a fraud as Mr. Hume said they all had done to his knowledge—Ragunath Row rejected the paper, throwing it aside with disgust. They all believed in the Mahatmas—he said, and the phenomena they had witnessed *personally*, but would have no more their names desecrated. Phenomena must be, hereafter, prohibited, and if they did happen independently, *must not be talked about* under penalty of expulsion. They declined to ask the Founders to resign. They saw no reason for it. Mr. Hume is a queer " Saviour! "

Ergo, no more phenomena, at least here in India. While Mas[kelyne] and Cook produce theirs far better and are paid for it, we come out second best and are kicked for them.

Mr. Hume is more liberal than the Padris. These call Olcott " a credulous fool but undeniably an honest man "; and *he* declares, that since Olcott swears to have seen the Masters he must be a dishonest man, and since he got his pearl-pin at the pawnbroker's at Bombay he must be (by implication) a thief too, though Hume denies this.

Such is in brief the present situation. It began at Simla opening with the first act and now comes the *Prologue* that will soon finish with my death. For though, doctors notwithstanding (who proclaimed my four days' agony, and the impossibility of recovery) I suddenly got better, thanks to Master's protecting hand, I carry two mortal diseases in me which are not cured— heart, and kidneys. At any moment the former can have a rupture, and the latter carry me away in a few days. I will not see another year. All this is due to five years of constant anguish, worry and repressed emotion. A Gladstone may be called a " fraud " and laugh at it. I—can't, say what you may, Mr. Sinnett.

And now to your business. I have never, before beginning the service for you and Mr. Hume, transmitted and received letters to and from Masters except for myself. If you had any idea of the difficulties, or the *modus operandi* you would not have consented to be in my place. And yet I never refused. The shrine was thought of to facilitate the transmission, as now dozens and hundreds come to pray and beg to put their letters inside. As you know, and is proved to all except Mr. Hodgson, who finds *contradictions*, all received answers without my leaving the room and often in different languages. It is this, that unable to account for, Mr. Hume calls a wholesale collective fraud for, since the Masters in his idea do not exist, and that they *have never written one single of the letters ever received*—then the logical conclusion is that it is the whole staff—everyone in the Headquarters—Damodar, Bowaji, Subba Row, all, all who helped me to write the letters and passed them through the *hole*. Even Hodgson finds the idea preposterous.

And now to the " deception " practised on Mr. Arthur Gebhard, of which I learned from the Mahatma and A.G.'s own letter sent to me. This "fraud," coupled to the revelations and hints about others insinuated by kitten-like Mrs. Holloway, must have impressed a figure of H.P.B. of exquisite honourability and honesty on poor, dear Mrs. Gebhard!!

Well, persons who are on the eve of their death do not generally fib and say lies. I hope you will give me credit for speaking the truth. Ar. G. is not the only one to suspect and accuse me of fraud. Say then to the " friends " who may have received letters from the Master through me that I never was a deceiver; that I never played tricks upon them. I have often facilitated phenomena of letter-transmission by easier but still occult means. Only as none of the Theosophists, except occultists, know anything of either difficult or easy means of occult transmission, nor are they acquainted with occult laws, everything is suspicious to them. Take for instance this illustration as an instance: transmission by *mechanical* thought transference (in contradistinction with the conscious). The former is produced by calling first the attention of a chela or the Mahatma. The letter must be open and every line of it passed over the forehead, holding the breath and never taking off the part of the letter from the latter until bell notifies it is read and noted. The other mode is to impress every sentence of the letter (consciously of course) still mechanically on the brain, and then send it phrase by phrase to the other person on the other end of the line. This of course if the sender permits you to read it, and believes in your honesty that you read it mechanically, only reproducing the *form* of the words and lines on your brain— and not the meaning. But in both instances the letter must be open and then burnt with what we call *virgin fire* (lit neither with matches, brimstone nor any preparation but rubbed with a resinous, transparent little stone, a ball that no naked hand must touch.) This is done for the ashes, which, while the paper burns become immediately invisible, which they should not, if the paper were lit otherwise; because they would remain by their weight and grossness in the surrounding atmosphere, instead of being transferred instantaneously to the receiver. This double process is done for double security: for the words transmitted from one brain to another, or to the *akasa* near the Mahatma or chela may, some of them be omitted, whole words slip out etc., and the ashes be not perfectly transmitted; and in this way one corrects the other. I cannot do that, and therefore speak of it only as an example how deception can be easily fathered. Fancy A. giving a letter for the Mahatma to B. B. goes in the adjoining room and opening the letter—not one word of which will he remember if he is a true chela and an honest man—transmits it to his brain by one of the two methods, sending one sentence after the other on the current and then proceeds to burn the letter; perhaps—he has forgotten the " virgin stone " in his room. Leaving inadvertently the opened letter on the table, he absents himself for a few minutes. During that time A. impatient and probably suspicious enters the room. He sees his letter opened on the table. He will either take it and make an EXPOSÉ (!!) or leave it and then ask B. after he has burnt it whether he sent his letter. Of course B. will answer he has. Then will come the *exposé* with consequences you may imagine, or A. will hold his tongue and do as many do: hold for ever B. for a fraud. This is one instance out of many, and a real one, given to me as a caution by Master.

There's a funny thing in Mr. A.G.'s letter, very funny and suggestive. For instance, recounting in it how he gave me the letter and six hours later I had told him " it was gone " he adds: " four days later Colonel wrote to H.P.B. saying that his Master appeared and said that K.H. had said: (see original sent back to you.) But then the good " Colonel must also be a fraud," a confederate of mine, an accomplice? Or is it my Master who mystifies him, Mr. A. G., Arthur Gebhard, or what? And then again: " H.P.B. is a fraud although I will never deny her excellent qualities." The ' excellent qualities ' of a fraud is something startling and original at all events.

Thus you will please tell Mr. A. R. Gebhard that we are *two* " frauds—" if any; and also this: Mahatma K. H. has received *but never read his letter*, for the simple reason that he was prevented by his promise to the Chohan never to read a letter from any theosophist until his return from his mission to China where he then was. This He condescended now to tell me to help to my justification, as he says. He had forbidden me most strictly to send him any more letters until further orders. Since Master at Arthur G.'s urgent prayer took it upon Himself for reasons best known to Himself, I had nothing to say but to obey. I took the letter and put it in a drawer full of papers. When I looked for it, I found it was gone, at least I did not see it, and said so to him. But before going to bed, taking out an envelope I found his letter still there, though in the morning it was really gone. Now if my remembrance is right I showed to Madame Gebhard Olcott's letter in which he speaks of what Master said. *I had not read Gebhard's letter* and may have taken the words as an answer to this letter. As it is I have not now the faintest recollection of the whole of the message. One thing I know and Madame Geb. will corroborate it; she spoke of the terrible quarrels between Arth. G. and his father to me in London, before going to Paris, and to Olcott repeatedly. She had expressed the hope that the Mahatma would interfere on her behalf, and these words may have related to this and not at all to the letter. How can I remember? Olcott may have heard imperfectly, or I muddled up the thing. Hundred combinations may have happened. The only *fraud* is, then, in my telling him an unconscious untruth about the letter going six hours later when it was taken only in the morning. To this I plead " guilty."

But as in the Hume " pearl-pin " affair there is something more implied than mere fraud in the production of phenomena. If I have bamboozled in this Mad. G. and himself then I become right away a black leg, a SWINDLER. I have received hospitality at their house for months; they have nursed me through out my sickness, and even not permitted [me] to pay the doctor, covered me with rich presents, honours and kindnesses, for all of which I repay with—DECEPTION. Oh powers of heaven, Truth and Justice! May Mr. Arthur Gebhard's Karma prove light to him. I forgive him for the sake of his mother and father whom I will love and respect to my last hour. Please give these my parting words to Mad. Gebhard; I have nothing more to say.

It is useless, Mr. Sinnett. The Theosophical Society shall live here, in India, for ever—it seems doomed in Europe, *because I am doomed*. It hangs on your *Esoteric Buddhism* and the *Occult World*. And if Mahatmas are myths, I—the author of all those letters, a proclaimed FRAUD and worse by the P.R.S. how can the London Lodge live? I told you—for I felt it, as I always feel that this investigation of Mr. Hodgson will be fatal. He is the most excellent, truthful, expert young man. But how can he recognise truth from lie when there is a thick net of conspiracy around him? At first, when he visited the Headquarters, and the padris could not well get hold of him, he seemed all right. His accounts were favourable. And then he was caught. We have our informants who followed the missionaries sharply. You, in England may laugh—we do not.

We know that the conspiracy is not one to laugh at. The 30,000 padris of India are all leagued against us. It is their last card they play—either *they* or *we*. There was 72,000 rupees collected in one week in Bombay—" to conduct the investigations against the so-called Founders of the T.S." All the Judges of the land (think of Sir C. Turner!) are against us. Sceptics and nominal Christians, free thinkers and C.S. snobs—my very name stinks in their nostrils. And now comes the old sleeping beauty again on the scene. I am, after all, A RUSSIAN SPY. Last night the Oakleys dined with Hume at the Garstins and were told very seriously that the Government was to *over-shadow* me once more; that they had information (the Coulombs?) and that I had " to be watched." Vainly did Hume laugh and the Oakleys protest. It was " very serious " in view of the Russians crossing Cabul, Afghanistan, or something of that sort.

An old and a *dying* woman, confined to her room; forbidden to mount a few steps lest her heart bursts; never reading a paper for fear of finding there the most vile personal abuse; receiving letters from Russia but from relatives—a spy, a dangerous character! Oh Britishers of India where is your valour?

Notwithstanding Hume, their friend Hodgson and all the evidence, the Oakleys do *not* believe me a fraud. They have full confidence in the Masters; nothing, they say, will make them doubt their existence and, apart [from] some little unpleasantness due to gossip upon private affairs, they are staunch theosophists and as they say my best friends. Well, and good. I believe O Lord, help thou my unbelief. How can I believe *anyone* my friend at such a moment? It is only *he* who knows, as he knows that he lives and breathes, that our Mahatmas exist and phenomena are real, who can sympathise with me, who do, and look upon me as a martyr. Pamphlets by Reverends, books and articles *exposing* me from top to foot appear every day. "Theosophy Unveiled—" "Madame Blavatsky Exposed—" "The Theosophical Humbug Before the World—" "Christ against Mahatmas " etc. etc.: you who knew India well, Mr. Sinnett, do you think it difficult to get *false witnesses* here? They have all the advantages over us. They (the enemies) work night and day, flooding the country with literature against us, and we sit motionless and only quarrel within the Theos: Headquarters. Olcott is held finally a fool, detested by the Oakleys (for some mistakes that really he could not help,) and adored by the Hindus. And now after the arrival of Hume I come for my share. Though my friends, the Oakleys, advise me to resign, the Hindus say they will all leave if I do. *I* must resign because being thought a " Russian spy " I endanger the Society. Such is *my* life during my convalescence when every emotion, says the doctor, *may prove fatal.* So much the better. I will then *resign de facto.* But then they forget that so far I am the only link between the Europeans and the Mahatmas. The Hindus do not care. Dozens of them are chelas, hundreds *know* Them, but as in the case of Subba Row they will sooner die than speak of their Masters. Hume could get *nothing* from Subba Row, though everyone knows what he is. The other night he received a long letter from my Master in the meeting room when Hume voted my resignation. They had just voted there should be no phenomena any more and Mahatmas never spoken about; the letter was in Telugu, they say. Though they stand by me and will stand to the last, they accuse me of having desecrated the Truth and the Masters by having been the means of the *Occult World* and *Esoteric Buddhism.* Do not count upon the Hindus, you of the L.L. I—dead, say Society good bye to the Masters. Say even now—all perhaps with one exception —for I have pledged my word to my Hindu Brothers, the occultists, *never* to mention except among ourselves Their names, and that I will keep it.

This will probably be my last letter to you, dear Mr. Sinnett. It took me a week nearly to write this one—I am so feeble; and then I do not think I will have an opportunity. I cannot tell you why: most probably, you will not regret it. You cannot remain faithful much longer, living as you do in the world. Myers and P.R.S. will laugh you to scorn. Hume, who goes to London in April will set all against the Mahatmas and me. It takes a different kind of men and women than you have in the L.L. with the exception of Miss Arundale and two or three others—to withstand such a persecution and storm. And all this because we have profaned Truth by giving it out indiscriminately—and forgot the motto of the true Occultist: To know, to dare, and to KEEP SILENT.

Good-bye then, dear Mr. Sinnett and Mrs. Sinnett. Whether I die in a few months or remain two or three years in solitude I am as good as dead—already. Forget me, and try to deserve *personal* communication with the Master. Then you shall be able to preach him, and if you succeed as I succeeded you shall be hooted and insulted as I was, and see whether you can stand it. The Oakleys urge me to write to my aunt and sister and ask her to send me the design of the pearl brooch I sent them in 1880. I refuse. Why, should I? The brooch phenomenon proven, then will come out some other proved fraudulent by false witnesses. I am tired, tired, tired and so disgusted that Death herself with her first hours of horror is preferable to this. Let the whole world, with the exception of a few friends and my Hindu Occultists, believe me a fraud. I will not deny it—even to their faces. Say so to Mr. Myers and others.

Good-bye, again.   May your life be happy and prosperous and Mrs. S.'s old age more healthy than her youth.   Forgive me the annoyances I may have caused you and—forget.

Yours to the end

H. P. BLAVATSKY

LETTER No. 139 [1]

Wednesday.

My dear Mr. Sinnett,

I asked you (*I* myself) in my letter to you " Do, please do *try* and have intuition." You have succeeded but only for one portion. You *felt* that a page or so of it had been dictated to me, and that it was by no *sham* K.H. But you have failed again to feel in what an unalloyed spirit of kindness, sympathy for and appreciation of yourself He dictated those few sentences. You mistook it for *criticism*. Now, hear me. Except a vague recollection that I have been writing under His dictation, I could not, of course, remember one line of it correctly, though I have read it carefully before I closed the letter. But what I can swear to is that there was *not a shadow of criticism* against yourself personally meant or in the Mahatma's thought when passing this to me. I was writing *my* letter to you and had written about three or four pages when the Countess came in and read to me out of your letter those desponding lines in which you said that you are inclined to suspect that the " Higher Powers " do not wish the Society to live any longer and that it is useless for you to try, or something like that. I had not had time to open my mouth for an answer and protest when I saw His reflection over the writing desk and heard the words " Now write, pray." I did not listen to the words dictated except in a mechanical sort of way, but I know with what attention and intense interest I watched the " thought and feeling-lights " and aura, if you understand my meaning. The Mahatma wanted me to, I suppose; otherwise His thoughts and inner working would have remained impenetrable. And I say, that NEVER, since you know Him, never was there so much kindness, genuine feeling for you, and an utter absence of " criticism " or reproach directed to yourself as this time. Don't be ungrateful; don't misunderstand. Open your *inner* heart and feeling entirely and do not judge through your world and cold reason spectacles. Ask the Countess to whom the letter was read and to whom I told what I say to you now, and to hear which she was so glad for

[1] It would seem that this Letter is a reply to Mr. Sinnett's reply to Letter 141, p. 474. At the end of that Letter Mr. Sinnett is asked to rouse his intuitions (p. 479). At the beginning of Letter 139 above H.P.B. refers to this.—EDS.

you, for she does sympathise with you and your position and appreciates as much as I do, all you have done. All you say is perfectly true, and just what I thought I had discerned in the Mahatma's aura. The yellow-grayish streaks were directed all to Olcott, (London period, not *now*), Mohini, Finch (more reddish); and to others I will not name. Your full size portrait, or *scin-lecca*, received a whole torrent of blue, clear silvery light—the Prince's Hall, Kingsford incident, and even Holloway were all far, far away from you in a mist—hence a *proof* undeniable that you were implicated in it by no fault of yours *personally*, but drawn into it irresistibly by the *general* Karma. Where then is the " criticism " or reproach? No man living can do more in this world than is in him. You could not *avoid*—Prince's Hall meeting, for the Society had chosen a path, in which it had to come. But all of you, you the first, had you prepared for it as it ought to have been done long before, would have saved the situation by each of you delivering—even reading it would have been better—a speech that would have gone home to the public instead of what it has done. Your speech was the only one against which nothing could be urged but, on account of your ill-will, you having been dragged into it—so cold, so devoid of enthusiasm or even earnestness that it became like a key-note to the others. Olcott's was a regular Yankee flapdoodle, one of the worst. The " Angel Mohini's " was a remarkably stupid one, Babu-like flowers of rhetoric etc. But that's things of the past. Of course it *was* a failure; but it *might have been a success* notwithstanding everything adverse, had it been prepared beforehand. The public reception *was* on the *path chosen* and had to take place, for it would have been worse still had it rot come off. Holloway *was* sent, and was in the programme of trials and destruction. She has done *you* ten times more harm than to the Society but this is your fault entirely and now she is dancing the war-dance around Olcott, who is as fast friends with her and more than you were. It is a *weekly correspondence* incessant and endearing, charming to behold; she is his *dear* agent in Brooklyn, for things occult etc. Let that go. About " chelas "—it is a more serious question. They are no fools either of them. They *feel*, if they do not know yet, that the abyss between them and Masters is being made wider daily. They *feel* they are on the wrong *left* side, and feeling that, they will turn towards that to which all such " failures " turn. If Masters *ordered* them to go back to India I do not think they would *now* under Bowajee's *inspiration*. Mohini *is* ruined by him, there's no mistake about it. And Miss——is going to pots in their company. You have to act independently of them; not to break visibly, but to do your own work as though they did not exist. Look here, I want you to write to Arthur Gebhard a serious letter and tell

33

him all you know about Bowajee. He is in full correspondence with the Americans, and getting round them as he got round the Gebhards. I wrote to him and the Countess did. But he will not believe us unless corroborated by you. He was surely told by this time that the Countess is entirely *under my psychology*. Franz is certain of it, poor man. Unless you warn him, the two, or one of " chelas " are sure to go to America. If you could bring the Leonard to clamour for his departure to India, as a *settlement* then he would have no excuse to stop. But *how* to do it! If I could only see, approach the hussy, I would be ready to sacrifice myself, anything to weed the Society from all this poisonous vegetation. But you *can work* independently of all [of] them—that's sure.

Before the 15th of April we will be near you, across the stream. The Countess comes with me and takes her chances until about the middle of May. I *have* to be near you in case something should happen, for save herself I do not think I have a friend, a *real* friend in this wide world besides yourself and Mrs. Sinnett. The " semblance," the theosophical Mr. Hyde (Dr. Jekyll) has done his best. I could stop it in one hour if I could only pounce on them *unexpectedly*. This I swear. But how to do it. If I could only arrive and stop in London for two days unknown it would be done. I would go to them at 8 in the morning. But I must see you and think over it first. If I had *health* only— which I have not. The " two years life and no more " of the London doctor brought by Mr. Gebhard and of my doctor at Adyar—are drawing near the end. Unless Master interferes once more—Good-bye.

You have said nothing of Gladstone's little tricks. Don't you believe in it? Funny. I am told you received a letter upon that subject so far back as during the Ilbert Bill row. Well I can tell you nice things about the Jesuits and their doings. But of course its no good. Yet indeed, indeed it *is* serious.

Well, good-bye, *do* write.

Yours ever faithfully,

H. P. B.

Love to Mrs. Sinnett.

LETTER No. 140

Jan. 6. 1886. Wurzburg.

My dear Mr. Sinnett,

I am impressed to give you the following: First let me tell you that the dear Countess went off to Munich like a shot to try and save Hübbe from his weakness and the Society from crumbling down. She was the whole evening in a trance, getting out and in from her body. She saw Master and felt him all the night. She *is* a great clairvoyant. Well, after reading a few pages of the *Report* I was so disgusted with Hume's gratuitous lies and Hodgson's absurd inferences that I nearly gave up all in despair. *What could I* do or say against evidence on the natural worldly plane! Everything went against me and I had but to die. I went to bed and I had the most extraordinary vision. I had vainly called upon the Masters—who came not during my waking state, but now in my sleep I saw them both, I was again (a scene of years back) in Mah. K.H.'s house. I was sitting in a corner on a mat and he walking about the room in his riding dress, and Master was talking to someone behind the door. " *I remind can't* "—I pronounced in answer to a question of His about a dead aunt.—He smiled and said " Funny English you use." Then I felt ashamed, hurt *in my vanity*, and began thinking (mind you, in my *dream* or *vision* which was the *exact* reproduction of what had taken place word for word 16 years ago) " now I am here and speaking *nothing but English* in verbal phonetic language I can perhaps learn to speak better with Him." (To make it clear with Master I also used English, which whether bad or good was the same for Him as he does not speak it but understands every word I say out of my head; and I am made to understand Him—*how* I could never tell or explain if I were killed *but I do*. With D.K. I also spoke English, he speaking it better even than Mah. K.H.) Then, in my dream still, *three months after* as I was made to feel in that vision—I was standing before Mah. K.H. near the old building taken down he was looking at, and as Master was not at home, I took to him a few sentences I was studying in Senzar in his sister's room and asked him to tell me if I translated them correctly—and gave him a slip of paper with these sentences written in English. He took and read them, and correcting the interpretation read them over and said " Now your English is becoming better—*try to pick out of my head even the little I know of it*." And he put his hand on my forehead in the region of memory and squeezed his fingers on it (and I felt even the same trifling pain in it, as then, and the cold shiver I had experienced) and since that day He did so with my head daily, for about two months. Again, the scene changes and I am going away with Master who is sending me off, back to Europe. I am bidding good-bye to his sister and her child and all the chelas. I listen to what the Masters tell me. And then come the parting words of Mah. K.H. laughing at me as He always did and saying " Well, if you have not learned much of the Sacred Sciences and practical Occultism—and *who could expect a* WOMAN to—you have learned, at any rate, a little English. You speak it now *only a little worse* than I do! " and he laughed.

Again the scene changes. I am 47th St. New York writing *Isis* and His voice dictating to me. In that dream or *retrospective* vision I once more *rewrote* all *Isis* and could now point out all the pages and sentences Mah. K.H. dictated—as those that Master did—in my bad English, when Olcott tore his hair out by handfuls in despair to ever make out the meaning of what was intended. I again saw myself night after night in bed—writing *Isis* in my dreams, at New York, positively *writing it in my sleep* and felt sentences by Mah. K.H. impressing themselves on my memory. Then, as I was awakening from that vision (in Wurzburg now) I heard Mah. K.H.'s voice—" and now put two and two together, poor blind woman. The bad English and the construction of sentences you *do* know, even that you have learned *from me* . . . take off the slur thrown upon you by that misguided, conceited man (Hodgson): explain the truth to the few friends who will believe you—for the public never will to that day that the Secret Doctrine comes out." I awoke, and it *was* like a flash of lightning; but I still did not understand what it referred to. But an hour after, there comes Hübbe Schleiden's letter to the Countess, in which he says that unless I explain how it is that such a similarity is found and proven by Hodgson between my faulty English and Mah. K.H.'s certain expressions, the construction of sentences and peculiar Gallicisms—I stand accused for ever of deceit forgery (!!) and what not. Of course I have learned my English from Him! This Olcott even shall understand. You know and I told it to many friends and enemies—I was taught dreadful Yorkshire by my nurse called *Governess*. From the time my father brought me to England, when fourteen, thinking I spoke beautiful English— and people asked him if he had me educated in Yorkshire or Ireland—and laughed at my accent and way of speaking—I gave up English altogether, trying to avoid speaking it as much as I could. From fourteen till I was over forty I never spoke it, let alone writing and forgot it entirely. I could read—which I did very little—in English—I could not speak it. I remember how difficult it was for me to understand a well written book in English so far back only as 1867 in Venice. All I knew when I came to America in 1873 was to speak a little, and this Olcott and Judge and all who knew me then can testify to. I wish people saw an article I once attempted to write for the *Banner of Light* when instead of sanguine I put *sanguinary*, etc. I learned to write it through *Isis*, that's sure, and Prof. A. Wilder who came weekly to help Olcott arranging chapters and writing *Index* can testify to it. When I had finished it (and this *Isis* is the *third part only* of what I wrote and destroyed) I could write as well as I do now, not worse nor better. My memory and its capacities seem gone since then.

What wonder then that *my* English and the Mahatma's show similarity! Olcott's and mine do also in our Americanisms that I picked up from him these ten years. I, translating mentally all from the French, would not have written sceptic with a *k*, though Mahat. K.H. did and when I put it with a *c* Olcott and Wilder and the proof reader corrected it. Now Mah. K.H. has preserved the habit and stuck to it and I never did since I went to India. I would have never put *carbolic* instead of " carbonic "—and I was the first to remark the mistake when [1] Hume Mahatma's letter, at Simla, in which it occurs. It is *mean* and stupid of him to publish it, for, if he says this referred to a sentence found in some magazine, then the word correctly written was there before *my* eyes or those of any chela who precipitated the letter, and therefore it *is* evidently a *lapsus calami* if there were any *calami* in precipitation. " Difference in handwriting "—oh the great wonder! Has Master K.H. written himself all *His* letters? How many chelas have been precipitating and writing them—heaven only knows. Now if there is such a marked difference between letters written by the same identical person *mechanically*, (as the case with me for instance who never had a *steady* handwriting) how much more in *precipitation*, which is the *photographic* reproduction from one's head, and I bet anything that no chela (if *Masters* can) is capable of *precipitating* his own handwriting twice over in precisely the same way—a difference and a marked one there shall always be, as no painter can paint twice over the same likeness (see Schmiechen with his (Master's) portraits). Now all this shall be easily understood by theosophists (not all) and those who have thought over deeply and know something of the philosophy. Who shall believe all I say in this letter outside of the few? No one. And yet, I am *demanded* an explanation, and when it comes out (*if you* write it out from facts I can give you) no one shall believe it. Yet you have to show at least one thing: occult transactions, letters, handwriting etc. *cannot* be judged by the daily standard, experts, this that and the other. There are no *three* solutions but *two*: Either I have invented the Masters, their philosophy, written their letters etc., or, *I have not*. If I have and the Masters do not exist, then their handwritings *could not have existed*, either: I have *invented* them also; and if I have—how can I be called a " forger "? They are *my* handwritings and I have the right to use them if I am so clever. As for philosophy and doctrine invented the S.D. shall show. Now I am here alone with the Countess for witness. I have no books, no one to help me. And I tell you that the *Secret Doctrine* will be 20 times as learned, philosophical and better than *Isis* which will be *killed* by it. Now there are hundreds of things I am permitted to say and

---

[1] Query, ' when ' should be ' in '.—Eds.

explain. It will show what a Russian *spy* can do, an alleged *forger plagiarist* etc. The whole Doctrine is shown the *mother stone*, the foundation of all the religions including Xty, and on the strength of *exoteric* published Hindu books, with their symbols explained *esoterically.* The extreme lucidity of *Esoteric Buddhism* will also be shown and its doctrines proven correct mathematically, geometrically, logically and scientifically. Hodgson is very clever, but he is not clever enough for *truth and it shall triumph,* after which I can die peacefully.

Babula writing my Master's letters indeed! Hume finding out five years later that the envelope from the municipality had been " tampered " by me brought by Babula. What good memory his Mahomedan bearer must have, to remember that it was *precisely that envelope!* And Garstin's letter taken to him by Mohini 2½ hours after his letter had been placed inside and disappeared from the shrine. His letter *sealed glued* with every precaution, bearing no such marks as now described on the night of the delivery, and now two years later, after having passed through 1000 hands, been tampered by Garstin and experts themselves, trying to see *how* it could have been opened—now it all goes *against* me! And Hume's *lies.* Such Tibetan or Nepaul paper he learned could be procured near Darjeeling. Masters *never* wrote he said on *such* paper before I had gone to Darjeeling. Indeed. Now I enclose a slip of such paper for your perusal, that with your memory you are *sure to recognise.* It is the original bit from which the first lessons of Master were given to you and Hume in his *Museum* at Simla. You looked at it many times. Please when recognised send it back to me. It is *private and confidential* and I ask you on your honour not to let it go out of your hands, not to give it to any one. No expert or Orientalist would find or understand anything in it but letters which have *a meaning for me,* for no one else. But what I want you to see and remember is that I went to Darjeeling a year later after Hume had quarrelled with K.H. and this paper I had at Simla when the first lessons were begun. And all throughout the whole *Report* the same *lies,* false testimony etc.

Yours—*No more broken down.*

H. P. BLAVATSKY.

LETTER No. 141 [1]

March 17th, 1886.

My Dear Mr. Sinnett,

Do anything you like. I am in your hands. Only I cannot see what harm there could be were the lawyers to be told that it is a lie my being Mme Metrovitch or Mme any one except myself.

[1] See Note to Letter 139, ante., p.468.—EDS.

It would prevent them and put a stop to their addressing letters to me in that name; for surely they are not such fools as not to know that this *open* libel *is* against law.   It is because the Bibiche bamboozle them into the belief that I was really a bigamist and a *trigamist* that they did it.   Well, very soon I may receive a letter addressed to me in the name of Mrs. Leadbeater or Mrs. Damodar or perhaps be accused of having had a child by Mohini or Bowajee. Who can tell unless *something* is refuted.

But this is all trifles.   There is something unutterably disgusting and sickening to me in the idea of any concealment of names. I hate incognitos and changing names.   Why should I give you more bother than you already have with me?   Why should you lose time and money to come and meet me?   Don't do this.   I will send the things before hand and come out with Louise quietly second class, passing the night at Bonn or at Achen (Aix la Chapelle) or somewhere on the road.   Lodgings will be dear at Ostende in June, not before.   Besides I can go somewhere near-by. I do not know when I will leave here.   May be on the 1st, may be on the 15th.   I have paid till that date.

Why shouldn't Mrs. Sinnett come with Dennie?   Where's the harm and why should she not stop with me if I find good lodgings? I would never be happy unless she was with me for what's the use of her being in other lodgings?   Only discomfort for her and vexation of spirit for me.

I have written to my aunt and sister giving them Redway's address.   The letters will all be addressed to you to his care, only for Madame B: under your name.   However, I really care little for letters or no letters.   There's a long article in my praise and glorification in the Russian papers in which I am called " the *martyr* of England."   That's comforting and makes me feel as though I were indeed a " *grand* Russian *Spy*! "   Say, do you know —but then you will never believe it—Well don't, but some day you will be forced to, Gladstone is a *secret Roman Catholic convert*. That's sure.   Make of it what you will, you cannot change FACTS. Ah, poor England; and foolish, blind are those who seek the destruction of the T.S.!

Well, I must say a few words in this respect.   You say " we are almost past praying for . . . paralyzed and helpless.   The French and German branches of the T.S. are practically dead. The London movement can only be revivified at some future period, etc."   You are asked: How is this? *You* are not dead. The Countess lives.   Two or three fellows around you breathe, so far.   The Society in India is flourishing and can NEVER die. In America it is becoming a grand movement.   Dr. Buck, Prof. Coues, Arthur Gebhard with a few others *are helped* because they move, and show their utmost contempt for whatever is said, printed, howled in the streets. Oh, do try and be intuitional—for pity's sake do not shut your eyes and because you cannot see *objectively* do not paralyze *subjective* help which *is* there living, breathing, evident. Does not all around you show the indestructibility of the Society, if we see how the fierce waves raised by the Dugpa-world have been for the last two years heaving and spreading and beating ferociously around the Society to break, what? only the *rotten* chips of the "Ark of the Deluge." Have they carried away anyone really worthy of the movement? Not one. You suspect that the "Masters" want to put an end to the movement? They see you do not understand what they are doing and *feel sorry* for it. Are *they* to be blamed for what happened, or *we*, ourselves? If the Founder of the Society and the Founders or Presidents of the Branches had ever kept in view the fact that it is not so much the quantity we are in need of, but the quality, to make the Society a success half of the disasters would have been avoided. There were two paths before the L.L. as before any other branch when you took up its mangled fragments and rebuilt them into the growing successful body it was: that which led to the formation of a secret, arcane Society of studying *practical* occultists; the other an open and fashionable body. You have always preferred the latter. A chance was given to all of you in the formation of an inner group: you *would not* assert your authority and left it to the *nominal* President—who shook on his legs at every gentle breeze from within and without, ruined and then deserted it. Every such attempt was either repelled or, if realized, had such a strong element of *sham* in it that it proved a failure. It was found *impossible* to help it and *it was left to its fate.* There is an Asiatic proverb: "You may cut the serpent of wisdom in a hundred pieces; so long as its heart, which is in its head, remains untouched, the serpent will join its bits and live again." But when the heart and head seem everywhere and are nowhere, what can be done? The L.L. having taken its rank and place among public bodies it had to be judged by its appearances. It is not enough to laud the Body and Branches, as schools of morality and wisdom and benevolence, for they will always be judged by the outward world by their *fruits*, not by their pretensions—not by what they *say* but by what they *do.* The Branch was always in need of efficient workers; and, as in all organizations the work devolved upon the very few. Out of those few *one* only had a definite object in view, pursued it firm and unwavering—YOURSELF. Yet your natural reserve and the strong element of *worldly* Society within the Occult body, the sense of English individuality and propriety in each member, prevented you on the one hand from asserting your rights as you ought to have done, and caused the rest to separate from you wide and apart, each determining to act as he or she thought best, to secure his own salvation and satisfy his aspirations, " working Karma out on a higher plane " as the foolish phrase goes now among them. You are *right* in saying that " the blows that have been struck at the movement " have been " all emanating from the consequences of the deputations from India "; you are *wrong* in thinking that (1) these consequences would have been as disastrous, had not the Hindu element been mixed up with the European and strongly helped and urged on toward mischief by the female element in the L.L.; and (2) that " the higher powers wish to arrest the growth of the Society." Mohini was sent, and at first won the hearts and poured new life into the L.L. He was spoiled by male and female adulation, by incessant flattery and his own weakness— your reserve and pride left you passive when you ought to have been active. The first bomb-shell from the Dug-pa world came from America; you welcomed and warmed it in your own breast, you drove the writer of this more than once to the verge of despair, your thorough-going, sincere earnestness, your devotion to truth and the " Masters " having been made powerless for the time being, for discerning the *real* truth, for sensing that which was left unsaid *for it could not be said* and thus leaving the widest margin for suspicion. The latter was not unfounded. The Dugpa element triumphed fully at one time—why? because you believed in one who was sent by the opposing powers for the destruction of the Society and permitted to act as she and others did by the " higher powers," as you call them, whose duty it was not to interfere in the great probation save at the last moment. To this day you are unable to say what was true, what false—because there is no spot made apart, separated from the Society and consecrated to the one pure element in it, love and devotion to the truth whether abstract or concreted in the " Masters "—a spot in which no element of individuality or selfishness would enter—a real *inner* group is here meant. The Oriental group has proved a *farce*. Miss——cares more for the chelas(?) than the Masters; she is blind to the fact that those who were (and yet think they still are) most devoted to the Cause, Masters, Theosophy, call it by what-ever name—*are those that are the most tried*; that she is now being tried, that it is her *last trial* and that she does not come out of it as a conqueror, it seems. " In the absence of any means of communicating directly with them I can only judge by signs"— you say. The signs are evident. It is the great supreme trial all round. He who remains *passive* will lose nothing, but *will not gain* one tittle, when it is over. He may even cause his Karma to slide him gently back on the path he has already been climbing. What you sorely lack is Olcott's blessed self-confidence and— pardon—his vulgar but all powerful *cheek*. One need not give up tact and culture to have it. It is a many faced Proteus that can have either of his faces or *cheek* turned to the enemy and *force* him to cover. If the L.L. is composed only of six members —the President the *seventh*; and this daring "vieille garde" faces the enemy coolly, not allowing him to know how many you are, and impressing him with outward signs of a multitude by the number of pamphlets, convocations and other distinct, material proofs that the Society has not been shaken, that it *has not felt the blows*, that it snaps its fingers in the enemy's face, you will soon win the day; you will have exhausted the enemy before it tires out the Society to its last member. All this can be easily achieved and no "smashing disasters" would really affect it, if its members had intuition enough to see what "the higher powers" really wish, what they can or cannot prevent. Spiritual discernment is what is most wanted. "It is not so much a question of saving what remains of the Society—as of recommencing the movement *at some future time*." Fatal policy. Follow it, and you will have broken by that (*future*) time every invisible yet powerfully vital thread that links the L.L. with the *ashrams* beyond the great mountains. NOTHING CAN KILL THE L.L. *except that one thing—Passivity*. Know this, you who confess that you " have no heart for the present to be giving lectures and addresses." "WORK UNDERGROUND"—it is the best you can do—but *not in silence*—if you would not kill the Society and your own personal aspirations with your own hand. All are not speakers in the L.L. and very lucky, or it would be a Babel. All are not wise, but those who are ought to share with the rest. Combine to make things complete. Make your activity commensurate with your opportunities and do not turn your face away from the latter, even from those that are created for you. "Fling the burning brands apart, and they will quickly go out; rake them together and they will glow, burst into flame, and shoot sky-ward with ruddy brightness." So shall the L.L. shine out if demoralization is kept at distance, if its lights are not allowed to burn and die out as isolated and intermediate points of light, but are clustered and focalized into full ruddiness by the hand of its President, and if this hand is not allowed to drop the banner entrusted to it. Human dirt never sticks, nor does it soil the flame it is flung against. It only sticks hard to the marble, to the cold heart that has lost the last spark of the Divine flame. Yes indeed, the "Masters" and the "Powers that be" would call and guide many and many a sad, lonesome and weary one in this fair land of occult, psychic *theosophy* to gather with them around their altars. Two are bodily there already, who have won their day and found the alleged "Invisibles"—each by his own path. For the teachings of the "Order" are like precious stones—whatever way turned, light and truth and beauty flash forth, and *will guide* the weary traveller in search of them, if he but stops not on his way to follow the will-o'-wisps of the illusive world, and remains deaf to public rumour.

Now do, for pity sake—do try to arouse for once your intuitions if you can. I do suffer for you and would do anything to help you. But you *prevent* me. Pardon this and try to recognize the foreign from my own words.

H. P. B.

LETTER No. 142 A

THE THEOSOPHICAL SOCIETY

With reference to the Rules and Organization of the Society, I beg to make the following suggestions. The points I urge, appear to me very necessary as I have had conversation with many Natives and have a claim to know the Hindu character better than a foreigner can.

A general impression appears to prevail that the Society is a religious sect. This impression owes its origin, I think, to a common belief that the whole Society is devoted to Occultism. As far as I can judge, this is not the case. If it is, the best course to adopt would be to make the entire Society a secret one, and shut its doors against all except those very few who may have shown a determination to devote their whole lives to the study of Occultism. If it is not so, and is based upon the broad Humanitarian principle of Universal Brotherhood, let Occultism, one of its several Branches, be an entirely secret study. From time immemorial this sacred knowledge has been guarded from the vulgar with great care, and because a few of us have had the great fortune to come into contact with some of the custodians of this invaluable treasure, is it right on our part to take advantage of their kindness and vulgarize the secrets they esteem more sacred than even their lives? The world is not yet prepared to hear truth about this subject. By placing the facts before the unprepared general public, we only make a laughing stock of those who have been kind to us and have accepted us as their co-workers for doing good to humanity. By harping too much upon this subject, we have made ourselves in a measure odious in the eyes of the public. We went even to such an extent that, unconsciously to ourselves, we led the public to believe that our Society is under the sole management of the Adepts, while the fact is that the entire executive management is in the hands of the Founders, and our Teachers give us advice only in rare exceptional cases of the greatest emergency. The public saw that they must have misapprehended the facts, since errors in the Management of the Society—some of which could have been very well avoided by the exercise of ordinary common sense—were from time to time exposed. Hence they came to the conclusion that

(1) Either Adepts do not exist at all; or

(2) If they do, they have no connection with our Society, and therefore we are dishonest impostors; or

(3) If they have any connection with the Society, it must be only those of a very low degree, since, under their management, such errors occurred.

With the few noble exceptions who had entire confidence in us, our Native Members came to one of these three conclusions. It is therefore necessary in my opinion that prompt measures should be adopted to remove these suspicions. For this, I see only one alternative:—(1) Either the entire Society should be devoted to occultism, in which case it should be quite as secret as the Masonic or the Rosicrucian Lodge or, (2) Nobody should know anything about occultism except those very few who may have by their conduct shown their determination to devote themselves to its study. The first alternative being found inadvisable by our " Brothers " and positively forbidden, the second remains.

Another important question is that of the admission of Members. Until now, any one who expressed a desire to join and could get two sponsors was allowed to come into the Society, without our enquiring closely what the motives in joining were. This led to two evil results. People thought or pretended to think that we took in Members simply for their Initiation Fees on which we lived; and many joined out of mere curiosity, as they thought that by paying an Initiation Fee of Rupees Ten, they could see phenomena. And when they were disappointed in this, they turned round on us, and began to revile our CAUSE for which we have been working and to which we have pledged our lives. The best way to remedy this evil would be to exclude this class of persons. The question naturally arises how can this be done, since our Rules are so liberal as to admit every one? But, at the same time our Rules prescribe an Initiation Fee of Rupees Ten. This is too low to keep out the curiosity seekers, who, for the chance of being satisfied, feel they can very well afford to lose such a paltry sum. The fee should therefore be so much increased that those only would join who are really in earnest. We need men of principle and serious purpose. One such man can do more for us than hundreds of phenomena-hunters. The fee should in my judgment be increased to Rs: 200 or Rs: 300. It might be urged that thus we might exclude really good men who may be sincere and earnest but unable to pay. But I think it is preferable to risk the possible loss of one good man than take in a crowd of idlers, one of whom can undo the work of all the former. And yet, even this contingency can be avoided. For, as now we admit some to membership, who appear especially deserving, without their paying their own fees, so could the same thing be done under the proposed change.

DAMODAR K. MAVALANKAR, F.T.S.

Respectfully submitted to the consideration of Mr. Sinnett.

LETTER No. 142 B

Respectfully submitted for the consideration of Mr. Sinnett, under the direct orders of Brother Koot Hoomi.

DAMODAR K. MAVALANKAR.

With the exception of fee—too exaggerated—his views are quite correct. Such is the impression produced upon the native mind. I trust, my dear friend, that you add a paragraph showing the Society in its true light. Listen to your *inner voice*, and oblige once more, yours

Ever faithfully,

K. H.

LETTER No. 143

Would you wish the pillow phenomenon described in the paper? I will gladly follow your advice.

Ever yours,

A. P. SINNETT.

It certainly would be the best thing to do, and I personally would feel sincerely thankful to you on account of our much ill-used friend. You are at liberty to mention my first name if it will in the least help you.

KOOT HOOMI LAL SING.

LETTER No. 144

Impossible: no power. Will write thro' Bombay.

K. H.

LETTER No. 145

Courage, patience and *hope*, my brother.

K. H.

INDEX

INDEX

A

go to, 289-90; crucial meeting at, 368

Book, K. H., on Sinnett's idea for, 21, 27, 31-2, 34, 50, 237; of lives, 101, 125; of Life, 359

Boothia, 165

"Bottomless Pit," 193

Bowajee, 469, 477

Boyle, Robert, 2

"Boys," the, Olcott's name for Masters, 32

Bradlaugh, 130, 399

Brahm, man as an integral, 27; the creative architect of the world, 60; nights of, 73

Brahmā, the vivifying expansive force, 71; nights of, 135; purush as, 340-1; lokas, 367

Brahman, and Sakti, 89

Brahmana, the meditating, 59

Brahmanical esoteric teaching, 370

Brahmanism, Orthodox, 455

Brahmin, 58, 327; initiated, 88; Subba Row a, 370

Brain, 22, 144; molecules of the, 56; Bible stuffed, 116; after death, 124; physical, 134; organised, 136; ecstatic, 159; and memory at death, 167; and the shell, 171; of adept, 177; spiritual, 228; versus heart, 263; active and passive, 416; and letter-transmission, 464

Branches, of T.S., 20; on Western continent, 207; may perish, 242; and parent body, 314

Branchlet Races, 116-7

Brewster, 170

Bridge, "golden," 106; of woven grasses, 217; of Sighs, 446

Brih, root of Brahma, 71

"Brilliant," the, cf. Taijasa

British, see English

British Island, fate of, 153

British (London Branch) T.S., 9, 14, 20, 208, 299, 330-2, 336, 414; members of, 199; danger to, 261; future of, 324; state of, 364; Mrs. Kingsford and, 394-6, 399-402

British Theosophists, 302

Bronze Age, 150

Brooch incident, 5, 10, 13, 209, 214, 461, 467

Brookes, 234

Brother, semi-European Greek, 64; "Blessed," 219, 224; "Lha," or, 261; Greek, 267; what is a, 303

Brotherhood, 32; universal, 8, 9, 17, 20, 23-4, 207, 211, 213, 313; versus phenomena, 24, 360; discredit to our, 240; M. on, 248; the whole, and its ramifications, 268; of Initiates, 272; respect for the, 369; three centres of, 393; and personalities,

395; and Hume, 435; fresh blood poured into, 458; T.S. a, 460-1

Brothers, 7, 10, 19, 244, 278, 299; not heartless, 32; of the Shadow, 40, 42, 49, 51, 280, 332; individual, 49; using power, 112; "Asiatic savages," 183; addressed first by Sinnett, 208; versus Jesuits, 228; M. on, and brotherhood, 248; not to be judged by worldly experience, 255; re H.P.B. and Olcott, 258-9, 305; question of, kept up, 289; not slave of, 307; and phenomena, 319; Hume on their system, 327; K.H. on, 409; prolong life, 456; H. P. B. foretells withdrawal of, 459

Brown, Mr., 421

Buck, Dr., 475

Buddh, Divine Wisdom, 456

Buddha, 33, 58, 134, 277, 354; and planetary spirit, 43-4; patron of all adepts, 43; man may become a, 75; a sixth rounder, 83; mystery of, 95; describes Devachan, 97-8; teaching re Avitchi, 106; will incarnate on next planet, 114; of last seventh race, 154; wisdom of a, 193; misunderstood, 277; his teaching, 455

Buddha Gaya, 290

Buddhahood, 67

Buddhangams of Creation, the interlaced triangles, 340

Buddhas, are rare, 43; the first, 49; those who succeed, 77

Buddhi, of Universe, 90; Maha, 90; or spiritual soul, 92; in man, 93; spiritual attributes reborn, 169; paralysed in madman, 169-70; when wedded to Atman, 336; when galvanised by Manas, 336; and curative talisman, 337; Universal, 338; error caused by Manas, 342; enlightenment or wisdom, 393; evolution of, 398; never within man, 447

Buddhism, and Masters, 58; seven mysteries of, 107; opponents of, 108; Rhys Davids on, 154, 182, 337, 339; criticisms of, 312; chronology, 339; metaphysics, 367, 396

Buddhist, scriptures, 54, 104; teaching, 58; philosophers, 89; sutra, 104; metaphysics, 107, 340, 370; priest, 107; books, 108; logic, 108; principal philosophical school in India, 136; Lama, 154; delegates, 251; exegesis, 337; Esoteric System, 392, 396

Buddhistic atheism, 135

Buddhists, 393; deny God, 52

Bulwer-Lytton, 32, 42, 292

Burke and Hastings, 290

Burnouf, 104

Burton, Mrs., of Simla, 460

154; every purified ego has chance
to exist as a, 154

Dhyan Chohans, 168, 195, 409; infallibility of, 54; are planetaries, 55,
316; silence regarding, 63-4; return
of animal soul to, 71; those who
succeed become, 77; "failures"
among, 86; hosts of the, 89; correspondence with lower kingdoms, 95;
at beginning of solar manwantara,
96; Tathāgatas, 97, 100, 105; rupa
and arupa, 104; and disincarnated
ego, 128; protectors of our race, 154;
devas are servants to, 316; and
Avalokiteshwara, 338-9; and "Chohans of Darkness," 455; their
opposites, 455-6

Dhyanis, 367

Diagram of "man on a planet," 84;
explanatory notes on, 85

Diatonic scale and Swabhavat, 96

Dichromatic body, 30

Diet, 57, 65, 448; (see Vegetarianism)

Diffraction spectrum, 163

Dikshita (initiated), 95, 216

Diogenes' Lantern, 208

"Direct communication" between
Sinnett and Masters impossible,
26-9, 50

Disciples, H.P.B., and Subba Row, 237

Discipleship, drawbacks of, 6; terms
and conditions of, 8, 9, 31; pathway,
254; passions not for, 270; fighting
our battles, 311; and Crookes, 336

Discord is the harmony of the universe,
395

Discretion, test of, for Sinnett, 256

Disease, origin of, 57

Disembodied spirits, 40-1, 47, 49, 271,
281

"Disinherited," Humanity as, 32;
"the," 33-4, 36, 110, 247, 251, 434,
443; See Djual Khool

Djual Khool, or D.K., 133, 266,
298-300, 351; will transmit letters,
66; diagram by, 85; accident to,
177-8; precipitation of K.H.'s portrait, 181, 295, 308; chela of K.H.,
200; can hardly be sacrificed, 239;
and Oxley, 270-1; footnote to
Oxley's article, 271, 289; and Col.
Chesney, 283; preparing for initiation, 293; tried to penetrate Rothney Castle, 293; interested in
Sinnett's progress, 331; "Lal Sing"
nom de plume invented by, 358;
would have to deputize, 383; and
H.P.B. quarrel, 434; borrowing from,
438; letter to Sinnett, 446-7; appears
on the "Clan Drummond," 460

Doctor, the little, 368

Doctrine, of occultism, fundamental,
138; septenary, not revealed in

Isis, 180; recorded in figures, 276;
dissemination of, 370; whole, not
told to Sinnett, 457

Dog, memory of a, 170

Domination over others, 40, 214, 427

Dondoukoff, Prince, 251, 456

Donnelly, 147, 152

Doppelganger, the independent, 43

Double, fluidic, of globe, 92

Doubt, to, is to risk insanity, 31; territory of, 105

Dreams, land of, 100

Druze brethren, 113

Dualities, struggle between upper and
lower, 101; struggle between upper
and middle, 168; final severance,
171; higher must become triad,
341

Dugpas, E[glinton] would make a
superb, 119; -Shammar, 130, 269;
given carte blanche to deceive chelas,
229; and Fern, 266, 292, 294; and
Gelukpas, fight in England, 268;
imitate M.'s handwriting, 289; ex-,
294; in Bhootan and Vatican, 317;
traps for chelas, 363; who provoke
vanity, 365; attracted by Hume,
375; occult forger, 412; opposition
to H.P.B., 438; and Chohans of
Darkness, 455; element in London
Lodge, 477; bomb-shell from, world,
477

Dumb Races, 86, 116

Dunraven, Lord, 424

Dupotet, an English, 27

Dust, meteoric, 158

Dutch Theosophist at Penang, letters
of, 66

Duty precedence of, 345, 366

Dwarf, 94; -race, 76

Dweller of the Threshold, 42

Dwellers in the subjective world, 105

"Dzing Dzing visionary," 183

E

EARTH, axis of, 4; and Planetaries, 41;
"Spirits that hover about the,
sphere," 41; cycle of, spirit-man
performs, 47, 117; our, the lower
turning point, 78; inner kingdom
below crust, 78; crust of, 80; history
of, missing pages, 87; our, 92-3, 96;
-particles, tidal wave of, 97; -rings
and ego, 98; "-walkers," 106, 109;
aura of, 107; an electrified conductor, 156; magnetism of, 158

East and West, only minute point of
contact, 13, 15.

East India Company, treatment of
ryots, 383; corruption in, 383-4

I

upon Adepts, 336; Prakriti and, 341; made of K.H., 346; self deception, 379; in mesmerism, 416

Mayavi rupa, 125, 195, 446

Mayer, Dr. J. R., 60, 63

Meat-eating; even craving is an impediment, 65; " savages," 118; barrier to vision, 272; abstinence from, 423 (see Vegetarianism)

Meditation, 29, 59

Medium, Mediums, persecution of a, 4; without aid of, 6; American, 27; Home a true skunk, 37; " Adept, no antagonism with," 42; pure spirits cannot use, 47; uninitiated, 99; incarnate, 99; moral state of, 99; easy-going, 106; and victim of accident, 107, 132; helps to awaken desire, 109; multiply causes for misery in " angel guides," 110, 118; soulless physical, 115; great, 149; most reliable of, 170; in California or London, 172; material shells, 172; hallucinated, 231; chief, 251; invitation to the lion's den, 259; the wounded vanity of a, 262; Tappan woman, 268; obstacles in way, 272; K. H. about, 272-3; Mrs. Billing a, 301; Billing and his wife, 301-2; fumigation against, 318; on same level with, 332; Russian, 409; impersonating adepts, 414; and chela, diametrically dissimilar, 417; professional, 424; forgery of handwriting, 425; and three secret words, 447

Mediumistic, dogmatism, 35; current, 48; message, 99; communications, 119; phenomena, 412; temperament, 417

Mediumship, proofs of, 34; K. H. on why we oppose, 41-3, 65, 110, 170-1, 202, 420; indiscriminate, 110; vortex of, 133; illusory, 409; heavy Karma of Spiritualists who entice men and women into, 425

Medusa, Head of, 444

Meerut, 17

Megatherium, 212

Mejnour, 32; of Baroda, 234

Melomans, Melomaniac, 185-6

Members, personal opinion of individual, 239

Memnon, 73

Memory, 101; of the Ego, 102; in Kama Loka and Devachan, 124-5, 184; dislodged by dying brain, 167; " full " remembrance, 167; K. H. on the, of a dog, 170; complete recollection at the end of 7 rounds, 195 (see Recollection)

Men, ex- and future, 104-5

Mendicants, 108, 238

Mental, perversity, 75; annihilation, 184

Mephitis, a true shunk, 37

Mercurial, intra-Mercurial planets, 166

Mesmer, 277

Mesmeric, powers, 214; cures, 342; K. H. about, healing, 416-7

Mesmeriser, a true adept or juggler, 214

Mesmerism, 97, 130; modern works on, 246

Messiah, 147

Messiahship, latent sense of, 324

Metals, metallic substances, 164; fusion of, 166

Metaphysics, Kant's, 56

Metaphysicians, Western, 57; British, 333

Meteor, 62, 158; " moral," 378

Meteoric, continent, 163; dust, 158, 162; matter, 162; masses, 163

Methods, of the Brothers, 305, 327; of Occultism, 393

Metrovich, Mme., H. P. B., is not, 474

Mexico, 146

Michelet, 16

Microcosm, 27, 46, 54, 134, 340; septenary, 89

" Micrographia," 3

Microscope, 86

Mills, John Stuart, 236

Milton, quoted by K. H., 415

Mind, Universal, 54-5, 72, 133, 338, 398; mystery of, 56; Western, 58; Adi-Buddha and, 89; the most spiritualised portion of its, 101; human, in connection with body, 134; the infinite, 134; state of, on earth, 189; state of, outside earth's sphere, 190; reading, 226

Mineral, evolution, 74; Spirit in every, 91; kingdom, 92; entities, 96; every, 149; life, 155

Minerva, 220

Miocene period, 151

Miracles, age of, 23; worker of, 140

Misconceptions of terms, 194

Misery, selfishness and religion the causes of, 57

Missionaries, 356, 465

Missions, hell-hounds of, 251

" Moggy," 23, 294

Moguls, 118

Mohini, 346, 350, 352, 368, 469; M, about, 344; must earn living, 344; and letter, 345; left in a very cold room, 348; not quite correct, 351; re Mrs. Holloway, 355, 362; as amanuensis, 360; to accompany Olcott to London, 391-2; a chela of K. H., 392; -Babu, K. H. sends on a mission, 443; H. P. B., about, 469; spoilt by adulation, 477

Moksha, 32

Northern current, 282
Note, seventh, 73
Nous, 285, 448
Now, an eternal, 24
Numbers, 276
Nutrition, Mayer's organic motion in
its connection with, 63

O

OAKLEYS, 462, 466-7; do not believe
H. P. B. a fraud, 466
Object, Objects, a Brotherhood of
Humanity, 24; branches to choose
some, 313; dissemination of TRUTH,
392; of Occultism, 393; of T.S.
Loyalty to, 402
Objective cannot mirror the subjective, 191
Obscuration, Obscurations, 95, 105,
122, 130, 174, 331, 333, 386; questions on, 145; of planet, 153, 166;
K. H. about, 444
Obscurities, the five, 261
Obstacles from those who know
best, 276
Occult, Science, Sciences, 4, 31, 54, 105,
118, 207, 210, 238, 336, 451;
mysteries, 6; proof of, 7; domain of
nature, 16; powers, 19, 35; phenomena, 23; Kosmos, 29; powers of
air, 29; Light, 30; law, 35; psychical
energies, 39; philosophy, 39, 267;
system, reformer and codifier of, 43;
doctrine, 64, 340; sounds, 65;
osmosis, 80; sciences, knowledge of,
105; fame, 150; science vindicated,
163; science sacrificed on altar of
modern science, 164; power requires
an effort, 177; sciences, laws of, 178;
"faculties," 244; students warned
against phenomena, 258; Free
Masonry, 262; research led Crookes,
268; rules, 269; truths, 274; Indian
knowledge, 277; schools, common
mistakes about, 278; amusing incident, 315-6; instrument, mind as,
318; training, K. H. about, 345-6;
teachings, those who can write on,
351; knowledge, K. H. about Sinnett obtaining, 355; instruction
comes to an end, 357; knowledge
the treasure, 361; Brotherhood, three
centres of, 393; instructions re
sealed paper, 397; science the
extinguisher of all superstitions, 405;
" occult " forger, 412; science, the
real aim of, 452; path of error, 455
Occultism, path of, 8; study of, 8, 13;
Sinnett has chances to learn, 20;
"professor of," 21; truths and

mysteries of, 23; realities of, 40;
S. M., turns his back on, 41; fundamental doctrines of, 138; exact
science, 140; a student of, 146; and
mediums, 251-2; word was unknown in America, 268; an act of,
283; keystone of, 341; practical,
345; how to obtain success in, 349;
Ocean of, 352; laws of, 357; mistakes
in T.S. about, 358; Universal
Brotherhood not, 368; Aryan, 378;
methods of, 393; truth through
unpopular channel, 404; and Spiritualism incompatible, 408; demands
all, 453; new blood poured into,
458; to be a secret study, 479
Occultist, Occultists, Macrocosm and
microcosm, 46; practical, 81; and
immortality, 110; in Egypt, 113;
Eliphas Levi an, 125; must be, to
solve the problem of life, 155; have
no intention to conceal from earnest
students, 275; M., a pukka orthodox,
294; an, who dies, 358
Occult Truth, Fragments of, 83
Occult World, The, 107, 318, 322, 353,
361, 417, 467; author of, 199;
discussed in Lamasery, 282; K. H.
about, 351; printed before sending
it to K. H. for revision, 358
Occult World Series, 1-37
Odessa, 250, 254; Old Lady, 250
Odic, Od force, 97; properties of plants
etc., 140; emanations, 378
Odylised, 101
Odyllic influences, 137
Olcott, Colonel H.S., 9, 10-2, 14-6,
19-20, 26, 28, 32, 37, 39, 112, 218,
234, 251, 267, 318, 325, 352, 378,
390, 445, 454; K. H. about, 36,
349; helps with *Isis*, 77, 472; his
sister starving, 199; the blunders of,
204; Hume says "stick to your,"
211; Hume's letter to, 218, 219, 221,
327-8; and Hume, 225; appeals to
M., 233; quoted by K. H., 239, 288;
in presence of, 242; signature to
letter to " Pioneer," 250; ridiculed
and libelled, 251; M. sees, 258; M.
about 259; eccentricity of, 269;
coming to Sinnett, 275; accused by
Dr. Billing, 302; sacrificed by
Dayanand, 308; compliments to
Founders, 313; K. H.'s warning to,
318; and Indian Branches, 336; in
London, 345; to stay with Arundale
ladies, 345; Sinnett wrong about,
347; treated in cruel way by Sinnett, 347; Sinnett's unjust suspicions
about, 349; the other victim, 356;
and H.P.B. far from perfect but
both unselfish, 364; Maha Chohan
to say when, can go to the Punjab,

Primary colours, 30
Primordial man, 47
Primrose, 268, 456
Prince's Hall, Kingford incident, 469
Principia of Newton, 31
Principle, active, 46, 60, 67, 101, 163; Passive, 71-2, 105; fifth, 72, 74, 347; sixth, 72, 89, 90, 341; seventh, 72, 74, 341, 452; fourth, 77; creative, 89; immutable, 90; igneous, 90; no abiding, 108; life, 124; causative, of all, 163; Universal 340; that one, 448
Principles, seven, 71, 73-4, 90, 92; man, 74, 77, 80, 97, 101-2, 106, 111, 117, 120, 124-5, 128, 131, 154, 168, 170-1, 173, 180, 336, 338-9, 341; of nature, 78, 90-2; universal, 80, 97, 340; of Globe, 92; one, developed fully in each round, 93; 5th, the soul, 108; of the Ego, 168-9, 185, 193; seven, referred to as a trinity, 285; of Theos, Socy., 313; K.H. about, in man, 447
Prismatic colours, 30
Pritchard, 116
Probation, lives of, 168; a chela under, 227-9; K.H. about, 233, 283; K.H. and, of Fern, 234; term of, will end, 260; period, 311; Eastern, the laws of, 325; Masonic, 359; drawn into the vortex of, 361
Probation and Chelaship, 201-370
Problem, the Great, 260
Procyon and invisible stars, 444
Programme of BEING, perverted the, 359
Progress, of man, 46-7; individuals can only outstrip general, by one remove, 94; of Theosophy paralysed by misconception, 248; of human race, 359
Prohibition removed in Sinnett's case, 390
Prophecy by K.H., 166, 382
Prophets, 269; English, 271
Proprietors, Sinnett's 22, 375; K.H. has his, also, 22
Prospect Hill, 10
Protean manifestations of spirit-matter, 138
Protegés are tested, 256
Protest, joint, of chelas, 239; of chelas, the order of the Chohan, 288
Protestant, 313; Theology, 116; Bills aimed at, England, 385
Protestantism, 37
Proteus, 56, 155; universal, 63, 161
Prototype, the Great is the, of the smaller cycles, 46
Proverb, Tibetan, 28, 134, 299
Providence, 107
Prshu (repulsion), 35

Pseudo Spirits, 40
Psyche, 285
Psychic, communication, 45; vampires, 107; phenomena, 111; secret of, phenomena, 111; impulse and Devachan, 197; idiosyncrasy, 244; power to be unfolded, 243; Society, 261; chemistry, 415; printing machine, 417
Psychical, powers of hearing, 28, 65; Research Society oracle, 461
Psychical Research, the Society for, 336, 356, 416, 454, 465-7
Psycho-physiological, tamasha, 28; peculiarities, 202
Psychography, 99
Psychological, observer, 185; aspirant now tested on the, side of his nature, 359
Psychologists, 79
Psychology, 27, 51
Psychometrical "delineation of character," 27
Psychopathist, 337
Ptolemy, 30
Publication, of letters, 350-1
Pundit, universal, 152
Punjab, 118, 447
Punjabi Singhs, 15
Pupil, 9, 10; our greatest trouble to teach, not to be befooled by appearances, 257; "pupil," 366
Purity, personal, 102
Purusha, -Sakti, 89; the Divine Essence, 117; Vedantic, 138; cannot manifest without Prakriti, 139; triangles on T.S. seal, 340
Pyramids, 138; of intellectual energy misspent, 246
Pythagoras, 341, 448
Pythagorean, Monad, 63; MSS., 150; doctrines, 276

Q

QUALIFICATIONS of aspirant, 270, 278-9, 334-5, 346
Quarrel, M. says "we never," 215; M. wrongly accused, 347
Quaternary, 101; loses recollection at death, 184
Quichote, Don, 219
Quick thinkers are hard to impress, 36
Quietism—that utter paralysis of the Soul, 208
Quintessence of Good, 101

R

RABBIS, initiated, 339
Rabelais, 38; "quart d'heure de," 381

Sex, a mere accident, 114
Sexual relations, 57
Shaberon, Shaberons, 8; Holy, 15;
  of Than-La, 20
Shadow-world, our natural allies in
  the, 264
Shakespeare quoted by K.H., 343;
  and Bacon, 320, 420
Shakya K'Houtchoo, 277
" Shamballah," 152
Shammars, 269; infamous, 130, 280
Shandba, mis-spelling of Skandha,
  107
Shan-Mun-Yih-Tung, 97
Shapa-tung Lama, 130
Sharp, Becky, 188
Shastra, Abhidharma, 106
Shastras, 455
Sheep, 150
Shell, Shells, 104, 106, 109, 120, 121,
  125, 128-9, 133, 144, 168, 172-3,
  184, 186, 196, 272; empty, 101; 1½
  principled and 2 principled, 120;
  self-consciousness of, 168, 170; may
  be a perfect Sinnett, 171; on same
  level with, 332
Shelley, 193
Shere-Ali, 322
Sherry, bars the way, 37
Shigatse, 118, 251, 288, 333, 361
Ship, the good, is sinking, 360
Shishir Koomar Gosh, Hume complains
  to, 298
Shiva, 86; the Creator, the Destroyer
  and Regenerator, 238; the ideal,
  238; the source of truth, 238; and
  Ma-Mos, 456
Shloma, 258
Shrine, letters put in, 463
Siberia, and fourth race, 150-1
Siberian coast, islands, 150
Sibyls and sirens of the Theosophical
  establishment, 421
Siddhas, ways of, 274; the perfected,
  367
Siddhi, of hearing, 65; powers trans-
  cended, 182
Siemens, 143; truth uttered by, 164
Signatures, our, 14
Sikhs, 12
Sikkim and dugpas, 438
Silence, oath of, about Masters and
  Lodge, 260; a part of the neophyte's
  training, 279
Simeon Stylites, Indo-Tibetan, 183
Simla, 3, 12, 13, 17, 21, 34, 39, 59,
  118, 133, 183, 225, 265, 274, 278,
  293, 343, 460-2; " period," 148;
  Eclectic Socy., 203-4; municipality
  row, 221; Lamas in, 234; hills, 237;
  instructions to the, Sage, 258; pam-
  phlet from, 263; Nawab, 266; phe-
  nomena at, 293; standard of gentle-

men, 330; Col. Gordon and, 371;
  Yogi, 377
Simpson, Mrs. of Boston, 379, 410
Sincere beliefs a barrier, 455
Sinnett, A.P., 15, 18, 30, 33, 52, 59,
  65, 70, 80, 85, 87, 97, 112, 113,
  121, 123-4, 131-2, 133, 140-1,
  144, 185, 206, 208-9, 213, 221, 236;
  shell of, 171-2; not an absolute new
  invention, 171; friend and brother
  of K.H., 172; praise for, 198-9;
  offer to, 202; his idea a " school of
  magic," 207; mind of, 217; room of,
  218; refusal to accept, as chela, 227;
  messages from Masters, 247; warned
  by M. to remember promise to
  K.H., 252; his feeling for K.H.,
  255; lack of perception, 257-8;
  warning to, 258; indiscretions of,
  261; and ignoramus of our Tibetan
  customs, 267; shocked by H.P.B.'s
  letter to C.C. Massey, 285; objection of, to chela test, 294; not to
  interfere between punishment of
  Hume's pride and fate, 295; elected
  President, 298; asked to write re
  work of Branches and oblige M.
  and K.H., 313; house of, 318; alone
  of the four worthy of trust, 323;
  may find himself in Massey's attitude, 330; to go to London, 330;
  does not have a vision, 331; departs
  from India, 331; his good work in
  London, 333; " looks down from
  on high," 338; threatens to leave
  London Lodge, 363; hints to,
  about checks on the Phœnix project,
  365; cares only for K.H. personally
  and phenomena, 369; advice re
  Phœnix project, 375; as good as
  tested, 390; instructions from K.H.
  to, 392; Mrs. Kingsford and, 394;
  beliefs and rights of, 396; " -Kings-
  ford incident," 401; to keep silence,
  406; beginning to attract the Chohan's attention, 424; warned by
  K.H., 431; to see K.H.'s astral self,
  445; told by H.P.B. he is deceiving
  himself, 453; H.P.B.'s best friends
  are Mr. and Mrs., 457; H.P.B.'s
  prophecy about, accusing K.H. of
  deception, 459; H.P.B. asks, to
  try to deserve personal communication with Masters, 467; H.P.B. says,
  please do try and have intuition,
  468; H.P.B. sees scin-lecca of, 469;
  H.P.B. about, 478
Sinnett, K.H. on, 172, 262-3, 269,
  274-5, 281, 317, 334, 346-51, 394;
  on methods and duties, 241; his
  friendship for, 261; his increased respect for, 261; appeals to,
  261; about his attitude, 278; does

36

Withdrawal of Masters, 51; " you may whistle then for the Brothers," 459

Witnesses, two, for the Founders, 288

Woman, 46; hysterical, 5; H.P.B. a, 234, 422; Chela, 288; K.H. about, 297; vanity, 324; anger or fury, 372: a calamity in this fifth race, 415; element in London Lodge, 477

Women, 36, 50; enrolment of, 248

Wood fires as fumigators, 318

Word, Lost, 272

World, Essence, 45; Soul, 45; star-, 46; of causes, 47-8, 71-2, 100, 103; atmosphere of, 47; of effects, 47-8, 71; one, Life principle, 73; rings, 79-81; phenomenal, 89; scattered remnants of material, 96; of Desire, 101-2; of Forms, 101-2; of bliss, 103; subjective, 105; each has a protector, 105; of force, 140; of Occultism, 140; knowledge given to Sinnett to be shared with the, 239

Worldly, the last, enterprise for K.H., 372

Worlds, inhabited, 45; interlinked, 46; evolution of, 72; string of, 78, 96; local variations in, 81; application of diagram, 85; visible and invisible, 86; man-bearing, 92; systems of, 97; seven, 126; in spiritualized state, 135; planets in our system, 145

Woven grasses, a bridge of, 217

Wranglers, scientifically logical, 136

Wren, 324

Writing, M.'s hatred for, 247

Wyld, Dr., 21, 33, 39, 261, 299; grim idol of the Jewish Sinai, 267

Y

Yak, -drivers, 56; Tibetan, 265

Yankee editors, 50

Yankees, 127

Ye-dhamma, 124, 176

" Yellow Cap," laymen, 130

Yin-Sin, 88, 340

Yog Vidya, 12, 15

Yoga, 15, 302; -Shastras, 238; Raja-, 359

Yogees, 12, 33; -Dayanand, 308

Yogi, powers of, 134; of Yogis, 238; Hume claims to be a, 329

Yogi-Arhat, M. calls K.H. a perfect, 264

Yogis, method of, 244

Yorkshire, H.P.B. learnt dreadful, 472

Young, Prof., 160

Yugs, Yugas, the four, 117

Z

Zanoni, 440; his Dweller, 42

Zemindar, intrigues against Rent Bill, 382; K.H. traces the history of their claims, 383-4; terms of Phœnix project, 383; failed to fulfil agreement, 384; wealthy, 389

Zenana women, 442

Zergvan Bey, 208

Zetetic, 64

Zodiacal tables, 146

Zöllner, 170

Zoologist, 80

Zoonizations, 80

Zoophagous friend, 65

Zoroastrian system, Ahriman in, 300